Depression in Young People

DEVELOPMENTAL AND CLINICAL PERSPECTIVES

Depression in Young People

DEVELOPMENTAL AND CLINICAL PERSPECTIVES

Edited by

Michael Rutter
Carroll E. Izard
Peter B. Read

THE GUILFORD PRESS
New York   London

© 1986 The Guilford Press
A Division of Guilford Publications, Inc.
200 Park Avenue South, New York, N.Y. 10003

PRINTED IN THE UNITED STATES OF AMERICA
Second printing, May 1986

Library of Congress Cataloging in Publication Data
Main entry under title:

Depression in young people.

Includes index.
1. Depression in children.   2. Youth—Mental health.
I. Rutter, Michael.   II. Izard, Carroll E. (Carroll
Ellis), 1923–   .   III. Read, Peter. [DNLM: 1. De-
pression—in adolescence.   2. Depression—in infancy &
childhood.   3. Depressive Disorder—in adolescence.
4. Depressive Disorder—in infancy & childhood.
WM 171 D424195]
RJ506.D4D48   1986   618.92′8257   85–870
ISBN 0–89862–660–9

List of Contributors

William R. Beardslee, MD. Department of Psychiatry, Massachusetts General Hospital, Boston, Massachusetts.

A. Bifulco, PhD. Department of Sociology, Bedford College, Inner Circle, Regent's Park, London, England.

G. W. Brown, PhD. Department of Sociology, Bedford College, Inner Circle, Regent's Park, London, England.

Gabrielle A. Carlson, MD. Department of Psychiatry, State University of New York at Stony Brook, Stony Brook, New York.

Dante Cicchetti, PhD.* Department of Psychology and Social Relations, Harvard University, Cambridge, Massachusetts.

Leon Cytryn, MD. Laboratory of Developmental Psychology, National Institute of Mental Health, Bethesda, Maryland.

Judy Dunn, MD. Medical Research Council, Unit on the Development and Integration of Behaviour, University of Cambridge, Cambridge, England.

Leon Eisenberg, MD. Department of Medicine and Health Policy, Harvard Medical School, Boston, Massachusetts.

Robert N. Emde, MD. Department of Psychiatry, University of Colorado School of Medicine, Denver, Colorado.

*Present address: Department of Psychology and Psychiatry, Rochester University, Rochester, New York.

Judy Garber, PhD. Department of Psychology and Human Development, George Peabody College, Vanderbilt University, Nashville, Tennessee.

Norman Garmezy, PhD. Department of Psychology, University of Minnesota, Minneapolis, Minnesota.

Elliot S. Gershon, MD. Unit of Psychogenetics, Biological Psychiatry Branch, National Institute of Mental Health, Bethesda, Maryland.

William V. Good, PhD. Department of Psychiatry, University of Colorado School of Medicine, Denver, Colorado.

T. O. Harris, PhD. Department of Sociology, Bedford College, Inner Circle, Regent's Park, London, England.

Robert J. Harmon, PhD. Department of Psychiatry, University of Colorado School of Medicine, Denver, Colorado.

Carroll E. Izard, PhD. Department of Psychology, University of Delaware, Newark, Delaware.

Maria Kovacs, PhD. Department of Psychiatry, University of Pittsburgh School of Medicine and Western Psychiatric Institute and Clinic, Pittsburgh, Pennsylvania.

Helen Block Lewis, PhD. Department of Psychology, Yale University, New Haven, Connecticut.

Donald H. McKnew, MD. Laboratory of Developmental Psychology, National Institute of Mental Health, Bethesda, Maryland.

John M. Neale, PhD. Department of Psychology, State University of New York at Stony Brook, Stony Brook, New York.

Christopher Peterson, PhD. Department of Psychology, University of Pennsylvania, Philadelphia, Pennsylvania.

Joaquim Puig-Antich, MD. Division of Child Psychiatry, Western Psychiatric Institute and Clinic, Pittsburgh, Pennsylvania.

Peter B. Read, PhD. Social Science Research Council, New York, New York.

Michael Rutter, MD, FRCP, FRCPsych. Department of Child and Adolescent Psychology, University of London Institute of Psychiatry, London, England.

Karen Schneider-Rosen, PhD. Department of Psychology, Boston College, Boston, Massachusetts.

Gail M. Schwartz, PhD. Department of Psychiatry, Medical College of Pennsylvania, Philadelphia, Pennsylvania.

Martin E. P. Seligman, PhD. Department of Psychology, University of Pennsylvania, Philadelphia, Pennsylvania.

David Shaffer, MB, BS, MRCP, FRCPsych. New York State Psychiatric Institute, Columbia University–College of Physicians and Surgeons, New York, New York.

Sheldon Weintraub, PhD. Department of Psychology, State University of New York at Stony Brook, Stony Brook, New York.

Ken C. Winters, PhD. Office of Research and Statistics, Amherst H. Wilder Foundation, St. Paul, Minnesota.

Carolyn Zahn-Waxler, MD. Laboratory of Developmental Psychology, National Institute of Mental Health, Bethesda, Maryland.

Preface

Prior to the 1970s, conventional wisdom held that children rarely exhibited depression. During the last decade the growing acceptance that depressive disorders can and do occur in childhood has been followed by an explosion of clinical and research papers. In some quarters this has been accompanied by an assumption that childhood depression is the same as adult depression, with perhaps only a few minor modifications that derive from children's immaturities in emotional expression or conceptualization. That assumption ignores, however, the evidence that there are quite striking changes with age in both the frequency and form of affective disturbances. Moreover, many clinical writings on depressive disorders have not taken account of developmental research or theory on affective expression. Similarly, most developmental writings have not considered the clinical distinctions between depressive *feelings* as an affective phenomenon and depressive *disorders* as psychopathological conditions.

This unfortunate separation of developmental and clinical approaches led the Social Science Research Council's Committee on Social and Affective Development during Childhood, to hold a symposium in 1982 that would initiate a dialogue between researchers from both "camps." The meeting was fruitful to the extent that it generated a greater appreciation of the important contributions to be made by both developmentalists and clinicians with respect to depression in children. It also resulted in a recognition of the extent to which the two approaches used different concepts and different language (or, more seriously, the *same* language to describe different phenomena). The meeting provided a unique opportunity to advance interdisciplinary dialogue and the editors of this volume, who were participants, decided that this approach should be shared with other interested clinicians and researchers. The authors of papers circulated prior to the meeting were asked to prepare new chapters that would take account of discussions during the symposium and comments made in subsequent correspondence. Several additional chapters were invited that would incorporate issues that could not be covered adequately in the original presentations. This volume is the final result of these endeavors.

The book offers a convenient summary of current thinking and empirical findings with respect to depression in young people. It is not, however, a "state of the art" review, but rather, an exploration of the connections between developmental and clinical theory and research as they apply to depressive feelings and disorders in childhood and adolescence. The objective has been to identify promising avenues for new inquiry, with a focus on empirical and conceptual issues that require further study. The chapters should be useful to both researchers and practitioners in the fields of child development, clinical psychology and psychiatry.

In the first part, Rutter indicates what is meant by a developmental psychopathology perspective, and briefly surveys age changes in depressive feelings and disorders. He outlines issues that require a combination of developmental and clinical approaches which provide a framework for the various themes explored by authors in the remaining sections of the book.

Part II is composed of three chapters that consider different theoretical approaches to development of depressive feelings and disorders. Izard and Schwartz selectively review general and developmental theories of emotion with particular attention to the affective phenomenology of depression. They note that while some theories postulate that emotions derive from cognitive processes, others view emotions as motivational and adaptive with biological, social and experiential components. Cicchetti and Schneider-Rosen outline some developmental issues involved in moving from concepts of adult depression to depressive phenomena in childhood. They argue for the importance of incorporating biological reorganizations and emerging competencies in the social, emotional and cognitive domains. In the third conceptual chapter, Emde, Harmon, and Good adopt a podition in which individual case studies are used to highlight the extent to which depressive feelings both change and remain constant over the course of development. They emphasize the communication dimension of depression and advocate a transactional approach for research in which the clinical researchers' empathic response to children's depressive feelings plays a major role.

The third part focuses on parental depression as a risk factor for depression in children. Cytryn and his colleagues review developmental approaches to affective illness with respect to genetic and environmental components. In their own studies of infants of parents with bipolar affective disorder, they found disturbances in attachment behavior, affective regulation, and interpersonal relations. Beardslee discusses the value of studying children's adaptation to parents who are depressed or bipolar and considers possible syndromes. Weintraub and his colleagues also note the mixture of competence and vulnerability in children brought up in high risk families and make the point that to a substantial extent children's susceptibilities may be unrelated to the particular diagnostic type of parental mental disorder.

In the fourth part of the book a variety of risk indices and mechanisms are related to depressive disorders. Seligman and Peterson present empirical findings suggesting that the learned helplessness model of depression applies to childhood depression as well as to adult depression. Beginning with the finding that the loss of a mother in childhood appears to increase the chances of depression in adult life, Brown and his colleagues proceed to use their research data to explore mechanisms that might account for this effect. They conclude that loss is important, not so much as an acute stress factor, but rather through its tendency to lead to situations involving a serious lack of affectionate care. This lack of care creates a vulnerability and Brown et al. examine the developmental chain of circumstances that might create such vulnerability. Garmezy surveys the concept of stress, and reviews literature on the effects of loss, separation and failure in childhood. Like Beardslee and Weintraub et al. he draws attention to the importance of emerging resilience in children under stress. Based upon her psychoanalytic experience and research on field-dependent cognitive style, Lewis argues that there is a network of congruent connections between feelings of personal helplessness, field dependence, and the state of shame and depression. Puig-Antich provides an authoritative review of psychobiological research into childhood depression and evaluates the findings in light of current knowledge of biological markers in adult affective illness. He notes that age and puberty have major modifying effects on most psychobiological markers of depressive illness and considers the implications that flow from observation. In the final chapter of this section, Shaffer outlines the dramatic age trends in child and adolescent suicide and considers why suicide may be so rare among children.

Throughout the book frequent reference is made to problems of methods and measurement. These are considered in greater detail in Part V. Carlson and Garber focus primarily on developmental issues inherent in any attempt to classify disorders as may arise in childhood. Their discussion of the issues reflects an integrative combination of their respective skills as a clinician and a developmentalist. Kovacs also provides an effective integration of developmental and clinical perspectives in her appraisal of the clinical interview as a tool for the diagnosis of depression in childhood. Her review reveals the implications of developmental issues for the ways in which children are interviewed and for the kinds of information they can be expected to provide.

The last three chapters use some of the concepts and findings discussed in earlier chapters to raise issues and to make suggestions for future research. Eisenberg addresses the disease concept of depression and uses knowledge on conditions as diverse as thalassemia and tuberculosis to consider what is implied by the notion of a qualitatively distinct "illness." He argues that it would be most unwise to bring premature closure to the debate about the nature and causes of childhood depression as a clinical entity; both disease and dimensional models are needed. Dunn, writing as a developmental researcher, offers a critical appraisal of three issues that are crucial to both clinical problems and an understanding of children's emotional development: stress and the need to study its long-term effects on family interaction; the relationships between a child's cognitive capacity to appreciate the meaning of events and their response to stress or their vulnerability to depression; and the role that "stressful" events may play in developmental advances. In the last chapter, Rutter critically surveys some of the clinical concepts and findings on depression in order to suggest possible directions for future research into childhood depression.

Our task as editors has brought immense rewards in fostering a continuing dialogue between clinicians and developmentalists. We hope that some of the liveliness of this interchange is equally rewarding to readers of this book. We must conclude this preface, however, with a special expression of thanks to those authors who responded so patiently and constructively to the editorial review of their chapters and particular thanks are also due to Joy Maxwell and Jenny Smith in London, and to Peggy Randall at SSRC in New York, for their skilled clerical assistance.

MICHAEL RUTTER
CARROLL E. IZARD
PETER B. READ

Contents

VI

SOME OUTSTANDING ISSUES

Depression in Young People

DEVELOPMENTAL AND CLINICAL PERSPECTIVES

I

SOME DEVELOPMENTAL ISSUES

The Developmental Psychopathology of Depression: Issues and Perspectives

Michael Rutter

DEVELOPMENTAL PSYCHOPATHOLOGY

Child psychiatry differs most obviously from adult psychiatry in terms of the fact that it deals with a developing organism. Yet, surprisingly and regrettably, research into the process of development and research into clinical psychiatric disorders have remained rather separate endeavors until quite recently (Achenbach, 1978). This volume seeks to bring the two together by taking a *developmental psychopathology* perspective. Such a perspective comprises three main components:

1. As the adjective "developmental" implies, it is concerned with the processes and mechanisms of development through childhood and into adult life, with an interest in discontinuities as well as continuities, and especially with a focus on the possibility that experiences or processes in one phase of development may modify an individual's set of responses at a later point—through either "sensitizing" or "steeling" effects.
2. As the noun "psychopathology" indicates, the interest does not lie in normality or abnormality as such but rather in the links or lack of links between normal emotions or behavior and clinical disorders or illnesses; similarly, there is a focus on the parallels or lack of parallels between the "normal" processes of adaptation and change and "abnormal" responses to stress or adversity.
3. The conjunction of noun and adjective emphasizes a concern to

Michael Rutter. Department of Child and Adolescent Psychiatry, University of London Institute of Psychiatry, London, England.

understand both the effects of developmental features on psycho-pathology (as reflected, for example, in age-dependent susceptibili-ties to stress or age-differentiated forms of disorder) and the effects of psychopathology on the course of development.

Developmental Perspectives

Eisenberg (1977) has argued eloquently that a developmental view-point constitutes an essential unifying concept in the psychiatry of both adults and children. Development encompasses not only the roots of behavior in prior maturation, in physical influences (both internal and ex-ternal), and in the residues of early psychosocial experiences, but also the modulations of that behavior by the circumstances of the present. But what does the taking of a developmental perspective imply, and in what ways does that perspective in the field of psychopathology differ from that in developmental psychology as a whole? Obviously, there are shared features crucial to any developmental approach. There is a concern with the general course of development. Thus, with respect to depressive feel-ings we might ask whether there are changes with age in children's ability to experience or to express such feelings, or we might want to know whether the manner of expression alters with development. However, also, insofar as developmental changes occur, it will be essential to inquire as to why they occur, in the way they do, when they do. In other words, what are the basic processes or mechanisms that underlie the developmental transi-tions? The developmentalist will seek to understand, as variants of this same general set of questions, the implications of these transitions. In this context, research will be needed to determine whether there are age-dependent variations in susceptibility to stress; whether the expression of depressive feelings at one age is dependent upon prior maturational changes or prior experiences at an earlier age; and whether there are points in development at which personality qualities associated with affect become stabilized such that although affective functions may still be vulnerable to change they can no longer be totally transformed. All of these matters are fundamental to any developmental approach.

Perhaps, too, there are differences in emphasis associated with the view of development taken in developmental psychopathology. The most obvious is the concern to understand individual differences. Much of developmental psychology has been based on the overriding perspective of universality—of the developmental progressions that occur in all normal children (McCall, 1981; Plomin, 1983). Thus, Kagan, Kearsley, and Zelazo (1978) have emphasized the consistency with which separation anxiety emerges in all infants by 8–10 months of age, reaches a peak at 15–18 months, and then declines in frequency and intensity throughout the sec-ond and third years. They note that this developmental progression seems to occur in similar fashion in a wide variety of cultures (including those in developing countries) and irrespective of whether the children are reared at home within the family or in group settings of various kinds. Similarly, Kagan (1981) has noted the consistency with which, toward the end of the second year, children develop a self-consciousness associated with an appreciation of the meaning of standards and of concepts of right and wrong. This growth function seems to be evident whether the children are brought up in the isolated Fiji islands or in affluent middle-class homes in the United States. In both cases, Kagan has used the evidence on consistency of developmental progression to argue that the changes reflect physiological maturation rather than any particular set of social experiences. It should be noted in this connection that the developmental issues concern discontinuities, at least as much as continuities, in psychological growth (Kagan, 1981; Rutter, 1983).

Knowledge of these universals, of course, is fundamental to any understanding of the developmental process, but the developmental psychopathologist will want equally to ask about the *variations* and individual differences in this process. Why does separation anxiety persist into later childhood in a few children, whereas in most it fades away during the preschool years? Why do people vary so greatly in their moral behavior in spite of the fact that all develop the sense of right and wrong so early in their development? The distinction between the perspectives of individuality and universality is important not only because of the contrasts in the questions that they pose but also because the two approaches require different methodologies (Plomin, 1983). Questions regarding individuality require measures that differentiate within broad domains. Thus, in the field of attachment, distinctions are now being drawn between secure and insecure attachments, or between generalized undiscriminating attachment behavior and selective bonding that is person-specific and persists over time and space (Rutter, 1980b). Similarly, in the field of depressive feelings we must identify those differentiations that have significance. Everyone feels low in mood at times, but that does not mean that everyone's experience of depressive feelings is identical or even directly comparable. An emphasis on individuality also has implications for sample selection and sample size in the research strategies to be pursued. Unless the effects of particular variables on individual differences are very strong (they rarely are), quite large samples will be required. Also, it will be necessary to choose samples that vary sufficiently on the features thought to influence individuality. Often, this means a comparison of normal populations and samples that constitute high-risk groups for one reason or another (Rutter, 1982b).

Perhaps a second characteristic of the developmental approach of the psychopathologist is the wish to extend the developmental perspective into adult life. In recent years, this emphasis has become somewhat fashionable under the banner of life-span development (Baltes & Brim, 1979). Life-span psychologists emphasize that developmental tasks and crises occur in adult life as well as in childhood, and that the ways in which early developmental issues are handled may influence the impact of later ones. As discussed elsewhere (Rutter, 1981b; 1983), there are at least seven main ways in which early experiences might be linked with psychiatric disorders occurring some years later:

1. They may lead to immediate disorder, with this disorder persisting into adult life for reasons that are largely independent of the initial causation or provocation.
2. They may lead to bodily changes, which in turn influence later functioning. The changes in the neuroendocrine system following acute physical stresses in infancy constitute a case in point.
3. They may lead directly to altered patterns of behavior, which although changed at the time of the event, take the form of overt disorder only some years later. The long-term social sequelae of an institutional unbringing may represent an example of this kind (Rutter, 1981a; Rutter, Quinton, & Liddle, 1983).
4. They may lead to changed family circumstances, which then in turn predispose to later disorder.
5. They may operate through their action in altering sensitivities to stress or in modifying styles of coping, which then protect from, or predispose toward, disorder in later life only in the presence of later stress events.
6. They may alter the individual's self-concept or attitudes or cognitive set, which then in turn influence the response to later situations.
7. Finally, they may have an impact on later behavior through effects on the selection of environments or on the opening up or closing down of opportunities.

These issues all have relevance to the topic of depression. Thus, Brown and Harris' (1978) concept of vulnerability factors in the genesis of adult depressive disorder suggests that the loss of mother in childhood predisposes to depressive conditions in adult life. Their theory does not suggest any direct connection between early loss and depression, but rather hypothesizes the development of a particular cognitive set, involving low self-esteem, that makes it more likely that the individual will develop depression following later stresses, but only if such stresses occur. In other words, the postulated developmental process concerns self-perception and social cognition and not altered affect as such. At present, the suggested process remains speculative; there is circumstantial evidence that makes it plausible but so far it lacks direct verification. The point here is that any adequate testing of this theory requires developmental research that goes well beyond the topic of affective disturbance in childhood.

Of course, the developmental precursors of adult disorders need not lie at all in the field of external stressors. The case of schizophrenia provides a good illustration (see Rutter & Garmezy, 1983). It has been found that about half the cases of adult schizophrenia have been preceded by nonpsychotic abnormalities in childhood. These abnormalities were not schizophrenic in form, nor were they recognizable as prepsychotic at the time. Nevertheless, the continuities over time make clear that the disturbances of emotions, behavior, and relationships in childhood did indeed represent the beginnings of the schizophrenic process—whatever that may be. Other research has emphasized the importance of a particular type of attentional deficit as a precursor of schizophrenia. The understanding of these atypical developmental processes is dependent on a knowledge of the outcome in adult life. Any study of child development that stops when physical maturity is reached is a peculiarly limited kind of developmental psychology.

In arguing that a developmental perspective is necessary in adult as well as in child psychiatry, it is not, of course, suggested that all adult disorders have their origins in childhood, nor that psychiatric conditions arising during the years of adulthood can only be understood by reference to the process of development as it took place during the early years (Rutter, 1980a). Far from it. It is evident that many mental illnesses arise for reasons that have little to do with happenings during childhood. Nevertheless, that is of interest in its own right. A developmental perspective must take account of continuities and discontinuities between childhood and adult life. The empirical data make clear that both occur (Rutter, 1983).

Moreover, it should not be thought that development comes to a halt with the ending of childhood. Of course, physical maturation in the strict sense does cease. On the other hand, physical growth following injury does not. Even the central nervous system (CNS) shows some cellular proliferation and the sprouting of neuronal axons following damage to the brain in adult life (Lynch & Gall, 1979; van Hof, 1981). This "rewiring" of the brain after trauma is much more marked in early childhood than at maturity but it does occur to some extent even in adults. Nevertheless, this plasticity of functioning with the continuing potential for some new development does not necessarily facilitate functional recovery (Rutter, 1982a)—the "rewiring" is just as likely to lead to abnormal neuronal connections as to the restoration of normal networks.

Also, it would be unduly limited to regard development solely in terms of physical growth. It is clear from other evidence that important changes in psychological development take place well after childhood has been left behind. For example, this was apparent in our own prospective study of girls reared in institutions in which they were followed into their mid-20s (Quinton, Rutter, & Liddle, 1984; Rutter et al., 1983). Not surprisingly, adverse experiences in childhood were associated with substantially worse psychosocial outcomes in early adult life. However, it was also found that marriage to (or a stable cohabitation with) a well-functioning man who provided a supportive relationship was associated with a marked improvement in functioning. Good experiences in adult life can lead to important psychosocial gains. The study of development, then, must encompass both continuities and discontinuities and also the developmental processes as they occur in adult life as well as in childhood.

Psychopathological Issues

The word "psychopathology" emphasizes a rather different facet of the perspective to be followed. Developmental psychologists tend to assume an essential continuity in functioning so that, for example, severe depressive feelings would be regarded as on the same continuum as "normal" sadness or unhappiness, with both extending to equable mood and on to cheerfulness and happy feelings. Clinical psychiatrists, in contrast, tend to study "conditions" or "disorders," so that there is the implicit assumption of discontinuity, with illness on one side of the demarcation line and normality on the other. Of course, both viewpoints may be valid in different circumstances. Doubtless, there are frank mental illnesses that are qualitatively distinct from normality. Equally, it is clear that many disorders in people referred to psychiatric clinics represent no more than quantitative departures from a health state. The use of the term "psychopathology" means that there is no prior assumption that either must be the case. Rather, the central interest concerns both the connections and the lack of connections between normality and disorder. The focus is on both the parallels between the normal processes of adaptation and change on the one hand, and "abnormal" responses to stress, trauma, or adversity on the other; and on the discontinuities between the two.

These issues are particularly critical in the study of depression. Epidemiological studies of the adult general population have produced prevalence rates for depressive conditions varying from 2% to 25% (Eastwood & Kramer, 1981), with the differences largely explicable in terms of variations in the criteria used in deciding what is a "case." Tennant and Bebbington (1978) have criticized the Brown and Harris (1978) work on the grounds (among other criticisms) that their concept of depression in community samples is not the same as depressive illness as seen in psychiatric hospital practice. Similarly, Clayton and her colleagues have argued that although bereavement is associated with depressed mood, sleep disturbance, anorexia, and loss of concentration (Clayton, Halikas, & Maurice, 1972), nevertheless grief is different from clinical affective *illness* and should not constitute a model for this illness (Bornstein, Clayton, Halikas, Maurice, & Robins, 1973). Or again, Link and Dohrenwend (1980) prefer to separate what they term "demoralization" from clinical depression. But what is the difference between "normal" depression and "abnormal" depressive illness? Indeed, what is meant by the very concept of "disease"?

Valiant attempts have been made to provide criteria for diseases in the field of psychiatry (see Kendall, 1975; Taylor, 1979; Wing, Bebbington, & Robins, 1981) but it cannot be said that any of them is entirely satisfactory. Sometimes it is assumed that this is a problem peculiar to psychiatry, which is not shared by other branches of medicine. Equally, sometimes it is thought that psychiatric classifications differ from psychological class-ifications in their reliance on a disease model and on categorical, rather than dimensional, distinctions. However, both assumptions are false. Scad-ding (1980, 1982), arguing from the perspective of respiratory disease and internal medicine, has shown clearly that the same issues apply there, even with diseases known to be caused by some specific etiological agent. Is tuberculosis to be regarded as present when there is a positive tuberculin reaction, when the mycobacterium has been isolated, or when there are clinically detectable signs and symptoms of illness? Similarly, chronic bronchitis and emphysema constitute categorical disease categories but much research has shown that chronic respiratory disease may more usefully be considered in dimensional terms (Fletcher, Peto, Tinker, & Speizer, 1976). Almost certainly, the search for a "unified concept of disease" will prove to be unprofitable.

Accordingly, we have no ready means by which to decide which types of depression constitute quantitative variations from normality and which represent qualitatively distinct disease entities. The psychopathologist seeks to capitalize on these difficulties by making the empirical study of the "gray area" between normal sadness and psychotic depression as the main focus of interest. Are the two linked and, if so, how? To what extent are the mechanisms similar or different and do they vary according to develop-mental level? These issues are far from resolved in adult psychiatry and they have only just begun to be explored in child psychiatry.

As noted in the beginning of this chapter, the third feature specifies a concern for the effects of developmental features on psychopathology and conversely for the effects of psychopathology on development. The first rubric would include, for example, age-dependent susceptibilities to stress, age-differentiated forms of response to adversity, or age-determined pat-terns of psychopathology. The second rubric emphasizes the need to ex-amine the ways in which psychopathology of varied types may be associ-ated with impairments or distortions in the normal course of psychosocial development.

As we shall see, social scientists, clinicians, and biologically oriented investigators have begun to turn their attention to the syndrome of depression as it occurs in childhood. As a result of their research, evidence is accumulating on the reality of the phenomenon and on some of the parallels with depressive conditions in adult life. The resulting increase in knowledge is both theoretically important and practically useful. However, it is not sufficient to know that depression somewhat similar to that which occurs in adult life may arise in childhood. Nor is it sufficient to identify the biological and psychosocial origins of childhood depression. The adjective "developmental" in the term "developmental psychopathology" demands that we ask other and different questions. Insofar as there are differences between childhood and adult life in the frequency of depression and in the manner of its presentation, why do these differences occur? What mechanisms and processes provide an explanation of the developmental changes that take place? So far, these crucial developmental questions have been rather neglected. However, it is that neglect and the need to fill the gap that constitutes the main justification for this volume. The main goals comprise the delineation of knowledge on the developmental psychopathology of depression where it exists, the determination of the key issues that constitute the most important challenges of the moment, and the identification of the research avenues that most need to be explored in the future.

With these general considerations in mind, some of the specific issues that arise in applying the developmental psychopathology perspective to the study of depressive feelings and depressive disorders in childhood may be considered. This discussion does not focus primarily either on the normal developmental course of affective expression or on depressive disorders as such as they appear in clinical practice. Both issues are important but, as they are discussed in other chapters, most attention is paid here to the interface between the two.

AGE CHANGES IN DEPRESSIVE FEELINGS
AND DISORDERS

It is appropriate to concentrate on the important age changes that occur in the frequency and sex ratio of depressive feelings and depressive disorders and related conditions. There are obvious difficulties in the assessment of depression in young children because of their limited ability to describe the emotions they are feeling. This is so with any emotion (as the feeling state and its personal meaning to the individual are essential components), but some (such as fear) can be fairly readily identified on the basis of facial expression, behavior, and autonomic activity (Ekman & Friesen, 1978; Izard, 1982). Depression is particularly difficult because it is generally held to involve not only misery and unhappiness (which perhaps may be observed), but also a lowering of vigor and energy, a sense of rejection (Sandler & Joffe, 1965), and a negative self-image (Poznanski & Zrull, 1970). Empirical studies have shown that psychiatrists find it more difficult to agree on ratings of depression than on those of anxiety (Rutter & Graham, 1968), this being especially so with intellectually dull, unresponsive, or uncommunicative children. Even with adolescents, it has been found that parents and teachers frequently fail to notice depression, even when the young people themselves report quite severe depressive (even suicidal) feelings at a personal psychiatric interview (Rutter, Graham, Chadwick, & Yule, 1976). It is apparent that there are substantial methodological problems in the study of age changes in depressive feelings, but also that an interview with the child (or some other form of self-report) is likely to constitute an essential element in any adequate assessment. Nevertheless, in spite of these difficulties, it is clear that important changes occur around the time of puberty.

Depressive Feelings in the General Population

For example, in the Isle of Wight general population study of 10- to 11-year-old children (Rutter, Tizard, & Whitmore, 1970/1981), 13% showed a depressed mood at interview, 9% appeared preoccupied with depressive topics, 17% failed to smile, and 15% showed poor emotional responsiveness. On the parent and teacher questionnaires, too, about 10–12% of children were said to be very miserable. The same children were reassessed at age 14–15 years with very different findings (Rutter, 1979/1980; Rutter et al., 1976), depressive feelings being considerably more prevalent (see Fig. 1). Over 40% of the adolescents reported substantial feelings of misery and depression during a psychiatric interview, 20% expressed feelings of self-depreciation, 7–8% reported that they had suicidal feelings, and 25% described ideas of reference. Self-ratings on a questionnaire gave much the same picture, and also showed that depressive feelings were more frequent in the adolescents than in their parents. Thus, it is necessary to explain both a rise in depressive feelings during early adolescence and also a fall in early adult life.

Because boys at age 14–15 years include both those who are prepubescent and those who have passed puberty, it was possible in this study to relate the frequency of depressive feelings to the stage of puberty within a group of similar age (Rutter, 1979/1980). It was striking that scarcely any of the 19 prepubescent boys showed depressive feelings, whereas about one-third of the 19 post-pubertal boys did so—the 45 pubescent boys were intermediate on all measures. Whether this surprisingly strong association with puberty was a function of endocrine changes, psychological responses to sexual maturation, or indeed some other influence remains unknown.

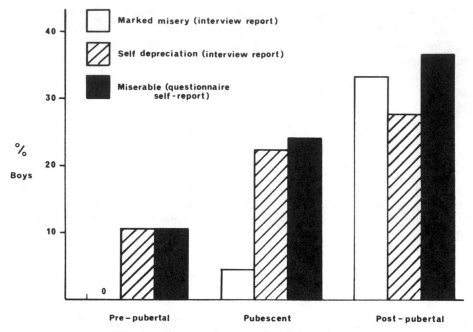

Fig. 1. *Depressive feelings and stage of puberty.*

Unfortunately, no comparable data are available for girls (virtually all the girls were postpubertal by 14–15 years) and it is not known if the same would apply. Nevertheless, it is obvious that further exploration of the possible links between puberty and depressive feelings is indicated.

Depressive Disorders

The same study on the Isle of Wight provided evidence on overt depressive conditions. Psychiatric disorder was diagnosed on the basis of abnormal psychological functioning associated with persisting social impairment or handicap (Rutter *et al.*, 1970/1981). All cases of disorder (diagnosed on the basis of systematic information from parents, teachers, and the young people themselves) were further classified according to type, using a simplified psychiatric classification appropriate to general population usage. At age 10 years there were only three cases of depressive disorder in a sample of some 2000 children. In sharp contrast, at age 14–15 years there were nine cases of "pure" depressive disorder and a further 26 cases of mixed affective disorder—a huge increase (Rutter, 1979/1980; Rutter *et al.*, 1976). These overall depressive disorders in adolescence were much more frequent in girls than in boys.

Clinic data provide a similar picture. For example, J. Pearce (1978, personal communication, 1982), in an investigation of 547 children who first attended the Maudsley Hospital during the years 1968 and 1969 found that whereas only one in nine prepubertal children showed depressive symptomatology, about one-quarter of postpubertal children did so—a more than twofold increase in rate. However, the marked change in sex ratio that took place across the period of puberty was equally striking (see Fig. 2). Among the prepubertal children depressive symptoms were twice as common in boys, whereas after puberty they were twice as common in girls. As these data were based on codings made at the time (and recorded on punch cards) by a diverse group of clinicians none of whom had any particular interest in depression, it is most unlikely that the swing during adolescence from a male preponderance to a female preponderance in depressive symptomatology was due to any kind of rating bias.

Most other studies of depression in children and adolescents either fail to report whether the sex ratio alters with age (Kuperman & Stewart, 1979),

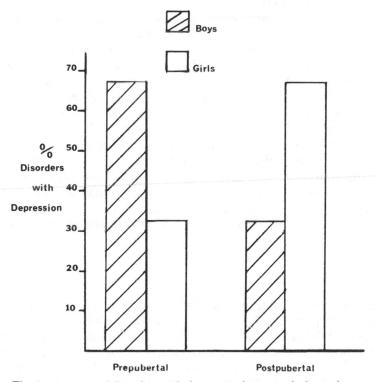

Fig. 2. *Sex ratio of disorders with depression before and after puberty.*

or describe changes in terms of age rather than sexual maturity (Carlson & Cantwell, 1980; G. A. Carlson & D. P. Cantwell, personal communication, 1980). This general preference for age indicators rather than physiological maturity indicators is regrettable both because of the evidence (already discussed) that puberty may constitute the key transition variable and because the two variables are hopelessly confounded in studies of early adolescence when most of the girls are likely to be pubertal but most of the boys prepubertal because of the substantially later onset of puberty in boys. Even so, such evidence as there is (e.g., Albert & Beck, 1975; G. A. Carlson & D. P. Cantwell, personal communication, 1980) tends to support the finding of an increase in depressive disorders and a change in sex ratio during adolescence for such disorders (although not necessarily for depressive feelings unconnected with any overall disorder).

Mania

Much less is known regarding age changes in the occurrence of mania or bipolar manic–depressive disorders, and there are no systematic data on prevalence at different stages of childhood and adolescence. Nevertheless, although claims have been made that mania may be more frequent in childhood than usually thought (Weinberg & Brumback, 1976), most reports of studies of children (Anthony & Scott, 1960; Lowe & Cohen, 1980) as well as retrospective histories of adults with bipolar affective illness (Loranger & Levine, 1978) suggest that mania rarely occurs before puberty, although it becomes more frequent during the midteens (Hassanyeh & Davison, 1980). It seems then that a further change in adolescence constitutes the more frequent appearance of mania. It remains uncertain whether this observation means that bipolar disorders usually begin after puberty although unipolar disorders more often have an earlier onset; that bipolar disorders can begin in childhood but that the manic component appears only during or after adolescence; or that mania occurs in childhood but takes a form different from that seen in adult life. However, whatever the explanation, it appears that some kind of change in the manifestation of mania occurs during adolescence.

Grief

Many writers have drawn parallels between grief and depression and Bowlby (1980), particularly, has argued that mourning has a central role in the genesis of depression. Accordingly, it is pertinent to enquire whether there are developmental changes in people's responses to bereavement. There is no one study that provides adequate and comparable general population data on the severity and persistence of grief reactions at different ages. Nevertheless, such data as are available (see Bowlby, 1980;

Kliman, 1968; Rutter, 1966; van Eerdewegh, Bieri, Parilla, & Clayton, 1982) are consistent in suggesting that immediate grief reactions are both milder and of shorter duration in young children compared with those in adolescents or adults. Usually it is suggested that the reasons for the age difference lie in the age-dependent variations in children's ability to conceptualize both the past and the meaning of death. This may be so, but the implication that children are therefore less affected by bereavement does not necessarily follow. Perhaps children have a more limited capacity to grieve or show depression in the manner typical of adults, but instead suffer in other ways. In that connection, it may be relevant that although the immediate grief reactions seem to be short-lived in younger children, the delayed consequences may actually be greater (Rutter, 1966). On the other hand, the evidence suggests that these long-term sequelae probably stem as much from factors consequent upon the death as from the death itself. These other factors include such hazards as the break-up of the home, frequent changes of caretaker, changes in family roles, financial and material disadvantage, the effects of bereavement on the surviving parent, and the arrival of a stepparent (Furman, 1974; Rutter, 1966). Once again, there is evidence of important age changes around the time of adolescence but also a lack of knowledge on what the changes mean or what mechanisms they reflect.

Suicide and Attempted Suicide

Studies in adults (Barraclough, Bunch, Nelson, & Sainsbury, 1974) have been consistent in indicating that most suicides occur in the context of psychiatric disorder, and that the most common diagnosis is depression. Hence, it might be thought that age differences in rates of suicide and attempted suicide should throw light on development progressions in affective disturbance. United States statistics show that suicide before age 12 years is excessively rare but that the rate rises rapidly during the midteens, from 0.06 per million below age 10 years, to 8 per million at 10–14 years, to 76 per million at 15–19 years—more than a 1000-fold increase (Eisenberg, 1980; Shaffer & Fisher, 1981)! British statistics show much the same (Shaffer, 1974).

On the other hand, it would be quite wrong to regard suicide as an adolescent phenomenon, as the rate continues to rise throughout life to reach a peak in old age (see Fig. 3). Hence, any explanation must account for both the extreme rarity of suicide before puberty (usually accounted for in terms of the infrequency of depression plus the protection of family support plus the lack of cognitive abilities required to plan a successful suicidal act (see Shaffer & Fisher, 1981), and also the continuing increase in rates of suicide that persists for the whole of adult life.

Attempted suicide, or parasuicide, is also relatively infrequent before

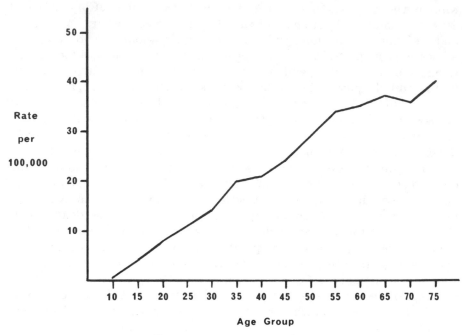

Fig. 3. *Suicide rates by age, 1966.*

puberty and shows the same massive increase during middle and later adolescence (Hawton & Goldacre, 1982). However, apart from that, the pattern is quite different in three key respects:

1. As shown in Fig. 4, the peak age is 15–19 years, with a progressive decline thereafter (Kreitman, 1977).
2. Whereas suicide is much more frequent in males, attempted suicide is far commoner in females.
3. It seems that attempted suicide is less likely than completed suicide to be associated with an overt depressive disorder (Hawton, O'Grady, Osborn, & Cole, 1982; Lumsden Walker, 1980).

It is obvious that something more than age changes in depressive disturbance must be invoked to account for the peak rate of parasuicide in late adolescence.

Age Differences in Historical Trends

The findings considered thus far all deal with age differences as shown at any one point in time. One further perspective needs to be added:

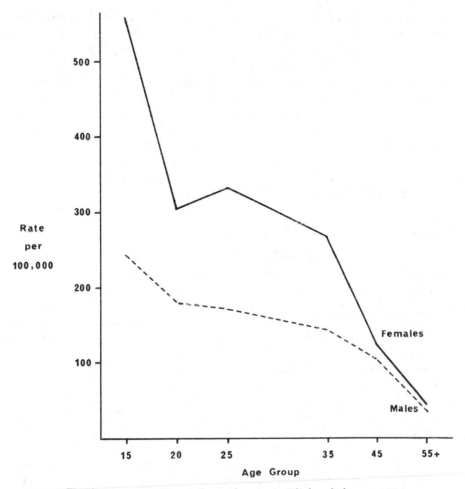

Fig. 4. *First-ever attempted suicide rates in Edinburgh, by age, 1974.*

namely, age differences in changing patterns over time. Such data are available only for suicide but these show a surprising picture (Rutter, 1979/1980). During the last few decades there has been a gradual but steady decline in the suicide rate for adults. Thus, in the U.K. the standardized mortality rate for male suicide fell from 117 in 1961 to 86 in 1976 and from 115 to 80 for female suicide during the same period (Central Statistical Office, 1978). However, the pattern for 15–19-year-olds has been quite different. In spite of a fall in other age groups, suicide in young people has continued to increase (Adelstein & Mardon, 1975), so that the suicide rate among adolescent girls has doubled over the last 20 years (Office of Population Censuses and Surveys, 1978). The pattern in the U.S. has been somewhat similar but the increase has included young adults as well as adolescents, so that Shaffer and Fisher (1981) have suggested that it represents a general "cohort" effect (i.e., one applying to people born since World War II) rather than an age-specific effect. It is too early to be able to decide between these two alternatives; but either way, it is clear that some explanation must be found for the observation that suicide rates in old people have been declining during the last two decades at the same time as suicide rates in adolescents and young adults have been increasing. It should be added that account must also be taken of the immense variations in suicide rates between different countries (Bakwin, 1957) such that, for example, the suicide rate among adolescent girls in Japan during the 1950s was more than 10 times that in the U.K. or the U.S.!

Depression during the Preschool Years

All the changes considered up to this point have concerned the adolescent age period, and it is necessary to ask whether changes in affective disturbance are evident also in earlier childhood. It is paradoxical that although more is known about affective and emotional development in the early years than in later childhood, the reverse applies to depressive disorder. Very few systematic data are available on developmental changes with respect to depression in early childhood.

Spitz (1946), in an influential paper, described "anaclitic depression" as a syndrome arising in institutionalized children about 6–12 months of age and characterized by weeping, withdrawal, apathy, weight loss, sleep disturbance, and a decrease in developmental quotient. The syndrome was attributed to the loss of a mother figure. Spitz' 1946 paper came under considerable methodological criticism (Pinneau, 1955), particularly with respect to the suggestion that the depression often led to death (it was argued by his critics that physical disease had not been taken into account) and to the suggestion that maternal loss led to developmental retardation. Nevertheless, the term and concept entered the literature and continue to be quoted in textbooks despite a paucity of other evidence on the validity of the syndrome. Emde, Harmon, and their colleagues (Emde, Plak, & Spitz, 1965; Harmon, Wagonfeld, & Emde, 1982) have provided one of the very few detailed clinical accounts of an apparently depressive syndrome in a young child—although their case concerned an institutional child who lacked a preexisting maternal bond. It seems from these accounts that depression *can* arise in infancy and early childhood but it seems equally probable that it is a relatively rare phenomenon—at least as compared with depression in later childhood or adolescence.

On the other hand, Spitz (1946) described it as a fairly common occurrence in institutional children; Freud and Burlingham (1974) in their wartime studies of children in the Hampstead nursery reported the frequency with which young children grieved for their absent mothers; and the Robertsons and Bowlby have documented the protest–despair–detachment sequence seen in many toddlers admitted to hospital or to a residential nursery (Bowlby, 1969, 1980). This seems to constitute an understandable response to the combination of loss of a loved person and the absence of personal parenting (it is much less likely to occur if the loss is not accompanied by a lack of personal parenting, even if this is provided by a stranger; Robertson & Robertson, 1971). However, it is questionable on two grounds whether this should be regarded as a depressive disorder: (1) it is a very common and apparently "natural" occurrence in young children placed in these circumstances; (2) the descriptions indicate that in most (but not all) cases rapid recovery tends to follow return to the family without the self-perpetuating autonomous course generally associated with an abnormal affective state. At least in some instances, it is evident that the syndrome does represent a significant disorder that is more than a transient response, solely reactive to environmental circumstances.

Whether or not it is the "same" as depression in later childhood and adolescence remains a matter of controversy. Yet, it can scarcely be disputed that it constitutes some form of affective response, which, at least in some children, can be relatively persistent and disabling. Insofar as that is the case, it poses further developmental questions, for the evidence indicates that this protest–despair–detachment sequence is most frequently seen between about 6 months and 4 years of age (Rutter, 1981a). Circumstantial evidence suggests that this age period of greatest risk is a consequence of two rather different factors (Rutter, 1981b). Children below the age of about 6 months are relatively immune because they have not yet developed enduring selective attachments and therefore are not able to experience the separation anxiety thought to underlie the syndrome. Children above the age of about 4 years, on the other hand, are less vulnerable probably because they have the cognitive skills needed to appreciate that separation does not necessarily mean abandonment or loss of a relationship and to understand better what is involved in hospitalization or admission to an institution.

However, if that is so, we have yet to account for the very different age trend for grief reactions following bereavement. Moreover, if loss is crucial to depression and if these syndromes in institutionalized children represent depressive disorders, as Bowlby (1980) has suggested, why does depression fall again in frequency during middle childhood only to rise once more in adolescence? Perhaps these infantile disorders are not the same as depression in later life, in which case it may be that different explanations are required for the changes during the preschool years and those during adolescence.

Possible Explanations for Developmental Changes

Although we still have much to learn regarding developmental progressions and changes in the expression of depressive feelings and in the manifestations of depressive disorder, it is apparent already that there are some reasonably well-documented phenomena that require explanation. This overview has highlighted three phases of transition: (1) that occurring toward the middle of the first year of life when infants first begin to manifest the protest–despair–detachment sequence following admission to hospital or some other institution; (2) the phase about age 4 or 5 years when this response becomes both less frequent and less intense; and (3) the period of puberty, which is characterized by a sharp rise in depressive feelings and disorder and by a change in the sex ratio of affective disorders. Also, adolescence is accompanied by a massive increase in the frequency of suicide and parasuicide and probably, too, by an intensification of grief reactions following bereavement and by a rise in the occurrence of mania. This third phase has been least researched from a developmental perspective and poses the greatest challenges. Other chapters provide data and ideas that deal with the issues in greater detail. However, this discussion of age changes may be concluded by briefly noting a few of the possible types of developmental changes that require consideration in any determination of the mechanisms that underlie this third phase (see Gove & Tudor, 1973; Radloff, 1975; Rutter, 1970, 1979/1980, 1980c; Weissman & Klerman, 1977).

The fact that the phase seems to coincide with puberty immediately raises the possibility that hormonal changes are responsible for the rise in depression and the reversal of the sex ratio. There are various pointers suggesting that sex hormones may have an impact on affect. For example, there is the well-documented substantial increase in psychiatric disorder during the puerperium (Kendell, Wainwright, Hailey, & Shannon, 1976); the irritability and depression experienced by many women during the premenstrual phase (Dalton, 1977; Kessel & Coppen, 1963; Sommer, 1978); and the rather inconsistent and contradictory evidence that, in a few women (but not most), oral contraceptives may predispose to depression (see Fleming & Seager, 1978; Weissman & Klerman, 1977). The findings on hormonal effects do not lead to any clear-cut implications for affective change, but it is possible that the hormonal changes experienced by girls at puberty may have emotional consequences.

Genetic factors, too, require consideration. Certainly, there is reasonably good evidence for the existence of a hereditary component in affective disorders, although both the mode of inheritance and what is inherited remain matters for dispute and controversy (see, e.g., Baron, Klotz, Mendlewicz, & Rainer, 1981; Jakimow-Venulet, 1981; Kidd & Weissman,

1978). But how could genetic factors explain the change in sex ratio and the rise in frequency of depressive disorders during adolescence? Several possibilities immediately present themselves. Perhaps the disorders arising after puberty differ genetically from those with an onset in childhood—a possibility suggested by the apparent increase in mania during adolescence. Thus, it could be that bipolar disorders rarely develop before puberty (of course, the occurrence of genetic disorders that do not become manifest until middle life is well-established—Huntington's chorea being the most obvious example of this kind). However, not only is there continuing uncertainty on whether unipolar and bipolar affective disorders are genetically distinct (Baron et al., 1981), but also they do not seem to differ markedly in sex distribution (Depue & Monroe, 1978). Another possibility is that the affective disorders of childhood are more often reactive to environmental adversity or stress whereas those of adult life have a stronger genetic component. In this connection, it may be relevant that psychiatric disorders in girls are less obviously associated with family disturbance than are those of boys (Rutter, 1970), and that disorders arising during adolescence do not have the clear associations with environmental difficulties seen with disorders beginning earlier in childhood (Rutter et al., 1976). Also, although the evidence is fragmentary and inconclusive, it may be that antidepressant medication is less effective with children and adolescents than it is with adults (Kramer & Feiguine, 1981; Puig-Antich, 1980). However, the findings on the importance of acute stresses in the precipitation of adult depression (Brown & Harris, 1978) make this a somewhat dubious explanation; moreover, although we have no systematic data on the importance of genetic factors in childhood depression, several studies have pointed to the heavy family loading of depressive disorders (see Puig-Antich, 1980).

A third type of explanation for the affective changes at puberty concerns possible alterations in the frequency of environmental stressors. Insofar as depression in adult life often follows acute stressors (Brown & Harris, 1978), perhaps the "loss" types of stressor most strongly associated with depression (Finlay-Jones & Brown, 1981) become more prevalent in adult life than they were in childhood. Certainly the possibility warrants exploration, but so far we have no satisfactory data on age changes in the frequency of stress events; indeed, we lack good data altogether on the importance of stress factors in childhood and on whether the events most stressful in adult life are also those most stressful during the earlier years (Rutter, 1981b). However, if changes in stressors are to be postulated as the explanation, it will be necessary to find a means to account for the change in sex ratio. Do women experience more stressors than men, whereas girls and boys do not differ in their exposure to loss events? Or, during adolescence, is there a sex-linked change in people's perception of stress

(Burke & Weir, 1978)? Or does puberty mark a change in vulnerability to stress, a change that is greater in females than males?

A fourth kind of explanatory hypothesis might invoke developmental variations in the availability of either vulnerability (Brown & Harris, 1978) or protective factors (Rutter, 1981b; Tennant, Bebbington, & Hurry, 1981). Perhaps the attenuations of family support associated with leaving home and becoming independent make older adolescents and young adults more susceptible to stress. Perhaps, too, women are more prone to depression whereas girls are not, because on reaching adulthood females experience disadvantages that were not operative during the years of childhood (Gove & Tudor, 1973). In this connection, it may be relevant that whereas marriage serves as a protective factor for men it does not seem to do so for women (see Rutter, 1970; Weissman & Klerman, 1977). Also, there is evidence that, at least among working-class women in inner-city areas, the risk of depression is associated with having to remain at home to look after dependent children (Brown & Harris, 1978). Moreover, paid employment outside the home may also be protective, with this lacking for many mothers of young children (Bebbington, Hurry, Tennant, Sturt, & Wing, 1981; Brown & Harris, 1978)—although the protection may well depend on both the nature of the work and the satisfaction it brings as well as on the extent of personal work involvement (Parry, 1982; Warr, 1982). That these factors play a part seems plausible but it is unlikely that they can account for the change in rate and sex ratio of depression among young people still at school.

A fifth reason suggested for the change in sex ratio of depression during adolescence concerns the possible role of cognitive sets associated with "learned helplessness" (Abramson, Seligman, & Teasdale, 1978). Whereas boys tend to respond with greater efforts when they receive feedback from adults that they are failing, girls are more likely to give up and attribute their failure to their own lack of ability (Dweck & Bush, 1976). One of the reasons for girls being more likely to give up seems to be in the sex-differentiated pattern of feedback from adults. Dweck, Davidson, Nelson, and Enna (1978) found that teachers were more critical of boys than girls but also that they were more critical of boys in a diffuse way, which could readily be perceived as irrelevant to their intellectual performance. In contrast, almost all criticisms of girls referred specifically to their intellectual failings. Conversely, positive feedback tended to be work specific for boys but diffuse for girls. The pattern is one likely to increase girls' tendency to feel that they cannot succeed. The increasing experience of feedback of this kind may lead girls to show an increase in "learned helplessness" during the later years of childhood and adolescence—an increase less evident in boys. The potential importance of this change lies in the evidence that experience with events felt to be outside one's control (learned helplessness) may predispose a person to depression.

Developmental changes in children's attributional capabilities may also play a part in the rise in the rate of depression during adolescence (Rholes, Blackwell, Jordan, & Walters, 1980). It seems that younger children may be less susceptible to feelings of helplessness because they do not view failure as implying a stable and lasting limitation on their performance. Although an awareness of standards and distress over failure to meet them develops during the preschool years (Kagan, 1981), it may be the cognitive component required for a pervasive sense of helplessness and hopelessness are a much later development.

Finally, explanations may be expressed in terms of developmental changes in children's concepts of emotions and in their ability to express affect, to be aware of emotions in others and to appreciate the emotional connotations of social situations (Chandler, 1977; Harris, Olthof, & Terwogt, 1981). Doubtless, all these changes are relevant to developmental progressions in the manifestations of depressive feelings but it is not readily apparent why they should lead to alterations in the frequency of depression at puberty, for the greatest developmental changes in emotional concepts and cognition appear in early and middle childhood. Nor is it obvious why they should lead to a shift in sex ratio.

There are many possible domains of explanation to be explored in attempts to account for age and sex changes in depression (those mentioned do not exhaust the possibilities), but it remains uncertain which will prove to be the most valid. It is all too clear that our understanding of the developmental mechanisms remains incomplete.

DEVELOPMENTAL CONTINUITIES IN DEPRESSION

The last issue to mention concerns the important, but very little studied, question of developmental continuities in depression. What is the course of childhood depression; does the occurrence of depression have implications for personality development; do depressed children become depressed adults? These are not easy questions to answer, for a variety of reasons, but perhaps the most immediate problem concerns the diagnosis and definition of depressive syndromes. Should they be defined solely in terms of the presence of severe and persistent depressive symptomatology, or should the presence or absence of other forms of disturbance also be taken into account? The question arises most strikingly in terms of the substantial overlap with conduct disorder. Whereas other types of emotional problems (such as anxiety, phobias, and obsessions) are relatively infrequent in children with conduct disturbances, depression is as common as it is in those with "pure" emotional disorders (Rutter et al., 1970/1981). The overlap was also apparent in Puig-Antich's in-patient studies of severely depressed children. For example, all five depressed boys aged over 10 years in one of their first reports presented disturbances of conduct with fire-setting, lying, and stealing (Puig-Antich, Blau, Marx, Greenhill, & Chambers, 1978). In their latest paper (Puig-Antich, 1982) based on 43 cases of major depression in prepubertal boys, one-third also met the DSM-III criteria for conduct disorder. Of the 13 boys with depression and a conduct disorder who showed a full response to antidepressant medication, 11 lost their conduct disturbance. However, it appears that the disturbed peer relations did not remit with the restoration of normal mood (Puig-Antich & Gittelman, 1982). The findings imply that in some cases conduct disturbance may arise as a result of depression, but how often is this the case and can the association arise the other way round?

Knowledge of the adult outcome of depressive disorders in childhood is much needed, but remains lacking. Dahl (1972) reported, in her long-term follow-up, that very few children with psychiatric disorder go on to develop manic–depressive psychosis. However, that observation does not take us very far, since depressive conditions in childhood were not identified as a separate group and because manic–depressive psychosis is, in any case, a relatively uncommon disorder even in adulthood (it accounts for only a minority of cases of depression). Zeitlin's (1972, 1985) studies are rather more informative. He investigated a group of individuals who had been under psychiatric care at the Maudsley Hospital in London, England, as both children and adults. The focus, therefore, was on continuities and discontinuities in the form of disorder—rather than on whether disorder persisted. However, for purposes of comparison, he had a group of children who had not reattended as adults and a group of adults whose disorders had begun in adult life. He found that many cases of adult depression were not preceded by any form of disorder in childhood.

Moreover, when adult depression had been preceded by psychiatric problems in childhood, in only a few cases were the disorders predominantly depressive. Conversely, of the children diagnosed as depressive (using Pearce's, 1974, operational criteria) most were not diagnosed as suffering from depression in adult life. On the other hand, when depression was diagnosed in both childhood and adult life solely in terms of operational criteria based on the presence of specified symptoms of affective disturbance, surprisingly high continuity was found. Thus, there were 37 cases of childhood depression on Pearce's criteria, 31 of which met the criteria for a depressive syndrome in adult life! This link between childhood depression and adult depression was highly significant and showed a strength of continuity rivaled only by obsessional symptomatology. However, we need to ask why this continuity was not apparent when the clinical diagnoses made at the time were employed. The answer is that in most cases the people had *other* symptoms of a nondepressive variety, and often these so dominated the clinical picture that depression was not diagnosed.

Zeitlin's findings are reasonably clear-cut, but the inferences to be drawn from them are not. Do the results imply that depressive disorders are better diagnosed entirely in terms of the presence of depressive symptomatology, irrespective of the rest of the clinical picture? Or, rather, do the findings mean that the depressive feelings represent a style of response to life crises that is better considered in personality terms rather than illness categorizations? The evidence to decide between these (and other) alternatives is not available. Clearly, it would be helpful to know what happens to the supposedly nondepressive symptoms (such as enuresis, fire-setting, aggression, and delinquency) when the depression remits (Rutter, 1972). If a depressive illness is supposed to be primary, presumably when the person ceases to be depressed the other problems ought to diminish in parallel. But do they? Unfortunately, apart from Puig-Antich's (1982) study of conduct disturbance in depressed children, the published studies do not provide data on this crucial point. The few snippets of available information on developmental continuities in depressive feelings raise tantalizing issues but further research is needed for their resolution.

IMPLICATIONS AND ISSUES

This brief overview of some of the most outstanding age changes in the frequency and sex ratio of depressive feelings and disorders, of course, provides but one crude index of developmental progressions in affective expression and disturbance. Quite deliberately, I have not attempted to review the course of affective development during childhood; nor have I sought to consider clinical studies of affective disease in childhood. Rather, my purpose has been to take just a few aspects of affective psychopathology in order to highlight the crucial developmental issues that they present. It is not enough to extend adult concepts downward into childhood (Achenbach, 1974), nor is it enough to consider disorders during the preadolescent years sui generis. Adult concepts may be applicable to the early years and, equally, it may be that disorders in childhood will prove to have their own distinctive features. Nevertheless, the perspective of developmental psychopathology requires that the questions to be posed include those concerning reasons for age differences in frequency, pattern, or manifestation; and those referring to continuities and discontinuities across age periods. The answering of such questions necessitates that knowledge of affective development and affective disorders be linked with that of other developmental phenomena. It is that need for linking that provides both the agenda and justification for this volume.

REFERENCES

Abramson, L. Y., Seligman, M. E. P., & Teasdale, J. D. (1978). Learned helplessness in humans: Critique and reformulation. *Journal of Abnormal Psychology, 87,* 49–74.

Achenbach, T. M. (1974). *Developmental psychopathology.* New York: Ronald Press.

Achenbach, T. M. (1978). Psychopathology of childhood: Research problems and issues. *Journal of Consulting and Clinical Psychology, 46,* 759–776.

Adelstein, A., & Mardon, C. (1975). Suicides 1961–74. *Population Trends, 2,* 13–18.

Albert, N., & Beck, A. T. (1975). Incidence of depression in early adolescence: A preliminary study. *Journal of Youth and Adolescence, 4,* 301–307.

Anthony, J., & Scott, P. (1960). Manic–depressive psychosis in childhood. *Journal of Child Psychology and Psychiatry, 1,* 53–72.

Bakwin, H. (1957). Suicide in children and adolescents. *Journal of Pediatrics, 50,* 749–769.

Baltes, P. B., & Brim, O. G., Jr. (Eds.). (1979). *Life-span development and behavior* (Vol. 2.). New York & London: Academic Press, 1979.

Baron, M., Klotz, J., Mendlewicz, J., & Rainer, J. (1981). Multiple-threshold transmission of affective disorders. *Archives of General Psychiatry, 38,* 79–84.

Barraclough, B., Bunch, J., Nelson, B., & Sainsbury, P. (1974). A hundred cases of suicide: Clinical aspects. *British Journal of Psychiatry, 125,* 355–373.

Bebbington, P., Hurry, J., Tennant, C., Sturt, E., & Wing, J. K. (1981). Epidemiology of mental disorders in Camberwell. *Psychological Medicine, 11,* 561–580.

Bornstein, P. E., Clayton, P. J., Halikas, J. A., Maurice, W. L., & Robins, E. (1973). The depression of widowhood after thirteen months. *British Journal of Psychiatry, 122,* 561–566.

Bowlby, J. (1969). *Attachment and loss: I. Attachment.* London: Hogarth Press.

Bowlby, J. (1980). *Attachment and loss: III. Loss, sadness and depression.* New York: Basic Books.

Brown, G. W., & Harris, T. (1978). *Social origins of depression.* London: Tavistock.

Burke, R. J., & Weir, T. (1978). Sex differences in adolescent life stress, social support and well-being. *Journal of Psychology, 98,* 277–288.

Carlson, G. A., & Cantwell, D. P. (1980). A survey of depressive symptoms, syndrome and disorder in a child psychiatric population. *Journal of Child Psychology and Psychiatry, 21,* 19–25.

Central Statistical Office. (1978). *Social Trends* (No. 9). London: H. M. Stationery Office.

Chandler, M. J. (1977). Social cognition: A selective review of current research. In W. F. Overton & J. M. Gallagher (Eds.), *Knowledge and development: Vol. 1. Advances in research and theory* (pp. 93–147). New York & London: Plenum Press.

Clayton, P. J., Halikas, J. A., & Maurice, W. L. (1972). The depression of widowhood. *British Journal of Psychiatry, 120,* 71–78.

Dahl, V. (1972). A follow-up study of child psychiatric clientele with special regard to manic-depressive psychosis. In A. Annell (Ed.), *Depressive states in childhood and adolescence* (Proceedings of the 4th UEP Congress, Stockholm, 1971) (pp. 534–541). Stockholm: Almqvist & Wiksell.

Dalton, K. (1977). *The premenstrual syndrome and progesterone therapy.* London: Heinemann Medical.

Depue, R. A., & Monroe, S. M. (1978). The unipolar-bipolar distinction in the depressive disorders. *Psychological Bulletin, 85,* 1001–1029.

Dweck, C. S., & Bush, E. S. (1976). Sex differences in learned helplessness. I. Differential debilitation with peer and adult evaluators. *Developmental Psychology, 12,* 147–156.

Dweck, C. S., Davidson, W., Nelson, S., & Enna, B. (1978). Sex differences in learned helplessness. II. The contingencies of evaluative feedback in the classroom. III. An experimental analysis. *Developmental Psychology, 14,* 268–276.

Eastwood, M. R., & Kramer, P. M. (1981). Epidemiology and depression. *Psychological Medicine, 11,* 229–234.

Eisenberg, L. (1977). Development as a unifying concept in psychiatry. *British Journal of Psychiatry, 131,* 225–237.

Eisenberg, L. (1980). Adolescent suicide: On taking arms against a sea of troubles. *Pediatrics, 66,* 315–320.

Ekman, P., & Friesen, W. V. (1978). *The facial action coding system (FACS).* Palo Alto, CA: Consulting Psychologists Press.

Emde, R. N., Plak, P. R., & Spitz, R. A. (1965). Anaclitic depression in an infant raised in an institution. *Journal of the American Academy of Child Psychiatry, 4,* 545–553.

Finlay-Jones, R., & Brown, G. W. (1981). Types of stressful life events and the onset of anxiety and depressive disorders. *Psychological Medicine, 11,* 803–816.

Fleming, O., & Seager, C. P. (1978). Incidence of depressive symptoms in users of the oral contraceptive. *British Journal of Psychiatry, 132,* 431–440.

Fletcher, C., Peto, R., Tinker, C., & Speizer, F. E. (1976). *The natural history of chronic bronchitis and emphysema.* London & New York: Oxford University Press.

Freud, A., & Burlingham, D. (1974). *Infants without families and reports on the Hampstead Nurseries, 1939–1945.* London: Hogarth Press.

Furman, E. (1974). *A child's parent dies: Studies in childhood bereavement.* New Haven, CT: Yale University Press.

Gove, W. R., & Tudor, J. F. (1973). Adult sex roles and mental illness. *American Journal of Sociology, 78,* 812–835.

Harmon, R. J., Wagonfeld, S., & Emde, R. N. (1982). Anaclitic depression: A follow-up from infancy to puberty. *Psychoanalytic Study of the Child, 37,* 67–94.

Harris, P. L., Olthof, T., & Terwogt, M. M. (1981). Children's knowledge of emotion. *Journal of Child Psychology and Psychiatry, 22,* 247–262.

Hassanyeh, F., & Davison, K. (1980). Bipolar affective psychosis with onset before age 16 years: Report of 10 cases. *British Journal of Psychiatry, 137,* 530–539.

Hawton, K., & Goldacre, M. (1982). Hospital admissions for adverse effects of medicinal agents (mainly self-poisoning) among adolescents in the Oxford region. *British Journal of Psychiatry, 141,* 166–170.

Hawton, K., O'Grady, J., Osborn, M., & Cole, D. (1982). Adolescents who take overdoses: Their characteristics, problems and contacts with helping agencies. *British Journal of Psychiatry, 140,* 118–123.

Izard, C. E. (Ed.). (1982). *Measuring emotions in infants and children.* London & New York: Cambridge University Press.

Jakimow-Venulet, B. (1981). Hereditary factors in the pathogenesis of affective illness. *British Journal of Psychiatry, 139,* 450–456.

Kagan, J. (1981). *The second year.* Cambridge, MA: Harvard University Press.

Kagan, J., Kearsley, R. B., & Zelazo, P. R. (1978). *Infancy: Its place in human development.* Cambridge, MA: Harvard University Press.

Kendell, R. E. (1975). *The role of diagnosis in psychiatry.* Oxford: Blackwell Scientific Publications.

Kendell, R. E., Wainwright, S., Hailey, A., & Shannon, B. (1976). The influence of child birth on psychiatric morbidity. *Psychological Medicine, 6,* 297–302.

Kessel, N., & Coppen, A. (1963). The prevalence of common menstrual symptoms. *Lancet, 2,* 61–64.

Kidd, K. K., & Weissman, M. M. (1978). Why we do not yet understand the genetics of affective disorders. In J. O. Cole, A. F. Shatsberg, & S. H. Frazier (Eds.), *Depression, biology, psychodynamics and treatment* (pp. 107–125). New York: Plenum Press.

Kliman, G. W. (1968). *Psychological emergencies of childhood.* New York: Grune & Stratton.

Kramer, A. D., & Feiguine, R. J. (1981). Clinical effects of amitriptyline in adolescent depression. *Journal of the American Academy of Child Psychiatry, 20,* 636–644.

Kreitman, N. (Ed.). (1977). *Parasuicide.* London: Wiley.

Kuperman, S., & Stewart, M. A. (1979). The diagnosis of depression in children. *Journal of Affective Disorders, 1,* 213–217.

Link, B., & Dohrenwend, B. P. (1980). Formulation of hypotheses about the true prevalence of demoralization in the United States. In B. P. Dohrenwend, B. S. Dohrenwend, M. S. Gould, B. Link, R. Neugebauer, & R. Wunsch-Hitzig (Eds.), *Mental Illness in the United States: Epidemiological estimates* (pp. 114–132). New York: Praeger.

Loranger, A. W., & Levine, P. M. (1978). Age at onset of bipolar affective illness. *Archives of General Psychiatry, 35,* 1345–1348.

Lowe, T. L., & Cohen, D. J. (1980). Mania in childhood and adolescence. In R. H. Belmaker & H. M. van Praag (Eds.), *Mania: An evolving concept* (pp. 111–117). New York: Spectrum Press.

Lumsden Walker, W. (1980). Intentional self-injury in school age children. *Journal of Adolescence 3,* 217–228.

Lynch, G., & Gall, C. (1979). Organization and reorganization in the central nervous system. In F. Falkner & J. M. Tanner (Eds.), *Human growth: Vol. 3. Neurobiology and nutrition* (pp. 125–144). London: Baillière Tindall.

McCall, R. (1981). Nature-nurture and the two realms of development: A proposed integration with respect to mental development. *Child Development, 52,* 1–12.

Office of Population Censuses and Surveys. (1978). *Trends in mortality 1951–75.* London: HM Stationery Office.

Parry, G. (1982, April). *Paid employment and mental health in working class mothers.* Paper read at the British Psychological Society annual conference, University of York.

Pearce, J. (1974). *Childhood depression.* M. Phil. (Psychiatry) Thesis, University of London.

Pearce, J. (1978). The recognition of depressive disorder in children. *Journal of the Royal Society of Medicine, 71,* 494–500.

Pinneau, S. R. (1955). The infantile disorders of hospitalism and anaclitic depression. *Psychological Bulletin, 52,* 429–452.

Plomin, R. (1983). Childhood temperament. In B. Lahey & A. Kazdin (Eds.), *Advances in clinical child psychology* (Vol. 6, pp. 45–92). New York: Plenum Press.

Poznanski, E., & Zrull, J. (1970). Childhood depression: Clinical characteristics of overtly depressed children. *Archives of General Psychiatry, 23,* 8–15.

Puig-Antich, J. (1980). Affective disorder in childhood: A review and perspective. *Psychiatric Clinics of North America, 3,* 403–424.

Puig-Antich, J. (1982). Major depression and conduct disorder in prepuberty. *Journal of the American Academy of Child Psychiatry, 21,* 118–128.

Puig-Antich, J., Blau, S., Marx, N., Greenhill, L. L., & Chambers, W. (1978). Prepubertal major depressive disorder: A pilot study. *Journal of the American Academy of Child Psychiatry, 17,* 695–707.

Puig-Antich, J., & Gittelman, R. (1982). Depression in childhood and adolescence. In E. S. Paykel (Ed.), *Handbook of affective disorders* (pp. 379–392). Edinburgh & London: Churchill-Livingstone.

Quinton, D., Rutter, M., & Liddle, C. (1984). Institutional rearing, parenting difficulties, and marital support. *Psychological Medicine, 14,* 107–124.

Radloff, L. (1975). Sex differences in depression: The effects of occupation and marital status. *Sex Roles, 1,* 249–267.

Rholes, W. S., Blackwell, J., Jordan, C., & Walters, C. (1980). A developmental study of learned helplessness. *Developmental Psychology, 16,* 616–624.

Robertson, J., & Robertson, J. (1971). Young children in brief separation: A fresh look. *Psychoanalytic Study of the Child, 26,* 264–315.

Rutter, M., (1966). *Children of sick parents: An environmental and psychiatric study* (Institute of Psychiatry Maudsley Monographs No. 16). London & New York: Oxford University Press.

Rutter, M. (1970). Sex differences in children's responses to family stress. In E. J. Anthony & C. Koupernik (Eds.), *The child in his family* (pp. 165–196). New York: Wiley.

Rutter, M. (1972). Relationships between child and adult psychiatric disorder. *Acta Psychiatrica Scandinavica, 48,* 3–21.

Rutter, M. (1979/1980). *Changing youth in a changing society: Patterns of adolescent development and disorder.* London: Nuffield Provincial Hospitals Trust, 1979. (Cambridge, MA: Harvard University Press, 1980)

Rutter, M. (1980a). Introduction. In M. Rutter (Ed.), *Scientific foundations of developmental psychiatry* (pp. 1–8). London: Heinemann Medical.

Rutter, M. (1980b). Attachment and the development of social relationships. In M. Rutter (Ed.), *Scientific foundations of developmental psychiatry* (pp. 267–279). London: Heinemann Medical.

Rutter, M. (1980c). Emotional development. In M. Rutter (Ed.), *Scientific foundations of developmental psychiatry* (pp. 306–321). London: Heinemann Medical.

Rutter, M. (1981a). *Maternal deprivation reassessed* (2nd ed.). Harmondsworth, Middlesex, England: Penguin Books.

Rutter, M. (1981b). Stress, coping and development: Some issues and some questions. *Journal of Child Psychology and Psychiatry, 22,* 323–356.

Rutter, M. (1982a). Developmental neuropsychiatry: Concepts, issues and prospects. *Journal of Clinical Neuropsychology, 4,* 91–115.

Rutter, M. (1982b). Epidemiological-longitudinal approaches to the study of development. In W. A. Collins (Ed.), *The concept of development: Proceedings of the 15th Minnesota Symposium on Child Psychology* (pp. 105–144). Hillsdale, NJ: Lawrence Erlbaum Associates.

Rutter, M. (1983). Continuities and discontinuities in socio-emotional development: Empirical and conceptual perspective. In R. Emde & R. Harmon (Eds.), *Continuities and discontinuities in development* (pp. 41–68). New York: Plenum Press.

Rutter, M., & Garmezy, N. (1983). Developmental psychopathology. In E. M. Hetherington (Ed.), *Socialization, personality, and social development: Vol. 4. Mussen's Handbook of child psychology* (pp. 775–911). New York: Wiley.

Rutter, M., & Graham, P. (1968). The reliability and validity of the psychiatric assessment of the child. I. Interview with the child. *British Journal of Psychiatry, 114,* 563–579.

Rutter, M., Graham, P., Chadwick, O., & Yule, W. (1976). Adolescent turmoil: Fact or fiction? *Journal of Child Psychology and Psychiatry, 17,* 35–56.

Rutter, M., Quinton, D., & Liddle, C. (1983). Parenting in two generations: Looking backwards and looking forwards. In N. Madge (Ed.), *Families at risk.* London: Heinemann Educational. 1983, (pp. 60–98).

Rutter, M., Tizard, J., & Whitmore, K. (1970/1981). *Education, health and behaviour.* Krieger: Huntington, NY. (Original work published 1970, London: Longmans)

Sandler, J., & Joffe, W. (1965). Notes on childhood depression. *International Journal of Psychoanalysis, 1965, 46,* 88–96.

Scadding, J. G. (1980). The concepts of disease: A response. *Psychological Medicine, 10,* 425–428.

Scadding, J. G. (1982). What is a case? *Psychological Medicine, 12,* 207–208.

Shaffer, D. (1974). Suicide in childhood and early adolescence. *Journal of Child Psychology and Psychiatry, 15,* 275–292.

Shaffer, D., & Fisher, P. (1981). The epidemiology of suicide in children and young adolescents. *Journal of the American Academy of Child Psychiatry, 20,* 545–565.

Sommer, B. B. (1978). Stress and menstrual distress. *Journal of Human Stress, 4,* 5–10, 41–47.

Spitz, R. (1946). Anaclitic depression. *Psychoanalytic Study of the Child, 2*, 313–342.

Taylor, F. K. (1979). *The concepts of illness, disease and morbus*. London & New York: Cambridge University Press.

Tennant, C., & Bebbington, P. (1978). The social causation of depression: A critique of the work of Brown and his colleagues. *Psychological Medicine, 8*, 565–575.

Tennant, C., Bebbington, P., & Hurry, J. (1981). The short-term outcome of neurotic disorders in the community: The relation of remission to clinical factors and to 'neutralizing' life events. *British Journal of Psychiatry, 139*, 213–220.

van Eerdewegh, M. M., Bieri, M. D., Parilla, R. H., & Clayton, P. (1982). The bereaved child. *British Journal of Psychiatry, 140*, 23–29.

van Hof, M. W. (1981). Development and recovery from brain damage. In K. Connolly & H. F. R. Prechtl (Eds.), *Maturation and development: Biological and psychological perspectives* (Clinics in Developmental Medicine Nos. 77/78, pp. 186–197). London: Heinemann Medical/SIMP.

Warr, P. (1982). Psychological aspects of employment and unemployment. *Psychological Medicine, 12*, 7–11.

Weinberg, W. A., & Brumback, R. A. (1976). Mania in childhood: Case studies and literature review. *American Journal of Diseases of Children, 130*, 380–385.

Weissman, M. M., & Klerman, G. L. (1977). Sex differences and the epidemiology of depression. *Archives of General Psychiatry, 34*, 98–111.

Wing, J. K., Bebbington, P., & Robins, L. N. (1981). *What is a case? The problem of definition in psychiatric community surveys*. London: Grant McIntyre.

Zeitlin, H. (1972). *A study of patients who attended the children's department and later the adults' department of the same psychiatric hospital*. M. Phil. dissertation, University of London.

Zeitlin, H. (1985). *The natural history of psychiatric disorder in children*. Institute of Psychiatry Maudsley Monograph. London: Oxford University Press (in press).

II

DEVELOPMENTAL PERSPECTIVES: THEORY AND RESEARCH

Patterns of Emotion in Depression

Carroll E. Izard
Gail M. Schwartz

There are a number of theories of emotion, but no one complete, general theory of emotional development. Several developmentalists have made substantial contributions to emotion theory and these will be noted. Our review of general and developmental theories of emotion will be selective, attending to concepts and issues we consider most relevant to depression.

EMOTION CONCEPTS IN GENERAL AND DEVELOPMENTAL THEORIES

Issues that are of concern to both general and developmental theories are (a) definition of emotions, (b) the instigation or activation of emotion, (c) the ontogenesis of emotions, and the functions of emotions at the (d) biological, (e) social, (f) cognitive, and (g) temperament–personality levels. At the temperament or motivation–systems level we shall consider the role of emotions in personality development and in psychopathology, particularly depression.

Definition of Emotions

There are two major types of emotion definitions. One type emphasizes the role of cognition and context, and the other focuses more on emotions

Carroll E. Izard. Department of Psychology, University of Delaware, Newark, Delaware.

Gail M. Schwartz. Department of Psychiatry, Medical College of Pennsylvania, Philadelphia, Pennsylvania.

as biosocial phenomena, considering them more as motivational/temperamental variables than as merely cognitive–behavioral reactions to events.

Much of the literature relating to the cognitive–contextual view of emotions places more emphasis on emotions as response and tends to characterize emotions as reactive, transient, and disrupting or disorganizing. This view is consistent with the widely held belief that the disruptive and disorganizing aspects of emotions contribute to psychological disorder and psychopathology. Most theorists in this tradition have little to say about the adaptive and motivational functions of emotions (Mandler, 1975; Schachter, 1971). However, a few investigators who give a prominent role to cognitive processes in emotion attribute motivational functions to them (e.g., Schwartz & Trabasso, 1984) or to "feeling states," provided they are detected (Kagan, 1984).

Biosocial definitions of emotions are set in evolutionary perspective. Emotions are considered as active, on-going processes that are motivational, organizing, and adaptive. In this view, emotions can also be studied as responses to internal and external events. Theorists who adopt a biosocial definition recognize the importance of cognitive processes in generating and regulating emotions. They do not, however, see any cognitive process as sole or necessary antecedent of emotion, and they do not assume that feeling states have to be detected (Kagan) or labeled (Schachter) in order to influence thought and action.

Of course, intense emotion as in rage or panic can lead to maladaptive behavior, but the emotions of anger and fear intensify to rage and panic because of a genetic predisposition or lack of coping skills in stressful situations, or both. Thus the primary causes of depression and other psychopathology must be sought in genetic, biochemical, and experiential factors. Analysis of the pattern of emotions (motivations) in depression is essential to understanding depressive behavior and symptomatology. Whereas emotions are considered as the principal motivators (causes) of human behavior, they are not thought to be *basic* causes of maladaptive behavior and psychopathology.

EMOTIONS AS COGNITIVE–BEHAVIORAL REACTIONS

The cognitive–behavioral view of emotion is represented by Schachter (1971) and Mandler (1975), who propose that emotion is a function of undifferentiated arousal plus cognition. Arousal is a function of autonomic nervous system (ANS) response to an incentive event (most typically external), and the cognition is an appraisal or evaluation of the event-in-context. Mandler holds that the arousal determines the intensity of emotion and the cognitive evaluation its quality. The empirical evidence for this view of emotion (e.g., Schachter & Singer, 1962) has recently been called into question on conceptual and methodological grounds and by failures to replicate the original findings (Marshall & Zimbardo, 1979; Maslach, 1979). Further, the notion that undifferentiated arousal is the physiological basis for all emotions has received a new challenge. The early evidence of differences in ANS activity associated with different emotions (Ax, 1953; Funkenstein, King, & Drolette, 1954; Wolf & Wolff, 1942) has been substantiated by the recent work of Schwartz and his colleagues (Schwartz, 1982) and Ekman, Levenson, and Friesen (1983). These new data suggest that part of the failure of past researchers to find consistent relationships among the physiological, expressive, and experiential components of emotions may have been due to problems in eliciting and maintaining a specific discrete emotion in the laboratory. Another shortcoming of most of the earlier research was failure to index somatic nervous system (SNS) activity.

The view of emotion that emphasizes cognition and context is represented among developmentalists by Kagan (1984; Kagan, Kearsley, & Zelazo, 1978). He defines emotion as a set of relations that involve cognitive evaluation of incentive events (real or constructed) and changes in feeling state. He acknowledges that differences in feeling, thinking, and acting are compelling phenomenologically, but he sees these phenomena as essentially inseparable. For this reason he is reluctant to adopt the common terms for emotions such as joy, sadness, anger, and fear as the starting place for investigation. Rather, he advocates the search for coherence in event–evaluation–feeling–action relationships. Identity of emotion states must be made in terms of the "incentive-cum-feeling" unit, that is, the name of the emotion should contain a reference to the incentive event.

EMOTION AS MOTIVATIONAL AND ADAPTIVE

A biosocial view of emotion is represented in general emotion theory by Izard (1977) and Plutchik (1980), and in developmental theory by Campos and Stenberg (1980), Cicchetti and Pogge-Hesse (1981), Emde, Gaensbauer, and Harmon (1976), Izard (1978; Izard & Buechler, 1980), Derryberry and Rothbart (1984), and Sroufe (1979; Sroufe, Schork, Motti, Lawroski, & LaFreniere, 1984). Differential emotions theory (Izard, 1977) defines emotion as having biological (neurophysiological/biochemical), social (expressive), and experiential (feeling) components. Emotions are viewed as part of the human evolutionary heritage. The biological component is the storehouse for the neural programs that subserve the motor–expressive patterns, and these motor–expressive patterns contribute to the feeling components of emotion through sensory feedback and to the social component through their signal value. Emotion expressions or signals have been shown to constitute effective motivation for the perceiver (Campos & Stenberg, 1980; Huebner & Izard, 1983) and the feeling state has motivational and cue-producing or informational functions (Izard, 1971, 1977) that have been shown to influence the individual's perception, memory, and intellectual performance (Bower, 1981; Izard, Wehmer, Livsey, & Jennings, 1965).

Instigation/Activation of Emotions

The cognitive–contextual view of emotions holds that some kind of cognitive process—appraisal, evaluation—is a necessary antecedent of emotion. This view is represented in general emotion theory by Arnold (1960), Lazarus (1968, 1982), Lazarus, Kanner, and Folkman (1980), Plutchik (1980), and the Schachter–Mandler model previously discussed.

Among these theorists, Lazarus has perhaps the most extreme position on emotion as a function of cognition. He is also the most extreme in his emphasis on the dependency of emotion on context. Lazarus *et al.* (1980) hold that emotion "arises from how a person construes the outcome, actual or anticipated, of a transaction with the environment" (p. 192). Emotion is a function of cognitive appraisal, which comes in three forms: primary appraisal is the evaluation of the organism–environment transaction as irrelevant, benign–positive, or stressful; secondary appraisal evaluates coping resources for a stressful encounter; and reappraisal capitalizes on feedback processes that can lead to changes in primary and secondary appraisals and hence to changes in emotional response.

Some theorists in this group define cognition or appraisal in such a way as to make it difficult to distinguish them from sensory or sensorimotor processes. For Arnold, appraisal is immediate, automatic, intuitive, and similar to what she calls a "sense judgment" (Arnold, 1960, chap. 9). On the other hand Plutchik includes in his concept of cognition phenomena such as imprinting and courtship rituals in lower animals (which seems inconsistent with his statement that "cognition will be considered as more or less synonymous with thinking"), and Lazarus acknowledges that appraisal may be unconscious.

Differential emotions theory holds that emotion expressions and feelings are activated by changes in the activities of the underlying neurochemical substrates. Such changes may be instigated by any internal or external event that creates a different intensity or pattern of neural activity. Receptors associated with particular discrete emotions are selectively sensitive to certain inputs or environmental conditions. The upshot of this for the present discussion is that emotion activation is closely tied to sensory processes and that cognition is but one of many phenomena that can trigger the neural events that lead to emotion. Physiological need or drive states (such as those associated with mating, feeding, elimination, fatigue, sleepiness) and ongoing emotion can activate a new emotion state.

One important difference between the two models of emotion activation concerns the source of feeling state in emotion. In the Schachter–Mandler view the quality of emotion is solely a function of the cognitive evaluation of the context. Differential emotions theory holds that for each fundamental emotion there is an innate neurochemical motor–expressive (or neuromotor program), and once the neuromotor program is activated, emotion *feeling* derives directly from the subsequent neurochemical and motor–expressive activities independent of any cognitive process. As already indicated, cognition is one of several sources of events that can trigger the neuromotor programs, and as neural and cognitive development proceed the individual becomes more capable of regulating (inhibiting, attenuating, amplifying) the innate–reflexive neuromotor programs.

Of course, the images, symbols, thoughts, and memories associated with emotion *feelings* derive from cognitive processes. These emotion–cognition associations over time result in mental structures that we have labeled affective–cognitive structures. In the course of development from presymbolic infant to the child with symbolic, reflective, and imaginal capacities these affective–cognitive structures come to be activated in a similar way as the neuromotor programs of early infancy, but the cognitive component of the affective–cognitive structures renders it more flexible and controllable than innate–reflexive emotion.

Ontogenesis of Emotions and Affective–Cognitive Structures

Among general theories of emotion, only differential emotions theory (Izard, 1977, 1978) has addressed the issue of ontogenesis. Several developmentalists have had something to say about the problem, but no one has produced anything near a complete map of this domain.

The two most common views of the ontogenesis of emotion expressions in infancy are the differentiation hypothesis (Bridges, 1932) and the discrete-emotions approach (Izard, 1978). The differentiation hypothesis holds that the infant is born with one or possibly two emotions—undifferentiated distress and excitement—and that other emotions differentiate from these in the course of the first 18 months of life as a function of maturation and experience, with conditioned responses or learning playing a significant role.

The discrete-emotions view (Izard, 1978) maintains that the infant is born with neural substrates for each of the fundamental emotions. The facial expressions of some fundamental emotions are fully functional at birth, and the others emerge largely as a function of maturation. The expressions of most of the fundamental emotions are present by 7–9 months of age and all are functional before the end of the second year. This view holds that each emotion plays a special role in personality development and that styles of emotion expression in infancy predict later adaptation.

In discussing the ontogeny of emotions, it is necessary to specify the definition of emotion or the emotion component being considered. For example, one can discuss the ontogeny of observable emotion expressions, as in the foregoing paragraphs, or one can consider the ontogeny of hormonal or autonomic functions, or self-reported feeling state (emotion labeling). The ontogeny of emotions can also be considered in general terms or in relation to specific events.

For psychology, we think the greatest challenge is the ontogeny of affective–cognitive structures, the study of the development of links between the feelings generated by the neuromotor emotion programs on the one hand and the images, symbols, and ideas that derive from cognitive processes on the other. In other words, a young infant has emotion feelings and action tendencies, but developmental processes must proceed for a time before the infant has images, words, and thoughts. Therefore, feelings, actions, and thought are neither automatically connected nor connected only in adaptive ways. The basic issue then is how these links are formed and what contributes to adaptive and maladaptive linkages.

Kagan (1984) has outlined an ontogeny of emotion-related phenomena with reference to some specific incentive events. He assumes that *cognitive evaluations* and *internal feelings* are absent in the first half year of life, yet he names several coherent relations between incentive events and affectlike phenomena during this period—closing eyes and heart rate acceleration to physical deprivation, excitement to assimilation of the unexpected, and attentive smiling to the moderately familiar.

Kagan chronicled a number of incentive-cum-feeling units from later infancy through adolescence. Those in the second half-year include behavioral inhibition to some discrepant events and resistance and protest to interruption or loss of an object of interest. In the second year, these are protest followed by inhibition and apathy to prolonged absence of attachment object and anxiety to possible task failure. In the fifth and sixth years, evaluation of self's properties in comparison with others can lead to emotional reactions commonly called insecurity, inferiority, humility, pride, and confidence. In the 12-year-old and in adolescents a discovery of an inconsistency in existing beliefs can lead to doubt and skepticism.

Note that Kagan's ontogeny is pegged to cognitive development, with important changes in affective phenomena following upon the emergence of a new cognitive ability such as object permanence (memory), ability to seriate self with others, and ability to examine the logic and consistency of existing beliefs. One can take issue with Kagan regarding the absence of feeling in early infancy and the dependence of emotion on cognition, but the relationships he describes between cognitive attainments and emotion experiences seem to match common observation. We think his theory is more applicable to the ontogeny of event–emotion relationships and affective–cognitive structures than to emotion expressions or emotion feelings.

Emotions as Motivational and Adaptive: Biological Functions

Theorists who view emotion primarily as a response or response syndrome and tend to reject or discount the concept of emotion as motivation (Lazarus, 1968; Mandler, 1975) either deny or give little attention to the possible adaptive functions of emotions. More recently Lazarus seems to be changing his position regarding the motivational properties of emotions (Lazarus et al., 1980). Like Izard (1971, 1977) and Plutchik (1980), he now attributes to emotions a signal function ("emotions can signal the need for coping," p. 206) and the capacity to arouse and sustain coping activities. Further, he sees positive emotions as alleviating stress by serving as "breathers" and "restorers."

The theory and evidence relating to the concept of emotions as motivational and adaptive has been presented in detail by Izard and Plutchik and need not be repeated here. Rather we shall note briefly two of the more obvious motivational–adaptive functions of emotions: energy mobilization and the regulation of sensory and motor systems.

Cannon (1929) provided physiological evidence for the effectiveness of anger and fear in mobilizing energy for defense or escape. Piaget (1981) argued that affectivity is the energy source for cognitive development and intelligence. Developmental research is beginning to address this issue. Langsdorf, Izard, Hembree, and Rayias (1983) showed that infants who displayed more facial signals of interest sustained their visual fixation of a variety of stimuli for a significantly longer period of time.

There is little hard evidence on the role of emotions in regulating other organismic systems, and most of the existing evidence relates to the regulatory function of emotion (facial) expressions. Several experiments by Lanzetta and his colleagues (e.g., Lanzetta, Cartwright-Smith, & Kleck, 1976; Vaughan & Lanzetta, 1980) have shown that overt affect expression influences autonomic reactivity as well as pain sensitivity. For example, in one experiment subjects who attenuated ("hid") their affect expressions while anticipating painful electric shock showed less autonomic arousal (as indexed by skin conductance) and reported less pain than subjects who did not suppress their facial expressions. That regulating or manipulating facial expressions, under certain conditions, can be tantamount to activating or regulating emotion experience has been demonstrated in a number of experiments (see Laird, Wagener, Halal, & Szegda, 1982). Our interpretation of this "expression effect" is that sensory feedback from the facial behavior is transformed by the limbic system and limbic–cortical interactions into emotion feeling or the experience of felt emotion. This research on the expression effect also shows the motivational impact of emotion on a variety of behaviors.

In the Izard et al. (1983) study of emotion responses to acute pain, the age-related changes in expressions could be said to serve a biologically adaptive function. In early infancy (first half-year of life) the predominant response to pain was a physical distress facial–vocal expression that apparently canalizes all the infant's energy into a compelling signal to the caregiver. The fact that this signal elicits mothers' tendencies to satisfy the infants' physical needs (Huebner & Izard, 1983) suggests that it has survival value. After early infancy pain no longer canalizes all available energy into a distress–emergency signal. The predominance of the anger expression to pain in 19-month-olds suggests that anger may be functioning in the more mature, mobile infant to mobilize energy for instrumental coping behaviors. Consistent with this interpretation of the different functions of the two expressions in the first half-year of life is the fact that in the physical distress expression the eyes are tightly closed [presumably to protect the eyeballs (Brash, 1948; Darwin, 1872/1965)] while in anger the eyes are open, providing another sensory modality to facilitate coping.

Emotions as Motivational and Adaptive:
Social Functions

Darwin (1872/1965) made a strong case for the adaptive functions of emotions, particularly emotion expressions and their social significance. He observed that emotion expression was the first means of communication between mother and infant and that expressions were the first vehicle of socialization. He also noted the use of expression in facilitating prosocial interaction and defense.

The systemic nature of emotions is underscored by the fact that the motor–expressive component that contributes to emotion experience through sensory feedback is also the chief mechanism subserving the social function of emotions. In the prelingual child the expressions are the sole means of emotion communication and account for virtually all social communication.

Throughout life, emotion expressions play an important role in social interactions—words from expressionless faces are difficult to interpret. In summary, the social functions of emotion expressions are (a) signaling the individual's feelings and intentions, (b) providing data for making inferences about the environment, and (c) facilitating social interactions that facilitate the development of attachment to the caregiver and affective bonds in the wider social surround. Main, Tomasini, and Tolan (1979) have shown that mothers judged as higher on emotion expressiveness tend to rear infants who are securely attached as measured by the Ainsworth Strange Situation procedure (Ainsworth, Blehar, Waters, & Wall, 1978).

We have shown that infants in the first 7–9 months of life have some 21 facial behaviors that have signal value. These 21 appearance changes are components of eight expressive configurations that signal the affect of physical distress and the emotions of interest, joy, surprise, sadness, anger, disgust, and fear (Izard, Huebner, Risser, McGinnis, & Dougherty, 1980).

Huebner and Izard (1983) have shown that mothers report significantly different behavioral tendencies when viewing infant expressions of interest, physical distress, sadness, and anger. Mothers tend to respond to distress by caring for physical needs, to sadness with positive affective responses, and to anger with discipline and behavior-control techniques.

In an ongoing study we have found support for our general hypothesis that emotion experiences and emotion expressions influence the mother–infant relationship. We found a significant correlation between mothers' rating of their infants' anger expressiveness in daily life and the amount of objectively coded anger expressed by the infant in response to the pain of inoculation. We found that mothers' self-reported anger experiences when their infants were 12 months old correlated significantly with mothers' rating of their infants' anger expressiveness at 19 months. Further, mothers' ratings of their infants' anger expressiveness at 12 months correlated even more strongly with mothers' anger experiences at 19 months.

Sroufe et al. (1984) reviewed a number of studies that support the hypothesis that emotion and the expression of emotion play a central role in the organization of individual behavior and the development of social competence. In recent studies of preschool children they showed that children who were more frequently involved in positive affective interactions with others were assessed as more competent in terms of observer and teacher ratings and sociometric data. They also found that children's positive adjustment index (based on several types of measures and including a positive affect index) was significantly correlated with teacher ratings of social competence.

Emotion and Cognition: Studies of Perception and Memory in Adults

That emotion influences the way we see the world, think, and act is a commonly held belief. Yet only a few empirical studies have attempted to establish the veracity of this assumption. A few experiments done in the early 1960s demonstrated the effect of emotion on various cognitive processes. Induced joy and anger differentially affected the resolution of binocular rivalry, such that angry subjects saw significantly more angry expressions in stereoscopically presented pairs of happy and angry expression photos and vice versa for happy subjects. Other experiments showed that induced joy, as compared to induced anger, yielded more favorable perceptions of the experimenter and experiment and better performance on three different types of cognitive tasks—naming multiple uses of common objects, digit span, and problem solving (Izard et al., 1965).

Bower and his colleagues (Bower, 1981; Bower, Gilligan, & Monteiro, 1981) conducted a series of experiments demonstrating the effects of hypnotically induced emotion on memory. This first set of studies produced evidence for emotion-state-dependent learning or mood-congruity effect. For example, subjects who learned while in a hypnotically induced sad state remembered better when they were put back in a sad state at time of recall.

Bower explained these effects in terms of a network theory of memory, a neoassociationist view, arguing that emotion events because of their psychological centrality have a greater network of associations than nonemotion events. In terms of specific hypotheses he favored the concept of selective reminding and emotion intensity—a sad event is more likely than a happy event to remind one of a similar sad event in the past and the more intense the emotion the greater the selectivity and thus the greater the mood-congruity effect. Figure 1 illustrates this effect. He also found the mood-congruity effect when normal subjects were asked to recount incidents from their childhood. Subjects who recounted while in a sad mood reported significantly more sad or unpleasant incidents and subjects recounting in a happy mood recalled more happy or pleasant events. They also found that the amount recalled or the magnitude of the mood-congruity effect was a function of the intensity of the emotion associated with the original event or learning situation, confirming the intensity hypothesis mentioned above.

Some of those affects were recently confirmed and extended by Hettena and Ballif (1981). Instead of inducing moods in the laboratory, they compared students who were naturally elated or depressed at the time of the experiment. Nondepressed subjects made much clearer differentiations between the positive and negative affective statements in the material studied, and they recalled significantly more information. Apparently inconsistent with Bower's mood-congruency effect, elated and depressed subjects did not recall more of the information that matched their emotion

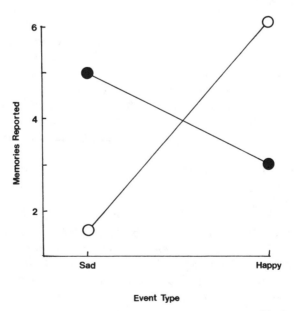

Fig. 1. *Number of happy and sad memories of recent events reported by happy (○) and sad (●) subjects. (Adapted from Bower, 1983, with permission.)*

state at the time of learning. Differences in methodology and possible differences in the complexity or intensity of the moods across experiments may help explain the discrepancy with Bower's findings.

Bower has marshalled substantial support for the mood-congruity effect, but Hettena and Ballif's finding of poorer learning and recall by depressed subjects is consistent with clinical observation of a reduction in speed and efficiency of information processing or mental functions in depression. It should be remembered that Bower induced sadness hypnotically and did not consider the induced sadness to be very intense. On the other hand, Hettena and Ballif used subjects who were currently experiencing naturally occurring depressive feelings. Further research is necessary to resolve this issue. Hettena and Ballif's conclusion that their data fail to support "the concept of the cue function of moods" (p. 507) deserves further consideration.

Emotions, Temperament, and Personality

Common language testifies to a relationship between emotions or mood and temperament. We describe ourselves and others as jolly or gloomy, suggesting that we experience joy or sadness sufficiently frequently to consider a particular emotion experience as a characteristic of our personality. The empirical research of Wessman and Ricks (1966) tends to confirm the validity of our common observations. In their intensive study of college men and women they found individuals who were characteristically happy or unhappy. They found that characteristically unhappy or depressed individuals had fewer success experiences in childhood, less intimacy and trust in their relationships, and were less committed to their work or study.

The recent investigations of Thoman and Acebo (1984) showed that babies have characteristically different cry patterns in response to routine care-giving activities. In the Izard, Hembree, Dougherty, and Spizzirri (1983) study of infants' emotion responses to the pain of diphtheria–pertussis–tetanus (DPT) inoculation, it was found that some babies were slow to soothe and some fast. Slow and fast soothers had characteristically different patterns of pain-instigated affect expressions, with slow soothers showing proportionately more anger expression than fast soothers. We interpreted the data as consistent with our hypothesis of individual differences in emotion thresholds, and in particular we speculated that slow soothers had lower anger thresholds and that pain–anger interactions prolonged perturbation.

Derryberry and Rothbart (1984) have established a productive line of research on temperament, emotion, and cognition. They defined temperament as constitutional differences in reactivity and self-regulation. By constitutional they mean the relatively enduring biological makeup of the individual. Reactivity is measured in terms of threshold, latency, intensity, rise time, and recovery of various endocrine, autonomic, somatic, and central nervous system functions. Self-regulatory processes are defined in terms of emotions or affective–motivational processes. They found, for example, that the average number of sleep–wake transitions in infants at 3 months of age correlated negatively with smiling and laughing at 3, 6, and 9 months of age, with distress to limitations at 6 months, and with duration and activity level at 9 months. These findings of Rothbart, like those of Thoman and Izard and their colleagues, are promising, but they are only a beginning in the study of the development of temperament. That it may be an important beginning is suggested by a central conclusion of the New York Longitudinal study of Thomas and Chess (1977): "temperament must be considered as an independent determining variable in itself, and not just an *ad hoc* modifier used to fill the gaps left unexplained by other mechanisms" (p. 205).

THE ROLE OF EMOTIONS IN DEPRESSION

The foregoing section does not provide a very firm grip on the problem of emotional development. Both theory and research are scarce, particularly for the span of years between toddlerhood and adulthood. Before discussing emotions and depression, we need to consider the important question of what develops in normal and abnormal emotional development.

What Develops in Emotional Development?

The models we use to describe cognitive development do not apply to the emotions. The main reason for this is that compared with the cognitive system, relatively more of the emotions system is either present at birth or is a function of maturational processes that are virtually complete by the end of the third quarter of the first year of life. The possible exceptions are the emotions of contempt, shame, shyness, and guilt, whose substrates seem more dependent on interaction with later developing cognitive capacities.

For differential emotions theory the developmental processes of central importance are of two sorts. The first kind are a function of biological and experiential factors and relate to the neural structures whose development increases the organism's capacity to regulate emotion. Of particular importance here is the development of the ability to use one emotion to regulate or shut off other emotions that are less appropriate to the situation. The second kind of emotion-related developmental processes of central importance are those that bridge and integrate the functions of the various systems of the individual organism. They are the integrative processes that link emotion and cognition in affective–cognitive structures and that organize the activities of the emotion, perceptual, cognitive, and motor systems so as to facilitate the development of skills and competencies for adapting to life's demands.

Possible Developmental Changes in Patterns of Emotions in Depression

It is clear from clinical descriptions since the turn of the century that sensory and social deprivation in the first year of life creates a behavioral syndrome that in some respects resembles an adult retarded depression. Infants are described as listless, immobile, unresponsive, and as having sleeping and eating disorders (Bakwin & Bakwin, 1972; Malmquist, 1971; Spitz, 1946). Spitz (1946) described "anaclitic depression" in the second half of the first year of life with symptoms similar to those listed above. Bowlby's (1969) observations of infants separated from caregiver in this time period include a three-phase response in which different emotions may predominate. The first phase, protest, seems dominated by anger and anger-related coping behaviors. The second phase, "despair," is characterized by sadness, withdrawal, and lack of interest. In the third phase, detachment, interest increases and sadness decreases. More recently, Gaensbauer (1980) has described a similar pattern of apathy, lack of interest, and lack of engagement in play. He described a 3½-month-old girl who smiled little and was easily upset. Her facial expression met objective criteria (Ekman & Friesen, 1975; Izard, 1979) for the "sad" expression, and she was judged to be sad by both naive and clinically sophisticated viewers.

Absent from these descriptions of depression in infancy are the emotions of fear, shame, and guilt. The studies by Scarr and Salapatek (1970), Campos and colleagues on the visual cliff (Campos & Stenberg, 1980), as well as observations of infants in the Human Emotions Laboratory at Delaware indicate that fear normally does not emerge until about 7–8 months of age. Also there is no objective evidence of shame and guilt in the first year of life. The development of fear, shame, and guilt responses may be relatively more dependent on the attainment of higher cognitive skills and on a more stable self-image than is possible in early infancy (Groh, 1980).

Although anger plays a complex role in depression, it, too, is absent from descriptions of depression in infancy. Infants can exhibit the facial display of anger as early as 2 months (Izard et al., 1983), but it is highly unlikely that it is either clearly object oriented or inner directed, because of the absence or instability of the infant's cognitive representation of object and self. In summary then, the pattern of emotions in depression during early infancy is one in which sadness predominates and varies inversely with interest.

The groundwork for the next major change in the predicted pattern of emotions in depression is laid at about 18 months of age. By about that age children have begun to show an awareness of parental demands and are able to comply and to monitor their own behavior somewhat (Kopp, 1982). M. Lewis and Brooks (1978) suggest that with the emergence of representational thinking the infant develops a sense of self as continuous in time. By 18 months, memory has improved but for the most part remains tied to environmental cues. Thus behavior control and self-awareness is, at this age, more a function of, or limited to, external cues and demands than internal ones (Kopp, 1982). This is also a crucial juncture as described in the object relations and psychosocial developmental literature. This is about the time the child faces toilet training, the "terrible twos," and "insult to infantile omnipotence." Erikson (1950/1963) saw this as the stage of dealing with autonomy versus doubt. Thus the job of the 1½–3-year-old seems to be to gain self-control and autonomy in the face of increasing parental and societal demands. The cognitive and social developments of this period set the stage for the experience of shame and for learned fear responses. In the adult literature shame was described by H. Lewis (1971), Izard (1977), and others as implying heightened self-awareness and the sense that one has been a public disappointment, a failure, or stupid in one's actions.

Although the child after toddlerhood is capable of a wider variety of the negative emotion experiences that characterize depression, the epidemiological studies report that depression is rare in the 2–5-year group. For example, Mendelson, Reid, and Frommer (1971) found among 210 children in a psychiatric clinic population 12 whose sole symptom was persistent weepiness and misery; however, 110 children displayed that symptom mixed with anxiety (defined as certain fear behaviors) and/or aggressive behavior. Others (Caplan & Douglas, 1969; Poznanski & Zrull, 1979) who have included the preschool groups in their studies have found few children who would qualify as depressed.

Lack of interest is mentioned in the 2–5-year group (e.g., Barker, 1971) but seems less crucial to investigators except as it may be reflected in withdrawal. None report shame or guilt as a part of depressive symptomatology in this age period. There may be a number of factors that account for this. Although speech is developing, children are not good at expressing feelings in words. The concepts of self and time are less stable and moods are more closely tied to external events, and thus occasions of shame and guilt (and other emotions) may be more fleeting. If the investigator does not observe the actual event, the emotion may not be detected. Denial, grandiosity, and involvement in fantasy may protect the child from high-level awareness of certain negative emotions.

Glasberg and Aboud (1981) reported that their 5-year-old group evaluated sad children negatively (as did the 7-year-olds) but did not extend that negative rating to themselves in those situations. The older children did rate themselves more negatively. The 5-year-olds also denied sadness.

A frequent response to pain and frustration is anger and tantrums (Glasberg & Aboud, 1981; Sandler & Joffee, 1965). The pervasive push of growth coupled with the frustrations of adapting to an expanding social and physical environment and apparent lack of the concept of hopelessness (J. Garber, personal communication) may contribute to anger and anger-motivated coping strategies at the 2–5-year level. The pattern of emotions in depression would thus be sadness with a lack of joy or interest. This appears to alternate with or follow upon more active coping and the experience of anger (Cytryn & McKnew, 1972; Sandler & Joffee, 1965). As in early infancy, guilt is not reported in this age group.

In the 6–9-year-old group the pattern again undergoes some change, and variations are added. The shame component is more salient in reports of low self-esteem, excessive self-criticism, and masochistic behavior (Brumback, Dietz-Schmidt, & Weinberg, 1977; Brumback & Weinberg, 1977a, 1977b; Carlson & Cantwell, 1980a; Cytryn & McKnew, 1972; Glasberg & Aboud, 1981; Green, 1972; Kashani & Simonds, 1979; Sandler & Joffe, 1965). McConville, Boag, and Purohit (1973) noted a decrease in the prevalence of "feeling–thought" or affect-predominant depression and increase in "thought–feeling"-type depressive disorders. In this latter type, self-deprecatory thoughts and negative self-esteem predominate.

The important developmental changes that occur at this stage (6–9 years) include significant changes in moral development (Freud, 1968) and the movement into the operational stage of cognitive development (Piaget, 1936/1963). Entry into formal schooling places increased demands on the child for self-mastery and provides more opportunities to observe one's public behavior. Erikson (1950/1963) viewed the tasks at this age as including initiative versus guilt. All of these may contribute to the increased prevalance of shame and guilt in depressed children of this age.

At 9–11 years the child is increasingly able to internalize standards of behavior. As children progress in the concrete operations stage (Piaget, 1936/1963), their thinking becomes more independent of concrete environmental cues or less dependent on the iconic mode (Bruner, 1964). Verbalization is steadily improving as a resource for problem solving and expression of feeling. Both the conscience and the ego ideal are solidifying. This sets the groundwork for the emergence of guilt as failure to live up to internalized standards. Achenbach and Zigler (1963) reported that with age there is awareness of greater discrepancy between real and ideal self. Thus with increasing cognitive sophistication the 9–11-year-old is able to perform the coordination and matching of the observed self and ideals that are independent of immediate environmental cues. Guilt may be experienced in the absence of any action. Self has consolidated to the extent that these self-ideal discrepancies can also be internalized and generalized across situations. McConville *et al.* (1973) found a "guilt-type depression" that was relatively rare but was more prevalent in this 9–11-year-old group than in younger children. It seems that Cytryn and McKnew (1974) also predicted that depressive disorders that involve awareness of violation of internal standards were more likely to be found in this older group.

Another frequent pattern for this age group, as well as for 6–9-year-olds, is the combined symptom picture of anger/acting out and alternately sadness/withdrawal. The two emotion complexes may coexist in some dynamic balance until events call, for example, for mobilization of the anger/action component fueled by the child's push for growth and basic optimism. Children react until fatigued, rewarded (punished), or temporarily without hope that their actions will restore what has been lost, and then sadness may dominate over anger/acting out. Carlson and Cantwell (1980b) suggested that with enough questions and measures, both these aspects of the depressive reaction may be observed simultaneously. Our empirical study of emotions in 10–11-year-olds (reported in the next section) tends to support the concept of an anger and sadness symptom picture in this age group.

The Affective Symptomatology of Depression

A number of years ago we undertook a series of studies on the phenomenology of emotions (Izard, 1972). We used imagery and recall techniques to induce each of 10 fundamental emotions. For each emotion, subjects were asked to imagine or recall a situation that elicited the emotion and then to complete the Differential Emotions Scale (DES), which measures self-reported subjective experience of interest, joy, surprise, sadness, anger, disgust, contempt, fear, shyness, and guilt. Thus we obtained DES profiles for a sadness situation, anger situation, etc. We also obtained profiles for an anxiety and a depression situation.

Two of our general conclusions from these studies are important for our discussion of depression: (1) emotions always occurred in patterns, that is, the imagery of each emotion-eliciting situation yielded a different pattern or *profile* of emotion scale scores; (2) the pattern of emotions for a particular (e.g., sadness-eliciting) situation as imaged by the subjects was stable across groups.

Before we present our findings from these and more recent studies, we want to emphasize that our data bear on the affective symptomatology of depression, not on its etiology. Because differential emotions theory (Izard, 1977) assumes that emotions are inherently adaptive, they are not considered the basic cause of maladaptive behavior. The principal functions of emotions are to motivate adaptive cognition and action and to facilitate social communication, and emotions do these things naturally. To understand the reasons for emotion being too intense, too weak, or inappropriate in a specific situation or syndrome, it is necessary to examine the appropriateness of the concurrent cognitive, social, and motor processes. The probability of finding disorder is much more likely in acquired knowledge and behavior and in the matchups between cognition, action, and situation than in the more biologically determined emotion process. The cognitive patterns associated with discovery in the laboratory may not be effective on the tennis court, and the thoughts and behaviors appropriate to a personal loss will soon become maladaptive in the workplace.

There surely are maladaptive emotion–behavior sequences, and so we must ask what deviant developmental or socialization processes produce such sequences. There may be rare genetic or ontogenic conditions that result in abnormal emotion mechanisms, but we hypothesize that most maladaptive behavior and most functional psychopathology is a result of missing or defective links or bridges between emotion, cognition, and action. Following this assumption, one could argue that the term "emotional disorder" is never fully descriptive of any psychological or mental health problem.

We do not mean that every individual's emotion system is equally adaptive in all circumstances. We have presented some evidence suggestive of individual differences in thresholds for negative emotions, in particular, differences in infants' anger thresholds. A low anger threshold in an infant may create a problem for the parents and jeopardize the infant–parent attachment. Data presented in the next section will show that anger turned inward, presumably during socialization, contributes to the symptomatology of depression.

While we do not consider emotions as basic etiological factors in depression, we recognize that they are a large part of the affective symptomatology of depression and thus may be considered as secondary causes. The primary causes of depression are multiple and little understood. We believe the most basic cause is failure to develop skills and competencies that buffer the self from sadness–discouragement, one's own hostility (anger, disgust, contempt), and shame. Continual vulnerability to these emotions may in turn lead to detrimental cognitive styles (negative views of self, world, and future) as described by Beck (1967) and Seligman and Peterson (Chapter 8 of this volume) and to biochemical disturbances as described by Davis (1970) and Puig-Antich (Chapter 12 of this volume). In searching for the causes of the failure to develop skills, competencies, and a concept of self-as-adequate, we must look both at genetic processes and at socialization and individual differences in responses to critical life events.

We are left with a seeming paradox: Emotions operate as both secondary causes and as sources of motivation for controlling and ameliorating depression. But how can emotions be part of both "cause" and "cure"? The answer in brief is that while the feeling states associated with emotions in depression contribute to the subjective misery and possibly to cognitive and biochemical disturbances, they are also the source of motivation for the coping behavior that counteracts depression. We shall try to support this proposition when we discuss the role of each of the depression-related fundamental emotions.

PATTERNS OF EMOTIONS IN DEPRESSED ADOLESCENTS AND ADULTS

In our early studies, the instrument for studying the affective phenomenology of depression (DES + D) was derived from a series of factor-analytic investigations of a pool of items drawn from Izard's Differential Emotions Scale (DES) (Izard, Dougherty, Bloxom, & Kotsch, 1974), Zuckerman's Mood Affect Adjective Checklist (MAACL) (Zuckerman & Lubin, 1964), and Beck's Depression Inventory (BDI) (Beck, 1967). Table 1 presents the DES + D factors and the items that resulted from both the factor analyses of large high school and college samples. For some studies additional trial items were added to the set shown in Table 1. The emotion adjectives were put on 5-point intensity scales and randomly arranged, with the restriction that no two items from the same factor would be adjacent.

Table 1
Factors and Items Common to Both High School and College Students

Distress	A/D/C[a]: Hostility, outer-directed
discouraged	disdainful of others
gloomy	revulsion toward others
forlorn	contemptuous of others
downhearted	mad at others
blue	angry at others
(sad)	others as distasteful
A/D/C[a]: Hostility, inner-directed	Physical well-being
mad	active
angry	fit
enraged	strong
Fear	Shyness
scared	bashful
afraid	shy
fearful	Surprise
Fatigue	astonished
sleepy	surprised
fatigued	amazed
sluggish	Joy
Guilt	happy
guilty	joyful
blameworthy	delighted
repentant	

Note: From Izard (1972).
[a]A, anger; D, disgust; C, contempt.

Since most of the data that we shall present come from normal or non-clinically depressed subjects, let us begin by comparing the emotion profiles of hospitalized depressives and adolescent high school students who report that they suffer from depression. The high school subjects indicated that they were "fairly often" so depressed that it interfered substantially with their schoolwork. Their emotion scale scores were obtained while they recalled and visualized a time when they were depressed. Table 2 compares the rank order of the emotion scale means for the high school students and the hospitalized depressives. We shall discuss aspects of these profiles later. The central point here is that the pattern of emotions in "normal" and "abnormal" depression are quite similar. This adds to the credibility of our analysis of the emotions in depression based on data from normal high school and college students imaging or recalling their periods of depression.

One other study contributed to our confidence in the imagery technique. Figure 2 presents the mean MAACL depression scores derived from subjects experiencing imagery-induced depression and depression-related emotions. It can be seen that the rank order of mean depression scores in the depression-related emotion situations conforms reasonably well with the description of depressive affect in both differential emotions theory (Izard, 1972) and psychoanalytic theory (Abraham, 1968; Freud, 1968; H. Lewis, 1979; Rado, 1968). Although the depression score is substantially elevated in the specific emotion situations, an analysis of variance showed that it was significantly higher in the depression situation than in the sadness situation, which had the highest of the specific emotion–situation means.

In summary, there is substantial evidence that the affective symptomatology of depression can be described as a complex pattern of emotions. The pattern is illustrated by the DES profile in Fig. 3, data obtained from high school students imaging depression.

It is important to emphasize that we have presented the "average" or

Table 2
Rank Order of Emotion Scales for Depressive Affect and Depressive Disorder

Factor	High school (N = 313)	Depressive patients (N = 40)
Sadness	1	1
Inner-directed hostility	2	3
Fear	3	2
Fatigue	4	7
Guilt	5	4.5
Outer-directed hostility	6	8
Physical well-being	7	6
Shyness	8	4.5

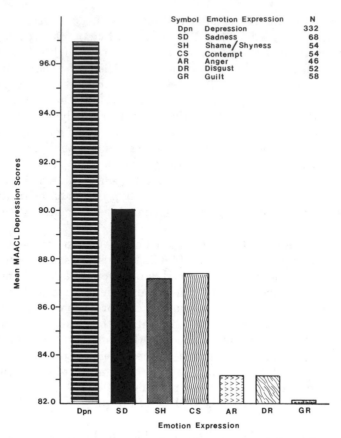

Fig. 2. *MAACL depression scores derived from imagery-induced depression.*

"modal" profile of emotions in depression. Profiles vary with type of depression and eliciting situation. This is illustrated in Figs. 4, 5, and 6 in terms of individual differences in the profiles of two depressed clients and a contrasting one for an anxious client.

Comparisons of Affective and Cognitive Correlates of Depression

The work of Seligman and his colleagues (Chapter 8 of this volume) suggests that there are some similarities in the cognitive correlates (attribution styles) of depressed children and depressed adults. In some ongoing studies we are repeating and extending some of the work of Seligman et al., examining both affective and cognitive correlates of depressed adults and children.

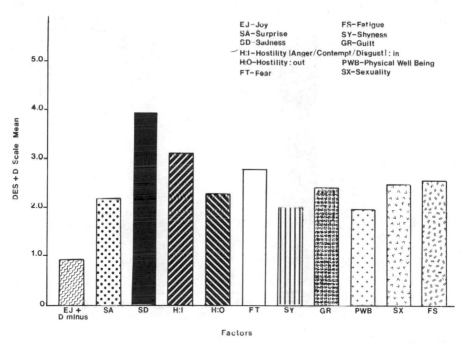

Fig. 3. *DES profile for high school students imaging depression.*

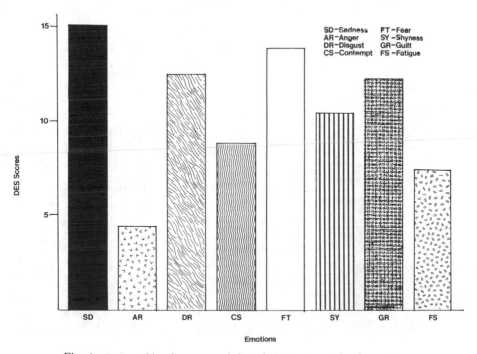

Fig. 4. *DES profile of a young adult male in treatment for depression.*

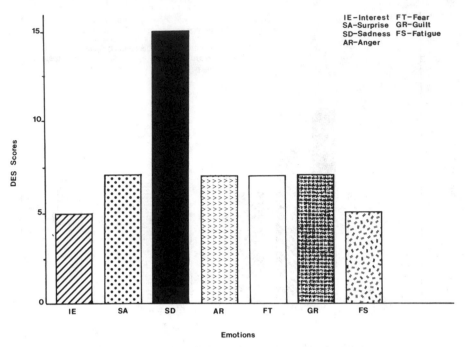

Fig. 5. *DES profile of a young adult female in treatment for depression.*

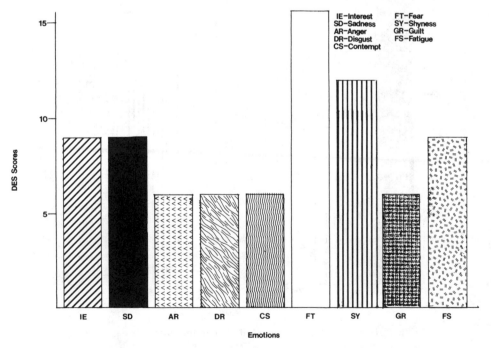

Fig. 6. *DES profile for young adult male in treatment for anxiety disorder.*

AFFECTIVE AND COGNITIVE FACTORS IN ADULT DEPRESSION

We began the studies of affective and cognitive correlates of depression with adults so we could compare results from a new form of the DES (DES IV) with results from the form used in the studies described above.

Izard, Oyster, Lelwica, and Blumberg (in preparation) examined the relationship of DES IV scores and Attribution Style Questionnaire (ASQ) scores (see Seligman & Peterson, Chapter 8, this volume) to depression as measured by the BDI (Beck, 1967). The DES IV contains the 10 scales of the DES III, a revision of the DES + D inner-directed hostility scale, and a new shame scale. The ASQ yields several subscale scores, but we used only the two most reliable overall (composite) positive (ASQ+) and overall negative (ASQ−).

In addition to the BDI total score (BDI-T) we derived two part scores by having judges classify the items as affective (BDI-A) or nonaffective (BDI-N). BDI-A consists of items that clearly connote affect (e.g., sadness) and BDI-N of items that describe nonaffective (mainly somatic) symptomatology (e.g., sleep disturbances, changes in body weight).

The DES, ASQ, and BDI were administered to 103 college students (72 females, 31 males) on two occasions approximately one month apart. (At Time 1, the children's version of ASQ, the CASQ, was administered and at Time 2 both ASQ and CASQ were included in the battery.)

To analyze the Time 1 data, the 12 DES variables and the 2 CASQ variables were regressed on the BDI-T, BDI-A, and BDI-N in three separate equations. The multiple Rs were .73, .73, and .55 for the regressions on BDI-T, BDI-A, and BDI-N, respectively. Significant unique variance in BDI-T was accounted for by the DES sadness, hostility inward (HI), and interest scales, in BDI-A by the DES sadness, joy, and interest scales, and in BDI-N by the DES HI scale. The CASQ did not account for any unique variance in any of the three BDI scores. (The possibility that for college students ASQ would do better than CASQ was examined in the analyses of the Time 2 data.)

Of particular interest were the findings that the DES HI scale accounted for a significant amount of unique variance in BDI-N, the index of nonaffective (including somatic) symptomatology in depression. In the hierarchical regression for BDI-N, the DES sadness, shyness, and HI scales accounted for a significant amount of variance.

The results of the analyses of the Time 2 data were similar to those for Time 1, with the exception that ASQ+, ASQ−, and CASQ− as well as the DES sadness, shyness, fear, and HI scales accounted for unique variance in the BDI-T ($R = .81$). Results for BDI-A were similar. Four of the DES scales (sadness, shame, shyness, and fear) accounted for unique variance in BDI-N ($R = .67$); as in Time 1 data, none of the ASQ or CASQ variables accounted for unique BDI-N variance.

That CASQ accounted for unique variance in BDI-T and BDI-A encouraged us to keep the CASQ variables in the analyses of Time 1 independent variables as predictors of Time 2 dependent (BDI) variables. In this analysis, the DES interest and joy scales at Time 1 accounted for significant unique variance in BDI-T at Time 2. Results were similar for the prediction of BDI-A at Time 2 (R = .66). For the latter, stepwise regression results showed that CASQ− and the DES sadness and HI scales were significant predictors. The DES sadness scale was the only variable that accounted for significant unique variance in BDI-N. In the stepwise regression, DES sadness and fear were significant predictors. It is noteworthy that some of the DES scales were significant predictors of the somatic symptomatology of depression as measured by the BDI nonaffective items.

AFFECTIVE AND COGNITIVE FACTORS IN CHILDHOOD DEPRESSION

Our studies of the development of depression in childhood are just beginning. We can only report the results of a single study of elementary school children, of which only about 16 were considered to be moderately depressed. Blumberg and Izard (in press) administered the DES IV, CASQ, and Childhood Depression Inventory (CDI) (Kovacs & Beck, 1979), to 150 (82 boys, 64 girls) fifth-graders (10–11 years old) in a rural Pennsylvania middle school. Preliminary analyses showed that boys and girls with high CDI scores responded differentially on some of the other measures, and so separate analyses were run for the two sexes. The DES profiles for depressed (CDI score > 19) boys and girls differed substantially, as shown in Figs. 7 and 8. Girls had lower positive emotion scores and higher negative emotion scores except for anger and contempt, where boys were higher. Although by comparison with depressed girls the depressed boys had generally lower negative emotion means and thus looked less depressed on the DES, depressed boys had substantially higher means than nondepressed boys (CDI score < 2) on sadness, anger, disgust, contempt, shame, and shyness. That depressed girls were much higher on inner- and outer-directed hostility and depressed boys higher only on outer-directed hostility (anger, contempt) suggests that depressed boys may be more likely to show conduct disturbance. Consistent with this notion were the relatively lower scores for boys on fear and shyness.

The product moment correlations between the CASQ scores and the CDI were lower than those reported by Seligman and Peterson (Chapter 8 of this volume). The correlation of CASQ+ with CDI was − .21 for boys, − .50 for girls; the corresponding correlations for CASQ− were .43 and .33. Correlations between the DES scores and the CDI were generally higher than those for the CASQ. For girls the DES sadness, HI, shame, guilt, and anger scores correlated with CDI .75, .82, .77, .67, and .59, respectively. The corresponding correlations for boys were .37, .30, .42, .06, and .45. Both the magnitude and the patterns of correlations were quite different for boys and girls.

Of more interest are the results of the regression analyses, with DES

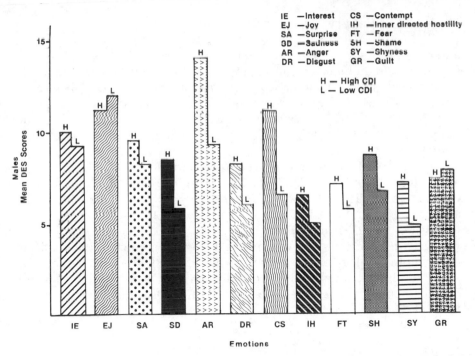

Fig. 7. DES profile for depressed 10–11-year-old boys.

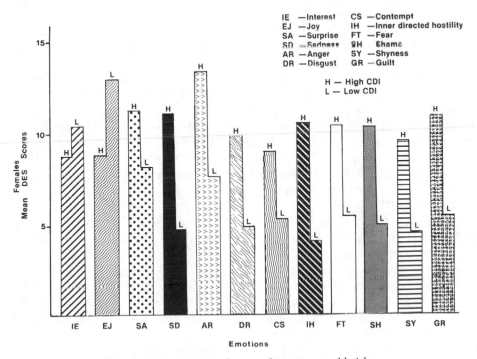

Fig. 8. DES profile for depressed 10–11-year-old girls.

and CASQ scores as predictors and CDI as criterion. The Rs for girls and boys were .90 and .69, accounting for 81 and 48% of the variance in the CDI, respectively. The unique variances accounted for by the DES were 53 and 26% for girls and boys, respectively. The corresponding figures for the CASQ were 1.2 and 7%. Several of the DES scales accounted for some unique variance in CDI, but the DES scales in combination were much more impressive.

Separate CDI scores were derived from the affective (CDI-A) and nonaffective (CDI-N) items. The DES and CASQ predicted the CDI-N virtually as well as they predicted the total CDI scores; the Rs were .89 and .67 for girls and boys, respectively. The results overall were almost identical for the regressions on CDI-T and CDI-N scores.

As with adults, the DES was quite effective in predicting the nonaffective symptomatology of depression, as measured by the CDI. It should be noted that in this initial study with children we have only shown "concurrent prediction" because the DES, CASQ, and CDI were administered on the same day.

Similarities and Differences in Depressive Emotion Profiles across Ages, Sexes, and Levels of Severity

A review of the emotion profiles in Table 2 and Figs. 2, 7, and 8 indicates that there are both continuities and discontinuities in patterns of emotions across levels of depression and age and sex groups. DES means on sadness, inner-directed hostility, and one or both of the emotions of shame and shyness were elevated in both severity levels (hospitalized, nonhospitalized) and in all age groups. Most group differences were in terms of the relative prominence of depression-related emotions, but there were some categorical differences in peak emotions. Hospitalized depressives reported relatively more outer-directed hostility and shyness than did nonhospitalized depressives. Sadness was the peak emotion for hospitalized and nonhospitalized adolescent and adult depressives, whereas anger was the peak emotion for children.

Sex differences were most pronounced in depressed children. Depressed girls' emotion profiles looked somewhat more like adults than did boys, particularly in regard to the sadness and hostility components, with boys showing relatively less sadness and more outward hostility. Also, depressed girls were more like adolescents and adults in the amount of fear and shyness reported.

Although the DES profiles of depressed girls resembled those of adults more than did those of boys, there were clear age differences. For example, relatively more guilt was reported by all adolescent and adults groups than by depressed 11–12-year-olds.

In the early studies of depression in college students sex was not considered as a factor. In the more recent studies, separate emotion profiles for male and female college students revealed some similarities and some differences between the sexes. While there were no significant sex differences for the nondepressed, depressed females reported somewhat more joy experiences and quite substantially more shame experiences than depressed males, supporting H. Lewis's (1971) notion of the importance of shame in women's depression.

Compared to depressed college males, depressed college females reported greater frequency of both positive and negative emotions, indicating greater emotional lability or more frequent and wider mood swings. Another possible source of sex differences lies in the differential socialization of sadness for men and women and subsequent sex differences in sadness phenomenology (Block, 1957; Izard, 1977).

On the Adaptiveness of Emotions in Depression

Evidence from depressed college students identified by high scores on the BDI, from primary school students who score high on the CDI, and from hospitalized depressives showed that the affective symptomatology of depression has features that cut across normal–abnormal and child–adult categories. In all of these groups depression tended to involve a characteristic set of emotions although there were developmental changes in the relative prominence of some emotions. We acknowledge the contribution of negative emotions to the subjective misery of depression. Yet, we maintain that these emotions, even in depression, have some adaptive function.

In all of our studies of the phenomenology of depression in adolescents and adults, the mean for sadness was always elevated. Thus, the feelings of dejection, downheartedness, discouragement, and loneliness are unquestionably a prominent feature of depressive experiences. Further, Bartlett and Izard (1972) found that subjects characterize the sadness experience as low on feelings of pleasantness, moderately low on feelings of self-assurance and impulsiveness, and relatively high on tension. The profiles of emotions and affective dimensions in the sadness situation are shown in Figs. 9 and 10.

Some investigators have raised the question as to whether sadness was a prominent feature of childhood depression, and others have questioned whether prolonged sadness could be distinguished from depression in children. Our data show that sadness is a prominent characteristic of girls who score high on the CDI, but the case is not so clear for boys, who are characterized by relatively more anger and outward hostility.

We found substantial differences between depression and sadness in adolescents and young adults. These data are summarized in Fig. 11. An analysis of variance revealed significant main effects for the DES + D fac-

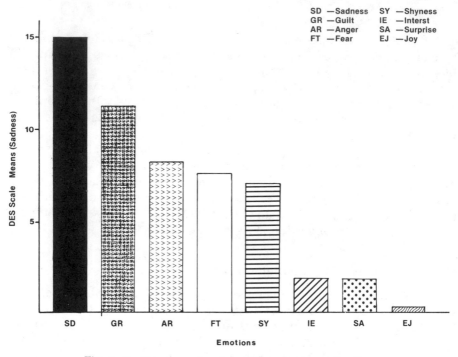

Fig. 9. *Profile of emotions in an imaged sadness situation.*

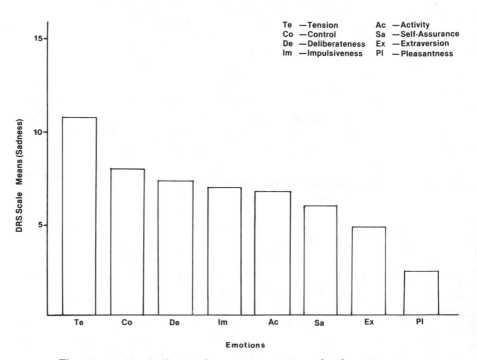

Fig. 10. *Profile of affective dimensions in an imaged sadness situation.*

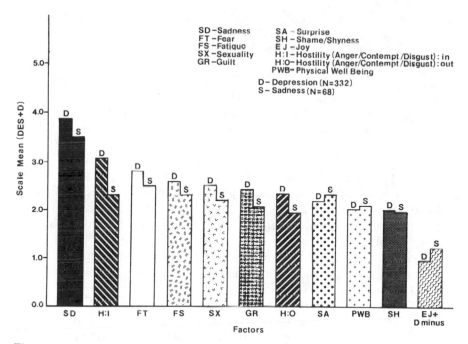

Fig. 11. *Differences in DES profiles for depression and sadness in adolescents and young adults.*

tors and for situations (depression versus sadness), and a significant Emotion × Situations (depression, sadness) interaction. The latter *F* indicated that subjects in the depression and sadness situations responded differentially to the various DES + D factors, indicating that the two emotion profiles in Fig. 11 are significantly different. Thus in adolescents and young adults sadness does not equal depression.

SADNESS

That sadness is different from depression enables us to consider the functions of sadness as a discrete emotion. As described earlier, Bower and his colleagues (Bower, 1981; Bower *et al.*, 1981) have demonstrated the mood-congruency effect for sadness. Other investigators (Hettena & Ballif, 1981) have shown that sadness interferes with learning or the processing of new information, such that people in a sad mood learn and remember significantly less than people in a happy mood. We shall call this effect the main effect of sadness.

Let us consider the possible maladaptive and adaptive influences of the mood-congruency effect and the main effect for sadness. A possible maladaptive consequence of the mood-congruency effect is that the enhanced memory for sad events can be reasonably expected to amplify and prolong the sad mood. However, enhanced memory for sad events might prove an adaptive resource by providing the individual a means of recalling and rehearsing coping strategies that have worked in past sadness-eliciting situations. It may also help the individual gain a more favorable perspective on the present situation. In one respect this is merely further testimony that sadness, like any emotion, has a powerful influence on mental events. If sadness has an adaptive function it must have some durability in consciousness, and the mood-congruency effect can produce the required durability.

The main effect for sadness guarantees that the sad person will have a reduced rate of learning and storage of new material in memory. This decrease in information processing provides the individual more time to evaluate and rectify the loss or failure that triggered the sadness. The slowing down of mental and physical processes that occurs in sadness can thus enable the individual to reconnoiter and make plans for recovery.

In addition to these characteristics of sadness identified through psychological experiments, a characteristic identified by common observation and clinical investigation is that sadness tends to create a feeling of loneliness or social isolation. At the same time, however, sadness expression serves as a stimulus for prosocial behavior and social bonding. Huebner and Izard (1983) have shown that the sadness expression in infants elicits positive affective response tendencies in the mother. Also, as adults we tend to empathize with the person who is sad from loss or failure. Shared sadness over loss of a loved one has a strong bonding effect, and one can argue that grief, which normally consists mainly of sadness, is a significant determinant of social cohesiveness (Averill, 1968). Everyone who has gathered for the last rites of a loved one has experienced a sense of increased affiliation with family and friends. What does this have to do with depression? Sadness is the key emotion in depression, and we are maintaining that its affiliative and empathic–prosocial functions are adaptive.

ANGER

The profile of emotions in the imaged anger situation is depicted in Fig. 12. Let us assume that this anger situation occurs in the context of depression. Note that with anger elevated (along with the rest of the hostility triad—disgust and contempt), sadness and fear are diminished. That this emotion–emotion dynamic—anger suppressing sadness/fear—occurs as a lawful emotion–emotion relationship is suggested by the repeatability of the profile in Fig. 12 (see Fig. 13) and by clinical observation. This sadness/fear suppression effect can be seen as the first adaptive function of anger in depressive disorders.

A second adaptive value of anger in depression comes from its energy mobilization function. Since Darwin and Cannon we have known that anger increases sympathetic discharge and creates strong tendencies to ac-
that any viable comprehensive model of depression will have to take a

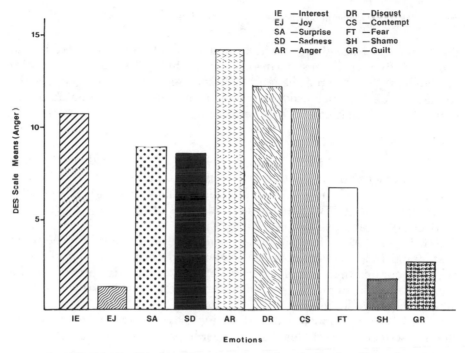

Fig. 12. *Profile of emotions in an imaged anger situation: Group I.*

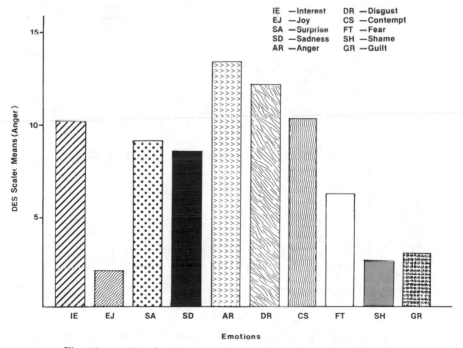

Fig. 13. *Profile of emotions in an imaged anger situation: Group II.*

tion. That anger affects energy and impulse to action is supported by the profile of affective dimensions in anger shown in Fig. 14. Anger not only increases tension and impulsiveness, it is associated with an elevated sense of self-assurance. The increased energy and self-assurance can facilitate constructive action that ameliorates depression.

SHAME

Darwin (1872/1965), H. Lewis (1971), and others (Izard, 1977) have noted that the experience of shame or humiliation is characterized by confusion of mind and inarticulateness. This shame experience shares with depression the cognitive deficiencies and sense of helplessness described by Beck (1967) and Seligman (1975).

H. Lewis (1979) cited empirical evidence for a connection between shame and field dependence—the tendency to be relatively more influenced by context than by self-generated affective–cognitive processes. She reviewed other empirical evidence for a relationship between field dependence and depression.

Izard (1977) hypothesized that shame or reflection on having been shamed activates anger. This shame–anger hypothesis is consistent with H.

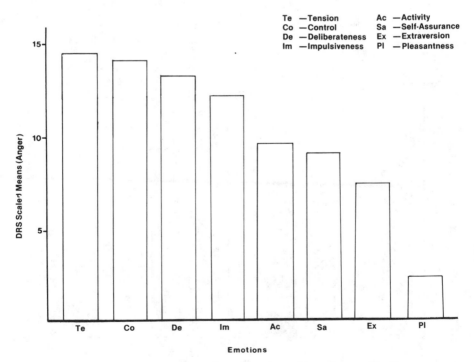

Fig. 14. *Profile of affective dimensions in an imaged anger situation.*

Lewis's (1971) observation from psychotherapy and clinical investigation that shame-prone field-dependent patients are more prone than field-independent patients to inner-directed hostility. The latter certainly contributes to the affective symptomatology of depression and can in extreme cases lead to suicide. As Lewis noted, shame is often experienced as rejection or hostility, including contempt–scorn from the "other," and thus outer-directed hostility is frequently generated toward the rejecting "other." She aptly described this outer-directed hostility as shame–rage, with the shamed self still being experienced as the object of the "other's" scorn.

These are persuasive arguments and evidence for shame and shame–anger interaction as part of the affective symptomatology of depression. Yet we maintain that shame and shame–anger interactions motivate behaviors that ameliorate depression and help prevent its recurrence. H. Lewis (1971), Izard (1977), and others have argued that shame and shame anticipation operate as a protector of the self and personal integrity. Shame increases the individual's sensitivity and responsiveness to criticism, contempt, rejection, or any indication that the self is overextended and overexposed. In depression the individual relies too much on the defense mechanisms of denial (or the significance of the source of criticism or scorn) and repression (of the shaming ideation). The fight against depression involves harnessing constructively the motivational and informational functions of shame–anticipation and shame-induced anger in developing social, cognitive, and motor skills and competencies that strengthen the self and make it less vulnerable to further shame and the pattern of emotions in depression.

Although we have argued that the emotions are basically adaptive, we recognize that intense emotion can be part of a vicious circle of maladaptively functioning systems. That is, biochemical disorders, environmental stress, negativistic perceptions and cognitions, irrational beliefs, and deficient coping skills can combine with intense emotion and result in maladaptive behavior and psychopathology. We also recognize that depressive and manic disorders are highly maladaptive. What we have highlighted in the foregoing arguments is that depression involves not only emotions but biochemistry, cognitive processes, and coping skills, and that the potential adaptive functions of the emotions in depression have been relatively neglected.

CONCLUDING REMARKS

We have focused on the affective phenomenology of depression and have left it to other contributors to address the other components of depression. We recognize that depression is multidimensional. We are convinced systems perspective and integrate information from the neurochemical, emotion, cognitive, motor, social, and ecological domains. Evidence in the other chapters of this volume makes it clear that depression involves all the systems of the individual and the larger social systems of the family and community.

The emotion-as-motivation theorists argue that missing or defective connections between certain emotions on the one hand and adaptive social and cognitive processes on the other play a critical role in depression. We need to determine whether there are stages of development in which the emotions identified as part of the symptomatology of depression are more likely to be linked to maladaptive styles of coping.

Our review of the clinical literature and the empirical evidence that are presented showed that some aspects of the affective symptomatology of depression are common to different levels of severity and to different age and sex groups. In our empirical studies of middle school through college and adult groups, the common core of emotions consisted of sadness, inner-directed hostility, and shame or shyness. The data also revealed some differences across severity, age, and sex groups that may help explain some of the difficulties in delineating stable criteria for depression. For example, the prominence of sadness, anger, and inner-directed hostility varies substantially with age and sex. The emotion profile for depressed boys (CDI > 19) was more consistent with possible aggressive or acting-out behaviors than were the profiles of depressed girls or adults.

We believe differential emotions theory and the empirical data we presented offer some fruitful leads for further research. However, we hasten to sound a note of caution. The work we reported was done over a 12-year period. Depression was identified in some of the studies by different criteria (psychiatric diagnosis, BDI, CDI, mood induction), and sex was not considered as a factor in some of the early studies. We recognize the need for multiple criteria and are initiating studies accordingly. We also recognize the inadequacy of sole reliance on self-report inventories (DES, CASQ) as predictor variables or for assessment of the affective and cognitive factors in depression. Judging from the amount of variance in the nonaffective symptomatology of depression that we can account for with these instruments, however, we do have a substantial beginning.

Obviously much remains to be discovered before a systems model of depression can integrate our knowledge of the role of biological, social, cognitive, ecological, and emotion processes in development. What we want to emphasize is that a recognition of the plurality of systems and causal factors should help us better understand the etiology of depression. The etiology of depression can be generally understood in terms of defective or missing links between the biochemical, emotion, cognitive, motor, and social systems, and the sources of the breakdowns in intersystem interaction and integration lie in the various biological and social processes of human development.

REFERENCES

Abraham, K. (1968). Notes on the psycho-analytical investigation and treatment of manic-depressive insanity and allied conditions. In W. Gaylin (Ed.), The meaning of despair (pp. 26–49). New York: Science House.

Achenbach, T., & Zigler, E. (1963). Social competence and self-image disparity in psychiatric and non-psychiatric patients. Journal of Abnormal and Social Psychology, 63, 197–205.

Ainsworth, M. D., Blehar, M. C., Waters, E., & Wall, S. (1978). Patterns of attachment: A psychological study of the strange situation. Hillsdale, NJ: Erlbaum.

Arnold, M. B. (1960). Emotion and personality: Vol. I. Psychological aspects. New York: Columbia University Press.

Averill, J. R. (1968). Grief: Its nature and significance. Psychological Bulletin, 70, 721–748.

Ax, A. F. (1953). The physiological differentiation between fear and anger in humans. Psychosomatic Medicine, 15, 433–442.

Bakwin, H., & Bakwin, R. M. (1972). Behavior disorders in children (4th ed.). Philadelphia: Saunders.

Barker, P. (1971). Basic child psychiatry. New York: Science House.

Bartlett, E. S. & Izard, C. E. (1972). A dimensional and discrete emotions investigation of the subjective experience of emotion. In C. E. Izard (Ed.), Patterns of emotions: A new analysis of anxiety and depression (pp. 129–173). New York: Academic Press.

Beck, A. T. (1967). Depression. New York: Harper & Row.

Block, J. (1957). Studies in the phenomenology of emotions. Journal of Abnormal and Social Psychology, 54, 358–363.

Blumberg, S., & Izard, C. E. (in press). Distinguishing patterns of emotions in anxious and depressed ten and eleven year old children. Journal of Personality and Social Psychology.

Bower, G. H. (1981). Emotional mood and memory. American Psychologist, 36(2), 129–148.

Bower, G. H. (1983). Affect and cognition. Philosophical Transactions of the Royal Society of London, Series B, 302, 387–402.

Bower, G. H., Gilligan, S., & Monteiro, K. P. (1981). Seloutivity of learning caused by affective states. Journal of Experimental Psychology: General, 110, 451–473.

Bowlby, J. (1969). Attachment and loss: Vol. I. Attachment. New York: Basic Books.

Brash, J. C. (1948). Cunningham's manual of practical anatomy. London & New York: Oxford University Press.

Bridges, K. M. B. (1932). Emotional development in early infancy. Child Development, 3, 324–341.

Brumback, R. A., Dietz-Schmidt, S. G., & Weinberg, W. A. (1977). Depression in children referred to an educational diagnostic center: Diagnosis, treatment, and analysis of criteria and literature review. Diseases of the Nervous System, 38, 529–535.

Brumback, R. A., & Weinberg, W. A. (1977a). Childhood depression: An explanation of behavior disorder in children. Perceptual and Motor Skills, 44, 911–916.

Brumback, R. A., & Weinberg, W. A. (1977b). Relationship of hyperactivity and depression in children. Perceptual and Motor Skills, 45, 247–251.

Bruner, J. S. (1964). The course of cognitive growth. American Psychologist, 19, 1–15.

Campos, J. J., & Stenberg, C. R. (1980). Perception, appraisal and emotion: The onset of social referencing. In M. Lamb & L. Sherrod (Eds.), Infant social cognition (pp. 273–314). Hillsdale, NJ: Erlbaum.

Cannon, W. B. (1929). Bodily changes in pain, hunger, fear and rage: An account of recent researchers into the function of emotional excitement (2nd ed.). New York: Appleton-Century-Crofts.

Caplan, M. G., & Douglas, V. I. (1969). Incidence of parental loss in children with depressed mood. Journal of Child Psychology and Psychiatry, 10, 225–232.

Carlson, G. A., & Cantwell, D. P. (1980a). A survey of depressive symptoms, syndrome and disorder in a child psychiatric population. Journal of Child Psychology and Psychiatry, 21, 19–25.

Carlson, G. A., & Cantwell, D. P. (1980b). Unmasking masked depression in children and adolescents. *American Journal of Psychiatry, 137*, 445–449.

Cicchetti, D., & Pogge-Hesse, P. (1981). Affect and intellect: Piaget's contributions to the study of infant emotional development. In R. Plutchik & H. Kellerman (Eds.), *Emotion: Research and theory* (Vol. 2, pp. 115–169). New York: Academic Press.

Cytryn, L., & McKnew, D. H., Jr. (1972). Proposed classification of childhood depression. *American Journal of Psychiatry, 129*, 63–69.

Cytryn, L., & McKnew, D. H., Jr. (1974). Factors influencing the changing clinical expression of the depressive process in children. *American Journal of Psychiatry, 131*, 879–881.

Darwin, C. R. (1965). *The expression of emotions in man and animals.* London: John Murray. (Original work published 1872).

Davis, J. (1970). Theories of biological etiology of affective disorder. *International Review of Neurobiology, 12*, 145–175.

Derryberry, D., & Rothbart, M. (1984). Emotion, attention and temperament. In C. E. Izard, J. Kagan, & R. Zajonc (Eds.), *Emotions, cognition, and behavior* (pp. 132–166). London & New York: Cambridge University Press.

Ekman, P., & Friesen, W. V. (1975). *Unmasking the face.* Englewood Cliffs, NJ: Prentice-Hall.

Ekman, P., Levenson, R. W., & Friesen, W. V. (1983). Autonomic nervous system activity distinguishes among emotions. *Science, 221*, 1208–1210.

Emde, R. N., Gaensbauer, T. J., & Harmon, R. J. (1976). *Emotional expression in infancy.* New York: International Universities Press, 1976.

Erikson, E. (1963). *Childhood and society.* New York: Norton. (Original work published 1950).

Freud, S. (1968). Mourning and melancholia. In W. Gaylin (Ed.), *The meaning of despair* (pp. 50–69). New York: Science House.

Funkenstein, D., King, S., & Drolette, M. (1954). The direction of anger during a laboratory stress-inducing situation. *Psychosomatic Medicine, 16*, 404–413.

Gaensbauer, T. J. (1980). Anaclitic depression in a three-and-one-half-month child. *American Journal of Psychiatry, 137*, 841–842.

Glasberg, R., & Aboud, F. E. (1981). A developmental perspective on the study of depression: Children's evaluative reactions to sadness. *Developmental Psychology, 17*, 195–202.

Green, M. R. (1972). The interpersonal approach to child therapy. In B. B. Wolman (Ed.), *Handbook of child psychoanalysis* (pp. 514–566). Princeton, NJ: Van Nostrand-Reinhold.

Groh, L. S. (1980). Primitive defenses: Cognitive aspects and therapeutic handling. *International Journal of Psychoanalytic Psychotherapy, 8*, 661–683.

Hettena, C., & Ballif, B. (1981). Effect on learning. *Journal of Educational Psychology, 73*(4), 505–508.

Huebner, R. R., & Izard, C. E. (1983). *Mothers' responses to infants' facial expressions of sadness, anger, and physical pain.* Unpublished manuscript.

Izard, C. E. (1971). *The face of emotion.* New York: Appleton.

Izard, C. E. (1972). *Patterns of emotion: A new analysis of anxiety and depression.* New York: Academic Press.

Izard, C. E. (1977). *Human emotions.* New York: Plenum Press.

Izard, C. E. (1978). On the development of emotions and emotion-cognition relationships in infancy. In M. Lewis & L. A. Rosenblum (Eds.), *The development of affect* (pp. 389–413). New York: Plenum Press.

Izard, C. E. (1979). *The maximally discriminative facial movement coding system (Max).* Newark, DE: University of Delaware, Instructional Resources Center.

Izard, C. E., & Buechler, S. (1980). Aspects of consciousness and personality in terms of differential emotions theory. In R. Plutchik & H. Kellerman (Eds.), *Theories of emotion* (pp. 165–187). New York: Academic Press.

Izard, C. E., Dougherty, F. E., Bloxom, B. M., & Kotsch, W. E. (1974). *The differential emotions scale: A method of measuring the subjective experience of discrete emotions.* Unpublished manuscript. Vanderbilt University, Nashville, TN.

Izard, C. E., Hembree, E. A., Dougherty, L. M., & Spizzirri, C. L. (1983). Changes in 2- to 19-month-old infants' facial expressions following acute pain. Developmental Psychology, 19, 418–426.

Izard, C. E., Huebner, R. R., Risser, D., McGinnis, G., & Dougherty, L. (1980) The young in fant's ability to produce discrete emotion expressions. Developmental Psychology, 16(2), 132–140.

Izard, C. E., Oyster, C. K., Lelwica, M. B., & Blumberg, S. H. (Unpublished). Cognitive and emotional factors in depression.

Izard, C. E., Wehmer, G. M., Livsey, W., & Jennings, J. R. (1965). Affect, awareness, and performance. In S. S. Tomkins & C. E. Izard (Eds.), Affect, cognition, and personality (pp. 2–41). New York: Springer.

Kagan, J. (1984). The idea of emotion in human development. In C. E. Izard, J. Kagan, & R. Zajonc (Eds.), Emotions, cognition, and behavior (pp. 38–72). London & New York: Cambridge University Press.

Kagan, J., Kearsley, R. B., & Zelazo, P. R. (1978). Infancy: Its place in human development. Cambridge, MA: Harvard University Press.

Kashani, J. & Simonds, J. F. (1979). The incidence of depression in children. American Journal of Psychiatry, 136, 1203–1205.

Kopp, C. B. (1982). Antecedents of self-organization: A developmental perspective. Developmental Psychology, 18, 199–214.

Kovacs, M., & Beck, A. T. (1979). Cognitive-affective processes in depression. In C. E. Izard (Ed.), Emotions in personality and psychopathology (pp. 415–442). New York: Plenum Press.

Laird, J. D., Wagener, J. J., Halal, M., & Szegda, M. (1982). Remembering what you feel: Effects of emotion on memory. Journal of Personality and Social Psychology, 42, 646–657.

Langsdorf, P., Izard, C., Rayias, M., & Hembree, E. (1983). Interest expression, visual fixation, and heart rate changes in 2- to 8-month old infants. Developmental Psychology, 19, 375–386.

Lanzetta, J. T., Cartwright-Smith, J. E., & Kleck, R. E. (1976). Effects of nonverbal dissimulation on emotional experience and autonomic arousal. Journal of Personality and Social Psychology, 33, 354–370.

Lazarus, R. S. (1968). Emotions and adaptation: Conceptual and empirical relations. In W. Arnold (Ed.), Nebraska symposium on motivation (Vol. XVI, pp. 175–266). Lincoln: University of Nebraska Press.

Lazarus, R. S. (1982). Thoughts on the relations between emotion and cognition. American Psychologist, 37, 1019–1024.

Lazarus, R. S., Kanner, A. D., & Folkman, S. (1980). Emotions: A cognitive-phenomenological analysis. In R. Plutchik & H. Kellerman (Eds.), Theories of emotion (Vol. 1, pp. 189–217). New York: Academic Press.

Lewis, H. (1971). Shame and guilt in neurosis. New York: International Universities Press.

Lewis, H. (1979). Shame in depression and hysteria. In C. E. Izard (Ed.), Emotions in personality and psychopathology (pp. 371–396). New York: Plenum Press.

Lewis, M., & Brooks, J. (1978). Self knowledge and emotional development. In M. Lewis & L. A. Rosenblum (Eds.), The development of affect (pp. 205–226). New York: Plenum Press.

Main, M., Tomasini, L., & Tolan, W. (1979). Differences among mothers of infants judged to differ in security. Developmental Psychology, 15, 472–473.

Malmquist, C. P. (1971). Depressions in childhood and adolescence. I, II. New England Journal of Medicine, 284, 887–893, 955–961.

Mandler, G. (1975). Mind and emotions. New York: Wiley.

Marshall, G. D., & Zimbardo, P. G. (1979). Affective consequences of inadequately explained physiological arousal. Journal of Personality and Social Psychology, 37, 970–988.

Maslach, C. (1979). Negative emotional biasing of unexplained arousal. Journal of Personality and Social Psychology, 37, 953–969.

McConville, B. J., Boag, L. C., & Purohit, A. P. (1973). Three types of childhood depression. *Canadian Psychiatric Association Journal, 18,* 133–137.

Mendelson, W. B., Reid, M. A., & Frommer, E. A. (1971). Some characteristic features accompanying depression, anxiety, and aggressive behavior in disturbed children under five. In A. L. Annell (Ed.), *Depressive states in childhood and adolescence* (pp. 151–158). Stockholm: European Congress of Pedopsychiatry.

Piaget, J. (1963). *The origins of intelligence in children.* New York: Norton. (Original work published 1936).

Piaget, J. (1981). *Intelligence and affectivity.* Palo Alto, CA: Annual Reviews.

Plutchik, R. (1980). *Emotion: A psychoevolutionary synthesis.* New York: Harper & Row.

Poznanski, E., & Zrull, J. P. (1970). Childhood depression: Clinical characteristics of overtly depressed children. *Archives of General Psychiatry, 23,* 8–15.

Rado, S. (1968). Psychodynamics of depression from the etiologic point of view. In W. Gaylin (Ed.), *The meaning of despair* (pp. 96–107). New York: Science House.

Sandler, J., & Joffe, W. G. (1965). Notes on childhood depression. *International Journal of Psychoanalysis, 46,* 88–95.

Scarr, S., & Salapatek, P. (1970). Patterns of fear development during infancy. *Merrill-Palmer Quarterly, 16,* 53–90.

Schachter, S. (1971). *Emotion, obesity and crime.* New York: Academic Press.

Schachter, S., & Singer, J. E. (1962). Cognitive, social, and physiological determinants of emotional states. *Psychological Review, 69,* 379–399.

Schwartz, G. E. (1982). Psychophysiological patterning and emotion revisted: a systems perspective. In C. E. Izard (Ed.), *Measuring emotions in infants and children* (pp. 67–93). London & New York: Cambridge University Press.

Schwartz, G. E., & Trabasso, R. (1984). Children's understanding of emotions. In C. Izard, J. Kagan, & R. Zajonc (Eds.), *Emotions, cognition, and behavior* (pp. 409–437). London & New York: Cambridge University Press.

Seligman, M. E. (1975). *Helplessness.* San Francisco: Freeman.

Spitz, R. (1946). Anaclitic depression. *Psychoanalytic Study of the Child, 2,* 113–117.

Sroufe, L. A. (1979). Socioemotional development. In J. D. Osofsky (Ed.), *Handbook of infant development* (pp. 462–516). New York: Wiley.

Sroufe, L. A., Schork, E., Motti, F., Lawroski, N., & LaFreniere, P. (1984). The role of affect in social competence. In C. E. Izard, J. Kagan, & R. Zajonc (Eds.), *Emotions, cognition, and behavior* (pp. 289–319). London & New York: Cambridge University Press.

Thoman, E. B. & Acebo (1984). Affective communication as the prelude and context for language learning. In R. L. Schiefelbusch & D. Bricker (Eds.), *Early language: Acquisition and intervention.* Baltimore: University Park Press.

Thomas, A., & Chess, S. (1977). *Temperament and development.* New York: Bruner/Mazel.

Vaughan, K. B., & Lanzetta, J. T. (1980). Vicarious instigation and conditioning of facial expressive and autonomic responses to a model's expressive display of pain. *Journal of Personality and Social Psychology, 36,* 909–923.

Wessman, A. E., & Ricks, J. H. (1966). *Mood and personality.* New York: Holt.

Wolf, S., & Wolff, H. G. (1942). Evidence on the genesis of peptic ulcer in men. *Journal of American Medical Association, 120,* 670–675.

Zuckerman, M., & Lubin, B. (1964). Measurement of experimentally induced affects. *Journal of Consulting Psychology, 23,* 418–425.

An Organizational Approach
to Childhood Depression

Dante Cicchetti
Karen Schneider-Rosen

THE NEED FOR A DEVELOPMENTAL PERSPECTIVE

It is a sensible scientific strategy to investigate and to interpret a new domain of inquiry using theories and methods that have been successfully employed in a similar but better known domain. One should expect that, insofar as the new domain differs from the familiar one, the theories and methods will need to be adapted to these differences. Furthermore, if the new domain differs systematically, then it is likely that more extreme modifications and adjustments in both theory and method will be required. The adaptations and developments that will characterize the conceptualization of the new domain will be guided by an understanding of the need for the formation of a new domain for scientific inquiry, an appreciation of the differences between the familiar and the new domains, and a theoretically and empirically based rationale for the proposition, development, and subsequent organization of the new domain.

The study of depression in childhood represents a clear illustration of this scientific strategy. In the past two decades, remarkable advances have been made in the understanding of the epidemiology, symptomatology, etiology, psychobiology, and treatment of adult depression. Concomitantly, there has been a proliferation of interest in childhood depression since the publication of Rie's (1966) comprehensive review. However, while impressive theoretical and empirical advances have been made in the development and organization of this "new domain" (for reviews see,

Dante Cicchetti and Karen Schneider-Rosen. Department of Psychology and Social Relations, Harvard University, Cambridge, Massachusetts. Author Cicchetti is now at the Department of Psychology and Psychiatry, University of Rochester, Rochester, New York.

e.g., Arieti & Bemporad, 1978; Kashani *et al.*, 1981; Puig-Antich, 1980b), there still exists a great deal of disagreement over many important issues crucial to the formulation of a comprehensive theory of childhood depression. Thus, for example, there is disagreement regarding what criteria should be used in the diagnosis of childhood depression; whether childhood depression can be divided into subtypes according to classifications such as primary versus secondary or endogenous versus nonendogenous; the role of genetic and biological factors in childhood depression; and the continuity of childhood with adult depression.

Given this state of affairs, it is probably best to work backward from adult depression, extending the models, concepts, and theories that have been useful there to childhood affective disorders (cf. Gittelman-Klein, 1977; Kovacs & Beck, 1977). However, their application to children is not a straightforward matter, because of the biological and psychological differences between children and adults, and because of the orderly, systematic progression that can be observed in the development of infants and children. It is therefore necessary to take into account how the presence of this orderly development may be expected to alter, affect, or limit the extension of adult theories of depression to children. Thus, the integration of extant work on adult depression and of developmental theory provides the appropriate basis for the formulation of a developmental perspective in order to understand the symptomatology, etiology, prognosis, assessment, and treatment of childhood depression. Therefore, one must rely upon knowledge of normal development in order to understand the forms depressive psychopathology can take throughout development. Furthermore, one must conceive of psychopathology as a process that develops through time and that is in a sense embedded in developmental changes approximating those found in the healthy child (see Cicchetti, 1984).

Development and Symptomatology

In recent years, many attempts have been made to apply adult criteria for the diagnosis of depression to children (Kashani *et al.*, 1981; Puig-Antich, 1980a). In fact, the DSM-III criteria (American Psychiatric Association, 1980) for diagnosis of major depressive episodes in childhood are substantially the same as those specified for adults. A growing number of empirical studies of childhood depression have relied upon the use of unaltered Research Diagnostic Criteria (RDC) (Puig-Antich, 1980a, 1980b; Spitzer, Endicott, & Robins, 1978) and upon the application of the DSM-III criteria. This research strategy may be flawed for a number of reasons. The criteria may be too narrow, excluding some cases that should be classified as depression. Some or all of those children who satisfy DSM-III or RDC criteria may have disorders whose etiology differs from that of adult depression. Moreover, if there are childhood precursors to or prototypes of adult depression, they may take a different, and as yet unknown, symptomatological form. Perhaps most importantly, age-appropriate limitations in children's cognitive, emotional, and social development may make the expression of specific depressive symptoms beyond their repertoire. Thus, the delineation of those characteristics relevant to the overt manifestation of depression at different ages can probably only be accomplished by means of longitudinal prospective studies that measure skills and capacities in a variety of developmental domains.

This research strategy is likely to be most fruitful if a developmental perspective is adopted. It is especially important in this regard to distinguish between similarities and differences in molar and molecular symptomatology during different developmental periods. Because of the reorganization of behavioral systems that takes place at each new level of development, one should not expect to see, for any symptom, behavioral isomorphism at the molecular level, even if there is isomorphism at the molar level. For example, the child whose depressive episode spans the transition from preoperational to concrete-operational thought may display excessive and inappropriate guilt, a loss of self-esteem, and a decrease in activity throughout the episode. Consequently, at a molar level, the depressive symptoms at the later period will be isomorphic to those of the earlier. Nonetheless, the particular manifestation of the guilt feelings, loss of self-esteem, and psychomotor retardation may change and develop during the transition, when the child's cognitive, affective, and behavioral competencies undergo a rather radical development (Flavell, 1977; S. H. White, 1965). In this way there may be noteworthy differences at the molecular level (cf. Dweck, Gittelman-Klein, McKinney, & Watson, 1977).

It is probably the case that most clinicians and researchers who apply DSM-III criteria to children to varying ages draw upon their knowledge of normal development and of the histories of the children being diagnosed in order to adapt and to adjust the criteria to the particular developmental levels of the children. They thus intuitively render the criteria age appropriate and sensitive to behavioral differences at the molecular level. That clinicians and researchers understand the diagnostic criteria differently and translate them into developmentally appropriate criteria in different ways probably explains a large portion of the lack of interjudge reliability in the diagnosis of major depressive illness using such criteria in children (Achenbach & Edelbrock, 1983). However, if one adopts a developmental perspective, one may then attempt to formulate more precise criteria by referring to the normal sequence of development and by specifying how the expression of the molar symptoms of depression may remain relatively stable while there may be significant changes at the molecular level with development. This we may expect would lead in turn not only to greater diagnostic reliability, but also to a clearer understanding of the etiology of childhood depression.

Development and Etiology

A range of opinions has been expressed concerning the etiology of childhood depression from a developmental point of view. The usual strategy adopted by theorists is to choose some psychological or psychobiological mechanism as being essential to depression and then to speculate concerning whether this mechanism can operate in children of various ages, given their levels of cognitive, affective, social, and moral development. For example, Rie (1966), taking an orthodox psychoanalytic view (cf. Beres, 1966; Rochlin, 1959), argues that it is not possible for genuine depressive illness to exist prior to puberty, due to the prepubertal child's lack of a well-developed superego and because of the absence of any structure by means of which anger can be retroflexed against the ego. Malmquist (1971, 1975) proposes the children's lack of ego differentiation limits their range of potential affective expressions, that their weaker ego and superego controls result in a greater intensity and fluctuation of moods, and that their less stable object relations result in greater mood swings that are of briefer duration than those experienced by adults. Anthony (1975) supports this view and contends that because children are more susceptible to external environmental influences, their depressive reactions are more likely to be transient and to represent relatively brief responses to their surroundings.

Perhaps the most sophisticated theoretical study of this type is that of Bemporad and Wilson (1978), who bring together Sandler and Joffe's (1965) notion of depression as a primary, psychobiological affect with a cognitive–structuralist view. Bemporad and Wilson (1978) argue that since the emotions that children can experience are determined by their level of cognitive development, the primary affect of depression will develop parallel with children's cognitive development. Bemporad and Wilson (1978) then describe precursors to adult depression that one may observe at various levels of cognitive development. In their opinion, because of the limited cognitive abilities of children, the primary affect of depression cannot take the form of a depressive syndrome until late childhood.

The notion that a mechanism of depression will manifest itself differently according to the cognitive capacities of the child seems sound to us, and we advocate that in a similar way the child's developing affective, social, and social–cognitive abilities should be taken into account in any theoretical formulation with regard to the etiology of depression. It is clear that, in order to do this, one will need to draw upon theories of normal cognitive, emotional, social, and social–cognitive development. It should be added that there is nothing methodologically problematic in hypothesizing that the same mechanism may have varying phenotypical manifestations. This could be established both by the construct validation of the mechanism involved (Cronbach & Meehl, 1955) and by the observation of a causal continuity between manifestations at successive developmental periods (J. H. Block & Block, 1980; Sackett, Sameroff, Cairns, & Suomi, 1981; Sroufe, 1979b).

Development, Prognosis, and Treatment

There have as yet been few published long-term, longitudinal, prospective studies of children suffering from depression. There are thus no clear and convincing data on whether depression in childhood is more than a transient sign of adjustment, whether it is episodic in nature and, if so, what the duration and period of episodes are, whether depression occurs both as a primary disorder and as secondary to other disorders, and whether symptoms secondary to depression remit after the depression remits (Costello, 1980; Tesiny & Lefkowitz, 1982). The only long-term study that we are aware of that is relevant in this respect (Poznanski, 1980–1981; Poznanski, Krahenbuhl, & Zrull, 1976) is methodologically flawed (e.g., small sample size, ratings were not made blindly, the symptoms as specified may not satisfy recognized criteria, no interrater reliability was obtained, there was no control group, and there is a paucity of developmental information). However, it is clear that if the natural course of childhood depression were known and charted against relevant developmental factors there would be a firmer basis both for prognoses to be made and for determining the relationship between severity and kind of symptoms and later functioning.

Finally, a developmental perspective seems especially relevant to the treatment of childhood depression. It would seem important to chart the normal ontogenesis of the biological substrates of depression as well as developmental changes in the neurobiological and biochemical anomalies reported in childhood depression (Puig-Antich, 1980b; Rapoport, 1977), which would be relevant to drug therapy. Moreover, the affective and especially cognitive, social, and social–cognitive developmental level of the child is particularly important for choosing and designing appropriate therapeutic intervention.

THE ORGANIZATIONAL APPROACH TO DEVELOPMENT

Since it is apparent that a developmental perspective should be adopted, we shall discuss how a developmentalist would view childhood depression. We shall first expound the particular developmental framework that we believe will be most helpful—the organizational approach.

The organizational approach to development (Cicchetti & Sroufe, 1978; Sroufe, 1979a, 1979b)—also sometimes referred to as the "organismic" or "structuralist" approach—consists of a set of regulative principles that can guide research into and theorizing concerning human behavior (Santostefano, 1978; Sroufe & Rutter, 1984). In calling these principles "regulative" we follow Werner (1948, 1957), who denied that they are themselves to be taken as empirical laws or that, in research and theory, one should necessarily attempt to find laws that can be seen as simple translations of these principles into empirical terms. Rather, these regulative principles are to be taken as heuristic tools, by means of which one can look for meaningful patterns in the great variety and quantity of data often accumulated in contemporary studies of human development and developmental psychopathology (Cicchetti, 1984; Sroufe & Rutter, 1984). With the aid of this heuristic, investigators may formulate empirical laws with greater confidence that they have uncovered lawful relations rather than merely accidental correlations.

According to the organizational approach, development may be conceived as a series of qualitative reorganizations among and within behavioral systems, which take place by means of differentiation and hierarchical integration. Variables at many levels of analysis determine the character of these reorganizations: genetic, constitutional, neurobiological, biochemical, behavioral, psychological, environmental, and sociological. Moreover, these variables are conceived as being in dynamic transaction with one another.

"Normal" development—one might say "healthy" development—is not defined in terms of the mean, since it is not necessarily the case that the mean defines mental health. Rather, it is defined in terms of a series of interlocking social, emotional, and cognitive competencies. Competence at one period of development, which tends to make the individual broadly adapted to his or her environment, prepares the way for the formation of competence at the next (Sroufe & Rutter, 1984). Moreover, normal development is marked by the integration of earlier competencies into later modes of functioning. It follows then that early adaptation tends to promote later adaptation and integration.

Pathological development, in contrast, may be conceived of as a lack of integration of the social, emotional, and cognitive competencies that are important to achieving adaptation at a particular developmental level (Cicchetti & Schneider-Rosen, 1984a; Kaplan, 1966; Sroufe, 1979a). Because early structures often are incorporated into later structures, an early deviation or disturbance in functioning may ultimately cause much larger disturbances to emerge later on.

However, just as early competence may lead to later adaptation and incompetence to later maladaptation, this isomorphism in functioning may not be the only expectable outcome. It is necessary to engage in a comprehensive evaluation of those factors that may influence the nature of individual differences, the continuity of adaptive or maladaptive behavioral patterns, and the different pathways by which the same developmental outcomes may be achieved. It is important to map out the processes whereby the normal course of development in the social, emotional, and/or cognitive domains, in dynamic transaction with the "inner" (i.e., biological) constitutional and "outer" (i.e., familial conditions, stresses, support systems, peer groups) environmental characteristics of the child, may lead to outcomes that either inhibit or exacerbate early deviations or maintain or disrupt early adaptation. Therefore, it is essential to look for prototypes and precursors of pathology by considering the continuity or discontinuity of adaptive or maladaptive behavioral patterns, the individual's level of functioning in relation to age- and stage-appropriate expectations, the quality and stability of the caregiving environment, and the nature of the early experiences to which the child is exposed.

The Orthogenetic Principle of Development

In the organizational approach, the qualitative reorganizations characteristic of development are conceived as proceeding in accordance with the orthogenetic principle (Werner, 1948), which states that the developing organism moves from a relatively diffuse and globally undifferentiated state, by means of differentiation and hierarchical integration, to a state of greater articulation and organized complexity. The orthogenetic principle may be seen as a solution to the problem of the individual's continuous adaptation to the environment and to the question of how integrity of function may be maintained in the face of change. Continuity in functioning can be maintained via hierarchical integration despite rapid constitutional changes and biobehavioral shifts (J. Block, 1971; J. H. Block & Block, 1980; Sackett et al., 1981; Sroufe, 1979a).

One major manifestation of the orthogenetic principle evident in normal psychological development is in the changes that take place in the relationship between the individual and the environment. Very young infants may be conceived of as relatively psychologically undifferentiated from their environment. They are governed largely by physiological processes and their actions are bound closely to particular stimulus situations, so that temperamental and biological rather than cognitive factors play the largest role in guiding their behavior. However, as development proceeds, infants and children play a greater role in interpreting, filtering, and thus "constructing experience;" therefore, cognitions and cognitive styles become more important in determining children's contemporary adjustments and later adaptation. Consequently, behavior and thought are no longer directly dependent upon changes in the external environment. Moreover, with this differentiation children develop greater flexibility in responding to their surroundings and become able to substitute various means for attaining a desired goal.

The psychological differentiation of children from their surroundings can be studied as a social phenomenon—the differentiation and integration of various bonds between children, caregivers, and peers in development—and as an affective–cognitive phenomenon—children's developing conception of their selves and of their emotions. Both of these processes are directly relevant to childhood depression, and they will be discussed below.

Because development typically involves the organization through integration of previously differentiated behaviors, we can predict that the expression of childhood depression will indeed be characterized by molar continuities but additionally by molecular discontinuities and changes. At the molar level, continuity will be preserved by an orderly development in the organization of behaviors; however, at the molecular level, the behaviors that are present at different periods may vary (J. Block, 1971; J. H. Block & Block, 1980; Kagan, 1980; Sackett et al., 1981; Sroufe & Waters, 1977).

The organization, and not frequency or duration, of behaviors is of the greatest importance in development because any behavior can have different functions in different organizational contexts, whereas the same function within one context can be served by many different behaviors (Werner & Kaplan, 1963). The significance of a behavior must then be inferred from its context, and meaningful interrelationships among behaviors, if they are to be detected, may be found among behaviors that play the same or related functions. This principle has at least two consequences for the study of childhood depression:

1. Concerning the occurrence of any symptom or expression of depression in childhood, there is a need to examine and to analyze both situational variables and antecedent and consequent events. The behaviors of interest must be examined in terms of how they reflect motivational, emotional, and biological needs of the individuals as well as influence those needs as a result of their occurrence. In particular, we may expect that developmental advances in various behavioral domains will influence the mode of expression and meaning of these behaviors.
2. Because what is sought is an evaluation of the organization of various capacities of the child at different periods of development, rather than a mere catalog of these capacities, the analysis of process becomes as important as the study of outcome (cf. Werner, 1937). The continuity of adaptation and the use of alternative

pathways to achieve adaptation are especially significant, and so it becomes essential to investigate individual as well as group differences.

Finally, it is necessary to mention the notion of *hierarchic motility:* that those early structures that are incorporated into later ones by means of hierarchical integration may remain accessible, ready to be activated and utilized during times of stress, crisis, novelty, and creativity. It has been suggested (Werner, 1957) that all problem-solving behavior involves first a regression via hierarchic motility to a relatively immature level of functioning in the relevant domain, and then renewed differentiation and integration, which takes the "problem" into account. It may be fruitful to consider environmental stressors as presenting "problems" to be "solved" by the child. We would expect that children who have a great deal of hierarchic motility would in general best be able to cope with stressors, by means of a strategy that may at first appear regressive and immature, but is later seen to be effective. Pathology in turn may result or partly be caused by a lack of motility or else an inability to redifferentiate after regression in response to stressors. An illuminating analogy here would be Teitelbaum's (1971, 1977) work on the parallels between loss of functions after brain damage and the normal ontogenesis of those functions. In the successful response of children to environmental stressors we may expect to see a process that parallels earlier, normal development. Moreover, we would expect that, with development and increased experience, the child becomes more competent at negotiating minor regressions in response to stress so that integrity of functioning may be more easily maintained with a concomitant decrease in the overt manifestation of disorganization or anxiety.

Behavioral Systems

The organizational approach conceptualizes human psychology in terms of a hierarchical organization of interacting and interrelated behavioral systems. These systems are constructs, hypothesized to account for the organization of behavior observed in naturalistic settings and in the laboratory. The concept of behavioral systems should be seen as an outgrowth of three scientific advances in fields other than psychology:

1. Advances in neurophysiology indicate that the nervous system is hierarchically organized (Bronson, 1965; Kandel, 1979; Kandel & Schwartz, 1981; Luria, 1980; Nauta & Feirtag, 1979). In proposing behavioral systems to explain behavior, one implicitly accepts that the systems have a neurophysiological instantiation that is likewise hierarchical.
2. It has become clear in computer science that a hierarchically organized computer program consisting of various subroutines is

best able to simulate the directedness of human behavior. Such programs provide a useful metaphor for understanding human behavior as likewise organized into subsystems that are hierarchically arranged (Miller, 1978; von Bertalanffy, 1968).

3. In ethology the notion of a fixed-action pattern (Lorenz, 1953; Lorenz & Tinbergen, 1938) has been elaborated and modified in order to explain behavior seemingly motivated by "drives." Ethologists have had success in describing the goal-directed behavior of animals by means of hierarchically organized control systems (see, for example, Dethier, 1976).

By adopting similar notions, psychologists can avoid awkward assumptions about metapsychological entities while integrating their findings with coordinate results in neurophysiology, ethology, ecology, and evolutionary theory.

In psychology three general behavioral systems—cognitive, affective, and social—have been proposed by investigators adopting an organizational approach. The hierarchical integration that occurs with development takes place *within* each behavioral system; additionally, competencies in each system become integrated *between* behavioral systems (see, for example, Bischof, 1975; Bronson, 1972; Cicchetti & Serafica, 1981). The organization of these behavioral systems in normal development and the observed lack of organization in pathology then become two of the most central concerns of developmental psychopathologists. Of particular importance are advances and lags in one behavioral system with respect to the others, because the presence of capacities of one behavioral system may be a necessary condition for the development or exercise of capacities of another system. For example, in infancy certain social capacities (that is, those associated with a secure attachment) may be necessary for the age-appropriate development of cognitive abilities. Likewise, certain cognitive skills may be necessary for the development of particular affectual expressions and experiences (Cicchetti & Sroufe, 1976, 1978; Hesse & Cicchetti, 1982). Lags in these systems may then result in compensatory development, which may in some instances leave the child vulnerable to pathology (see Cicchetti & Schneider-Rosen, 1984a, 1984b).

A Dynamic, Transactional Model

The organizational approach implies a transactional model of development (cf. Sameroff & Chandler, 1975), which recognizes the importance of the transacting genetic, constitutional, neurobiological, biochemical, psychological, and sociological factors in the determination of behavior, and which states that those factors change through their dynamic transaction. A transactional model thus denies reductionism (see also Engel, 1977;

Marmor, 1983); in particular, it denies that the pathological process of depression can be seen as an emerging characteristic of, for example, some biological process or some history of reinforcement *alone*. Rather the various factors that operate in a pathological process all operate together through a hierarchy of dispositions. For example, a genetic diathesis may constitute a disposition to biochemical anomalies only given the action of some psychological mechanism; these biochemical anomalies in turn may constitute a disposition to the development of psychological anomalies only given a particular pattern of socialization (cf. Meehl, 1962). Thus, some factors act as *permissive* causes by constituting dispositions; others act as *efficient* causes by realizing these dispositions. Moreover, it need not be the case that, as in the traditional diathesis–stress model (Gottesman & Shields, 1972; Zubin & Spring, 1977), only genetic or biological factors act as permissive causes, whereas psychological or environmental factors function only as efficient causes. For example, long-standing patterns of social interaction in a child's immediate social environment may constitute a permissive cause for depression, or what may be called a "vulnerability factor," whereas transient biological or biochemical changes during the course of development may be efficient causes of depression, or "challengers" (Cicchetti & Schneider-Rosen, 1984b). Furthermore, the particular vulnerability factors and challengers may vary in significance over time, as well as in relative importance with regard to the operation of alternative permissive or efficient causes. Similarly, with development, the organization of competencies in each of the behavioral systems, and the integration between the systems, may introduce protective factors or buffers against the overt manifestation of depression.

The transactional model, because it denies reductionism and emphasizes the potential role of a variety of factors in childhood depression, provides a place for the activity of children themselves in the pathological process. Attention and perception thresholds, cognitive styles, and interpretive presuppositions will alter the influence that environmental and even biological factors may have. Perception itself is conceived as a transaction between subject and object. Here the notion of *microgenesis* (Werner, 1948) becomes especially important. Microgenesis refers to the transient psychological processes and events that actually display in a telescoped manner a developmental process. For example, a child who perceives and interprets a previously unencountered stimulus moves from formulating a global and diffuse representation of the stimulus to then integrating it into a unified conception. It would seem important to study processes that display microgenesis in depressed children in order to see if these develop in an anomalous fashion, perhaps in some way corresponding to the anomalous development of depressive pathology. Perception is of particular significance, since it is in a sense children's front line of encounter with the world. The manner in which the depressed child selects and organizes stimuli may be related to the broader cognitive distortions observed in depression (Beck, 1967) and may resemble classic accounts of the operation of defense mechanisms (cf. Bowlby, 1980).

CHILDHOOD DEPRESSION AND THE ORGANIZATION OF NORMAL DEVELOPMENT

Below, we shall consider three topics drawn from contemporary developmental research that we believe play a particularly important role in the understanding of childhood depression. The theme that will be elaborated in these sections is that the theory of and research into the organizational changes in normal development can lead to a better understanding of the pathological process of depression.

Competence

DEFINITION AND VALIDITY OF THE CONSTRUCT

The concept of competence (Harter, 1978; R. White, 1959) is of the greatest relevance to psychopathology because of the important interrelations between affect and social relations (Erikson, 1950; Sroufe, 1979b). The concept of competence has a potential of playing a wide-ranging integrative role in theories of social, emotional, and cognitive development. Hence, through investigating the relationship between competence and childhood depression, it may be possible to place theories of the pathogenesis of depression squarely within an integrative framework of normal ontogenesis. However, it is precisely because competence is such a broad and integrative concept that care must be taken in assessing competence at various developmental periods and in determining how various means of achieving competence may both affect and be affected by depressive symptomatology.

Waters and Sroufe (1983) define the competent child as one who is able to use internal and external resources in order to attain a satisfactory developmental adaptation. *Internal resources* include both specific skills and also broad characteristics of an individual, which would be subsumed under general constructs such as self-esteem. *External resources* include anything else that may serve to help the developing child coordinate affect, cognition, and behavior in order to attain short- and long-term adaptation (e.g., relations with others, appropriate imitation of models). Adaptation at a particular developmental level implies the successful resolution of the developmental task or tasks most salient for that period. It is part of the Waters and Sroufe (1983) conception of competence that early competence is predictive of later competence, given that there are no irregularities in development (e.g., changes in the quality of care the child receives, increased stress in the environment). This notion of competence requires that the successful resolution of a stage-salient developmental task by the child should be correlated with the resolution of other tasks salient for that stage as well as those salient for the next stage; that is, there should be concurrent and predictive correlations among measures of competence. Of course, the possibility of circularity and a lack of openness to experimental falsification enters in at this point: if putative measures of competence fail to correlate in this way, does the child change in competence, are the measures poor, or should the construct of competence itself be rejected? As with any construct, there is no simple way of deciding which of these alternatives is correct (cf. Cronbach & Meehl, 1955; Meehl, 1972). However, Waters and Sroufe (1983) argue that the choice will be a clearer and easier one if multiple measures are used to assess competence. These measures should be broadband and they should be employed in both naturalistic and experimental settings. In addition, they should tax the adaptive capacity of the child by requiring the child to coordinate affective, cognitive, and social behavioral systems (Waters & Sroufe, 1983).

There has been a good deal of research in the past few years on the continuity of competence in normal children based upon a series of stage-salient developmental issues that have been proposed and agreed upon by a number of developmentalists (Erikson, 1950; Greenspan, 1981; Sander, 1962; Sroufe & Rutter, 1984). These issues are presented chronologically in Table 1. The delineation of these issues is not exhaustive; rather, it is intended to be illustrative of several of the major developmental themes of infancy and childhood. Instead of construing development as a series of unfolding tasks that need to be accomplished and then decrease in importance, we perceive development as consisting of a number of important age- and stage-appropriate tasks that, upon emergence, remain critical to the child's continual adaptation but decrease in salience relative to other newly emerging developmental tasks. For example, we do not perceive of attachment as a developmental issue of the first year of life alone; rather, once an attachment relationship develops, it continues to undergo transformations and reintegrations with subsequent accomplishments such as emerging autonomy and entrance into the peer world. As a result, children are continually renegotiating the balance between being connected to others and being independent and autonomous as they encounter each new developmental issue. Consequently, each of the issues portrayed in Table 1 represent life-span developmental tasks that require continual coordina tion and integration in the individual's adaptation to the environment.

The general developmental trend represented in Table 1 is a familiar one in theories of socioemotional development: social ontogenesis begins with an undifferentiated state of arousal, from which attachment and later a distinct sense of self and of autonomy are first differentiated. Subse-

Table 1
Developmental Scheme for Conceptualizing the Ontogenesis of Competence

General developmental issue	Approximate age			
	0–12 months	12–30 months	30 months–7 years	7–12 years
Attachment	Modulation of arousal Physiological regulation Formation of secure attachment relationship with primary caregiver Differentiation and integration of emotional reactions	→		
Autonomy		Differentiation of persons Awareness of self as distinct entity Exploration of environment Regulation and control of emotional reactions Problem solving, pride and mastery motivation Capacity to delay gratification and to tolerate frustration Awareness of standards Development of language and communicative skills	→	

Establishing peer relationships

Hierarchical integration of attachment, autonomy, and peer relationships

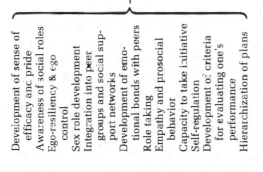

Development of sense of efficacy and pride
Awareness of social roles
Ego-resiliency & ego control
Sex role development
Integration into peer groups and social support networks
Development of emotional bonds with peers
Role taking
Empathy and prosocial behavior
Capacity to take initiative
Self-regulation
Development of criteria for evaluating one's performance
Hierarchization of plans

Hierarchization of social networks and multiple attachment figures
Formation of feelings of volition and agency of the self
Awareness of and ability to express multiple emotions
Internalization of standards of right and wrong and development of morality
Capacity to assume responsibilities and to accomplish tasks
Awareness of internal psychological processes

quently, peer relations develop, and finally the social and affective bonds with principal attachment figures and peers are organized and integrated, together with a more consolidated conception of the self. Therefore, with development, there is a continuing differentiation between self and other, paralleled by a reorganization of connections between children and their expanding social world.

Recent studies have indicated that, for normal middle-class children raised in relatively stable, stress-free environments—that is, those in which the parents have no mental illness and where there are few significant deleterious life events—there is considerable continuity of adaptation and maladaptation (Sroufe, 1979a, 1983; Sroufe, Schork, Motti, Lawroski, & LaFreniere, 1984). One of the first stage-salient developmental tasks, establishing an attachment relationship, has been assessed primarily by Ainsworth and Wittig's (1969) Strange Situation paradigm, according to which infants can be judged as securely or insecurely attached (Ainsworth, Blehar, Waters, & Wall, 1978). Ainsworth *et al.* (1978) distinguish three kinds of attachment relationships—avoidant, secure, and resistant—which they label Groups A, B, and C, respectively. Approximately 70% of normal mother–infant dyads are securely attached, while 30% are insecurely attached (20% avoidant and 10% resistant). Quality of attachment in normal infants raised in a relatively stress-free environment has been shown to be highly stable between 12 and 18 months (Waters, 1978). In addition, quality of attachment is predicted by the quality of the earlier mother–infant interaction (Ainsworth *et al.*, 1978; Blehar, Lieberman, & Ainsworth, 1977), which is itself related to the specific issues of modulation of arousal and physiological regulation. Moreover, Waters, Wippman, and Sroufe (1979) have shown that there are good concurrent correlations among quality of attachment and various measures of affectivity.

Matas, Arend, and Sroufe (1978) have proposed that observational studies of problem-solving behavior in the presence of an attachment figure can be used to assess competence in toddlers. Since the securely attached infant is one who uses the caregiver as a secure base for exploration and returns to the caregiver when distressed, Matas *et al.* (1978) reasoned that the secure attachment in the toddler should take a similar form. They thus posited not behavioral isomorphisms between competent toddler and infant, but rather a similar organization of behavior. It was hypothesized that competent toddlers would show flexibility, resourcefulness, and perseverance (internal resources); moreover, they would be able to rely on the attachment figure for assistance when necessary without becoming dependent (external resources). A high correlation between quality of attachment at 18 months and competence thus defined at 24 months was discovered.

Finally, the assessment of competence has been extended into early and middle childhood by the finding that quality of attachment predicts peer relations (Waters et al., 1979), ego-resiliency (Arend, Gove, & Sroufe, 1979), and behavior in the nursery school setting (Sroufe, 1983; Sroufe et al., 1984).

COMPETENCE IN DISADVANTAGED CHILDREN

Is competence as continuous in disadvantaged children (i.e., those reared in chaotic, stressful homes) as it is among middle-class children in stable environments? That is, among disadvantaged children, does the competent child remain competent and the incompetent child incompetent over time? Recent studies concerning the quality of attachment in disadvantaged children (Schneider-Rosen, Braunwald, Carlson, & Cicchetti, in press; Vaughn, Egeland, Sroufe, & Waters, 1979) and in highly stressed middle-class families (Thompson, Lamb, & Estes, 1982) have indicated that this is not the case. These results have led Schneider-Rosen et al. (in press), following Cicchetti and Rizley's (1981) model of the etiology, intergenerational transmission, and sequelae of child maltreatment, to propose a transactional model of the attachment bond—a model that can be extended to measures of competence throughout childhood.

According to this model, in studying qualitative differences in the attachment relationship in any population, one must consider the dynamic interplay among a variety of factors. Some of these factors are enduring and others are transient, and they may tend either to promote or to inhibit the development of a secure attachment relationship as well as to maintain or interfere with the quality of the relationship as it develops over time. Enduring factors are "protective" or "vulnerability" factors as they tend to promote or to inhibit a secure attachment, respectively. Likewise, transient factors are either "buffers" or "challengers," promoting or inhibiting a secure attachment, respectively. Thus, given this transactional analysis, one would not expect that early competence would predict later competence in a rigid, deterministic way. Nor is it the case that if, at an early age, children do not adequately resolve a stage-salient developmental task, such as forming a secure attachment with the primary caregiver, that they are destined to "fail" at each of the subsequent tasks.

Instead, this transactional analysis incorporates the notions of stability and change over time, while simultaneously attempting to account for those factors that may maintain, or lead to alterations in, the child's capacity to resolve developmentally salient tasks. In extending this analysis to the assessment of competence at various stages of the life span, several points need to be emphasized:

1. Competence at one developmental period will exert a positive influence toward achieving competence at the next period.
2. Early competence also exerts a subtle influence toward adaptation throughout the life span since each developmental issue, although

perhaps most salient at one developmental period, is of continuing importance throughout the life cycle.

3. The failure to achieve adaptation at one period makes adaptation that much more difficult at the next and, in a lesser way, more difficult throughout the life span since each issue continues to assume importance throughout the individual's development.

4. Many factors that may mediate between early and later adaptation or maladaptation may permit alternative outcomes to occur; that is, early problems or deviations in the successful resolution of a developmental task may be countered by major changes in the child's experience that could result in the successful negotiation of subsequent developmental tasks.

Given these assumptions, it seems that children who are reared in chaotic or stressful home environments may be less well-equipped to negotiate successfully the critical developmental tasks that need to be accomplished; they may be more prone to becoming incompetent, thereby placing them at a greater risk for encountering problems in the resolution of subsequent issues throughout childhood. This in turn may make them more vulnerable to developing alternative modes of functioning that permit their own unique way of adapting to their environmental conditions. Thus, for example, as Schneider-Rosen et al. (in press) suggest, physically abused children may be more likely to manifest an anxious-avoidant (Type A) attachment relationship with the caregiver as a means of protecting themselves against future incidents of maltreatment. While this mode of resolving the developmental task of achieving a secure attachment relationship may not appear to be competent, according to generally accepted standards for "normal" patterns of development, it may be extremely adaptive for a child reared in such adverse conditions. Therefore, it becomes necessary to consider alternative modes of resolving stage-salient issues in populations of disadvantaged children for whom what may appear to be incompetent is rather highly adaptive.

Perhaps more importantly, it becomes critical to examine the question of whether the use of alternative or less commonly employed pathways to achieving competence makes the child more vulnerable to manifesting deviations or delays in development (Schneider-Rosen et al., in press). In particular, are there certain developmental tasks that, if resolved in an alternative manner (i.e., one that may be adaptive although not competent according to generally accepted criteria), make the child more prone to developing pathology in later life? Unfortunately, no studies have been done on how depressed children resolve the stage-salient developmental issues. Nevertheless, from what is known from empirical and theoretical investigations into competence, it is possible to formulate hypotheses concerning its relationship to childhood depression. We shall want to consider first the possible impact that a depressive episode might have on those skills that constitute a child's competence and that predict later competence. We would want to identify those protective or buffering factors that may promote competence, or those vulnerability factors or challengers that inhibit the development of competence, following a depressive episode. Moreover, and perhaps more importantly, we shall want to investigate how incompetence may play a role in the etiology of depression. These points correspond to a similar distinction made by Rutter (this volume) that, in any study of developmental psychopathology, one needs to look at the impact not only of the pathology on development, but also of development on the pathology (see also Cicchetti, 1984).

IMPACT OF DEPRESSION UPON COMPETENCE

Our concern here is for how depression expresses itself in terms of competence, how it may lead to deviations in adaptation at various developmental periods, and how such deviation may be assessed. In particular, the following questions are of importance:

1. Does a depressive symptomatology manifest itself at every developmental level in terms of a lack of competence?
2. Does depression result in a lack of competence within one domain (e.g., affective), which then influences the other domains, or does depression result in a lack of integration of competencies across domains?
3. If so, in what manner does depression, as opposed to some other form of psychopathology, manifest itself as a lack of competence?
4. Does a depressive episode at one developmental level affect a child's ability to attain competence at later periods?
5. How might a genotype that predisposes for depression or biological abnormalities that constitute a diathesis for depression manifest themselves in terms of the resolution of stage-salient developmental tasks, especially in infancy and early childhood?

Questions (1), (2), and (4) are related and are relevant to the possibility of a positive feedback effect leading to the perpetuation of a depressive episode. It is probable that the depressed child lacks competence; therefore, if incompetence serves as a vulnerability factor to depression (discussed below), then a depressive episode may tend to perpetuate itself, through affecting competence. The process by which this may occur is schematized in Fig. 1. Obviously, there may be developmental-level-specific etiological ramifications of incompetence, and this would dictate the importance of determining time of onset in order to determine both the developmental sequelae of the depressive episode and the role these sequelae may play in perpetuating the depression.

However, because it is likely that every form of psychopathology

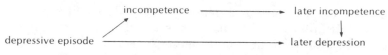

Fig. 1. *Positive feedback effect of a depressive episode.*

manifests itself as incompetence in the developmental period in which it occurs, there is a need to develop finer measures of competence and incompetence. This follows from the maxim that the organization of behavior is most important in development (Sroufe & Waters, 1977). Therefore, it is important to study how competent and incompetent behavior is organized. Ainsworth's (Ainsworth *et al.*, 1978) distinction of insecurely attached infants into Types A (anxious-avoidant) and C (anxious-resistant) is an example of a laudable first attempt to characterize different forms of incompetence. Once such a characterization is made, then it may be possible to study the different ways in which various pathologies manifest themselves in incompetence.

This finer characterization of various means of resolving the stage-salient developmental tasks necessary for adaptation would provide us with an answer to question (3), and this would be relevant for both the treatment and etiology of depression. For example, it is likely that both a depressed toddler and an autistic toddler would be assessed as incompetent in the problem-solving paradigm of Matas *et al.* (1978), but they probably are incompetent for different reasons. A depressed toddler would perhaps lack the enthusiasm, zest, and interest necessary for persevering when thwarted, whereas the autistic toddler, among other things, would not turn to the attachment figure for assistance when necessary. If it is true that a positive feedback relationship exists between a depressive episode and incompetence, then a fruitful approach to therapy in childhood depression may consist of training the child to complete tasks that exercise skills relevant to attaining competence at that developmental period. Such therapy could be better devised and planned if the manner in which depression affects competence were better known.

Moreover, it is possible that true depression simply does not exist in infancy and early childhood, and that one can only find at these periods potential precursors (or prototypes) of later childhood or adult depression (e.g., Gaensbauer, 1980; Zahn-Waxler, Cummings, Iannotti, & Radke-Yarrow, 1984). If this is the case, then a finer grain characterization of different modes (or pathways) of attaining competence or incompetence would possibly lead to a better detection of these precursors and a better understanding of how they develop into depression. Thus, it becomes important to investigate how genetic or biological diatheses may manifest themselves in terms of the organization of the cognitive, affective, and motivational behavioral systems in the resolution of stage-salient developmental issues. The study of these diatheses may be especially crucial in infancy and early childhood when, according to the orthogenetic principle, one would expect genetic and biological factors to be exerting a more explicit influence over development. So, for example, it would be interesting to study the possible role of inborn emotional display patterns or the influence of temperamental characteristics upon the early caregiver–infant interaction and how these may influence the developing organization of attachment behavior; the relationship between possible early deviations in the ontogenesis of the diencephalic reward system and early caregiver–infant interaction; or the relationship between deviations in amine levels in young children and variations in the role of affect in the mediation of attachment behavior according to contextual cues (Akiskal & McKinney, 1975; Schildkraut & Kety, 1967; Zis & Goodwin, 1982).

THE ETIOLOGICAL SIGNIFICANCE OF INCOMPETENCE

It is of course not the case that early incompetence always leads to later depression, since about 30% of infants are insecurely attached (Ainsworth et al., 1978) and the prevalence of childhood depression is much lower than this (Kashani et al., 1981; Rutter, 1972 and Chapter 1 of this volume). Moreover, incompetence, and especially insecure attachment, has been implicated in the developmental sequelae of child maltreatment (Egeland & Sroufe, 1981; Gaensbauer & Sands, 1979; Schneider-Rosen & Cicchetti, 1984; Schneider-Rosen et al., in press) and in the failure-to-thrive syndrome (Gordon & Jameson, 1979), which could in turn lead to later disorders. Therefore, it is most important to consider why incompetence leads to one form of psychopathology rather than another, or perhaps to none at all.

Rutter's conceptualization of the role that early events may play in the development of psychopathology is relevant here (Rutter, 1981; also this volume). Early incompetence may lead to a depressive disorder either directly or else indirectly, by first leading to intervening bodily changes, to altered patterns of behavior, to a changed family situation, to altered sensitivity to stress, or to an altered cognitive set. These intervening changes would result in a vulnerability to depression, and the depressive episode would be precipitated by some stressor (Cicchetti & Schneider-Rosen, 1984b). These alternatives are schematized in Fig. 2.

The stressor would represent some significant event that interferes with the child's capacity to regulate behavior or that creates anxiety of a sufficient magnitude to interfere with the child's current level of adaptive functioning. This would influence the organization of the cognitive, affective, social, and motivational systems and lead to a temporary regression in behavior that reflects developmentally earlier forms of responding in the organizational hierarchy. The severity of the stressor, and the degree to which it impacts upon the child, will depend upon a variety of factors such as the child's prior experiences with similar stressors, the personal meaning of the stressful event, the child's individual resiliency and flexibility of

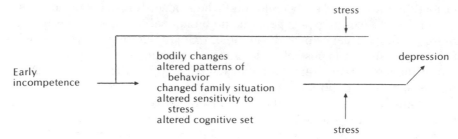

Fig. 2. *Schematic representation of the relationship between early incompetence and later depression.*

coping mechanisms, the availability of social supports, and the outcome of the stressful experience. Thus, while early incompetence may result in a greater vulnerability to experiencing stress, the specific impact of the stressor, and the role that the stressor may play in mediating between early imcompetence and the overt manifestation of depression, will depend upon several factors that may be unrelated to incompetence (see Cicchetti & Schneider-Rosen, 1984b).

However, in considering competence, this conceptualization must be amplified by taking into account the different effects of the child's failure to resolve issues at different stages: maladaptation at one period of development may have very different consequences for depression from that at another developmental period. The resulting causal network will be very complex. Early incompetence will have a variety of effects, some of which will tend to perpetuate incompetence, others of which may constitute a vulnerability to depression, and still others of which may potentiate later adaptation. A depressive episode, if it occurs, would lead to maladaptations, and these again would lead to a variety of effects, some perhaps maintaining the depression, others predisposing for future maladaptation, and still others leading to adaptation which may buffer against the experience of subsequent depressive episodes. A sketch of these causal interdependencies is presented in Fig. 3, which illustrates the complex feedback relationships that we might expect to obtain. Of course it should also be mentioned that maladaptation and depression will have sequelae dependent upon the ontogenesis of those neurophysiological and biochemical systems that serve as the biological bases of depression.

Obviously, what is needed is a longitudinal, prospective study, using broadband, naturalistic measures like those discussed by Waters and Sroufe (1983). Offspring of depressed parents who have a family history of depression could be studied along with normal matched controls (e.g., Zahn-Waxler et al., 1984; Zahn-Waxler, Cummings, McKnew, & Radke-Yarrow, 1984). It might be worthwhile to ensure greater homogeneity by dividing the offspring of depressives into those whose parents suffer from unipolar as opposed to bipolar depression, since bipolar depression is

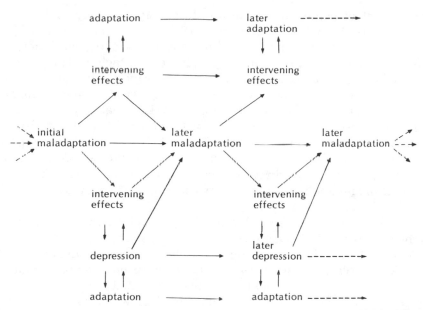

Fig. 3. *Causal relationships between early maladaptation as it may result in depressive episodes, later maladaptation, or later adaptation.*

rarely seen before puberty (Depue & Monroe, 1978; Perris, 1982). These children could be followed over time, and their pattern of adaptation and maladaptation charted and related to episodes of depression.

However, in the absence of such a study, it is possible to formulate some rough, preliminary hypotheses regarding the etiological role of incompetence. As we noted, insecurely attached infants may be classified as either avoidant (Type A) or resistant (Type C) babies. Type A infants avoid their caregiver upon reunion from brief separations and display anger toward the caregiver. Sroufe (1983) has discovered that Type A classification predicts excessive dependency in the preschool, as rated by teachers and peers. Excessive dependency has been implicated as a possible risk factor in depression (Bemporad & Wilson, 1978); moreover, it may perhaps be construed as one form of what Arieti considers to be an excessive investment of self-esteem in others (Arieti, 1982). This would suggest the causal sequence Type A infant → dependent child → depression. Obviously this model needs to be elaborated upon by determining the mechanisms that operate between each of these steps and by specifying in greater detail the nature of the dependency and the manner in which it manifests itself at different developmental periods.

Type C infants are ambivalent toward the caregiver, explore passively and very little, and have difficulty being comforted by their caregiver upon reunion. Each of these characteristics is suggestive. Ambivalent feelings toward the attachment figure constitute a necessary condition for the development of depression, according to classic psychodynamic theory (Abraham, 1911/1960; S. Freud, 1917/1968). Since the formation and maintenance of attachment relationships to principal caregivers is actually a life-span issue, it is possible that Type C insecure attachment may predict later maladaptive responses to the loss of a principal caregiver, either through death or divorce (cf. Bowlby, 1980). That Type C infants explore little suggests that they may fail to develop some skills that may be helpful in coping with stress, but this would seem to be a vulnerability factor for many forms of psychopathology. That Type C infants fail to find comfort in the principal caregiver when distressed would seem to be a vulnerability factor for depression both directly, because a means of coping with distress is absent, and indirectly, because later social support networks are likely to be weak (Waters et al., 1979).

Moreover, a close relationship has been found between quality of attachment and the earlier emergence of visual self-recognition, an early precursor of the developing sense of self, in 19-month-old infants (Schneider-Rosen & Cicchetti, 1984). This relationship may be paralleled and extended in later development in such a way that those children who are securely attached to their primary caregiver will also have a more secure sense of self. Qualitative differences in one's sense of self may in turn influence the manner in which one responds to major life events. Finally, Ainsworth et al. (1978) have shown that noncontingency of maternal caregiving predicts insecure attachment. This noncontingency suggests that an interference effect typical of learned helplessness may be at least in part responsible for the poor quality of attachment. The avoidance of Type A babies and the failure to explore of Type C babies may perhaps be construed as a decrease in the emission of behaviors that would usually be rewarded, because of an interference effect (cf. Lewinsohn, 1974; Maier, Seligman, & Solomon, 1969; Seligman, 1975; Watson, 1977). Thus, insecure attachment may be the manifestation of a developmental deviation that, at a later time, may manifest itself as a depression or as a prototype of depression.

These remarks are admittedly speculative; however, the attachment relationship is the most thoroughly studied of those state-salient issues relevant to competence. What can be said of issues that arise later in ontogenesis must at this point be very limited. The failure to resolve adequately the developmental issue of autonomy could, it seems, lead to depression in two ways.

1. By a lack of differentiation between self and others, the process of identification with the lost object by which anger is introjected may be enhanced, as suggested by object relations theorists (Fairbairn, 1952; Kernberg, 1976; Mahler, 1968).
2. As Bemporad and Wilson (1978) suggest, the failure to develop

autonomy may put a toddler in a bind between manipulative parents who at once encourage dependency and then castigate the child for immature behavior—a state of affairs that these theorists consider to be a vulnerability factor for childhood depression.

The failure for the child to develop good peer relations, the next major developmental issue, could predispose to later depression, because a means of coping with stress would be absent and peers could not serve as substitute love objects in case of loss. Furthermore, it is conceivable that the child may perhaps be prone to develop peer relationships with an accompanying intensity and overmeasurement of the self such that the expectations that the child might have for the role such relationships should play (e.g., to substitute for a lost or psychologically unavailable parent) will never be fulfilled. This disappointment could represent a vulnerability factor for depression. In addition, the absence of good peer relations could result in a greater tendency to make more disparaging social comparisons when engaged in self-evaluation.

As the child continues to renegotiate the balance between autonomous functioning and an expanding social world, the way in which the earlier developmental issues were resolved will loom large in determining the child's sense of self-esteem, a crucial factor in depression (Bibring, 1953; Jacobson, 1971). The child begins to develop a sense of self extended through time; however, at the same time, various relations with others are integrated into a concept of the self (Damon & Hart, 1982). Accordingly, children who perceive themselves as deficient in comparison to others may be more prone to developing poor self-esteem, another consequence of incompetence that may predispose to depression.

Self-Understanding and Self-Esteem

The loss of self-esteem has often been considered a defining characteristic of depression, especially by theorists of the psychoanalytic, cognitive, and behavioral schools (Abramson, Seligman, & Teasdale, 1978; Beck, 1967; Bibring, 1953; S. Freud, 1917/1968; Jacobson, 1971). S. Freud (1917/1968) claimed that feelings of self-depreciation and self-devaluation were crucial for differentiating depression from normal mourning. Bowlby (1980), partly following in this tradition, has likewise argued that mourning characterized by self-reproach is a disordered form of grief, which is prone to develop into later pathology. Bibring (1953) and Jacobson (1971) have both argued that lowered self-esteem gives the dysphoric mood of depression its distinctive character and serves to distinguish depression from other affective disorders. Taking a similar position, Beck (1967) proposed that the cognitive structure of a depressed person's thought endows depression with its essential characteristics and that, in particular, a loss of self-esteem is the central cognitive manifestation of depression. One could plausibly maintain that the cognitions involved in the loss of self-esteem constitute a large part of those negative cognitions of self, world, and future that make up the "negative cognitive triad" of depression (Beck, 1967). Moreover, this traditional theoretical characterization of depression as a dysphoric mood marked by a loss of self-esteem finds contemporary expression in clinical work and research in the form of the RDC and DSM-III criteria, which refer to "feelings of worthlessness, self-reproach, or excessive or inappropriate guilt" in major depressive episodes (DSM-III) (American Psychiatric Association, 1980).

It would thus seem that psychological research on self-esteem in normal children would be of special relevance for the study of depression. In particular, when investigating childhood depression, it would seem important to consider studies on the development of self-esteem and its relationship to other indices of psychological "well-being" in normal children. However, a recent and comprehensive review of the literature on self-esteem (Wylie, 1979) has indicated that, contrary to intuitive expectations, few studies have succeeded in establishing any strong relationship between self-esteem and important variables involving achievement, ability, and social-relations.

Damon and Hart (1982) have argued convincingly that the disarray of the literature on self-esteem stems from a failure of researchers and investigators to attend to the development of self-understanding on the part of the child. They argue that self-esteem is basically an affect, which may have either a positive or negative valence, and which has as its object the self, as the child conceives it. They therefore conclude that any measures of self-esteem must be based upon prior research on the development of self-understanding: in particular, measures of self-esteem used in developmental research must be age appropriate and must be adapted to the kind of understanding of the self that the child may have at his or her particular age.

This strategy seems sound to us, and so we propose that any developmental study of the role that loss of self-esteem plays in the development of childhood depression must rely upon prior studies concerning the possible relevance of the development of self-understanding to depression. The loss of self-esteem that occurs in depression may be understood as an enduring affect of negative valence that has as its object the child's concept of self. The "structure" of this affect and also the reasons why this affect has developed may perhaps be highlighted by an understanding of how the child's understanding of self changes in normal ontogenesis.

Unfortunately, while there is a substantial body of research (albeit of questionable merit) that has examined positive or negative self-esteem (Wylie, 1979), there have been few studies of developmental changes in self-understanding (Brim, 1976). However, such studies as there have been are suggestive (Damon & Hart, 1982) and are of some relevance to childhood depression. In what follows we shall delineate how these studies may be relevant; a common theme of our discussion will be that an account of the development of self-understanding provides us with an understanding of the structure underlying those changes in self-esteem that may be important for childhood depression.

DISTINCTIONS AND DEFINITIONS

Self-understanding is a cognitive skill or ability. It is basically the person's representation of the self. A self-cognition is a particular exercise of this skill or ability; a self-schema is a structuralized representation of the self that may endure over time. Self-schemata may be formed after repeated and intense self-cognitions have emerged that possess similar character, meaning, or affective quality (i.e., positive or negative), and they may be conceived of metaphorically as mental habits (Beck, 1967). Furthermore, they may be seen as a direct parallel to Bowlby's (1980) description of "internal working models" or internal representational models of one's attachment figures and of the organization of attachment behaviors.

Self-esteem is an affect, which may have either a positive or negative valence or polarity, and which is distinguished from other affects primarily by its object, which is the self, or, more precisely, a representation of the self (Damon & Hart, 1982).

Because self-esteem is an affect, it can be measured by means of graded, quantitative scales. Self-cognitions, on the other hand, must be assessed by measures that tap both style and content: style, insofar as they measure the procedures by which a person arrives at a particular representation of the self; content, insofar as they measure what is embodied in that representation (Damon & Hart, 1982). This distinction in how self-esteem and self-cognition should be assessed suggests a possible resolution of the problem of whether the dysphoric mood of a depressive episode associated with a loss of self-esteem should be considered only quantitatively or rather qualitatively different from normal sadness. To the extent that the dysphoric mood differs from sadness in intensity of negative affect, it is only quantitatively different; to the extent that it differs from sadness because it is mediated by distorted cognitive processes and has as its object a deviant conception of the self, it is qualitatively different.

The relationship between self-cognitions and self-esteem may be conceptualized as a particular instance of the relationship between cognition and affect. We embrace an interactionist view of the latter (cf. Cicchetti & Hesse, 1983; Cicchetti & Schneider-Rosen, 1984a; Hesse & Cicchetti, 1982) and propose that self-cognitions and affects of self-esteem interact in a similar way. In particular, it may be expected that certain self-cognitions cause specific feelings of self-esteem to arise and that these feelings will have a positive or negative polarity depending upon the content of the cognition. In a reciprocal manner, an intense or enduring affect of self-esteem may be expected to lead to congruent self-cognitions. This view can be seen to be compatible with the cognitive theory of depression (Beck, 1967). Furthermore, it may be useful in accounting for the relationship between cognition and affect the development as well as in the maintenance or recurrence of depressive episodes.

Because self-cognitions are representations of the self, it is important to mention, if only briefly, various characteristics of the self that may be represented. In accordance with Damon and Hart (1982), who follow James (1892), we can distinguish four:

1. *Material characteristics* include a person's possessions and body.
2. *Social characteristics* are the roles, relations, and personality of a person.
3. *Active characteristics* are the typical activities and skills a person may engage in or have (e.g., running, typing, writing, piano playing).
4. *Psychological characteristics* include the consciousness, thoughts, emotions in their inward aspects, and psychological processes of a person.

Thus, persons can conceive of themselves in any of these terms. Again, a person may invest more affect into self-esteem in one of these characteristics than another, thereby significantly influencing self-esteem. Moreover, a person may tend to think of one of these characteristics rather than others as constituting that person's essential identity and as serving to distinguish that person from other persons.

THE NORMAL DEVELOPMENT OF SELF-UNDERSTANDING

A person's conception of self changes markedly from infancy to childhood through adolescence (Damon & Hart, 1982; Harter, 1983). Moreover, these changes seem to take place in an orderly fashion and appear to do so in accordance with integrative concepts of development, such as the orthogenetic principle. However, it should be observed that these orderly changes have not yet been studied in cross-cultural, longitudinal studies, and so at this point it is too premature to postulate the presence of universal developmental stages in the ontogenesis of self-understanding.

Damon and Hart (1982) conclude that the development of self-understanding displays four general trends:

1. There is a trend, most apparent in childhood, from conceiving of the self in terms of material characteristics to conceiving of it in terms of psychological ones.
2. The child, mainly in adolescence, but to some extent in childhood, increasingly conceives of the self in terms of stable social characteristics, such as relations and personality traits.

3. The self is conceived of increasingly as active, self-reflective, and volitional.

4. Finally, as the child conceives of the self increasingly in terms of a variety of characteristics, and as the child's understanding of each of those characteristics becomes more complex and differentiated, there is a tendency for these various characteristics to be brought together into a unified and hierarchically integrated conception of the self, with some characteristics assuming greater salience than others. This last trend is most marked in adolescence, but, as with the others, it can also be seen throughout all of the periods of development.

We contend that, in conceptualizing these general developmental trends, the study of atypical patterns of development or of manifest psychopathology (such as depression) illuminates another significant feature of self-understanding. Following the orthogenetic principle, it seems probable that while these various components of one's understanding of the self (i.e., material, social, active, psychological) become increasingly differentiated and integrated with time, there is also the possibility of regression (i.e., hierarchic motility) to earlier levels of functioning. Thus, one's understanding of the self may become more well articulated and may increasingly reflect the integration of active and psychological conceptions, rather than only material and social aspects. However, during periods of stress or frustration, circumstances may challenge sufficiently the individual's level of self-understanding so as to increase the salience of relatively less mature features or to prevent the operation of a well-integrated understanding of the self, thereby focusing on those qualities primarily associated with negative affect. Thus, it is possible that the relationship between affect and cognition becomes more apparent when one is constrained to rely upon a single, less well articulated characteristic of self-understanding (e.g., only material, social, active, or psychological) or when one is less able to integrate these different components of self-understanding. However, this does not imply that the other components are not available in the future or disappear from one's cognitive repertoire; rather, their decreased salience makes it more difficult for the person to have access to the various features of the self and may have significance in the perpetuation of the negative affect.

SELF-UNDERSTANDING IN INFANCY AND DEPRESSION

There has been a remarkable concordance among studies relevant to the development of self-understanding in infancy (cf. Amsterdam, 1972; Kagan, 1981; Lewis & Brooks-Gunn, 1979). Modifying the account provided by Lewis and Brooks-Gunn (1979), we can divide infancy roughly into five phases. Before 3 months, infants display an unlearned attraction to images of other infants. From 3 to 8 months, infants develop the ability to recognize their own image in a mirror by means of contingency clues, that is, from observed correspondences between the infant's own movement, known by proprioceptive feedback, and the movements of the mirror image, known visually. After 8 months, infants begin to discriminate their own image from those of opposite sex babies and of older children and adults. After 12 or 13 months, infants begin to develop the ability to recognize their own image on the basis of the features of that image alone, not relying solely on contingency clues. Finally, from approximately 20 to 24 months, one sees the emergence of behaviors and expressions that imply that toddlers are aware, not only of their appearance, but also of their activities; thus, self-admiring behaviors (such as strutting and preening), embarrassment, and coyness may be observed. Kagan (1981) has demonstrated that it is also at about this age that the frequency of a child's self-descriptive statements increases drastically (see also Bretherton & Beeghly, 1982). Moreover, the child cries after seeing a stranger perform a task that the child knows it is incapable of doing, perhaps implying that the child has developed a "sense of standards" (Kagan, 1981). We think that the affective reaction accompanying the child's recognition of its own limitations may also reveal the beginnings of shame and guilt.

While these results are clear, their interpretation is equivocal. In particular, one wants to know to what extent cognitions mediate in early visual self-recognition, and thus to what extent the discriminating behavior reported in infants can be construed as elementary or prototypical self-recognition. Moreover, there have been no longitudinal studies looking at the relationship between these early behaviors and the more developed self-recognition seen in childhood.

We enter uncharted territory when we consider the relevance of such studies to childhood depression and must be constrained simply to formulating questions the answers to which would be important in this regard. Again, since the existence of true clinical depression before 6 or 7 years is questionable, we must concentrate on how the prototypical forms of visual self-recognition seen in infancy may be related to prototypical forms of childhood depression. Also, it should be stressed that, in order to investigate such prototypes, prospective longitudinal studies of genetically homogeneous offspring of depressed persons are necessary.

The development of contingency recognition seems especially important for two reasons. First, it depends upon the infant's coordination of proprioceptive feedback and, in particular, of the relationship between felt proprioceptive clues and visual clues (cf. Butterworth & Cicchetti, 1978; Izard, 1977). Quality of mother–infant interaction likewise depends in part upon a similar coordination (Stern, 1977). It is possible that the delayed development of contingency recognition may indicate a difficulty in the infant's ability to coordinate proprioceptive and visual clues. This may be especially important to study in children of depressed mothers, for whom contingency of maternal responsiveness may be deficient or absent, thereby making the child more prone to manifesting delays in this ability. Second, it depends upon the ability of infants to perceive contingency in their environment, and a deficiency here could render a child vulnerable to experiencing learned helplessness (cf. Watson, 1977).

We may also ask what the relationship is between visual self-recognition and later self-esteem. In normal, lower-class infants, secure attachment seems to be associated with earlier visual self-recognition, but this relationship does not obtain in maltreated, lower-class infants (Schneider-Rosen & Cicchetti, 1984). Does the relationship also break down in offspring of depressed persons, in infants separated from their principal caregivers (e.g., through illness), or in infants whose home environment is marked by life events implicated in depression (Paykel, 1982)? It would be interesting to study individual differences in the emergence of the capacity for visual self-recognition in children of depressed parents. This would help to illuminate the potential role that cognitive factors play in mediating early visual self-recognition behavior. For example, children of depressed parents may be delayed in their use of contingency clues that are based on proprioceptive feedback and facilitate the discrimination of one's own image from those of others. In addition, following Schneider-Rosen and Cicchetti's (1984) findings with maltreated infants, infants of depressed parents would be important to study because they are less likely to be cared for by supportive, available, emotionally sensitive, and contingently responsive caregivers. Thus, based upon the positive association reported between these early caregiving behaviors and subsequent attachment classifications (Ainsworth et al., 1978), one would expect that these children would be less likely to manifest a secure attachment relationship. If these infants also demonstrate delays in the development of visual self-recognition, or if their affective reactions to their mirror image reflect developmentally less mature and less well articulated responses in comparison to normal infants as has been found in maltreated infants (Schneider-Rosen & Cicchetti, 1984), then these findings would be particularly relevant in a first attempt to address the hypothesized relationship between early visual self-recognition and the development of one's self-esteem.

The development of a certain self-consciousness in late infancy seems especially important, because of its greater proximity to and similarity with childhood forms of depression. For example, Kagan (1981) argues that infants who cry when shown a difficult task by a stranger have a sense of standards that they feel they cannot attain. What is the relationship between these standards and the development of later standards, which, in being unrealistic or unattainable, may predispose to depression (cf. Jacobson, 1971; Sandler & Joffe, 1965)? It would also be interesting to study the success caregivers have in comforting infants who, as a result of a sense of standards, cry in the Kagan modeling paradigm. In the Strange Situation paradigm for young infants (Ainsworth et al., 1978), the caregiver's success in comforting the distressed infant may best be interpreted as restoring the infant's "sense of felt security" (Sroufe & Waters, 1977). However, in any problem-solving task in later infancy, the caregiver may be seen not only as providing assistance when necessary (Matas et al., 1978), but also as playing the role of restoring the toddler's prototypical sense of self-esteem when the child is unable to attain felt standards. Perhaps the ability of the child to be comforted by the caregiver after falling short of the child's sense of standards may indicate the presence of a factor that would protect against depression.

SELF-UNDERSTANDING IN CHILDHOOD AND DEPRESSION

A number of empirical investigations have documented a major change in self-understanding that occurs at about 8 years of age (Broughton, 1978; Guardo & Bohan, 1971; Keller, Ford, & Meacham, 1978; Selman, 1980). Before this age, children tend to conceive of themselves in what Selman (1980) has called "physicalistic" terms, focusing on the *material* and *active* characteristics of the self. Children before 8 years of age tend to conceive of themselves in terms of what they own, what they do, and what their bodies are like. Moreover, they believe that their continuity through time—their connectedness with themselves at earlier times in their life—is constituted by such physical factors as well (Guardo & Bohan, 1971). After 8 years, however, the self is conceived of as being essentially psychological. At this time, children develop the ability to conceptualize conflicts and incongruities between their inner thoughts and outer actions (Selman, 1980); they conceive of their distinctness from others in terms of psychological differences; and they locate the source of their diachronic continuity in psychological factors (Guardo & Bohan, 1971). It is noteworthy that these changes occur almost simultaneously with the transition from preoperational to operational thought (S. H. White, 1965). It is understandable why operational thought might be a necessary precondition for drawing a distinction between two kinds of characteristics of the self, material, and psychological, and for being able to coordinate awareness of and representations of both. That the transition takes place about 1 year after the development of concrete operations may perhaps be explained as an instance of *décalage:* psychological processes, thoughts, and emotions in their inward aspect, because they are less tangible than weights, volumes, and numerical size, may be one of the last areas in which concrete operations develop (cf. Harter, in press).

Another transition, this one concerning self-evaluations, has been reported by Secord and Peevers (1974) and Livesly and Bromley (1973). It seems that before age 7 or so, when children are asked to evaluate themselves, they tend to do so in absolute terms; that is, in terms of some standard, rather than in terms of what others do. After age 7, however, children tend to evaluate their performances or characteristics by comparison with others (e.g., "I'm a better baseball player than my brother, but worse at schoolwork than my friend").

Secord and Peevers (1974) also observe a transition in that children at this time move from thinking of themselves only in terms of habitual actions—that is, in terms of what they are wont to do at various times and in various places—to thinking of themselves more frequently in terms of what their actual abilities are, what Secord and Peevers (1974) call "action competencies."

Each of these transitions—from physicalistic to psychological self-understanding, from absolute to comparative self-evaluations, and from action-based self-cognitions to competency-based ones—is potentially important for childhood depression. We believe that the association with childhood depression comes via Abramson et al.'s (1978) reformulation of the learned helplessness theory of adult (Seligman, 1975) and childhood (Dweck, 1977) depression. According to this reformulation, since learned helplessness is the expression of a person's perception of noncontingency between responses and rewards or punishments, one must inquire into what factors in the environment the person attributes the noncontingency before one can determine the extent to which the perceived noncontingency is recalcitrant to modification. Abramson et al. (1978) delineate three orthogonal dimensions governing the attribution: noncontingency can be attributed to personal versus universal, global versus specific, and stable versus unstable factors. If the attribution is personal rather than universal—that is, if noncontingency is attributed to some failing of the individual not possessed by others, so that others are thought not to experience the same noncontingency—then the depressed affect occasioned by perceived helplessness will be accompanied by a loss of self-esteem. If the attribution is global, then the affect will be depressed across situations. If the attribution is stable, then the depression will endure through time.

We believe that it becomes possible to conceptualize a relationship between developmental changes in self-understanding and one's position on each of the three dimensions governing the attribution of noncontingency and to speculate as to how these hypothesized associations relate to the development of depression in childhood. Table 2 illustrates the associations that may be relevant.

The transition from a physicalistic to a psychological conception of the self is relevant to the dimension of stable versus unstable. If the child before age 8 conceives of the self principally in terms of actions or physical factors such as possessions, then any attribution of noncontingency to features of the self would be an unstable one, since these physicalistic factors are usually transient. The transition to psychological cognitions of the self would be a kind of necessary precondition for attributing noncontingency

Table 2
Developmental Changes in Self-Understanding as They Relate to Personal Attributions of Noncontingency

Developmental changes in conceptions of the self[a]	Characteristics of personal attributions of noncontingency[b]		
	Stable vs. unstable	Personal vs. universal	Global vs. specific
Physical → psychological	Physical → unstable Psychological → stable	Physical → universal Psychological → personal	Physical → specific Physical → global
Absolute → comparative	Absolute → unstable Comparative → stable	Absolute → universal Comparative → personal	Absolute → specific Comparative → global
Action based → competency based	Action based → unstable Competency based → stable	Action based → universal Competency based → personal	Action based → specific Competency based → global
Resulting self-schemata	Psychological, comparative, competency based, and relatively stable	Psychological, comparative, competency based, and personal	Psychological, comparative, competency based, and global

[a]Lively and Bromley (1973); Ruble (in press); Secord and Peevers (1974).
[b]Abramson et al. (1978).

to stable characteristics of the self, and hence for an enduring depressed state. Furthermore, the transition from physical to psychological conceptions of the self reflects the integration of more personal and meaningful factors into one's self-representation (e.g., "I am very intelligent") rather than more general universal factors (e.g., "I don't steal or murder"). These psychological characteristics are more likely to represent global features of the person such as predispositions or intrapsychic conflicts rather than specific qualities such as physical appearance or material possessions. Thus, the physicalistic conception of the self common before age 8 is relatively unstable and refers to more specific but highly universal qualities.

The transition from absolute to comparative self-evaluations, which occurs at about the same time, may be a requisite precondition for personal attributions of helplessness that are relatively stable and global. Before the age of 8, children tend to conceive of successes or failures in terms of absolute standards of which they have fallen short. Their evaluations are relatively unstable in that the standards are not well integrated as personally relevant nor are they internalized into an enduring concept of the self; they are therefore more likely to relate to specific characteristics of the individual rather than to their general being. When children are capable of simultaneously discerning whether others would have succeeded in situations where they have failed, they are more likely to make personal attributions that reflect relatively stable conceptions of their global character.

Finally, the transition from cognitions of self centering on habitual actions to those centering on competencies (Secord & Peevers, 1974) is relevant to our conceptualization. Particular habitual actions are specific, are more likely to be shared by others, and are amenable to change through conscious efforts to modify their overt display. Competencies are more stable in that they tend to reflect relatively enduring capacities or skills that are already present but may be enhanced or repressed (e.g., artistic ability or athletic powers); they are unique or personal to each individual and they are global in that they tend to become manifest in a variety of perhaps very different contexts.

We believe that this hypothesized association between developmental changes in self-understanding and personal attributions of noncontingency has relevance to various theoretical positions on childhood depression. Clearly, the etiological significance of the specific associations needs to be examined more carefully. However, we contend that the conceptual power of these associations warrants further investigation. Studies of the development of self-understanding indicate that, at about 7 or 8 years, children develop the ability to make attributions to personal, stable, and global characteristics of the self. Theorists of childhood depression often doubt whether depression can occur before 6 or 7 years (Bemporad & Wilson, 1978). We believe that the conception of the nature of self-cognitions presented here may help to elucidate this issue. Prior to the transition from physicalistic to psychological, from absolute to comparative, or from action-based to competency-based self-cognitions, the mood of young children tends to be unstable and specific to context; thus, this helps to account for one of the features of children's overt mood (i.e., its variability and relatively global and undifferentiated nature) that has led some to call into question the veridicality of the diagnostic category of depression in childhood (e.g., Anthony, 1975; Lefkowitz & Burton, 1978; Malmquist, 1971, 1975). In addition, we contend that it is only following the transition in the nature of self-cognitions at about age 8 that it becomes possible for a child to experience a loss of self-esteem accompanying depressed affect that is associated with personal comparisons (based on global, psychological qualities) resulting in negative valuations of the self. This loss of self-esteem reflects an affective concomitant to the cognitive activity that may introduce a positive circular relationship between affect and cognition as they serve to maintain the depressed state. Furthermore, this capacity for engaging in negative evaluations of the self occurs at just the age at which McConville, Boag, and Purohit (1973) found a transition from "affectual" depression to depression characterized by negative self-esteem. According to these investigators, at about age 8, the kinds of childhood depression seen change from those typified by dysphoric "feeling–thought," akin to Sandler and Joffe's (1965) primary affect, to those typified by "thought–feeling," with more of the properties that cognitivists like Beck (1967) ascribe to depression. Similarly, we maintain that the transitions from physical to psychological, from absolute to comparative, and from action-based to competency-based conceptions of the self, when considered in the framework of those orthogonal dimensions proposed by Abramson *et al.* (1978) in their reformulation of learned helplessness theory, provide the means for conceptualizing developmental changes in self-understanding as they relate to the development of depression as a syndrome, rather than as a symptom or a psychobiological reaction.

SELF-COGNITIONS, SELF-SCHEMATA, AND THE ETIOLOGY
OF CHILDHOOD AND ADULT DEPRESSION

It is possible to extend the proposed relationship between self-understanding and personal attributions of noncontingency beyond its application to learned helplessness theory. While it is clear that a certain capacity for self-cognition is a necessary precondition for the perception of noncontingency in the learned helplessness model, developmental changes in self-understanding must be considered in a broader characterization of the role that self-cognitions play in the development and perpetuation of a depressive disorder. Specifically, at this point we want to introduce the concept of self-schemata and to speculate with regard to the role that these internal, structural representations of the self play in the etiology and sequelae of childhood depression.

The development of self-understanding in general and of self-schemata in particular is extremely important for Beck's (1967) theory of depression for four reasons:

1. Negative cognitions about the self constitute one of the three kinds of negative cognitions in the "cognitive triad" held to be central in the etiology of depression, and indirectly they are related to negative cognitions about the world and the future as well. Therefore, in order to know the content of these negative cognitions in childhood depression, it is necessary first to know the kinds of cognitions about the self that a child of a particular age would be likely to have.

2. Kovacs and Beck (1978) maintain that the depressive self-schemata seen in later childhood and adult depression appear to have been structuralized at an earlier age: "[the] formal characteristics of most depressogenic schemata, including the psychologically simplistic and 'childish' content of the premise, the rigid directives, and their apparent lack of differentiation, all combine to create the impression that we are dealing with relatively stable, developmentally early constructions" (p. 529). If the development of self-understanding were more thoroughly understood, one might then be able to specify better the characteristics of depressogenic schemata observed later in life. Ideally, from a consideration of the content and character of later schemata, one would like to be able to locate the approximate place in the developmental sequence where they were first formed and structuralized—information important for more effective cognitive therapy.

3. Beck's theory emphasizes the circular, positive feedback that can obtain between depressed affect and negative cognitions. This circular feedback can take the particular form of a feedback between depreciatory representations of the self and low self-esteem. However, it would seem that, in order to delineate the mutual influence that cognition and affect have on each other in this case, it would be important first to know the degree of differentiation and content of the self-cognitions, since as these factors change the influence that they may have on depressed affect or that depressed affect may have on self-cognitions may change as well.

4. Recent investigations of self-reference and of the encoding of personal information have shown that self-schemata operate in the encoding and interpretation of incoming information, and that these internal cognitive structures seem to be most influential in the selection and organization of information concerning the self (Davis, 1979; Kandzierski, 1980; Markus, 1977; Rogers, Kuiper, & Kirker, 1977; Rogers, Rogers, & Kuiper, 1979). The developmental changes regarding how negative self-cognitions and self-schemata can

operate in this way seem especially important. For example, as the child moves from a physicalistic to psychological conception of the self in midchildhood, we could expect that any negative cognitions of the self would operate to distort incoming information differently. Furthermore, the child would selectively attend to that information that is congruent with existing self-schemata, thereby preserving the stability of these internal cognitive representations and making them less susceptible to modification over time.

In general, it would seem that each of the three major transitions in midchildhood concerning the child's conception of the self—from physicalistic to psychological, from absolute to comparative, from action based to competency based—would entail that negative self-schemata occurring after the transition would extend to more basic and enduring traits of the child and would apply to a wider range of circumstances. This would seem to imply that, in midchildhood and beyond, cognitive factors may begin to take a more prominent role in mood disturbances, either by maintaining depression as a result of the preservation of negative self-schemata or by reactivating the "relatively stable, developmentally early constructions" (Kovacs & Beck, 1978, p. 529) that have been unconscious or previously less readily accessible.

Of particular interest to the developmentalist is the relationship between earlier and later negative self-schemata. Are the negative cognitions in adult depression merely reactivations of negative self-schemata structuralized in early childhood (Beck, 1967; Kovacs & Beck, 1978)? Or, as Davis (1979) maintains, do the negative schemata of a depressive episode arise only after the depression has existed for some period of time? Clearly, longitudinal work on the development of self-schemata would help to illuminate the role that they play in the development or sequelae of depression. Our position, though speculative, is congruent with Piaget's (1954) notion of the diachronic development of schemata through assimilation and accommodation. We contend that early loss, inadequate maternal care, lack of a secure attachment relationship, an impoverished environment, maternal depression, or a temperamental predisposition to heightened awareness (which Bronson [1972] suggests may be a precursor to the development of social unease) may lead to the formation of depressogenic schemata which make an individual *vulnerable* to depression. Through time, these cognitive structures may then be elaborated and organized by experiences congruent with them. Though the basic cognitive distortions may remain relatively stable, new information can be systematically integrated and organized into them. These structures can then be activated either by stress (either "specific" or "general" stress [Beck, 1967]), or by a prolonged depressed affect. And it should be noted that one need not understand the activation of schemata in terms of an infusion of some doubtful "psychic energy" (cf. Mendelson, 1982); rather, schemata are activated by means of an affect, which serves as a "force" for which the cognition is a "structure" (Piaget, 1981), and which causes the schemata to play a larger role in the processing of information and motivation of action.

Emotional Development

When one turns to consider the relationship between normal emotional development and childhood depression, one encounters a threefold absence of knowledge. First, it is unknown precisely what role emotions play in the etiology and expression of childhood depression. For example, now that theories of "masked depression" (Cytryn & McKnew, 1972; Glaser, 1967) have been either rejected or repudiated (Carlson & Cantwell, 1980; Cytryn, McKnew, & Bunney, 1980; Puig-Antich, 1980a, 1980b) it is no longer possible to conceive of symptoms such as enuresis or encopresis as "masking" an underlying dysphoric mood. Similarly, delinquency, probably an expression of anger or frustration, is a common symptom in childhood depression (e.g., Kashani et al., 1981; Puig-Antich, 1980a, 1982; Shaffer, 1974). However, it is still necessary to provide a clear account of how emotions such as the anger or frustration expressed in these symptoms are related to the dysphoria of childhood depression. Second, the study of normal emotional development, long neglected in psychology, is presently in a state of infancy (Hesse & Cicchetti, 1982). Thus, the database against which one may chart the disordered emotional development evidenced in childhood depression is sketchy and incomplete. Third, the precise nature of the interrelationships between emotional and cognitive development in normal (Cicchetti & Pogge-Hesse, 1981) or atypical (Cicchetti & Schneider-Rosen, 1984a) populations is equivocal and the influence that each domain may exert upon the other in the etiology and sequelae of depression remains unclear. Consequently, in this section, we will discuss the ways in which research in normal emotional development can lead to a better understanding of the expression, etiology, course, and treatment of childhood depression.

THE DEFINITION OF EMOTION

There is virtually no agreement in contemporary psychology as to how to define emotion: what the components of an emotion are, how they are related, and what their role is in thought, motivation, and personality (see Cicchetti & Hesse, 1983; Izard, 1977). Since it is common to define mood in terms of emotion (cf., for example, American Psychiatric Association, 1980), this definitional disagreement extends also to mood, its components, and their relationship. Therefore, it is obvious that attempts to delineate more precisely what an emotion is may have immediate consequences for the understanding of mood, and, in particular, the dysphoric mood of depression. However, it is necessary to clarify the distinction between emotion and mood before describing their relationship to one another.

An emotion, considered structurally, can be described in terms of its subject, object, valence (or polarity), intensity, and cause (Hesse & Cicchetti, 1982). The *subject* of an emotion is the person who experiences it, and this experience can in turn be divided into several components: nonverbal expressive, verbal expressive, phenomenological (or inner experiential), and biological (Hesse & Cicchetti, 1982; Izard, 1977). The *object* of an emotion is the person or thing at which the emotion is directed; for example, a person may be angry at someone or desirous of something. An emotion may also have as its object a representation in the mind of the person who has the emotion. Thus, a person may fear, be anxious about, or desire some nonexistent or imagined person or event. The *valence* of an emotion may be described as either positive or negative; generally, emotions having a positive valence are pleasant, whereas those with a negative valence are associated with mental pain. The *cause* of an emotion is the reason, perhaps unconscious, why the emotion has arisen at all; for example, a boy may (perhaps unconsciously) hate his mother because she has divorced his father and married another man. The *intensity* of an emotion is a quantitative rating of the emotion's valence; for example, a person whose emotions vary from the mean in intensity is described clinically as having either flattened affect or elevated, expansive affect.

A mood differs structurally from an emotion in that it lacks an object, whereas it does have a subject, valence, cause, and intensity: a person may be depressed; and the depressed mood may have a cause, but the mood itself is not directed at any real or represented object. That emotions have objects implies that cognitions play a more important role in emotions than in moods. It follows then that if cognitions do play a causal role in the etiology of childhood depression (Kovacs & Beck, 1977) they perhaps do so largely indirectly, precipitating dysphoria by means of intense, disordered emotions, which may be directed at unrealistic objects (cf. Abramson *et al.*, 1978; Sandler & Joffe, 1965).

Each of the components of emotion—nonverbal expressive, verbal expressive, experiential, and biological—is potentially relevant to childhood depression. Izard and Schwartz (Chapter 2 of this volume) discuss these components in terms of their implication for the symptomatological expression of depression. In this regard, it may be added that emotional display rules (Ekman, Friesen, & Ellsworth, 1972; Malatesta & Haviland, 1982) would seem to be very important. Emotional display rules, which may be classified as either social, reflecting generally accepted and socially defined rules for the display of emotions, or personal, representing individual standards that regulate the overt expression of emotions, concern how, when, and where emotions are displayed; they describe the conventions that govern the use of emotional expressions as signaling systems in a social group. Emotional display rules are a function of the temperament of the persons involved, their repertoire of emotional expressions (dependent upon developmental age), their particular life experiences, the prevailing social conventions, and also the genetic heritage of the human "environment of evolutionary adaptedness" (Ekman et al., 1972). For this reason, the study of the relationship between the development of the depressed person's personal display rules in interaction with the social display rules of the immediate social environment (family, peers) as well as those of the culture at large may be a way of integrating some of the genetic, constitutional, personality, familial, and sociological factors that may converge in the etiology of childhood depression.

The examination of those personal rules that regulate the display of emotions raises the possibility of integrating, at least in part, the psychoanalytic and behavioral theories of the etiology of depression, since personal display rules may often be conceived as the behavioral expression of defense mechanisms (Hesse & Cicchetti, 1982). Defense mechanisms have been held to play an imporant role in both normal and pathological development (Elkind, 1976; A. Freud, 1946, 1965; Vaillant, 1978). The role of these defense mechanisms in the pathogenic process of childhood depression may then be conceived of in one of two ways: (1) as a maladaptation between the individual's emotions and the display rules governing the immediate social environment; (2) as a means of successfully adapting to the unconscious awareness of, and resulting anxiety from, the perceived incongruity between one's internal emotional experiences and societal regulations and norms. Consequently, a longitudinal, observational study of the development of personal display rules could draw upon the resources of ethological models of nonverbal signaling and its social function (Charlesworth, 1982), thus bringing to bear an explicit evolutionary perspective. Furthermore, the examination of the association between the development of personal and social display rules over time would help to illuminate adaptive and maladaptive processes involved in resolving discrepancies between subjective and conventional rules regarding the appropriateness of emotional displays.

In contrast to the nonverbal expression of emotion, its verbal expression seems especially important for the treatment of childhood depression, if one grants that children's ability to express the emotions that they feel is crucial to successful treatment—an operating assumption of dynamically oriented therapy. Moreover, it would seem necessary to understand the biological component of emotion in order to delineate more clearly the manner in which emotional disturbances can precipitate a depressive episode, which in turn has a kind of biochemical inertia of its own (Akiskal & McKinney, 1975). The study of the ontogenesis of the biological substrates of emotional development may be important for understanding the age-dependent neurobiological, endocrinological, and biochemical correlates of childhood depression (Adamec, 1978; Nauta & Domesick, 1980; Panksepp, 1982).

It should be added that much more attention needs to be given to the notion of an unconscious emotion, and to the role that such emotions may play in the etiology of childhood depression. Can emotions operate unconsciously at developmentally earlier periods before they may be consciously experienced? Would these "unconscious" emotions operate in a similar manner, at different developmental periods, in precipitating a depressive episode? Can one describe nonverbal expressive components of unconscious emotions? In particular, what is the biological basis of an unconscious emotion, and how does it relate to that of the same emotion when consciously experienced and expressed? Many psychoanalytic theorists of depression have considered the role of unconscious emotions such as ambivalence, anger, and aggression to be of the greatest importance: perhaps by uncovering the biological component of unconscious emotions one may find a concrete referent for the metapsychological notion of an unconscious arena of emotions.

THE ONTOGENESIS OF EMOTIONS

There are two major, competing theories of the ontogenesis of emotions, which differ most importantly in the relationship they describe as obtaining between affect and cognition and which have different implications for the symptomatology, etiology, and treatment of childhood depression. The first view is basically that the full range of emotions found in a normal adult is differentiated throughout childhood from two or three primary affects, differing in valence, that are present at birth (Bridges, 1932; Sroufe, 1979b). This view ascribes to cognition a central role in this process of differentiation, and, indeed, some theorists attribute the differentiation of emotions solely to the differentiation of cognitive structures, arguing that cognitions determine the content of an emotion (Mandler, 1975). The other view, called "differential emotions theory," argues that the biological and expressive components for a wide range of emotions are already present and differentiated at birth and that, throughout infancy and childhood, various associations develop, linking these discrete biological units with cognition (Izard, 1977; Izard & Schwartz, Chapter 2 of this volume). On this view, cognitions are not essential to the experience or feeling state of any emotions; however, cognitions are associated with emotions in most important ways. Emotions are essentially biosocial, playing motivational and adaptational functions. The normal ontogeny of emotion *expressions*, as they occur in infancy, is mainly biological.

In order to understand the pathology of childhood depression, it is important first to know, in normal development, whether the expressions of emotions remain phenotypically similar over time, what the range of emotions is at each developmental period, and what role cognitions play in emotional experience at each developmental period. The two main theories of emotional ontogenesis predict different answers to the questions. On the first view, that emotions are differentiated as cognitive structures differentiate, we may expect that the phenotypic expression of emotions will change over time and that, more importantly, the contexts that elicit various emotions will change; therefore, great care would be necessary in designing methods of assessment of childhood depression that were adapted to the level of cognitive development of the child. Moreover, because emotions are differentiated over time, one would expect that some emotions that may be necessary for a true depressive episode to occur, such as self-reproach or entrenched guilt feelings, may not be able to be experienced or expressed until certain cognitive advances are first made. Finally, because on this view cognitions play an essential role in determining the content of an emotion, cognitive behavior therapy (Beck, 1967) may be expected to be very effective.

However, according to differential emotions theory, one may expect a phenotypical continuity of emotion feeling states over time. If this is not the case, at least phenotypical changes in the expression of emotion might be expected to reflect largely maturational changes in the biological substrates of emotions. Again, the range of emotions in the child's repertoire would vary less over time, while the range of affective–cognitive structures increases immensely. In particular, those emotions that are thought to play a central role in the etiology of depression (anger, guilt, sadness, shame, and fear) would be present from an early age (i.e., by infancy). However, cognitive associations with these emotions would at this time not have developed to a very great extent. In differential emotions theory, one may expect that, if cognitions play an important role in the etiology of depression, then they may operate in two distinct ways. First, the cognitive interpretations that may be associated with certain emotional reactions differ as the individual's cognitive structures become more developed; thus, while the discrete emotion of anger may be present from early infancy, the association between the anger and its direction toward a specific object (such as a psychologically unavailable parent) may not be possible for an infant or a young child to make until the concrete operational period when the child is able to focus on more than one aspect of a situation simultaneously and to reason about experiences not immediately present. It is only when the child is capable of experiencing the emotional reaction to an object that the anger may be seen to assume etiological significance in depression. Second, cognitions may play a role in the development of depression through the formation of deviant associations between emotions and cognitions, such that particular cognitions might lead to maladaptive emotional (and hence motivational) responses, and particular emotions might occasion associated unrealistic or distorted cognitions. However, in differential emotions theory, the possibility—not present in the view according to which cognitions essentially constitute emotions—exists that emotions can become disordered via some biological or biochemical dysfunction, apart from any cognitive distortions or deviations. It thus admits the possibility that some forms of depression have a predominantly biological basis, follow a classic disease course, and do not in any way develop in accordance with cognitivist theories of depression. Again, this view would have implications for appropriate therapeutic intervention, perhaps ascribing greater value to psychopharmacological treatment in addition to more traditional therapeutic approaches.

Two additional, specific issues in the ontogenesis of emotions seem worthy of notice. First, it would appear to be important to study the range of dysthymic mood at different developmental stages in nonclinical populations, since these conditions may represent either precursors to or vulnerability factors for major depression and manic–depressive disorder, respectively. A second and related issue involves the specification, for each developmental period, of normal ranges of emotional responses and of intensity of emotional reactions in a variety of contexts. This would seem to be a necessary preliminary step to characterizing disordered or inappropriate affect in early childhood, which again may be either a precursor to or vulnerability factor for depression in late childhood, adolescence, and adulthood.

SOCIALIZATION OF AFFECT AND DEPRESSION

The degree to which caregivers exert an influence upon their children's overt display, modulation, or control of emotions has not been clearly addressed to date. The role that caregivers assume in socializing affect could impact upon the types of affects the child is capable of expressing, the range and variation of affective expressions, their intensity and duration, the regulation of emotional displays, and the contexts in which emotions are expressed. Furthermore, particular problems may arise in the socialization process if the child displays atypical developmental patterns (see Cicchetti & Schneider-Rosen, 1984a, for an elaboration) or if the caregiver is experiencing some form of pathology. In particular, children of depressed parents seem to represent a group vulnerable to manifesting deviations or delays in emotional development (Beardslee, Bemporad, Keller, & Klerman, 1983). Therefore, several issues need to be investigated in order to achieve a more comprehensive understanding of the relationship between socialization of affect and depression.

1. While the language that a caregiver employs to label certain affective states may impact on the intensity, frequency, or type of the child's affective displays, it is unclear as to what role such emotional language might

have on the child's developing ability to modulate internal emotional experiences or to respond appropriately to environmental stimuli. Furthermore, it would seem likely that a depressed parent would tend to respond differentially to different classes of affects (e.g., negative but not positive affects). This could influence the child in that it may result in a greater tendency for the child to inhibit those affects to which the parent does not respond, or to ignore the caregiver as a source of information or emotional support. This could, in turn, create a certain degree of helplessness in the child; parental noncontingency or inconsistency of responsiveness could result in the child's feeling ineffectual in acquiring parental attention, support, or care.

2. Empirical investigations of children's reactions to caregivers' affective expressions would help to illuminate the relationship between qualitative differences in caregivers' affect and behavior of the child. Several studies have demonstrated that infants respond differentially to natural variations in maternal expressions (e.g., Brazelton, Koslowski, & Main, 1974; Field, 1980; Stern, 1977). Experimentally induced maternal affective behavior, such as appearing motionless (Carpenter, Tecce, Stechler, & Friedman, 1970) or displaying a still face (Fogel, Diamond, Langhorst, & Demos, 1982; Tronick, Als, Adamson, Wise & Brazelton, 1978), results in increased proportions of negative affect and gaze aversion in infants as young as 2 months of age. Tronick (1982) suggests that because these infant behaviors usually follow an overt display of positive affect, the distress and gaze aversion represent an adaptive response to the infants' inability to reinstitute normal patterns of interaction.

There is empirical evidence suggesting that infant development is strongly related to qualitative differences in caregiver's affect (e.g., Tronick, Ricks, & Cohn, 1982; Weissman & Paykel, 1974). However, to date, there are few investigations of the contingency of infant behavior in response to normal (e.g., Kaye & Fogel, 1980) or simulated depressed (e.g., Cohn & Tronick, 1983) maternal expressions. Certainly, these investigations will help to illuminate the relationship between the organization and structure of infant behaviors following qualitative variations in caregiver affective displays. Furthermore, they will have implications for our understanding of the socialization process whereby affect and behavior develop and become integrated over time. Specifically, with children of depressed caregivers, it is likely that depressed affect will result in a pattern of adaptation in the child that could represent a helpless response; that is, children unable to alter the caregiver's affect may, as Cohn and Tronick (1983) suggest, modify their own affective display (e.g., gaze avert or become wary) in response to a lack of positive affect in the caregiver. One would expect that the degree of the child's experience of helplessness would vary according to the quality, duration, and severity of the caregiver's depression. However, the critical point with regard to the socialization of affect is that children appear to be capable of assuming an active role in the socialization process, altering their own affect and behavior in response to the detection of and meaning ascribed to stimuli (e.g., maternal affect) in a particular context.

3. It is necessary to explore the characteristic patterns of verbal and nonverbal emotional expressiveness in the caregiver and their relationship to the availability, responsivity, and sensitivity of the caregiver. Research has demonstrated that there is a significant relationship between these maternal characteristics and the subsequent development of the attachment relationship (e.g., Ainsworth, Bell, & Stayton, 1974; Main, 1977; Main, Tomasini, & Tolan, 1979). If depressed caregivers tend to be less available and responsive, as well as less affectively expressive or less capable of modulating their own emotional displays, then their children may develop aberrant patterns of emotional expressiveness that reflect the nature of the early relationship with the caregiver (cf. Zahn-Waxler et al., 1984). Therefore, there is a need to explore not only qualitative differences in the way emotions are socialized via nonverbal emotional displays of the caregiver, but also the relationship between the early quality of the attachment relationship as it influences later differential affective responsiveness in the child.

4. Finally, the relationship between the development of *social referencing* and the quality of the early parent–child relationship is one that warrants future investigation. Social referencing may be defined as the process whereby a person seeks emotional information from another in order to appraise an ambiguous situation that evokes uncertainty (Campos & Stenberg, 1981; Feinman & Lewis, 1983; Klinnert, Campos, Sorce, Emde, & Svejda, 1983). The relationship between the development of this self-regulatory mechanism and qualitative differences in parent–child interaction would be important to study in "normal" dyads. However, it would be especially important to examine the role that a depressed parent may assume as a source of emotional information for a child. Specifically, it would be necessary to understand whether children of depressed parents are more likely to exhibit deviations or delays in their capacity for social referencing due to the likelihood of problems in the caregiver's ability to reduce uncertainty by providing appropriate cues for the evaluation of and response to environmental stimuli. If the depressed parent tends to be psychologically unavailable, then it becomes critical to determine whether this fosters deviant or developmentally immature social referencing skills in the child, which will interfere with the child's developing capacity to learn about affectively arousing stimulus situations. The etiological significance of this acquired pattern of responding for the later development of a depressive disorder necessitates empirical examination.

THE ONTOGENESIS OF THE AWARENESS OF EMOTION

Perhaps of greater importance to childhood depression than the onto-genesis of the child's emotional repertoire is the metaproblem of the onto-genesis of the child's awareness of the emotions in that repertoire. In particular, we are interested in children's ability to understand their own emotions and to use language to express this understanding. There are at least four reasons why this is important to childhood depression:

1. It is obviously relevant to the treatment of childhood depression us-ing psychotherapy, since the ability to be aware of, to express, and to understand an emotion may be a necessary condition for achiev-ing both insight into the emotion and some conscious control over it. If the child's awareness of emotions follows a developmental course, then therapeutic programs that took this into account would probably be more effective (see Harter, in press).
2. An asymmetry exists between affect and cognition, in that it is possi-ble to have a cognition about an affect, but not possible to have an affect about a cognition (Cicchetti & Pogge-Hesse, 1981). Because of this, it would seem that certain cognitive developments may be necessary for being aware of particular emotions or groups of emo-tions, even if they are not necessary for the experience or expression of those emotions.
3. It seems to be important to understand the child's capacity to be aware of an emotional response directed toward another real or in-ternally represented object since the presence of an object toward which a feeling is directed represents the major structural dif-ference between an emotion and a mood. This issue is especially relevant to childhood depression, since it may be that a clinical depression may not become manifest before the child is capable of experiencing an intense emotional reaction toward a specific object (e.g., anger toward a psychologically unavailable parent). This emo-tional response toward the object may be conscious or unconscious. Then, therapeutic intervention may not be successful until a person is able to and willing to acknowledge this emotional reaction. If the emotional response is unconscious, then this process may involve the breaking down of well-formed defenses that have prevented such an awareness from being achieved. As an example, it seems particularly important to study the child's capacity to experience and to be aware of emotional ambivalence, since this has been held to play an important role in the pathogenesis of depression (Abraham, 1911/1960; S. Freud, 1917/1968). It would seem that the

child's response to an ambivalently loved object would differ markedly, depending upon whether the child is or is not capable of being aware of this ambivalence.

4. Finally, the child's ability to be aware of multiple emotions seems relevant because of the role that complex combinations of emotions such as anger, sadness, shame, fear, and hostility (either self- or other-directed), directed either at the same or at different objects, may play in a depressive episode. In particular, it would seem important first to know the ages at which children can become aware of multiple, even conflicting emotions, for then it would be possible to determine whether the child's lack of awareness was due either to a natural, developmental lack of ability or to the employment of defense mechanisms.

The development of the awareness of multiple emotions has been studied by Harter (in press). Harter observed in her clinical work that children who, to the clinician, were obviously ambivalent about some person, lacked an awareness of the ambivalence. These children would sometimes say that they hated this person and at other times they professed only love. They seemed incapable of being aware of the two conflicting emotions that they experienced simultaneously.

Harter (in press) postulated that the ability to conceptualize multiple, conflicting emotions would develop soon after the development of concrete operational thought. Various Piagetian experiments have demonstrated that preoperational children are unable to conceptualize simultaneously more than one dimension of their environment; moreover, their ability to use reason is limited to judgments concerning concrete, immediate experience (Flavell, 1977). Harter (in press) hypothesized that these developments would be necessary for the simultaneous conceptualization of two different emotions, which she likened to two different dimensions. Moreover, she argued that, because of the intangible, psychological nature of emotional experience, décalage would occur. She also employed the orthogenetic principle to describe the change that may be expected to take place with the development of concrete operations. Before concrete operations, ambivalent children's awareness oscillates almost violently between emotional extremes, as their emotion is directly dependent upon contextual factors. Afterwards, the child can coordinate these two emotions, being able to be aware, for instance, of momentary emotions superimposed upon enduring, possibly opposite ones. These hypotheses were confirmed in a cross-sectional study of 45 children, aged 3–13 years (Harter, in press). However, since the study was not longitudinal, and since no cross-cultural work has been done, one cannot yet postulate a necessary developmental sequence.

The work by Harter raises the question of the relationship between awareness of emotions, the use of emotional language to describe them, and skills helpful in coping with maladaptive emotions. Katan (1961) and Furman (1978) have suggested that the use of language referring to emotions facilitates one's control over nonverbal emotional expressions, which may in turn facilitate control over the emotions themselves (Izard & Schwartz, Chapter 2 of this volume). It may then be the case that parents who frequently use emotional language to refer to their own and to others' emotional expressions may in fact provide their children with a means of controlling these expressions and, indirectly, emotions. Here it would be important to study parents' emotional speech and their socialization of emotional language in their children as being potential protective or vulnerability factors in childhood depression. It has been proposed that children, in assimilating their parents' emotional language, assimilate their parents' coping skills (Hesse & Cicchetti, 1982). The emotional language of a depressed parent may thus serve as a means of transmission of depression. Of particular importance in this regard would be the parents' inappropriate or maladaptive labelings of emotion (Cicchetti & Schneider-Rosen, 1984a) and the natural history of their emotional taxonomies (Hesse & Cicchetti, 1982).

A related, and perhaps more basic question, concerns whether children's ability to conceptualize another person's having multiple, conflicting emotions develops before or after the ability to conceptualize their own multiple, conflicting emotions. This issue bears upon the question of whether emotions are differentiated essentially through cognitive development or at birth. According to the former, structuralist view, the ability to conceptualize multiple emotions in others could not precede the same ability with respect to oneself. Certain cognitive structures must develop prior to the emergence of this capacity; once these structures develop, they will be employed with respect to oneself and to others. According to the latter, differential emotions theory view, it is possible that one learns how to conceptualize multiple emotions through a social learning process (cf. Harter, in press). Maturational changes will underlie the ability to understand how several emotions may exist simultaneously, but social learning experiences will determine whether an individual will be capable of applying this ability to oneself and/or to others. This view is more compatible with the preceding hypothesis regarding the role of emotional language in the intergenerational transmission of depression since individual differences in the tendency of parents to use emotional language, and in the quality of their emotional speech, may bear directly on the development of the child's capacity to understand others' experience of discrete or multiple emotions.

Finally, the study of the ability to conceptualize multiple emotions is directly relevant to the development of self-cognitions, which was discussed above. Harter (in press) proposed that preoperational children would evaluate themselves in terms of extremes (e.g., "all good" or "all bad") and these extremes would vacillate with context. The concrete operational child would have the ability to coordinate favorable and unfavorable self-cognitions that may exist simultaneously. We maintain that it is this characteristic of concrete operational thought that may represent a significant factor in one's vulnerability to, or capacity to defend against, depression. That is, the ability to maintain simultaneously several emotions with the self as the object is a feature of concrete operational thought that allows for the integration of these various emotions into an organized conception of the self. The transition to concrete operations also makes possible self-attributions that are stable, enduring and global. This illustrates how developments in different domains can compensate for each other and be mutually adaptive. That is, a child may make a stable, enduring, and global negative attribution of the self that makes them vulnerable to experiencing entrenched learned helplessness. At the same time, they should be able to coordinate simultaneously opposite-valence self-evaluations. Thus, a vulnerability factor is matched by a protective factor. The breakdown of this protective factor—the child's becoming unable to coordinate a transient or specific positive self-evaluation with an enduring and global negative self-evaluation—might lead to the development of depression.

THE DEVELOPMENT OF GUILT FEELINGS

The role of guilt feelings in the symptomatology of adult depression is widely acknowledged. Rado (1928) has provided what is perhaps the classic explanation for such guilt: the punitive superego of the depressed patient reproduces in an internalized fashion the love of the parents, and thus constitutes a means by which the depressed person can both identify with the parents and win again their approval. However, it is unclear what role guilt feelings can play in childhood depression, especially when they are conceived according to such a model. It would seem that one could argue here, as did early theorists of childhood depression in general (e.g., Malmquist, 1971, 1975; Rie, 1966), that because the child younger than age 11 or so has neither a well-developed superego nor a fully integrated ego, the process described by Rado cannot obtain, and so one should expect not to see guilt feelings in affective disorders of infancy and early to middle childhood. This conclusion finds support in the study of McConville *et al.* (1973), which found almost no instances of guilt-type depressive symptoms before age 11. However, guilt feelings are included in the RDC, DSM-III, and Dweck *et al.* (1977) criteria for depression without any qualification, implying the possibility of guilt feelings in childhood depression at any age. It would therefore seem imperative first to trace the development of the capacity to experience guilt in normal children, before determining what role guilt can play in the symptomatology of child depression.

In order to address this issue, it would be necessary to understand more comprehensively the process whereby parental and societal standards become internalized. Furthermore, the relationship between the internalization of these standards and the extent to which parents actively socialize and encourage this internalization would be important in order to address the significance of guilt in the symptom picture of the depressive disorder. If parents adopt discipline techniques such as love withdrawal or physical aggression as a means of ensuring that their child is obedient and is upholding their standards and values, then the child may be less likely to disobey or to act in a manner that would deviate from parental expectations. This conditional nature of the parent–child relationship (i.e., "I will love you as long as you do what you are supposed to") would undoubtedly lead to the experience of more intense guilt and self-doubt if the child acts in a manner contrary to parental expectations. Without parental approval, the child may fear that the threat of the loss of love would be too overwhelming; therefore, depression with associated guilt may represent, in part, the child's efforts to deal with the perceived parental loss that results from the failure to fulfill their expectations.

It may be fruitful here to follow Kohlberg (1969) and Hoffman (1982a) who argue that the quality of the guilt feelings a child is able to experience changes with the cognitive development of the child. Both Kohlberg (1969) and Hoffman (1982a) follow Piaget (1954/1981) in taking cognition to determine the structure of guilt feelings. Since guilt results from the perception of having transgressed one's norms or standards, it follows that the types of incidents that will occasion guilt, and even the way in which guilt feelings present themselves phenomenologically, will vary with developments in the system of norms or standards that the person accepts. In this regard, Kohlberg's (1969) theory of six developmental stages of moral development, even if these stages are not invariable and universal, provides a rough outline of such development. Research into the role that environmental stressors or life events may have in the formation of guilt feelings in childhood, which may in turn lead to depression, should take into account the moral stage of the child, which will determine what stressors or events could lead to guilt feelings.

By taking such a developmental perspective on the development of guilt feelings, one avoids the metapsychological notion of a superego, and thus one maintains a kind of continuity between early, prototypical forms of guilt and later, more developed, forms of guilt feelings, which may play a larger role in depression. Hoffman (1982a) argues that guilt is basically the result of cognitive structure plus felt empathy. Hoffman argues that the distress of a person who empathizes with another person in distress is transformed into guilt feelings via a causal attribution, by the person feeling empathy, of being responsible for the other's distress. Obviously, a necessary precondition for a person's having guilt feelings would then be the ability to be aware of one's control over one's own actions and of the consequences that one's actions have for others. Moreover, as one's ability to make more complex causal attributions develops, so does one's ability to experience guilt feelings of particular kinds.

Thus, for example, Hoffman (1982a) argues that the cognitive ability to imagine the effect of one's action on another person will give rise to "anticipatory guilt" as well as "guilt of omission or inaction" (as opposed to guilt over having done something wrong in the past). Again, the cognitive ability to engage in social comparison is required for feelings of guilt to arise as a result of perceiving that one is in a more advantageous position than someone else. Since these and related cognitive abilities develop at different periods, we would expect that the manifestation of excessive or inappropriate guilt will take a different form at different developmental stages, even if the mechanism underlying the production of guilt feelings (a transformation of felt empathetic distress through a causal attribution) is the same. Here the literature on the development of self-understanding may be relevant. Studies by Broughton (1980) and Selman (1980) indicate that it is in late childhood and early adolescence that the child begins to conceive of the self more as a self-determining, volitional agent. The child's sense of will and agency takes on a greater importance at this time. This change in cognitive abilities may mark a transition to a period in which children will make causal attributions to their own agency with greater frequency and intensity, and through such attributions empathetic distress would be more frequently transformed into a more intense guilt. Therefore, according to Hoffman's model, it is in late childhood that one may expect to see the development of a capacity to experience more enduring and more intense guilt feelings. This conclusion is supported by the McConville et al. (1973) study, which reported an increase in guilt-type depression at about this time.

Finally, guilt feelings have been found to be potent sources of motivation (Hoffman, 1978, 1982b). This suggests that the relationship between guilt feelings and the actions that they motivate may be an important factor in the etiology of depression. We may hypothesize that there are both adaptive and maladaptive responses to guilt feelings. For example, the child who is in a state of learned helplessness and expects noncontingency may not respond to feelings of guilt with adaptive action. If those feelings were originally the result of a perceived failure to act so as to prevent another's or one's own distress ("guilt of omission or inaction"), the guilt feelings may then be exacerbated by the lack of response. In this way initially appropriate guilt, which occurred in the context of a depressive episode, could be transformed into execessive and inappropriate guilt feelings.

HEDONIC CAPACITY AND DISAPPOINTMENT

It is worthwhile to mention briefly two other areas deserving closer investigation from a developmental point of view: hedonic capacity and disappointment. A decrease in hedonic capacity, or anhedonia, is commonly observed in adult depression. However, although Sandler and Joffe (1965) include anhedonia in their description of the basic psychobiological affect of childhood depression, little is known about the ontogenesis of either the biological basis or the cognitive basis of anhedonia (see Meehl, 1975). The former seems particularly relevant to childhood depression, given the suggested role that the diencephalic reward system plays in its etiology (Akiskal & McKinney, 1975; Meehl, 1975; Kashani et al., 1981). It would seem necessary to ascertain, through a longitudinal study, the nature and extent of pleasure typically derived from particular activities by children. It may then be possible to determine the qualitative changes in the depressed child's ability to engage in those activities with enthusiasm, persistence, and vigor. Ideally, one would also study possible correlations between these changes and changes in central urinary and cerebrospinal fluid amine metabolites. Moreover, since it has been demonstrated that cognition plays an important role in the child's derivation of pleasure from an activity or task (Harter, 1978) the depressed child's inability to derive pleasure may be related to cognitive distortions or dysfunctions, and these may vary with developmental level.

Similarly, the experience of disappointment, which is so often experienced by adult depressives as the result of failing to achieve aspirations for oneself or of failing to have expectations for other's behavior or responses toward oneself fulfilled, must be studied developmentally. In particular, it seems important to determine the effect of cognitive advances upon the formulation of expectations for oneself and others, as well as to illuminate the particular cognitive skills that are necessary for individuals to be able to perceive incongruities or discrepancies between goals that they have formulated and the extent to which those goals have or have not been met. An analysis of how realistic those goals or expectations are, either for oneself or for another to fulfill, would seem essential in understanding the significance of the experience of disappointment.

Furthermore, the relationship between disappointment and anger needs to be better understood developmentally. Then it may be possible to illuminate those cognitive capacities that enable children to experience and to express anger toward the self, that is, in the form of disappointment felt over expectations failing to be met, as opposed to anger explicitly directed toward another individual. It may be that this distinction between the direction in which anger is directed is crucial for understanding a feature that differentiates between depressed and nondepressed children, if it in fact may be determined that depressed individuals are more likely to direct their anger inward, as suggested by psychoanalytic writings, or at inappropriate objects, while nondepressed individuals are more capable of expressing their anger externally to the appropriate objects. Moreover, it seems to be important to highlight developmental changes in the experience of disappointment and anger that may be related to cognitive advances.

CONCLUSION

The basic tenets and principles of the organizational perspective provide the guiding assumptions for formulating research questions and for designing the appropriate empirical designs for testing theoretical propositions when one is interested in considering the coherence of development in both normal and atypical populations of children (Cicchetti & Pogge-Hesse, 1982; Cicchetti & Schneider-Rosen, 1984a). Researchers who adapt this perspective examine the ways in which behaviors become hierarchically organized into more complex patterns within developmental systems, the manner in which later modes and functions evolve from earlier prototypes, and the processes by which global and diffuse part functions become integrated into wholes. This developmental approach emphasizes the relationships between cognitive, social, emotional, and neurophysiological systems, as well as the consequences of advances or lags within one system for the functioning of other systems. Moreover, an attempt is made to understand the effects of early experiences for later adaptation, while simultaneously considering the individual's current level of functioning and the influence of extraorganismic, environmental factors.

We believe that greater progress will be made in unraveling the conundrum of childhood depression when this developmental approach is adopted. More specifically, it is our contention that this developmental perspective will provide essential information for the appropriate delineation of diagnostic criteria, for the understanding of course and prognosis, for the assessment of competence or incompetence in the different behavioral domains, and for the application of therapeutic interventions that are congruent with the child's age and stage-level of functioning.

In this chapter, we have introduced and discussed several issues that are relevant to the application of a developmental approach to childhood depression. We maintain that it would be very surprising if any consistent picture of early behavioral patterns specific to depression in children were found to emerge. Instead, we argue that children of different ages, at different developmental stages, from diverse environments, and with differing constitutions and experiences, are likely to manifest vulnerabilities and symptomatology in a wide variety of specific, age-appropriate ways. One would not expect to find behavioral isomorphism in the observed signs or symptoms of depression in children of different ages, nor would one predict that the child's internal cognitive structures would enable children of varying ages to interpret, express, or even defend against their affective experiences or internal emotional states in the same way. Therefore, when one considers the manner in which depression manifests itself in childhood, it is not possible to define symptom characteristics that comprise the diagnostic picture for depression that may be applicable across ages.

We have argued that developmental changes in cognitive structures and functions impact upon the manner in which children experience and express emotions. Consequently, the manifest characteristics of depression are influenced by parallel advances in logical operations, language, symbolism, and representation. Furthermore, the child's intellectual growth is paralleled by evolving affective schemata that progress from the elementary emotional expressions to more complex and intricate schemata reflecting more advanced modes of regulation, modulation, and control. Thus, there will be individual differences in the manner in which increasing cognitive sophistication impacts upon and influences children's capacities for emotional regulation, for the differentiation of various affective expressions in oneself and others, and for the ability to perceive, interpret, and respond to one's own and others' emotional experiences and expressions.

Motivational and interpersonal factors, as well as internal psychological mechanisms such as the operation of defense mechanisms or the reliance upon social display rules to modulate one's expressed emotions, may interact with cognitive development to create individual variation in children's affective growth. Developmental changes in competence and in self-understanding may have implications for the etiology of depression, and the ontogenesis of emotions and of the awareness of emotions may significantly influence the overt manifestations of depression. Throughout this chapter, we have developed our position that it is only when descriptive and theoretical formulations of depression take into account the biological reorganizations and the changing integration of competencies in the social, emotional, and cognitive domains that a more comprehensive understanding of the etiology and sequelae of childhood depression may be achieved and that methods for diagnosis and therapeutic intervention may be improved.

ACKNOWLEDGMENTS

This manuscript was supported by grants from the Foundation for Child Development (Young Scholar in Social and Affective Development), the W. T. Grant Foundation (83089400), the National Center for Child Abuse and Neglect (90-C-1929), and the National Institute of Mental Health (1-R01-MH37960-01) to author Cicchetti. In addition, we would like to thank Drs. Cal Izard, Peter Read, and Michael Rutter for their extremely thoughtful and helpful comments on an earlier version of this chapter. Finally, Dante Cicchetti would like to extend his appreciation and gratitude to Drs. Marjorie Beeghly, Jules Bemporad, Vicki Carlson, Norman Garmezy, Sanford Gifford, Philip Holzman, Maria Kovacs, Joseph Lipinski, Paul Meehl, and Alan Sroufe, and to Michael Pakaluk.

REFERENCES

Abraham, K. (1960). Notes on the psychoanalytical investigation of manic-depressive insanity and allied conditions. In *Selected papers on psychoanalysis*. New York: Basic Books. (Original work published 1911)

Abramson, L. Y., Seligman, M. E. P., & Teasdale, J. D. (1978). Learned helplessness in humans: Critique and reformulation. *Journal of Abnormal Psychology, 87*, 49–74.

Achenbach, T. M., & Edelbrock, C. S. (1983). Taxonomic issues in child psychopathology. In T. H. Ollendick & M. Hersen (Eds.), *Handbook of child psychopathology*. New York: Plenum Press.

Adamec, R. (1978). Normal and abnormal system mechanisms of emotive biasing. In K. Livingston & O. Hornykiewicz (Eds.), *Limbic mechanisms*. New York: Plenum Press.

Ainsworth, M. D. S., Bell, S., & Stayton, D. (1974). Infant-mother attachment and social development: "Socialization" as a product of reciprocal responsiveness to signals. In M. P. Richards (Ed.), *The integration of a child into a social world*. London & New York: Cambridge University Press.

Ainsworth, M. D. S., Blehar, M., Waters, E., & Wall, S. (1978). *Patterns of attachment: A psychological study of the strange situation*. Hillsdale, NJ: Lawrence Erlbaum Associates.

Ainsworth, M. D. S., & Wittig, B. A. (1969). Attachment and exploratory behavior of one year olds in a strange situation. In B. M. Foss (Ed.), *Determinants of infant behavior* (Vol. 4). New York: Wiley.

Akiskal, H. S., & McKinney, W. T., Jr. (1975). Overview of recent research in depression: Integration of ten conceptual models into a comprehensive clinical frame. *Archives of General Psychiatry, 32*, 285–305.

American Psychiatric Association (1980). *Diagnostic and statistical manual of mental disorders* (3rd ed.). Washington: American Psychiatric Association.

Amsterdam, B. (1972). Mirror self-image reactions before age two. *Developmental Psychobiology, 5*, 297–305.

Anthony, E. J. (1975). Childhood depression. In E. J. Anthony & T. Benedek (Eds.), *Depression and human existence*. Boston: MA: Little, Brown.

Arend, R., Gove, F. L., & Sroufe, L. A. (1979). Continuity of individual adaptation from infancy to kindergarten: A predictive study of ego-resiliency and curiosity in preschoolers. *Child Development, 50*, 950–959.

Arieti, S. (1982). Individual psychotherapy. In E. Paykel (Ed.), *Handbook of affective disorders*. New York: Guilford Press.

Arieti, S., & Bemporad, J. (1978). *Severe and mild depression*. New York: Basic Books.

Beardslee, W. R., Bemporad, J., Keller, M. B., & Klerman, G. L. (1983). Children of parents with major affective disorder: A review. *American Journal of Psychiatry, 140*, 825–844.

Beck, A. T. (1967). *Depression: Causes and treatment*. Philadelphia: University of Pennsylvania Press.

Bemporad, J., & Wilson, A. (1978). A developmental approach to depression in childhood and adolescence. *Journal of the American Academy of Psychoanalysis, 6*, 325–352.

Beres, D. (1966). Superego and depression. In R. M. Lowenstein, L. W. Newman, M. Scherr, &

A. J. Solnit (Eds.), *Psychoanalysis—A general psychology*. New York: International Universities Press.

Bibring, E. (1953). The mechanism of depression. In P. Greenacre (Ed.), *Affective disorders*. New York: International Universities Press.

Bischof, N. (1975). A systems approach toward the functional connections of attachment and fear. *Child Development, 46*, 801–817.

Blehar, M., Lieberman, A. F., & Ainsworth, M. D. S. (1977). Early face-to-face interaction and its relation to later infant-mother attachment. *Child Development, 48*, 182–194.

Block, J. (1971). *Lives through time*. Berkeley, CA: Bancroft Books.

Block, J. H ., & Block, J. (1980). The role of ego-control and ego resiliency in the organization of behavior. In W. A. Collins (Eds.), *Minnesota symposium on child psychology* (Vol. 13). Hillsdale, NJ: Lawrence Erlbaum Associates.

Bowlby, J. (1980). *Attachment and loss. Vol. III. Loss*. New York: Basic Books.

Brazelton, T. B., Koslowski, B., & Main, M. (1974). The origins of reciprocity: The early mother-infant interaction. In M. Lewis & L. Rosenblum (Eds.), *The effect of the infant on its caretaker*. New York: Wiley.

Bretherton, I., & Beeghly, M. (1982). Talking about internal states: The acquisition of an explicit theory of mind. *Developmental Psychology, 18*, 906–921.

Bridges, K. M. (1932). Emotional development in early infancy. *Child Development, 3*, 324–341.

Brim, O. G. (1976). Life-span development of the theory of oneself: Implications for child development. In H. W. Reese (Ed.), *Advances in child development and behavior* (Vol. 2). New York: Academic Press.

Bronson, G. (1965). The hierarchical organization of the central nervous system. *Behavioral Science, 10*, 7–25.

Bronson, G. (1972). Infants' reactions to unfamiliar persons and novel objects. *Monographs of the Society for Research in Child Development, 37* (Serial No. 148).

Broughton, J. (1978). Development concepts of self, mind, reality, and knowledge. *New Directions for Child Development, 1*, 75–100.

Broughton, J. (1980). The divided self in adolescence. *Human Development, 24*, 13–32.

Butterworth, G., & Cicchetti, D. (1978). Visual calibration of posture in normal and Down syndrome infants. *Perception, 7*, 513–525.

Campos, J. J., & Stenberg, C. R. (1981). Perception, appraisal and emotion: The onset of social referencing. In M. Lamb & L. Sherrod (Eds.), *Infant social cognitive*. Hillsdale, NJ: Lawrence Erlbaum Associates.

Carlson, G. A., & Cantwell, D. P. (1980). A survey of depressive symptoms, syndrome and disorder in a child psychiatric population. *Journal of Child Psychology and Psychiatry, 21*, 1019–1025.

Carpenter, G. C., Tecce, J. J., Stechler, G., & Friedman, S. (1970). Differential visual behavior to human and humanoid faces in early infancy. *Merrill Palmer Quarterly, 16*, 91–108.

Charlesworth, W. R. (1982). An ethological approach to research on facial expressions. In C. E. Izard (Ed.), *Measuring emotions in infants and children*. Cambridge, MA: Cambridge University Press.

Cicchetti, D. (1984). The emergence of developmental psychopathology. *Child Development. 55*, 1–7.

Cicchetti, D., & Hesse, P. (Eds.) (1982). *Emotional development*. San Fransicso: Jossey-Bass.

Cicchetti, D., & Hesse, P. (1983). Affect and intellect: Piaget's contributions to the study of infant emotional development. In R. Plutchik & H. Kellerman (Eds.), *Emotion: Theory and research* (Vol. 2). New York: Academic Press.

Cicchetti, D., & Pogge-Hesse, P. (1981). The relation between emotion and cognition in infant development: Past, present, and future perspectives. In M. Lamb & L. Sherrod (Eds.), *In-*

fant social cognition: Empirical and theoretical considerations. Hillsdale, NJ: Lawrence Erlbaum Associates.

Cicchetti, D., & Pogge-Hesse, P. (1982). Possible contributions to the study of organic retardates to developmental theory. In E. Zigler & D. Balla (Eds.), Developmental and difference theories of mental retardation. Hillsdale, NJ: Lawrence Erlbaum Associates.

Cicchetti, D., & Rizley, R. (1981). Developmental perspectives on the etiology, intergenerational transmission, and sequelae of child maltreatment. New Directions for Child Development, 11, 31–55.

Cicchetti, D., & Schneider-Rosen, K. (1984a). Theoretical and empirical considerations in the investigation of the relationship between affect and cognition in atypical populations of infants: Contributions to the formulation of an integrative theory of development. In C. Izard, J. Kagan, & R. Zajonc (Eds.), Emotions, cognition, and behavior. London & New York: Cambridge University Press.

Cicchetti, D., & Schneider-Rosen, K. (1984b). Toward a transactional model of childhood depression. In D. Cicchetti & K. Schneider-Rosen (Eds.), Childhood depression. San Francisco: Jossey-Bass.

Cicchetti, D., & Serafica, F. (1981). The interplay among behavioral systems: Illustrations from the study of attachment, affiliation, and wariness in young Down syndrome children. Developmental Psychology, 17, 36–49.

Cicchetti, D., & Sroufe, L. A. (1976). The relationship between affective and cognitive development in Down's syndrome infants. Child Development, 47, 920–929.

Cicchetti, D., & Sroufe, L. A. (1978). An organization view of affect: Illustration from the study of Down's syndrome infants. In M. Lewis & L. Rosenblum (Eds.), The development of affect. New York: Plenum Press.

Cohn, J. F., & Tronick, E. Z. (1983). Three-month-old infants' reaction to simulated maternal depression. Child Development, 54, 185–193.

Costello, C. G. (1980). Childhood depression: Three basic but questionable assumptions in the Lefkowitz and Burton critique. Psychological Bulletin, 87, 187–190.

Cronbach, L. J., & Meehl, P. E. (1955). Construct validity in psychological tests. Psychological Bulletin, 52, 281–302.

Cytryn, L., & McKnew, D.H., Jr. (1972). Proposed classification of childhood depression. American Journal of Psychiatry, 129, 149–155.

Cytryn, L., McKnew, D.H., Jr., & Bunney, W. E., Jr. (1980). Diagnosis of depression in children: A reassessment. American Journal of Psychiatry, 137, 22–25.

Damon, W., & Hart, D. (1982). The development of self-understanding from infancy through adolescence. Child Development, 53, 841–864.

Davis, H. (1979). Self-reference and the encoding of personal information in depression. Cognitive Therapy and Research, 3, 97–110.

Depue, R. A., & Monroe, S. M. (1978). The unipolar-bipolar distinction in the depressive disorders. Psychological Bulletin, 85, 1001–1029.

Dethier, V. (1976). The hungry fly: A physiological study of the behavior associated with feeding. Cambridge, MA: Harvard University Press.

Dweck, C. S. (1977). Learned helplessness: A developmental approach. In J. G. Schulterbrandt & A. Raskin (Eds.), Depression in childhood: Diagnosis, treatment, and conceptual models. New York: Raven Press.

Dweck, C. S., Gittelman-Klein, R., McKinney, W. T., & Watson, J. S. (1977). Summary of the subcommittee on clinical criteria of the diagnosis of childhood depression. In J. G. Schulterbrandt & A. Raskin (Eds.), Depression in childhood: Diagnosis, treatment, and conceptual models. New York: Raven Press.

Egeland, B., & Sroufe, L. A. (1981). Attachment and early maltreatment. Child Development, 52, 44–52.

Ekman, P., Friesen, W., & Ellsworth, P. (1972). *Emotion on the human face.* Oxford: Pergamon Press.

Elkind, D. (1976). Cognitive development and psychopathology: Observations on egocentrism and ego defense. In E. Schapler & J. Reichler (Eds.), *Psychopathology and child development.* New York: Plenum Press.

Engel, G. (1977). The need for a new medical model: A challenge for biomedicine. *Science, 196,* 129–135.

Erikson, E. (1950). *Childhood and society.* New York: Norton.

Fairbairn, W. R. (1952). *Psycho-analytic studies of the personality.* London: Tavistock.

Feinman, S., & Lewis, M. (1983). Social referencing at ten months: A second-order effect on infants' responses to strangers. *Child Development, 54,* 878–887.

Field, T. M. (1980). Interaction of high-risk infants: Quantitative and qualitative differences. In D. B. Swain, R. C. Hawkins, L. O. Walker, & J. H. Penticuff (Eds.), *Exceptional infant: Psychosocial risks in infant-environment transactions.* New York: Brunner/Mazel.

Flavell, J. H. (1977). *Cognitive development.* Englewood Cliffs, NJ: Prentice-Hall.

Fogel, A., Diamond, G. R., Langhorst, B. H., & Demos, V. (1982). Affective and cognitive aspects of the two-month-old's participation in face-to-face interaction with its mother. In E. Tronick (Ed.), *Social interchange in infancy: Affect, cognition, and communication.* Baltimore: University Park Press.

Freud, A. (1946). *The ego and the mechanisms of defense.* New York: International Universities Press.

Freud, A. (1965). *Normality and pathology in childhood: Assessments of development.* New York: International Universities Press.

Freud, S. (1968). Mourning and melancholia. In J. Strachey (Ed.), *The standard edition of the complete works of Sigmund Freud* (Vol. 14). London: Hogarth Press. (Original work published 1917)

Furman, R. (1978). Some developmental aspects of the verbalization of affects. *The psychoanalytic study of the child, 33,* 187–211.

Gaensbauer, T. (1980). Anaclitic depression in a three-and-one-half-month-old child. *American Journal of Psychiatry, 137,* 841–842.

Gaensbauer, T. J., & Sands, K. (1979). Distorted affective communication in abused/neglected infants and their potential impact on caretakers. *American Journal of Child Psychiatry, 18,* 236–250.

Gittelman-Klein, R. (1977). Definitional and methodological issues concerning depressive illness in children. In J. G. Schulterbrandt & A. Raskin (Eds.), *Depression in childhood: Diagnosis, treatment, and conceptual models.* New York: Raven Press.

Glaser, K. (1967). Masked depression in children and adolescents. *American Journal of Psychotherapy, 21,* 565–574.

Gordon, A., & Jameson, J. (1979). Infant-mother attachment in patients with nonorganic failure-to-thrive syndrome. *Journal of the American Academy of Child Psychiatry, 18,* 251–259.

Gottesman, I. I., & Shields, J. (1972). *Schizophrenia and genetics: A twin study vantage point.* New York: Academic Press.

Greenspan, S. I. (1981). *Psychopathology and adaptation in infancy and early childhood.* New York: International Universities Press.

Guardo, C. J., & Bohan, J. B. (1971). Development of a sense of self-identity in children. *Child Development, 42,* 1909–1921.

Harter, S. (1978). Effectance motivation reconsidered: A developmental model. *Human Development, 21,* 34–64.

Harter, S. (1983). Developmental perspectives on the self system. In E. M. Hetherington (Ed.), *Handbook of child psychology.* New York: Wiley.

Harter, S. (in press). Children's understanding of multiple emotions: A cognitive-developmental approach. In *Proceedings of the Jean Piaget Society*. Hillsdale, NJ: Lawrence Erlbaum Associates.

Hesse, P., & Cicchetti, D. (1982). Perspectives on an integrated theory of emotional development. *New directions for child development, 16*, 3–48.

Hoffman, M. (1978). Empathy, its development, and prosocial implications. In C. B. Keasey (Ed.), *Nebraska symposium on motivation* (Vol. 25). Lincoln: University of Nebraska Press.

Hoffman, M. (1982a). Affect and moral development. In D. Cicchetti & P. Hesse (Eds.), *Emotional development*. San Francisco: Jossey-Bass.

Hoffman, M. (1982b). Development of prosocial motivation: Empathy and guilt. In N. Eisenberg-Berg (Ed.), *Development of prosocial behavior*. New York: Academic Press.

Izard, C. (1977). *Human emotions*. New York: Plenum Press.

Jacobson, E. (1971). *Depression: Comparative studies of normal, neurotic, and psychotic conditions*. New York: International Universities Press.

James, W. (1892). *Psychology: The briefer course*. New York: Holt.

Kagan, J. (1980). Perspectives on continuity. In O. G. Brim & J. Kagan (Eds.), *Constancy and change in human development*. Cambridge, MA: Harvard University Press.

Kagan, J. (1981). *The second year. The emergence of self-awareness*. Cambridge, MA: Harvard University Press.

Kandel, E. R. (1979). Small systems of neurons. *Scientific American, 241*, 67–76.

Kandel, E. R., & Schwartz, J. H. (1981). *Principles of neural science*. New York: Elsevier/North-Holland.

Kandzierski, D. (1980). Self-schemata and scripts: The recall of self-referent and scriptal information. *Personality and Social Psychology Bulletin, 6*, 23–29.

Kaplan, B. (1966). The study of language in psychiatry: The comparative developmental approach and its application to symbolization and language in psychopathology. In S. Arieti (Ed.), *American handbook of psychiatry*. New York: Basic Books.

Kashani, J. H., Husain, A., Shokim, W. O., Hodges, K. K., Cytryn, L., & McKnew, D. H. (1981). Current perspectives on childhood depression: An overview. *American Journal of Psychiatry, 138*, 143–153.

Katan, A. (1961). Some thoughts about the role of verbalization in early childhood. *Psychoanalytic Study of the Child, 16*, 184–188.

Kaye, K., & Fogel, A. (1980). The temporal structure of face-to-face communication between mothers and infants. *Developmental Psychology, 16*, 454–464.

Keller, A., Ford, L. H., Jr., & Meacham, J. A. (1978). Dimensions of self-concept in preschool children. *Developmental Psychology, 14*, 484–489.

Kernberg, O. (1976). *Object relations theory and clinical psychoanalysis*. New York: Jason Aronson.

Klinnert, M. D., Campos, J. J., Sorce, J. F., Emde, R. N., & Svejda, M. (1983). Emotions as behavior regulators: Social referencing in infancy. In R. Plutchik & H. Kellerman (Eds.), *Emotion: Theory, research, and experience* (Vol. 2). New York: Academic press.

Kohlberg, L. (1969). Stage and sequence: The cognitive-developmental approach to socialization. In D. A. Goslin (Ed.), *Handbook of socialization theory and research*. Chicago: Rand McNally.

Kovacs, M., & Beck, A. T. (1977). An empirical clinical approach toward a definition of childhood depression. In J. G. Schulterbrandt and A. Raskin (Eds.), *Depression in childhood: Diagnosis, treatment, and conceptual models*. New York: Raven Press.

Kovacs, M., & Beck, A. T. (1978). Maladaptive cognitive structures in depression. *American Journal of Psychiatry, 135*, 525–533.

Lefkowitz, M. M., & Burton, N. (1978). Childhood depression: A critique of the concept. *Psychological Bulletin, 85*, 716–726.

Lewinsohn, P. M. (1974). A behavioral approach to depression. In R. J. Freidman & M. M. Katz (Eds.), The psychology of depression: Contemporary theory and research. Washington, DC: Winston.

Lewis, M., & Brooks-Gunn, J. (1979). Social cognition and the acquisition of self New York: Plenum Press.

Lively, W. J., & Bromley, D. B. (1973). Person perception in childhood and adolescence. New York: Wiley.

Lorenz, K. (1953). Die Entwicklung der vergleichenden Verhaltensforschung. In den letzten 12 Jahren. Zoologischer Anzeiger Supplement, 16, 36–58.

Lorenz, K., & Tinbergen, N. (1938). Taxis und Instinkthandlung in der Eirollbeweguns der Graugans. Zeitschrift für Tierpsychologie, 2, 1–29.

Luria, A. R. (1980). Higher cortical functions in man. New York: Basic Books.

Mahler, M. (1968). On human symbiosis and the vicissitudes of individuation. Vol. 1, Infantile psychosis. New York: International Universities Press.

Maier, S. F., Seligman, M. E. P., & Solomon, R. L. (1969). Pavlovian fear conditioning and learned helplessness. In B. A. Campbell & R. M. Church (Eds.), Punishment. New York: Appleton-Century Crofts.

Main, M. (1977). Analysis of a peculiar form of reunion behavior seen in some day-care children: Its history and sequelae in children who are home-reared. In R. Webb (Ed.), Social development in childhood: Daycare programs and research. Baltimore: Johns Hopkins University Press.

Main, M., Tomasini, L., & Tolan, W. (1979). Differences among mothers of infants judged to differ in security. Developmental Psychology, 15, 472–473.

Malatesta, C. Z., & Haviland, J. M. (1982). Learning display rules: The socialization of emotion expression in infancy. Child Development, 53, 991–1003.

Malmquist, C. P. (1971). Depressions in childhood and adolescence. New England Journal of Medicine, 284, 887–893, 955–961.

Malmquist, C. P. (1975). Depression in childhood. In F. F. Falch & S. C. Draghi (Eds.), The nature and treatment of depression. New York: Wiley.

Mandler, G. (1975). Mind and emotion. New York: Wiley.

Markus, H. (1977). Self-schemata and processing information about the self. Journal of Personality and Social Psychology, 35, 63–78.

Marmor, J. (1983). Systems thinking in psychiatry: Some theoretical and clinical implications. American Journal of Psychiatry, 140, 833–838.

Matas, L., Arend, R., & Sroufe, L. A. (1978). Continuity of adaptation in the second year: The relationship between quality of attachment and later competence. Child Development, 49, 547–556.

McConville, B. J., Boag, L. C., & Purohit, A. P. (1973). Three types of childhood depression. Canadian Psychiatric Association Journal, 18, 133–138.

Meehl, P. E. (1962). Schizotaxia, schizotypy, schizophrenia. American Psychologist, 17, 827–838.

Meehl, P. E. (1972). Specific genetic etiology, psychodynamics, and therapeutic nihilism. International Journal of Mental Health, 1, 10–27.

Meehl, P. E. (1975). Hedonic capacity: Some conjectures. Bulletin of the Menninger Clinic, 39, 295–307.

Mendelson, M. (1982). Psychodynamics of depression. In E. Paykel (Ed.), Handbook of affective Disorders. New York: Guilford.

Miller, J. (1978). Living systems. New York: McGraw-Hill.

Nauta, W., & Domesick, V. (1980). Neural associations of the limbic system. In A. Beckman (Ed.), Neural substrates of behavior. New York: Spectrum.

Nauta, W., & Feirtag, M. (1979). The organization of the brain. Scientific American, 241, 88–111.

Panksepp, J. (1982). Toward a general psychological theory of emotions. *Behavioral and Brain Sciences, 5*, 407–467.

Paykel, E. (1982). Life events and early environment. In E. Paykel (Ed.), *Handbook of affective disorders*. New York: Guilford.

Perris, C. (1982). The distinction between bipolar and unipolar affective disorders. In E. Paykel (Ed.), *Handbook of affective disorders*. New York: Guilford.

Piaget, J. (1954). *The construction of reality in the child* (2nd ed.). New York: Basic Books.

Piaget, J. (1981). *Intelligence and affectivity: Their relationship during child development*. Palo Alto, CA: Annual Reviews. (Original work published 1954)

Poznanski, E. (1980–1981). Childhood depression: The outcome. *Acta Paedopsychiatrica, 46*, 297–304.

Poznanski, E., Krahenbuhl, V., & Zrull, J. P. (1976). Childhood depression: A longitudinal perspective. *Journal of the American Academy of Child Psychiatry, 15*, 491–501.

Puig-Antich, J. (1980a). Affective disorders in childhood: A review and perspective. *Psychiatric Clinics of North America, 3*, 403–424.

Puig-Antich, J. (1980b). The use of RDC criteria for major depressive disorder in children and adolescents. *Journal of the American Academy of Child Psychiatry, 19*, 291–293.

Puig-Antich, J. (1982). Major depression and conduct disorder in prepuberty. *Journal of the American Academy of Child Psychiatry, 21*, 118–128.

Rado, S. (1928). The problem of melancholia. *International Journal of Psychoanalysis, 9*, 420–438.

Rapoport, J. L. (1977). Pediatric psychopharmacology and childhood depression. In J. G. Schulterbrandt & A. Raskin (Eds.), *Depression in childhood: Diagnosis, treatment, and conceptual models*. New York: Raven Press.

Rie, H. E. (1966). Depression in childhood: A survey of some pertinent contributions. *Journal of the American Academy of Child Psychiatry, 5*, 653–685.

Rochlin, G. (1959). The loss complex. *Journal of the American Psychoanalytic Association, 7*, 299–316.

Rogers, T. B., Kuiper, N. A., & Kirker, W. S. (1977). Self-reference and the encoding of personal information. *Journal of Personality and Social Psychology, 35*, 677–688.

Rogers, T. B., Rogers, P. J., & Kuiper, N. A. (1979). Evidence for the self as a cognitive prototype: The "false alarms effect." *Personality and Social Psychology Bulletin, 5*, 53–56.

Ruble, D. (in press). The development of social comparison processes and their role in achievement-related self-socialization. In E. T. Higgins, D. Ruble, & W. W. Hartup (Eds.), *Social cognition and social behavior: Developmental perspectives*.

Rutter, M. (1972). Relationships between child and adult psychiatric disorders. *Acta Psychiatrica Scandinavica, 48*, 3–21.

Rutter, M. (1981). Stress, coping and development: Some issues and some questions. *Journal of Child Psychology and Psychiatry, 22*, 324–356.

Sackett, G., Sameroff, A., Cairns, R., & Suomi, S. (1981). Continuity in behavioral development: Theoretical and empirical issues. In K. Immelmann, G. Barlow, L. Petrinovich, & M. Main (Eds.), *Behavioral development*. Cambridge, MA: Cambridge University Press.

Sameroff, A., & Chandler, M. (1975). Reproductive risk and the continuum of caretaking causalty. In F. Horowitz (Eds.), *Review of child development research* (Vol. 4). Chicago: University of Chicago Press.

Sander, L. (1962). Issues in early mother-child interaction. *Journal of the American Academy of Child Psychiatry, 1*, 141–166.

Sandler, J., & Joffe, W. G. (1965). Notes on childhood depression. *International Journal of Psychoanalysis, 46*, 88–96.

Santostefano, S. (1978). *A biodevelopmental approach to clinical child psychology*. New York: Wiley.

Schildkraut, J. J., & Kety, S. S. (1967). Biogenic amines and emotions. *Science, 156*, 21–30.

Schneider-Rosen, K., Braunwald, K., Carlson, V., & Cicchetti, D. (in press). Current perspectives in attachment theory: Illustration from the study of maltreated infants. In I. Bretherton & E. Waters (Eds.), Growing points in attachment theory and research. Monographs of the Society for Research in Child Development.

Schneider-Rosen, K., & Cicchetti, D. (1984). The relationship between affect and cognition in maltreated infants: Quality of attachment and the development of visual self-recognition. Child Development, 55, 648–658.

Secord, P., & Peevers, B. (1974). The development and attribution of person concepts. In T. Mischel (Ed.), Understanding other persons. Oxford: Blackwell Scientific Publications.

Seligman, M. E. P. (1975). Helplessness: On depression, development, and death. San Francisco: Freeman.

Selman, R. (1980). The growth of interpersonal understanding. New York: Academic Press.

Shaffer, D. (1974). Suicide in childhood and early adolescence. Journal of Child Psychology and Psychiatry, 15, 275–291.

Spitzer, R. L., Endicott, J., & Robins, E. (1978). Research diagnostic criteria: Rationale and reliability. Archives of General Psychiatry, 35, 773–782.

Sroufe, L. A. (1979a). The coherence of individual development. American Psychologist, 34, 834–841.

Sroufe, L. A. (1979b). Socioemotional development. In J. Osofsky (Ed.), Handbook of infant development. New York: Wiley.

Sroufe, L. A. (1983). Infant–caregiver attachment and patterns of adaptation in preschool: The roots of maladaptation and competence. In M. Perlmutter (Ed.), Minnesota symposia in child psychology. Hillsdale, NJ: Lawrence Erlbaum Associates.

Sroufe, L. A., & Rutter, M. (1984). The domain of developmental psychopathology. Child Development, 55, 17–29.

Sroufe, L. A., Schork, E., Motti, F., Lawroski, N., & LaFreniere, P. (1984). The role of affect in social competence. In C. Izard, J. Kagan, & R. Zajonc (Eds.), Emotions, cognition, and behavior. London & New York: Cambridge University Press.

Sroufe, L. A., & Waters, E. (1977). Attachment as an organizational construct. Child Development, 48, 1184–1199.

Stern, D. (1977). The first relationship: Infant and mother. Cambridge, MA: Harvard University Press.

Teitelbaum, P. (1971). The encephalization of hunger. In E. Stellar & J. Sprague (Eds.), Progress in physiological psychology (Vol. 4). New York: Academic Press.

Teitelbaum, P. (1977). Levels of integration of the operant. In W. K. Horig & J. Staddon (Eds.), Handbook of operant behavior. Englewood Cliffs, NJ: Prentice-Hall.

Tesiny, E. P., & Lefkowitz, M. M. (1982). Childhood depression: A six-month follow-up study. Journal of Consulting and Clinical Psychology, 50, 778–780.

Thompson, R. A., Lamb, M. E., & Estes, D. (1982). Stability of infant-mother attachment and its relationship to changing life circumstances in an unselected middle-class sample. Child Development, 53, 144–148.

Tronick, E. (1982). Social interchange in infancy: Affect, cognition, and communication. Baltimore: University Park Press.

Tronick, E., Als, H., Adamson, L., Wise, S., & Brazelton, T. B. (1978). The infant's response to entrapment between contradictory messages in face-to-face interaction. Journal of the American Academy of Child Psychiatry, 17, 1–13.

Tronick, E., Ricks, M., & Cohn, J. F. (1982). Maternal and infant affective exchange: Patterns of adaptation. In T. Field & A. Fogel (Eds.), Emotion and interaction: Normal and high risk infants. Hillsdale, NJ: Lawrence Erlbaum Associates.

Vaillant, G. (1978). Adaptation to life. Boston: Little, Brown.

Vaughn, B., Egeland, B., Sroufe, L. A., & Waters, E. (1979). Individual differences in infant-mother attachment at 12 and 18 months: Stability and change in families under stress. Child Development, 50, 971–975.

von Bertalanffy, L. (1968). *General systems theory: Foundations, development, applications.* New York: Braziller.

Waters, E. (1978). The reliability and stability of individual differences in infant and mother attachment. *Child Development, 49,* 483–494.

Waters, E., & Sroufe, L. A. (1983). Competence as a developmental construct. *Developmental Review, 3,* 79–97.

Waters, E., Wippman, J., & Sroufe, L. A. (1979). Attachment, positive affect, and competence in the peer group: Two studies in construct validation. *Child Development, 50,* 821–829.

Watson, J. S. (1977). Depression and the perception of control in early childhood. In J. G. Schulterbrandt & A. Raskin (Eds.), *Depression in childhood: Diagnosis, treatment, and conceptual models.* New York: Raven Press.

Weissman, M. M., & Paykel, E. S. (1974). *The depressed woman: A study of social relationships.* Chicago: University of Chicago Press.

Werner, H. (1937). Process and achievement: A basic problem of education and developmental psychology. *Harvard Educational Review, 7,* 353–368.

Werner, H. (1948). *Comparative psychology of mental development.* New York: International Universities Press.

Werner, H. (1957). The concept of development from a comparative and organismic point of view. In D. Harris (Ed.), *The concept of development.* Minneapolis: University of Minnesota Press.

Werner, H., & Kaplan, B. (1963). *Symbol formation: An organismic-developmental approach to language and the expression of thought.* New York: Wiley.

White, R. (1959). Motivation reconsidered: The concept of competence. *Psychological Review, 66,* 297–333.

White, S. H. (1965). Evidence for a hierarchical arrangement of learning processes. In L. Lipsett & C. Spiker (Eds.), *Advances in child development and behavior* (Vol. 2). New York: Academic Press.

Wylie, R. C. (1979). *The self concept: Theory and research on selected topics* (rev. ed.). Lincoln, NE: University of Nebraska Press.

Zahn-Waxler, C., Cummings, E. M., Iannotti, R., & Radke-Yarrow, M. (1984). Young offspring of depressed parents: A population at risk for affective problems. In D. Cicchetti & K. Schneider-Rosen (Eds.), *Childhood depression.* San Francisco: Jossey-Bass.

Zahn-Waxler, C., Cummings, E. M., McKnew, D., & Radke-Yarrow, M. (1984). Affective arousal and social interactions in young children with a manic-depressive parent. *Child Development. 55,* 112–122.

Zis, A., & Goodwin, F. (1982). The amine hypothesis. In E. Paykel (Ed.), *Handbook of affective disorders.* New York: Guilford.

Zubin, J., & Spring, B. (1977). Vulnerability: A new view of schizophrenia. *Journal of Abnormal Psychology, 56,* 103–126.

Depressive Feelings in Children: A Transactional Model for Research

Robert N. Emde
Robert J. Harmon
William V. Good

Recent reviews have documented the increasing awareness that depression in childhood constitutes a significant clinical problem (Anthony, 1975; Cytryn & McKnew, 1979, 1980; Cytryn, McKnew, & Bunney, 1980; Kashani et al., 1981; Kovacs & Beck, 1977; Malmquist, 1971, 1976). This chapter deals with depressive feelings, a topic that has received insufficient attention.

Two clarifying perspectives are important to share at the outset. First, it is necessary to distinguish between depressive feelings and the diagnostic syndrome of depression (Carlson & Cantwell, 1979; Hersov, 1977; Rutter, Tizard, & Whitmore, 1970). The syndrome includes more than depressive feelings (Cytryn et al., 1980), is necessarily more restrictive, and is intended to have implications for prognosis and treatment. In this chapter, we will view depressive feelings as a general response; it should be understood that such feelings are not only present in the diagnostic syndrome but occur in all of us. Second, in considering depressive feelings in children, one must also consider the reactions of others. This is a simple strategic fact, which emerges from reviewing clinical experience and recent research, yet this has not been addressed systematically in research or in theoretical discussions of childhood depression. Because of this, we have adopted a transactional approach for considering research needs and opportunities.

The chapter will begin with a statement of the transactional approach and its justification. Following this, discussion will center around a single question: "Do depressive feelings develop?" Curiously, there is evidence

Robert N. Emde, Robert J. Harmon, and William V. Good. Department of Psychiatry, University of Colorado School of Medicine, Denver, Colorado.

for both a positive and a negative answer; there is evidence for depressive feelings changing across development and for depressive feelings being similar across development. The chapter will describe the need for research in both areas. Finally, we will discuss promising research directions concerning the nature of depressive feelings and their communication.

A TRANSACTIONAL APPROACH FOR UNDERSTANDING DEPRESSIVE FEELINGS

A transactional approach has been useful in the study of perception (Ittelson, 1962) in developmental psychology (Sameroff & Chandler, 1975) and in psychiatry (Grinker, 1971). We believe that such an approach can also be useful for investigating and understanding childhood depression. A transactional approach directs us to look at the experience of depressive feelings, not only in the identified patient but also in others who are with that patient. Such "intersubjective feelings" mutually influence each other in significant ways. We may respond to children's depressive feelings with depressive feelings of our own and then react in various ways to that. We may feel sad or even helpless but then, recognizing those feelings, respond with understanding, availability, and caring. In contrast, we may restrict our feelings, pull back, and remove ourselves from such painful transactions. Either way, a depressed child will resonate with the other's response, and the interactive process will continue at a new level. Significant transactions of this sort are prominent, both with family members and with clinician–researchers.

Family Members

Transactional processes are increasingly complex for the parent who is with the child day in and day out. Parental feelings will be added to the child's feelings in ever new mixtures and combinations. There is apt to be much distress in the parent, the child, and in their relationship. Thus, in assessment, the clinician–researcher must directly tap the experiential world of the parent, in addition to that of the child, even though this might be painful. A quotation from the recent review of Cytryn and McKnew (1980) is remarkably pointed:

> our own experience as well as that of other investigators indicates a frequent disparity between material gathered from the child and that reported by the other people. . . . Parents are seldom aware of even severe affective disorders, but their children are acutely aware of even mild changes in their own moods. That disparity seems relatively unique to affective disorders in children and, in the authors' experience, is seldom seen in other disorders. The phenomenon has probably con-

tributed as much to the controversy surrounding childhood depression as has the lack of uniform diagnostic criteria. (p. 2801)

The evidence for direct transactional effects with children is extensive. Reviews of childhood depression have pointed to the prominence of depression in a parent. Indeed, in the opinion of Cytryn and McKnew (1980), depression in a parent is "the most prevalent etiological factor" in episodic affective disorders. They go on to note that parental depression may affect the child either through the child's identification with the parent or through the parent's loss of involvement with the child as a result of the depressive illness. Oftentimes, in such cases, children improve as soon as they are separated from their parents such as may occur through a brief hospitalization or placement in a more affectively attuned foster home. One can imagine other mechanisms for this transaction of depression, including emotional resonance, lack of emotional availability, lack of rewards, and the creation of a pervasive transactional mood state. These are not mentioned in any of the reviews, but clearly, when depression is formulated in terms of a transactional process, these possibilities emerge; there are many hypotheses awaiting research.

Transactional effects are also suggested by data from studies involving children of parents with a major affective disorder (bipolar or unipolar). In two studies of Cytryn and McKnew (1979) and Cytryn, McKnew, Bartko, Lamour, and Hamovit (1982; also see Chapter 5 in this volume), the authors point to the remarkably high incidence of childhood depression in these offspring. In one study, 16 of 30 children (from 26 families) were depressed, according to the Weinberg criteria, on at least one of two psychiatric interviews held 4 months apart, and 9 of 30 were diagnosed as depressed on both interviews. In the other study, 11 of 19 children (from 13 families) were diagnosed as depressed on at least one of two psychiatric interviews held 4 months apart. These results dramatically extend observations of others that child and adult depressions tend to aggregate in families (Puig-Antich, 1982). Such a high incidence may reflect more than what would be expected from a simple genetic determination for this disorder. While environmental influences could be due to general factors such as hospitalization of a parent who is chronically ill (Rutter, 1966), more specific effects through parental transactions are also a distinct possibility. A depressed and depressing parent often coexists with the development of a depressed and depressing child.

A variety of other parental transactional effects are worth noting. One such effect is implied by the prevalence of parental deprecation and rejection in cases of childhood depression (Cytryn & McKnew, 1980). This occurs when parents deprecate the child over a period of time by stressing the child's inadequacy or worthlessness or, more subtly, by indicating a lack of respect, involvement, or caring. This may occur through frequent criticism and humiliation or through emotional unavailability. Cytryn and McKnew emphasize that parents may not be aware of this behavior and that deprecation can be shown through overprotection as well as through overt rejection. The point is that mutual influences are the rule, and the painful feelings of both parent and child must be understood in research and clinical assessment.

Other transactional effects follow from a parent or loved one withdrawing interest in the child while maintaining a physical presence. This may occur in the midst of illness, divorce, remarriage, or sometimes with the birth of a new child. Clinicians have noted the frequent occurrence of a mild depression in a young child after the birth of the next sibling (Berman, 1979; Brazelton, 1969). The detailed observations of Dunn concerning the reactions of such children to the birth of a sibling begin to illuminate the conditions under which such responses might occur (Dunn & Kendrick, 1981, 1982).

Clinician–Researchers

Transactional processes are also prominent in clinician–researchers who deal with depressed children. We feel this is a reflection both of a general scientific principle and of particular problems with empathy.

The general principle is highlighted by the recent history of science. Before the twentieth century, Newtonian physics assumed that the observer was outside the system being observed, that an observation was independent of the observing process. Now the limitations of this view are realized. Physics led the way to our appreciating that the act of our observing influences what is observed (Bohr, 1928; Heisenberg, 1927). This principle is no less true for our clinical sciences and for studying the complexities of developmental psychopathology. Clinician–researchers participate as they observe; they influence and are influenced by what they are observing (Ittelson, 1962). Thus, the task of the researcher is not only to acknowledge these mutual influences but to make use of them; above all, the researcher must discern what is generalizable from each transaction and what is unique (Ittelson, 1962). It seems to us that more explicit attention needs to be given to understanding this process. But there is more.

Depressive feelings are a universal experience. Anthony (1975) wrote convincingly of this truth, citing Burton's *Anatomy of Melancholy*, written some 350 years ago, as well as the corpus of recorded human experience since that time. Over the past 10 years, a number of clinical reviews have noted that children become depressed in ways that bear common features to adults who are depressed and that diagnostic systems, such as the one established in DSM-III for adults, can be applied to children (Cytryn *et al.*, 1980; Kashani *et al.*, 1981). It appears that depressive feelings are not only a universal experience across people, but across development.

In spite of this universality, depression, especially childhood depression, is not easily appreciated. The reviews cited at the beginning of this chapter document that depression in children was not widely acknowledged among clinicians until the past decade. What accounts for this fact? Considering our own clinical experiences and the facts before us, we wondered if clinicians, as well as parents, were not subject to major transaction effects. Putting the question in another way, is there something about the experience of childhood depression that blocks our empathy or makes it unavailable? By empathy, we refer to the general use of the term, derived etymologically from the Greek (en + pathos, 'feeling')—in other words, the process of appreciating another's feelings.

There would appear to be important issues here for clinical research. Is there something about the way depression is communicated that makes it more difficult to acknowledge than other dysphoric affects? Do adults have particular problems empathizing with depressive feelings because of past experiences with depression, because of past relationships, or because of particular losses? Similarly, do some clinicians have particular problems being empathic with childhood depression because of such factors? Perhaps there are reasons for an empathy block in our early development, related to the subculture of our families of origin and the ways we have been taught to mask or inhibit sadness. Perhaps, in order to be empathic, it is necessary to have experienced sadness, to have felt helplessness and depression in the midst of illness or loss.

Appreciating depressive feelings in children appears to be a difficult and painful process. Clinicians, like parents, are responsive, but, unlike parents, it is easier for us to remove ourselves. There is an implication that unless we, as clinicians, work at it, we may have a tendency to lose our sensitivity to the experience of depression in our patients. This may be particularly relevant as clinical research leads to increasing biological advances in our understanding and in our treatment of depression. Even in the most "biological" forms of depression, if we are not in tune with our patients, we can be misled in evaluations of treatment response, and we can contribute, however inadvertently, to patient loneliness and isolation. Further, as clinician–researchers, we need to maintain a sensitivity to the experience of depression so that our measures do not mislead us. There may be a related transactional tendency to bypass the experience of depression and concentrate on "objective" and less difficult measures. In drug studies of childhood depression, for example, there is a tendency for rating instruments to be used to "define depression." It would seem obvious that any such instrument requires not only external sources of validation (i.e., other behavioral measures) but something that taps the domain of inner experience. As painful as it might be, clinician–researchers need to collect data by communicating with patients as directly as possible. All of us must pay attention to, and make use of, our own empathic personal "instrument." The observational field of one's own resonating and dynamic inner affective life cannot be neglected.

The tendency to bypass the experience of depression is illustrated in the recent resurgence of emotions research in early development. In this area, researchers appear to be concentrating, quite understandably, in those areas where measurement advances have taken place, in facial and vocalic expressions of emotion, and in techniques for measuring behavioral regulation (Emde, 1980; Izard, 1982; Izard, Huebner, Risser, McGinnis, & Dougherty, 1980; Klinnert, Campos, Sorce, Emde, & Svejda, 1983; Sroufe, 1979). Yet these advances in the realm of expression and action make us more aware of the gap in our understanding of feelings.

Ask anyone what he considers to be the most compelling or human aspect of depression, and it is likely that he will talk about hurt, pain, and wanting to help. It seems clear that there is an urgent need for basic knowledge about the development of empathic processes, not only in children but in parents, and not only in parents but in clinicians—in those who are responding to and helping children and parents.

It is noteworthy, as Hoffman has pointed out (1978), that, in the general area of empathy research, the same tendency has been evident. Investigators more often see problems as cognitive in nature rather than in terms of the transmission of feelings; furthermore, it seems easier to research prosocial behavior (from the outside), as opposed to urges, intentions, and conflicts (from the inside).

DEPRESSIVE FEELINGS ACROSS DEVELOPMENT: TWO VIEWS

Do depressive feelings develop? There are two contrasting views. Both of these views pose promising questions for research.

Depressive feelings seem to be universal. Across people and, by implication, across development, there seems to be an organized aspect of inner life that can experience and resonate with depressive feelings. This universal pattern of experience is presumably rooted both in biology and in the human condition. However, it also seems true that depressive feelings change with development. The meaning, the dynamics, and the cognitive context for experiencing depressive feelings increase in complexity as the child develops. Thus, across development, depressive feelings are the same, and they are also different. In the following discussion, we will highlight developmental differences by discussing four periods of childhood. Although the periods represent major qualitative differences in the organization of experience, the reader may also wish to think of this discussion as the developmental dimension of depressive feelings.

*Developmental Change in the Expression
of Depressive Feelings*

Until recently, the prevailing developmental view of depression was psychoanalytic with an emphasis on two periods, before superego development and after it (see Rie, 1966; Rochlin, 1959; also the discussion in Malmquist, 1976). Since the superego (an internalized self-critical mental agency) was thought to be necessary for depression, it was assumed that, before its development (that is, before 4–6 years of age), depression was either nonexistent or fundamentally different; beyond this age, depression was assumed to be possible. Clinicians have now documented the existence of childhood depression before 5 years (see recent reviews of Anthony, 1975; Cytryn & McKnew, 1979; Kashani et al., 1981), including rather extensive documentation of depressive responses in infancy (Bakwin, 1942; Bowlby, 1963; Emde, Polak & Spitz, 1965; Fraiberg, 1981; Gaensbauer, 1980; Goldfarb, 1955; Spitz, 1946). In addition, Cytryn and McKnew (1972, 1974), in the early 1970s, gave vivid clinical descriptions of "masked depressions," which seemed characteristic of school-aged children prior to adolescence. In this age period, depressive symptoms tended to be expressed in action, aggressiveness, and fantasy life. Obvious depression in mood and verbal expression were less apparent and often defended against. Although these authors have recently recommended dropping the designation of "masked depression" (Cytryn et al., 1980) in favor of using DSM-III criteria for affective disorders in both adulthood and childhood, their clinical descriptions of the depressive response in this childhood period between infancy and adolescence remain valid.

We choose to distinguish four periods of childhood: *infancy, preschool, school age*, and *adolescence*. Although these periods have logical relevance to clinical experience, they also correspond to (1) traditional divisions with respect to society's role expectations, (2) theoretical divisions based on major transformations in cognitive development as demarcated by Piaget (Piaget & Inhelder, 1969), and (3) theoretical divisions of psychosexual development as demarcated by Freud (1905/1953) and Erikson (1950).

Several case vignettes are presented to illustrate the changing meaning of depressive feelings as a function of these developmental periods. Many complex relationships need to be investigated. From a transactional viewpoint, the picture changes, not only for the child, but for those around the child. Adopting a view of depression that is both developmental and transactional raises many issues in need of empirical investigation.

INFANCY

A 7-month-old, reared in a foster home since 2 weeks of age, thrived under the care of an excellent foster mother. When the foster mother developed an acute depression due to life circumstances and became less emotionally available to him, the infant gradually developed a full syndrome of anaclitic depression: a sad face, immobility, and loss of appetite. He wept when others approached him and seemed inconsolable. When the foster mother was observed with the infant, a painful series of interactions were noted. At those few times when the infant was able to respond to the mother's attempts at interaction, the mother's depression would interfere with her ability to respond appropriately. Often in irritation and out of touch with her infant's needs, she would push the child away, generating a cycle of frustration and distress. With sensitive clinical intervention and slow resolution of the mother's depression, the depressive response of the infant also resolved.

Clearly, a depressive response in infancy can result from a loss of the mothering function, not just the physical loss of the mother, be she biological or foster mother. Furthermore, this case illustrates that depression in infancy is expressed and recognizable in facial expression and behavior. Those around the infant are likely to perceive and feel some sadness.

Spitz has described how infant depressive responses can result from prolonged separation from the mother, following an earlier satisfactory period of attachment. Subsequent observations have extended this clinical picture to include depression after a marked diminution or interference with the mothering function (Emde *et al.,* 1965; Fraiberg, 1981) into depression at ages earlier than 6 months (Gaensbauer, 1980). Current research issues include what mothering functions are involved and how much deficit is required under what circumstances for depression to occur.

PRESCHOOL

A 3-year-old boy was referred for psychiatric evaluation due to increased withdrawal in the hospital following accidental burns to his legs and feet. He had been transferred from home to the Burn Center, and his parents were unable to visit regularly. Although the burns were severe, they were not considered life threatening. The child's quiet apathy and withdrawn behavior initially were interpreted by the hospital staff as cooperative behavior. Staff became increasingly concerned, however, by the contrast between their optimistic view and the child's apparent negative attitude, which seemed to express a "giving up."

During the initial consultation, it became clear that the child was depressed. The nurses had noticed that when he was left alone, he was less irritable and was less demanding as compared with times when someone was with him; as a consequence, he was left alone for long periods. A self-perpetuating cycle then developed wherein occasionally people tried to interact with him, but they did not persist when he became more irritable. Many felt that they should leave him alone. What was difficult to appreciate was the fact that he was becoming severely depressed and that his protestations were an attempt to engage the environment around him. As this became apparent in the course of consultation with a child psychiatrist, the child was assigned a primary care nurse and a consistent foster grandmother, in addition to being seen by the psychiatrist and a developmental specialist. When the foster grandmother noticed that he became more upset when his legs were uncovered, the staff became aware of the shame he felt concerning his burns when others were around. Exploration of this led to appreciation of a deeper humiliation he felt concerning his having to wear a diaper and have it changed by others, since his burn had followed his having recently mastered toilet training. He was reassured that once his legs were feeling better, he could again use the toilet; the staff helped him understand his temporary need for diapers because of the physical problem. As a result of these interventions, his depressive mood improved.

This vignette shows how the environment around young children can miss depression when it takes a quiet form. In the hospital and in the school, the quiet child with prolonged sadness frequently goes unnoticed or is regarded as cooperative and "good." The active "conduct problem" draws attention and concern. Additionally, depressed children can drive away those who are attempting to respond to their depression. In this "protest phase," irritable behavior may appear to signal that efforts are "making the child worse" when, in fact, the child is attempting to interact. By 2 years of age, children have developed a sense of self-awareness and are, under most circumstances, willful and active. More than previously realized, they have a sense of what is expected of them and a beginning sense of adult standards for what is "right and wrong" (Kagan, 1981). The preschool age is a time when children learn what emotional expressions are permitted and encouraged and in what circumstances. Many questions remain to be investigated in this domain, however. For example, from the clinician's view of depression, the preschool age is an important period because of the appearance of shame. Shame appears to play a major role in the feeling of depression at this age, but much remains to be investigated concerning its relationship to experiences of success or failure, to the development of self-esteem, and to later manifestations of depression.

SCHOOL AGE

A 7-year-old boy was referred to the Child Psychiatry Clinic for school problems —temper tantrums and hyperactivity. The family was reluctant to take the child to see a psychiatrist but went at the school's insistence. They claimed the boy was "manageable at home." During the course of taking a history, the family described their strict management of the child's behavior, including washing his mouth out with soap when he was "bad." With some self-righteous indignation, they emphasized how they kept him in line. The child was interviewed in several sessions. At first, he seemed quiet and compliant. He was not overtly sad and denied feelings relating to sadness and depression. In the third session, he began describing his family life and, in fantasy and play, he indicated he felt rotten inside; he was concerned about sinfulness and had a preoccupation with dying and banishment to hell. He remarked that sometimes he felt incapable of doing anything right, and it became evident that he was quite depressed.

When the diagnosis of depression was discussed with the family, both parents responded with indignation. For them, depression was impossible. How could a child who played actively and who went to school regularly be depressed? He did not look like a depressed adult, they stated. Further, how could their child be unhappy? For them, only terrible parents could have an unhappy 7-year-old. Unfortunately, the parents could not appreciate the child's suffering, and they discontinued treatment.

Although the symptoms may differ from older individuals, school age children are not less vulnerable to feelings of depression. This case illustrates how complicated the picture can be. Not only do defenses against affects become prominent during this age period (Cytryn & McKnew, 1974), but there may be special complicating circumstances in the family environment. Why is it that children during this age period so often mirror the conflicts of their parents? In this case, for example, it was discovered that the child's aggressive behavior at school, in part, expressed the mother's covert hostility toward authority figures. Similar family dynamics have been studied for delinquent behavior (Johnson & Szurek, 1957), but systematic research is needed in the case of childhood depression. The above case also illustrates the trouble parents may have, both in appreciating depression in a child this age and in empathizing with it. In addition, their stopping their son's therapy represented a continuation of the transaction that prevented their child from making contact with others.

ADOLESCENCE

> A 14-year-old adolescent girl asked to see a psychiatrist after many discussions with friends. She felt distressed about her parents' divorce. But, more than this, visiting back and forth between her parents was getting her down. It was especially difficult when she visited her father who, himself, was increasingly feeling unhappy and lonely. She felt unable to tell him of her discomfort, and he denied depression or the need for help. The girl described her depression to the psychiatrist as a full feeling in her chest that was "hard to take." She cried more than usual. As discussions continued over the course of brief psychotherapy, she was able to feel less depressed and increasingly talked about what was meaningful to her in her current life with friends and at school. She also talked about plans for the future. Although there were many uncertainties, she showed many strengths and seemed to develop an increasingly solid sense of herself as separate from her father's problems.

This vignette illustrates that teenagers are also vulnerable to depressive responses and to participation in transactions of depressive feelings with other family members. Often, depressive feelings seem more understandable to those around adolescents, with moods more characteristic of what we have all experienced. Although they are often mixed with anger, hostility, rebelliousness, or self-destructiveness, there is now a capacity for understanding and communicating feelings verbally. There is also more capacity for self-reflection.

This case poses several important research questions concerning the transaction of depression. Under what circumstances are adolescents susceptible to feelings of sustained depression from a parent or another family member? If a depressed parent talks about such feelings to the adolescent, does that decrease or increase the risk for depression? Are certain blocks in empathic communication (such as the parent refusing to believe his child can be depressed) associated with increased acting out? How is adolescent depression related to family life cycle dynamics—with parents dealing with such issues as "the empty nest," the "midlife crisis," and the anticipation of retirement?

Developmental Constancy in the Expression
of Depressive Feelings: A Biological Patterning

In discussing developmental constancy, we will emphasize a biological patterning for depressive feelings. There seem to be important questions with respect to three areas: moods, an alternative response to stress, and discrete emotions.

In what follows, we will emphasize research in infancy. Later developmental influences are important (particularly with biological mechanisms influencing the major affective disorders), but the rationale for studying early development seems compelling, not only for early identification of individuals at risk but also for identifying species-typical patterns before the complex influences of culture supervene. The question may well arise: How can we relate infant data about biological patterning to the domain of feelings? There are two strategic answers to this question: (1) We can make use of our transactional approach. We can use our own empathy and the empathy of caregivers as data for understanding the infant's feelings, particularly if we supplement these with convergent measures. (2) We can make use of longitudinal study, wherein we can identify individual differences and attempt to trace what leads to what under what circumstances.

MOODS

Is it possible to identify a predisposition for sad or depressed mood states in infancy? A mood state seems to involve not only increased duration with respect to emotional tone, but also pervasiveness. Interestingly, Thomas, Chess, Birch, Hertzig, and Korn (1963) used "mood" as one of their nine categories of behavioral functioning in studying individual differences among infants. With data derived from mothers' reports, they defined mood as "the amount of pleasant, joyful, and friendly behavior" (p. 41). Not only did they find that most babies were regarded as preponderantly positive in mood; but that from one period to another (from 6 to 27 months), the patterning of infant moods showed more stability than their other categories. Currently, infant "temperament" (usually measured through maternal perceptions) is an area of fervent research activity (although the degree of stability is not high, all current research programs employ measures of some aspects of emotionality) (see Goldsmith & Campos, 1982; Plomin, 1982). Whether individual differences in a bias toward sadness or depressive feelings can be identified remains to be seen.

Overall, we might suppose that it would be adaptive for the species-typical individual to be born predisposed toward a basic ongoing mood of happiness with some ongoing engagement with the world. Yet it is also true that mood may vary within each day. This raises research questions, even in infancy, concerning behavior fluctuating according to biological rhythms, including metabolic rhythms, hunger rhythms, endogenous sleep–wakefulness rhythms, and basic rest–activity rhythms (for example, see Emde, Swedberg, & Suzuki, 1975; Gaensbauer & Emde, 1973; Kleitman, 1963; Sander, 1975; Sterman & Hoppenbrouwers, 1971). Do these biological rhythms in some prototypic prepsychological way influence what later will become psychological mood conditions? There is evidence that the 45-minute basic rest activity cycles of the newborn continue to have an influence as 90-minute rhythms in adults in daytime as well as night (see Globus, 1966; Kripke, 1972; Othmer, Hayden, & Segelbaum, 1969; Sterman & Hoppenbrouwers, 1971). Although the amount of variance of adult behavior that can be accounted for by these rhythms is small, could they not trigger or influence mood states? In the newborn, considerable amounts of behavioral variation can be accounted for by them. Is it not probable that between the newborn age period and the adult stage such rhythms may have an intermediate role in influencing behavioral and affective predispositions?

AN ALTERNATIVE RESPONSE TO STRESS

Another area of biological patterning relevant for the development of depressive feelings is suggested by the infant's organismic response to stress. Engel and his collaborators (Engel, 1962a, 1962b; Engel, Reichsman, & Segal, 1956; Engel & Schmale, 1972) have postulated two basic patterns of biologic response to stress, reflecting the way the CNS is organized at birth: (1) the fight–flight pattern and (2) the conservation–withdrawal pattern, the first involving activity and engagement of the environment (serving to avoid or control the stress) and the second involving inactivity and withdrawal from the environment (conserving energy when stress cannot be managed). These reaction patterns are presumed to be biological precursors of later "affect states" or "moods" of anxiety and depression. The distress, or fight–flight reaction, had been well known since Cannon's work (1932); Engel's original observations for the addition of conservation–withdrawal came from an infant, Monica, who had a gastric fistula and who, when approached by a stranger, had a diminished amount of gastric secretion of hydrochloric acid and fell asleep. Other instances of infant sleep or a profound lowering of arousal in response to stress have been reported (Bernstein, Emde, & Campos, 1973; Brazelton, 1969; Emde, Harmon, Metcalf, Koenig, & Wagonfeld, 1971; Papousek & Papousek, 1980; Ribble, 1943). Systematic longitudinal exploration of the conservation–withdrawal phenomenon in infancy and childhood still remains to be done. Perhaps research, up to this time, has been hampered because conservation–withdrawal seems elusive, occurring in a small minority of infants and under a limited range of stressful circumstances. As an illustration of this, in a 1-year-long study (Emde, Gaensbauer, & Harmon, 1976), we observed 1 of 15 normal infants who, on two separate occasions, during the latter part of the first year, became drowsy instead of overtly distressed when a stranger approached. Tennes, Downey, and Vernadakis (1977) encountered a similar pattern of findings in a study of 1-year-olds correlating cortisol excretion with separation distress. Of their 20 infants, they found 2 who, when mother left, became drowsy and went to sleep instead of become distressed. Unlike the distressed infants who had increased excretion of cortisol, these withdrawn infants had a diminished excretion of cortisol. Thus, individual differences are important. The investigator must be prepared to seize opportunities in the midst of observing large numbers of infants and young children under a variety of naturally occurring stress encounters. Furthermore, in order to understand the relationship of conservation–withdrawal responses to depressive feelings, a great deal of longitudinal clinical investigation must be carried out.

DISCRETE EMOTIONS

The third area relevant to the biological patterning of depressive feelings is one we shall treat in more detail. This concerns the organization of emotional response systems. Virtually all studies that have scaled emotional expressions have found similar results for their organized relationships, namely, a primary dimension of hedonic tone and a secondary dimension of activation. A third dimension is often suggested but is usually difficult to interpret. Such findings have come from adult judgment studies using facial expressions and verbal responses (Abelson & Sermat, 1962; Frijda, 1970; Frijda & Philipszoon, 1963; Gladstone, 1962; Osgood, 1966; Woodworth & Schlosberg, 1954) and are consistent with earlier thinking (Freud, 1915/1968; Spencer, 1890; Wundt, 1896). Our work on the facial expression of emotion in infancy has yielded similar results (Emde, Kligman, Reich, & Wade, 1978) and, most recently, the age gap between infancy and adulthood in scaling studies has been filled by Russell and Ridgeway (1982), who have reported a similar organization of emotion expression in school age children.

The consistency of these results would seem to imply a biological organization for emotional responding that is similar across development. However, much of the excitement for today's emotional research has come from the cross-cultural evidence for discrete emotions. Even though Darwin (1872/1904) had long ago advanced the idea of species-wide discrete emotional expression, and although Tomkins's work (1962, 1963; Tomkins & McCarter, 1964) had revived this idea, it remained for the separate investigative teams of Ekman and Izard to provide a systematic test of it. A number of studies (Eibl-Eibesfeldt, 1979; Ekman & Friesen, 1971; Ekman, Sorenson, & Friesen, 1969; Izard, 1971) showed that not only are facial expression patterns similar across Western and preliterate cultures, but individuals can recognize and express facial expressions of basic emotions. The implication of this work is quite profound. For such discrete emotions as happiness, sadness, fear, surprise, disgust, anger, interest, and shame, there may be species-wide, "prewired" neural programs (Ekman, 1972; Izard, 1971) that provide an adaptive readiness for their expression, experience, and recognition. These findings have stimulated considerable research, not only with the face, but with the vocal expression of emotion (see reviews in Izard, 1982). Developmental investigation has mainly occurred with infants, and consistent conclusions now seem to be emerging. Facial patterns of discrete emotions can be judged by those who know nothing about eliciting circumstances; furthermore, such patterns fit the specifications of discrete emotions suggested from theoretical analyses of Tomkins, Izard, and Ekman. Thus far, this is the case for emotional patterns in happiness, fear, sadness (or distress), surprise, anger, disgust, and pain (Emde *et al.*, 1978; Hiatt, Campos, & Emde, 1979; Izard *et al.*, 1980; Stenberg, Campos, & Emde, 1983).

Explicit studies on the feeling level for discrete emotions have not been done in early development although one would assume that this domain is being tapped when various judgment studies are employed, especially when global judgments of the face or voice are ascertained. In our studies of maternal reports, between one-third and one-half of mothers who have been surveyed responded that they had seen sadness in their infants, with many having seen this in early infancy. This approach makes use of the transactional model for gaining data about sad feelings in infancy and needs to be explored even more systematically. Interestingly, we know from the studies of Stein and Jewett (1982) that by 5 years, children connect sadness with an experience of loss and the overcoming of sadness with restitution.

But how is sadness related to depression? Izard (1972) conceptualized depression and anxiety as separate patterns of discrete emotions. Based largely on studies of college and high school students who either recalled or imagined a depression situation, Izard obtained results from self-reports using a paper and pencil test (the Differential Emotion Scale, DES); these results were consistent with his theory that depression was a complex pattern of discrete emotions and bodily feelings. Sadness (which Izard refers to as "distress") is central in depression, and other prominent discrete emotions making up the pattern of depression include anger, disgust, contempt, fear, guilt, and shyness. The combination of emotions that occur with sadness varies across individuals and situations, thus giving depression a different quality, depending upon where it is encountered.

The theory of depression and anxiety as separate patterns is quite similar to one proposed by Plutchik (1970) and strikes us as extremely important and needing further research. Not only is it consistent with the theory of two alternative modes of response to stress already mentioned, but it also deals with feelings, as well as expressions, and is consistent with current psychoanalytic thinking about signal affect systems (see below).

Unfortunately, Izard's empirical approach is analytic rather than synthetic; consequently, his theory of depression does not deal with questions about coherence. (What is the minimal coherence necessary among discrete emotions for the experience of depression? How organized is the depression pattern?) Further, the theory does not deal with the developmental onset for depression in terms of emotion patterning. When and under what circumstances do depressive feelings come into awareness? These questions remain for research.

Needed Research on the Nature of Depressive Feelings

The discrete emotions approach has opened up an enormous amount of research activity, not only because of its intuitive appeal but also because of measurement advances, especially in facial and vocal expression (see Izard, 1982; Scherer, 1979). Not only can emotional expressions in childhood be examined experimentally as dependent variables, which can be looked at in relation to a variety of other behavioral and physiological measures, but emotional expressions can be manipulated and controlled as independent variables (Klinnert et al., 1983). Still, there is a poverty of research on the relationship of discrete emotions to various forms of depression in various childhood contexts. This is especially so at the level of feelings. Below are some examples of questions needing research.

In childhood, what is the relationship of sadness to depression? Do children who express more sadness early in life in response to similar environmental events have any greater or lesser propensity for depression? Is sadness always the central emotion for depression? One would think from the extensive documentation of masked forms of depression and the tendency of school-aged children to express depression with aggressiveness and increased activity that this need not be so. Perhaps there can be childhood depression without sadness. We need to ask the children about this directly and also indirectly with a variety of research probes. Trying the transactional approach, we need to ask ourselves about our sadness as we work with children.

There are a host of other questions about discrete emotions. Can there be depression without guilt? This has apparently been answered in the affirmative for adults since in at least one study a surprisingly large percentage of depressed patients were found to be free of excessive guilt feelings (Prosen, Clark, Harrow, & Fawcett, 1983). Given the different appearances of depression in childhood, one would expect that children would also show depression without guilt. Many have referred to the syndrome of prolonged expressed sadness and withdrawal in infancy as depression, even though there may not be any capacity for guilt. Research questions abound, however, as to the differences between depression with and without guilt in later childhood. The same questions abound concerning forms of childhood depression with and without anger and for childhood depressions with and without shame. Do these different forms of depression have different natural histories? Are they characteristically found in different contexts? What about depressions with and without disgust? Interestingly, this latter discrete emotion is mentioned prominently both by Izard (1972) and by Plutchik (1970) but does not receive much attention in clinical or research discussions of depression.

It would also seem important to study childhood depression with and without grief, to compare the depressive feelings that follow the loss of a parent or sibling with feelings that do not occur in this context. Equally important, what are the different forms of feeling states that occur in the childhood grieving situation itself? As Horowitz, Wilner, Marmar, and Krupnick (1980) have reviewed, in adults, depressive states that follow upon loss are apt to take the form of one of four ego states. These can be labeled by predominant emotional tone and include: (1) fear or helplessness, (2) rage at others and at self, (3) deflated self-esteem or shame, and (4) withdrawn numbness (a sort of conserving hibernation response). All of these states can be found in normal grief. But in pathological grief, thought of as depression, there is an intensification to a level of feeling overwhelmed; there is also maladaptive behavior or prolonged inhibition. What are the conditions under which these forms of depression occur in children? What are the developmental parameters of such ego states? Related questions emerge from the work of Seligman (1975; Seligman *et al.*, in press) and Beck and Kovacs (Beck, 1976; Kovacs & Beck, 1977). These works theorize how different depressive states can be related to different cognitive views. Thus, sadness and frightened helplessness could be initiated from a change in thinking, a change from seeing oneself as strong and competent to seeing oneself as weak and helpless. Rage states could occur when one thinks of oneself as evil instead of good, and states of self-disgust could result from changes in thinking of oneself as inferior instead of worthy and lovable. Loss can initiate such changes in terms of thoughts about the meaning of the lost relationship or the failure to prevent the loss (Horowitz *et al.*, 1980). This line of theorizing generates many useful research questions for childhood since the child's world of meaning can change so dramatically, both as a function of development and as a function of environmental context. Following the induction of repeated failures, Rholes, Blackwell, Jordan, and Walters (1980) found a shift in cognitive performance between 9- and 11-year-old normal school children, a finding these authors interpreted as an effect of "helplessness" at the later age; however, the relevance of these results to depression and the specific cognitive context employed needs to be determined. Similarly, the report of Weisz (1979) raises the question of the learned helplessness effect increasing with mental age in normal and mentally retarded children. The latter report also reminds us of the need for research concerning depressive feelings in mentally retarded children. These studies, as well as those initiated by the Seligman and the Beck–Kovacs groups, offer considerable promise in exploring children's depressive feelings and cognitions, both directly and indirectly.

There are still further developmental dimensions to these questions. How does the feeling of sadness develop? Does the balance of discrete emotions in a depressive feeling pattern shift as a function of development? How are the child's feelings and the meaning of the depressive experience related to the organization of self-experience? Recent experimental and clinical evidence converges on the conclusion that the representational self has its developmental onset between 15 and 20 months. [For examples of mirror recognition studies, see Lewis and Brooks-Gunn (1979); for examples of cognitive studies, see Kagan (1981); for clinical observations about willfulness, see Freud (1905/1953); for autonomy, see Erikson (1950) and Mahler, Pine, and Bergman (1975); and for the onset of the "semantic no," see Spitz (1957).] Research now needs to be done on fundamental questions related to self-esteem, shame, and depressive feelings in relationship to self-awareness development.

Another clinical case reminds us of the dynamic nature of depressive feelings and poses further questions for research. The case illustrates recurrent depressions in a child seen intermittently for psychotherapy from preschool to school age and demonstrates how depressive feelings may change during the course of therapy. In addition, the case illustrates the complex role of shame and anger in the experience of depression and some of the transactional complexities of provocativeness.

A 7-year-old boy was again referred to a child psychiatrist because of recurrent problems at school with aggressiveness, temper tantrums, and an inability to get along with peers and teachers. He had been seen on several occasions for similar problems when the clinical picture seemed to indicate a conduct disorder. On this occasion it became clear that he had a lowered self-esteem. During one session he began to play with puppets, and one puppet blurted out, "I hate myself. . . . I wet my bed and fight in school." The therapist said he could understand how bad this could make a boy feel, and he was interested in trying to help with these kinds of problems. The child talked of feeling bad about bed wetting. His younger brother was now dry throughout the night. Puppet play continued, with a "therapist puppet" reassuring another puppet that these kinds of problems could be overcome. The child began to discuss problems more openly, school behavior improved, and therapy was no longer necessary.

A year later the child was again seen in consultation because of a recurrence of school problems. During the first two sessions, he seemed more open than before, but at the beginning of the third session, he was provocative. The therapist surmised that he must have had a bad day at school and said it seemed easier to fight than talk. The child then began discussing his sense of failure with friends at school. As therapy continued, the pattern of provocativeness in the midst of feelings of sadness and depression diminished but was seen on two additional occasions. One was related to a change in school and another to a maternal hospitalization. In these instances, however, the trusting relationship with the child's therapist and the additional work conducted with the child's parents enabled the child to interrupt the previous pattern. He no longer had to make people angry and confirm he was bad by their rejecting him. Instead, his feelings of sadness and anger could be discussed with others who could now "listen."

There will always be investigative questions related to the dynamics and integration of feelings in an individual case, but this case also illustrates research questions related to reactivation of depression. What are the conditions under which an early experience of depression makes one more likely to have reactivations of that depression? In one case followed prospectively (Harmon, Wagonfeld, & Emde, 1982), we observed that depressions recurred after sudden decreases in nurturing that recapitulated the early experience, which had been associated with an infantile anaclitic depression. Do processes involved in affective memory have a special role in reactivation forms of depression? The recent work inaugurated by Rovee-Collier and her colleagues (Rovee-Collier & Fagen, 1981; Rovee-Collier, Sullivan, Enright, Lucas, & Fagen, 1980) is most promising in this regard. These investigators have shown that reinstatement of the contextual cues under which original learning took place is a potent mechanism by which early experiences persist to influence behavior after relatively long time periods—even within infancy. The role of affect in reinstatement learning remains to be researched, but we would think it must be central.

A final area concerns developmental questions about feelings in those around the depressed child. For example, what does the experience of depression mean to the caregiver and family when the child is depressed at different ages? An adequate answer to this question requires knowledge of how different forms of childhood depression are expressed at different ages and how they influence empathic and transactional responses of adults and siblings. In addition to understanding children's social, cognitive, and emotional capacities at different ages, we need to understand the development of adults who surround the child. The adult who is getting established in a career or beginning to generate a family of youngsters is apt to experience a child's depressive feelings differently than the adult who is going through a midlife crisis or one who is beginning to think about retirement. We also need to understand about family development, in addition to individual development. The family "reconsolidating," as children are beginning to leave home, will respond differently from the family with young children or the family with children beginning college.

Needed Research on the Communication of Depressive Feelings

A transactional approach draws attention to the need for research on the communication of depressive feelings. Are there systematic ways that others perceive and deal with such communications? Does the communication process differ depending on different combinations of discrete emotions? One would assume that this would be the case, but no systematic data exist. One would also assume that such communications are affected by family style (whether anger or sadness are tolerated or encouraged, for example), by previous experiences with loss, and by variations in caregiving relationships.

Three research areas concerning the communication of feelings seem especially promising. All concern the child's development toward the end of the first year and throughout the second year. The first area concerns the instrumental use of affect expressions. This occurs when the infant offers an expression in order to get another to act in a certain way on his behalf. The smile, intended to propitiate or as a "bid" to begin an interaction during the nonresponsiveness of another, has been observed by many. Similarly, expressions of pouting or sadness have been observed by mothers as a child's way of getting attention under certain circumstances. Systematic research is needed on the development of these and other affect expressions (such as the instrumental use of anger, disgust, fear, surprise, and shame). In addition to descriptions, we need a variety of convergent measures to understand the relationships to the internal state of the child in various contexts, and we need to know more about individual differences in the feeling responses of others when these expressions occur.

The second area of research promise concerns the "socialization" of expressions of sadness and depression. Indications are that such expressions get shaped in a fairly dramatic fashion with masking and distortion often being learned during the second and third years of life. Individual differences seem prominent. Some families allow and encourage such expressions while others inhibit them. Cross-cultural research would be helpful since we know that marked systematic differences exist in the extent to which cultures allow the free expression of such emotions. Again, particular questions will emerge concerning depressive feelings as such data are accumulated. How are depressive feelings affected when the expression of sadness or depression is masked, distorted, or inhibited? Izard's facial feedback hypothesis (Izard, 1982) would suggest that, with an inhibition of such emotional expression, the experience of that emotion would become less intense. Does this occur with sadness and depression? Or, alternatively, as many clinicians would suggest, would the depressive experience become more painful in the absence of its expression and sharing with others? What about families who give double messages? (For example, "It's O.K. to feel sad but not around me; I can't take it.") Variations in socializing experience are considerable and await systematic description.

A third area of research promise concerns the form of emotional signaling that we refer to as social referencing. This also begins toward the end of the first year and continues to have major importance during the second year. Social referencing is a general process whereby a person of any age seeks out emotional information from a significant other in order to make sense of an event that is otherwise ambiguous or beyond that person's own intrinsic appraisal capabilities. From our research, social referencing appears especially salient at the dawn of self-awareness when infants regularly experience more uncertainty about the impact of environmental events. In the midst of a new toy propelling itself into the room or in the midst of encountering an ambiguous drop-off on the visual cliff, an infant will look to the face of mother or an experimenter. If there is an expression of joy or interest, approach and exploration are likely. On the other hand, if the infant sees an expression of fear or anger, retreat or cessation of activity is likely (Klinnert et al., 1983; Sorce, Emde, Campos, & Klinnert, 1985). Social referencing, although unstudied until recently, appears to be common at the beginning of the second year in a variety of playroom, experimental, and naturalistic circumstances. A range of research questions is now before us. What about the infant's use of vocalic signals of emotion? What about facial expressions of varying intensities and at varying blends? What about sadness? Thus far, we have found that adult sadness expressions produce a mixed result. Sadness seems to communicate a negative hedonic tone as evidenced by the infant's sober face, although sometimes fleeting smiles occur as if the infant is attempting to initiate an interaction or change the expression of the other. Some infants approach the person who is expressing the sadness, and others cease activity and do not approach. It would seem that individual differences in sadness transactions begin early in life. Longitudinal study is needed to understand how this is related to transactions involving depressive feelings. Such forms of emotional signaling are complex. It may be that many young children can tell the difference between an adult who is acting a sadness expression from an adult who is actually experiencing sadness. The ongoing research of Main, Weston, and Wakeling (1979), Zahn-Waxler, Radke-Yarrow, and King (1979), and Dunn and Kendrick (1981) on comforting behaviors of 2-year-olds in response to distress are important in this regard.

Besides external (or social) signaling of emotions, there are internal (or psychological) signaling processes. These have been familiar to psychoanalysts and a variety of other psychotherapists who facilitate anticipatory functions wherein small doses of some feelings mobilize coping before extreme distress supervenes. "Signal anxiety" has received the most attention in this regard. That there is a developmental childhood sequence involving signal depression or "helplessness" bearing analogy to Freud's original developmental sequence involving anxiety (Freud, 1926/1961) and that this signal depression system evolves to regulate self-esteem and avoid depression has been suggested by a line of thinking that began with Bibring (1953) and has included Engel (1962a), Anthony (1975), Brenner (1975), and Kaufman (1977). As previously mentioned, the work of Engel and his collaborators has concluded that there are two alternative response patterns to stress, which are precursors of later states of anxiety and depression. In addition, these investigators have postulated that anxiety and depression have their own hierarchical developmental histories and result in separate signal affect systems. More recently, Brenner (1975) also proposed a dual signal affect system based on his clinical experience. For Brenner, anxiety is associated with the idea that something bad is about to happen. Depression, on the other hand, is associated with the idea that something bad has happened. Since the something bad may be at any state of development and may be a humiliation, narcissistic injury, loss, bad deed, or punishment, the individuality of the experience is reflected. Signal depression can act much as signal anxiety as a motive for defense or action. Brenner puts forth the following formula for defense: for anxiety it is, "If I do A, then B will not happen;" for depression it is, "If I do A, then B will change; it will stop happening or will stop making me suffer so or both" (Brenner, 1975, p. 17).

As useful as these theories are for organizing and explaining clinical data of psychotherapy and psychoanalysis, they require developmental research for confirmation or rejection. To what extent do children make use of anticipatory feelings of depression in coping? To what extent do interferences with such capacities lead to particular problems? Are children who do not develop adequate internal emotional signaling more reliant on external signals and therefore more vulnerable to environmental precipitants of depression? Are there hierarchical arrangements and developmental stages for such signaling capacities? Can a discrete emotions approach be brought to this area such that one could investigate "patterns of emotions" in various forms of signal anxiety and signal depression? At this point, there is considerable theory for generating hypotheses but little research.

CONCLUSION

In this chapter, we have attempted to raise some promising research questions concerning depressive feelings in infants and children. New questions arise because of the recent appreciation of childhood depression as a significant clinical problem and because of recent advances in the field of emotion research. In addition, questions arise because of the recognition that depressive feelings change over the course of development while, paradoxically, they remain constant in some respects. Finally, promising research questions arise with respect to understanding the nature of depressive feelings and their communicative aspects.

We have proposed that a transactional approach is useful for research. Such an approach takes into account both the child with depressive feelings and those who encounter the child. The approach, therefore, includes child vis-à-vis family member and child vis-à-vis clinical researcher as part of the investigative field. Whatever else, it is apparent that problems of empathy are prominent in those around the depressed child.

Throughout our chapter, we have highlighted individual case study. This seems important for several reasons. First, it puts us in touch with the complexity of the human individual, a complexity that can often be lost sight of in research studies that generalize across numbers. Second, it is the individual who experiences and suffers these feelings. Third, as clinical researchers, there is no more direct way to encounter depressive and other feelings than by interacting with our individual patients. Further, if we make use of our own feelings in response to another who is troubled, we can often find new meanings, raise new questions, and envision broader research horizons.

REFERENCES

Abelson, R. P., & Sermat, V. (1962). Multidimensional scaling of facial expressions. *Journal of Experimental Psychology, 63,* 546–554.

Anthony, E. J. (1975). Childhood depression. In E. J. Anthony & T. Benedek (Eds.), *Depression and human existence* (pp. 231–277). Boston: Little, Brown.

Bakwin, H. (1942). Loneliness in infants. *American Journal of the Disabled Child, 63,* 30–40.

Beck, A. T. (1976). *Cognitive therapy and emotional disorders.* New York: International Universities Press.

Berman, S. (1979). The psychodynamic aspects of behavior. In J. A. Noshpitz (Ed.), *Basic handbook of child psychiatry* (Vol. 2, pp. 3–28). New York: Basic Books.

Bernstein, P., Emde, R., & Campos, J. (1973). REM sleep in 4-month old infants under home and laboratory conditions. *Psychosomatic Medicine, 34*(4), 322–329.

Bibring, E. (1953). The mechanism of depression. In P. Greenacre (Ed.), *Affective Disorders* (pp. 13–48). New York: International Universities Press.

Bohr, N. (1928). Das Quantenpostulat und Die neurere Entwicklung der Apomistik. *Naturwissenschaften, 16,* 245.

Bowlby, J. (1963). Pathological mourning and childhood mourning. *Journal of the American Psychological Association, 11,* 500–541.

Brazelton, T. B. (1969). *Infants and mothers: Differences in development.* New York: Delacorte Press.

Brenner, C. (1975). Affects and psychic conflict. *Psychoanalytic Quarterly, 44,* 5–28.

Cannon, W. (1932). *The wisdom of the body.* New York: Norton.

Carlson, G. A., & Cantwell, D. P. (1979). A survey of depressive symptoms in a child and adolescent psychiatric population. *American Academy of Child Psychiatry, 18,* 587–599.

Cytryn, L., & McKnew, D. H., Jr. (1972). Proposed classification of childhood depression. *American Journal of Psychiatry, 129,* 149–155.

Cytryn, L., & McKnew, D. H., Jr. (1974). Factors influencing the changing clinical expression of the depressive process in children. *American Journal of Psychiatry, 131*(8), 879–881.

Cytryn, L., & McKnew, D. H., Jr. (1979). Affective disorders of childhood. In J. Noshpitz (Ed.), *Basic handbook of child psychiatry* (Vol. 2, pp. 321–340). New York: Basic Books.

Cytryn, L., & McKnew, D. H., Jr. (1980). Affective disorders of childhood. In H. I. Kaplan, A. M. Friedman, & R. Sadock (Eds.), *Comprehensive textbook of psychiatry* (3rd ed., pp. 2798–2809). Baltimore: Williams & Wilkins.

Cytryn, L., McKnew, D., Bartko, J., Lamour, M., & Hamovit, J. (1982). Offspring of patients with affective disorders. II. Journal of the American Academy of Child Psychiatry, 18, 389–391.

Cytryn, L., McKnew, D. H., Jr., & Bunney, W. E. (1980). Diagnosis of depression in children: A reassessment. American Journal of Psychiatry, 137(1), 22–25.

Darwin, C. (1904). Expression of emotions in man and animals. London: John Murray. (Original work published 1872)

Dunn, J., & Kendrick, C. (1981). Siblings and their mothers: Developing relationships within the family. In M. Lamb & B. Sutton-Smith (Eds.), Sibling relationships: Their development and significance (pp. 39–59). Hillsdale, NJ: Lawrence Erlbaum Associates.

Dunn, J., & Kendrick, C. (1982). Siblings. Cambridge, MA: Harvard University Press.

Eibl-Eibesfeldt, I. (1979). Human ethology: Concepts and implications for the science of man. Behavioral and Brain Sciences, 2, 1–57.

Ekman, P. (1972). Universal and cultural differences in facial expressions of emotion. In J. Cole (Ed.), Nebraska Symposium on Motivation. Lincoln: University of Nebraska Press.

Ekman, P., & Friesen, W. (1971). Constants across cultures in the face and emotion. Journal of Personality and Social Psychology, 71, 124–129.

Ekman, P., Sorenson, E., & Friesen, W. (1969). Pan-cultural elements in facial displays of emotion. Science, 164, 86–88.

Emde, R. (1980). Toward a psychoanalytic theory of affect: The organizational model and its propositions. In S. Greenspan & C. Pollack (Eds.), The course of life: Psychoanalytic contributions toward understanding personality development: Vol. I. Infancy and early childhood (pp. 63–83). Washington, DC: U.S. Government Printing Office.

Emde, R. (1982, March). The pre-representational self and its affective core. Paper presented to the symposium on "Early Life and the Roots of Identity," University of California at Los Angeles Extension.

Emde, R., Gaensbauer, T., & Harmon, R. (1976). Emotional expression in infancy: A biobehavioral study. Psychological Issues, Monograph Series, 10 (Monograph No. 37).

Emde, R., Harmon, R., Metcalf, D., Koenig, K., & Wagonfeld, S. (1971). Stress and neonatal sleep. Psychosomatic Medicine, 33, 491–497.

Emde, R., Kligman, D., Reich, J., & Wade, T. (1978). Emotional expression in infancy. I. Initial studies of social signaling and an emergent model. In M. Lewis & L. Rosenblum (Eds.), The development of affect (pp. 125–148). New York: Plenum Press.

Emde, R., Polak, P., & Spitz, R. (1965). Anaclitic depression in an infant raised in an institution. Journal of Child Psychiatry, 4, 545–553.

Emde, R., Swedberg, J., & Suzuki, B. (1975). Human wakefulness and biological rhythms during the first two postnatal hours. Archives of General Psychiatry, 32, 780–783.

Engel, G. (1962a). Anxiety and depression-withdrawal: The primary affects of unpleasure. International Journal of Psychoanalysis, 43, 89–97.

Engel, G. (1962b). Psychological development in health and disease. Philadelphia: Saunders.

Engel, G., Reichsman, F., & Segal, H. (1956). A study of an infant with gastric fistula. I. Behavior and the rate of total HCl secretion. Psychosomatic Medicine, 18, 374–398.

Engel, G., & Schmale, A. (1972). Conservation-withdrawal: A primary regulatory process for organismic homeostasis. Physiology, emotion and psychosomatic illness (Ciba Foundation Symposium No. 8). Amsterdam: Elsevier.

Erikson, E. H. (1950). Childhood and society. New York: Norton.

Fraiberg, S. (Ed.). (1981). Clinical studies in infant mental health. New York: Basic Books.

Freud, S. (1953). Three essays on the theory of sexuality. In J. Strachey (Ed.), The standard edition of the complete works of Sigmund Freud (Vol. 7, pp. 125–244). London: Hogarth Press. (Original work published 1905.)

Freud, S. (1961). Inhibitions, symptoms and anxiety. In J. Strachey (Ed.), The standard edition of the complete works of Sigmund Freud (Vol. 20, pp. 87–172). London: Hogarth Press. (Original work published 1926.)

Freud, S. (1968). Instincts and their vicissitudes. In J. Strachey (Ed.), The standard edition of the complete works of Sigmund Freud (Vol. 14, pp. 111–140). London: Hogarth Press. (Original work published 1915.)

Frijda, N. (1970). Emotion and recognition of emotion. In M. B. Arnold (Ed.), Feelings and emotions (pp. 241–250). New York: Academic Press.

Frijda, N., & Philipszoon, E. (1963). Dimensions of recognition of expression. Journal of Abnormal and Social Psychology, 66, 45–51.

Gaensbauer, T. (1980). Anaclitic depression in a three-and-one-half-month-old child. American Journal of Psychiatry, 137(7), 841–842.

Gaensbauer, T., & Emde, R. (1973). Wakefulness and feeding in human newborns. Archives of General Psychiatry, 28, 894–897.

Gladstone, W. H. (1962). A multidimensional study of facial expressions of emotion. Australian Journal of Psychology, 14, 95–100.

Globus, G. (1966). Rapid eye movement cycle in real time. Archives of General Psychiatry, 15, 654–659.

Goldfarb, W. (1955). Emotional and intellectual consequences of psychological deprivation in infancy: A reevaluation. In P. Hoch & J. Zubin (Eds.), American Psychopathological Association Publication: Proceedings, Vol. 9, Psychiatry and the Law, 43rd meeting (pp. 105–119). New York: Grune & Stratton.

Goldsmith, H., & Campos, J. (1982). Toward a theory of infant temperament. In R. N. Emde & R. J. Harmon (Eds.), The development of attachment and affiliative systems (pp. 161–193). New York: Plenum Press.

Grinker, R. R. Sr. (1971). Biomedical education as a system. Archives of General Psychiatry, 24, 291–298.

Harmon, R., Wagonfeld, S., & Emde, R. (1982). Anaclitic depression: A follow-up from infancy to puberty. Psychoanalytic Study of the Child, 37, 67–94.

Heisenberg, W. (1927). Uber den anschaulichen Inhalt der quantentheoretischen Kinematik und Mechanik. Zeitschrift fuer Physik, 43, 172.

Hersov, L. (1977). Emotional disorders. In M. Rutter & L. Hersov (Eds.), Child psychiatry: Modern approaches (pp. 428–454). London: Blackwell Scientific Publications.

Hiatt, S., Campos, J., & Emde, R. (1979). Facial patterning and infant emotional expression: Happiness, surprise, fear. Child Development, 50(4), 1020–1035.

Hoffman, M. L. (1978). Toward a theory of empathic arousal and development. In M. Lewis & L. Rosenblum (Eds.), The development of affect (pp. 227–256). New York: Plenum Press.

Horowitz, M. J., Wilner, N., Marmar, C., & Krupnick, J. (1980). Pathological grief and the activation of latent self-images. American Journal of Psychiatry, 137(10), 1157–1162.

Ittelson, W. H. (1962). Perception and transactional psychology. In S. Koch (Ed.), Psychology: A study of a science (pp. 660–704). New York: McGraw-Hill.

Izard, C. (1971). The face of emotion. Meredith, NY: Appleton-Century Crofts.

Izard, C. (1972). Patterns of emotion: A new analysis of anxiety and depression. New York: Academic Press.

Izard, C. (1982). Measuring emotions in human development. In C. Izard (Ed.), Measuring emotions in infants and children (pp. 3–18). London & New York: Cambridge University Press.

Izard, C., Huebner, R., Risser, D., McGinnis, G., & Dougherty, L. (1980). The young infant's ability to produce discrete emotional expressions. Developmental Psychology, 16(2), 132–140.

Johnson, A. M., & Szurek, A. A. (1957). Etiology of antisocial behavior in delinquents and psychopaths. Journal of the American Medical Association, 154, 814–817.

Kagan, J. (1981). The second year. Cambridge, MA: Harvard University Press.

Kashani, J., Husain, A., Shekim, W., Hodges, K., Cytryn, L., & McKnew, D. (1981). Current perspectives on childhood depression: An overview. American Journal of Psychiatry, 138(2), 143–153.

Kaufman, I. C. (1977). Developmental considerations of anxiety and depression: Psychobiological studies in monkeys. In T. Shapiro (Ed.), Psychoanalysis and contemporary science (Vol. 4, pp. 317–363). New York: International Universities Press.

Kleitman, N. (1963). Sleep and wakefulness. Chicago: University of Chicago Press.

Klinnert, M , Campos, J., Sorce, J., Emde, R., & Svejda, M. (1983). The development of social referencing in infancy. In R. Plutchik & H. Kellerman (Eds.), Emotion in early development (Vol. 2, pp. 57–86). New York: Academic Press.

Kovacs, M., & Beck, A. T. (1977). An empirical-clinical approach toward a definition of childhood depression. In J. Schulterbrandt & A. Raskin (Eds.), Depression in childhood: Diagnosis, treatment, and conceptual models (pp. 1–25). New York: Raven Press.

Kripke, D. F. (1972). An ultradian biologic rhythm associated with perceptual deprivation and REM sleep. Psychosomatic Medicine, 34, 221–234.

Lewis, M., & Brooks-Gunn, J (1979). Toward a theory of social cognition: The development of self. In I. Uzgiris (Ed.), New directions in child development: Social interaction and communication during infancy (pp. 23–33). San Francisco: Jossey-Bass.

Mahler, M., Pine, F., & Bergman, A. (1975). The psychological birth of the human infant. New York: Basic Books.

Main, M., Weston, D., & Wakeling, S. (1979, March). "Concerned attention" to the crying of an adult actor in infancy. Presentation at the bi-annual meeting of the Society for Research in Child Development, San Francisco.

Malmquist, C. (1971). Depressions in childhood and adolescence. New England Journal of Medicine, 284(2), 887–893.

Malmquist, C. (1976). The theoretical status of depressions in childhood. In E. J. Anthony & D. C. Gilpin (Eds.), Three clinical faces of childhood (pp. 173–204). New York: Spectrum.

Osgood, C. (1966). Dimensionality of the semantic space for communication via facial expression. Scandinavian Journal of Psychology, 7, 1–30.

Othmer, E., Hayden, M., & Scgelbaum, R. (1969). Encephalic cycles during sleep and wakefulness in humans: A 24-hour pattern. Science, 164, 447–449.

Papousek, H., & Papousek, M. (1980, March–April). Interactional failures: Their origins and significance in infant psychiatry. Presented at the first World Congress on Infant Psychiatry, Cascais, Portugal.

Piaget, J., & Inhelder, B. (1969). The psychology of the child: I. The semiotic function and imitation (pp. 52–57). New York: Basic Books.

Plomin, R. (1982). Childhood temperament. Advances in Clinical Child Psychology, 6, 1–78.

Plutchik, R. (1970). Emotions, evolution, and adaptive processes. In M. B. Arnold (Ed.), Feelings and emotions (pp. 3–24). New York: Academic Press.

Prosen, M., Clark, D., Harrow, M., & Fawcett, J. (1983). Guilt in conscience in major depressive disorders. American Journal of Psychiatry, 140, 839–844.

Puig-Antich, J. (1982). Major depression and conduct disorder in prepuberty. Journal of the American Academy of Child Psychiatry, 21(2), 118–128.

Rholes, W. S., Blackwell, J., Jordan, C., & Walters, C. (1980). A developmental study of learned helplessness. Developmental Psychology, 16(6), 616–625.

Ribble, M. (1943). The rights of infants: Early psychological needs and their satisfactions. New York: Columbia University Press.

Rie, H. E. (1966). Depression in childhood: A survey of some pertinent contributions. Journal of the American Academy of Child Psychiatry, 5, 653–685.

Rochlin, G. (1959). The loss complex. Journal of the American Psychoanalysis Association, 7, 299–316.

Rovee-Collier, C. K., & Fagen, J. W. (1981). The retrieval of memory in early infancy. In L. P. Lipsitt & C. K. Rovee-Collier (Eds.), Advances in infancy research (Vol. I, pp. 226–254). Norwood, New Jersey: Ablex.

Rovee-Collier, C. K., Sullivan, M. W., Enright, M., Lucas, D., & Fagen, J. W. (1980). Reactivation of infant memory. Science, 208, 1159–1161.

Russell, J. A., & Ridgeway, D. (1982). Structure of Affect in Children. Preprint.

Rutter, M. (1966). *Children of sick parents*. London & New York: Oxford University Press.

Rutter, M., Tizard, J., & Whitmore, K. (Eds.). (1970). *Education, health and behaviour*. London: Longman.

Sameroff, A. J., & Chandler, M. (1975). Reproductive risk and the continuum of caretaking casualty. In F. Horowitz (Ed.), *Review of child development research* (Vol. 4, pp. 187–244). Chicago: University of Chicago Press.

Sander, L. (1975). Infant and caretaking environment: Investigation and conceptualization of adaptive behavior in a system of increasing complexity. In E. J. Anthony (Ed.), *Explorations in child psychiatry* (pp. 129–166). New York: Plenum Press.

Scherer, K. (1979). Nonlinguistic indicators of emotion and psychopathology. In C. Izard (Ed.), *Emotions in personality and psychopathology* (pp. 495–529). New York: Plenum Press.

Seligman, M. (1975). *Helplessness: On depression, development, and death*. San Francisco: Freeman.

Seligman, M., Peterson, C., Alloy, L. B., Abramson, L., Kaslow, N. J., Tanenbaum, R., Karpf, S., Semmel, A., Talmon, M., & von-Baeyer, C. (1982). Depressive symptoms, attributional style and helplessness deficits in children. Ms. submitted for publication.

Sorce, J. F., Emde, R. N., Campos, J., & Klinnert, M. D. (1985). Maternal emotional signaling: Its effect on the visual cliff behavior of 1-year-olds. *Developmental Psychology, 21*(1), 195–200.

Spencer, H. (1890). *The principles of psychology*. New York: Appleton.

Spitz, R. (1946). Anaclitic depression: The psychoanalytic study of the child (Vol. 2, pp. 313–342). New York: International Universities Press.

Spitz, R. (1957). *No and yes: On the genesis of human communication*. New York: International Universities Press.

Sroufe, A. (1979). Socioemotional development. In J. Osofsky (Ed.), *Handbook of infant development* (pp. 462–516). New York: Wiley.

Stein, N. L., & Jewett, J. (1982, January). *Children's understanding of emotional reactions: The antecedents and resulting plans of anger, fear and sadness*. Presentation at the SSRC Workshop on the Socialization of Anger and Related Affects. New York: Social Science Research Council.

Stenberg, C., Campos, J., & Emde, R. N. (1983). The facial expression of anger in seven-month-olds. *Child Development, 54*, 178–184.

Sterman, M., & Hoppenbrouwers, T. (1971). The development of sleep-waking and rest–activity patterns from fetus to adult in man. In M. Sterman, D. McGinty, & A. Adinolfi (Eds.), *Brain development and behavior* (pp. 203–225). New York: Academic Press.

Tennes, K., Downey, K., & Vernadakis, A. (1977). Urinary cortisol excretion rates and anxiety in normal one-year-old infants. *Psychosomatic Medicine, 39*, 178–187.

Thomas, A., Chess, S., Birch, H., Hertzig, M., & Korn, S. (1963). *Behavioral individuality in early childhood*. New York: New York University Press.

Tomkins, S. S. (1962). *Affect, imagery, consciousness: The positive affects*. New York: Springer.

Tomkins, S. S. (1963). *Affect, imagery, consciousness: The negative affects*. New York: Springer.

Tomkins, S. S., & McCarter, R. (1964). What and where are the primary affects? Some evidence for a theory. *Perceptual and Motor Skills, 18*, 119–158.

Weisz, J. R. (1979). Perceived control and learned helplessness among mentally retarded and nonretarded children: A developmental analysis. *Developmental Psychology, 14*(3), 311–319.

Woodworth, R. S., & Schlosberg, H. S. (1954). *Experimental psychology*. New York: Holt.

Wundt, W. (1896). *Grundriss der psychologie* (C. H. Judd, trans.) As quoted in Izard (1971).

Zahn-Waxler, C., Radke-Yarrow, M., & King, R. A. (1979). Child rearing and children's prosocial initiations toward victims of distress. *Child Development, 50*, 319–330.

III

PARENTAL DEPRESSION
AS A RISK FACTOR

Developmental Issues in Risk Research: The Offspring of Affectively Ill Parents

Leon Cytryn
Donald H. McKnew
Carolyn Zahn-Waxler
Elliot S. Gershon

INTRODUCTION

The major studies relevant to developmental approaches to affective illness will be reviewed considering several issues central to a developmental scheme, namely, the genetic component and the role of the environment as seen in family studies of children at different ages, the epidemiology as well as the biological concomitants at various ages. Child studies have tended to follow the leads provided by the study of adults. However, recent investigations of infants and toddlers at risk, as reported later in the chapter, point to areas in which child studies may contribute to our understanding of adult affective illness: that is, the developmental approach to psychopathology (Rutter, Chapter 1 of this volume), the development of normal and abnormal emotions (Izard & Schwartz, Chapter 2 of this volume), the study of cognitive, affective, and social precursors of depressive illness (Gaensbauer, Harmon, Cytryn, & McKnew, 1984; Zahn-Waxler, Chapman, Cummings, & Cytryn, 1982; Zahn-Waxler, McKnew, Cummings, Davenport, & Radke-Yarrow, 1984) and the attempts to understand the nature of vulnerability or invulnerability in children (Anthony, 1974, 1975) at risk for affective illness.

Probably the most important and most difficult issue is the question of continuity and discontinuity of affective disorders: Are these disorders,

Leon Cytryn, Donald H. McKnew, and Carolyn Zahn-Waxler. Laboratory of Developmental Psychology, National Institute of Mental Health, Bethesda, Maryland.

Elliot S. Gershon. Unit of Psychogenetics, Biological Psychiatry Branch, National Institute of Mental Health, Bethesda, Maryland.

seen and diagnosed in childhood, identical with the same disorders diagnosed by the same criteria in adults? Are the prodromal disturbances seen in infants and toddlers at risk for affective illness part of a continuum of such illness, stretching from infancy into adult life, or do the psychopathological phenomena seen at different ages represent similar but independent disease entities?

We shall first concentrate on the salient features of research on affective disorders in adults, and then consider the same features in children of parents with affective illness. Child genetic studies are not included since rigorous studies in this area are not as yet available. We shall present our recent data on infants and toddlers of affectively ill parents, and we shall discuss the entire material from a developmental view, with particular emphasis on the issue of continuity versus discontinuity.

STUDIES OF ADULT AFFECTIVE DISORDERS

Genetics

Recently Gershon, Nurnberger, Nadi, Berrettini, and Goldin (1983) summarized evidence that genetic predisposition exists in a substantial proportion of patients with manic–depressive illness and major depression. This conclusion is based largely on the numerous twin and adoption studies of affective illness carried out in the last half-century. In a recent review Nurnberger and Gershon (1982) stressed the fact that, although findings indicate a genetic transmission of affective illness, the possibility remains that nongenetic influences such as infection with a slow virus, acting prior to the age of adoption (i.e., during infancy), could mimic genetic transmission.

Three major areas are unsettled and to some extent controversial in the field of genetic studies:

1. What is the genetic relationship of unipolar (UP) to bipolar (BP) illness? This is part of the general issue of whether there is a spectrum of disorders genetically transmitted with BP illness, or whether there are discrete and independent genetic entities defined by clinical diagnosis.
2. What is the mode of genetic transmission? In particular, does any X chromosome or autosomal single major gene inheritance exist in affective disorders?
3. Are there biological markers of genetic vulnerability?

The genetic vulnerability perspective implies first that persons who become ill have a continuous and chronic constitutional vulnerability that is present even when the persons are well. Second, it is implied that the etiological importance of any specific biologic factor can be tested by observing whether it is genetically transmitted in pedigrees along with the illness, instead of independently of it.

Two major classes of models have been proposed for affective illness, which for this discussion we shall call "unitary" and "heterogeneous." In the unitary models, all patients with a given diagnosis are hypothesized to be part of a genetic liability distribution. With heterogeneous models, on the other hand, we can hypothesize that within a diagnostic entity some cases are caused by one genetic disorder and others by a second (and distinct) disorder. The well-known hypothesis that some proportion of bipolar pedigrees show X linkage, and others do not have X-linked transmission (Mendlewicz, Linkowski, Guroff, & van Praag, 1979), represents a model of genetic heterogeneity.

The multiple-threshold multifactorial model of Reich, James, and Morris (1972) has been applied to prevalences of affective illness in first-degree relatives (Gershon, Bunney, Leckman, van Eerdewegh, & Debauche, 1976; Gershon, Goldin, Weissman, & Nurnberger, 1981; Gershon et al., 1982). This model can be understood to test whether the familial transmission of the different diagnostic entities can be fit to a single dimension of underlying vulnerability. Greater liability is associated with more transmission of illness and more transmission of the higher liability forms of illness. The key question tested by this model is whether there is shared or independent transmission of several disease entities under multifactorial inheritance. By and large, this model fits observed prevalences of affective illness in relatives of patients and of controls where bipolar is the more severe form of illness and unipolar is the less severe form.

LINKAGE STUDIES

Mendlewicz and his co-workers (Mendlewicz, Fleiss, & Fieve, 1972, 1975; Mendlewicz et al., 1979), combining theirs and Winokur's data (Reich, Clayton, & Winokur, 1969; Winokur & Tanna, 1969), concluded that, in families of BP patients, affective illness is closely linked to color blindness and that linkage to the Xg blood group is also present. Mendlewicz, Linkowski, and Wilmette (1980) reported linkage between manic–depressive illness and glucose-6-phosphate dehydrogenase (G6PD) deficiency. HLA (human leukocyte antigen) associations with bipolar affective illness have also been reported.

All of the above linkage studies are a matter of controversy. Some data have not proven to be replicable or have lacked statistical significance (Beckman et al., 1978; Gershon, Targum, Kessler, Mazure, & Bunney, 1977; Gershon, Targum, Matthysse, & Bunney, 1979; Leckman, Gershon, McGinnis, Targum, & Dibble, 1979; Smeraldi et al., 1978; Targum, Gershon, van Eerdewegh, & Rogentine, 1979; Temple, Dupont, & Shopsin, 1979).

ETIOLOGIC MARKERS

Relatively few studies have attempted to identify biological factors that are inherited in these disorders. To do this would require a genetic marker that, applied to each individual in a pedigree, successfully predicts who is at risk and who is not.

Rieder and Gershon (1978) proposed certain criteria for a genetic vulnerability to an illness:

1. The characteristic must be associated with an increased likelihood of the psychiatric illness. (The converse, that persons with the illness should generally show the characteristic, need not be true since there may be biologic heterogeneity in the illness.)
2. It must be heritable and must not be a secondary effect of the illness. Phenomena that are demonstrable only in the presence of active illness have limited usefulness in the genetic investigation of an illness with incomplete penetrance. For example, if a urinary metabolite is decreased only during episodes of illness, it is impossible to determine whether well relatives or controls would have the same finding.
3. It must be observable (or evocable) in the well state, so that it is possible to determine its presence independently of the illness and to evaluate well relatives.

Stable characteristics that have been examined in adults in the hope of identifying a marker include measures related to neurotransmitter chemistry: monoamine metabolism (enzymes and metabolites) (Gershon, Goldin, Lake, Murphy, & Guroff, 1980; Sedvall et al., 1980; van Praag and de Haan, 1979), cholinergic pharmacologic response (Janowsky, Risch, Parker, Huey, & Judd, 1980; Sitaram, Moore, & Gillin, 1978; Sitaram, Nurnberger, Gershon, & Gillin, 1982), cholinergic receptor density (Nadi, Nurnberger, & Gershon, 1984), plasma GABA (Berrettini, Nurnberger, Hare, Gershon, & Post, 1982), [^{3}H] imipramine binding, which is related to serotonin transport (Berrettini, Nurnberger, Post, & Gershon, 1982), indices of cation transport (Dorus et al., 1979), and a brain protein variant (PC 1 Duarte) (Comings, 1979).

Only two of these characteristics have suggestive data on segregation of a biological abnormality with illness. Lithium erythrocyte/plasma ratio has a higher mean value in ill relatives of BP patients than in well ones (Dorus et al., 1979), but a large proportion of ill relatives overlap the controls (Nurnberger, Pandey, & Gershon, 1982). Muscarinic cholinergic receptor density on fibroblasts is considerably higher in patients than in normal controls, with only modest overlap between the two groups (Nadi et al., 1984). Ill relatives were very similar to the patients. This corroborates the cholinergic hypothesis of affective disorders (Janowsky et al., 1980;

Sitaram *et al.*, 1982) and is compatible with receptor density as a necessary (primary) genetic vulnerability factor.

Family Studies

The foregoing remarks were based on many family studies of patients with affective illness, reviewed by Nurnberger *et al.* (1982). As pointed out by Weissman *et al.* (1984), many of the older studies of adults had certain shortcomings:

1. Since rigorous diagnostic criteria have become available only recently, most of the older studies lacked diagnostic precision, resulting in variability between studies.
2. Most studies investigated families of only severely ill, hospitalized patients, ignoring the family histories of patients with milder forms of affective illness, who represent the majority of the affected population. Specifically we may add, there is a virtual absence of family studies of patients with minor depression (dysthymic disorder).
3. Save for several recent investigations, most family studies did not include matched normal control groups. Properly executed family studies can provide important information of epidemiology, demographic, and social factors, etiology, differential analysis, and primary and secondary prevention.

Following are the results of two affective family studies that satisfy the above mentioned criteria. The findings of the first one (Gershon *et al.*, 1982) are as follows: The lifetime prevalence of major affective disorder (including schizoaffective) was 37, 24, 25, 20, and 7% in first-degree relatives of schizoaffective, BP I (mania and depression), BP II (hypomania and depression), UP, and normal controls, respectively. UP illness is the most frequent disorder in relatives of all types of probands (patients). These data are compatible with a model in which different affective disorders represent thresholds on a continuum of underlying vulnerability rather than separate disorders genetically independent of each other. Neither of the proband groups differed from normal controls as to the frequency of alcoholism, drug abuse, and sociopathy. There were no significant sex differences in a relative's morbid risk. Minor depression and depressive personality were not found in excess in relatives of patients with BP affective illness. The mean ages of onset were for UP, 29.9 years; for BP I, 26.1; and for BP II, 29.9. The findings of overall risk for major affective illness in the adult children of affectively ill parents (27% if one parent is ill, 74% if both parents are ill) is especially relevant to the offspring studies in child psychiatric literature, which deal only with children of parents with affective disorders.

The findings of the second major recent family study (Weissman *et al.*, 1984), done in collaboration with the aforementioned NIMH team (Gershon *et al.*, 1982), are as follows: the probands (all adults) included three groups: major depression–severe (hospitalized), major depression–mild (outpatient), and a normal control group. The most frequent disorders in the relatives of all affective proband groups as compared to normal controls were major and minor (UP) depressions. The relatives of probands with severe and mild major depressive disorders showed no difference in their frequency of affective and other psychiatric disorders. Depressive personality and minor depression aggregate in the relatives of patients with major depressive personality. However, antisocial personality and alcoholism did not distinguish between relatives of probands and normal controls. The incidence of major depressive UP disorders was significantly higher in female relatives of all probands, while the incidence of BP illness was unrelated to sex. Finally, the rates of affective and most other psychiatric disorders in the relatives of affectively ill probands were comparable to the findings of Gershon *et al.* (1982).

Epidemiology

A recent review of the vast literature on this subject (Hirschfeld and Cross, 1982) revealed estimates of a lifetime prevalence of affective disorders in adult populations in the range 17–20%, and a 1-year prevalence of 5–8%. The reported prevalence in the general population may vary widely, depending on the criteria used for assessment (Gershon *et al.*, 1982).

Hirschfeld's review focused on the psychosocial risk factors in three categories: BP and UP illness, and depressive symptoms. The latter term indicates a dysphoric mood combined with other characteristics of depression, which does not meet the criteria for a full depressive syndrome.

SEX

The majority of studies report a higher rate of depressive symptoms in women than in men (Comstock & Helsin, 1976; Craig & Van Natta, 1976, 1979; Radloff & Rae, 1979; Steele, 1978; Weissman & Klerman, 1977; Weissman & Myers, 1978), with an average female:male ratio of 2:1. This sex ratio exists in unipolar depressive syndromes, although the ratio is almost equal in bipolar depressive syndrome (Clayton, 1978). The explanations offered for the greater susceptibility of women to depression (Weissman & Klerman, 1977) include endocrine factors, higher reactivity to stress, and an inferior social status resulting in greater passivity and dependency. Contrary to this general trend, a recent study of depression in the Amish (Egelund, 1980) failed to show the sex difference found in the above groups.

AGE

Depressive symptoms and syndromes (BP and UP) are more prevalent in young adults (18–44 years) than in older ones. This is especially true of women (Weissman & Myers, 1978). The age of onset of the initial episode is reported to be earlier on the average in BP illness (late 20s), than in UP illness (middle to late 30s) (Bebbington, 1978; Clayton, 1978; Weissman & Myers, 1978).

RACE AND RELIGION

No racial differences were found in either the depressive symptoms or syndromes. As to religious factors the prevalence of BP illness was found to be higher in Hutterities (Mendels, 1970) and Ashkenazi Jews as compared with the general population (Grewel, 1967).

SOCIAL CLASS

The rate of depressive symptoms is significantly higher in the lower socioeconomic population than in other class groups (Comstock & Helsin, 1976; Steele, 1978; Warheit, Holzer, & Arey, 1975). Findings on the relation between the socioeconomic status (SES) and UP illness are equivocal (Brown, Bhrolchain, & Harris, 1975; Hoover & Fitzgerald, 1980; MacMahon & Pugh, 1970; Weissman & Myers, 1978). BP illness is more prevalent in people of higher SES (Bebbington, 1978; Weissman & Myers, 1978).

LIFE EVENTS

This term is usually applied to stressful environmental stimuli in the area of social relationships ("social stressors"). There is some evidence that number and intensity of stressful life events are positively related to the number of depressive symptoms (Ilfeld, 1977; Warheit, 1979). Such a relationship is, however, less clear with regard to depressive syndromes. BP versus UP patients, and patients with endogenous versus reactive depression, did not differ significantly in their rates of life events (Patrick, Dunner, & Rieve, 1978; Thomson & Hendrie, 1972). Brown (Chapter 9 of this volume) stresses the risk of adult depression attendant on the presence of life events with high contextual threat, especially in conjunction with the early loss of a parent. Paykel, Myers, and Dienelt (1969) and Paykel and Tanner (1976) stressed the importance of undesirable "exit" events (loss of an important person). He estimated that 9–10% of such events are followed by depression (Paykel, 1978). These figures indicate that most undesirable life events are not followed by depression, and other causative factors may be of importance.

Summary

There is considerable evidence, based on family and epidemiological studies, that a genetic predisposition exists in a substantial proportion of patients with major mood disorders. However, biological evidence for such a genetic factor in these illnesses, such as linkage studies and genetic markers, is still inconclusive.

STUDIES OF CHILDHOOD AFFECTIVE DISORDERS

Trait and State Markers

Less research has been done in this area. Puig-Antich, Chambers, Halpern, Hanlon, and Sachar (1979) and Puig-Antich *et al.* (1981, 1982), and Puig-Antich (this volume) concentrated on prepubertal major depression of endogenous type. They have reported hypersecretion of cortisol in 10% of this group and have found a positive dexamethasone suppression test (DST) in two-thirds of the cases. Similar DST results have been reported by Poznanski, Carroll, Bemejas, Cook, and Grossman (1982). However, both cortisol hypersecretion and positive DST return to normal upon recovery. Other important findings concern the secretion of growth hormone: There is hypersecretion of growth hormone in sleep (especially during delta stage of sleep) in prepubertal children with major depression, but there is also a diminished growth hormone secretion in responses to an insulin tolerance test. Both findings are similar to those in adults but are more pronounced in prepubertal children. Although the growth hormone data are quite suggestive of a trait, they do not yet fulfill all the criteria of a genetic marker as enumerated above by Rieder and Gershon (1978), especially the state independence and the relative absence of such a trait in nonill relatives of prepubertal children with major depression.

Cytryn, McKnew, Logue, and Desai (1974) and McKnew and Cytryn (1979) examined urinary metabolites in chronically depressed children and found that they excreted significantly less 3-methoxy-4-hydroxyphenyl-ethylene glycol (MHPG) in 24 hr than normal controls, paralleling the findings of Maas, Dekirmenjian, and Fawcett (1971) and Maas, Fawcett, and Dekirmenjian (1968) in adults. The same authors in a study of children with a BP affective disorder (McKnew *et al.*, 1981) found the children to have a clear-cut response to lithium and a strongly augmented average evoked response (AER) to sensory stimuli, again paralleling findings in adults (Buchsbaum, 1978, 1979; Buchsbaum, Goodwin, Murphy, & Borge, 1971). However, both the alteration in the MHPG urinary excretion, as well as that of the AER have to be considered state markers, since they return to normal once the child has recovered.

Family Studies

Family studies of affective disorders in childhood lag behind adult studies in many ways. In the methodology of the child studies, the following questions can be raised:

1. Childhood studies have involved small and nonrepresentative samples.
2. Diagnostic criteria differ from study to study and only in a minority of studies have well-defined operational criteria been used.
3. Use of normal controls and controls with other psychiatric or non-psychiatric pathology is rare.
4. Even when proper diagnostic criteria have been used with the parents, the timing of parental illness in the life of the child, especially at the time of the child's psychiatric evaluation, is usually unreported.
5. The mental state of the spouse of the ill proband is equally ignored.
6. Association of a depressive disorder in children with an antecedent undesirable life stress is even less clear than in adults. In both children and adults the findings in the life events literature are hampered by the fact that life events may be the consequence of, the cause of, or confounded with a psychologic disorder (Hirschfeld & Cross, 1982).
7. There is a broad range of nonspecific psychopathology existing in infants and toddlers at risk for affective illness (Gaensbauer et al., 1984; Zahn-Waxler et al., 1984), with a diagnosable depressive picture usually not emerging until age 6–7 (Cytryn, McKnew, Zahn-Waxler, Radke-Yarrow, Gaensbauer, Harmon & Lamour, 1984).
8. There are no well-conducted studies that follow children at risk for affective illness past adolescence and especially into adulthood until they pass the age of morbid risk in adults.
9. Currently available genetic models have not yet been applied to affective disorders in childhood and adolescence.

It is difficult to estimate precisely the number of offspring studies of affectively ill parents—involving children and adolescents—because of the widely divergent criteria used to characterize the parents and their offspring. Probably the earliest study of parents with depressive illness was in Rutter's pioneering work "Children of Sick Parents" (1966). Of the 137 children of 43 depressed parents, nearly 50% had a diagnosable psychiatric disorder. The disorders included conduct disturbances, neurotic behavior disturbances, mixed behavior disturbances, and neurotic illness. None of the children was diagnosed as depressed. Other studies, whose number exceeds 20, date since the early 1970s. Interestingly, only four of those (Cytryn, McKnew, Bartko, Lamour & Hamovit, 1982; McKnew, Cytryn, Efron, Gershon, & Bunney, 1979; Orvaschel, Weissman, Padian, & Lowe, 1981; Welner, Welner, McCrary, & Leonard, 1977) used affective diagnoses in the children. The incidence of depressive disorders ranged from 7% to 65%; however, most of these studies did not clearly distinguish between major and minor depressions. There was also a conspicuous absence of mania and depressive psychosis in those children, consistent with the findings of Anthony and Scott (1960). Depressive symptoms that did not satisfy precise diagnostic criteria were reported in a number of investigations (Greenhill & Shopsin, 1979; Kuyler, Rosenthal, Igel, Dunner, & Fieve, 1980; O'Connell, Mays, O'Brien, & Mirsheidaie, 1979; Weissman & Siegel, 1972; Welner et al., 1977). Rutter (1966) found no difference between the diagnostic pattern of children of parents with affective illness and that of children of parents with nonaffective psychiatric illness. Behavior disturbances, adjustment reactions, various personality disorders, minimal brain dysfunction, sociopathic behavior, and drug problems were reported in several studies (Conners, Himmelhoch, Goyette, Ulrich, & Neil, 1979; El-Guebaly, Offord, Sullivan, & Lynch, 1978; Greenhill & Shopsin, 1979; Kuyler et al., 1980; Weissman & Siegel, 1972), in addition to the whole gamut of psychiatric symptoms that did not satisfy diagnostic criteria. Several investigators used children of normal controls (Cytryn et al., 1982; Orvashel et al., 1981; Weissman & Siegel, 1972; Welner et al., 1977). Although the rates of depression varied in these studies, it is significantly lower in the control group than in children of parents with affective disorders. One study (Weissman & Siegel, 1972) reported significantly more defiant behavior, rebellion, and withdrawal in adolescents with depressive mothers as compared to those with well mothers.

USE OF NONAFFECTIVE PSYCHIATRIC CONTROLS

Most of these studies have used schizophrenic parents as control groups. There are conflicting findings. Some investigators (Rolf, 1972, 1976; Rolf & Garmezy, 1974) have reported that children of depressed mothers have more appropriate peer relationships and school behavior (similar to normal controls) than children of schizophrenic mothers. Other investigators (Weintraub, Neale, & Liebert, 1975; Weintraub, Prinz, & Neale, 1978) have reported that children of depressed as well as schizophrenic mothers were rated by teachers and peers as more disturbed than children of normal controls on such measures as impatience, defiance, disturbed behavior in the classroom, withdrawal, lesser creativity, initiative, comprehension, aggression, and unhappiness.

FOLLOW-UP STUDIES

With some evidence that affective illness occurs at a higher rate in the children of these families, a question of interest is that of the continuity or discontinuity of this phenomenon over time. All the children of parents with a major affective illness who were seen in our earlier offspring studies were contacted to arrange for a follow-up study. We studied the 18 children who responded to our contacts (Apter *et al.*, 1982). The mean age of the children when first seen was 10 years; the mean age at follow up was 14 years. The interviewers and diagnostician were blind as to the original diagnosis. Of the 12 originally diagnosed as depressed by the Weinberg criteria, only two were asymptomatic 4 years later. Of the remaining 10, seven retained their diagnostic depressive label using the DSM III criteria (mostly dysthymic), and three switched to other psychopathology. Of the six who were originally diagnosed as Weinberg negative, five remained asymptomatic at follow-up, while one had a major depressive disorder.

Poznanski, Krahenbuhl, and Zrull (1976) in a long-term follow-up of their depressed children found that about 50% of them remained depressed as young adults and the remainder had other psychopathology.

Zeitlin, as discussed by Rutter (Chapter 1 of this volume), reported that when both children and adults were diagnosed by his operational criteria for depressive syndromes, an impressive continuity was found, that is, of 37 children diagnosed as depressed by Pearce's criteria, 31 were diagnosed as having a depressive syndrome in adulthood, using the same criteria. Rutter speculates that the contrast between this impressive continuity and the lack of it when traditional clinical diagnoses rather than the recently employed strict operational criteria were used may be explained by the concomitant nondepressive disorders that overshadowed the presence of a depressive syndrome.

One group of investigators examined 12 adolescents whose mothers had been psychotic during the child's infancy (Grunebaum, Cohler, Kauffman, & Gallant, 1978; Kauffman, Grunebaum, Cohler, & Gamer, 1979). They found significantly less competence in the children with depressed mothers than in those with mothers with nonaffective diagnoses. Another follow-up study of children (Kokes, Harder, Fisher, & Strauss, 1980) of depressed mothers indicated a general increase of emotional disturbance during adolescence as measured by the rate of school dropout and overall adjustment.

All the findings suggest that depression or related psychological problems in childhood are not evanescent phenomena but often a precursor of significant psychopathology in adolescence.

Epidemiology of Childhood Depression

The frequency of childhood depression among the general population has been studied by relatively few investigators. Just as in the adult epidemiological studies, the wide variance in reported prevalence is probably due to the different diagnostic instruments used. Rutter, Tizard, Yule, Graham, Whitmore (1976) and Rutter, Tizard, and Whitmore (1981), in the Isle of Wight study reported that three out of 2199 prepubertal children were depressed. This study was the first to report the existence of childhood depression among the general population. However, the study was not specifically designed to investigate depression, and the reported prevalence therefore might have been underestimated. Kashani and Simonds (1979) reported a frequency of 1.9% of depression, using DSM-III criteria (1980), in a sample of children (N = 53) born at the University of Missouri—Columbia Hospital and a sample (N = 50) whose parents were attending a family practice clinic for a medical condition. Although distinguishing among children who had a major depression and children who had only a dysphoric mood, this study did not address the issue of major and minor subtypes of depression.

A representative sample of 641 9-year-old New Zealand children was studied by Kashani, McGee, Clarkson, Anderson, Walton, William, Silva, Robins, Cytryn, and McKnew (1983). The methods used to assess the prevalence of depression included (1) a parent's questionnaire based on DSM-III criteria (1980); (2) teachers' report of school behavior based on Rutter's Child Scale B (Rutter *et al.*, 1981); (3) the K-SADS-E (Puig-Antich & Chambers, 1978). The diagnoses of major and minor depression, present or past, were based on the child's meeting the criteria of minor or major depression of the Research Diagnostic Criteria (RDC). In addition the child's K-SADS-E interview, information obtained from the parents and teachers was used to corroborate the child's statements and especially the timing of the past depressive episodes. The current prevalence of major and minor depression was estimated as 1.7 and 3.6%, respectively. The past prevalence of major depression was estimated at 1.0% and of minor depression as 8.5%.

Summary

Most of the numerous studies of the offspring of parents with a major mood disorder were methodologically inadequate. However, the few offspring studies that used normal controls did show a significantly higher rate of mood disorders in the offspring of patients versus controls. The studies of biological markers in mood disorders in children gave some support for the similarities of mood disorders in adults and children. However, most of these are state rather than trait markers and hence do not resolve the issue of genetic vulnerability in depressed children.

OUR OFFSPRING STUDIES TO DATE

Studies of Children

The authors have been involved for many years in the study of the offspring of parents with a major affective illness. The children have been seen at various stages of development. We have chosen this strategy because affective illness tends to aggregate in families, placing such children at high risk for affective illness. Thus, such families provide an opportunity to study affective disorders and other psychopathology at all stages of development and ultimately to discover the genetic and rearing practices that may be at the root of their illnesses.

Our first offspring study (McKnew, Cytryn, Efron, Gershon, & Bunney, 1979) was exploratory, open, and without controls. We saw 30 children (ages 6–15) of 14 families in which one parent was hospitalized at NIMH for manic depressive (M-D) illness (12 BP, 2 UP). Sixteen of the 30 children were found to meet the Weinberg criteria (Weinberg, Rutman, Sullivan, Penick, & Deitz, 1973) for depression on at least one of two structured interviews done 4 months apart.

In our second offspring study (Cytryn et al., 1982), we saw 19 children (ages 5–15) of 13 hospitalized (at NIMH) M-D parents (7 BP, 6 UP) and 21 children (also ages 5–15) of 13 normal parents. The control group was matched to the index group on (1) age within 2 years, (2) sex, (3) socioeconomic status, within one point on the Holingshead–Redlich scale. Parents were assessed by the Life Schedule of Affective Disorder and Schizophrenia (L-SADS) (Endicott & Spitzer, 1978) and diagnosed using the RDC (Spitzer, Endicott, & Robins, 1978) as modified by Mazure and Gershon (1979). All children were interviewed and rated by a member of our team who was blind to parental diagnosis and the purpose of the study. The children were seen at 4-month intervals and were interviewed each time by a different interviewer using the previously mentioned structured interview, which elicits all types of psychopathology. The results were analyzed in two ways: (1) using the individual children as a unit of analysis, (2) using the families as units of analysis:

1. Of the 19 children of manic–depressive parents, 12 were depressed at one or both interviews, using the Weinberg criteria and only 5 of 21 control children were depressed at one or both interviews using the same criteria. The difference was statistically significant.

2. When using the families as units of analysis we employed both the Weinberg and DSM III criteria: of the 13 index (patient) families 11 had at least one child who was depressed as measured by Weinberg criteria and of the 13 control families three had a depressed child as measured by the Weinberg criteria. The difference was statistically significant. When the DSM-III criteria were used the following results were obtained: In the 13 index families, nine families had at least one depressed child, four families had none. In the 13 control families, three families had at least one depressed child, while 10 had none. The difference was statistically different. In the index group, three families had children with major depressive disorder, while one control family had a child with such a disorder. The remaining children with affective illness in both groups had dysthy-

mic disorder. In addition to affective disorders, the DSM-III diagnoses of overanxious disorder were made in the children of two proband families and in one of the control families. Another index family had a child with a simple phobia. No child had manic or psychotic symptoms.

Studies of Infants and Toddlers of Bipolar Parents

DESCRIPTION OF THE SAMPLE

Seven male children with a BP parent were studied longitudinally, beginning at age 1. A matched control sample of seven male children of normal parents was initially selected but later expanded to $N = 20$ (10 males and 10 females) in order (1) to make statistical group comparisons possible and (2) to be able to generalize results to young girls as well. Extensive recruitment efforts were expended to obtain a sample of 1-year-old females from BP families. The BP disorder itself is not common, however, and the search failed to yield any young female offspring. Therefore, sex of child was controlled for in statistical analyses. None of the children had significant physical health problems. Control and index families were equated in socioeconomic status, race, religion, ethnicity, and parental age. They were predominantly white middle-class families, with an average parental age in the early to mid 30s. The SADS (Schedule for Affective Disorders and Schizophrenia) (Endicott & Spitzer, 1978) was used to diagnose parents. In four of the index families the mother was BP; the father was manic–depressive in the remaining three families. BP patients were on lithium and considered to be in remission at the time of the study. Hence any observed impact of the parental illness at this point in the child's development would be due to subclinical manifestations of the symptoms.

We studied at different time periods the following four aspects of the behavior of probands and controls:

1. Attachment behavior and the nature of affiliative expression and quality of social relationships were investigated in the seven proband infants and seven normal controls (Cytryn et al., 1984). A modified Ainsworth paradigm (Gaensbauer & Harmon, 1981) was used at 12, 15, and 18 months of age. In addition, a developmental and neurological examination was performed at 18 months. The study of average evoked potential was attempted, but too few infants would cooperate in this procedure to make the results meaningful. The ratings of attachment were based on traditional measures developed by Ainsworth and her colleagues (Ainsworth & Wittig, 1969). Ratings of emotional expression were measured by the methods developed by Gaensbauer and Harmon (1981; Harmon & Culp, 1981; Gaensbauer et al., 1984).

Results of the study most relevant to a developmental perspective are (1) an increase over time, from 12 to 18 months, of insecure, ambivalent attachment, in the proband infants (at 12 months two of seven proband infants showed insecure attachment, while at 18 months six of seven demonstrated this pattern); (2) a significantly lesser capacity of these infants for self-regulation of their emotional equilibrium, especially in handling fear and anger; and (3) one of the proband infants showed at times a predominantly depressive mood. We found no neurological deficit, and no abnormalities in developmental milestones in any of the infants.

2. Beginning at age 1, staff visits to the home were made monthly. When the subjects reached age 2, home visitors made assessments of problem behaviors in the children (Zahn-Waxler, McKnew, et al., 1984). Based on their cumulative observations and mothers' reports, the home visitors identified psychological symptoms in the child. These included phobias, sleep disturbances, eating problems, excessive shyness, passivity, hyperactivity, poor impulse control, self-punitive behaviors (head banging), excessive dependency, social language problems, disturbances in regulation of affect, temper tantrums, echolalia, and resistance to physical contact. Children with a BP parent were coded as having significantly greater numbers of these types of problems ($\overline{X}$ proband = 4.3 symptoms, $\overline{X}$ control = 1.71 symptoms; $t(25) = 5.28$ $p < .001$). Also, the proband children were particularly likely to show problems thought to be reflective of more serious disturbance such as head banging, echolalia, and resistance to physical contact ($\overline{X}$ proband = 1.57 serious symptoms, $\overline{X}$ control = .33; $t(25) - 3.57$, $p < .001$). Because observers were not blind to parental diagnosis and because psychiatrically ill mothers had input to the symptom reports, the highly significant findings may reflect an exaggeration of the differences. In subsequent analyses (see below) significant differences between the groups of children continued to emerge when data were coded and analyzed by persons blind to parent diagnosis and when mothers had no involvement in the children's interactions.

3. Peer interactions were investigated (Zahn-Waxler, Cummings, McKnew, & Radke-Yarrow, 1984). At age 2½ years, the children seen in Study II came to the laboratory for two sessions with their mother and same-age playmates and their mothers. Observations of peer interactions took place in a living room–kitchenette area that was part of a small apartment equipped for research observations.

    a. A novel environment. Children's initial play in a new room and situation (5 min).

    b. A background climate of affection and sharing. Two female adults entered the adjoining kitchen. They greeted the mothers and children, and then cooperated with each other in a warm and friendly fashion while getting coffee for the mothers and juice for the children, and straightening up the kitchen (5 min).

  c. A neutral context. There were no experimental interventions (5 min).
  d. A background climate of hostility, anger, and rejection. The two women returned and had a verbal argument while washing dishes. Each bitterly accused the other of not doing her share of work around the building (5 min).
  e. A second neutral context (5 min).
  f. A reconciliation. The adults returned, greeted each other with affection, and apologized for their unpleasant behavior (5 min).
  g. A friend's separation experience. The mother of the child's friend was asked to leave the room (1 min).
  h. Separation from mother. The child's own mother was also called from the room (1 min).
  i. Reunion with the mother. Both mothers returned to the room (4 min).

Mothers were asked not to initiate peer activities or to interrupt interactions between the children unless something made mothers uncomfortable or was dangerous. The above procedure was repeated 1 month later. Aggression, altruism, and emotional expressiveness were coded.

No differences were found in total aggression toward peers. However, children from BP homes showed more inappropriate displayed aggression, hurting their friends with greater frequency than controls during the period of reunion following separation from the mother. Children from BP families showed substantially less altruism toward their peers, most noticeably reflected in less sharing. Children from BP families showed heightened emotion during the argument between two adults and little emotion following the fight, while controls showed the reverse pattern. The high level of emotion shown by proband children following exposure to the climate of anger consisted primarily of distress, while the high level of emotion of controls following anger consisted primarily of positive emotion.

   4. Zahn-Waxler et al. (1982) investigated the development of object relations in infants and toddlers. Object relations were assessed in four tests of cognitive and/or social functioning:

  a. Object permanence, that is, understanding that the temporary disappearance of physical objects does not constitute permanent absence, was measured using the Uzgiris-Hunt (1975) test of object constancy.
  b. Self-awareness was assessed using a test of self-recognition developed by Bertenthal and Fischer (1978).
  c. Self–other differentiation was measured by the Agent-Use test developed by Watson and Fischer (1977). This procedure provides knowledge of children's rudimentary role-taking abilities in the context of imaginative, pretend play with other symbolic agents.

d. Interpersonal object relations were assessed in terms of the child's attachment relationship to the mother. Attachment was judged as secure versus insecure (anxious or ambivalent/avoidant) using a variant of the separation–reunion paradigm developed by Ainsworth, Blehar, and Waters (1978). The first three tests were administered to children in their homes at 14, 18, and 24 months of age. Attachment to the mother was measured in the laboratory at 26 months.

Children from BP and normal families performed similarly on tests of object permanence and self-recognition, each group showing normal developmental patterns of cognitive growth. However, on the Agent–Use test, where children from control families showed the normal developmental transition from a preference for imitating self-oriented actions during play to a preference for pretend play involving others in the environment (e.g., pretending to put self to sleep vs. putting a doll to sleep), children from BP families failed to show the normal developmental age changes. Children from BP families also were more frequently judged insecure in their attachment relationship to the mother at age 26 months (86% in bipolar families vs. 30% in controls, $p < .05$). Early impairments in object relations were thus manifested in tasks that involved interactions with real or symbolic others.

DISCUSSION

The data presented (which include material on genetics, family studies, epidemiology, and biological studies in samples of adults and children) provide material germane to the central theme of this chapter, namely, continuity and discontinuity of affective illness, that is, are these disorders seen and diagnosed in childhood identical with the same disorders seen in adults? Since our sample of infants of BP parents was small, the findings are only preliminary. Nevertheless, definite trends are evident. Already at the age of 12 months the infants of manic–depressive parents show disturbances in attachment behavior and dysregulation of affect, which become more pronounced with advancing age and are similar to the central characteristics of adults with affective illness. The characteristics include disturbed interpersonal relations marked by conflict, instability, and dissatisfaction as well as difficulties in handling emotions, particularly sadness and anger, and in maintaining emotional homeostasis. The above characteristics of infants, toddlers, and adults may be related to the quintessential clinical features of depressive disorders: anhedonia and dysphoria.

By the age of 5–6 years, we can begin to make diagnoses of mood disorders using modified adult assessment instruments and unmodified adult diagnostic criteria. In addition to the clinical similarity, there are certain biological features common to both child and adult mood disorders as previously mentioned. These include hypersecretion of cortisol, positive dexamethasone suppression test, hypersecretion of growth hormone in sleep, diminished growth hormone response to an insulin tolerance test, and diminished 24-hr MHPG excretion in the urine. The BP children, like their adult counterparts, had a strongly augmented AER to sensory stimuli.

Additionally, children with major UP or BP disorders respond to the same medication as do adults, although the evidence is still preliminary. There have been only several sound studies of the efficacy of tricyclic antidepressants in children (Geller, Perel, Knitter, & Lycak, in press; Preskorn, Weller, & Weller, 1982; Puig-Antich *et al.*, in press). These reports show that clinical responses of children with major depressive disorders to tricyclic antidepressants are significantly related to plasma levels of these drugs, as is true in adults with depressive illness. BP or manic–depressive disorder is rare in childhood (Anthony & Scott, 1960), but there are well-documented case reports describing good clinical response to lithium in children with manic–depressive disorders (Berg, Hullen, Allsopp, O'Brien, & MacDonald, 1974; Feinstein & Wolpert, 1973; Kelly, Koch, & Bulgel, 1976; McKnew *et al.*, 1981; Warneke, 1975; Youngerman & Canino, 1978). Compared to the rich if sometimes conflicting material available on the epidemiology of affective illness in adults, similar information on children is relatively modest. However, the study of children in New Zealand indicates the occurrence of depressive disorders in young children. In addition, our offspring studies indicate that prepubertal children of parents with affective illness are at a similar risk to develop mood disorders as adult offspring of such parents. Although the follow-up of children has generally been inadequate, the few studies done suggest that in prepubertal children mood disorders often continue into adolescence. Finally, the issue of loss is one that runs through discussions of the etiology of depression in all age groups (see Bowlby, 1980; Brown, Harris, and Bifulco (Chapter 9 of this volume); Freud, 1917/1957; McKnew & Cytryn, 1973; Spitz, 1946).

The concept of discontinuity, that is, that the affective disorders as seen in infancy and childhood are clinically similar but fundamentally independent from those disorders in adulthood, also finds support in the evidence presented in this chapter. During infancy, depressive illness as we know it in older children and adults does not occur. However, when life stresses are overwhelming and of long duration, then the infant may develop a primitive depressive state, characterized by a sad face, withdrawal, failure to interact, and even refusal of food. Spitz described such extreme response to separation from mother in the second half of the first year as "anaclitic depression" (Spitz, 1946). George Engel, in his famous study of Monica, named her affective withdrawal to threatening situations "conservation–withdrawal," which he conceptualizes as a biological response akin to hibernation (Engel & Reichsman, 1956). Finally Bowlby (1980) in analyzing the behavior of children ages 6 months to 3 years who were separated from their mothers noticed that following a period of vigorous protest, there ensued a period he termed "despair," associated with social withdrawal, sad facial expression, whimpering, and refusal to eat. All the aforementioned disorders followed massive traumata. In toddlers we still fail to see depressive illness diagnosable by standard operational criteria; although the possible precursors, difficulty with attachment behavior and affect dysregulation, do occur. Finally, even though there is a fascinating putative connection between precursors of affective illness in infants and toddlers and their adult counterparts, there are no studies demonstrating a true and consistent link between such precursors and later adult affective illness, or any other form of psychopathology.

Despite the fact that affective disorders can be properly diagnosed after the age of 5, psychotic and manic states prior to adolescence are only rarely seen. In contrast to the generally accepted higher prevalence of depression in females over males (except in BP) in adults, no such sex disparity has yet emerged from either epidemiological or offspring studies in children. Although suicidal ideation is frequently present in depressed children, suicidal attempts almost never occur prior to adolescence.

Many of the issues reviewed concerning continuity and discontinuity can probably be explained from a developmental perspective. The absence of a true affective illness (as we know it in children and adults) in infants and toddlers may be due to cognitive and emotional immaturity. The lack of a sex disparity of affective illness prior to adolescence may be due to sex hormones which exert a major influence on the sex differences at a later age, playing a relatively minor role prior to adolescence. Alternatively, it may reflect the emergence, during adolescence, of strong differential socialization pressures for boys and girls.

In conclusion, despite a gratifying increase in research on affective illness (as evidenced by all the contributions to this volume), the central issue of continuity and discontinuity of affective disorders in children and adults must still await definitive answers, which seems to require at least two crucial developments: (1) the discovery of a reliable genetic marker already detectable in infancy and early childhood and phenotypically independent; (2) well-designed longitudinal, developmental studies of children at risk, based on valuable information already furnished by largely cross-sectional studies reviewed in this chapter. We agree with Garmezy (1974a, 1974b) that only follow-up or rather follow-through studies may bring us closer to the solution of the continuity versus discontinuity issue in all psychiatric risk studies.

REFERENCES

Ainsworth, M. D. S., Blehar, M. C., & Waters, E. (1978). *Patterns of attachment: A psychological study of the strange situation.* Hillsdale, NJ: Lawrence Erlbaum Associates.

Ainsworth, M. D. S., & Wittig, B. (1969). Attachment and explanatory behavior of one-year-olds in a strange situation. In B. Foss (Ed.), *Determinants of infant behavior* (Vol. 4). London: Methuen.

American Psychiatric Association. (1980). *Diagnostic and statistical manual of mental disorders* (3rd ed.). Washington, DC: American Psychiatric Association.

Anthony, E. J. (1974). The syndrome of the psychologically invulnerable child. In E. J. Anthony & C. Koupernik (Eds.), *The child in his family: Children at psychiatric risk.* New York: Wiley.

Anthony, E. J. (1975). Childhood depression. In E. J. Anthony & T. Benedek (Eds.), *Depression and human existence.* Boston: Little, Brown.

Anthony, E. J., & Scott, P. (1960). Manic–depressive psychosis in childhood. *Journal of Child Psychology and Psychiatry, 1,* 53–72.

Apter, A., Borengasser, M. A., Hamovit, J., Bartko, J. J., Cytryn L., & McKnew, D. H. (1982). A four-year follow-up of depressed children. *Journal of Preventive Psychiatry, 1,* 331–335.

Bebbington, P. E. (1978). The epidemiology of depressive disorders. *Culture Medicine and Psychiatry, 2,* 297–341.

Beckman, G., Beckman, L., Cedergren, B., Perris, C., Strandman, E., & Wahlby, L. (1978). Genetic markers in cycloid psychosis. *Neuropsychobiology, 4,* 276–282.

Berg, I., Hullen, R., Allsopp, M., O'Brien, P., & MacDonald, R. (1974). Bipolar manic–depressive psychosis in early adolescence. *British Journal of Psychiatry, 125,* 416–417.

Berrettini, W. H., Nurnberger, J. I., Jr., Hare, T., Gershon, E. S., Post, R. M. (1982). Plasma and CSF GABA in affective illness. *British Journal of Psychiatry, 141,* 483–488.

Berrettini, W. H., Nurnberger, J. I., Jr., Post, R. M., & Gershon, E. S. (1982). Platelet ^{3}H-imipramine binding in euthymic bipolar patients. *Psychiatry Research, 7,* 215–219.

Bertenthal, B. I., & Fischer, K. W. (1978). The development of self-recognition in the infant. *Developmental Psychology, 14,* 44–50.

Bowlby, L. (1980). Attachment and loss. In *Loss, sadness and depression* (Vol. 3). New York: Basic Books.

Brown, G. W., Bhrolchain, M. N., & Harris, T. (1975). Social class and psychiatric disturbance among women in an urban population. *Sociology, 9,* 225–254.

Buchsbaum, M. S. (1978). The average evoked response technique in differentiation of bipolar, unipolar and schizophrenic disorders. In H. Akiskal (Ed.), *Psychiatric diagnosis: Exploration of biological criteria.* New York: Spectrum.

Buchsbaum, M. S. (1979). Neurophysiological reactivity, stimulus intensity modulation and the depressive disorders. In R. A. Depue (Ed.), *The psychobiology of the depressive disorders: Implications for the effects of stress.* New York: Academic Press.

Buchsbaum, M. S., Goodwin, F. K., Murphy, D. L., & Borge, G. (1971). AER in affective disorders. *American Journal of Psychiatry, 128,* 19–25.

Clayton, P. (1978). Bipolar affective disorder: Techniques and results of treatment. *American Journal of Psychotherapy, 32,* 81–92.

Comings, D. E. (1979). Pc 1 Duarte, a common polymorphism of a human brain protein, and its relationship to depressive disease and multiple sclerosis. *Nature (London), 277,* 28–32.

Comstock, G. W., & Helsin, K. J. (1976). Symptoms of depression in two communities. *Psychological Medicine, 6,* 551–563.

Conners, C. K., Himmelhoch, J., Goyette, C. H., Ulrich, R., & Neil, J. F. (1979). Children of parents with affective illness. *Journal of the American Academy of Child Psychiatry, 18,* 600–607.

Craig, T. J., & Van Natta, P. A. (1976). Presence and persistence of depressive symptoms in patient and community populations. *American Journal of Psychiatry, 133*, 1426–1429.

Craig, T. J., & Van Natta, P. A. (1979). Influence of demographic characteristics on two measures of depressive symptoms: The relation of prevalence and persistence of symptoms with sex, age, education, and marital status. *Archives of General Psychiatry, 36*, 149–154.

Cytryn, L., McKnew, D. H., Logue, M., & Desai, R. B. (1974). Biochemical correlations of affective disorders. *Archives of General Psychiatry, 31*, 659–661.

Cytryn, L., McKnew, D. H., Bartko, J. J., Lamour, M., & Hamovit, J. (1982). Offspring of patients with affective disorders. II. *Journal of the American Academy of Child Psychiatry, 21*, 389–391.

Cytryn, L., McKnew, D. H., Zahn-Waxler, C., Radke-Yarrow, M., Gaensbauer, T. J., Harmon, R. J., & Lamour, M. (1984). Affective disturbances in the offspring of affectively ill patients—a developmental view. *American Journal of Psychiatry, 141*, 219–222.

Dorus, E., Pandey, G. N., Shaughnessey, R., Gaviria, M., Val, E., Eriksen, S., & Davis, J. M. (1979). Lithium transport across the red cell membrane: A cell membrane abnormality in manic–depressive illness. *Science, 205*, 932–934.

Egelund, J. A. (1980, December). *Affective disorders among the Amish: 1976–1980.* Presented at the annual meeting of the American College of Neuropsychopharmacology, Puerto Rico.

El-Guebaly, N., Offord, D. R., Sullivan, K. T., & Lynch, G. W. (1978). Psychosocial adjustment of the offspring of psychiatric inpatients: The effect of alcoholic, depressive and schizophrenic parentage. *Journal of the Canadian Psychiatric Association, 23*, 281–289.

Endicott, J., & Spitzer, R. L. (1978). A diagnostic interview: The schedule for affective disorders and schizophrenia. *Archives of General Psychiatry, 35*, 837–844.

Engel, G. L., & Reichsman, F. (1956). Spontaneous and experimentally induced depression in an infant with gastric fistula. *Journal of the American Psychoanalytic Association, 4*, 428–452.

Feinstein, S., & Wolpert, E. (1973). Juvenile manic–depressive illness. *Journal of the American Academy of Child Psychiatry, 12*, 123–136.

Freud, S. Mourning and melancholia. In J. Strachey (Ed.), *The standard edition of the complete psychological works of Sigmund Freud* (Vol. 14). London: Hogarth Press. (Original work published 1917).

Gaensbauer, T. J., Harmon, R. J., Cytryn, L., McKnew, D. H. (1984). Social/affective development in proband infants: Study of infants of parents with bipolar illness. *American Journal of Psychiatry, 141*, 223–230.

Gaensbauer, T. J., & Harmon, R. J. (1981). Clinical assessment in infancy utilizing structured playroom situations. *Journal of the American Academy of Child Psychiatry, 20*, 264–280.

Garmezy, N. (1974a). Children at risk. The search for the antecedents of schizophrenia. Part I. *Schizophrenia Bulletin, 8*, 14–91.

Garmezy, N. (1974b). The search for the antecedents of schizophrenia. Part II. *Schizophrenia Bulletin, 9*, 55–126.

Geller, B., Perel, J., Knitter, E., & Lycak, H. (in press). Nortryptiline in major depressive disorders in children. *Psychopharmacology Bulletin.*

Gershon, E. S., Nurnberger, J., Nadi, N. S., Berrettini, W. H., Goldin, L. R. (1983). *The origins of depression: Current concepts and approaches.* New York: Springer-Verlag. (Berlin: Dahlem Konferenzen, 1982.)

Gershon, E. S., Bunney, W. E., Jr., Leckman, J. F., van Eerdewegh, M., & Debauche, B. A. (1976). The inheritance of affective disorders: A review of data and of hypotheses. *Behavior Genetics, 6*, 227–261.

Gershon, E. S., Goldin, L. R., Lake, C. R., Murphy, D. L., & Guroff, J. J. (1980). Genetics of plasma dopamine-B-hydroxylase (DBH), erythrocyte catechol-O-methyltransferase (COMT), and platelet monoamine oxidase (MAO) in pedigrees of patients with affective disorders. In E. Usdin, P. Sourkes, & M. B. H. Youdim (Eds.), *Enzymes and neurotransmitters and mental disease*. London: Wiley.

Gershon, E. S., Goldin, L. R., Weissman, M. M., & Nurnberger, J. I., Jr. (1981, July). *Family and genetic studies of affective disorders in the Eastern United States: A provisional summary*. Presented at the third World Congress on Biological Psychiatry, Stockholm, Sweden.

Gershon, E. S., Hamovit, J., Guroff, J. J., Dibble, E. D., Leckman, J., Sceery, W., Targum, S. D., Nurnberger, J. I., Jr., Goldin, L., & Bunney, W. E., Jr. (1982). A family study of schizo-affective, bipolar I, bipolar II, unipolar probands and normal controls. *Archives of General Psychiatry, 39,* 1157–1167.

Gershon, E. S., Targum, S. D., Kessler, L. R., Mazure, C. M., & Bunney, W. E., Jr. (1977). Genetic studies and biologic strategies in the affective disorders. *Progress in Medical Genetics, 2,* 101–164.

Gershon, E. S., Targum, S. D., Matthysse, S., & Bunney, W. E., Jr. (1979). Color blindness not closely linked to bipolar illness. *Archives of General Psychiatry, 36,* 1423–1434.

Greenhill, L. L., & Shopsin, B. (1979). Survey of mental disorders in the children of patients with affective disorders. In J. Mendlewicz & B. Shopsin (Eds.), *Genetic aspects of affective illness*. New York: Spectrum.

Grewel, F. (1967). Psychiatric differences in Ashkenazim and Sephardim. *Psychiatria, Neurologia, Neurochirurgia, 70,* 339–347.

Grunebaum, H., Cohler, B. J., Kauffman, C., & Gallant, D. (1978). Children of depressed and schizophrenic mothers. *Child Psychiatry and Human Development, 8,* 219–228.

Harmon, R. J., & Culp, A. M. (1981). The effects of premature birth on family functioning and infant development. In I. Berlin (Ed.), *Children and our future*. Albuquerque: University of New Mexico Press.

Hirschfeld, R. M. A., & Cross, C. K. (1982). Epidemiology of affective disorders. *Archives of General Psychiatry, 39,* 35–46.

Hoover, C. F., & Fitzgerald, R. G. (1980). Marital conflict of manic–depressive patients. *Archives of General Psychiatry, 198,* 65–67.

Ilfeld, F. W. (1977). Current social stressors and symptoms of depression. *American Journal of Psychiatry, 134,* 161–166.

Janowsky, D. S., Risch, C. D., Parker, D., Huey, L., & Judd, L. (1980). Increased vulnerability to cholinergic stimulation in affective disorder patient. *Psychopharmacology Bulletin, 16,* 29–31.

Kashani, J. H., McGee, R. D., Clarkson, S. E., Anderson, J. C., Walton, L. E., William, S., Silva, P. A., Robins, A. J., Cytryn, L., & McKnew, D. H. (1983). Depression in a sample of nine year old children: Prevalence and associated characteristics. *Archives of General Psychiatry, 40,* 1217–1227.

Kashani, J. H., & Simonds, J. F. (1979). The incidence of depression in children. *American Journal of Psychiatry, 136,* 1203–1205.

Kauffman, C., Grunebaum, H., Cohler, B., & Gamer, E. (1979). Superkids: Competent children of psychotic mothers. *American Journal of Psychiatry, 11,* 1398–1402.

Kelly, J., Koch, M., & Buegel, D. (1976). Lithium carbonate in juvenile manic–depressive illness. *Diseases of the Nervous System, 37,* 90–92.

Kokes, R. F., Harder, D. W., Fisher, L., & Strauss, J. S. (1980). Child competence and psychiatric risk. *Journal of Nervous Mental Disorders, 168,* 348–352.

Kuyler, P. L., Rosenthal, L., Igel, G., Dunner, D. L., & Fieve, R. R. (1980). Psychopathology among children of manic–depressive patients. *Biological Psychiatry, 15,* 589–597.

Leckman, J. F., Gershon, E. S., McGinnis, M. H., Targum, S. D., & Dibble, E. D. (1979). New data do not suggest linkage between the Xg blood group and bipolar illness. *Archives of General Psychiatry, 36*, 1435–1441.

Maas, J. W., Dekirmenjian, H., & Fawcett, J. (1971). Catecholamine metabolism, depression and stress. *Nature (London), 230*, 330–331.

Maas, J. W., Fawcett, J., & Dekirmenjian, H. (1968). 3-methoxy-4-hydroxy-phenylglycol (MHPG) excretion in depressive states. *Archives of General Psychiatry, 19*, 129–134.

MacMahon, F., & Pugh, T. F. (1970). *Epidemiology: Principles and methods.* Boston: Little, Brown.

Mazure, C., & Gershon, E. S. (1979). Blindness and reliability in lifetime psychiatric diagnosis. *Archives of General Psychiatry, 36*, 521–525.

McKnew, D. H., & Cytryn, L. (1973). Historical background in children with affective disorders. *American Journal of Psychiatry, 130*, 1278–1279.

McKnew, D. H., & Cytryn, L. (1979). Urinary metabolites in chronically depressed children. *Journal of the American Academy of Child Psychiatry, 18*, 608–615.

McKnew, D. H., Cytryn, L., Efron, A. M., Gershon, E. S., & Bunney, W. E., Jr. (1979). Offspring of manic–depressive patients. *British Journal of Psychiatry, 134*, 148–152.

McKnew, D. H., Cytryn, L., Rapoport, J., Buchsbaum, M., Gershon, E. S., Lamour, M., & Hamovit, J. (1981). Lithium in children of lithium responding parents. *Psychiatry Research, 4*, 171–180.

Mendels, J. (1970). *Concepts in depression.* New York: Wiley.

Mendlewicz, J., Fleiss, J. L., & Fieve, R. R. (1972). Evidence for x-linkage in the transmission of manic–depressive illness. *JAMA, Journal of the American Medical Association, 222*, 1624–1627.

Mendlewicz, J., Fleiss, J. L., & Fieve, R. R. (1975). Linkage studies in affective disorders. The Xg blood group and manic–depressive illness. In R. R. Fieve, D. Rosenthal, & H. Brill (Eds.), *Genetics and psychopathology.* Baltimore: Johns Hopkins University Press.

Mendlewicz, J., Linkowski, P., Guroff, J. J., & van Pragg, H. M. (1979). Color blindness linkage to bipolar manic–depressive illness. *Archives of General Psychiatry, 36*, 1442–1449.

Mendlewicz, J., Linkowski, P., & Wilmette, J. (1980). Linkage between glucose-6-phosphate dehydrogenase deficiency and manic–depressive psychosis. *British Journal of Psychiatry, 137*, 337–342.

Nadi, N. S., Nurnberger, J. I., & Gershon, E. S. (1984). Mascarinic cholinergic receptors on skin, fibroblasts in familial affective disorder. *New England Journal of Medicine, 311*, 225–230.

Nurnberger, J. I., Jr., & Gershon, E. S. (1982). Genetics. In E. S. Paykel (Ed.), *Handbook of affective disorders.* Edinburgh & London: Churchill-Livingstone.

Nurnberger, J. I., Jr., Pandey, G., & Gershon, E. S. (1982, May). *Lithium ratio in psychiatric patients: A caveat.* Presented at the annual meeting of the American Psychiatric Association, Toronto, Canada.

O'Connell, R. A., Mays, J. A., O'Brien, J. D., & Mirsheidaie, F. (1979). Children of bipolar manic–depressives. In J. Mendlewicz & B. Shopsin (Eds.), *Genetic aspects of affective illness.* New York: Spectrum.

Orvaschel, H., Weissman, M. M., Padian, N., & Lowe, T. L. (1981). Assessing psychopathology in children of psychiatrically disturbed parents: A pilot study. *Journal of the American Academy of Child Psychiatry, 20*, 112–122.

Patrick, V., Dunner, D. L., & Rieve, R. R. (1978). Life events and primary affective illness. *Acta Psychiatrica Scandinavica, 58*, 48–55.

Paykel, E. S. (1978). Contribution of life events to causation of psychiatric illness. *Psychological Medicine, 8*, 245–254.

Paykel, E. S., Myers, J. K., & Dienelt, M. N. (1969). Life events and depression: A controlled study. *Archives of General Psychiatry, 21*, 753–760.

Paykel, E. S., & Tanner, J. (1976). Life events, depressive relapse, and maintenance treatment. *Psychological Medicine, 6*, 481–485.

Poznanski, E. O., Carroll, B. J., Bemejas, M. C., Cook, S. C., & Grossman, J. A. (1982). The dexamethasone suppression test in prepubertal depressed children. *American Journal of Psychiatry, 139*, 321–324.

Poznanski, E. O., Krahenbuhl, V., & Zrull, J. P. (1976). Childhood depression: A longitudinal perspective. *Journal of the American Academy of Child Psychiatry, 15*, 491–501.

Preskorn, S., Weller, E. B., & Weller, R. A. (1982). Depression in children; Relationship between plasma imipramine levels and response. *Journal of Clinical Psychiatry, 43*, 450–453.

Puig-Antich, J., & Chambers, W. (1978). *KIDDIE SADS—Schedule for affective disorders and schizophrenia for school-age children (6–16 years)* (2nd working draft). New York: New York State Psychiatric Institute.

Puig-Antich, J., Chambers, W., Halpern, F., Hanlon, C., & Sachar, E. J. (1979). Cortisol hypersecretion in prepubertal depressive illness: A preliminary report. *Psychoneuroendocrinology, 4*, 191–197.

Puig-Antich, J., Lupatkin, W., Chambers, W. J., King, J., Tabrizi, M., Davies, M., & Goetz, R. (in press). Imipramine effectiveness in prepubertal major depressive disorders. II. A double-blind placebo-controlled study. *Archives of General Psychiatry.*

Puig-Antich, J., Novacenko, H., Davies, M., Chambers, W. J., Tabrizi, M. A., Krawiec, V., Ambrosini, P. J., & Sachar, E. J. (1982, October). *Growth hormone secretion in prepubertal major depressive children in response to insulin induced hypoglycemia.* Paper presented at the annual meeting of the American Academy of Child Psychiatry, Washington, DC.

Puig-Antich, J., Tabrizi, M. A., Davies, M., Goetz, R., Chambers, W. J., Halpern, F., & Sachar, E. J. (1981). Prepubertal endogenous major depressives hyposecrete growth hormone in response to insulin-induced hypoglycemia. *Biological Psychiatry, 16*, 801–818.

Radloff, L. S., & Rae, D. S. (1979). Susceptibility and precipitating factors in depression: Sex differences and similarities. *Journal of Abnormal Psychology, 88*, 174–181.

Reich, T., Clayton, P. J., & Winokur, G. (1969). Family history studies. V. The genetics of mania. *American Journal of Psychiatry, 125*, 1358–1369.

Reich, T., James, J. W., & Morris, C. A. (1972). The use of multiple threshold in determining the mode of transmission of semi-continuous traits. *Annals of Human Genetics, 36*, 163–184.

Rieder, R., & Gershon, E. S. (1978). Genetic strategies in biological psychiatry. *Archives of General Psychiatry, 35*, 866–873.

Rolf, J. E. (1972). The social and academic competence of children vulnerable to schizophrenia and other behavior pathologies. *Journal of Abnormal Psychology, 80*, 225–243.

Rolf, J. E. (1976). Peer status and the directionality of symptomatic behavior: Social competence predictors of outcome for vulnerable children. *American Journal of Orthopsychiatry, 46*, 74–88.

Rolf, J. E., & Garmezy, N. (1974). The school performance of children vulnerable to behavior pathology. In M. Roff (Ed.), *Life history research in psychopathology* (Vol. 3). Minneapolis: University of Minnesota Press.

Rutter, M. (1966). *Children of sick parents: An environmental and psychiatric study* (Institute of Psychiatry Maudsley Monographs No. 16). London & New York: Oxford University Press.

Rutter, M., Tizard, J., & Whitmore, K. (1981). *Education, health and behaviour.* Huntington, NY: Krieger.

Rutter, M., Tizard, J., Yule, W., Graham, P., & Whitmore, K. (1976). Isle of Wight studies 1964–1974. *Psychological Medicine, 6*, 313–332.

Sedvall, G., Fyro, B., Gullberg, B., Nyback, H., Wiesel, F. A., & Wode-Helgodt, W. (1980). Relationships in healthy volunteers between concentrations of monoamine metabolites in cerebrospinal fluid and family history of psychiatric morbidity. *British Journal of Psychiatry, 136,* 366–374.

Sitaram, N., Moore, A. M., & Gillin, J. C. (1978). Experimental acceleration and slowing of REM sleep ultradian rhythm by cholinergic agonist and antagonist. *Nature (London), 274,* 490–492.

Sitaram, N., Nurnberger, J. I., Jr., Gershon, E. S., & Gillin, J. C. (1982). Cholinergic regulation of mood and REM sleep: Potential model and marker of vulnerability to affective disorder. *American Journal of Psychiatry, 139,* 571–576.

Smeraldi, E., Negri, F., Melica, A. M., Scorza-Smeraldi, R., Fabio, G., Bonara, P., Belledi, L., Sachetti, E., Sabbadini-Villa, M. G., Cazzullo, C. L., & Zanussi, C. (1978). HLA typing and affective disorders: A study in the Italian population. *Neuropsychobiology, 4,* 344–352.

Spitz, R. A. (1946). Anaclitic depression: An inquiry into the genesis of psychiatric conditions in early childhood. II. *Psychoanalytic Study of the Child, 2,* 313–324.

Spitzer, R. L., Endicott, J., & Robins, E. (1978). Research diagnostic criteria. *Archives of General Psychiatry, 35,* 773–782.

Steele, R. E. (1978). Relationship of race, sex, social class, and social mobility to depression in normal adults. *Journal of Social Psychology, 104,* 37–47.

Targum, S. D., Gershon, E. S., van Eerdewegh, M., & Rogentine, N. (1979). Human leukocyte antigen (HLA) system not closely linked to and associated with bipolar manic–depressive illness. *Biological Psychiatry, 14,* 615–636.

Temple, H., Dupont, B., & Shopsin, B. (1979). HLA antigen and affective disorders: A report and critical assessment of histocompatibility studies. *Neuropsychobiology, 5,* 50–58.

Thomson, K. C., Hendrie, H. C. (1972). Environmental stress in primary depressive illness. *Archives of General Psychiatry, 26,* 130–132.

Uzgiris, I. C., & Hunt, J. Mc. (1975). *Assessment in infancy.* Urbana: University of Illinois Press.

van Praag, H. M., & de Haan, S. (1979). Central serotonin metabolism and frequency of depression. *Psychiatry Research, 1,* 219–224.

Warheit, G. J. (1979). Life events, coping, stress and depressive symptomatology. *American Journal of Psychiatry, 136,* 502–507.

Warheit, G. J., Holzer, E. E., & Aroy, S. A. (1975). Race and mental illness: An epidemiologic update. *Journal of Health and Social Behavior, 16,* 243–256.

Warneke, L. (1975). A case of manic–depressive illness in childhood. *Canadian Psychiatric Association Journal, 20,* 195–200.

Watson, M. W., & Fischer, K. W. (1977). A developmental sequence of agent use in late infancy. *Child Development, 48,* 828–836.

Weinberg, W. A., Rutman, J., Sullivan, L., Penick, E. C., & Deitz, S. G. (1973). Depression in children referred to an educational diagnostic center: Diagnosis and treatment. *Journal of Pediatrics, 83,* 1065–1072.

Weintraub, S., Neale, J. M., & Liebert, D. E. (1975). Teacher ratings of children vulnerable to psychopathology. *American Journal of Orthopsychiatry, 45,* 839–845.

Weintraub, S., Prinz, R. J., & Neale, J. M. (1978). Peer evaluations of the competence of children vulnerable to psychopathology. *Journal of Abnormal Child Psychology, 6,* 461–473.

Weissman, M. M., Gershon, E. S., Kidd, K. K., Prusoff, B. A., Leckman, J. F., Thompson, W. D., Pauls, D., Dibble, E. D., Guroff, J. J., & Hamovit, J. (1984). Psychiatric disorders in the relatives of probands with affective disorders. *Archives of General Psychiatry, 41,* 13–21.

Weissman, M. M., & Klerman, G. L. (1977). Sex differences and the epidemiology of depression. *Archives of General Psychiatry, 34,* 98–111.

Weissman, M. M., & Myers, J. K. (1978). Rates and risks of depressive symptoms in a United States urban community. *Acta Psychiatrica Scandinavica, 57,* 219–231.

Weissman, M. M., & Siegel, R. (1972). The depressed woman and her rebellious adolescent. *Social Casework, 53*, 563–570.

Welner, Z., Welner, A., McCrary, M. D., & Leonard, M. A. (1977). Psychopathology in children of inpatients with depression: A controlled study. *Journal of Nervous and Mental Disease, 164*, 408–413.

Winokur, G., & Tanna, V. L. (1969). Possible role of x-linked dominant factor in manic–depressive disease. *Diseases of the Nervous System, 30*, 87–94.

Youngerman, J., & Canino, I. (1978). Lithium carbonate use in children and adolescents. Archives of General Psychiatry, 35, 217–227.

Zahn-Waxler, C., Chapman, M., Cummings, E. M., & Cytryn, L. (1982). *Cognitive and social development in infants and toddlers with a bipolar parent.* Presented at the annual meeting of the American Academy of Child Psychiatry, Washington, DC.

Zahn-Waxler, C., Cummings, E. M., McKnew, D. H., & Radke-Yarrow, M. (1984). Affective arousal and social interaction in young children of manic–depressive parents. *Child Development, 55*, 112–122.

Zahn-Waxler, C., McKnew, D. H., Cummings, E. M., Davenport, Y. B., & Radke-Yarrow, M. (1984). Problem behaviors and peer interactions of young children with a manic–depressive parent. *American Journal of Psychiatry, 141*, 236–240.

The Need for the Study of Adaptation in the Children of Parents with Affective Disorders

William R. Beardslee

INTRODUCTION

From the perspective of a clinical child psychiatrist, much of the interest in childhood depression derives not so much inductively from the study of children, but rather from the application to children of advances in the study of adult affective disorder. Such advances have made possible a remarkable growth in the knowledge of the epidemiology of affective illness (Boyd & Weissman, 1981), its genetics (Nurnberger & Gershon, 1982), its naturalistic course and outcome (Keller, Lavoie, Endicott, Coryell, & Klerman, 1983; Keller & Shapiro, 1981; Shapiro & Keller, 1981), its biological substrata, and above all, its treatment using tricyclic antidepressants and lithium salts in combination with psychotherapy. A cornerstone of these advances is the assessment of affective disorder according to strict diagnostic criteria such as the Research Diagnostic Criteria (RDC) (Spitzer & Endicott, 1977; Spitzer, Endicott, & Robins, 1978) using standardized interview instruments such as the Schedule of Affective Disorders and Schizophrenia (SADS). Similar structured research interviews, such as the KIDDIE SADS (Puig-Antich & Chambers, 1978) or the Diagnostic Interview for Children and Adolescents (Herjanic & Campbell, 1977; Herjanic, Herjanic, Brown, & Wheatt, 1975) have recently been developed for the assessment of psychopathology in children and adolescents.

Researchers have begun the examination of the biological and interpersonal manifestation of depressive disorder in children and ado-

William R. Beardslee. Department of Psychiatry, Massachusetts General Hospital, Boston, Massachusetts.

lescents in the areas similar to those in which abnormalities have been described in adults. A fundamental underlying hope is that pharmacologic treatment regimes that have proven successful with adults can be applied to children with severe affective disorder. The interest in depression in children and adolescents, combined with the repeated clinical observation that depressed children frequently have parents who are depressed (Beardslee, Bemporad, & Famularo, 1984; McKnew & Cytryn, 1979; Philips, 1979) has led researchers in several centers, including our own, to study children at particular risk for affective disorder because of having a parent with affective disorder. This research focuses on the presence or absence of diagnostic entities, particularly affective disorders, as the main outcome variable.

However, there is much to be learned in studying dimensions besides the presence or absence of diagnoses in these children. The study of adaptation is one such dimension. This chapter will explore the proposition that while the investigation of affective disorder and its precursors is essential in this risk population, the study of the child's or adolescent's adaptation is a necessary complement to the study of diagnosis. Adaptation refers to both adaptive behavior evident in cross-sectional assessment and the traits, or coping processes, that underlie the behavior. To focus on one outcome, the diagnosis of depression, is too narrow and specific. It is true that the study of adaptation is complicated. Further, widely used and standardized interview instruments and rating scales are not available. However, children and adolescents may respond in a wide variety of ways to the actions of a depressed parent and may establish a range of traits and interactive patterns that lead to later adaptive, or maladaptive behavior and various clinical states in later life.

The study of depression and of adaptation proceeds from somewhat different conceptual bases. The concept of vulnerability to depression in the child requires the study of the genetics of the disorder, precursor states of childhood depression, possible manifestations of the depression other than those contained in the diagnostic criteria, and the course and outcome of the disorder. The concept of adaptation to the stress of parental illness implies an interest in the factors that mitigate against the development of illness and enable the child to withstand the impact of parental disorder.

PREDICTIONS OF LATER OUTCOME
AND LIMITATIONS OF DIAGNOSIS

The risk researcher inherently must have a longitudinal interest as well as a cross-sectional one. Researchers would like to know not only how many children are impaired at a particular point in time and in what ways, but also the predictive value of that impairment, or the lack of it, for the later occurrence of affective disorder. In any sample of children at risk for depression because of parental illness much of the sample will not have passed through the age of morbid risk for the occurrence of depression itself when studied, and thus an interest in follow-up is necessary. The long-term predictive validity of DSM-III diagnostic categories in childhood remains to be demonstrated. This is especially true for the diagnostic category of depression. There is quite limited evidence about the long-term implications of childhood and adolescent depression as it has only recently been recognized as a valid diagnostic entity in childhood and adolescence. Various kinds of withdrawing behavior in childhood and adolescence have been recognized as forms of childhood psychopathology for a much longer time. However, follow-up studies have shown that symptoms and states of withdrawal behavior are exremely poor predictors for later difficulties. There is evidence from the work of Robins (1966), Glueck and Glueck (1950), McCord and McCord (1966), and others that antisocial symptoms best identify children who will have difficulty in later life. This is not to suggest that childhood depression in its current, carefully defined state is similar to the older category of withdrawn behavior, but rather to emphasize that much remains to be learned about the course of the diagnostic entity of childhood depression.

The study of overall psychosocial functioning would appear to be a more known predictor of later outcome than an actual diagnostic category. Kohlberg, in his classic review, observed that the best predictors of good adult mental health and absence of maladjustment are the presence of various forms of competence in childhood, rather than the lack of difficulties in childhood and adolescence.

Data from Vaillant's 35-year longitudinal study of normal development are particularly relevant, since this study focused on observable behavioral outcomes, or competencies, in childhood and behavioral and diagnostic outcomes in adulthood (Vaillant & Vaillant, 1981). This focus on competence is similar to the approach risk researchers have used, as will become evident. Vaillant studied 456 men who were identified in the years 1940–1945 as controls for a study by Glueck and Glueck (1950) of juvenile delinquency. The men were identified as inner-city junior high school youngsters from poor or underprivileged backgrounds at the time of entry into the study. They were followed for more than 25 years with multiple, objective outcome measures. Scales were developed by Vaillant to rate competence, or adaptive behavior, in adolescence and included such areas as success in part-time jobs, participation in household chores, participation in extracurricular activities, good work in school, and demonstration of the ability to plan. An overall competence rating from these scales correlated significantly with positive adult outcomes as measured by indices of both physical and mental health and of productivity in work. Multiple regression analyses of a wide variety of variables demonstrated that, according to this measure, competence in childhood and adolescence, the presence of childhood environmental strengths, and the absence of emotional problems accounted for the majority of the explained variance as to who succeeded and who did not, although, of course, in the 35-year follow-up study this explained a small percentage of the overall variance. Vaillant concludes that "things that go right in our lives do not predict future successes and the events that go wrong in our lives do not forever damn us" (Vaillant & Vaillant, 1981, p. 1438).

Aside from the predictive issue, another limitation of using diagnosis as the sole outcome variable is the fact that diagnosis per se does not take account of the severity of an impairment. Some diagnoses carry with them the implication of major severe impairment (childhood schizophrenia, or anorexia nervosa, for example), while others (the anxiety states or enuresis) do not. Finally,the occurrence of symptomatology in the affective area takes a place on a continuum of both severity and chronicity, while diagnosis involves a specific threshold or cutoff point for both, a dichotomy for those who have it and those who do not. We simply do not know where that cutoff point should be set for childhood depression. Indeed, recurrent short episodes of affective symptomatology may be both more impairing and better predictors of later disorders than a single longer episode. The study of adaptive behavior offers a continuum along which to describe the youngsters, rather than the presence–absence dichotomy of diagnosis.

THE OPPORTUNITY IN RISK RESEARCH

Risk research offers an opportunity for the study of adaptation because of the population studied, namely, the entire sample at risk. In any risk sample there will be children who are manifesting difficulties, but there will also be many who, at any one point in time, are not. The investigation of parameters beyond the presence or absence of diagnosis offers an opportunity to describe how they are adapting or dealing with stress, in this case having an ill parent. More importantly, the underlying aim of risk research is to develop strategies for the primary prevention of illness. Studying what is *in vivo* protective, that is, what characterizes those children who are at high risk and are doing well, is a first step in understanding what is needed in intervention strategies. Moreover, it may well be that intervention strategies should, in part, try to encourage or develop in children those behaviors and traits which characterize children at high risk who are doing well.

A PERSPECTIVE ON THE RISK RESEARCH LITERATURE

A full review of the literature on children at risk because of parent illness is beyond the scope of this chapter, but selected studies are relevant for the inclusion of the study of adaptation. It has been conclusively demonstrated that the children of parents with major psychiatric disorder do manifest significant dysfunction in a variety of ways, more so than control groups (Buck & Laughton, 1959; Cooper, Leach, Storer, & Tonge, 1977; Ekdahl, Rice, & Schmidt, 1962; Landau, Harth, Othray, & Sharfhertz, 1972). Children at risk because of having a parent with schizophrenia have received special attention and have been reviewed by Garmezy (1974, 1978). Garmezy and Devine (1984) have described some youngsters doing unusually well in spite of the stress of having a schizophrenic parent. This literature on children of schizophrenic parents interests investigators studying children of parents with affective disorders.

The existing literature on children of parents with major affective disorder is much smaller. It consists of two kinds of studies—those in which the children were examined in cross-sectional designs as the primary focus of the study and those in which the children of affectively ill parents were included as a kind of comparison or control group for other risk groups. A review of this literature by our research team in Boston (Beardslee, Bemporad, Keller, & Klerman, 1983) has demonstrated that although the studies differ considerably in terms of the instruments employed, the severity and course of parental affective disorder, and the outcome measures, there is a convergence of findings. There is quite a high level of impairment in the children of affectively ill parents, both those with depression and manic–depressive disorder. The impairments the children manifest occur in many areas of functioning and occur at all stages and ages in development. Infancy and adolescence appear to be stages of particular difficulty for children. Some studies, involving young school-aged children, present evidence that the youngsters at risk turn out severely impaired.

Only a few studies have compared rates of difficulty in an experimental and a comparison group based on face to face interviews with mother and/or child. For example, according to Weissman and her associates (Weissman, Paykel, & Klerman, 1972; Weissman & Siegel, 1972), depressed mothers report having significant problems with their adolescents in 17–23 cases, while nondepressed mothers report difficulty in only three cases. Welner, Welner, McCrary, and Leonard (1977), in a study of children whose parents have been recently hospitalized for depression and in which there was a specific search for depression, found depression in 7% of the experimental group and none in the comparison group and also found significantly higher rates of depressive symptomatology in the experimental group.

The question of the difference in rate of impairment between the at-risk and comparison groups cannot be answered until more work is completed. There is a need for more systematic studies in the area that employ standard assessment techniques, so that results may be compared across studies. Such studies are now underway in a number of centers. Also, there is a need for studies that examine a range of outcomes in the youngsters.

Three studies deserve special mention. Rolf (1972, 1976) and Garmezy have examined extensively four groups of children in Minnesota: children of schizophrenics, children of internalizing (described as largely depressed) mothers, externalizing children, and internalizing children, using peer ratings, teacher ratings, and school records. These dimensions are combined into overall competency ratings. Their initial findings suggested the opposite of a number of other studies, namely, that the children of internalizing mothers most clearly resemble controls rather than the other risk groups. The children studied were ages 9–11. Follow-up of this cohort and another similar one presents opposing findings. The follow-up was conducted by Herbert under Garmezy's direction, using school records and interviews with school personnel from junior high schools, which were combined to an overall outcome rating (Garmezy & Devine, 1984). Only 48% of the children of depressed mothers received an overall good outcome score as opposed to 82% for the controls. The findings demonstrate that in adolescence the children of depressed mothers experience particular difficulty, while at earlier developmental stages they do not manifest difficulties.

In Boston, Grunebaum, Cohler, Kauffman, and Gallant (1978) have followed a cohort of children of psychotic mothers over many years, using both cognitive measures and measures of overall functioning. They have noted a particularly high risk to the children of psychotically depressed mothers. In a recent paper entitled "Superkids: Competent Children of Psychotic Mothers," the group reported on a follow-up of these children. (Kauffman, Grunebaum, Cohler, & Gamer, 1979). The children were ranked according to scores on psychological tests, interviews, and summary ratings derived from Anthony's six-point competency scale. Five of the six most competent children were children of schizoaffective or schizophrenic disordered mothers, while five of the six least competent children were children of depressed mothers. Five of the six most competent children reported extensive contact with adults outside the family. Each of the six had received caring attention from parents, while such attention was absent from the history of the less competent children. The highly competent children were more competent and creative than their controls. This research suggests important social dimensions beyond diagnosis that have implications for understanding how competent children develop in the population of children of mentally ill parents, while at the same time documenting risk to the children of depressed parents. It emphasizes the importance of the interactive view similar to that proposed by Emde for an earlier developmental stage.

The data from Wynne's project in Rochester emphasize somewhat different aspects of the nature of risk to the children, while also pointing to the risk to the children of depressed parents. It also raises a crucial question for risk research with depressed parents, which is the specificity or nonspecificity of risk to the child when the parent is depressed. Wynne and associates (Fisher, Harder, & Kokes, 1980; Fisher & Jones, 1980; Harder, Kokes, Fisher, & Strauss, 1980; Kokes, Harder, Fisher, & Strauss, 1980) have used teacher and peer rating measures of competence as outcomes, and parental diagnosis, family communication, deviance and interactive pathology, and severity and chronicity of illness as dependent variables. Four groups of children were studied in a short-term longitudinal design of children of affectively ill psychotic parents, mostly of narrow- and broad-band schizophrenic parents and children of nonpsychotic ill parents, many of whom have depression. The subjects were boys ages 7 and 10. The group that appears to be doing most well is the children of affectively ill psychotic parents, while those in most trouble are the children of nonpsychotic ill parents. Independent of diagnostic status in the parent, family communication deviance is consistent with the outcome of competence in the children. Moreover, it is the overall impairment in functioning of the parent, not diagnostic category, that most clearly relates to competence as an outcome. The aforementioned studies demonstrate the usefulness of measures of competence as a useful outcome. None has reported systematic diagnostic interviews with the children. The Minnesota group's findings emphasize the need for a developmental perspective and longitudinal follow-up. The Grunebaum group's work offers systematic evidence of adaptive behavior under high stress, albeit not with the children of depressed parents for the most part.

THE RELATIONSHIP OF RISK VARIABLES
AND ADAPTIVE VARIABLES

The Rochester group's research leads to an important observation about risk variables and, by analogy, about the study of adaptation. In terms of risk, in relation to the children of depressed parents or other risk groups, clearly there are specific and nonspecific risk factors. The specific risk factors are those that are unique to the diagnostic category of the parents, for example, the particular genetic risk associated with the pedigree of affective illness in the family , or the specific psychosocial impact on the child of depression in the parent versus other mental disorder in the parent. Such a specific psychosocial impact may be that the child of the depressed parent takes on the depressive stance of the parent through imitation or through the need to communicate with the ill parent by getting in touch with his/her world.

Nonspecific risk factors are those that operate generally to cause clinical psychopathlogy in children and are not related to a specific diagnostic category in parents. The Rochester group's finding about the importance of nonspecific factors such as family communication deviance in those children studied is an example of this. Another study involving nonspecific risk factors is Rutter's (1979), which is based on large-scale epidemiologic studies. Risk variables described by Rutter associated with disorder in children included severe marital discord, low social status, overcrowding of family size, parental criminality, maternal psychiatric disorder, and the child's being placed outside the home. In Rutter's work, the presence of two or more risk factors is associated with significant disorder, while one or fewer is not, and the risk factors potentiate one another rather than being simply additive.

ADAPTIVE VARIABLES

The identification and description of risk factors both specific and nonspecific beyond parental illness provide a model for what is needed in the study of adaptation. The study of adaptation should involve two main dimensions: (1) the inclusion of some measure of overall adaptive or psychosocial behavior as an outcome variable in addition to diagnosis; (2) beyond outcome, the study of the component parts of overall adaptation, of adaptational variables. These variables should be at the same level as, and analogous to risk factors. What is needed is to be able to identify individual domains that are descriptively clear and appear to make contributions to the overall outcome of adaptation. The analogy to risk variables goes further, because risk variables have predictive validity over time in identifying those who will become impaired from those who will not. The study of adaptation in general and of adaptation with a risk population in particular should reflect an interest in the identification of protective factors, that is, factors that in longitudinal perspective are demonstrated to protect against the development of illness in children in a high-risk or stress situation. In the broadest sense, adaptive variables may be genetic or constitutional in part (for example, temperament or physical ability), they may be inner traits (such as ego strength or self-esteem), or they may be in the social situation of the child (such as close confiding relationships with others outside the family). The enormous number of studies in this area of coping and adaptation that have recently appeared reflects in part the search for such adaptive variables. Lazarus and Golden's (1982) review provides a useful, organizing framework in which to think about the various types of coping and related variables.

There is a lack of consensus about how to measure adaptational variables, and more importantly a lack of conceptual clarity of what they should be. The problem is not one of lack of possibilities, but of an overabundance of risk conceptual framework about what adaptation is and how it should be described, from psychoanalytic thinking (particularly ego psychology), from the Piagetian tradition, from behavioral observation of highly stressed individuals, and from the longitudinal study of normal development.

To date, when examining the effect of parental illness, risk researchers have dealt with dilemmas of what to study largely by focusing on competence in behavioral function as an outcome variable through the use of teacher and peer ratings. Competence is defined as the accomplishment of major developmentally appropriate behavioral tasks such as forming relationships or doing well in school. As a major first-order outcome variable, in addition to diagnosis, it has much to recommend as it is relatively objective and not dependent on the reporting of inner states.

Risk researchers also have begun to explore the characterization of adaptive behaviors beyond competence in behavioral functioning. In Project Competence in Minnesota, investigators are exploring the role of humor, creativity, and social cognition in relation to outcome. From an epidemiological perspective, Rutter (1979) has described variables from very different domains that are associated with relatively good functioning when at risk. These include reasonable intelligence, the presence of bonds and relationships, and self-esteem. Within the broader social context, the scope of opportunities available to a child, the presence of clear structure within the family, and the nature of the school experience may also have a significant impact. Depending on the ages of the children studied, the population examined, and the aim of the study, domains within the child, the broader social context, and the biological and constitutional factors should be examined. A full examination of all these dimensions using a longitudinal design would be prohibitively costly in a single study.

CHILDREN AT RISK FOR AFFECTIVE DISORDER— THE MASSACHUSETTS GENERAL HOSPITAL STUDY

Our own study is an attempt to examine both diagnostic assessment and adaptive variables in examining children of parents with affective disorders. Our design is a cross-sectional assessment with a short-term longitudinal component.

We are studying the children (ages 7–19) of parents with major affective disorder and a comparison group of children whose parents have no major mental illness. The overall aims of our project are:

1. Epidemiological—relative risk: to establish the relative risk of psychiatric dysfunction in children of affectively ill parents and in a comparison group of children.
2. Identification of risk factors: to identify risk factors that significantly increase the probability that a child will manifest difficulty.
3. Clinical and developmental: to describe the course, severity, and nature of psychopathology in children who experience difficulties because of parental illness, and to determine the influence of developmental factors and changes in the parents' illness on the development of childhood and adolescent psychopathology.
4. Psychosocial mediating factors: to explore the role of factors that may augment or prevent the development of difficulties.

Risk factors include factors both in the parents and in the child. Risk factors that we hypothesize will be associated with higher rates of disorder in the children include the presence of assortative mating (both parents with diagnosable psychiatric disorder), chronicity of parental illness, severity of parental illness, early onset of parental illness in the course of the child's life, extensive family history of disorder, marital discord in the parents' marriage, learning disabilities or neuropsychiatric impairments in the child, and frequent negative events in the child's experience.

The psychosocial mediating factors we are studying are the presence of an open, confiding relationship with the non-ill parent where one parent is ill, the presence of reliable extrafamilial sources of social support (i.e., friends and extended family), high IQ in the absence of significant learning disabilities, the presence of varied extensive activities and outside interests, high levels of ego development as measured by the Loevinger scale (Loevinger, 1976), good self-esteem, and developmentally advanced negotiations strategies as measured by Selman's interviews (Krupa & Selman, 1982; Selman, 1982; Selman, Jacquette, & Lavin, 1977).

We are studying a group of parents already well studied through the Boston Center's part of the National Institute of Mental Health—Clinical Research Branch, Collaborative Psychobiology of Depression Study, thus benefiting from the rich source of already collected data and supplemented by the recruitment of additional samples. Our main instruments are in-depth interviews with parent and child to assess the child's overall adaptive functioning, presence of any diagnoses, and a battery of psychopathological and psychological tests for the child, and psychopathological and family history evaluation, past and present, of the parents and marital problems.

The design contains cross-sectional measures of adaptive behavior functioning from overlapping domains. The in-depth interviews with both parent and child, about the child's life, provide information about the child's overall work in school, pattern of friendships, function in the family, activities, and overall adjustment. School records scored blind to any other information provided an independent estimate of school function. The battery of psychological tests allows for measurement of cognitive ability and actual achievement. Self-esteem is assessed both through the interview and through a paper and pencil measure. The Loevinger scale of ego development provides a measure from a Piagetian cognitive developmental point of view, while the negotiation strategies interview provides a measure of actual strategies used in social situations by youngsters, again from a basic cognitive development point of view.

Obviously a central issue in all of this research is the possible circularity of measures. That is, are outcomes of psychopathology and psychosocial functioning simply different ways of describing the same phenomena? Our position is that there is some but by no means total overlap, and that both measures or areas are necessary for a full description. At the present time, our work in this area is correlational and descriptive. In terms of psychosocial mediating factors, or adaptive factors, we are describing what is associated with the absence of disorder and trying to see in children variations in patterns of adaptive variables without disorder. We do not feel we can call these variables protective factors until we can demonstrate longitudinally that they protect children against illness over time. We hope that we shall be able to describe the overlap and interrelationship of the adaptive variables.

Our own work and that of others (Beardslee, Keller, Lavori, & Klerman, 1983; Kestenbaum, Farber, Kvon, Gargan, Sackeim, & Fieve, 1983; Weissman, Prusoff, Gaumm, Merikangas, Leckman, & Kidd, 1982) has confirmed that there is a high degree of impairment in the youngsters of parents with major affective disorder. In our sample we have identified a small number of youngsters who are in the highest risk group but are coping extremely well. While the number is too small to present any quantitative findings, a brief case description of one of these young people gives some sense of how these individuals are functioning. As well, the case description will be useful in reporting the finding that a good outcome with depressed parents is rare.

CASE EXAMPLE

JG, his mother, and his father were interviewed separately when JG, age 18, was a student at a local college. The family lives in a housing project and all were interviewed at home. JG's father had met criteria for alcohol abuse for several years when JG was a young child, although the father claimed that this was no longer a problem. Because of work as a salesman, his father was absent during periods in JG's early childhood. There was also considerable marital discord and conflict and two separations during JG's growing up. A number of years prior to the interview, JG's father developed a medical illness and a major depressive disorder. He also lost his job. Both medical symptoms and symptoms of chronic depression persisted. The treating psychiatrist and others evaluating JG's father reported that his poor recovery from the medical illness was largely due to the depression. At the time of assessment he was in psychotherapy and was also being medicated with Valium and Elavil. JG's mother had major depressive episodes when JG was 5 and 11. At the time of interview she met criteria for chronic intermittent depressive disorder and also agoraphobia. She was described as secluding herself in a room, brooding, feeling sorry for herself, being pessimistic, self-doubting, irritable, and guilty.

JG was on full scholarship at a college when interviewed. He had always been active in organizations and pursuits outside the home, including doing art work, teaching at a local learning center, being a CCD teacher, being the president of a national society and of the local math club. He had always been an excellent student, graduating in the top 5% of his high school class of several hundred. He was described as demonstrating good self-esteem. In college he was doing reasonably well. He had had a number of jobs and handled them well. He had had at least one good friendship all through school, although his best friend and he had broken off the relationship in the previous year. He had a long-standing friendship with an older man and a number of acquaintances. He had had both homosexual and heterosexual relationships. He was assessed as having high intelligence, got along well with people, but was not gregarious. No medical problems or learning disabilities were reported by him or his mother.

In terms of the family, he reported that he got along extremely well with his mother, was very close to her, and confided in her. They talked about, "anything and everything" and spent considerable time together. The mother described the relationship in similar terms. JG was estranged from his father, did not confide in him, did not get along with him, and spent little time with him. JG's 12-year-old brother was an athletic youngster. He met diagnostic criteria for oppositional syndrome. He was found to have significant reading and other learning problems and a mild speech impediment. He was not close to JG at all. JG himself had no history of affective illness and at no time, past or present, met criteria for any DSM-III diagnosable illness.

In terms of the risk factor model, this young man and his family experience several risk factors beyond affective disorder in the parents; namely, both parents are ill, their illnesses are both chronic and severe, the marriage is characterized by severe discord, the family is quite poor, and they live in a housing project.

Of special interest among the adaptive variables are JG's relationships. Most important is the relationship to the mother. In spite of the mother's illness, her warmth and capacity to relate to this son, but not the other, is relatively spared. This young man's primary relationships have been with his mother, one older friend, and one friend his own age, not a huge variety.

It is important to realize that what is remarkable about this adaptation is adaptation against the background of stress or risk factors, not necessarily the adaptation itself. It would be premature to describe this young man as a "super" youngster or an invulnerable youngster. He is a young man functioning well at present under conditions of high risk for illness. There are certainly concerns for his future: the closest of his ties is with his mother, and his homosexual as well as heterosexual experiences may prove to cause difficulties later on, or they may not. The point is that, at the present time, he is functioning well. The sources of his adaptation, for example, his capacity for relationships, are various and certainly stem in part from earlier temperamental variables and prior positive experiences, and thus are not a function of the main experimental variable, the illness in the parents. However, his pattern of relationships has been influenced by that, and it is possible that the mastery of a difficult home situation has contributed to his capacity for relationships at home and elsewhere and his motivation and effort to succeed in obtaining an excellent education.

With the entire study, we expect the adaptational variables described to be useful in two rather different ways. First, for cross-sectional data analysis we shall use overall adaptation and some individual variables as an outcome independent of diagnosis. We expect those youngsters at highest risk overall to have statistically significant lower levels of adaptive functioning when compared to their nonstress colleagues. Second, we shall attempt to use the overlapping variables from different conceptual frameworks to begin to understand more fully underlying processes of adaptive variables. It is likely that these processes, naturally associated with good functioning while at high risk, should provide an important first step in the identification of and development of intervention strategy of present illness in the high-risk population.

Clearly, ours is only one among a number of approaches. There are certainly other instruments and other variables that could have been selected and are being studied in other projects across the country. Indeed, precisely because there is a wide diversity of opinion as to what constitutes the most important variables to study, adaptation is, at the same time, both intriguing and perplexing. However, the study of both is necessary for any full understanding of children at risk, and the design of study in risk research offers a unique opportunity to learn about adaptation as well as psychotherapy in children at risk.[*]

ACKNOWLEDGMENTS

This work was supported by the National Institute of Mental Health Grant "Children at Risk for Affective Disorder," RO-1-MH34780-1, in conjunction with the Boston Center of the National Institute of Mental Health—Clinical Research Branch, Collaborative Psychobiology

[*] The research group consists of Drs. William R. Beardslee, Martin B. Keller, Philip Lavori, and Gerald L. Klerman.

of Depression Study 2-U02-MH25475-09. Additional support was provided by the William T. Grant Foundation, the Harris Trust through Harvard University, the Overseas Shipholding Group, and the George P. Harrington Trust.

REFERENCES

Beardslee, W. R., Bemporad, J., & Famularo, R. (1984). Depression in childhood: Recent developments. In *Psychiatric medicine update: MGH reviews for physicians* (3rd ed., pp. 117–131). New York: Elsevier/North-Holland.

Beardslee, W. R., Bemporad, J., Keller, M. B., & Klerman, G. L. (1983). Children of parents with major affective disorder: A review. *American Journal of Psychiatry, 140*(7), 825–831.

Beardslee, W. R., Keller, M. B., Lavori, P., & Klerman, G. L. *Children of parents with affective disorders: The pathogenic influence of illness in both parents.* International Journal of Family Therapy, in press.

Boyd, J. H., & Weissman, M. J. (1981). Epidemiology of affective disorder. *Archives of General Psychiatry, 38,* 1039–1049.

Buck, C., & Laughton, K. (1959). Family patterns of illness. *Acta Psychiatrica et Neurologica Scandinavica, 39,* 165.

Cooper, S. F., Leach, C., Storer, D., & Tonge, W. L. (1977). The children of psychiatric patients: clinical findings. *British Journal of Psychiatry, 131,* 514–522.

Ekdahl, M. C., Rice, E. P., & Schmidt, W. M. (1962). Children of parents hospitalized for mental illness. *American Journal of Public Health, 52,* 428–435.

Fisher, L., Harder, D. W., & Kokes, R. F. (1980). Child competence and psychiatric risk. III. Comparisons based on diagnosis of hospitalized parent. *Journal of Nervous and Mental Disorder, 168,* 338–342.

Fisher, L., & Jones, J. E. (1980). Child competence and psychiatric risk. II. Areas of relationships between child and family functioning. *Journal of Nervous and Mental Disorders, 168,* 332–337.

Garmezy, N. (1974). Children at risk: The search for the antecedents of schizophrenia. Part II: Ongoing research programs, issues, and intervention. *Schizophrenia Bulletin, 9,* 55–125.

Garmezy, N. (1978). Current status of a sample of other high risk research programs. In L. Wynne, R. Cromwell, & S. Matthysse (Eds.), *The nature of schizophrenia: New approaches to research and treatment* (pp. 473–480). New York: Wiley.

Garmezy, N., & Devine, V. (1984). Project competence: The Minnesota studies of children vulnerable to psychopathology. In N. Watt, J. Rolf, & E. J. Anthony (Eds.), *Children at risk for schizophrenia.* London & New York: Cambridge University Press.

Glueck, S., & Glueck, E. (1950). *Unraveling juvenile delinquency.* New York: Commonwealth Fund.

Grunebaum, H., Cohler, B. J., Kauffman, C., & Gallant, D. (1978). Children of depressed and schizophrenic mothers. *Child Psychiatry and Human Development, 8,* 219–228.

Harder, D. W., Kokes, R. F., Fisher, L., & Strauss, J. S. (1980). Child competence and psychiatric risk. IV. Relationship of parent diagnostic classification and parent psychopathology severity to child functioning. *Journal of Nervous and Mental Disorders, 168,* 343–347.

Herjanic, B., & Campbell, W. (1977). Differentiating psychiatrically disturbed children on the basis of a structured interview. *Journal of Abnormal Child Psychology, 3,* 41–48.

Herjanic, B., Herjanic, M., Brown, F., & Wheatt, T. (1975). Are children reliable reporters? *Journal of Abnormal Child Psychology, 3,* 48.

Kauffman, C., Grunebaum, H., Cohler, B., & Gamer, E. (1979). Superkids: Competent children of psychotic mothers. *American Journal of Psychiatry, 11,* 1398–1402.

Keller, M. B., Lavori, P. W., Endicott, J., Coryell, W., & Klerman, G. L. (1983). Double depression: A two year follow-up. *American Journal of Psychiatry, 6,* 689–694.

Keller, M. B., & Shapiro, R. W. (1981). Initial results from a one-year prospective naturalistic follow-up study. *Journal of Nervous and Mental Disorders, 12,* 761–768.

Kestenbaum, C. J., Farber, S., Kvon, L., Gargan, M. Sackeim, H. A., & Fieve, R. R. (1983). Clinical and psychological assessment of children of bipolar probands. *American Journal of Psychiatry, 140*(5), 548–553.

Kokes, R. F., Harder, D. W., Fisher, L., & Strauss, J. S. (1980). Child competence and psychiatric risk. V. Sex of patient parent and dimensions of psychopathology. *Journal of Nervous and Mental Disorders, 168,* 348–352.

Krupa, M., & Selman, R. L. (1982). *Assessment of developmental level in adolescents' interpersonal negotiation strategies.* Unpublished scoring manual. Harvard University, Cambridge, MA.

Landau, R., Harth, P., Othray, N., & Sharfhertz, C. (1972). The influence of psychotic parents on their children's development. *American Journal of Psychiatry, 129*(1), 70–76.

Lazarus, R. S., & Golden, G. (1982). Coping and adaptation. In W. D. Gentry (Ed.), *The handbook of behavioral medicine.* New York: Guilford.

Loevinger, J. (1976). *Ego development.* San Francisco: Jossey-Bass.

McCord, W., & McCord, J. (1966) *Origins of alcoholism.* Stanford, CA: Stanford University Press.

McKnew, D. H., & Cytryn, L. (1979). Historical background in children with affective disorders. *British Journal of Psychiatry, 134,* 148–152.

Nurnberger, J. I., & Gershon, E. S. (1982). Genetics. In E. S. Paykel (Ed.), *Handbook of disorder.* Edinburgh & London. Churchill-Livingstone.

Philips, I. (1979). Childhood depression: Interpersonal interaction and depressive phenomena. *American Journal of Psychiatry, 136,* 511.

Puig-Antich, J., & Chambers, W. (1978). *KIDDIE SADS—Schedule for affective disorders and schizophrenia for school-age children (6–16 years)* (2nd working draft). New York: New York State Psychiatric Institute.

Robins, L. (1966). *Deviant children grown up.* Baltimore: William & Wilkins.

Rolf, J. E. (1972). The social and academic competence of children vulnerable to schizophrenia and other behavior pathologies. *Journal of Abnormal Psychology, 80,* 225–243.

Rolf, J. E. (1976). Peer status and the directionality of symptomatic behavior: Prime social competence predictors of outcome for vulnerable children. *American Journal of Orthopsychiatry, 47,* 74–88.

Rutter, M. (1979). Protective factors in children's response to stress and disadvantage. In J. Rolf, M. D. Kent (Eds.), *Primary prevention of psychopathology: Vol. III. Social competence in children* (pp. 49–74). Hanover: University Press of New England.

Selman, R. L. (1982). *The growth of interpersonal understanding.* New York: Academic Press.

Selman, R. L., Jacquette, D., & Lavin, D. R. (1977). Interpersonal awareness in children: Toward an integration of developmental and clinical child psychology. *American Journal of Orthopsychiatry, 47*(2), 264–274.

Shapiro, R., & Keller, M. B. (1981). Initial follow-up of patients with major depressive disorder: A preliminary report from the NIMH Collaborative Study of the Psychobiology of Depression. *Journal of Affective Disorders, 3,* 205–220.

Spitzer, R. L., & Endicott, J. (1977). *Research diagnostic criteria (RDC)* (3rd ed.), New York: Biometrics Research, New York State Psychiatric Institute.

Spitzer, R. L., Endicott, J., & Robins, E. (1978). The research diagnostic criteria: Rationale and reliability. *Archives of General Psychiatry, 35,* 773–782.

Vaillant, G. E., & Vaillant, C. O. (1981). Natural history of male psychological health. X. Work as a predictor of positive mental health. *American Journal of Psychiatry, 138*(11), 1433–1440.

Weissman, M. M., Paykel, E. S., & Klerman, G. L. (1972). (vers 5): The depressed woman as a mother. *Social Psychiatry, 7,* 98–108.

Weissman, M. M., Prusoff, B. A., Gaumm, G. D., Merikangas, K. R., Leckmen, T., & Kidd, K. K. (1982). *Psychopathology in the children (ages 6–18) of depressed and normal parents.* Presented at the American Academy of Child Psychiatry meetings, Washington, DC.

Weissman, M. M., & Siegel, R. (1972). The depressed woman and her rebellious adolescent. *Social Casework, 53*(9), 563–570.

Welner, Z., Welner, A., McCrary, M. D., & Leonard, M. A. (1977). Psychopathology in children in inpatients with depression: A controlled sutdy. *Journal of Nervous and Mental Disorders, 164*(6), 408–413.

Competence and Vulnerability in Children with an Affectively Disordered Parent

Sheldon Weintraub
Ken C. Winters
John M. Neale

INTRODUCTION

The study of children at risk for psychopathology is a promising research strategy designed to identify precursor signs of adult maladjustment and to open the door to possible early intervention and prevention of adult disorders. The high-risk design avoids many of the serious methodological confounds inherent in the study of already maladjusted adults. For example, recollections of adult patients and their families concerning possible etiological factors are suspect because of the notoriously low reliability and validity of data collected retrospectively (Burton, 1970; Yarrow, Campbell, & Burton, 1970). Psychological and biological laboratory research with adult patients and control groups fails to control adequately for the correlates of psychopathology such as institutionalization, medication, social failure, and personal suffering (Mednick & McNeil, 1968). Any difference found between the patient group and the control group may well represent a consequence of the disorder rather than a cause. The study of high-risk children prior to the development of manifest psychopathology is not biased by the consequences of the disorder or the distortions of retrospective reporting. Longitudinal follow-up of these children into adulthood may lead to the discovery of factors that identify those who break down.

Most high-risk researchers have identified children as vulnerable or at risk on the basis of parental psychiatric status. Children with a schizo-

Sheldon Weintraub, Ken C. Winters, and John M. Neale. Department of Psychology, State University of New York at Stony Brook, Stony Brook, New York.

phrenic parent, for example, have a 10–15 times greater risk for developing schizophrenia than children of normal parents. Although many investigators consider genetic factors to constitute the basis of this risk or vulnerability, in fact, it merely reflects an empirical or statistical finding. In addition to whatever genetic factors might be operative, children with a mentally ill parent are subject to a host of other influences, including birth complications, disruptions in the family due to parental hospitalization, and interaction with a disturbed parent. The concept of vulnerability or risk makes no assumptions about its cause, but only that it exists (Zubin & Spring, 1977).

While the high-risk method has many strengths, we should also mention some of its limitations. One problem is that a high-risk sample defined on the basis of parental psychopathology is unrepresentative of the disorder in general. For example, a high-risk study of schizophrenia must confront the fact that the great majority of schizophrenics (about 90%) do not have a schizophrenic parent (Zerbin-Rudin, 1967). Although we do not yet know the importance of differences between schizophrenics with and without a schizophrenic parent, the conclusions drawn from a high-risk study are nevertheless limited. Since schizophrenic men are less likely to marry and to have children, the schizophrenic fathers selected by high-risk studies are of higher premorbid social competence and thus unrepresentative of schizophrenic men in general.

Another shortcoming of this research strategy is that it may be difficult to interpret cross-sectional findings obtained prior to the age of risk. Differences between high-risk and control children could be due to the effects of a third variable, such as marital discord or family disorganization.

Finally, high-risk research is most vulnerable to the logistic problems that plague longitudinal research in general, foremost of which is sample attrition, a problem that is particularly serious for American investigators who have no central registry to track the whereabouts of a mobile sample.

Despite these limitations, the high-risk approach to the study of schizophrenia has already begun to provide data that attest to the method's promise. Children with a schizophrenic parent have shown deficits on a wide range of variables, including psychophysiological, cognitive, attentional, and social functioning (Erlenmeyer-Kimling et al., 1984; Mednick, Cudeck, Griffith, Talovic, & Schulsinger, 1984; Steffy, Asarnow, Asarnow, MacCrimmon, & Cleghorn, 1984; Weintraub & Neale, 1984; Worland, Janes, Anthony, McGinnis, & Cass, 1984).

Despite the potential richness in this vein of research, the high-risk method remains to be successfully mined in the area of depression. We have recently extended the focus of our own high-risk research to include affective disorders as well as schizophrenia, and have assembled a large sample of children with an affectively disordered parent. Our approach to the study of vulnerability in children is based on a diathesis–stress model and is directed toward assessing precursor variables and early signs of psychopathology as well as environmental stressors. Of course, the great task facing the researcher is to determine what the early signs might be and which variables are likely to be important in the development of psychopathology. Although depressive disorder is rare in childhood, it does occur (Cytryn & McKnew, 1973) and its incidence rises sharply in adolescence (Strober & Carlson, 1982). Moreover, it is possible that certain depression-related patterns, such as lowered competence, may be present from early childhood.

Moreover, there is evidence that children with an affectively ill parent are at risk for psychopathology. In one study of 30 children of 15 affectively ill parents, 77% were diagnosed as depressed on the basis of at least one of the two interviews conducted with the children (McKnew, Cytryn, Efron, Gershon, & Bunney, 1979). Cytryn, McKnew, Bartko, Lamour, and Hamovit (1982) also found high rates of depression in 19 children with an affectively ill parent. Other investigators not only found high rates of depression, but many other problems as well, such as attention deficit disorder, anxiety, impulsivity, and withdrawal (Conners, Himmelhock, Goyette, Ulrich, & Neil, 1979; Greenhill, Shopsin, & Temple, 1980; Robbins, Engström, Mrazek, & Swift, 1977; Welner, Welner, McCrary, & Leonard, 1977).

Clinicians have speculated about possible precursor patterns to affective disorder (e.g., Abramson, Seligman, & Teasdale, 1978; Akiskal & McKinney, 1975; Anthony, 1975; Kashani et al., 1981), and the following factors are among the ones that have been implicated: learned helplessness, depressogenic attributional styles, insecure attachments because of "psychological loss" of caretaker, exposure to deviant child-rearing, contagion, and modeling of parental depression. Clinical accounts of the parenting characteristics of affectively ill parents support the view that their children are subjected to a stressful environment (Anthony, 1975; Davenport, Adland, Gold, & Goodwin, 1979). A recent study of the parents of depressives, as described by their depressed offspring, found them to be characterized as rejecting, controlling, derisive, manipulative, and withdrawing of affection (Crook, Raskin, & Eliot, 1981). Of course, we do not know whether these descriptions are really accurate or merely a function of the depressed state of the respondent.

In schizophrenia, there has been a search for continuities from childhood to adulthood both in form, expressed in symptoms, and in function or process. An example of a developmental continuity in process is that found by Harvey, Winters, Weintraub, and Neale (1981) in children of schizophrenics. These children showed a particular vulnerability to distraction in the primacy position of a serial position task that was similar to findings with adult schizophrenics (Oltmanns, 1978). Since such a pattern could reflect deficits in memory rehearsal and retrieval, it could lead to disorders in thought and speech that are characteristic of schizophrenic patients. Despite the presence of purported continuities in emotions, cognition, behaviors, and relationships, which might represent the beginnings of a schizophrenic process, abnormalities in the childhood of schizophrenics that are actually schizophrenic or even psychotic in form are not common (Garmezy, 1974).

As Rutter (Chapter 1 of this volume) has pointed out, the search for developmental precursors to depression must extend well beyond childhood affective disorder and must take into account developmental discontinuities as well as continuities.

The strategy in the research reported here was to take a more descriptive approach and develop a detailed picture of the characteristics of children who are at risk for psychopathology. The central focus of this descriptive approach has been the assessment of *competence*. We regard competence as a construct with various links to a nomological network of multiple behaviors that are related to childhood adjustment. These behaviors have direct adaptational significance and are supported and rewarded by the environment. Measures of competence tend to show significant temporal stability, thus contributing to their success in the prediction of adult behavior (Kohlberg, LaCrosse, & Ricks, 1972). In addition, measures of competence prove to be among the best predictors of course and outcome for adult psychiatric patients (Klorman, Strauss, & Kokes, 1977). It is important not to neglect the transactional (Sameroff, 1982) linkages in the cause–effect chain of development between childhood competence and later depression, or other forms of psychopathology. Impaired competence can function both as a cause of later psychopathology as well as a consequence of earlier experiences.

The schools are a major source in our assessment of childhood competence. Children spend almost half of their waking hours in school, the most significant social and psychological arena encountered outside the family, representative as it is of the competitive, work, and social demands of adulthood.

Teachers, as educators and parent surrogates, are in a unique position to assess how children cope academically and socially, and to compare their adjustment with that of their classmates. Considerable evidence exists that teachers are able to appraise a child's current adjustment with considerable reliability and validity. Lambert and Bower (1961), for example, found that 90% of elementary school pupils rated as emotionally disturbed by teachers were so labeled by experienced clinicians following individual assessment. Weintraub, Neale, and Liebert (1975) found that teachers were able to identify vulnerable children at risk for psychopathology. In predicting later maladjustment, teachers have been found to be even more successful than clinicians (Kellam & Schiff, 1967).

Peers may also provide a sensitive index to a child's adjustment. Peer evaluations are obtained in the rich, nontest context of the child's real-life environment and are based on observations made over extended periods of time by multiple observers who have different personal relationships with the child, and consequently varying perspectives (Smith, 1967). Peer ratings are stable over time, across sex of raters, and over a wide age range (Minturn & Lewis, 1968), and are only minimally influenced by social desirability variance (Norman, 1963). Peer evaluations have been validated successfully against parental, clinician, and teacher ratings, as well as behavioral observations (Bower, 1969; Wiggins & Winder, 1961; Winder & Wiggins, 1964); have effectively predicted maladjustment (Roff & Sells, 1968); and have identified children at risk for adult psychopathology (Rolf & Garmezy, 1974; Weintraub, Prinz, & Neale, 1978). Cowen, Pederson, Babigian, Izzo, and Trost (1973) found that peer evaluations not only predicted later maladjustment, but did so more effectively than clinician or teacher ratings.

The purpose of this chapter is to assess the competence, as indexed by teachers and peers, of children with an affectively disordered parent contrasted with children with a schizophrenic parent and children whose parents are free of diagnosable psychopathology.

METHOD

Four groups of children were investigated: those with a parent diagnosed as unipolar depressed ($N = 113$), as having a bipolar disorder ($N = 73$), as schizophrenic ($N = 57$), and a normal control group ($N = 297$). The inclusion of multiple psychiatric groups assists in the interpretation of findings. A difference between the offspring of unipolars and normals, for instance, cannot be interpreted as specifically relevant to depression. Affective disorder and schizophrenia constitute excellent contrast groups since they appear to be distinct clinical and genetic entities (Kendler, Gruenberg, & Strauss, 1981). The inclusion of both unipolar and bipolar patient–parents reflects the current literature, which emphasizes a distinction between unipolar and bipolar disorders (Depue & Monroe, 1978).

Patient–parents were selected from the inpatient new admissions at four local psychiatric hospitals. Our diagnostic assessment battery included a semistructured diagnostic interview, the Current and Past Psychopathology Scales (Spitzer & Endicott, 1968); a short form of the MMPI, the Mini-Mult (Kincannon, 1968); interviews with the patient's spouse; and the hospital case history. Diagnoses met the criteria of DSM-III (American Psychiatric Association, 1980), and were assigned with high interrater reliability; kappa (Cohen, 1960) ranged from .84 to .92. The unipolar depressed group included both minor and major episodes. The bipolar group included both bipolar, depressed and bipolar, manic patients. The selection and diagnostic procedures have been described in detail elsewhere (Winters, Stone, Weintraub, & Neale, 1981).

The normal control group was obtained by selecting two children from each of the classrooms of the target children. One of these was a same-sex but otherwise randomly drawn child; the other was matched to the target child on sex, race, social class, and IQ. Matching was conducted to control for potential confounds or "nuisance variables," but matching involves the tacit assumption that the matching variables are merely peripheral correlates and unrelated to the development of psychopathology. This assumption may not be warranted with variables such as social class and IQ. In addition, matching on one variable often produces systematic unmatching on another (Meehl, 1970). For these reasons, we decided to include both matched and random controls.

Teacher ratings were obtained with the Devereux Elementary School Behavior Rating Scale (DESB) (Spivack & Swift, 1967). It consists of 47 behavior items, which the teacher rates on the basis of frequency or intensity, using a 5- or 7-point rating scale. The 11 scales are:

1. Classroom Disturbance: Extent to which child teases and torments classmates, interferes with others' work, is quickly drawn into noisemaking, and must be reprimanded or controlled.
2. Impatience: Extent to which child starts work too quickly, is sloppy and hasty in its performance, and is unwilling to review it.
3. Disrespect–Defiance: Extent to which child speaks disrespectfully to teacher, resists doing what is asked, belittles the work being done, and breaks classroom rules.
4. External Blame: Extent to which child claims not helped or called on by the teacher, blames external circumstances when things do not go well, and is quick to say the work assigned is too hard.
5. Achievement Anxiety: Extent to which child gets upset about test scores, worries about knowing the "right" answers, is overly anxious when tests are given, and is sensitive to criticism or correction.
6. External Reliance: Extent to which child looks to others for direction, relies on the teacher for direction, requires precise instructions, and has difficulty making decisions.
7. Comprehension: Extent to which child gets the point of what is going on in class, seems able to apply what has been learned, and knows material when called upon to recite.
8. Inattention–Withdrawal: Extent to which child does not pay attention, seems oblivious of what is happening in the classroom, and is preoccupied or difficult to reach.
9. Irrelevant Responsiveness: Extent to which child tells exaggerated

stories, gives irrelevent answers, interrupts when teacher is talking, and makes inappropriate comments.

10. Creative Initiative: Extent to which child brings things to class that
relate to current topics, talks about things in an interesting fashion,
initiates classroom discussion, and introduces personal experiences into class discussion.

11. Need for Closeness to Teacher: Extent to which child seeks out the
teacher before or after class, is friendly toward and offers to do
things for the teacher, and likes to be physically close to the
teacher.

Data from previous work with the DESB indicate that test–retest
reliabilities over a 1-week period range between .85 and .91 for the 11
scales, and interrater reliabilities between teachers and teacher-aides
range between .62 and .77 (Spivack & Swift, 1967). As regards validity, the
scales correlate significantly with grades, controlling for 10, and
discriminate among groups of problem children (Spivack, Swift, & Prewitt,
1972).

Our own cluster analysis of the DESB revealed four clusters: (1)
Aggressive–Disruptive (14 items); (2) Cognitive Competence (21 items); (3)
Social Competence (8 items); and (4) Achievement Anxiety (4 items). The
mean item to cluster correlation was .77 and coefficient alpha for the four
clusters was .72, .71, .70, and .77, respectively.

Peer ratings were obtained with a measure we developed, the Pupil
Evaluation Inventory (PEI) (Pekarik, Prinz, Liebert, Weintraub, & Neale,
1976). The format consists of an item-by-peer matrix in which the items appear as rows down the left side of the page and the names of the children in
the class across the top of the page. The subject checks each child believed
to be described by a particular item. This format permits every student to
be selected for each item; additionally, all students are rated item by item,
preventing a possible bias or set that may develop when all items are rated
for one person at a time. Only those students of the same sex as the target
child are rated by both the boys and girls in the class. The PEI consists of 34
items, and factor analysis has revealed three major dimensions: (1) Aggression–Disruptiveness; (2) Withdrawal; and (3) Likeability–Social Competence. Reliability of the PEI, in terms of internal consistency (split-half
reliability) and interrater agreement (between male and female raters) on
factor scores, is satisfactory. For a sample of third- and sixth-grade classes
tested over a 2-week period, all of the factor test–retest correlations were
greater than .80; for the items, the median test–retest correlation was .73.

In order to protect the confidentiality of the children and their families,
the reason for our choice of children was concealed from school personnel
who had contact with them, and the names of the participating children
were not identified to the teacher or the class members. As a further protec-

tion, testing was conducted as a class activity, and all of the same-sex classmates of the target child were assessed together with the peer and teacher measures.

RESULTS

Teacher Ratings

Our first analysis of the DESB is according to its clusters: (1) Aggressive–Disruptive (14 items); (2) Cognitive Competence (21 items); (3) Social Competence (8 items); and (4) Achievement Anxiety (4 items). Each of the four clusters was analyzed using a 4 (Parental Diagnosis: schizophrenic, unipolar, depressed, bipolar, normal) × 2 (Grade Level of Child: 2–5, 6–9) × 2 (Sex of Child) analysis of variance. Means and standard deviations may be found in Table 1. Significant main effects for Sex of Child were found on the Aggressive–Disruptive, Cognitive Competence, and Social Competence clusters; boys were rated as more deviant ($p <$ .01). There were no significant main effects for Grade Level. There were also no significant interactions beween Parental Diagnosis and Sex of Child or Grade Level.

For the Aggressive–Disruptive, the Cognitive Competence, and the Social Competence clusters, the three groups of children with patient–parents were reliably more deviant than the children of normal controls ($p <$ .05). The children in the patient–parent groups did not significantly differ from each other.

We also conducted a redundant analysis of the teacher DESB according to its 11 scales (see Table 1). Analyses of variance indicated that teachers rated the children with a patient–parent as significantly more deviant than the normal controls on all of the scales except Achievement Anxiety. There were no significant differences among the groups of children with a patient–parent.

Peer Evaluations

Distributions of the percentage scores for PEI items were found to be skewed, and so all item scores were transformed by computing the arcsine of the square root of the scores (Winer, 1971). The three factor scores—Aggression, Withdrawal, and Likeability–Social Competence—represent the average of the transformed scores of the items comprising each factor. Untransformed factor means and standard deviations may be found in Table 1.

Analyses of variance revealed significant main effects for Sex of Child on the Aggression and Likeability factors; boys were rated as more ag-

Table 1
Means and Standard Deviations for the Teacher DESB and Peer Evaluations

| | Offspring of | | | | | | | |
| | Schizophrenics | | Unipolars | | Bipolars | | Controls | |
	X	SD	X	SD	X	SD	X	SD
Teacher DESB clusters								
Aggressive–Disruptive	29.25	13.89	28.34	13.78	28.08	14.30	24.70	10.66
Cognitive Competence	36.52	21.78	38.72	22.44	35.64	25.30	31.24	22.22
Social Competence	20.96	6.72	20.80	6.64	21.68	8.00	22.88	7.52
Achievement Anxiety	9.52	4.88	9.28	3.84	9.16	4.28	9.04	4.04
Teacher DESB scales								
Classroom–Disturbance	11.46	5.46	10.91	5.45	10.65	5.42	9.72	4.77
Impatience	11.39	5.50	12.14	5.53	11.44	5.90	10.34	5.05
Disrespect–Defiance	7.61	3.77	7.60	4.34	7.58	4.52	6.26	3.00
External Blame	7.91	4.92	8.07	4.41	7.56	4.31	6.97	3.59
Achievement Anxiety	9.52	4.90	9.27	3.82	9.15	4.29	9.05	4.03
External Reliance	15.48	6.31	15.93	6.66	15.02	7.11	14.47	6.68
Comprehension	10.83	3.59	11.25	3.71	11.71	4.21	12.10	3.72
Inattention–Withdrawal	11.02	4.75	11.51	5.65	11.33	6.23	9.97	5.36
Irrelevant Responsiveness	8.39	3.78	7.94	3.49	7.87	3.83	7.21	3.29
Creative Initiative	8.78	3.65	8.86	3.45	9.65	4.13	9.82	4.22
Need for Closeness to Teacher	12.20	4.33	11.93	4.39	12.02	5.00	13.04	4.62
Peer evaluations								
Aggression–Disruptiveness	25.42	17.22	21.90	17.50	22.01	16.97	18.12	15.02
Withdrawal	18.54	14.98	15.40	9.77	14.13	10.08	14.43	10.75
Likeability–Social Competence	21.96	14.42	25.29	15.34	25.01	16.41	25.38	16.20

gressive ($p < .01$) and less likeable ($p < .01$). There was also a significant main effect for Grade Level on the Likeability factor; younger children were rated more positively.

On the Aggression factor, the children of normal controls were significantly less aggressive than the children with a schizophrenic parent ($p < .005$), the children with a unipolar depressed parent ($p < .05$), and the children with a bipolar parent ($p < .05$). There were no significant differences among the groups of children with a patient–parent.

On the Withdrawal factor, only the children with a schizophrenic parent were rated as significantly more deviant than the normal controls ($p < .05$). Additionally, they were more deviant than the children of unipolars ($p < .05$) and children of bipolars ($p < .02$).

On the Likeability factor, the diagnoses by Grade Level interaction approached significance. For the younger children (grades 2–6), those with a schizophrenic parent were rated as more deviant ($p < .05$) than the normal controls. There were no significant differences for the older children nor for any other diagnostic comparison.

DISCUSSION

Our school data strikingly indicate that children with an affectively ill parent show lowered competence along several dimensions. Teachers rated them as more deviant than their classmate controls on three of the four rational Devereux clusters, Aggressive–Disruptive, Cognitive Competence, and Social Competence, and 10 of the 11 Devereux scales, all but Achievement Anxiety. Children with such a pattern have been described as presenting a major behavioral disturbance (Spivack *et al.*, 1972). They manifest acting out and impulsive behavior and are in conflict with the behavioral demands of the school environment. They seem unable to make productive use of the classroom and achieve poorly. Their peers also perceive them to be different, describing them as abrasive, withdrawn, and unhappy. These children with an affectively ill parent may indeed be described as vulnerable.

Girls were rated as more socially competent and less aggressive than boys by both their teachers and their peers, and as more cognitively competent by their teachers, all findings consistent with the evidence that girls mature earlier than boys (Williams, 1977). We also found that younger children rated their peers as more likeable than did older children. It may be that younger children are less discriminating and critical in their assessment of others, or that they actually do have more friends.

It is notable that there was not a singular behavior pattern that characterized the children with an affectively ill parent. Rather, their deviance extended across a wide range of academic, social, and emotional behaviors. On the basis of these data, it is unlikely that only one childhood precursor pattern will be associated with adult affective disorder. It is also noteworthy that despite the major difficulties these children exhibited, depressive disorder of significant clinical proportions was not common at the time of our assessment. This finding is in contast to the work of others, who have found a high incidence of clinical depression in offspring of affectively ill parents (e.g., Cytryn et al., 1982; McKnew et al., 1979), and suggests that such children may show significant problems in the absence of diagnosable depression.

Our results are also at variance with psychosocial maturation theories that view depression-prone people as "oversocialized" (Phillips, 1968), but are quite consistent with the findings that children with an affectively ill parent show a variety of behavioral and cognitive impairments (Conners et al., 1979; Greenhill et al., 1980; Strober, Burroughs, Salkin, & Green, 1982; Winters et al., 1981).

Might lowered competence play a role in the development of depression? Recent cognitive theories of depression, based on studies with adult depressives, claim that depressogenic cognitions and attributional styles are instrumental in the development of lowered competence and depressed feelings. Our data suggest that lowered competence, and hence actual failure experiences, might precede the development of depression. That is, a depressed outlook might be a consequence rather than a cause of lowered competence. A high-risk study, with its prospective design, has the potential to unravel this causal chain.

We would like to emphasize that the children with a schizophrenic parent showed patterns of maladjustment similar to those exhibited by the children with an affectively ill parent. We did find a trend, however, for the varying perspectives of the teachers and peers to produce a different pattern of results. The teachers tended to rate the children with an affectively ill parent, and most particularly those with a unipolar depressed parent, as the most deviant. The peers, on the other hand, tended to rate the children with a schizophrenic parent as the most deviant, particularly on the Withdrawal factor. Such an interaction between risk status and type of rater requires replication for a proper interpretation, but it might be due to the differences in the type and extent of information available. The peers have the opportunity to observe the child in more varied situations, unstructured play as well as structured classroom settings, for example, than do teachers.

Nevertheless, there was considerable overlap between the children with an affectively ill parent and the children with a schizophrenic parent on almost every variable that we assessed. This is despite the considerable evidence that schizophrenia and affective disorder are two very distinct disorders, decisively, diagnostically, and genetically (Kendler et al., 1981). In addition, we found significant overlap between the children with a bipolar parent and those with a unipolar parent, again in contrast to studies of adult patients (Depue & Monroe, 1978).

There is one other study that reports on the classroom behaviors of the offspring of DSM-III affectives and schizophrenics (Janes, Weeks, & Worland, 1983). This well-conducted study, which is part of the St. Louis Risk Research Project (Anthony, 1975; Worland et al., 1983), included 11 children with an affectively ill parent (bipolars and unipolars) and 11 children with a schizophrenic parent among its sample of high school adolescents. Teachers rated these two groups as less motivated, less harmonious, less stable, more dogmatic, and more verbally negative. The two high-risk groups did not differ. What could account for the overlap and lack of specificity in this study and in our own?

One possibility is that the diagnoses of the parents were insufficiently differentiating; indeed, the reliability and validity of psychiatric diagnosis have been the bete noire of many a research project. Our data, however, on the reliability and validity of our diagnostic ratings and diagnostic assignments (Winters et al., 1981) provide considerable support for our differentiating diagnoses of unipolar, bipolar, and schizophrenic.

Another possibility is that the high-risk children are responding in some reactive way to their parent's illness and hospitalization. Data from our own studies document how a parent's problems, irrespective of diagnosis, can shake the equilibrium and stability of the entire family. A stable emotional climate, so important to a child's sense of security and conducive to growth and maturity, is often unavailable to the high-risk child. Our longitudinal follow-up of these children, which involves repeated assessments at intervals not linked to parental illness, will enable us to test more definitively the reactivity of the behavioral patterns that we have observed thus far.

Despite the similarities in behavioral patterns observed in the high-risk groups, there might well be significant differences in the mechanisms that produce these behavioral patterns. Indeed, analyses that we have recently conducted provide some support for this claim. Emery, Weintraub, and Neale (1982) evaluated two different mechanisms or paths that might account for the deviant school behaviors observed in our samples. One considered the possible influence that parental diagnosis might exert, perhaps reflecting a genetic diathesis. The second path evaluated the possible mediating influence of marital discord. Marital discord and deviant behavior in childhood are known to be correlated (Rutter, 1971), and the marriages of the affectively ill and schizophrenic patients participating in the Stony Brook Project are characterized by substantial discord, but not differentially (Weintraub & Neale, 1983). Using path analyses that can separately evaluate the relationships between parental diagnosis and child behavior, and between marital discord and child behavior, an interesting pattern was found. For the children with a schizophrenic parent, parental diagnosis had a direct effect on classroom behavior while marital discord did not. Among the children with an affectively ill parent, the pattern was reversed; marital discord and not parental diagnosis was the crucial variable.

We believe that our findings of extensive teacher-rated and peer-rated deviance in children with an affectively ill parent and children with a schizophrenic parent indicate that both groups of children are at risk and vulnerable to later psychopathology. Childhood vulnerability may, to some considerable extent, be unrelated to a parent's specific psychiatric diagnosis.

In summary, our findings of lowered levels of competence in children with an affectively ill parent reflects the impact of ill parents on their children's adjustment. Our challenge is to continue our search for precursor variables that relate childhood characteristics to adult outcome.

In closing we would like to note that many of the high-risk children and their families are adjusting quite satisfactorily, and demonstrate impressive degrees of strength and resilience. We hope to learn more about the coping strategies and support systems required for the "invulnerable" children who are able to survive and even thrive where others break down.

ACKNOWLEDGMENTS

This research was supported by grants from the National Institute of Mental Health and the William T. Grant Foundation.

REFERENCES

Abramson, L. Y., Seligman, M. E. P., & Teasdale, J. D. (1978). Learned helplessness in humans: Critique and reformulation. *Journal of Abnormal Psychology, 87,* 49–74.

Akiskal, H., & McKinney, W. (1975). Overview of recent research in depression: Integration of ten conceptual models into a comprehensive clinical frame. *Archives of General Psychiatry, 32,* 285–305.

American Psychiatric Association. (1980). *Diagnostic and statistical manual of mental disorders* (3rd ed.). Washington, DC: APA.

Anthony, E. J. (1975). The influence of a manic-depressive environment on the developing child. In E. J. Anthony & T. Benedek (Eds.), *Depression and human existence.* Boston: Little, Brown.

Bower, E. M. (1960). *Early identification of emotionally handicapped children in school.* Springfield, IL: Charles C Thomas.

Bower, E. M. (1969). *Early identification of emotionally handicapped children in school* (2nd ed.). Springfield, IL: Charles C Thomas.

Burton, R. V. (1970). Validity of retrospective reports assessed by the multitrait-multimethod analysis. *Developmental Psychology Monographs, 3*(Pt. 2).

Cohen, J. A. (1960). A coefficient of agreement for nominal scales. *Education and Psychological Measurement, 20,* 37–46.

Conners, C. K., Himmelhoch, J., Goyette, C. H., Ulrich, R., & Neil, J. F. (1979). Children of parents with affective illness. *Journal of the American Academy of Child Psychiatry, 18,* 600–607.

Cowen, E., Pederson, A., Babigian, H., Izzo, L., & Trost, A. (1973). A long-term follow-up of early detected vulnerable children. *Journal of Consulting Psychology, 41,* 438–446.

Crook, T., Raskin, A., & Eliot, J. (1981). Parent-child relationships and adult depression. *Child Development, 52,* 950–957.

Cytryn, L., & McKnew, D. H. (1973). Proposed classification of childhood depression. *American Journal of Psychiatry, 129,* 149–155.

Cytryn, L., McKnew, D. H., Bartko, J. J., Lamour, M., & Hamovit, J. (1982). Offspring of patients with affective disorders. II. *Journal of the American Academy of Child Psychiatry, 21,* 389–391.

Davenport, Y. B., Adland, M. L., Gold, P. W., & Goodwin, F. K. (1979). Manic-depressive illness: Psychodynamic features of multigenerational families. *American Journal of Orthopsychiatry, 49,* 24–35.

Depue, R. A., & Monroe, S. M. (1978). The unipolar-bipolar distinction in the depressive disorders. *Psychological Bulletin, 85,* 1001–1030.

Emery, R., Weintraub, S., & Neale, J. M. (1982). Effects of marital discord on the school behavior of children of schizophrenic, affectively disordered, and normal parents. *Journal of Abnormal Child Psychology, 10,* 215–228.

Erlenmeyer-Kimling, L., Marcuse, Y., Cornblatt, B., Friedman, D., Rainer, J. D., & Rutschmann, J. (1984). The New York high-risk project. In N. F. Watt, J. Anthony, L. C. Wynne, & J. E. Rolf (Eds.), *Children at risk for schizophrenia: A longitudinal perspective.* New York: Cambridge University Press.

Garmezy, N. (1974). Children at risk: The search for the antecedents of schizophrenia. Part I. Conceptual models and research methods. *Schizophrenia Bulletin, 8,* 14–91.

Greenhill, L. L., Shopsin, B., & Temple, H. (1980). Children of affectively ill parents: Psychiatric status determined by structured interview. *Psychopharmocological Bulletin, 16,* 23–24.

Harvey, P., Winters, K. C., Weintraub, S., & Neale, J. M. (1981). Distractibility in children vulnerable to psychopathology. *Journal of Abnormal Psychology, 90,* 298–304.

Janes, C. L., Weeks, D. G., & Worland, J. (1983). School behavior in children of parents with mental disorder. *Journal of Nervous and Mental Disease, 171,* 234–244.

Kashani, J. H., Husain, A., Shekim, W. O., Hodges, K., Cytryn, L., & McKnew, D. (1981). Current perspectives on childhood depression: An overview. *American Journal of Psychiatry, 138,* 143–153.

Kellam, S., & Schiff, S. (1967). Adaptation and mental illness in the first-grade classrooms of an urban community. *Psychiatric Research Reports, 21,* 79–91.

Kendler, K. S., Gruenberg, A. M., & Strauss, J. S. (1981). An independent analysis of the Copenhagen sample of the Danish adoption study of schizophrenia. *Archives of General Psychiatry, 38,* 973–990.

Kincannon, J. C. (1968). Prediction of the standard MMPI scale scores from 71 items: The Min-Mult. *Journal of Consulting and Clinical Psychology, 32,* 319–325.

Klorman, R., Strauss, J., & Kokes, R. (1977). The relationship of demographic and diagnostic factors to measures of premorbid adjustment. *Schizophrenia Bulletin, 3,* 214–225.

Kohlberg, L., LaCrosse, J., & Ricks, D. (1972). The predictability of adult mental health from childhood behavior. In B. E. Wolman (Ed.), *Manual of child psychopathology.* New York: McGraw-Hill.

Lambert, N., & Bower, E. (1961). *Technical report on in-school screening of emotionally handicapped children.* Princeton, NJ: Educational Testing Service.

McKnew, D. H., Cytryn, L., Efron, A. M., Gershon, E. S., & Bunney, W. E. (1979). Offspring of patients with affective disorders. *British Journal of Psychiatry, 134,* 148–152.

Mednick, S. A., Cudeck, R., Griffith, J. J., Talovic, S. A., & Schulsinger, F. (1984). The Danish high risk project: Recent methods and findings. In N. F. Watt, J. Anthony, L. C. Wynne, & J. E. Rolf (Eds.), Children at risk for schizophrenia: A longitudinal perspective. New York: Cambridge University Press.

Mednick, S. A., & McNeil, T. F. (1968). Current methodology in research on the etiology of schizophrenia: Serious difficulties which suggest the use of high-risk group method. Psychological Bulletin, 70, 681–693.

Meehl, P. E. (1970). Nuisance variables and the expost facto design. In M. Radner & S. Winokur (Eds.), Minnesota studies in the philosophy of science (Vol. 4). Minneapolis: University of Minnesota Press.

Minturn, M., & Lewis, M. (1968). Age differences in peer ratings of socially desirable and socially undesirable behavior. Psychology Reports, 23, 783–791.

Nuechterlein, K. H., Phipps-Yonas, S., Driscoll, R. M., & Garmezy, N. (1980). Attentional functioning among children vulnerable to adult schizophrenia; Vigilance, reaction time, and incidental learning. Paper presented at the Risk Research Consortium Plenary Conference, San Juan, Puerto Rico.

Norman, W. T. (1963). Toward an adequate taxonomy of personality attributes: Replicated factor structure in peer nomination personality ratings. Journal of Abnormal and Social Psychology, 66, 574–583.

Oltmanns, T. F., (1978). Selective attention in schizophrenic and manic psychosis: The effect of distraction on information processing. Journal of Abnormal Psychology, 87, 212–225.

Pekarik, E., Prinz, R., Liebert, D., Weintraub, S., & Neale, J. M. (1976). The pupil evaluation inventory. Journal of Abnormal Child Psychology, 4, 83–97.

Phillips, L. (1968). Human adaptation and its failure. New York: Academic Press.

Robbins, D. R., Engström, F. W., Mrazek, D., & Swift, W. (1977). Psychological characteristics of children of manic-depressive mothers. Presented at the annual meeting of the American Academy of Child Psychiatry, Houston, TX.

Roff, M., & Sells, S. (1968). Juvenile delinquency in relation to peer acceptance—rejection and socioeconomic status. Psychology in the Schools, 5, 3–18.

Rolf, J. E., & Garmezy, N. (1974). The school performance of children vulnerable to behavior pathology. In D. F. Ricks, A. Thomas, & M. Roff (Eds.), Life history research in psychopathology, (Vol. 3). Minneapolis: University of Minnesota Press.

Rutter, M. (1971). Parent-child separation: Psychological effects on the children. Journal of Child Psychology and Psychiatry and Allied Disciplines, 12, 233–260.

Sameroff, A. J. (1982). Biochemical factors and measurement: Discussant. Presented at the Conference on Depression and Depressive Disorders: Developmental Perspectives, Temple University, Philadelphia.

Smith, G. (1967). Usefulness of peer ratings of personality in education research. Educational and Psychological Measurement, 24, 967–984.

Spitzer, R., & Endicott, J. (1968). Current and past psychopathology scale (CAPPS). New York: Evaluations Unit, Biometrics Research, New York State Department of Mental Hygiene.

Spivack, G., & Swift, M. (1967). Devereux elementary school behavior rating scale manual. Devon, PA: Devereux Foundation.

Spivack, G., Swift, M., & Prewitt, J. (1972). Syndrome of disturbed classroom behavior: A behavioral diagnostic system for elementary schools. Journal of Special Education, 5, 269–292.

Steffy, R. A., Asarnow, R., Asarnow, J. R., MacCrimmon, D., & Cleghorn, N. (1984). The McMaster-Waterloo high-risk project: Multifaceted strategy for high-risk research. In N. F. Watt, J. Anthony, L. C. Wynne, & J. E. Rolf (Eds.), Children at risk for schizophrenia: A longitudinal perspective. New York: Cambridge University Press.

Strober, M., Burroughs, J., Salkin, B., & Green, J. (1982). Ancestral secondary cases of psychiatric illness in adolescents with mania, depression, schizophrenia, and conduct disorder. Biological Psychiatry.

Strober, M., & Carlson, G. (1982). Clinical, genetic, and psychopharmacological predictors of bipolar illness in adolescents with major depression: A three-to-four year prospective follow-up investigation. *Archives of General Psychiatry, 39*, 549–555.

Weintraub, S., & Neale, J. M. (1984). The Stony Brook high-risk project. In N. F. Watt, J. Anthony, L. C. Wynne, & J. E. Rolf (Eds.), *Children at risk for schizophrenia: A longitudinal perspective.* New York: Cambridge University Press.

Weintraub, S., Neale, J. M., & Liebert, D. (1975). Teacher ratings of children vulnerable to psychopathology. *American Journal of Orthopsychiatry, 45*, 838–845.

Weintraub, S., Prinz, R., & Neale, J. M. (1978). Peer evaluations of the competence of children vulnerable to psychopathology. *Journal of Abnormal Child Psychology, 4*, 461–473.

Welner, Z., Welner, A., McCrary, M. D., & Leonard, M. A. (1977). Psychopathology in children of inpatients with depression: A controlled study. *Journal of Nervous and Mental Disorders, 164*, 408–413.

Wiggins, J. S., & Winder, C. L. (1961). The peer nomination inventory: An empirically derived sociometric measure of adjustment in pre-adolescent boys. *Psychological Reports, 9*, 643–677.

Williams, J. (1977). *Psychology of women: Behavior in a biosocial context.* New York: Norton.

Winder, C. L., & Wiggins, J. S. (1964). Social reputation and behavior: A further validation of the Peer Nomination Inventory. *Journal of Social Psychology, 68*, 681–684.

Winer, B. J. (1971). *Statistical principles in experimental design.* New York: McGraw-Hill.

Winters, K. C., Stone, A. A., Weintraub, S., & Neale, J. M. (1981). Cognitive and attentional deficits in children vulnerable to psychopathology. *Journal of Abnormal Child Psychology, 9*, 435–453.

Worland, J., Janes, C. L., Anthony, E. J., McGinnis, M., & Cass, L. (1984). St. Louis risk research project: Comprehensive progress report of experimental studies. In N. F. Watt, J. Anthony, L. C. Wynne, & J. E. Rolf (Eds.), *Children at risk for schizophrenia: A longitudinal perspective.* New York: Cambridge University Press.

Yarrow, M. R., Campbell, J. D., & Burton, R. V. (1970). Recollections of childhood: A study of the retrospective method. *Monographs of the Society for Research in Child Development, 35*(5, Serial No. 138).

Zerbin-Rudin, E. (1967). Endogene psychosen. In P. Becker (Ed.), *Humangentik: Ein kurzes handbuch in funf baden* (Vol. 2). Stuttgart: Thieme.

Zubin, J., & Spring, B. (1977). Vulnerability—A new view of schizophrenia. *Journal of Abnormal Psychology, 86*, 103–126.

IV

RISK INDICES AND MECHANISMS

A Learned Helplessness Perspective on Childhood Depression: Theory and Research

Martin E. P. Seligman
Christopher Peterson

In this chapter, we describe the learned helplessness model of depression and illustrate how it can be applied to depression among children. Several empirical studies from our research group are described. For the most part, they parallel our previous work with depressed adults, and they show learned helplessness to be a useful model for depression across the life span. Because this chapter was originally prepared for a conference attempting to articulate some of the developmental issues inherent in the study of the depressive disorders, we begin and end here with some general comments about the place of learned helplessness in a developmental perspective on psychopathology.

INTRODUCTION: SOME IDEAS ABOUT DEVELOPMENTAL PSYCHOPATHOLOGY

Developmental psychopathology is a relatively new endeavor. Indeed, one of the field's few textbooks starts with the statement that it is "a field that hardly exists" (Achenbach, 1974, p. 3). This textbook goes on to describe a pervasive problem in defining the field, namely, that many workers studying psychopathology in children have simply applied "downward" theories and concepts from adult psychopathology. Progress

Martin E. P. Seligman. Department of Psychology, University of Pennsylvania, Philadelphia, Pennsylvania.

Christopher Peterson. Department of Psychology, Virginia Polytechnic Institute and State University, Blacksburg, Virginia.

toward defining the field cannot proceed, this text stresses throughout, until psychopathology in children is regarded as different in kind from psychopathology in adults.

We agree with this sentiment if it means that theories of childhood psychopathology should take into account not just the quantitative differences between children and adults but also the qualitative differences, such as those described by Piaget (1932). However, we disagree with this sentiment if it means that theories and concepts of adult psychopathology cannot *in principle* be applied to children. We feel strongly about this point because the learned helplessness model of depression has been proposed as a general theory (Seligman, 1974, 1975); although most research within the helplessness tradition has employed adults, we see no reason why the model cannot be profitably applied to children as well.

To be sure, many theories of adult psychopathology cannot be sensibly extended to children, but one can classify theories as more or less general. If the constructs of a theory can be invoked to explain the behavior of both children and adults, then that theory *may be* general. And if theory-guided research employing both children and adults yields convergent results, then that theory *is* general.

We recognize that children are in some ways different in kind from adults, particularly in the manner that they think about themselves and their world. Since the helplessness model is primarily a cognitive account of depression, it might seem particularly difficult for the theory to span different levels of cognitive development. On the other hand, the key constructs of helplessness theory probably apply to individuals at most stages of development. Stage of cognitive development should influence some of the constructs and processes of the helplessness model, but it need not preclude them.

If "developmental psychopathology" is placed in the context of "developmental psychology" in general, then the above discussion might be clarified. We are arguing that the different in kind versus different in degree argument is largely a false dichotomy, despite the fact that it looms as an important issue in developmental psychology. Attempts to explain how, why, and when behavior changes have taken two different directions; a generally accepted integration is still awaited.

The first may be dubbed a *learning approach*, and is characterized by the conception of development as continuous and gradual, occurring through interaction with the environment. This approach accounts for development with a few simple concepts, such as reward, punishment, and expectancy, and searches for theories of behavior that apply equally well to children and to adults, and even to animals. Such an approach puts great stock in laboratory experimentation, and is exemplified by reinforcement theory (e.g., Skinner, 1938), social learning theory (e.g., Bandura & Walters, 1963), and behavior modification (e.g., Bandura, 1969).

The second thrust within developmental psychology may be identified as a *stage approach*, and conceives development as a discontinuous process, occurring in quantum leaps. While interaction with the environment is acknowledged as important for normal development to occur, theoretical interest is in the unfolding of mental structures and schemata, which seem to be accorded a biological status. Children and adults pass through stages, and the psychological theories that "work" at one stage may be invalid at another stage. This approach has been less likely to use laboratory experiments, relying instead on ethological observations of individuals in naturalistic settings. Well-known examples of the stage approach include Freud (1953), Piaget (1932), Kohlberg (1963), and Erikson (1977).

Described so starkly, these two approaches can be seen in many ways as compatible—even complementary—once one allows each approach to have its own "focus of convenience" (Kelly, 1955). Unfortunately, theories in developmental psychology are often polarized and stand isolated from theories within the other general approach. A point we wish to emphasize here is that developmental psychopathology should avoid such polarization. The field should not be so zealous in creating its own identity that it refuses entry to theories and constructs that might prove useful.

We feel that learned helplessness might prove useful. It is a model that falls within the learning approach, but is sufficiently "uncluttered" to allow room for constructs identified as important by stage theorists. Although the research we describe here looks at similarities between children and adults, we could very well have attended additionally to differences. For instance, the attributional reformulation of helplessness theory (Abramson, Seligman, & Teasdale, 1978) proposes that the boundary conditions of helplessness and depression are under the sway of attributions. Children probably use attributions in a more "egocentric" fashion than do adults, and may offer "internal" attributions more readily and on the basis of different evidence than do adults. However, regardless of how internal attributions arise, the helplessness model proposes that they affect helplessness and depression similarly. Thus, the model allows for both differences and similarities across the life span.

THE LEARNED HELPLESSNESS MODEL OF DEPRESSION

Learned helplessness was first described systematically by animal learning researchers at the University of Pennsylvania (Overmier & Seligman, 1967; Seligman & Maier, 1967). These workers observed that mongrel dogs, following exposure to uncontrollable shocks, later showed several classes of deficits while attempting to learn a response that would terminate shock. First, the dogs showed a *motivational* deficit, failing to initiate as many escape attempts as animals not given prior shock. Second, they showed a *cognitive* deficit, failing to learn the response to terminate shock, even when an occasionally successful escape response was made. Third, they showed an *emotional* deficit, evidencing little overt emotionality while being shocked, instead sitting and enduring the shock without whimpering.

To describe these deficits, as well as to explain them, these workers coined the phrase "learned helplessness" (Maier, Seligman, & Solomon, 1969; Seligman, Maier, & Solomon, 1971), and proposed that the dogs learned during the uncontrollable shocks that responses and shock termination were unrelated. Regardless of what they did or did not do, the dogs were shocked. This learning of response–outcome independence was represented as an expectation of helplessness that was generalized to the new situation where learning was objectively possible to produce the observed deficits.

In a series of experiments reviewed by Maier and Seligman (1976), it was demonstrated that the key factor in producing helplessness deficits was the uncontrollability of the original shocks, and not their other traumatizing properties. Further, these experiments provided evidence with which the cognitive account of helplessness could be defended against alternative interpretations in peripheral and/or biological terms.

Although the cognitive explanation of animal helplessness has remained controversial (e.g., Maier & Jackson, 1979), numerous researchers interested in human behavior have used this explanation to account for a variety of failures of human adaptation (e.g., Garber & Seligman, 1980). Best known of these applications is by Seligman (1974, 1975) to depression; he has argued that the parallels between helplessness and depression, in terms of causes, symptoms, and cures, are strikingly similar, and that helplessness might serve as a laboratory model of depression.

Interestingly (at least to us), no one has suggested that helplessness theory when applied to people is too cognitive; indeed, most criticisms of helplessness as applied to people conclude that the "simple" cognitive explanation of learned helplessness fails to do justice to the complexities of people, including those with depressive symptoms. Thus, while uncontrollable events may indeed precede depression in a number of cases (e.g., Lloyd, 1980), helplessness theory as originally stated fails to address (1) the role of individual differences in response to uncontrollability, (2) the boundary conditions of the generality of helplessness, across time and situation, and (3) the frequent loss of self-esteem observed among depressives.

Recently, Abramson et al. (1978) reformulated the helplessness model as it applies to depression in order to handle these issues. Although the "reformulation" leaves intact the key constructs of the "original" theory, that is, still proposing that uncontrollability leads to an expectation of helplessness that in turn leads to deficits, it adds that *causal attributions* about the uncontrollable events are important determinants of the generality of induced deficits and of self-esteem involvement.

The reformulation suggests that three dimensions of attributions are important. If the uncontrollable events are attributed to characteristics of the individual (*internal* as opposed to external attributions), then self-esteem will diminish as helplessness develops. If the uncontrollable events are attributed to factors that persist over time (*stable* as opposed to unstable attributions), then helplessness is expected to be nontransient. Finally, if uncontrollability is attributed to causes present in a variety of situations (*global* as opposed to specific attributions), then helplessness is predicted to be pervasive.

Abramson et al. (1978) also suggested that people have characteristic attributional styles, habitual ways of explaining the causes of good and bad events. To the degree that a person points to internal, stable, and global causes of bad events, then that person is increasingly likely to be helpless and depressed once a bad event is encountered. Support for this suggestion has been found with mildly depressed college students and clinically depressed inpatients (see a review by Peterson & Seligman, 1981).

The attributional reformulation can be seen as a diathesis–stress model of depression. Depression results from characteristics of an individual (i.e., the "depressive" attributional style) in conjunction with characteristics of the environment (i.e., uncontrollable bad events). Neither the attributional style nor the uncontrollable events alone result in widespread helplessness and depression; only their co-occurrence leads to depression.

HELPLESSNESS THEORY IS IN PRINCIPLE APPLICABLE TO CHILDREN

The important constructs in the original helplessness theory and its attributional reformulation are mundane: contingency learning, expectations, and attributions. Numerous studies demonstrate that these constructs can be meaningfully used to explain the behavior of children as well as adults (see a review by Peterson, 1980). Watson (1972), for instance, has shown that young infants are sensitive to contingencies between their behaviors and environmental feedback. Dweck and Licht (1980) have shown that school children can be "helpless" in the face of failure and, further, that attributions play an important role in the development and maintenance of this helplessness.

These studies make the earlier point compelling: to apply helplessness theory to children is *not* to make the unthinking generalization decried by Achenbach (1974), since such an application makes sense. That helplessness theory "originated" in the animal learning laboratory, from which it traveled with such ease to the human laboratory (and beyond to the clinic, classroom, and hospital) shows that helplessness theory is a general statement about behavior, a status to which most learning theories aspire. Helplessness theory, at least in principle, can be applied to children without doing injustice either to the theory or to what is known about children.

CHILDHOOD DEPRESSION
FROM A LEARNED HELPLESSNESS VIEW

In this section, we report several empirical studies of depressive symptoms in children from the viewpoint of helplessness theory. These studies are preliminary ones, for the most part replicating our previous research with adults. More specifically, these questions guided our research:

1. Are depressive symptoms among children associated with the same cognitive deficits as they are among adults (e.g., W. R. Miller & Seligman, 1975; Price, Tryon, & Raps, 1978)?
2. Are depressive symptoms associated with the same insidious attributional style as they are in adults (e.g., Seligman, Abramson, Semmel, & von Baeyer, 1979)?
3. Does this style precede children's depressive symptoms as it does adults' (e.g., Golin, Sweeney, & Schaeffer, 1981)?
4. What are the origins of a child's attributional style?

Depressive Symptoms in Children

In contrast to the vast literature on adult depression, relatively little attention has been paid to depression in children—probably because some theorists doubt the very existence of childhood depression (e.g., Lefkowitz & Burton, 1978). However, we assume with Cantwell and Carlson (1979) that "if one looks for the clinical picture of depression in children in a way analogous to the way it is looked for in adults, it can indeed be found and may be much more common than people think" (p. 526). Recent research starting from this assumption agrees about the clustering of depressive symptoms in children and shows that these symptoms can be reliably measured (e.g., Cantwell & Carlson, 1979; Lefkowitz & Tesiny, 1980; Orvaschel, Weissman, & Kidd, 1980; Schulterbrandt & Raskin, 1977).

Kovacs and Beck (1977), for instance, developed the Childhood Depression Inventory (CDI), a self-report questionnaire modeled after the adult Beck Depression Inventory (BDI; Beck, Ward, Mendelson, Mock, & Erbaugh, 1961), a frequently employed and well-validated (Beck, 1967; Bumberry, Oliver, & McClure, 1978) measure of depressive symptoms. Kovacs (1979) found that clinicians' ratings of severity of depression correlate well with CDI scores ($r = .55$), and reported an internal reliability (estimated by Cronbach's [1951] coefficient alpha) of .86 for the CDI.

Similarly, Lefkowitz and Tesiny (1980) showed that multiple measures of depressive symptoms in children—such as peer nomination, teacher nomination, and self-report—converge. Thus, depressive symptoms among children analogous to the depressive symptoms of adults appear to cohere and may be measured reliably and validly. The present studies extend these investigations by asking if some of the consequences and causes of childhood depressive symptoms parallel those of adult depression.

Cognitive Deficits

A major prediction from the learned helplessness model is that individuals with naturally occurring depression as well as nondepressed individuals who experience uncontrollable events in the laboratory solve cognitive and instrumental problems poorly. Confirming the prediction, depressed adults, both hospitalized and nonhospitalized, solve anagrams poorly and learn to terminate noise poorly, and the extent of these deficits correlates highly with the severity of depression (Klein, Fencil-Morse, & Seligman, 1976; Klein & Seligman, 1976; W. R. Miller & Seligman, 1975; Price et al., 1978). Parallel deficits occur in nondepressed adults made helpless in the laboratory (Glass & Singer, 1972; Hiroto & Seligman, 1975; Klein et al., 1976; Klein & Seligman, 1976; W. R. Miller & Seligman, 1975). Investigators have recently found analogous deficits in children, unselected for depression, who are made helpless with prior unsolvable problems or uncontrollable noise (Dweck & Reppucci, 1973; Glass, 1977; Smith & Seligman, 1979). Taken together, these studies suggest that learned helplessness in children, as well as adults, is reflected by deficits in problem solving, and that these same deficits occur in adults with depressive symptoms. Do these deficits occur in children with depressive symptoms?

We attempted, in the first investigation reported here, to determine whether cognitive deficits, as measured by failure to solve Anagrams and Block Designs problems, are associated with depressive symptoms in children as measured by the CDI. To the extent that parallel deficits exist in both children and adults who are depressed, the hypothesis that depression among children parallels depression among adults is supported, and some usefulness of the learned helplessness model for childhood depression is implied.

Attributional Style as a Correlate of Depressive Symptoms

The reformulated learned helplessness hypothesis (Abramson et al., 1978) proposes that the expectation of uncontrollable bad events leads to depression when the person attributes them to internal, stable, and global causes. If such attributions are habitual, we speak of an attributional "style" that predisposes to depression (Seligman *et al.*, 1979). Empirical research (reviewed by Abramson *et al.*, 1978; Peterson & Seligman, 1981) suggests that the debilitating effects of uncontrollable bad events may be governed by subjects' attributions.

To date, only adults have been studied. It is not known if the same insidious attributional style correlates with depressive symptoms among children. In our second study, we measured attributional style in children with an instrument developed for this purpose. By a forced-choice technique, we obtained scores for the tendency to explain good or bad events with internal (as opposed to external) causes, with stable (as opposed to unstable) causes, and with global (as opposed to specific) causes. Depressive symptoms were measured with the CDI. According to the reformulated learned helplessness hypothesis, children with depressive symptoms should be inclined to make more internal, stable, and global attributions for bad events than their nondepressed peers. The learned helplessness model does not make an unequivocal prediction about depression and attributions regarding good events, but the research with adults (Seligman *et al.*, 1979) suggests that external, unstable, and specific attributions for good events might be associated with depressive symptoms.

Attributional Style as a Cause of Depressive Symptoms

The second purpose of the second study was to see whether attributional style precedes, "causes," or is a "risk factor" for depressive symptoms in children. The laboratory data reviewed by Abramson *et al.* (1978), I. W. Miller and Norman (1979), and Peterson and Seligman (1981) imply that attributional style is a risk factor for adult depression, and the studies showing that attributional style correlates with depressive symptoms are not inconsistent with a causal hypothesis (Peterson & Seligman, 1981). These demonstrations, however, are far from definitive, and, of course, these data are of unknown relevance to children.

It is possible to decide questions of causal priority among non-manipulated variables, at least tentatively, by using a longitudinal design and cross-lagged correlational analysis (Campbell & Stanley, 1963; Kenny, 1973, 1975). The measures of depressive symptoms and attributional style were therefore taken at each of two times, and the cross-lagged correlations between depression and attributional style were computed. Since causes work forward in time, a higher correlation between attributions at Time 1 and depression at Time 2 than between depression at Time 1 and attributions at Time 2 suggests a causal relation and disconfirms third variable explanations (for a pertinent example of the recent use of this inferential technique, see the study of Golin, Sweeney, and Schaeffer, 1981, investigating attributional style and depressive symptoms among college students). Therefore, we measured children's depressive symptoms and their attributional style at two intervals separated by 6 months to test whether attributional style is a risk factor for depressive symptoms.

Whence Attributional Style?

Do children learn their attributional style from parents? We attempted to gather preliminary evidence about the origins of attributional style by comparing the attributional styles of parents and their children, as well as by comparing their depressive symptoms. We used the adult and child versions of our attributional style questionnaire, the CDI, and the BDI.

STUDY 1

Method

SUBJECTS

Forty elementary school children (19 males and 21 females) in the fourth and fifth grades of three elementary schools in Philadelphia served as subjects. All children were white, middle class, between 9 and 11 years of age, had no diagnosed learning disability, and were not using antidepressive medication. All children took the CDI. Neither age nor grade correlated with CDI scores.

MATERIALS

The CDI contains 27 items, each consisting of three self-report statements graded in severity from 0 to 2. The items are drawn from the emotional, motivational, cognitive, and somatic symptoms of depression. A sample item is: I am sad once in a while (0); I am sad many times (1); I am sad all the time (2). No item refers to problem-solving abilities or performance. Children are instructed to complete the CDI based on how they have been feeling during the last 2 weeks. Scores may range from 0 (nondepressed) through 54 (extremely depressed).

The materials for the Block Designs task (from WISC-R) consisted of four blocks, all of which are red on two sides, white on two sides, and red and white on two sides. On each trial, the child is shown a sample design and asked to construct a match to the sample using the four blocks, with a time limit of 30 sec.

The Anagrams task consisted of 20 5-letter words with scrambled letters. The words were chosen from fourth and fifth grade spelling books. They were: "chair, place, women, brain, fight, plant, table, train, stamp, house, print, write, round, blind, story, water, child, dirty, mouse, and watch." All anagrams could be solved by a single pattern: 3-4-2-5-1; e.g., USOEH = HOUSE. There was a time limit of 2 min per anagram.

PROCEDURE

The CDI and experimental tasks were administered individually to each child in a quiet room. Following CDI administration, the child was given a series of Block Designs problems and Anagrams in counterbalanced order. The Block Designs task consisted of 5 practice trials followed by 10 test trials. On each trial, the child was shown the sample design and asked to construct a match to the sample using 4 blocks. In the Anagrams task, the child was given 3 practice anagrams followed by 20 test anagrams. The child was told that there might be a pattern to the letters of each of the scrambled words and that discovering the pattern would help.

A different experimenter was used for each of the two tasks, and the experimenter was counterbalanced with task. The experimenter was blind to the child's CDI score. Following completion of the two tasks, each of the children was given a digit span task designed so that everyone succeeded. Finally, all children were debriefed.

Because depressed adults do poorly on Block Designs tasks but not on verbal intelligence measures (Rapaport, Gill, & Schafer, 1968), the children were given the Peabody Picture Vocabulary Test within 1 month of their participation in this study. In this test, the experimenter reads a word, and the child chooses the picture that best illustrates the word. As expected, CDI scores did not correlate with performance on this test.

Results and Discussion

The more depressive symptoms on the CDI, the worse was the child's performance on both Block Designs and Anagrams. The relationships between CDI scores and latency measures were particularly strong: the more depressive symptoms, the slower was the child to complete the Block Designs ($r = .64$, $p < .001$) and to solve the Anagrams ($r = .67$, $p < .001$). Similar results were obtained for the number of failures on both tasks. In addition, "depressed" children (the upper third of the sample, stratified on CDI scores) "discovered" the anagram pattern less readily than did the "nondepressed" children (the lower third of the sample), where "discovering the pattern" is defined as three consecutive anagram solutions in less than 15 sec each (17 vs. 92%, $\chi^2 = 13.6$, $p < .0002$).

Along with poor problem solving, children with depressive symptoms made different kinds of spontaneous remarks during the tests than did nondepressed children. Typical comments made by depressed children were: "How many more problems are there?" "I never do well when I get timed." Comments typical of the other children were: "I am really smart." "I like the anagrams because they are more challenging." "It is easy once you get the pattern." At the end of the experiment, most of the children said they had enjoyed the "games," but many of the depressed children showed negative feelings and low mood during the tasks. In contrast, most of the nondepressed children showed bright affect throughout. (For parallel results with helpless children, see Dweck & Licht, 1980.)

The tasks at which the children with depressive symptoms did poorly are the same tasks at which both depressed adults and nondepressed adults and children made helpless by uncontrollable events also do poorly. To the extent that an expectation that future bad events will be uncontrollable is responsible for deficits in adult depression and in adult learned helplessness (Seligman, 1975), we speculate that a parallel expectation may be responsible for cognitive and instrumental deficits observed in helpless and depressed children. As Costello (1978) and Alloy and Abramson (1979) have pointed out, though, our methodology is not fine-grained enough to determine whether an expectation of uncontrollability causes these performances deficits. Future work is necessary to assess whether depressed children expect that their own responses fail to control outcomes and whether this expectancy mediates the deficits in their performance.

Anagrams and Block Designs are not unrepresentative of the cognitive tasks children face in school. Therefore, we suggest that when a school child does badly in class, the possibility that the child is depressed—rather than "dumb"—should be entertained.

STUDY 2

Method

SUBJECTS

Ninety-six children were obtained from two Philadelphia elementary schools. These schools consist predominantly of white, middle-class children. Approximately equal numbers of boys ($N = 50$) and girls ($N = 46$) and third, fourth, fifth, and sixth graders participated. (Five children who completed the questionnaires only at Time 1 or at Time 2, but not both, were excluded from the sample.) The questionnaires were filled out during classtime. The researcher read the questionnaires aloud while the children silently read their copies at the same time. The interval from Time 1 to Time 2 was 6 months.

INSTRUMENTS

The subjects completed the same two questionnaires at each of the two administrations: the CDI (see description in Study 1) and the Children's Attributional Style Questionnaire (CASQ). The CASQ has 48 items, each of which consists of an event followed by two possible causes. Respondents pick the sentence from the pair that better describes why the event happened. The two causes provided hold two of the attributional dimensions (and the valence) constant, while varying the third attributional dimension. Sixteen questions pertain to each of the three attributional dimensions. Half of each are about bad events, half about good events. Examples are shown in Table 1.

Thus, the 48 questions consist of eight items operationalizing each of the factorial combinations of attributional dimension (internal–external, global–specific, stable–unstable) and desirability of events (good, bad). The questions are arranged in a nonsystematic order, as is the sequence of the response alternatives (so that the internal alternative, for instance, is not consistently first or second).

Results

Attributional style and depressive symptoms were reliable and stable, attributional style correlated strongly with depressive symptoms as predicted, and evidence was found that attributional style for bad events may be a risk factor for later depressive symptoms, also as predicted.

SCORING, RELIABILITY, AND STABILITY

The CASQ is scored by assigning a 1 to each internal, stable, or global response chosen, and a 0 to each external, unstable, or specific response.

Table 1
Sample Items of the CASQ

Item	Dimension varied	Dimension held constant	Valence
A good friend tells you that he hates you.			Bad
A. My friend was in a bad mood that day.	External	Stability, globality	
B. I wasn't nice to my friend that day.	Internal	Stability, globality	
You get all the toys you want on your birthday.			Good
A. People always guess what toys to buy me for my birthday.	Stable	Internality, globality	
B. This birthday people guessed right as to what toys I wanted.	Unstable	Internality, globality	
You get an "A" on a test.			Good
A. I am smart.	Global	Internality, stability	
B. I am good in the subject that the test was in.	Specific	Internality, stability	

Subscales are formed by summing these scores across the appropriate questions for each of the three attributional dimensions, separately for good events and bad events. Thus, each of the six subscales has eight items, and scores could range from 0 to 8. Means, standard deviations, reliabilities, and stabilities of these subscales are presented in Table 2.

As can be seen, the instruments yielded similar means, standard deviations, and internal reliabilities at both administrations. The reliabilities tended to exceed the scale intercorrelations (see Table 3), indicating that the scales were empirically distinguishable, although the magnitudes of these reliabilities were not particularly high. Composites were formed by summing scores from the three dimensions, separately for good events and bad events, and reliability increased substantially. The subscales and composites were relatively stable across the time between administrations.

The CDI also yielded comparable means, standard deviations, and reliabilities at both administrations (see Table 2). Further, CDI scores were highly stable across the time between administrations. This stability implies that childhood depressive symptoms, at least as measured here, are not transient over 6 months.

MALE–FEMALE DIFFERENCES

Among adults, both depressive symptoms and affective disorder occur more frequently in women than in men, with a ratio estimated at somewhere between 1.5:1 and 3:1 (e.g., Radloff, 1975). Our data suggest that the difference may be present early in life. Among the 9- to 13-year-old school

Table 2
Means, Standard Deviations, and Reliabilities of Instruments (N = 96)

Instrument	Time 1			Time 2			
	$\overline{X}$	SD	r_{11}	$\overline{X}$	SD	r_{22}	r_{12}
Attributional style for good outcomes							
Internality	4.61	1.48	.32	4.71	1.61	.43	.53*
Stability	4.21	1.91	.55	3.91	1.89	.54	.61*
Globality	4.67	1.58	.40	4.81	1.78	.55	.54*
Composite	13.49	3.72	.66	13.43	4.10	.73	.71*
Attributional style for bad outcomes							
Internality	2.30	1.57	.43	2.47	1.73	.56	.63*
Stability	2.40	1.40	.42	2.01	1.17	.13	.52*
Globality	1.88	1.27	.31	1.61	1.26	.39	.64*
Composite	6.58	2.77	.50	6.09	2.80	.54	.66*
CDI	7.71	6.28	.86	7.16	5.92	.85	.80*

Note. r_{11} is internal reliability at Time 1, estimated by Cronbach's (1951) coefficient alpha; r_{22} is internal reliability at Time 2; r_{12} is product–moment correlation between scores at Time 1 and Time 2.
*$p < .001$.

Table 3
Intercorrelations of Attributional Style Subscales (N = 96)

Subscale	1	2	3	4	5	6
Attributional style for good outcomes						
1. Internality		.25*	.35*	−.24*	−.13	−.20
2. Stability	.26*		.57*	−.41*	−.23*	.03
3. Globality	.33*	.41*		−.14	−.16	.03
Attributional style for bad outcomes						
4. Internality	−.22*	−.45*	−.14		.25*	.05
5. Stability	−.22*	−.15	−.02	.18		.23*
6. Globality	−.01	−.02	−.27*	−.02	.27*	

Note. Intercorrelations below the diagonal (lower left-hand corner) are from Time 1; intercorrelations above the diagonal (upper right-hand corner) are from Time 2.
*$p < .05$.

children in our sample, girls reported more depressive symptoms than did boys ($p < .05$ at both administrations). Such early sex differences may be the substratum of adult differences in depression. This is consistent with the work of Dweck and Licht (1980), who reported that fourth grade girls were more susceptible to helplessness than were boys. Additionally, they found that girls were more likely than boys to make internal and stable attributions for their failures. In contrast, our girls reported only slightly more internal attributions for bad events than did boys ($p < .10$ at both administrations), and there were no significant sex differences in the use of the other attributional dimensions. Thus, it seems insufficient to interpret the sex difference in depression solely in terms of a sex difference in attributional style, although this may be partially an artifact of the lower reliability and stability of the CASQ than the CDI (see Amenson & Lewinsohn, 1981).

The remaining analyses are collapsed across sex, since separate analyses for boys and girls revealed identical patterns of results. Similarly, the school attended by the child and the grade of the child did not affect the other variables and are thus pooled across.

CORRELATIONS BETWEEN CASQ AND CDI

Table 4 presents the correlations of the CASQ subscales and composites with the CDI. As predicted, an attributional style in which bad events are attributed to internal, stable, and global causes correlated strongly with depressive symptoms, as did the reverse style for good events. The magnitudes of these associations were quite substantial, actually approaching the reliabilities of the instruments involved and accounting for the bulk of the reliable variance. Thus, depressive symptoms in school children are closely tied to attributional style.

Table 4
Correlations of Attributional Style Subscales with CDI Scores (N = 96)

Subscale	Correlation with CDI		Correlation corrected for attenuation	
	Time 1	Time 2	Time 1	Time 2
Attributional style for good outcomes				
Internality	−.34***	−.31**	−.64	−.52
Stability	−.47***	−.54***	−.69	−.79
Globality	−.35***	−.39***	−.59	−.57
Composite	−.53***	−.54***	−.71	−.68
Attributional style for bad outcomes				
Internality	.45***	.28**	.74	.41
Stability	.31**	.26**	.52	.79
Globality	.21*	.26**	.40	.46
Composite	.51***	.40***	.78	.59

$*p < .05.$ $**p < .01.$ $***p < .001.$

LOPSIDED ATTRIBUTIONS

Recent evidence surprisingly suggests that nondepressed individuals show optimistic distortions whereas depressed individuals are accurate at a variety of cognitive tasks. Among adults, nondepressed individuals (1) perceive more control than they actually have (Alloy & Abramson, 1979); (2) believe that they are more socially skilled than judges rate them to be (Lewinsohn, Mischel, Chaplin, & Barton, 1980); (3) misremember the number of successes and failures (e.g., Nelson & Craighead, 1977); and (4) show an optimistic "lopsidedness" in attributions for success versus failure (Raps, Peterson, Reinhard, Abramson, & Seligman, 1982). On the other hand, individuals with depressive symptoms (1) perceive noncontingency more accurately; (2) assess their social skills more accurately; (3) remember successes and failures more correctly; and (4) are evenhanded regarding attributions for success and failure, using the same forms of attributions to explain each (cf. Kelly, 1955; Rizley, 1978).

Our nondepressed children showed the same lopsidedness of attributional style that nondepressed adults do. Nondepressed children (those scoring below the median on the CDI at Time 1) were less likely than "depressed" children (those scoring above the median) to explain good and bad events evenhandedly. We calculated, for each of the three attributional dimensions, the absolute value of the difference between a child's attributions for good events and bad events. These differences were much larger among the nondepressed than among the depressed (see Table 5). Making internal, stable, and global attributions for success while making

Table 5
Lopsidedness of Attributions and Depression: Mean Absolute Value
of the Difference between Attributions for Good and Bad Events

Dimension	Depressed (N = 53)	Nondepressed (N = 43)	t(94)
Internality			
Time 1	1.91	3.70	5.12**
Time 2	2.53	3.33	2.10*
Stability			
Time 1	1.89	3.26	3.90**
Time 2	1.85	3.16	3.58**
Globality			
Time 1	2.34	3.77	4.30**
Time 2	2.64	4.35	5.23**

*p < .05.   **p < .001.

asymmetrical external, unstable, and specific attributions for failure may be lopsided and even "irrational," but it is probably important in sustaining hope for the future (cf. Lazarus, 1979).

CAUSALITY

Following the suggestions of Campbell and Stanley (1963) and the analytic procedures of Kenny (1973, 1975), the cross-lagged correlations between attributional style and depression were compared to see if causal priority could be assigned to one factor or the other. Because of the modest reliabilities of the subscales, we used only the attributional style composites. As can be seen in Fig. 1, the correlations between composite attributional style for bad events at Time 1 and depressive symptoms at Time 2 (r = .54) exceeded (p < .10) the correlation between depressive symptoms at Time 1 and attributional style at Time 2 (r = .34). This supports the prediction that the insidious attributional style puts one at risk for later depressive symptoms. For attributional style regarding good events, the cross-lagged correlations were essentially the same (r = −.47, −.54), implying no causal priority.

Rogosa (1980) has recently criticized the use of cross-lagged panel designs to draw causal inferences. An alternative means of answering our questions—correlating attributional style at Time 1 with depressive symptoms at Time 2, partialling out depressive symptoms at Time 1 (cf. Peterson, Schwartz, & Seligman, 1981)—yielded the same conclusions. Composite style for bad events predisposed later depressive symptoms (partial r = .27, p < .01), while composite style for good events did not (partial r = −.10, ns).

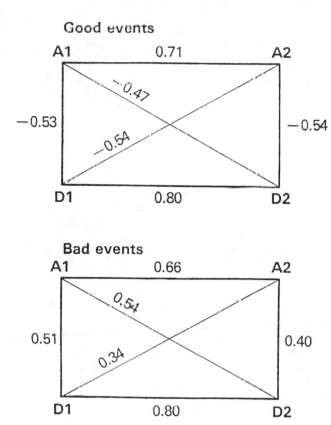

Fig. 1. *Cross-lagged correlations between attributional style composites and CDI scores (N = 96). A1 and A2 are attributions at Time 1 and 2, respectively; D1 and D2 are depression scores at Times 1 and 2, respectively.*

Discussion

There were six major findings of this study:

1. Self-report of depressive symptoms in 9- to 13-year-olds was highly stable (r = .80) across 6 months.
2. Girls reported more depressive symptoms than boys.
3. Composite attributional styles were reliably measured (r = .73, .54) in children of this age, and they were stable (r = .71, .66) over 6 months.
4. Attributional style correlated highly with depression in children, just as it does in adults. Compared to nondepressed children, children with depressive symptoms made more internal, stable, and global attributions for bad events (r = .51, .40) and more external, unstable, and specific attributions for good events (r = .53, .54).

5. Children with depressive symptoms, like their adult counterparts, were more evenhanded in causal attributions about bad versus good events.
6. An internal, stable, and global way of construing the causes of bad events may make children more vulnerable to depressive symptoms 6 months later.

STABILITY OF DEPRESSION

Depressive symptoms in childhood are often passed off as either a "transient developmental phenomenon" or a "reflection of inner turmoil," unworthy of being called "psychopathologic" (Lefkowitz & Burton, 1978). The fact that the same children who initially showed depressive symptoms also showed them 6 months later ($r = .80$) demonstrates that they are neither transient nor an isolated developmental event. The fact that these symptoms correlate so highly with poor cognitive performance (Study 1) suggests that they are maladaptive. Lefkowitz & Burton (1978) argued that childhood depressive symptoms should not be taken seriously as a form of psychopathology because of the statistical consideration that as many as 30% of children may show them at any given time. Surely debilitated performance, maladaptiveness, persistence, and misery outweigh considerations of frequency in terming a phenomenon "psychopathologic." Indeed, one of the notable characteristics of adult depression is its frequency. In their clinical and subclinical forms, the depressive disorders may affect between 20 and 50% of American adults at some point in their lives (Beck, 1967). Precise estimates of frequency of depression among children are not currently available, but we speculate that childhood depression also is quite frequent, affecting children's efforts in school and elsewhere to a greater degree than heretofore thought.

THE MEASUREMENT OF ATTRIBUTIONAL STYLE IN CHILDREN

In measuring attributional style in children, we departed somewhat from the method of Seligman et al. (1979) for measuring attributional style in adults. With adults, we asked open-ended questions, in which individuals provided their own cause for a specified situation and then rated that cause on internality, stability, and globality. Our pilot work suggested that younger children had some trouble understanding the adult questionnaire, particularly in rating the globality of causes. For this reason, we turned to a forced-choice method in which we held two dimensions constant while varying only the third. Our data indicated that attributional style in 9- to 13-year-old children can be measured this way, although reliability coefficients for the separate subscales were modest. In contrast, the reliability estimates for the composites (internal plus stable plus global subscales) were more satisfactory. Until the subscales are revised, ongoing work should either use the composite scales or add more items to them to bolster their reliabilities, if the individual dimensions are of interest.

CORRELATION OF ATTRIBUTIONAL STYLE AND DEPRESSION

The reformulated helplessness model of depression (Abramson et al., 1978) posits a depressive attributional style: Depressed individuals construe the causes of failure as more internal, stable, and global than nondepressed individuals. This prediction has been tested and confirmed in mildly depressed college students (Seligman et al., 1979) and in depressed inpatients (Raps et al., 1982). These studies have also shown that depressive symptoms are associated with external, unstable, and specific attributions about good events. The primary purpose of the second study was to test whether the same patterns existed among children with symptoms of depression. Each of the six expected relationships was strongly confirmed and then replicated 6 months later. The relationship between attributional style and depression was even stronger among children than it is among college students or adult inpatients. These data imply that the reformulated model may be applied to depressive symptoms in 9- to 13-year-olds. Whether the same relations hold with clinically depressed children is under investigation by our research group.

ATTRIBUTIONAL STYLE AS A CAUSE OF DEPRESSION

The reformulated helplessness model of depression predicts that when an individual with preexisting insidious attributional style for failure encounters actual failure, depression results. The mere correlation of depression and attributional style does not provide evidence for the causal hypothesis. Recent developments in the statistical analysis of longitudinal data, however, allow causal inferences to be drawn tentatively about nonmanipulated variables. Our cross-lagged analysis and partial correlations lead us to conclude that a child's attributional style for bad events may "cause" later depression. These data are not definitive, however, and we can give three reasons for caution:

1. Depression as operationalized here was somewhat more stable than was attributional style. The reformulation implies that attributional style should be more characteristic of a person than is depression, which is a sometimes consequence of an abiding attributional style. One possibility for resolving this problem is that the lower reliability of our attributional style measure accounts for the discrepancy, since reliability puts an upper limit on stability. Another possibility is that attributional style is a stable individual difference only for some individuals. Distinguishing between these possibilities, one at the level of operations and the other at the level of phenomena, is

impossible with only the present data, and we are attempting to develop converging and more reliable measures of attributional style, as well as an index of individual variability of style.

2. Attributional style for good events was as highly correlated with depression as was the style for bad events, but the cross-lagged procedure indicated causal priority only for attributional style for bad events. The resulting state of affairs—that positive attributional style appears inextricably bound up with depression, while negative attributional style seems more a cause of depression—awaits an explicit theory.

3. The cross-lagged panel technique is controversial, in part because computational procedures implementing the basic logic of the technique are still being developed. Further, the statistical power of these procedures seems low, and a sample size larger than the one employed here would be desirable. Although cross-lagged panel procedures cannot definitively rule out third variable arguments, they do represent an improvement over cross-sectional techniques. It seems likely that increasingly analytic means for handling longitudinal data will be developed in the future; we recommend their use to developmental psychopathologists.

STUDY 3

Method

SUBJECTS

In the third study, 47 mothers of the children who participated in the second study and 36 of the fathers completed the BDI and the adult Attributional Style Questionnaire (ASQ).

INSTRUMENTS

The BDI contains 21 items and measures the extent to which an adult reports a variety of depressive symptoms. Scores range from 0 (nondepressed) to 63 (extremely depressed).

The ASQ asks subjects to provide causes for each of 12 hypothetical events involving themselves, half good and half bad, and then to rate each provided cause along 7-point scales corresponding to its internality, stability, and globality. Internality, stability, and globality subscales are formed separately for good and bad events, by summing the appropriate scores over the events. Composite scores for good and bad events result from summing the appropriate subscales (Seligman *et al.*, 1979).

Results*

Overall, (1) a mother's attributional style for bad events correlated with her child's attributional style for bad events (r = .39) and with her child's depressive symptoms (r = .42); (2) a mother's depressive symptoms correlated with her child's depressive symptoms (r = .37) and weakly with her child's attributional style for bad events (r = .27); (3) a father's attributional style and depression were not related to scores of his mate or their children.

The correlations between the mothers' and children's composites are presented in Table 6. (The children's scores were obtained by averaging the scores from the two administrations.) The intercorrelations between mother's and child's scores for the individual dimensions (see Table 7) suggest that the bulk of the relationships among the composite measures resulted from the contributions of the internality and globality subscales.

Table 6

Means and Intercorrelations of Depression and Attributional Style Measures: Mother and Child (N = 47)

Measure	1	2	3	4	5	6
Mother						
1. Composite attributional style for good events (ASQ)	(.65)					
2. Composite attributional style for bad events (ASQ)	−.12	(.79)				
3. Depression (BDI)	−.34*	.60*	(.92)			
Child[a]						
4. Composite attributional style for good events (CASQ)	.08	−.07	−.03	(.82)		
5. Composite attributional style for bad events (CASQ)	−.09	.39*	.27	−.26	(.76)	
6. Depression (CDI)	−.27	.42*	.37*	−.48*	.49*	(.84)
X̄	15.10	12.22	5.85	13.26	6.00	6.62
SD	1.82	2.40	7.45	3.59	2.37	4.83

Note. Figures in parentheses, on the diagonal, are reliabilities estimated by Cronbach's (1951) coefficient alpha.

[a]Means from the two administrations (see text).

*p < .05.

*The pattern of results for boys and girls was identical, and so the data are pooled across this distinction. Another possible contrast, whether the parents were divorced/separated or not, also yielded the same pattern of results and thus is pooled across.

Table 7
Intercorrelations of Depression and Attributional Style Subscales for Bad Events: Mother and Child (N = 47)

	Mother			
Child	Internality (ASQ)	Stability (ASQ)	Globality (ASQ)	Depression (BDI)
Internality (CASQ)	.42*	.18	.24	.36*
Stability (CASQ)	.17	.10	−.06	.07
Globality (CASQ)	.35*	.06	.31*	.33*
Depression (CDI)	.48*	.18	.25	.39*

*$p < .05$.

Discussion

A mother's attributional style for bad events and depressive symptoms correlated with her child's corresponding attributional style and her child's depressive symptoms. This pattern is relevant to the learned helplessness model of depression in several ways. First, the central role it assigns to attributional style is supported, since attributional style was closely linked to the report of depressive symptoms, both by mother and child. Second, the results imply that the origins of attributional style may be in part familial (Cantwell & Carlson, 1979). Third, because the attribution–attribution correlation was as robust as the depression–depression correlation, attributional style is probably more than a mere by-product of depression.

Our results invite the speculation that the vicious circle describing the intrapsychic functioning of the depressive (Beck, 1967) may be embedded within an interpersonal vicious circle. The child may learn attributional style (or depressive symptoms) from its mother, and then the depressions of mother and child may maintain each other, particularly when each possesses the insidious attributional style. If so, the currently popular individual therapies used with depressives might be supplemented with family therapy, as has been done with other disorders in which family interaction is causal. More generally, the present results suggest that the depressed child is apt to be found in a family in which the mother is also depressed, and a depressed mother may well have a depressed child at home.

That fathers' depression and attributional style were not related to those of their wives or children may be due to the fact that mothers probably spend a good deal more time with the children than do fathers. In addition, Brown and Harris (1978) have argued that lack of social support is important in the development of depression, and so perhaps the support for the women and children in our sample was the family, while for the men, it was work or peer based.

The mechanisms by which mothers and children converge on attributional style and depressive symptoms are a matter of speculation. We have refrained from fully endorsing the likely hypothesis that causality flows from mother to child, since we suspect that the causality may be at least weakly bidirectional. Kelley's (1973) attribution theory proposes that attributions (and by extension, attributional styles) result from the abstraction of causal relationships from actual events (Cordray & Shaw, 1978) or from already abstract notions about causal relationships (Ajzen, 1977). Thus, the reason children and mothers have similar styles may be common experiences or common lore, but imitation is also likely.

Dweck and her colleagues (e.g., Dweck & Licht, 1980) have demonstrated that elementary school instructors accompany corrections, suggestions, and criticisms of students with attributions (e.g., "Robert, you're not trying hard enough at those long division problems"). The attributions made by instructors tend to be the ones that children themselves later employ (Dweck & Reppucci, 1973), suggesting that attributional styles can be transmitted as a whole. This important research should be extended from the classroom to other domains in which socialization occurs.

At any rate, our third study shows that mothers and children have similar attributional styles for bad events and similar depressive symptoms, and we speculate that depression may be prevented or ameliorated by changing the insidious attributional style of the whole family.

LEARNED HELPLESSNESS
AND DEVELOPMENTAL PSYCHOPATHOLOGY

In the preceding section, we have reviewed some evidence from our research showing that children with depressive symptoms share some of the characteristics of adults with depressive symptoms. Both show deficits at problem solving that parallel the deficits produced in depressed adults and children by uncontrollable events. Both have an attributional style in which bad events are seen as caused by internal, stable, and global causes. Both may be put at risk for future depression by processing causal information through this insidious attributional style.

Some general qualifications of our work to date should be acknowledged:

1. We have relied on questionnaires. This seems an acceptable strategy for preliminary work, but questionnaires should be supplemented with more sensitive techniques in future research.
2. A qualification related to the first is that we have studied depressive symptoms as a continuous variable. We have not studied depression as a clinical entity. Although our approach stresses the continuity

between clinical and subclinical depression, this is largely an empirical issue deserving explicit attention (cf. Raps *et al.*, 1982).

3. Our research participants did not include extremely young children. Whether learned helplessness aids in understanding depression among children younger than 8 or 9 years of age is not known.

4. Although we have argued that attributional style is particularly pertinent to depression, we have not shown this specificity with children, as we have with adults (Raps *et al.*, 1982). In other words, attributional style may predispose *other* childhood psychopathologies as well.

5. Several important "facts" about childhood depression are unanswered by our research to date. Most importantly, some researchers have found depressive symptoms among children to increase at puberty. Is this a helplessness phenomenon? Is this related to sex differences in depression?

6. As noted in our introduction, learned helplessness as a theory has yet to be fully melded with developmental theories. What we present here is more a juxtaposition than a merger, but helplessness theory seems compatible with both stage approaches to development and learning approaches.

Our hope in conducting these investigations—to show that helplessness theory could be profitably applied to childhood depression—has been realized. As we have elsewhere noted (Peterson & Seligman, 1981), the learned helplessness model is not a finished product. Further revisions will need to be made to incorporate new constructs within the model, including those with developmental implications. At the present time, we propose learned helplessness as a useful perspective for developmental psychopathologists interested in depression. Future studies might consider additional developmental factors that could influence depressive symptoms in relation to self-attributions, such as the nature of the self-concept at different ages and the capacities to perceive and attribute causality to various agents. It is clear that the repertoire of controlling responses and the manner in which attributional style is acquired and maintained are also relevant to understanding early manifestations of helplessness. We look forward to such elaborations of the helplessness model.

ACKNOWLEDGMENTS

The research reported here was supported by PHS MH-19604 to Martin E. P. Seligman. We acknowledge gratefully the assistance of our colleagues, particularly those in the Helplessness Seminar at the University of Pennsylvania. Michael Rutter and Peter Read made helpful comments on an earlier draft of this chapter.

REFERENCES

Abramson, L. Y., Seligman, M. E. P., & Teasdale, J. D. (1978). Learned helplessness in humans: Critique and reformulation. *Journal of Abnormal Psychology, 87,* 49–74.

Achenbach, T. M. (1974). *Developmental psychopathology.* New York: Ronald Press.

Ajzen, I. (1977). Intuitive theories of events and the effects of baserate information on prediction. *Journal of Personality and Social Psychology, 35,* 303–314.

Alloy, L. B., & Abramson, L. Y. (1979). Judgment of contingency in depressed and nondepressed students: Sadder but wiser? *Journal of Experimental Psychology: General, 108,* 441–485.

Amenson, C. S., & Lewinsohn, P. M. (1981). An investigation of the observed sex difference in prevalence of unipolar depression. *Journal of Abnormal Psychology, 90,* 1–13.

Bandura, A. (1969). *Principles of behavior modification.* New York: Holt, Rinehart, & Winston.

Bandura, A., & Walters, R. H. (1963). *Social learning and personality development.* New York: McGraw-Hill.

Beck, A. T. (1967). *Depression: Clinical, experimental, and theoretical aspects.* New York: Harper (Hoeber).

Beck, A. T., Ward, C. H., Mendelson, M., Mock, J., & Erbaugh, J. (1961). An inventory for measuring depression. *Archives of General Psychiatry, 4,* 561–571.

Brown, G. W., & Harris, T. (1978). *Social origins of depression.* New York: Free Press

Bumberry, W., Oliver, J. M., & McClure, J. N. (1978). Validation of the Beck Depression Inventory in a university population using psychiatric estimate as the criterion. *Journal of Consulting and Clinical Psychology, 46,* 150–155.

Campbell, D. T., & Stanley, J. C. (1963). Experimental and quasi-experimental designs for research and teaching. In N. L. Gage (Ed.), *Handbook of research on teaching.* Chicago: Rand McNally.

Cantwell, D. P., & Carlson, G. (1979). Problems and prospects in the study of childhood depression. *Journal of Nervous and Mental Disease, 167,* 522–529.

Cordray, D. S., & Shaw, J. I. (1978). An empirical test of the covariation analysis in causal attribution. *Journal of Experimental Social Psychology, 14,* 280–290.

Costello, C. G. (1978). A critical review of Seligman's laboratory experiments on learned helplessness and depression in humans. *Journal of Abnormal Psychology, 87,* 21–31.

Cronbach, L. J. (1951). Coefficient alpha and the internal structure of tests. *Psychometrika, 16,* 297–334.

Dweck, C. S., & Licht, B. (1980). Learned helplessness and intellectual achievement. In J. Garber & M. Seligman (Eds.), *Human helplessness: Theory and applications.* New York: Academic Press.

Dweck, C. S., & Reppucci, N. D. (1973). Learned helplessness and reinforcement responsibility in children. *Journal of Personality and Social Psychology, 25,* 109–116.

Erikson, E. (1977). *Toys and reasons: Stages in the ritualization of experience.* New York: Norton.

Freud, S. (1953). Three essays on sexuality. In J. Strachey (Ed.), *The standard edition of the complete psychological works of Sigmund Freud* (Vol. 7). London: Hogarth Press. (Original work published 1905)

Garber, J., & Seligman, M. E. P. (Eds.). (1980). *Human helplessness: Theory and applications.* New York: Academic Press

Glass, D. C. (1977). *Behavior patterns, stress, and coronary disease.* Hillsdale, NJ: Lawrence Erlbaum Associates.

Glass, D. C., & Singer, J. E. (1972). *Urban stress: Experiments on noise and social stressors.* New York: Academic Press.

Golin, S., Sweeney, P. D., & Schaeffer, D. E. (1981). The causality of causal attributions in depression: A cross-lagged panel correlational analysis. *Journal of Abnormal Psychology, 90,* 14–22.

Hiroto, D. S., & Seligman, M. E. P. (1975). Generality of learned helplessness in man. *Journal of Personality and Social Psychology, 31,* 311–327.

Kelley, H. H. (1973). The processes of causal attribution. *American Psychologist, 28,* 107–128.

Kelly, G. A. (1955). *The psychology of personal constructs.* New York: Norton.

Kenny, D. A. (1973). Cross-lagged and synchronous common factors in panel data. In A. S. Goldberger & O. D. Duncan (Eds.), *Structural equation models in the social sciences.* New York: Seminar Press.

Kenny, D. A. (1975). Cross-lagged panel correlation: A test for spuriousness. *Psychological Bulletin, 82,* 887–903.

Klein, D. C., Fencil-Morse, E., & Seligman, M. E. P. (1976). Learned helplessness, depression, and the attribution of failure. *Journal of Personality and Social Psychology, 33,* 508–516.

Klein, D. C., & Seligman, M. E. P. (1976). Reversal of performance deficits in learned helplessness and depression. *Journal of Abnormal Psychology, 85,* 11–26.

Kohlberg, L. (1963). The development of children's orientations toward a moral order. I. Sequence in the development of moral thought. *Vita Humana, 6,* 11–33.

Kovacs, M. (1979). *Interim information on the Children's Depression Inventory.* Unpublished manuscript, Western Psychiatric Institute and Clinic.

Kovacs, M., & Beck, A. T. (1977). An empirical clinical approach towards a definition of childhood depression. In J. G. Schulterbrandt & A. Raskin (Eds.), *Depression in children: Diagnosis, treatment, and conceptual models.* New York: Raven Press.

Lazarus, R. S. (1979). Positive denial: The case of not facing reality. *Psychology Today, 13,* 44–60.

Lefkowitz, M. M., & Burton, H. (1978). Childhood depression: A critique of the concept. *Psychological Bulletin, 85,* 716–726.

Lefkowitz, M. M., & Tesiny, E. P. (1980). Assessment of childhood depression. *Journal of Consulting and Clinical Psychology, 48,* 43–50.

Lewinsohn, P. M., Mischel, W., Chaplin, W., & Barton, R. (1980). Social competence and depression: The role of illusory self-perceptions. *Journal of Abnormal Psychology, 89,* 203–212.

Lloyd, C. (1980). Life events and depressive disorder reviewed. I. Events as predisposing factors. II. Events as precipitating factors. *Archives of General Psychiatry, 37,* 529–548.

Maier, S. F., & Jackson, R. L. (1979). Learned helplessness: All of us were right (and wrong): Inescapable shock has multiple effects. In G. H. Bower (Ed.), *The psychology of learning and motivation: Advances in research and theory* (Vol. 13). New York: Academic Press.

Maier, S. F., & Seligman, M. E. P. (1976). Learned helplessness: Theory and evidence. *Journal of Experimental Psychology: General, 105,* 3–46.

Maier, S. F., Seligman, M. E. P., & Solomon, R. L. (1969). Pavlovian fear conditioning and learned helplessness. In B. A. Campbell & R. M. Church (Eds.), *Punishment.* New York: Appleton-Century-Crofts.

Miller, I. W., & Norman, W. H. (1979). Learned helplessness in humans: A review and attribution theory model. *Psychological Bulletin, 86,* 93–119.

Miller, W. R., & Seligman, M. E. P. (1975). Depression and learned helplessness in man. *Journal of Abnormal Psychology, 84,* 228–238.

Nelson, R. E., & Craighead, W. E. (1977). Selective recall of positive and negative feedback, self-control behaviors, and depression. *Journal of Abnormal Psychology, 86,* 379–388.

Orvaschel, H., Weissman, M. M., & Kidd, K. K. (1980). Children and depression. *Journal of Affective Disorders, 2,* 1–16.

Overmier, J. B., & Seligman, M. E. P. (1967). Effects of inescapable shock upon subsequent escape and avoidance learning. *Journal of Comparative and Physiological Psychology, 63,* 28–33.

Peterson, C. (1980). Perceived control over one's life: A review of the literature. Unpublished manuscript, University of Pennsylvania, Philadelphia.

Peterson, C., Schwartz, S. M., & Seligman, M. E. P. (1981). Self-blame and depressive symptoms. Journal of Personality and Social Psychology, 41, 253–259.

Peterson, C., & Seligman, M. E. P. (1981). Helplessness and attributional style in depression. Tiddskrift for Norske Psykologforening, 18, 3–18, 53–59.

Piaget, J. (1932). The moral judgment of the child. New York: Harcourt.

Price, K. P., Tryon, W. W., & Raps, C. S. (1978). Learned helplessness and depression in a clinical population: A test of two behavioral hypotheses. Journal of Abnormal Psychology, 87, 113–121.

Radloff, L. (1975). Sex differences in depression: The effects of occupational and marital status. Sex Roles, 1, 249–265.

Rapaport, D., Gill, M. M., & Schafer, R. (1968). Diagnostic psychological testing (rev. ed., R. R. Holt, Ed.). New York: International Universities Press.

Raps, C. S., Peterson, C., Reinhard, K. E., Abramson, L. Y., & Seligman, M. E. P. (1982). Attributional style among depressed patients. Journal of Abnormal Psychology, 91, 102–108.

Rizley, R. (1978). Depression and distortion in the attribution of causality. Journal of Abnormal Psychology, 87, 32–48.

Rogosa, D. (1980). A critique of cross-lagged correlation. Psychological Bulletin, 88, 245–258.

Schulterbrandt, J. G., & Raskin, A. (Eds.). (1977). Depression in children: Diagnosis, treatment, and conceptual models. New York: Raven Press.

Seligman, M. E. P. (1974). Depression and learned helplessness. In R. J. Friedman & M. M. Katz (Eds.), The psychology of depression: Contemporary theory and research. Washington, DC: Winston.

Seligman, M. E. P. (1975). Helplessness: On depression, development, and death. San Francisco: Freeman.

Seligman, M. E. P., Abramson, L. Y., Semmel, A., & von Baeyer, C. (1979). Depressive attributional style. Journal of Abnormal Psychology, 88, 242–247.

Seligman, M. E. P., & Maier, S. F. (1967). Failure to escape traumatic shock. Journal of Experimental Psychology, 74, 1–9.

Seligman, M. E. P., Maier, S. P., & Solomon, R. L. (1971). Unpredictable and uncontrollable aversive events. In F. R. Brush (Ed.), Aversive conditioning and learning. New York: Academic Press.

Skinner, B. F. (1938). The behavior of organisms. New York: Appleton-Century-Crofts.

Smith, R., & Seligman, M. E. P. (1979). Black and lower class children are more vulnerable to impairment of problem solving following helplessness. Unpublished manuscript, University of Pennsylvania, Philadelphia.

Watson, J. S. (1972). Smiling, cooing, and "the game." Merrill-Palmer Quarterly of Behavior and Development, 18, 323–339.

Long-Term Effects
of Early Loss of Parent

G. W. Brown
T. O. Harris
A. Bifulco

INTRODUCTION

Three recent reviews have been skeptical regarding the possibility that parental loss in childhood plays any role in the etiology of clinical depression in adulthood (Crook & Eliot, 1980; Granville-Grossman, 1968; Tennant, Bebbington, & Hurry, 1980), although one group has since put its negative conclusions in less absolute terms, arguing that loss does "not appear to exert any substantial effect on adult psychiatric morbidity" (Tennant, Hurry, & Bebbington, 1982). Most reviews have concentrated on death of a parent but Richards and Dyson (1982) in a comprehensive review of the impact of separation and divorce on children state "if effects exist they must be relatively weak or the studies would have been able to demonstrate them much more consistently" (pp. 35–36). Only one recent review has come to more positive conclusions but even this admits that the evidence is "not overwhelming" (Lloyd, 1980, p. 534). Nonetheless, there are now good data to support the persistent belief of clinicians that there is an important long-term link: a tradition admirably reflected in Bowlby's third volume on *Attachment and Loss* (1980), relying a good deal as it does on case-history material.

Why then have recent reviewers been so skeptical? As implied by Richards and Dyson it would appear a straightforward enough matter to settle: depression is common and there should be no difficulty in establishing when a parent died or whether there has been a lengthy separation from

G. W. Brown, T. O. Harris, and A. Bifulco. Department of Sociology, Royal Holloway and Bedford New College, University of London, London, England.

one or both of them. However, this simplicity is only apparent: shortcomings in measurement and design have been very common. To add to the confusion, they appear to be as likely to produce positive as negative findings; and, indeed, their ubiquity has been one reason for the current skepticism—so many of the positive findings in the literature could have resulted from various kinds of bias, particularly stemming from the selection of unsuitable comparison series (see Granville-Grossman, 1968). However, the crudity of many efforts to measure early loss has almost certainly contributed to negative findings. One research report, for example, merely stated that separations from a parent of 2 weeks or more were unrelated to current psychiatric disorder (Tennant, Hurry, & Bebbington, 1980). There is nothing to suggest that a separation of a few weeks would be likely to lead to long-term consequences; it is in any case essential to consider a *range* of experiences. Moreover, even if attention is paid to such features as duration of separation, or whether the mother or father is involved, this may not account for the full complexity of the loss experience. Death or separation from a father, for instance, is not infrequently followed within a year or so by separation from a mother and it is essential to take account of both.

Undoubtedly the greatest shortcoming has been failure to consider the highly complex chain of experiences that must link loss of a parent with later depression. If factors that provide crucial intervening links are not studied, then the association between loss of a parent and depression in adult life is bound to be low. There has, for example, been a general failure to recognize the importance of a key final link—that most episodes of depression appear to result from *current* adversity, whatever the contribution of early experiences to vulnerability.

Recent research, concentrating on psychosocial influences, has suggested a three-factor model of depression:

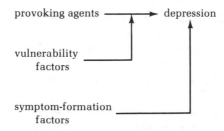

Certain current *provoking agents* determine when an episode of depression takes place. Most significant are severe events that usually involve an important loss or disappointment, if this is understood to encompass not only loss of a person but loss of a role or even an idea (Brown &

Harris, 1978). (Loss in the sense of bereavement forms only a small minority of events associated with onset of depression—at least among women in urban settings.) A second and somewhat less important agent concerns ongoing major difficulties such as might be brought about by poor housing or by a husband who drinks heavily. Evidence for the etiological role of such agents is now impressive. Many research centers have demonstrated the critical role of certain life events and have shown that onset usually occurs within a month or so of the event (e.g., Finlay-Jones, 1981; Paykel, 1973).

Such provoking agents probably bring about at least 60% of all episodes of depression among psychiatric patients and between 80 and 90% among women developing depression in the general population (Brown & Harris, 1978). However, the chance of such experiences bringing about depression is greatly influenced by the presence of *vulnerability factors,* such as lack of social support. The middle arrow in the diagram represents the fact that these factors increase risk only in the presence of the provoking agent, but have no impact without them. There is now reasonably good evidence that lack of an intimate tie with a husband and having three or more children under the age of 14 living at home act as vulnerability factors for women—that is, the risk of depression is increased in their presence once a provoking agent occurs (e.g., Brown & Harris, 1978; Campbell *et al.,* 1983; Martin, 1982; Murphy, 1982; Paykel, Emms, Fletcher, & Rassaby, 1980; Surtees & Ingham, 1980). There is some suggestion that lack of employment may play this role, under certain circumstances, but evidence, as yet, is less convincing. Which factors act in this way is bound to be influenced by the cultural setting of those studied (Brown & Prudo, 1981; Prudo, Brown, Harris, & Dowland, 1981).

The third factor in the model, *symptom-formation,* is different from the others in that rather than increasing risk of depression, it influences its form once it occurs—in terms, for instance, of the degree to which it is "psychotic" rather than "neurotic." The relevant experience leading to such an effect apparently may come from any point in a person's life, but so far early experience has been heavily implicated.

Although a number of research centers have produced evidence supporting parts of this model, we shall concentrate on two studies of women from our own research program as these have also dealt adequately with the etiological role of early loss of parent. The second one, carried out in Walthamstow, was designed specifically to tackle the question of early loss. It is important to relate such loss to the causal model as the impact of early loss may at times be masked if possible "counterbalancing" influences from current favorable circumstances are not taken into account. This can be illustrated by results from our first inquiry carried out among women living in Camberwell, an inner-city area of London, with the well-recognized social problems of such areas. In a random sample of women between 18 and 65 a definite association emerged between early loss of a parent and psychiatric "caseness" in the year before our inquiry, i.e., symptoms were of a severity comparable with those seen in out-patient practice. This was established by a clinical-type interview, Present State Examination (PSE). The PSE has as its core a glossary of terms and definitions about specific symptoms, and it has been established that medical and nonmedical interviewers can reach satisfactory reliability in rating specific items (Cooper et al., 1977; Wing, Nixon, Mann, & Leff, 1977). We added a number of further stages to these initial ratings. One of these was to rate women considered to have experienced a definite psychiatric syndrome in the year before interview as cases and those with lower disturbance as borderline cases.

In order for a woman to be considered a case there had to be both depressed mood and four or more of the following 10 symptoms: hopelessness, suicidal ideas or actions, weight loss, early waking, delayed sleep, poor concentration, neglect due to brooding, loss of interest, self-depreciation, and anergia. Usually many other PSE symptoms were also present. These items have been shown statistically to underlie our clinical criteria of depression (Finlay-Jones et al., 1980). The great majority of the conditions were entirely depressive or involved an important depressive component (Brown & Harris, 1978). For the purpose of this chapter we shall henceforth simply refer to depression, although this included a few disorders where anxiety was primary. In all instances the depression or anxiety was quite severe.

When type of loss was considered, only that of mother before age 11, by either death or separation (not due to war) lasting at least 1 year, had a clear association with depression in the year of our inquiry: the proportion with a loss of a father between birth and 10, or between 11 and 16, was not statistically different between depressed and other women. Of those with depression, 22% had lost a mother before age 11, compared with 6% of other women (see Brown, Harris, & Copeland, 1977, for details).

However, the most important result to emerge from this early study concerned evidence that one way in which early loss of a mother relates to onset of depression is through its role as a vulnerability factor. To test this it is essential to deal only with women not already depressed at the start of the year investigated and to consider how far increased risk of depression is associated with early loss of a mother only when a provoking agent has also occurred before onset. Table 1 shows that this is just what happened among women in the general population. As required by the concept of vulnerability, there was a much increased risk of depression in the year of inquiry among those who lost their mothers before the age of 11 in the presence of a provoking agent but no raised risk without one. In fact, none of the 15 women with an early loss of mother but without a provoking agent developed depression, compared with 7 of the 15 with such an agent.

Table 1
Percentage of Women in Camberwell Who Suffered Onset of Depression
in the Year (Chronic Cases Excluded)

	Loss of mother before 11 (%)		Loss of father before 11 (excluding 30 women with a loss of mother before 11) (%)	
	Yes	No	Yes	No
Severe event or major difficulty	47* (7/15)	17* (26/149)	20 (3/15)	17 (23/135)
None	0 (0/15)	2 (4/240)	0 (0/17)	2 (4/222)

*$p < .01$.

SOCIAL CLASS AND DEPRESSION

The fact that current adversity relates to risk of depression raises the question of the role of social class. Given that early loss of a parent acts as a vulnerability factor, it is likely to show a relatively low association with prevalence of depression in any population with a low rate of provoking agents. This is because a vulnerability factor cannot act without the presence of a provoking agent. Furthermore, since risk of depression increases with the number of vulnerability factors, early loss of a mother will be more highly associated with depression in any population in which such loss is correlated with other vulnerability factors such as having three or more children under 14 living at home. In Camberwell, at least, both points hold for working-class women—they more often experience provoking agents and vulnerability factors, and among them early loss of mother is more highly correlated with the other vulnerability factors. It is therefore perhaps not surprising that the link between early loss of mother and depression clearly held only among working-class women (58 vs. 20%, $p <$ .001, as against 14 vs. 8%, n.s., in the middle class). Very few other population surveys have considered the long-term effect of losing a parent, and the Midtown survey in New York reported by Langner and Michael (1963) is the only one to our knowledge that gives results in terms of social class. Only loss of mother, not of father, related to current psychiatric state, and the association for loss of mother by death held only for "lower-class" women. This social-class effect seen in London and New York is probably enough to explain the negative results obtained in a recent small but well-conducted survey by Birtchnell (1980) of women whose mothers had died in childhood and who were currently living in the Chichester area of West Sussex, a notably prosperous English county town. There was no greater rate of psychiatric symptomatology among the 42 with a loss than among the 42 women without, 4.7 and 4.7% with serious symptomatology, and

20.9 and 18.6% with at least moderate psychiatric symptomatology, respectively.

Given such effects, findings concerning early loss will almost certainly vary greatly with the social composition of the population studied—in general, the lower the rate of provoking agents and vulnerability factors (other than early loss), the lower will be the association between early loss and current depression. However, it is still necessary to consider another study with seemingly negative results, since it was carried out in the same location (Camberwell) and thus cannot be accounted for by varying rates of severe life events and different class compositions between populations (Bebbington, Hurry, Tennant, Sturt, & Wing, 1981). One complication in coming to terms with this study is that the results have been presented in at least five separate papers, often in rather differing ways, both in terms of the measures of loss and in terms of the statistical methods used.

In some of their more recent publications (Tennant, Bebbington, & Hurry, 1982; Tennant, Hurry, & Bebbington, 1982) the authors seem to be moving toward the conclusion that there are some effects of childhood loss of parent upon adult morbidity, especially depression. It would seem that their earlier failure to detect effects of separations could be due to their having taken too short a duration of separation at that time (Tennant, Hurry, & Bebbington, 1980). Moreover, their claim that early death of mother is unrelated to adult morbidity is contradicted by their own data. These show a higher rate among cases for maternal death at 0–10 and 11–18 but neither on its own reaches statistical significance (Tennant, Smith, Bebbington, & Hurry, 1981, Table 2, p. 311). However, if, as is statistically legitimate, the two loss groups are combined the difference between maternal-loss and maternal-no-loss groups is statistically significant ($\chi^2 = 5.67$, 1 df, 7% of noncases having a loss of mother versus 14% of cases).

PSYCHIATRIC PATIENTS AND EARLY LOSS OF PARENT

So far we have dealt with population studies of early loss: however, most research has relied for its depressive conditions on psychiatric inpatients and, to a lesser extent, out-patients. We also collected comparable material for 114 women living in Camberwell who had been treated by psychiatrists for depression of recent onset. Findings were less clear-cut than for the general population, which conforms to the generally inconsistent results of studies based on patient populations. There was only a very small association between early loss of parent and depression among both groups of patients when compared with women of much the same age and social class in the Camberwell general population. There was, however, a quite straightforward reason for this lack of association. It is easily overlooked that the comparison groups so far used in published studies of patient populations have included women who are themselves suffering from depression. Since we have seen that such women are likely to have a high rate of early loss of a parent, their inclusion in the comparison group will attenuate any association between early loss of a parent and depression.

The fact that no published study of depressed patients has made adequate allowance for this goes some way to explain the negative findings in the literature. This failure is probably related to a lack of appreciation of how common the experience of depression can be in the general population—during the 3 months before interview, 15% of women in Camberwell suffered from a definite psychiatric disorder, usually with an important depressive component. Only a small number of the women were seeing a psychiatrist.

When the findings were reanalyzed after exclusion of depressed women from the comparison group a difference was found. Almost double the proportion of patients had a loss of mother before the age of 11 when compared with women in Camberwell who were not depressed (Table 2). The finding confirms the etiological importance of early loss of a mother. Nonetheless, this difference (which falls short of significance) is still smaller than the fourfold difference obtained from women within the general population.

One possible explanation for this difference between patients and those depressed in the community is that vulnerability factors may increase risk but, once depression has occurred, decrease chances of contacting a psychiatrist. This is not as farfetched a possibility as at first might appear. There are two pieces of evidence. While having three or more children under the age of 14 clearly increased risk of depression among women in Camberwell, having young children was not more common among depressed patients drawn from the same population. Furthermore,

Table 2
Women with Loss of Parents before Age 17

Age at loss	Patients (%) (N = 114)	General population (Camberwell) (%) (N = 458)	General population excluding cases (%) (N = 382)
	Loss of mother		
0–10	10.5	8.7	6.0
11–16	3.5	1.7	2.1
	Loss of father		
0–10	15.8	12.4	11.5
11–16	5.3	4.3	5.0

Note. No differences are significant at the $p = .05$ level.

among those depressed in the general population, the presence of young children at home was associated with a reduced chance of being treated by a general practitioner for a depressive condition (Brown & Harris, 1978, p. 188). It makes sense that women with young children will be less well equipped to overcome the various barriers to medical care and moreover might be more likely to see their affliction as due to the life they are leading and thus not really of medical concern. Women with very marked symptoms of depression are often highly ambivalent about the appropriateness of seeking medical help (Ginsberg & Brown, 1982; Goldberg & Huxley, 1980). Second, while the frequency of depression was greater among working-class than middle-class women in the general Camberwell population, this association almost disappears when women receiving psychiatric treatment are considered (Brown & Harris, 1978). There is a tradition in the literature that selective factors will determine who receives treatment among those suffering from psychiatric disorder (Hollingshead & Redlich, 1958) and that conclusions based on treated populations alone can often prove misleading (Mechanic, 1978). Unfortunately there is little evidence on the particular treatment selection process at issue here other than the two findings we have mentioned concerning the presence of several children at home and working-class status. Since early loss of mother has related both to having three or more children under 14 living at home and to a working-class status, it is possible that some of the inconsistency of published research has been the result of studying only psychiatric patients. In other words, patients may tend to exhibit a lower rate of early loss of parent than would be expected from population surveys because, once depressed, women with such loss are less likely to receive psychiatric care. The problem is further complicated, however, by the distinction between types of childhood loss of parent, for there is recent evidence to suggest that, while the above line of argument may hold for maternal deaths, childhood separation from mother may in fact increase chances of reaching a psychiatrist, if not a general practitioner, due to its link with "acting out" behavior once depressed (Brown, Craig, & Harris, in press). Perhaps the best that can be said at present is that there are very powerful selective factors associated with childhood parental loss and until these are fully explicated it would be as well to be cautious about drawing firm conclusions from findings based on psychiatric patients.

SOME PRELIMINARY THEORETICAL CONSIDERATIONS

We have speculated that the importance of major loss and disappointment in depression may lie in the deprivation of important sources of value and reward, of good thoughts about ourselves, our lives, and those close to us, so that feelings of extreme hopelessness, set off by such deprivation, are critical in bringing about clinical depression (Brown & Harris, 1978). Particularly important is loss of faith in one's ability to obtain or retain an important and valued goal (Melges & Bowlby, 1969). Feelings of hopelessness as such are not enough: before the core psychological and physical symptoms of depression are set in train it is necessary for such feelings to generalize—an idea closely linked to Beck's discussion of a cognitive triad in depressed patients of hopelessness about circumstances, one's self and the future (Beck, 1967). The crucial role of cognitive processes in depression has recently been underlined by studies systematically examining the effectiveness of changing negative thought processes through cognitive therapy interventions with depressed patients (Beck, Rush, Shaw, & Emery, 1979; Teasdale & Fennell, 1982).

Relatively few people develop such generalized hopelessness following loss and disappointment because they are not susceptible to these cognitive processes. Such a vulnerability consists in the relative inaccessibility of positive memories that constitute evidence against the pessimistic generalizations being formulated; the level of self-esteem is intimately related to the size of such a fund of positive memories (and thus possibly their accessibility). Feelings of ongoing low self-esteem may include, say, a tendency to react to frustration with a sense of helplessness. We see an important link between mastery of problems and feelings of self-esteem, but any factor contributing to low mastery would be relevant. Our reference to self-esteem should, at present, be seen as no more than a way of highlighting core notions concerning the self and biographical factors that have contributed to them. We believe that the present simple indicators of vulnerability are significant because of their connection with these core notions of self. We have emphasized for women the importance of low intimacy with a husband, having three or more children under the age of 14, and lack of employment outside the home. It is easy to see how these might, in an urban setting at least, relate to enduring feelings of failure and low self-worth. However, early loss of a mother is more difficult to explain in such terms. There are two obvious possibilities. Such loss may lead to internal changes in "personality," say, in doubts about how lovable one is, and this may lead to a particular reaction to current losses and disappointments. Alternatively, early loss may increase the chance of certain external experiences occurring in adulthood. In turn these may increase the chance of experiencing one of the vulnerability factors. Of course, both possibilities may play a role.

This, however, deals only with the role of early loss of mother as a vulnerability factor. For a full picture it is essential to consider three other possibilities. The same experiences that may increase chances of experiencing certain vulnerability factors may also subject the person to a greater risk of experiencing provoking agents: membership of the unskilled manual classes may act in this way to increase rates of depressive illness. Indeed, the vulnerability factor of three or more children under 14 living at home is likely to be associated with a greater chance of experiencing a provoking agent if only because the greater the number of household members the greater the number of relevant people for whom events will be occurring. A second possibility is that early loss may influence chances of recovery and this would bring about a link between early loss and prevalence of depression irrespective of its etiological role. A third possibility is that early loss might increase risk of depression quite independently of the factors in our model.

Bowlby's recent review of childhood antecedents of disordered mourning and of clinical depression and anxiety (Bowlby, 1980; see also Bowlby, 1969, 1973) notes how the nature of attachment and how disruption of the initial bond with mother may influence subsequent personality development. In the third volume of his trilogy on attachment and loss he argues that even young children are capable of successful mourning, but that at any age mourning can take a pathological course in terms of either chronic mourning or the absence of conscious grieving. Children are particularly likely to experience pathological mourning because of their dependence on adults for comfort and for information to help them understand the reasons for the loss. Often this support is not forthcoming, perhaps as a result of the surviving parent's own grief, and the child finds it more difficult to accept the fact of the loss.

Bowlby considers a current sense of helplessness or hopelessness as the key characteristic of depression; he relates the likelihood of experiencing such feelings in adult life to three kinds of experience in childhood: never attaining a stable and secure relationship with parents; being told repeatedly that one is unlovable, inadequate, or incompetent; and experiencing loss of a parent with other disagreeable consequences that are not easily changed. His emphasis on the importance of pathological mourning fits in here, although these three types of experiences might occur before, or indeed without, the loss of parent. All are important in so far as they impart "cognitive biases" of a kind that lead to seeing later loss in terms of personal failure or to seeing oneself as doomed to frustration in restoring or replacing what has been lost.

In his final volume, Bowlby appears to change somewhat the emphasis of his earlier formulations by giving greater weight to external circumstances in determining whether or not mourning following loss is pathological. In childhood such "unfavorable" circumstances are stated to include poor family relationships before the loss, separation from the surviving parent after the loss, having to fend for oneself, and having to look after a parent.

Loss in childhood associated with such unfavorable circumstances increases the chance of disordered mourning; and a failure to complete the work of mourning means that the child does not withdraw attachment from the lost parent and therefore cannot reinvest in any substitute parent. The importance of unsuccessful mourning therefore lies not so much in a failure to express grief, but in a predisposition to distortion in subsequent relationships and to various cognitive biases that continue into adult life. It is through these cognitive biases that distortions in later attachment behavior tend to occur. Bowlby (1980) outlines three types of cognitive bias that result from disordered mourning in childhood: compulsive care-giving relationships, ambivalence and anxiety in relationships, and a show of independence from close ties ("compulsive self-reliance"). However, the perspective is far from being couched in deterministic terms. The impact of such bias can be avoided, or the bias corrected, if the person happens to make a secure attachment at some point. Bowlby suggests that favorable experience can push a person away from pathological development: unfortunately the circumstances that are conducive to such a reorientation are as yet poorly formulated and little documented.

Others emphasize far more the importance of the favorable circumstances dealt with by Bowlby. Rutter's review of research has been particularly influential. In *Maternal Deprivation Reassessed* (1981) he discusses research relating to parental loss, particularly in relation to institutional care and its link with childhood disorders such as affectionless psychopathy and delinquency. Rutter is critical of Bowlby's emphasis on the disruption of the bond with a mother as such and underlines the importance of social circumstances surrounding the loss that bring disruption and disturbance rather than the loss itself. The actual distress experienced by children when separated from their mothers can be moderated if adequate substitute care is provided. Rutter distinguishes failure to make the original bond with mother in the first place from the disruption of the relationship. He argues that the former is likely to be more damaging, pointing to evidence that very young children put into care show more signs of disturbance. He also emphasizes the critical importance of the nature of family relationships in the home before the loss. Where loss of a parent has come from separation, this is often linked to ongoing family tension and discord and in such instances delinquency among children is more likely to occur than in families where a parent has been lost by death and perhaps ongoing tension and discord have been relatively low. He also makes the important general point that it is necessary to characterize losses by their surrounding circumstances: that, for instance, separations due to holidays or physical illness have fewer disturbing effects than those of family break-up.

Indeed, both Rutter and Bowlby show a tendency to move away from the role of early loss to emphasize early experience in general. This may well be correct and we would also emphasize the importance of studying early loss as a way of introducing us to the general impact of childhood experience in adult depression. Rutter cites a study in London in which children from broken homes are less disturbed than those in intact but disturbed homes (Rutter, 1971). However, methodological pitfalls are everywhere in this research and as Richards and Dyson (1982) point out, the tension in the disturbed homes is contemporaneous while the separation may have taken place some time ago and the disturbance that followed it to some extent abated. For any conclusion about relative impact it would be essential to deal either with children coping with a recent separation or take account of the time element in some other way. Comparative studies of the quality reported by Rutter are extremely rare and it would therefore meanwhile be wise to retain the possibility that loss of a parent is still a peculiarly potent stress factor for a child.

This very brief overview is sufficient to make the point that differences between the views exemplified by Bowlby and Rutter are probably best seen as ones of emphasis. We see at present no reason why their formulations should not eventually prove compatible. Nonetheless, it is important to recognize that there are differences in emphasis that research will need to explore.

While we have been much influenced by Bowlby's formulation, we are much in favor of Rutter's central concern with the role of social circumstances leading to, surrounding, and following the loss. We are sympathetic not only because we believe it to be correct, but because we see no effective way for research to proceed in this extraordinarily complex field without the detailed documentation of the circumstances surrounding the loss and the subsequent biography of the person as child and adult up to the time of any depressive disorder. The cognitive biases emphasized by Bowlby will be difficult to study because their measurement is likely to be influenced by the very thing we wish to understand—depression in adult life. Emphasis on environmental circumstances is therefore critical if only because their documentation is less likely to be subject to bias due to the presence of current psychiatric disorder; and insofar as they can be shown to link to cognitive biases they are likely to provide the most convincing evidence, albeit indirect, of the presence of the intrapsychic processes emphasized by Bowlby. It may be useful to give an example of this point by anticipating some results we present later. The experience of premarital pregnancy is highly related to both loss of mother and depression in adulthood but only for working-class women. It is therefore of considerable interest that middle-class women on the whole reported quite different behavior at the time of the pregnancy—several, for instance, had the pregnancy terminated, but none of the working-class women had done so. Together with "softer" evidence that middle-class women were in general less "helpless" in their outlook both now and at the time of the pregnancy, such "hard" evidence makes a reasonably convincing case for the role of a long-term "cognitive set." Our general position will be that we require this kind of "triangulation" between soft and hard data both on methodological grounds and as a source of substantive insights about the complex processes at work.

While Bowlby's and Rutter's views are consistent with the cruder statements of our own concerning the role of early loss of mother, it may be useful to distinguish two possible chains of explanation inherent in their formulations. First, that it is the cognitive biases resulting from the experiences surrounding early loss that are the critical intervening factors: and that it is these which leave a woman vulnerable to later depression following a major loss or disappointment. Such biases will probably be reflected in the relationships she has formed, but it is the underlying cognitive sets that are critical. A second view would downplay cognitive bias as such and place overriding weight upon the external circumstances in later life—while not denying that cognitive biases may have played a significant role in creating these. Thus to continue our example, certain cognitive biases, perhaps expressed as a wish to be looked after, may increase chances of a premarital pregnancy. However, whether or not this leads to depression in adult life will entirely depend on how things turn out. How "suitable" is the man? Does she get married? How does the marriage turn out? Does the fact of the premarital pregnancy lead to a long history of adverse experiences, say, a series of pregnancies in a short space of time, unsuitable and overcrowded housing, continual tension with mother-in-law, and so on. Consistent with this emphasis would be the assertion that the experience of premarital pregnancy, whether or not there were associated enduring cognitive biases, would be associated with depression as long as the pregnancy resulted in adverse later experiences. Pushing this more sociological, less psychological strand of explanation further back in time, it could be argued that the premarital pregnancy itself need not in any way be the result of a cognitive bias, but could be entirely determined by untoward experiences in adolescence. Thus some women might be at greater risk of premarital pregnancy simply because through circumstances resulting from the loss, they find themselves at the time of finishing their schooling with no settled base—perhaps because they do not get on well with their stepmothers or because they have nowhere to go when they emerge from institutional life.

Figure 1 depicts these two strands of explanation, extending the original Camberwell etiological model of depressive onset to take account of the role of the inner world of the individual along the bottom line and the

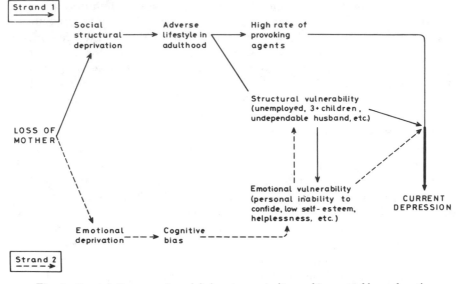

Fig. 1. *Speculative causal model showing main lines of impact of loss of mother.*

outer world along the top. The mutual interdependence of these worlds, in fact, persists throughout the person's life span, but for simplicity's sake the vertical arrows representing these influences have only been included at the time just before onset. This is the point where the level of ongoing self-esteem may prove critical in determining whether or not onset of depression occurs and it is the consequence of both strands. At this point the roles available to a woman in her particular social setting determine her ongoing level of self-esteem, and at this point also her self-esteem influences the use she chooses to make of the resources available to her in her social environment.

Our own view is that both processes are at work and that there is a great deal of interplay between enduring cognitive biases and later experience. For example, Bowlby has outlined more than one kind of bias including that of "compulsive caregiving." This involves a dependent helpless orientation in relationships, with a strong need to give care and nurturance. Such a woman may therefore find herself with a partner who is in some sense inadequate—for example, a man who is a heavy drinker. The result is then likely to be a highly unsatisfactory relationship—with one partner an alcoholic and the other too involved and dependent to leave. This will in turn leave the woman at risk to succumbing to the complex of provoking agents and vulnerability factors resulting from the bad marriage. However, circumstances may at some stage push the woman into taking action to end the relationship—for example, if when drinking her husband attacks the children. Having somehow propelled herself out of the situation the woman may then form a satisfactory relationship with someone else. The experience of having made the break and meeting someone new who is suitable could give sufficient impetus to change significantly the overdependent cognitive set.

We have noted Bowlby's discussion of certain kinds of cognitive bias to be found among many who have experienced early loss of a parent. However, since he studied men and women receiving psychological treatment, he might well at times have been misled about the degree to which they are neceessarily associated with psychopathology or some other adverse outcome. For instance, in our own research in the general population we have often noted, as Bowlby suggests, compulsive caregiving among women with an early loss of mother, but where there has been no hint as yet that it was linked with an "adverse" outcome. One woman who had two children of her own, although widowed, took on as a foster parent a series of children and had adopted two of them. She was much valued by the local Social Services Department and had frequent friendly contacts with social workers. Through these experiences she had decided, despite leaving school at 15, to obtain some training herself in "social work." She obtained an impressive range of "rewards," both through the care she gave and friendships she had developed in connection with her foster mothering, and it is difficult to see her behavior as in any way maladaptive or increasing basic vulnerability to depression. Although her drive to care for others could be seen as compulsive, her behavior lacked the anxious quality that emerges in the descriptions of Bowlby's examples. It may be the insecurity in attachment that often goes with such care-giving rather than the compulsion to give care itself that is the crucial determinant as to whether people become depressive cases rather than just grief stricken when they lose the person for whom they are caring. Bowlby would probably agree with this point, and we make it to emphasize the need for future research to "fill in" relevant experiences for the whole period between early loss and the occurrence of crises in adulthood, whether bereavement or other severe events, and to do so as well for women who have not developed psychiatric disorder following crises in their adult lives. It is possible, for instance, that the most relevant aspect of compulsive caregiving is simply that it increases the number of persons who can be lost, and thus increases the risk of experiencing loss: those who give more have more to lose.

CURRENT WALTHAMSTOW STUDY

With this last point in mind we embarked some years ago on a detailed exploratory study of the consequences of such loss among a large series of ordinary women. It involved screening about 3000 women registered with two general practices in Walthamstow, a district in North London, by

Table 3
Cases of Psychiatric Disorder (%) in the 12 Months before Interview

A. No "loss" of parent at all:		4 (2/45)**	

| | Age at loss | | |
	0–10	11–17	0–17
B. Loss of mother (including loss of father)			
Death	28 (14/50)	16 (5/31)	23 (19/81)
Separation due to divorce, illness, parent's employment, or child's choice[a,b]	13 (4/30) } 23	9 (1/11) } 14	12 (5/41) } 21
Separation due to other reasons[b]	43 (6/14)	33 (1/3)	41 (7/17)
Total	26 (24/94)	16 (7/45)	22 (31/139)**
C. Loss of father (including loss of mother)			
Death	6 (2/31)	13 (1/8)	8 (3/39)
Separation	20 (17/83)	18 (3/18)	20 (20/101)
Total	17 (19/114)	15 (4/26)	16 (23/140)
D. Loss of mother (without loss of father)			
Death	38 (5/13)	20 (5/25)	26 (10/38)
Separation[b]	14 (1/7)	25 (1/4)	18 (2/11)
Total	30 (6/20)*	17 (5/29)	22 (12/149)
E. Loss of father (without loss of mother)			
Death	0 (0/20)	not studied	
Separation	19 (4/21)	not studied	
Total	10 (4/41)*	not studied	

[a]There were 13 separations due to illness: 9% (1/11), 0% (0/2), and 8% (1/13), respectively; and 28 due to divorce, employment, etc.: 16% (3/19), 11% (1/9), and 14% (4/28), respectively.
[b]Excluding those with death of mother as well.
*$p < .05$.   **$p < .01$.   (Only two tests of significance are included in this table. For others see text.)

means of a postal questionnaire asking about various kinds of early loss and separation in childhood. On the basis of their answers we selected women with:

1. Loss of mother before the age of 17 either by death or by separation of 1 year or more (other than for wartime evacuations).
2. Loss of father in a similar way before the age of 11.
3. A group of women having no loss of parent of any kind before the age of 17 (separation due to evacuation or war service disqualified women from this group, as did all separations of 6–11 months).

This gave us 126 instances of loss of mother. In order to increase our numbers of women with certain types of loss we supplemented our sample with the next 13 women (selected alphabetically from a parallel Islington survey) with the types of loss we required (for further details, see Harris, Brown, & Bifulco, 1985).

One economy concerned our focus on contemporary intervening factors. We decided not to spend time on the collection of information about current life events and difficulties. The prime target of the study was exploratory, to investigate whole life histories and to rechart new areas, such as childhood experiences and previous psychiatric episodes.

Table 3 summarizes basic results concerning current psychiatric disorders for various kinds of loss of parent. As already noted, our term "depression" refers to affective disorder of a level of severity commonly encountered in out-patient psychiatric clinics. In almost every instance the disorder was, in fact, predominantly one of depression. One woman was a case of obsessional neurosis without depression. Although included among those with a loss of mother in Table 3, she has been counted as "not depressed" throughout our subsequent analyses.

Because the table is already complex, separate rows have not been given for every kind of possible "double" loss (e.g., a death of both parents versus separation from both versus a death of father with a separation from mother), but this should not prove misleading since results for these more specific groupings follow the pattern of the simpler groupings we do present. As expected, those without any loss had a much lower rate of depression in the year before interview, 4%.

Among those with a loss of mother by *death* before the age of 17, the rate of depression was 23%. That for women with a *separation* from a mother was almost identical, 21%. However, it is important to distinguish the 43 women where separation was due to a parent's divorce or marital separation (21), illness of mother or child (15), the parent's need to seek employment (5), and the teenage girl's choice (2), from the 18 instances where it was due to some other reason. In each of these 18, the child was sent away from both parents at a time when there had been no obvious socially accepted reason for the separation. In six of the 18 the little girls had been removed from their families where they were being neglected, battered, or interfered with sexually; in four instances the girls had been illegitimate and were left with the maternal grandmother, in four there was no clear reason why the mother had sent the child away, and in another four a miscellany of reasons of a rejecting nature applied. (For example, in one instance, the paternal grandmother and three single aunts wanted to have a child and "borrowed" the little girl for years.) In an attempt to characterize the rather unusual, one might even suggest stigmatizing, character of these 18 separations, we have called them *aberrant separa-*

tions, and the rate of depression of 44% (8/18) among them was significantly greater than the 12% (5/43) among the remaining separations (p < .05). (These figures include three women whose mothers later died.) Therefore, there is already the implication that it is not separation as such that is the critical factor leading to depression, but more the circumstances surrounding the loss.

Death of a father was unrelated to the rate of depression, but there is some hint in Table 3 that there may be an increased rate among those who had been separated from a father ($\chi^2 = 3.69$, p < .06, when comparing group E with group A). Separations from father lasting longer than 1 year as a sequel to the death of the mother were surprisingly common; there was, however, no difference in rate of disorder between those with and without separation from father among the mother-loss group. Taking those with loss of only one parent (groups D and E), the rate of depression is significantly higher among those who lost a mother before 11 than among those who lost a father.

To summarize, the original Camberwell finding concerning the overriding importance of loss of mother is confirmed; but in this larger series there is some suggestion that the influence of maternal loss on depression may extend beyond the age of 11 although its impact on later depression may be less strong than for losses before 11. In the way we have defined loss, there is no suggestion that death of a mother leads to a greater risk of subsequent disorder than separation, but there must be an important caveat. It is highly likely that the relative frequency of the various kinds of separation especially of the "aberrant" kind will differ between populations. It would therefore be hazardous to place much weight on the lack of a difference in prevalence of depression between deaths and separations as a general phenomenon. The important conclusion is that type of separation appears to be highly related to depression and that the rate for those with separations from a mother due to illness, marital separation, and the like appears to be surprisingly low. It was still greater than those without it, but the difference did not reach statistical significance, namely 4% (2/45) versus 12% (5/41). As in Camberwell, loss of a father was very much less important than that of a mother, although there was some hint that at times it does increase risk of depression, particularly if it was a separation. However, the numbers involved are too small for the difference between deaths and separations to reach statistical significance.

FURTHER CONFIRMATIONS OF THE ROLE
OF LOSS OF MOTHER

In designing this latest study we had not anticipated the recent spate of doubt about whether early loss can have any effect on a woman's chances of developing depression. We had seen it primarily as a vehicle for exploring biographical experiences bringing about such an increased risk of depression in adulthood following further loss experiences. One possible objection to the results we have reviewed stems from the size of the comparison series, which we deliberately kept small. Fortunately, it has been found possible to make two further tests, which provide a convincing confirmation of the significance of these results. The first is somewhat untidy. In the course of work on a different project, we interviewed 70 married women also living in Walthamstow, selected at random and aged between 18 and 45; and it is possible to use them to provide a second comparison series. When women who had lost a mother by death before the age of 17 are matched with this second series in terms of social class, age, marital status, and stage of family development, the rate of depression of those with a loss is again much higher: 37% (7/19) compared with 10% (6/59) ($p < .01$). The matching decreases the number of women who lost a mother by death from 81 to 19; many in the original early-loss series could not be matched exactly as they were either from Islington or over 45 years of age or unmarried.

A second check is possible from our entirely separate recent survey of wives of manual workers with a child at home living in the adjacent borough of Islington, but one that is poorer and has far more social problems. At the time of first interview, 35% of those who had lost a mother by death or a separation of one year or more before they were 11 were considered cases of depression in the year before interview compared with 19% of those without such a loss ($p < .02$). (War service and evacuation have not been included as losses.) Women with loss of mother between 11 and 17 also showed a significantly higher rate of depression when compared with those who never lost their mothers at all ($p < .05$). Death of father was not related to depression in either age group, nor was separation from father when separation from mother was controlled for.

We therefore conclude that there is an important link between early loss of a parent, most clearly a mother, and later depression, and we now examine the reasons for this in the Walthamstow sample. Of course, to the degree to which we are successful in finding *within* the early-loss group experiences that increase the risk of depression but that are uncommon in the groups without loss of mother, we help to confirm the validity of the overall link.

INTERVENING FACTORS

Number of Changes

We collected a wealth of material, using lengthy semistructured interviews, including "hard" material such as the circumstances surrounding the loss, dates spent in an institution or in foster care, and premarital pregnancy. If important links and continuities can be established by the use of such relatively trustworthy data, they could be used as a scaffolding from which to explore our "softer" material. One obvious starting point, and one which the predictive power of the aberrant separations from *both* parents had already suggested might prove important, was whether the child had not only lost her mother but also her father. In fact, one additional loss did not increase the association with adult depression. Among the 43 standard forms of separation from a mother, in only 11 was the child not separated from her father before 17 as part of the consequences of the initial separation. For these the rate of caseness was 18% (2/11) compared with 9% (3/32) among those with a double loss. When only those with a death of mother were taken, there was no higher rate of current depression among those subsequently separated for 1 year or more from fathers or from any surrogate mother with whom the girl had lived for a minimum of 1 year. Taking all losses of mother there was, however, a small but not significant tendency for women who had experienced three or more such losses before age 17 (for example, both parents and a subsequent surrogate parent) to have a higher rate of current depression than those with only one or two, 32% (6/19) and 20% (24/120), respectively.

Following this lead, we looked at some of our other measures that detailed the degree of change during childhood. Overall there was some hint of a relationship between the number of household arrangements after the loss of mother and current depression: those with four or more changes in household arrangements after the loss of a mother had a rate of depression of 29% (8/28) and those with less 20% (22/111). In order to try to increase this association we turned to the nature of the arrangements; much the most important experience relating to current depression turned out to be an institutional stay for any length of time. However, it is important to note that the relationship held only for working-class women among whom those with such an experience had double the rate of depression: 56% (9/16) of working-class women with experience of institutional care were depressed and 26% (10/39) without ($p < .05$), compared with 15% (2/13) and 13% (9/71) of middle-class women. This kind of association with *current* social class position emerges at several points of the analysis and will prove a critical issue in it.

Early Relationships with the Opposite Sex

An even greater contribution to depression came from two indicators of early relationships with the opposite sex. Premarital pregnancy and early marriage before the age of 20 were common among women with loss of a mother. Of the 139 women with a loss of a mother before the age of 17, 24% experienced a premarital pregnancy, compared with 10% of the remaining women in the Walthamstow sample ($p < .05$). Early marriage was experienced by 37 and 25% of the mother-loss and no-mother-loss groups, respectively ($p < .10$). Both measures were significantly related to depression among those with loss of a mother; 42% (14/33) and 15% (16/106) of those with and without premarital pregnancy were depressed in the year of our study and 31% (16/52) and 16% (14/87) of those with and without an early marriage ($p < .001$ and $p < .05$, respectively). In the no-mother-loss groups, premarital pregnancy was also related to depression, 33% (3/9) versus 4% (3/77) ($p < .01$); but early marriage showed no association with depression in the no-mother-loss group. However, there were again important social class differences: premarital pregnancy was only related to an increased risk of depression among working-class women and early marriage was modestly related among working-class women, but this disappeared when premarital pregnancy was controlled. Among middle-class women only early marriage was associated with depression, and this association only reached significance when those with premarital pregnancy were excluded. The association of this sexual–marriage index with depression was particularly strong among working-class women and was related to depression both among women with loss of mother by death and among those with a separation (Table 4).

At this point therefore, the hard measures showed an impressive association with depression. If premarital pregnancy is used for working-class women, early marriage for middle-class women, and aberrant separation for both social classes, there was a fivefold difference in rate of depression: 41% (24/59) with any of these three experiences were depressed compared with 8% (6/80) of those without ($p < .001$). However, it was clear that on the whole the hard measures were predicting better for working-class than for middle-class women, and, by reason of the restricted nature of the definition of "aberrant" we were predicting better for losses by separation than for those with losses by death. If we were ever able to study a larger series of middle-class women with death of mother, early marriage on its own would be unlikely to be sufficiently highly correlated with depression to provide a basis for an explanation.

Aspects of the Loss and Mourning

Following Bowlby's hypothesis that disorders of mourning at the time of childhood loss predict psychological disturbances, we explored the 40 or so aspects of the loss itself that we had measured, such as whether the child had witnessed the death, seen the corpse, attended the funeral, visited the

Table 4
Two Measures of Early Relationships with the Opposite Sex by
Depression (%) and Current Social Class for Women with
Loss of Mother

		Premarital pregnancy		Early marriage
		Depression		Depression
Working class	Yes	68 (13/19)*	Yes	42 (10/24)
	No	17 (6/36)*	No	29 (9/31)
Middle class	Yes	7 (1/14)	Yes	21 (6/28)
	No	14 (10/70)	No	9 (5/56)
All women	Yes	42 (14/33)*	Yes	31 (16/52)
	No	15 (16/106)*	No	16 (14/87)***

*$p < .001$.   ***$p < .05$.

grave, felt responsible for the loss, found it difficult to talk about the mother with siblings, surviving parents, and other relatives and many other facets. Of these, the only variable to show a relationship with depression in the year of our inquiry was the degree of anxiety shown by siblings at the time of the loss. Taking a clue from the fact that the predictive power of the aberrant separations was nearly as strong for middle-class as for working-class women, we decided to move on from facets of the loss itself and investigate our softer measures of the quality of care given in childhood; perhaps they might reflect the features of neglect, rejection, and even cruelty, which we suspected accounted for the differential rates of depression in the two types of separation. If we managed to measure these qualities in care given after any type of loss, and if they were indeed the features that accounted for the predictive power of the aberrant separation measure, then they ought also to explain depression in any series consisting purely of middle-class women who had lost a mother by death.

Quality of Care

We had devised numerous measures of the care given, ranging from estimates of warmth, companionship, and punitiveness of each surrogate and surviving parent to global ratings of rejection, and the amount of discord in any home. Each of the measures was rated twice, once exactly as reported by the subject and once as finally estimated by the interviewer and consensus rating team. This final estimate was only made after many probes: for example, if a woman claimed that her stepmother was very strict, such a rating would only be made on the "estimated punitiveness" scale if a good deal of description was also given by the woman about, say, smacking, locking in the bedroom, being made to wait to eat until all the other family members had finished. Interviewers were made aware of the possibility that women who were currently depressed might overreport unpleasant atmospheres in childhood. In order to combat this possibility, they probed particularly carefully and collected detailed descriptions of incidents rather than merely being content with general statements such as "she was never loving." While acknowledging the limitations inevitable in such data, we nevertheless felt there could be considerable exploratory value in these analyses. Two measures that captured the flavor of the aberrant separations were ratings of indifference by parent surrogates and of their lack of concern for discipline (or low control). Taking women whose childhoods showed evidence of either of these for a period of one year or more at any point after the loss of mother, we found both measures related to depression. Thirty-five percent (22/62) rated on either or both of these measures were currently depressed compared with only 11% (8/77) of those not so rated ($p < .001$). The impact was identical for the death and separation groups (for further discussion, see Harris, Brown, & Bifulco, 1985a).

Both measures represent material and emotional inadequacy in the way the surviving or substitute parent related to the child after the loss of her mother. *Parental indifference* reflects general neglect, lack of interest, and lack of attention. The rating is based on answers to questions about interest shown in friends, school work, jobs, and career, and also more gross areas such as whether or not she was fed and clothed properly. Only "marked" or "moderate indifference" was included in the index: in every instance there were examples of neglect that were clear enough to have been used by the child as undoubted evidence of indifference. Usually such clear-cut neglect was reported to stem from stepmothers, with fathers described as apathetic rather than indifferent. *Parental control* relates to the restrictions put on the child and to the establishment and enforcement of rules within the family. In common sense terms, an upbringing with a rating of "moderate" would probably be considered desirable by most people since it would provide enough structure to reduce chances of a child getting into trouble outside the home. "Marked" control may also have this effect but in common sense terms it is probably too constricting, allowing a child too little freedom of expression. "Low control" arose when the supervision of the child was so negligent that she was apparently allowed to do more or less what she liked. The phrase "we ran wild" recurred in the accounts of the childhood of such women. Typically "low control" most often occurred when the father alone was responsible and appeared to be too busy or preoccupied to be able to look after her properly. We asked about strictness and punitiveness in general, behavior at mealtimes, whether children were allowed to play out in the streets for long periods of time, restrictions on going out with boys in teenage years, and coming home late.

The joint index of parental indifference and low control shows a relationship with aberrant separation (gamma = .30). That it was not closer probably stems from the fact that the measures of indifference and control applied to the period *after* the initial loss, which for some who had experienced an aberrant separation was an improvement on the original family situation. The two measures had not been applied to the rather different situations obtaining in institutional care. Since many of the women with aberrant separations went into institutions, they had not been considered in terms of this measure and were scoring zero on lack of care when this was not in fact evidence that they had received adequate care. It thus seemed important to take account of this by including the experience of aberrant separation along with the other two measures in a trial threefold index, which we named *lack of care*. Before this was done, we checked among those with a death of mother the nature of any later separation to see if any were aberrant in type. In only six instances did they seem to have a similar flavor. Most had already been rated as examples of parental indifference, and we therefore felt justified in including the experience of aberrant separation in a joint index of lack of care. Lack of care defined by the index was highly related to depression—both for those with a loss by separation or by death and for those with no loss of mother (Table 5). This relationship with depression held equally for working-class and middle-class women [21% vs. 7% depression in the middle-class (p = .059); 53% vs. 9% in the working-class (p < .001)]; the results we are about to report emerge clearly even if only the hard component of index, aberrant separation, is used. Moreover, in a subsample of 20 pairs of sisters a high level of agreement (kappa = .89) between informants about lack of care was found (Bifulco, 1985).

Social Class and Loss of Mother

Social class proved to be of central significance throughout our analysis of the Walthamstow material. There was a large social class difference in prevalence of depression among those with loss of a mother—35% of working-class and 13% of middle-class women experienced depression in the year of our inquiry. However, this was complicated by the high rate of depression among those who had experienced a premarital pregnancy. For those without such a pregnancy there was no social class difference. For working-class women, lack of care and premarital pregnancy were both highly related to depression. However, most of the association of premarital pregnancy occurred in conjunction with lack of care. Without premarital pregnancy or lack of care no working-class woman was depressed (0/20). When there was both lack of care and premarital pregnancy, 69%

Table 5

Depression and Index of Lack of Care after Loss for Those with Loss of Mother and throughout Childhood for Those without Loss of Mother by Type of Loss

Lack of care index	Separation (%)	Death (%)	No loss of mother (%)
Yes	36 (12/33)	34 (13/38)	23 (3/13)
No	4 (1/28)	10 (4/40)	4 (3/73)

$p < .01$.

(11/16) were depressed, and when there was lack of care but without premarital pregnancy 38% (6/10) were depressed. There were only three women with premarital pregnancy without lack of care but two of them were depressed.

The other hard measure was an institutional stay, which related to depression only among working-class women. Since all 16 working-class women who experienced it were also rated as lacking care, it adds nothing to the overall association of lack of care with depression. However, it is of interest since its impact was largely mediated by premarital pregnancy, which occurred in 10 of the 16 (7/10 were depressed vs. 2/6 of those without premarital pregnancy).

For middle-class women the most important association concerned those with lack of care who had three times more depression than those without, 20% (8/39) versus 7% (3/45) ($p = .06$). We have already established that for middle-class women early marriage related to depression but it did so only among those also experiencing lack of care. Table 6 shows that in fact depression was more common only among middle-class women experiencing lack of care and early marriage, 38% versus 7% ($p < .01$). Therefore results are simpler for middle-class women: in essence they are that lack of care and early marriage are only of importance when they occur together.

The size of the associations involved in these two social class results is impressive, but the failure of premarital pregnancy to relate to any extent to depression among middle-class women needs to be explained. Turning back to our original speculative model (Fig. 1), it is not immediately apparent how this can be accommodated. For if the link between premarital pregnancy and depression were to follow strand 2—say an enduring personality feature such as helplessness both rendered a woman more liable to become premaritally pregnant and made her more vulnerable to depression later—then the link between such pregnancy and depression should occur equally in both social classes. If the link operated through strand 1—say a premarital pregnancy leads to more adversity in later life—then,

Table 6
Lack of Care, Early Marriage, and Depression among Currently Middle-Class Women with Loss of Mother

	Early marriage	Depression (%)
Lack of care	Yes	38 (6/16)
	No	9 (2/23)
No lack of care	Yes	7 { 0 (0/12)
	No	9 (3/33)

$p < .01$, 1 *df* (row 1 × rows 2, 3, and 4).

although one might expect (following the Camberwell results) even more adversity to occur to working-class women than to middle-class women with such earlier pregnancies, one would still expect some link among the latter.

We believe that the most plausible explanation for the absence of any such link among currently middle-class women is that the aspects of the premarital pregnancy that are linked with current depression are the same as those that determine current class position: in other words current class may be as much a result of other causes of depression as it is an independent cause of current depression in its own right. The same factors, whether located in the more internal arena of the woman's personality or in the more external arena of the kind of man she has married and the kind of roles in which the pregnancy has trapped her and her husband, determine both working-class status and depression. Given that class position is defined by husband's occupation, the last of these seemed the most obvious possibility, namely, that the sort of man who had allowed such a pregnancy to occur might not have the resources to maintain or achieve a higher class status. But the restrictions imposed by starting a family early could also play an important role:

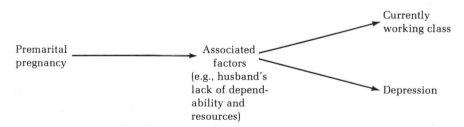

These associated factors linked to the pregnancy would thus be much less closely associated with pregnancy in the middle-class group, since where they did occur women would tend to be working-class. We knew that about one-third of our sample had had working-class fathers but were now themselves currently middle class (including some "higher level" skilled manual occupations); this proportion did not differ between women with and without childhood losses of parent. Downward social mobility was less common—about one-tenth had had middle-class fathers and were now working class. It seemed therefore quite plausible that the experience of premarital pregnancy might act to prevent a woman rising into the middle class along with her other contemporaries. The latter would have more freedom to maneuver themselves onto the conveyor belt of upward social mobility since they and their husbands would not have their occupational achievement restricted by the high expenditure and lack of opportunity for further training imposed by starting a family so early in life. These interpretations are supported in Table 7. For women whose fathers were middle class none of the early experiences such as premarital pregnancy were related to a current working-class status (Table 7, column 1). For women whose fathers were working class, lack of care, early marriage, and institutional stay also failed to relate clearly to current working-class status; but the experience of a premarital pregnancy was significantly related—74% of women with such a pregnancy were working class compared with 37% of the remainder ($p < .01$). Put another way, only 26% (6/23) of those women with a premarital pregnancy whose fathers were working class moved up into the middle class compared with 63% (43/68) of those without premarital pregnancy ($p < .01$). (None of the women with a

Table 7

Percentage of Women Who Are Currently Working Class by Father's Class and Whether Experienced after the Loss of Mother

	Father middle class (N = 48)	Father working class (N = 91)
A. Lack of care		
Yes	29 (6/21)	52 (26/50)
No	26 (7/27)	39 (16/41)
B. Experience of an institutional stay		
Yes	40 (2/5)	58 (14/24)
No	25 (11/43)	42 (28/67)
C. Experience of early marriage (with or without premarital pregnancy)		
Yes	35 (6/17)	51 (18/35)
No	23 (7/31)	43 (24/56)
D. Experience of premarital pregnancy		
Yes	20 (2/10)	74 (17/23)*
No	29 (11/38)	37 (25/68)*

$p < .01$.

working-class father and a premarital pregnancy who had experienced a rise in social class status were depressed, in contrast to half of the rest of such women with a premarital pregnancy.) As already noted, the proportions of those falling in status—that is, who had middle-class fathers and were currently working class—did not differ in early experience (column 1): it was failure to rise in class status that was critically related to early experience and then only clearly to premarital pregnancy.

Coping with Premarital Pregnancy

Obviously many factors might contribute to whether or not the consequences of a premarital pregnancy turn out to be oppressive and painful; among them could even be good luck in terms of marrying a man with a dependable character. Effective coping at the time of the pregnancy is, however, perhaps the most obvious possibility. The women who were currently middle class had reacted differently to the crisis at the time. For example, only one-half (7/14) had married the father as a result of the pregnancy, and one-third (5/14) had had the pregnancy terminated. In these ways the currently middle-class women could be said not to have allowed themselves to be trapped by the implications of the pregnancy. One woman, for instance, broke with the father of the child on the same day as she left hospital after the birth and later married a dependable old friend, thus saving herself at the eleventh hour from a marriage to someone who would have been likely to have constantly dented her self-esteem by his infidelities. None of the 19 women who had premarital pregnancies and who were now working class had had a termination.

A simple index was devised to reflect such coping with a premarital pregnancy. Supposedly "successful" coping included seeking terminations, marrying someone already intended as the future spouse, or deliberately choosing as a husband a man who was not the father of the child; "unsuccessful" coping included marrying the father only because of the illegitimate conception, becoming a long-term single parent, or bearing the child only to have it adopted later. Successful coping was twice as common among those currently middle class as among those currently working class, 71% (10/14) versus 32% (6/19) ($p < .05$). Furthermore, the rate of current depression was much lower among those who had coped successfully, 25% (4/16) versus 59% (10/17) ($p < .05$). This trend held both for those whose fathers were middle class (0/5 vs. 3/5) and for those whose fathers were working-class (4/11 vs. 7/12). The style of coping also appeared to provide the main mechanism by which premarital pregnancy had prevented upward social mobility: the women with working-class fathers who coped successfully had not only avoided being trapped in an unintended partnership but had also quite often moved out of the working class. Five times more successful than unsuccessful copers rose to the middle class ($p < .05$) (see Table 8). Of particular interest is the fact that there was no link between father's class and success in coping with the pregnancy. Rather it was the interaction between father's class position and success in coping with premarital pregnancy that was critical (see Fig. 2).

Low father's class was only very weakly associated with lack of care ($\gamma = .22$, n.s.), and although lack of care was highly linked with premarital pregnancy there was no association between father's class and premarital pregnancy as such [one-quarter of women with a working-class (23/91) and 21% (10/48) of those with a middle-class father had a premarital pregnancy (n.s.)]. Father's class was therefore important only in interaction with unsuccessful coping; with this combination almost all the women were currently working class. Why should this be so? Perhaps a limitation on the range and kind of social contacts may mean that the women fail to become involved with a man who will achieve middle-class status. However, the circumstances surrounding the birth and its consequences may also have hindered some of the men they married from achieving middle-class status.

It is notable that once current class is taken into account, success at coping with a premarital pregnancy is less clearly related to depression (Table 9). Irrespective of coping success, the mere fact of a premarital pregnancy strongly predisposes to depression in working-class but not in middle-class women. The increased rate of depression associated with unsuccessful coping is due entirely to the fact that women who cope poorly were more likely to be currently working class. Therefore, although such coping is important for our model, it does not explain the high rate of depression among currently working-class women who had a premarital pregnancy. Table 9 also serves as a reminder that there was no class link with depression when those with a premarital pregnancy were excluded.

Intimacy and Dependability of Husband

Some of the raised risk of depression following premarital pregnancy may stem from "shortcomings" in men with whom the women become in-

Table 8
Proportion Currently Middle Class by Premarital Pregnancy, Success in Coping with the Pregnancy and Father's Class (%)

	Premarital pregnancy		No premarital pregnancy
	Unsuccessful coping	Successful coping	
Father working class	8 (1/12)	45 (5/11)	63 (43/68)
Father middle class	60 (3/5)	100 (5/5)	71 (27/38)

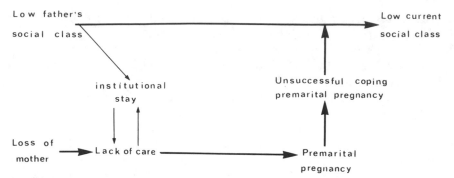

Fig. 2. *Relationship of father's class and premarital pregnancy. (Main links are shown in heavy lines; arrow from unsuccessful coping represents an interactive effect.)*

volved. Perhaps the pregnancy made them so keen to "settle down" that they were less discriminating in their choice of husband than the general run of women with working-class fathers. One reason for the link between unsuccessful coping with premarital pregnancy and current depression may be the association with the quality of the woman's current marital relationship. As already noted, lack of intimacy with a husband acts as a vulnerability factor, increasing the chances of current depression in those experiencing a provoking agent (Brown & Harris, 1978). Among working-class women, premarital pregnancy was highly related to low intimacy with a husband or boyfriend in the period just before onset for women currently depressed or, for those not depressed, at the time of interview. Of working-class women with a premarital pregnancy, 74% (14/19) were low on intimacy compared with 28% (10/36) of the remaining working-class women ($p < .01$). Even when those with current depression were excluded, the difference remained statistically significant [83% (5/6) vs. 20% (6/30), $p < .01$]. For middle-class women there was no suggestion of a link between premarital pregnancy and current intimacy. Therefore, one way in which early loss of a mother relates to depression is through the linkage be-

Table 9
Percentage with Depression by Current Social Class and Success with Dealing with Premarital Pregnancy

		Working class	Middle class	Totals
Premarital pregnancy	Unsuccessful coping	69 (9/13)	25 (1/4)	59 (10/17)
	Successful coping	66 (4/6)	0 (0/10)	25 (4/16)
No premarital pregnancy		17 (6/36)	14 (10/70)	15 (16/106)

tween premarital pregnancy and lack of later intimacy with husband. It may well be the characteristics of the husbands that influence both the women's liability to depression and their failure to rise above the working class. A measure of the estimated dependability of a husband (based on such items as regularity in homecoming time, bringing in the family income, absence of drinking, gambling, battering, infidelities, and criminal activity) related to social mobility and premarital pregnancy in exactly the same way as had depression and lack of intimacy (see Table 10).

Overall there was a link between depression and having an undependable husband: taking only those with a husband or boyfriend, 39% (11/28) of those who were depressed had undependable men compared with 11% (10/93) of those not depressed ($p = .001$). In the no-mother-loss group the figures were 50% (2/4) and 4% (3/67), respectively ($p = .022$, Fisher's Exact Probability). For working-class women the same higher rate of undependable husbands occurred in the premarital pregnancy group whether or not they coped successfully with it. Since this pattern repeated what we had found for the rates of depression, it is tempting to link the latter directly with the characteristics of the husband rather than with the successful coping with the pregnancy. However, the absolute numbers in the key cells were too small to examine this possibility further. Nevertheless, the rate of undependable husbands among working class women without a premarital pregnancy was no higher than among the middle class (see Table 10).

The Current Cognitive Set of Helplessness

Something akin to a masterful coping style may also have been operative in the complex of pathways involving premarital pregnancy, current class, and depression. The work of Seligman (1975), Seligman, Abramson, Semmel, and von Baeyer (1979), and Abramson, Seligman, and Teasdale (1978) suggested that helplessness could be as important as hopelessness in the development of depression: a continuation of a theoretical tradition that has stretched from Freud (1917) through Bibring (1953) and

Table 10
Undependability of Husband/Boyfriend by Father's and Subject's Social Class and Premarital Pregnancy

	Father working class		Father middle class	
	Premarital pregnancy (%)	No premarital pregnancy (%)	Premarital pregnancy (%)	No premarital pregnancy (%)
Currently working class	53 (8/15)	13 (3/23)	50 (1/2)	10 (1/10)
Currently middle class	0 (0/5)	10 (4/40)	14 (1/7)	16 (3/19)

Engel (1967) to current cognitive models of depression. We have explained elsewhere (Brown, 1974, 1981) our preference for semistructured verbal probing about specific social roles and situations over the open and shut generalizations of pencil and paper questionnaires favored by Seligman. We therefore designed our own measures of helplessness, based on detailed information about how the subject had behaved in a series of situations and key relationships (details of the measures are obtainable upon request). We asked, for instance, about examples of her behavior when someone pushed ahead of her in a queue and her influence on her husband's everyday decisions.

One problem in the measurement of cognitive sets is the potentially distorting effect of current mood—a woman with depression may report herself as having always been helpless just because her depressed state makes her feel helpless at the time of interview. In order to reduce this bias we questioned closely about changes in behavior after onset of previous as well as current episodes of affective disorder. It seemed that when asked about such changes, women were able to differentiate between their premorbid cognitive set and their current feelings. Since we were concerned to determine whether a long-term cognitive set of helplessness was related to a subsequent onset of depression, it was important to use an estimate of helplessness just before onset rather than during the current episode for those depressed at interview. There was a clear link between premorbid helplessness and current depression: 7% (6/81) of nonhelpless women with loss of mother were depressed at interview compared with 41% (24/58) of the more helpless ($p < .001$). Among those without loss of a mother the figures were 2% (1/49) and 14% (5/37), respectively ($p < .05$).

Of course, it is never possible completely to eliminate the possibility of bias in retrospective recall. Nevertheless, other data of ours suggest that such biases did not account for the association with depression. If women with current depression are excluded from analyses there should be no reporting bias due to depressed mood. Possible associations between cognitive set and previous episodes of depression can then be examined. In the whole sample (irrespective of whether there had been early losses) there were 188 women without psychiatric disorder of whom 61 had had a previous episode of affective disorder of severity amounting to caseness (for details of measurement of previous caseness, see Harris et al., 1985a). Of those with such a previous episode, 61% (37/61) were rated as helpless before that onset compared with only 34% (43/127) of those without a probable previous episode ($p < .02$). The latter were rated for their current helplessness since by definition this was before any first episode.

Thus both low intimacy with husband and helplessness were highly related to current depression and therefore capable of acting as critical intervening variables between depression and earlier experiences such as premarital pregnancy. Both were common, but among middle-class women helplessness was somewhat less frequent (Table 11) and was less often associated with low intimacy (γ = 0.25 compared with γ = 0.69 for working-class women).

The pattern of interrelations between variables linked with depression is summarized in Fig. 3. Among working-class women all three earlier experiences were highly associated with helplessness and low intimacy (average γ = .62); probably this explains the substantial correlation between these two intervening measures (γ = .69). Among middle-class women the three earlier experiences related only to helplessness and then only modestly (average γ − .20); hence the low correlation between the same two intervening measures (γ = .25).

These results, of course, parallel those obtained for early marriage and premarital pregnancy, institutional stay, and depression. It is clear that the links between early and later experiences are far stronger for working-class women; a tentative case can be made that helplessness largely stemming from experiences following (and perhaps also preceding) loss of mother plays a critical role, along with low intimacy, in the increased risk of depression among working-class women. The picture of middle-class women is different. We have seen that among them premarital pregnancy does not relate to an increased rate of depression, and it is therefore unsurprising that only 21% (3/14) of those with such a pregnancy were both helpless and low on intimacy with husband compared with 63% (12/19) of working-class women (p < .02). In general, childhood background and current factors were much less strongly related among middle-class women. This is consistent with our arguments on the role of selection in the determination of current social class.

Table 11
Helplessness, Lack of Intimacy, and Current Social Class

	Working class (%)	Middle class (%)
Helplessness	53 (29/55)	35 (29/84)*
Lack of intimacy with husband		
(1) all women	44 (24/55)	37 (31/84)
(2) those with husband/ boyfriend	38 (10/50)	25 (18/71)
Both helplessness and lack of intimacy with husband	33 (18/55)	15 (13/84)**

*p < .05.   **p < .01.

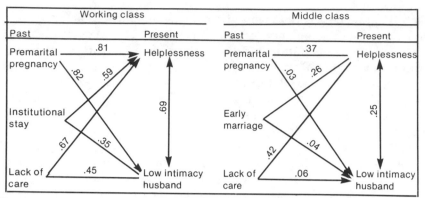

Fig. 3. *Pattern of interactions between variables linked with depression (gamma used).*

Cognitive Sets Antedating the Premarital Pregnancy

There is some hint that the almost complete lack of depression among middle-class women with a premarital pregnancy might be explicable, not only in terms of the consequences of the pregnancy but also of antecedent factors. Of those with a loss of mother, 70% of the women with a premarital pregnancy (23/33) were currently considered helpless compared with one-third (35/106) among the remaining women ($p < .01$). Possibly this helplessness might represent a continuing strand of personality that had contributed to the occurrence of the pregnancy, as well as to influences on social mobility. More than half of those with a premarital pregnancy became pregnant for reasons somewhat beyond their control (as with lack of contraceptive knowledge or failure of a generally reliable technique). The others had become pregnant for reasons suggesting some form of helplessness already present in the teenage years (e.g., failure to consider consequences or risk-taking with regard to sexual activities).

The fact that unsuccessful coping with a premarital pregnancy failed to relate to depression when current class was controlled strongly suggests that more than a continuation of cognitive set and coping style was operative. This was confirmed by our analysis of dependability of husbands. However, equally it seemed that a continuation into the present of the same cognitive sets and coping styles associated with premarital pregnancy was important in some instances. For example, one-half (8/16) of those who coped successfully with a premarital pregnancy were considered helpless currently compared with 88% (15/17) of those who did not cope effectively ($p < .02$). (Only one-third of those without a premarital pregnancy were considered helpless.) There is a second kind of evidence for some kind of continuity. Although originally we had not set out to measure helplessness in childhood, we had systematically collected information on the early teenage years similar to that used for rating helplessness in adulthood. We developed items such as confidence in meeting new acquaintances, mastery in trying to make plans for one's future, and helplessness in managing day-to-day matters, post hoc but blind to current factors, into a scale of childhood helplessness, aware of course that the retrospective biases mentioned earlier were, if anything, likely to apply even more to such an exercise. The results seem to confirm that the helplessness apparently involved in the development of later depression might in some instances have predated the premarital pregnancy rather than resulted from it. For example, 53% (9/17) of those who coped unsuccessfully with a premarital pregnancy had been rated as helpless on behavior exhibited well before the pregnancy compared with 13% (2/16) of those whose coping we considered adequate ($p < .01$). However, results summarized in Table 12 also suggest that this childhood helplessness did not harbinger depression in adulthood without lack of care in childhood.

Of those with childhood helplessness but without either lack of care or premarital pregnancy, none were depressed (0/9). For those who were not helpless in childhood (bottom row), there was a gradient of rates of current depression. Lack of care showed a modest association with childhood helplessness and perhaps played a role in its genesis—although the association did not reach statistical significance. Childhood helplessness related to depression only among those with lack of care. Particularly notable is the high rate of depression in this group even without premarital pregnancy—63% (5/8) compared with 21% (8/34) among comparable women without childhood helplessness ($p < .02$). Whatever interpretation is placed on this result, it indicates that something in the early experience of the woman antedating early relationships with the opposite sex played an important part in bringing about depression in adulthood.

The crucial role of our three-item index of lack of care will not surprise those familiar with Bowlby's (1980) case histories or Rutter's (1971) findings on the readjustment in more harmonious households of children who had experienced separation from a parent. Birtchnell, too, has noted that

Table 12
Percentage of Women with Depression by Lack of Care, Premarital Pregnancy, and Childhood Helplessness

| | Lack of care | | No lack of care | | |
	Premarital pregnancy (%)	No premarital pregnancy (%)	Premarital pregnancy (%)	No premarital pregnancy (%)	Totals (%)
Childhood helplessness	70 (7/10)	63 (5/8)	100 (1/1)	0 (0/9)	46 (13/28)
No childhood helplessness	36 (5/14)	21 (8/39)	13 (1/8)	6 (3/50)	15 (17/11)

poor mother–child relationships before and after mother loss influence the degree and character of depression and dependency that result (Birtchnell, 1980; Kennard & Birtchnell, 1982). Adam, Bouckoms, and Streiner (1982) found not only a significantly higher rate of parental loss before age 25 among those attempting suicide than among a comparison group, but also that this effect was potentiated by a "chaotic" family environment after the loss. He found the same association with suicidal intention and behavior in another sample selected this time on the independent variable (parental loss before 16). Perusal of his case descriptions suggests that what distinguishes his "chaotic" category from his "unstable" one is similar to our lack of care: it is emotional stability that seems crucial. In many ways, too, our index resembles Parker's measure of low care on his Parental Bonding instrument, which was found to relate significantly to depression and to anxiety in adults (Parker, 1979, 1981). If our index of lack of care proves methodologically acceptable, it is also theoretically appropriate within our cognitive model of depression; since the regard of others is often a source of one's own self-regard, those exposed to deficient care in childhood are likely to place a lower estimate on their own worth and will thus prove more vulnerable to depression in the face of provoking agents.

AN INTERPRETATION AND TENTATIVE MODEL

The evidence from the Walthamstow survey indicates that early loss of a mother can be powerfully linked to depression in adult life and this association was confirmed in a separate study in Islington, a more deprived area in North London. However, there is every reason to believe that the size of this link will be highly related to the kind of population studied. Thus, Birtchnell's finding of a lack of any association in middle-class Sussex is understandable in terms of the class distribution of the provoking agents and vulnerability factors in our causal model of depression. The same general point holds for the distribution of aberrant separation experiences. It is highly unlikely that the kind of extreme experiences involved are randomly distributed among those undergoing a separation from a mother in the general population; without a random sample it is not possible for us to give exact figures, but such separations are almost certainly far more frequent in just those areas where there are more provoking agents anyway. In the evaluation of any results in this area of research, therefore, it is essential to take account of the kind of population studied. (The study of psychiatric patients introduces additional perils; Brown, 1982.)

With respect to loss of mother, these results suggest two main lines of influence, which in practice may well interact to have a joint impact on feelings of self-esteem.

Strand 1 in Fig. 4 is best seen in terms of two components. First, there are the links between unsuccessful coping with a premarital pregnancy and current working-class status. Such a class status is known to increase the rate of experiencing provoking agents and vulnerability factors, and hence working-class status alone should be associated with a greater chance of depression. However, in the present study we found no social-class difference in depression once women with a premarital pregnancy were excluded. The most parsimonious explanation lies in the critical secondary effect of premarital pregnancy on choice of marriage partner and on the course of the marriage. A person's level of education is usually crucial for social mobility, but we found little relationship with subsequent social class and none with depression, helplessness, and low intimacy. This negative finding indicates that for women factors concerning husbands and marriages have a greater impact on their psychiatric state than their own educational and work achievements.

However, a case can also be made for the role of enduring personality characteristics comprising cognitive sets and coping styles (Strand 2). These personality features are influenced by experiences surrounding early loss, especially aberrant separations, indifference, and low control on the part of the remaining parent or parental surrogate. The links with depression are shown in the bottom half of Fig. 4 (dotted lines). When childhood helplessness is used to represent "early personality factors," all the associations are substantial except for that between lack of care and childhood helplessness. Particularly important is the fact that there is still a large association between childhood helplessness and current helplessness once premarital pregnancy is controlled (Table 13). This is important for our argument as the two strands are likely to be inextricably mixed after passing through premarital pregnancy. Moreover, it is highly likely that the chances of such a pregnancy are increased both by straightforward environmental factors (for example, lack of care from an indifferent stepparent from whom a girl wishes to escape) and by personality factors such as childhood helplessness. Nevertheless, even when those

Table 13
Proportions Currently "Helpless"

Childhood helplessness	Premarital pregnancy (%)	No premarital pregnancy (%)
Yes	82 (9/11)	65 (11/17)
No	64 (14/22)	27 (24/89)

Note. Logit analysis shows that both childhood helplessness and premarital pregnancy have a significant effect on those currently helpless, $p < .05$ for each.

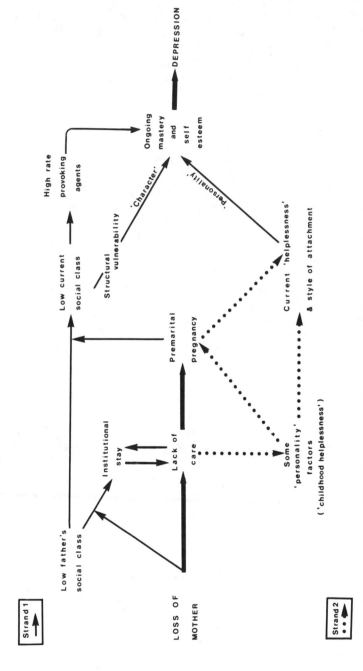

Fig. 4. *Causal model showing main lines of impact of loss of mother.*

with a premarital pregnancy are excluded, those with lack of care and current helplessness have a particularly high rate of depression (Table 14).

At present the evidence for the importance of the cognitive set of helplessness is no more than suggestive. However, our case vignettes show "cognitive biases" in interpersonal relationships that are remarkably close to those described by Bowlby (1980). We have long been aware that women with low intimacy include both those whose inability to confide in dependable men stems in part from some feature of their personalities (more Strand 2), and women whose lack of a confiding tie stems from the undependability of their husbands (more Strand 1). Therefore, as our analysis proceeds we do not expect to be able to distinguish any more tidily the two paths we have outlined. Undoubtedly "personality" and "experience" are intimately related; for example, women who blossom in personality once they have managed to break away from a disastrous marriage and have built up their lives again with a more dependable man. The helplessness that appears to have kept them locked for many years in a hopeless marriage is not beyond some change as a consequence of better things. There is a need to take heed of Machiavelli's dictum of the inevitable role of *Fortuna* in human affairs, the bitch–goddess of unpredictability. Not everything about the role of early loss in leading to later depression can be understood in terms of the kind of factors outlined. At times things will look up for the most handicapped and incompetent of us as a result of some lucky choice or decision, and some of the most resilient will succumb to just one more inexplicable disappointment. Nonetheless we believe that the two strands do represent in schematic terms possible paths following early loss of mother, and that despite their labyrinthine mingling in real life the effort to distinguish them as far as possible is likely to increase our chances of making theoretical progress.

From the results presented there can be little doubt that the particular circumstances surrounding and following early loss of mother markedly increase the risk of depression in adulthood. However, if the complex links are to be followed, it is necessary also to take into account social class influences, differentiating current class from class of origin, and differen-

Table 14
Women without Premarital Pregnancy

	Helplessness (%)	No helplessness (%)	Totals (%)
Lack of care	53 (10/19)*	11 (3/28)	28 (13/47)
No lack of care	6 (1/16)	5 (2/43)	5 (3/59)
Totals	31 (11/35)	7 (5/71)	15 (16/106)

*$p < .01$.

tiating factors leading to current working-class status from those leading to current depression. Second, interactive effects are crucial. Because father's working-class status is unrelated to success at coping with a premarital pregnancy, such coping cannot be reduced to a simple lack of resources. Moreover, within a working-class group, women who failed to cope successfully were no more likely to be depressed than were those who succeeded in coping. However, the combination of a father's working-class status and unsuccessful coping did relate highly to current working-class status. In turn it was the combination of current working-class status and premarital pregnancy (irrespective of coping) that related highly to current depression. Therefore, failure to cope well with the pregnancy is important for depression simply because it almost ensures an eventual working-class status.

This, in turn, would lead to an increased risk of provoking agents and vulnerability factors. However, clearly such a simple view would have to take into account the impact of the premarital pregnancy on the man's chances of achievement, its impact on material and economic circumstances, and perhaps also the behavior of the women on the development of the husband's "undesirable" behavior.

There is a tendency for women from "broken homes" to have higher rates of conception outside marriage (e.g., Wolkind, 1977) although the association is modest (e.g., Illsley & Thompson, 1961; Wadsworth, 1979). Moreover, premarital pregnancy is followed by an increased rate of subsequent marital disruption. Personal instability, lack of preparation for marriage, insufficiency of economic resources, and pressure from rapid family building may all play a part in this association (Furstenberg, 1979). However, it seems that it is those who remain trapped in marriages to undependable husbands rather than those who actually separate who have the highest rates of depression.

Early marriage forms part of a different, although comparable pathway. This relates to depression among those currently middle class, but does not itself relate to intimacy or dependability of husband, nor does it influence class position. There is, however, a modest association with current helplessness, suggesting that this pathway involves Strand 2 rather than Strand 1. The contrast between the differing paths early marriage → depression and premarital pregnancy → depression, serves to differentiate between young women who settle down early in marriage out of a cognitive set or a simple need to find someone to "belong with," and young women who do so only because they are compelled into settling down by a premarital pregnancy.

In this connection, it is necessary to contrast a person's *personality* and *character*. Personality refers to the source of our most personal intentions. By contrast, character is the tangible result of such intentions played out in terms of our social roles (Park, 1974, p. 83). Such performances give rise to our ideas about ourselves and the sense of our own worth. As Park emphasizes, the notions of character and social structure are intimately linked since the pursuit of self-respect is for the most part made among a network of others. It is the capital with which an actor enters each scene: "the current store of reputational and positional gains which he has built up, or to which he has fallen heir. So far as a man is an effective social agent, we conceive that it will be an overriding concern in all his involvements to maintain his character: defending what he has gained and adding, where he thinks he can add, to its ostensible value" (Park, 1974, p. 97). Therefore, while character is open to change, perhaps sudden and dramatic change, it usually exhibits a basic continuity and permanence, tending to fluctuate around a fairly fixed point, at best gaining or losing modest portions. Feelings of self-worth are important in the etiology of depression; such feelings are powerfully influenced by success in the social roles or identities to which we are committed. It is the sum of people's views of themselves in terms of those identity achievements that forms their characters. Since provoking agents often disrupt our plans and hence our identities, they may make a substantial impact on our feelings of self-worth. Women are particularly likely to be sensitive to such influences because so many of the roles they enact, particularly perhaps if working-class, validate the occupancy of roles that are heavily *ascribed* rather than *achieved* (Linton, 1936). The main conception underlying this distinction is the degree of choice prior to the entry into any particular status (Sarbin, 1970). Achieved status leads to esteem, whereas ascribed or granted roles tend not to do so. The relevance of such a distinction for the place of women in our society is obvious. Of course, it is a matter of degree; certainly there are ways of dealing with an ascribed role such as motherhood that emphasize its achievement. Nevertheless, broader social forces provide constraints on the rewards of esteem and respect and hence on character (Boulton, 1983).

In terms of the two strands in Fig. 4, character is particularly dependent on current environment or Strand 1. Of course, some influence from Strand 2, the internal cognitive sets, would also be expected, if only in the sense that they influence our intentions and so help create the current environment. There is a final common pathway involving feelings of self-worth to which both character and personality contribute; but the input from character, if things are going well in terms of role performance, may mask and overlay feelings of incompetence stemming from the cognitive set of helplessness. Such a balance may survive indefinitely, but failure in a significant role can quickly bring helplessness from the underlying set to the fore.

The most crucial measure in our model is lack of care in childhood, which spans both strands of explanation in Fig. 4. That this proved more discriminating than any of the measures surrounding the actual loss experience itself may mean no more than that our various measures failed to identify pathogenic childhood mourning experiences. However, even if such experiences can later be identified, inevitably they will be highly correlated with lack of care since this is so highly linked with depression. It may also be taken as a sign that of the two theoretical perspectives we contrasted earlier in terms of the work of Bowlby and Rutter, there is more evidence in our material for the role of family environment than for the impact of loss and mourning in producing disorder in adulthood. The softer measures of helplessness give an interpretation of the impact of early loss of mother that is less external or sociological, and more internal or social psychological, aspects of personality rather than character. At a minimum, long-term cognitive sets seem to be important links between loss experiences and the current situation. Moreover, a cognitive set of helplessness may well play a critical and continuing role in susceptibility to depression irrespective of vulnerabilities stemming from the current environment and particularly from "shortcomings" in a husband. A more extreme position still might emphasize the role of personality characteristics that were present in childhood before the loss but potentiated by it. However, the core role of the loss and the circumstances following it can hardly be denied, with the rate of such losses influenced by broader societal and environmental factors. Our own position is an intermediate one in which the role of enduring cognitive sets such as helplessness is recognized but in which plenty of room is left for social and environmental influences both past and present, which determine self-esteem and character in the here and now just as crucially as does early personality development.

SOME FINAL CONCLUSIONS

Three final, more general conclusions may be drawn. First, at least in urban working-class populations, the consequences of a loss of a mother considerably increase chances of depression occurring in adult life. However, since maternal loss in childhood is relatively uncommon in Western industrialized urban populations, the general rate of depression is probably not greatly augmented (probably a rise of no more than a fifth). However, if we were to take account of other experiences, the impact of childhood, as a whole might prove substantial. Nevertheless, in most instances, the vulnerability stemming from early experiences does not lead directly to depression; rather it requires interaction with current adversity before translation into an episode of depression. It is possible for there to be considerable vulnerability stemming from childhood experience and yet no depression because of an absence of current adversity.

Second, it is a mistake to view associations between childhood loss of mother and current depression as spurious simply because there is a further association with social class (see Crook & Eliot, 1980). This is because our findings show that childhood experiences may determine social class position in adult life; there is a pathway running through loss of mother, lack of subsequent care, and premarital pregnancy to adult class position. Social class, as defined by husband's occupation, may be more a dependent than an independent variable in terms of the effects of childhood experience.

Third, the question of whether early loss has a long-term impact cannot be settled one way or another by the latest inquiry. Necessarily results will be influenced by the nature of the population studied. Rutter (1981) recently made much the same point about the short-term effect of so-called broken homes. Failure to find an association in a particular population no more deals a fatal blow to the importance of loss of a parent than does the finding that water does not boil at 212°F on the top of Mont Blanc threaten generalizations about the boiling point of water. The need for such awareness emphasizes that psychiatry, whatever else it is, must be part of the social sciences.

REFERENCES

Abramson, L. Y., Seligman, M. E. P., & Teasdale, J. D. (1978). Learned helplessness in humans: Critique and reformulation. *Journal of Abnormal Psychology, 87,* 49–74.

Adam, K. S., Bouckoms, A., & Streiner, D. (1982). Parental loss and family stability in attempted suicide. *Archives of General Psychiatry, 39,* 1081–1085.

Bebbington, P., Hurry, J., Tennant, C., Sturt, E., & Wing, J. K. (1981). Epidemiology of mental disorders in Camberwell. *Psychological Medicine, 11,* 561–579.

Beck, A. T. (1967). *Depression: clinical, experimental and theoretical aspects.* London: Staples Press.

Beck, A. T., Rush, A. J., Shaw, B. F., & Emery, G. (1979). *Cognitive therapy of depression.* New York: Wiley.

Bibring, E. (1953). Mechanisms of depression. In P. Greenacre (Ed.), *Affective disorders: Psychoanalytic contributions to their study.* New York: International Universities Press.

Bifulco, A. (1985). *Death of mother in childhood and depression.* Doctoral thesis, University of London (to be submitted).

Birtchnell, J. (1980). Women whose mothers died in childhood: An outcome study. *Psychological Medicine, 10,* 699–713.

Boulton, M. G. (1983). *On being a mother: A study of women with preschool children.* London: Tavistock.

Bowlby, J. (1969). *Attachment and loss: Vol. 1. Attachment.* New York: Basic Books.

Bowlby, J. (1973). *Attachment and loss: Vol. 2. Separation: Anxiety and Anger.* New York: Basic Books.

Bowlby, J. (1980). *Attachment and loss: Vol. 3. Loss: Sadness and depression.* New York: Basic Books.

Brown, G. W. (1974). Meaning, measurement and stress of life events. In B. S. Dohrenwend & B. P. Dohrenwend (Eds.), *Stressful life events: Their nature and effects.* New York: Wiley.

Brown, G. W. (1981). Contextual measures of life events. In B. S. Dohrenwend & B. P. Dohrenwend (Eds.), *Stressful life events and their contexts.* New York: Neale Watson Academic Publications.

Brown, G. W. (1982). Early loss and depression. In C. M. Parkes & R. S. Hinde (Eds.), *The place of attachment in human behaviour.* New York: Basic Books.

Brown, G. W., Craig, T. K. J., & Harris, T. O. (in press). Depression: Disease or distress? Some epidemiological considerations. *British Journal of Psychiatry.*

Brown, G. W., & Harris, T. O. (1978). *Social origins of depression.* London: Tavistock and New York: Free Press.

Brown, G. W., Harris, T. O., & Copeland, J. R. M. (1977). Depression and loss. *British Journal of Psychiatry, 130,* 1–18.

Brown, G. W., & Prudo, R. (1981). Psychiatric disorder in a rural and an urban population: 1. Aetiology of depression. *Psychological Medicine, 11,* 581–599.

Campbell, E. A., Cope, S. J., & Teasdale, J. D. (1983). Social factors and affective disorder: An investigation of Brown and Harris' model. *British Journal of Psychiatry, 143,* 548–553.

Cooper, J. E., Copeland, J. R. M., Brown, G. W., Harris, T. O., & Gourley, A. J. (1977). Further studies on interviewer training and Inter-rater reliability of the Present State Examination (P.S.E.) *Psychological Medicine, 7,* 517–523.

Crook, T., & Eliot, J. (1980). Parental death during childhood and adult depression. *Psychological Bulletin, 87,* 252–259.

Engel, G. L. (1967). A psychological setting of somatic disease: The "giving up–given up complex." *Proceedings of the Royal Society of Medicine, 60,* 553–555.

Finlay-Jones, R. A. (1981). Showing that life events are a cause of depression—A review. *Australian and New Zealand Journal of Psychiatry, 15,* 229–238.

Finlay-Jones, R. A., Duncan-Jones, P., Brown, G. W., Harris, T. O., Murphy, E., & Prudo, R. (1980). Depression and anxiety in the community: Replicating the diagnosis of a case. *Psychological Medicine, 10,* 445–454.

Finlay-Jones, R. A., & Murphy, E. (1979). Severity of psychiatric disorder and the 30-item general health questionnaire. *British Journal of Psychiatry, 134,* 609–616.

Freud, S. (1971). Mourning and melancholia. In *Collected Papers, Vol. IV.* London: Hogarth. (Originally published 1917.)

Furstenberg, F. F. (1979). Premarital pregnancy and marital instability. In G. Levinger & O. C. Moles (Eds.), *Divorce and Separation.* New York: Basic Books.

Ginsberg, S. M., & Brown, G. W. (1982). No time for depression: A study of help-seeking among mothers of preschool children. In D. Mechanic (Ed.), *Symptoms, illness behavior, and help-seeking.* New York: Neale Watson.

Goldberg, D. P., & Huxley, P. (1980). *Mental illness in the community: The pathway to psychiatric care.* London: Tavistock.

Goldthorpe, J. H., & Hope, K. (1974). *The social grading of occupations: A new approach and scale.* London: Oxford University Press.

Granville-Grossman, K. L. (1968). The early environment of affective disorder. In A. Coppen & A. Walk (Eds.), *Recent developments in affective disorders.* London: Headley Brothers.

Harris, T. O., Brown, G. W., & Bifulco, A. (1985a). *Loss of parent in childhood and adult psychiatric disorder: The Walthamstow Study. 1. The role of lack of adequate parental care.* (Unpublished manuscript.)

Harris, T. O., Brown, G. W., & Bifulco, A. (1985b). *Loss of parent in childhood and adult psychiatric disorder: The Walthamstow Study. 2. The role of social class position and premarital pregnancy.* (Unpublished manuscript.)

Harris, T. O., Brown, G. W., & Bifulco, A. (1985c). *Loss of parent in childhood and adult psychiatric disorder: The Walthamstow Study. 3. The role of situational helplessness.* (Unpublished manuscript.)

Hollingshead, A. B., & Redlich, F. C. (1958). *Social class and mental illness.* New York: Wiley.

Illsley, R., & Thompson, B. (1961). Women from broken homes. *Sociological Review, 9,* 27–54.

Kennard, J., & Birtchnell, J. (1982). The mental health of early mother separated women. *Acta Psychiatrica Scandinavica, 65,* 388–402.

Langner, T. S., & Michael, S. T. (1963). *Life stress and mental health.* London: Collier-Macmillan.

Linton, R. (1936). *The study of man.* New York: Appleton-Century.

Lloyd, C. (1980). Life events and depressive disorder reviewed. 1. Events as predisposing factors. *Archives of General Psychiatry, 37,* 529–535.

Martin, C. J. (1982). *Psychosocial stress and puerperal psychiatric disorder.* Presented to the Marce Society.

Mechanic, D. (1978). *Medical sociology* (2nd ed.). New York: Free Press.

Melges, F. T., & Bowlby, J. (1969). Types of hopelessness in psychopathological process. *Archives of General Psychiatry, 20,* 690–699.

Murphy, E. (1982). Social origins of depression in old age. *British Journal of Psychiatry, 141,* 135–142.

Park, G. (1974). *The idea of social structure.* New York: Anchor Books.

Parker, G. (1979). Parental characteristics in relation to depressive disorders. *British Journal of Psychiatry, 134,* 138–147.

Parker, G. (1981). Parental representations of patients with anxiety neurosis. *Acta Psychiatrica Scandinavica, 65,* 33–36.

Paykel, E. S. (1973). Life events and acute depression. In J. P. Scott & E. C. Senay (Eds.), *Separation and depression* (Publ. 94) Washington, DC: American Association for the Advancement of Science.

Paykel, E. S., Emms, E. M., Fletcher, J., & Rassaby, E. S. (1980). Life events and social support in puerperal depression. *British Journal of Psychiatry, 136,* 339–346.

Prudo, R., Brown, G. W., Harris, T. O., & Dowland, J. (1981). Psychiatric disorder in a rural and an urban population. 2. Sensitivity to loss. *Psychological Medicine, 11,* 601–616.

Richards, M. P. M., & Dyson, M. (1982). *Separation, divorce and the development of children: A review.* London: Department of Health and Social Security.

Rutter, M. (1971). Parent–child separation. Psychological effects on the children. *Journal of Child Psychology and Psychiatry, 12,* 233–260.

Rutter, M. (1981). *Maternal deprivation reassessed* (2nd ed.). Hammondsworth, Middlesex, England. Penguin Books.

Rutter, M. (1982). Epidemiological-longitudinal approaches to the study of development. In W. A. Collins (Ed.), *Minnesota symposium on child psychology* (Vol. 15). Hillsdale, NJ: Lawrence Erlbaum Associates.

Sarbin, T. R. (1970). The culture of poverty, social identity, and cognitive outcomes. In V. L. Allen (Ed.), *Psychological factors in poverty.* Chicago: Markham.

Seligman, M. E. P. (1975). *Helplessness: On depression, development and death.* San Francisco: Freeman.

Seligman, M. E. P., Abramson, L. Y., Semmel, A., & von Baeyer, C. (1979). Depressive attributional style. *Journal of Abnormal Psychology, 88,* 242–247.

Surtees, P. G., & Ingham, J. G. (1980). Life stress and depressive outcome: Application of a dissipation model to life events. *Social Psychiatry, 15,* 21–31.

Teasdale, J. D., & Fennell, M. (1982). Immediate effects on depression of cognitive therapy interventions. *Cognitive Therapy and Research, 6,* 343–352.

Tennant, C., Bebbington, P., & Hurry, J. (1980). Parental death in childhood and risk of adult depressive disorders: A review. *Psychological Medicine, 10,* 289–299.

Tennant, C., Bebbington, P., & Hurry, J. (1982). Social experiences in childhood and adult psychiatric morbidity: A multiple regression analysis. *Psychological Medicine, 12,* 321–327.

Tennant, C., Hurry, J., & Bebbington, P. (1980). Parent–child separations during childhood: Their relation to adult psychiatric morbidity and to referral: Preliminary findings. *Acta Psychiatrica Scandinavica, 285,* 324–331.

Tennant, C., Hurry, J., & Bebbington, P. (1982). The relation of childhood separation experiences to adult depressive and anxiety states. *British Journal of Psychiatry, 141,* 475–482.

Tennant, C., Smith, A., Bebbington, P., & Hurry, J. (1981). Parental loss in childhood. *Archives of General Psychiatry, 38,* 309–314.

Wadsworth, M. (1979). *Roots of delinquency. Infancy, adolescence, and crime.* London: Martin Robertson.

Wing, J. K., Nixon, J. M., Mann, S. A., & Leff, J. P. (1977). Reliability of the P.S.E. (ninth edition) used in a population study. *Psychological Medicine, 7,* 505–516.

Wolkind, S. N. (1977). Women who have been "in care"—psychological and social status during pregnancy. *Journal of Child Psychology and Psychiatry, 18,* 179–182.

Developmental Aspects of Children's Responses to the Stress of Separation and Loss

Norman Garmezy

INTRODUCTION

The frequency with which the term "stress" is used by researchers masks the dissatisfaction with the concept. Critics condemn its multiple and imprecise definitions, the ineffectiveness of its measuring instruments including those termed "life events schedules," the heterogeneity of stimuli that are likely to potentiate the ill-defined state, and the complex aggregate of behavioral and somatic processes that reflect its presence.

Yet despite these shortcomings there continues to be an outpouring of research on the topic of stress—its antecedents, correlates, and consequences. Mason (1975) suggested that the very durability of usage warranted a "continuing search" for whatever was "solid and valid" in the concept.

The methods that characterize stress research are varied: clinical case studies, biographical retrospective reconstructions of life histories, naturalistic observations, and laboratory studies of biological and psychological processes have all been used in an effort to understand the effects of stressful experiences on adaptation. For the most part, adults have been the focus of research attention but an emergent literature on children's reactions to various types of stressors is now evident (see Garmezy & Rutter, 1983, 1985, for reviews).

However, the children's literature is a piecemeal one that is primarily empirical, atheoretical in conception, variable with regard to the different

Norman Garmezy. Department of Psychology, University of Minnesota, Minneapolis, Minnesota.

stressors studied, typically cross-sectional rather than longitudinal in method, with subject groups that vary with regard to age, gender, demographic, and other status factors. Thus, even the fundamental questions posed by the editors for consideration in this chapter ("To what extent are there developmental changes in how children respond to stress? What are the age changes in what is felt as stressful?") preclude a definitive reply because of the absence of systematic research cast in a developmental perspective.

In a recent review of the development of achievement motivation, an area with a far more active research history compared to children's reactions to stress, Heckhausen (1982) cautioned that his conclusions of a developmental progression were limited by the paucity of directly relevant data. That same justifiable tentativeness must be extended to any conclusions derived from the present review of developmental changes in children's reactions to loss or separation.

Stress research has undergone a series of significant shifts in emphasis. Early studies were focused on the effects on lower organisms of systemic stressors such as heat, cold, injury, shock, and infections (Selye, 1936, 1946), particularly in terms of physiological responses organized around the pituitary–adrenal axis. Later, psychological stressors were employed in laboratory studies of higher order animals. These investigations added to the catalog of evoking stimuli and the behavioral response systems that were activated. The latter came to be identified as "coping" patterns, while confusion on the stimulus scale was compounded by adding a multitude of both benign and damaging events as potentiators of the stress response.

Later, physiology and cognition became commingled with the effort to subsume, under the rubric of stress, such diverse constructs as frustration, arousal, emotion, conflict, and anxiety (Eysenck, Arnold, & Meili, 1972).

THE NATURE OF STRESS

Despite the definitional ambiguity, four components seem to comprise current conceptions of stress: (1) the presence of a stimulus event, which induces (2) an element of change that modifies the organism's systemic and/ or psychological equilibration, and (3) is capable of inducing a state of emotional arousal marked by concomitant neurophysiological, cognitive, and expressive components (see Izard & Buechler, 1979), which (4) has the potential of disrupting the organism's normative pattern of responding.

The categorization of those stimulus situations capable of energizing this sequence have come to be termed stressors, which can be viewed as varying along dimensions such as pleasant/unpleasant, mild/severe, brief/long term, and acute/chronic. These dimensions help to define the potential effects of an event but, in turn, are modified by a diverse set of subject factors such as age and gender of the affected individual, developmental status, degree of physical and social maturity attained, as well as the complexity of the physical and social environment (Emde & Robinson, 1976) and the presence or absence of other risk and protective factors (Garmezy, 1985; Rutter, 1979b).

The quartet of factors that structure the stress–response sequence is evidently capable of being elicited at various points in the human life span, including early infancy when emotional states are as yet undifferentiated and a more generalized pattern of arousal prevails. The point that follows, admittedly speculative, suggests one possible source of linkage of human response over time.

Infancy, Arousal, and Stress

First, a broad-based propositional statement: Stimuli that evoke very low or very high states of arousal tend to be associated with poor task performance, whereas a moderate level of stimulation tends to produce an optimal pattern of behavior. This relationship (Hebb, 1955) has its representation in the well-known, inverted U-shaped function depicted in Fig. 1. Is there an analogous relationship to be found in the first weeks of life of the newborn, at which time behavior is unconfounded by the vagaries of the stress concept or by the differentiation of emotional states that begins to take place by the third month of life?

Wolff (1966) provided a glimpse into this presumed relationship between generalized arousal and performance. He studied 12 healthy infants

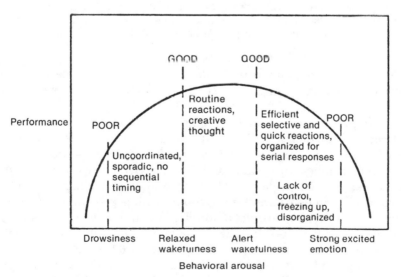

Fig. 1. *Behavioral arousal and performance (Cox, 1978, p. 43).*

during the first week of life, searching for gradations in the behavioral state of the newborn that could be equated with the concept of generalized arousal and that, in turn, would relate to behavioral effectiveness.

Based on his observations of newborns, Wolff reported a continuum of behavioral states ranging from regular sleep → irregular sleep → periodic sleep → drowsiness → alert inactivity → waking → inactivity → crying vocalization. Wolff's descriptions of these neonatal states seem to parallel the arousal continuum as initially suggested by Lindsley (1960), who sought to trace its representation in EEG patterns reflective of different behavioral states in adults. Lindsley, too, described a range of behavioral states extending from deep sleep → moderate sleep → light sleep → drowsiness → relaxed wakefulness → alert attentiveness → strong excited emotion (e.g., fear, rage, anxiety). With these data in hand, he sought to relate the concept of variations in the level of arousal to variations in the efficiency of performance as suggested earlier by Hebb (1955).

Wolff's observations, like those of others (Spears & Hohle, 1967), of the effect on responsivity of the neonate to pain, touch, auditory, and visual stimulation to changes in motility indicated that responsiveness in the form of an inverted U-shaped function appeared to be related to the state of alertness of the neonate. He noted:

> Except for pain, infants were generally unresponsive to stimulation in regular sleep, most responsive to the various modalities somewhere between irregular sleep and alert inactivity (the peak depending on the modality of stimulation), and unresponsive again while active or crying.
>
> These results are compatible with the clinical impression that the infant is sensitive to external stimuli at both ends of the arousal continuum, and that the direction of response for all modalities is to a large extent determined by the state of the organism. (pp. 35, 37)

Wolff concluded that it was "in states of mild or moderate activity that the effect of modality on responsiveness could be demonstrated most clearly."

Turning to results provided by other investigators, Reese and Lipsitt (1970) reported on those conditions of low stimulation that led the infant to engage in "diversive" exploration in an effort to change the situational context. Neonates appeared to show activity and irritability under conditions of relative stimulus deprivation. The presentation of a stimulus, whether a nonaversive monotone, variations in room lighting, providing a pacifier, or rocking the baby tended to quiet a bored infant and reduced its restiveness. Wolff, too, described the "dramatic" power of a monotone in influencing the behavior of a baby in irregular sleep. On 66 or 67 occasions white noise (80 db through a microphone 10–12 cm from the infant's ears) that was not painful converted an infant's irregular sleep to regular sleep within 1 min.

It also reduced activity in 87% of instances in which the babies were softly crying.

Criticism of the Arousal Formulation

Though the observations are provocative they are contained by a dispute that focuses on the arousal–performance formulation (Dunn, 1977). One objection centers on the concept of arousal itself with its implication that various states of alertness in the neonate reflect the presence of a continuum in central nervous system excitation, an inference that is neither consistent with the organization of the CNS, nor with intraindividual variations in the neonate's heart rate, breathing rate, and blood pressure when measured during a specific behavioral state.

A second major objection is drawn from the research of Hutt, Lenard, and Prechtl (1969). These investigators have disputed the assignment of descriptive, observable, behavioral states as indicators of levels of "arousal," "activation," or "consciousness." Furthermore, they fail to find a set progression in responsiveness from state to state. They observe that the neonate's spinal reflexes can be elicited strongly in one state but not in another; an optimal state for eliciting one reflex is not necessarily optimal for eliciting a different one. To these investigators therefore behavioral states reflect qualitatively different systems of organization in the neonate rather than variations on a continuum of arousal.

A third argument, counter to the notion of generalized arousal, is one related to the developmental nature of emotional states (Izard & Buechler, 1979). Currently, there are two theoretical views of the ontogenesis of human emotions. One, the differentiation hypothesis, views the separate emotions of the infant as derived from a single emotional or arousal state. In the early weeks of life, excitement or generalized distress serves as the precursor state to later emotional development. An alternative view, espoused by Izard, emphasizes the emergence of emotions as these become adaptive for the developing neonate. A basic factor influencing the emergence is the critical relationship that exists between infant and caregiver. Distress, powerful in the first months of life, is necessary as a signal to caregiver to enhance survival of the infant. Fear, powerful in the latter half of the first year, has importance for the development of self-protection and self-control. The inhibition of physical distress signals later in development, Izard asserts, is a function of maturation of cortical and subcortical mechanisms and the accompanying neurophysiological development that ensures learning derived from experience. Thus, C. E. Izard (personal correspondence) suggests that continuity of arousal patterns and sequences from the neonatal period to adulthood will be difficult to verify. If there is continuity, he argues, it is more likely to be found in affect thresholds and regulatory mechanisms that cannot be readily determined in the neonate.

I do not dispute the issues that surround the concept of "arousal" as a reflection of a form of CNS excitation. Dunn's urging that these states be recognized simply as descriptive is more neutral, less inferential, and consistent with what takes place in the CNS. Such state descriptions do not presume arousal or activation, whereas they more comfortably meet descriptions of the neonate's state of alertness (Brackbill, 1971; Dunn, 1977).

However, the point that deserves mention is that conditions of high distress or of markedly reduced stimulation (both of which may be precursors to stress states in the neonate) are not optimal conditions for an all-important activity, namely, the infant's early attempts to process information about the world. The signpost for that index of future competence is one typified by a more moderate state of alert inactivity.

Nor is it farfetched to suggest that alertness, under conditions of moderate arousal, may foster first efforts at adaptive learning in the infant, which can heighten the possibility of the development of more effective coping skills in early childhood. Why study the possibility that such continuity may exist? First, it might clarify the role of intra- and interindividual variability in responsiveness as mediated by fundamental biological predispositions that contribute to tendencies toward behavioral vulnerability or resilience under stress. Second, it gives centrality to the nature of the supportive environment with particular emphasis on the caregiver in alleviating distress; it thus emphasizes the critical role of maternal attachment, the disruption of which by separation or loss makes these the near universal stressors of human existence. Third, in emphasizing the interaction between infant and caregiver, it focuses on the beginnings of transactional processes that influence pathways to adaptation or maladaptation. Contributing to that transactional exchange is the emotional state of both infant and caregiver.

With regard to the latter consideration, Cohn and Tronick (1983) have reported that an infant 3 months of age and older, when faced with its mother who has briefly simulated a depressed state, will respond with protest, wariness, negative expression, and disorganized responsiveness. Such a finding, if replicable, would suggest a broad set of important questions related to risk factors in infancy. What consequences ensue for the infant of a truly depressed mother whose emotional state is of a long duration? Are infants differentially responsive to such maternal emotions? If so, what processes underlie this readiness of some infants to respond sensitively to discrepant maternal cues? Is the sensitivity to atypical maternal behaviors an at-risk factor that may be manifestly present in infants and young children born to mothers who are prone to depressive behaviors? Does habituation take place to such repetitive affective maternal behaviors more effectively in some infants than in others? To what extent do such sensitivities (see Bergman & Escalona, 1949) reflect a lower threshold to distress inputs that make for a more threatening and less receptive world in the orientation to others of the infant or the young child? Answers to such questions are not available but they should be a part of the scientific agenda for the study of stress responsiveness in children in relation to aberrant behaviors by their significant caregivers.

One can anticipate the ubiquitous issues of continuity and individual variability to arise in this context of risk for true psychopathology as well. In a recent review of children's prosocial dispositions and behavior Radke-Yarrow, Zahn-Waxler, and Chapman (1983) have reported clinical observations that some children reared by affectively disordered parents show "helpful, responsible, and sympathetic behavior." These investigators have affirmed these findings in observational studies of mothers who have had a depressive episode while interacting with their children in a simulated but realistic home setting. What, they ask, are the socialization processes, extending beyond traditional child development research, that children acquire for dealing with helplessness and need in others? One can extend the concept of "protective factors" to incorporate not only resistance to disorder in children, but to those altruistic motives of "required helpfulness" (Garmezy, 1985; Rachman, 1979) that children often display toward others in distress.

THE ROOTS OF LOSS AND SEPARATION AS STRESSORS

The remainder of this chapter will focus on one group of stressors that typically is assumed to fall at the severe end of the dimension of stress. These are loss events and they are marked by grief and bereavement induced by the severing of deep-seated attachments through death or loss of a significant figure, or by a failure to develop such attachments through profound neglect by uncaring parents or surrogates. Yet it is important to realize that even for extreme events, which presumably evoke a universal distress experience, one can only speak of a modal pattern of response, recognizing that severity and adequacy of reaction can vary considerably from individual to individual even under the most distressing circumstances.

To return to the earliest distress signal of the neonate, Wolff's observations that a high state of arousal is indexed by the crying vocalization of the newborn moves one toward the identification of "nonhunger fussiness" and the critical role it plays in ensuring the survival of the infant. Bowlby (1969) and others (e.g., Emde, Gaenbsbauer, & Harmon, 1976) have indicated its evolutionary role in fostering infant–mother attachment. Through distress reduction the infant is enabled to focus attention and to begin the act of information processing of sensory and social signals emanating from this all-important figure in the environment. Dunn (1977) writes:

The best possible state for the intimate exchange of gaze between mother and child is one where the baby is calm and alert. Our interest then in the calming effect of a mother's picking up a crying baby is not simply in the part this plays in removing a cause of distress 0 that in state X he was uncomfortable but in his mother's arms he is in state Y and is comfortable. Notice rather the way the baby stops thrashing, becomes calm and attentive, scans the world and gazes at his mother's face. She returns his intent gaze, smiles, nods, and talks to him. It is when he is in this calm attentive state that he can begin to know his mother's face and voice, can begin to take part in the reciprocal exchanges of looks, sounds and movements—in the "conversations" that are so important in the development of their relationship. (p. 19)

All theories of development emphasize the significance of this bonding between mother and baby, of reciprocal exchange, the induction of comfort, and the alleviation of distress through a loving and affectionate interaction. All the reason then to expect that one of the most powerful stress experiences for infant and child would be separation from or loss of mother or other attachment figures who have been primary caregivers.

In *Inhibition, Symptoms and Anxiety*, Freud (1925–1926/1959) provided a descriptive prototype of the contemporary *strange situation* (Ainsworth & Wittig, 1969):

Only a few of the manifestations of anxiety in children are comprehensible to us, and we must confine our attention to them. They occur, for instance, when a child is alone, or in the dark, or when it finds itself with an unknown person instead of one to whom it is used—such as its mother. These three instances can be reduced to a single condition—namely that of missing someone who is loved and longed for. . . .

The child's mnemonic image of the person longed for is no doubt intensely cathected, probably in a hallucinatory way at first. But this has no effect, and now it seems as though the longing turns into anxiety. . . . Here anxiety appears as a reaction to the felt loss of the object. . . .

But a moment's reflection takes us beyond this question of loss of object. The reason why the infant in arms wants to perceive the presence of its mother is only because it already knows by experience that she satisfies all its needs without delay. The situation, then, which it regards as a "danger" and against which it wants to be safeguarded is that of nonsatisfaction, of a *growing tension due to need,* against which it is helpless. (pp. 136–137)

Freud's commentary reflects part of the beginnings of a historical sequence of the growth of scientific interest in the problem of psychological deprivation in children. This sequence is marked too by the gradual introduction of better methods for identifying conditions of deprivation, their evocation, and measurement, and the range of the consequences that result from exposure to such deprivation events (see Langmeier & Matêjĉek, 1975).

DEVELOPMENTAL CHANGES IN CHILDREN'S RESPONSES
TO THE STRESS OF SEPARATION

A growing and systematic literature on attachment, stranger anxiety, infant wariness, and children's response to the "strange situation" has provided insights into the development of fear in children. Schaffer (1974) a prime contributor to that literature, has provided a summary of the points of agreement on the age sequencing of the infant's fear behaviors when exposed to strangers. The developmental sequence proceeds in this fashion:

1. The early months of life are a period of fearlessness to object and to person, in which there are no infant avoidance responses to unfamiliarity.
2. In the later stages of that period some degree of wariness enters in, marked by lessened responsiveness and some distancing from others.
3. The definitive onset of fear occurs in the third quarter of the first year with the mode represented by the eight month of life, when its initial appearance is quite marked.
4. However, initial differences exist both in the age of onset of fear as well as in the intensity of its expression. Although the precise nature of the interaction between gene and experience is not known, both undoubtedly have a role to play in the manifestation of fear behavior at this point in the infant's development.
5. The stability of fearfulness varies over both the short and long term with fluctuations a function of many state and situational variables.

In sum, a high degree of degree of group consistency in a modal sense is evident, but individual, situational, and state variables also operate to provide a high degree of inter-individual variation.

It seems evident that a part of the scientific agenda has been achieved, both in descriptive precision as well as in terms of comprehending fundamental developmental changes in affective and cognitive processes that underlie the patterning of the infant's response to strangers. Initially there is the reduction of impulsiveness in approach to others and the emergence of appraisal and inhibition prior to action. The infant learns to match object to standard and develops an appreciation of the significance of differences (from "sequential to simultaneous" consideration, in Schaffer's words) followed by the development of memory in which the infant moves from recognition to recall. It is from these developmental changes that the stressful experience of fear of strangers, emerges at the 8-month marker. Yet the factor of individual variation is also present, and this too requires explanation. Temperament factors such as activity level, approach–withdrawal, adaptability, intensity of reaction, threshold of responsiveness, quality of mood, attention span, and persistence (Thomas, Birch,

Chess, Hertzig, & Korn, 1963) would seem likely candidates as constitutional variables that may contribute to individual variation in social fearfulness, contributions which demand increasing attention from investigators.

The many studies of attachment that have been conducted in recent years have tended to focus on mother's behavior in fostering the bond between mother and child. Developmentalists, however, have been the prime contributors to the transactional view that mother and baby are reciprocal actors in the critical arena of bonding. Here, too, infant temperament factors undoubtedly play an important role in the quality of attachment that takes place (Rutter, 1979a). This is another area of research that is a requisite for understanding the attachment process. The importance of this relationship has been affirmed by Crockenberg (1981) in an evaluation of the complex relationships that obtain between (1) temperament ratings of infant irritability in the first weeks of life, (2) maternal responsiveness to infant distress signals at 3 months of age, (3) infant attachment to mother as adduced from the strange situation at 1 year of age, and (4) the magnitude of stress upon the mother and her availability of support from the spouse, older children, and others at that 1-year mark.

Results indicate that lack of social support of mothers is associated with unresponsiveness to irritable infants' distress signals at 3 months and in 10 of 11 cases to anxiety attachment in these infants when 1 year old.

The complexity of the interaction between infant temperament, maternal responsiveness, maternal stress, and available social supports, and the anxiety attachment of infants where support was lacking, offer important clues regarding both risk and protective factors that may interact to influence the subsequent adaptation of the infant-cum-child. The father's presence and the degree of support and intimacy he can provide point to another potentially protective factor that requires research, for his behavior too can markedly modify, enhance, or disrupt the child's adaptation to mother and others (Lamb, 1981).

In addition, there is a need for longitudinal research on the issue of the continuity of adaptation from infancy into childhood. The studies of Sroufe, Egeland, and their colleagues (Egeland & Farber, in 1984; Erickson, Sroufe, & Egeland, 1985; Sroufe, 1979; Sroufe & Waters, 1977) demonstrating that securely attached infants are more persistent and enthusiastic when engaged in problem-solving tasks at age 2, are more positive at age 3½ in their affective expression, more accepting of assistance, less oppositional, more involved, more curious, and actively engaged peer leaders in a nursery setting—in other words more *ego resilient*—suggest that these early experimental paradigms may offer clues to the qualities of stress resistance (the "steeling" effect) that some children exhibit in the presence of adversity.

CHILDREN'S FEARS AND SPECIFIC STRESSORS

Fear of loss and separation from loved ones are stressors that demonstrate marked staying power through the years of infancy, childhood, adolescence, and even adulthood. From the standpoint of both continuity and intensity, loss demonstrates the attributes of a near universal stress experience.

The emphasis on specific stressors coincides with a decline of interest in the more traditional mode of cataloguing various types of children's fears accompanied by a Gesell-like age profiling of the rise and fall of individual objects and situations that evoke a fear response. The prototype for this orientation was to be found in Jersild and Holmes's (1935) volume on *Children's Fears,* although more recent studies by Barnett (1969) and Miller, Barrett, Hampe, and Noble (1972) have also mapped variations in children's fears from ages 7 to 12. These studies demonstrate a reduction in concern about imaginary creatures and personal safety over that span, with a rise from age 9 onward of anxiety about school and social relationships, and concern over death and dying, illness, and disability. These shifts reflect in older children the appraisal of fears that are consistent with those exhibited by adults.

Miller *et al.* (1972) secured parent responses to a 60-item children's fear inventory. Their focus of inquiry was on 179 children from ages 6 to 16. Of the children, 78 had been diagnosed as phobic and were attending a clinic, while 101 constituted a normal control group. A factor analysis of the parents' responses revealed the emergence of three factors: Factor 1 comprised fears of physical injury stemming out of man-made dangers or threat of personal loss; Factor II fears consisted of natural and supernatural dangers; while Factor III reflected psychic distress ranging from fear of exams, schools, and social events to separation from parents and rejection by others. Factors I and III carry into adulthood and mark the entire life span; Factor II declines as childhood merges into adult status.

There has been a resurgence in the study of children's fears largely as a consequence of the development of fear schedules (Geer, 1965; Scherer & Nakamura, 1968) as devices for determining the presence of phobias that are to be treated by various behavior therapy methods (Sulzer-Azaroff & Pollack, 1982). Although fears, by inference, tap real or imagined stress experiences, this area of intervention has had only a tangential connection to current developments in the study of stress and coping in children. A fear schedule contains verbal contents related to one's fear of loss of parents or dissolution of families. Crisis life events reflect the actuality of such events and the consequences they hold for children and their adaptation. The literature on separation from and loss of parental figures is one based on actual rather than feared events. This literature is an extensive one and cannot be easily summarized in a brief chapter. Rutter's (1979a, 1981) reassessment of maternal deprivation suggests that there remain certain consistent findings with regard to stressful early life experiences that are associated with separation from significant caregivers:

1. Admission to hospital or residential nursery evokes an acute distress reaction in children. This is most marked in children between the ages of 6 and 48 months. Emotional disturbance in children is particularly acute if they have had poor relationships with their parents or if they come from homes marked by discord. Multiple hospital experiences enhance the probability of later psychiatric disorder. This outcome is greatest in children from disturbed or disadvantaged families.
2. Poor-quality institutions can produce intellectual and developmental retardation in children whose period of placement in such a setting is an extended one.
3. Multiple foster home and institutional placements in early childhood can contribute significantly to the development of later psychopathic and antisocial behavior.
4. The nature of significant attachments and hence of significant separations warrants extension beyond mothers or mother surrogates. Other important figures in the lives of infants and children also influence development, and these embrace fathers, sibs, teachers, peers, neighbors, etc.
5. One of the most important recent development in maternal deprivation has been the emphasis on individual differences in vulnerability to deprivation, disadvantage, and stress. Factors involved include temperament, sex differences, age at time of stress, and strength of prior relationships.
6. Long-range effects following separation experiences such as manifest psychological disturbance are not a typical outcome. Those children who do exhibit such consequences are the products of disturbed families prior to separation. When such effects do occur they are more likely to be exhibited by boys and to take the form of antisocial disorder.

These findings suggest several observations:

1. The foreboding predictions of dire outcomes attendant on separation have not been fulfilled on the basis of data gathered from carefully designed studies. A study of the long-term effects on children separated from their parents in the London blitz—20 years later—indicated that these persons, now adults, showed few instances of severe psychopathology.
2. This failure to predict the effective functioning of some children em-

phasizes the need for more research directed toward the study of healthy adaptation in stressed children rather than toward an exclusive concern with children who are manifestly vulnerable to stressful experiences.

3. There needs to be a greater emphasis on contextual factors that may be present during seemingly stress-arousing events. Thus, in the case of separation important protective factors are the attributes of significant adults in the new setting, whether it is a hospital, institution, or foster home.

In general, there would appear to be greater plasticity than has been anticipated in the adaptive capacities of children who have known separation experiences, but data on the age-related effects of separation are meager. Infants under 6 months of age seemingly are less affected than are those 6 months and older—a finding that is consistent with the observed wariness of children at that later age. However, more systematic age-related studies extending beyond early and middle childhood are needed.

Bereavement

Despite the tremendous stress placed on children by death of a parent, research on bereavement in childhood remains a markedly neglected area. Children's responsiveness to parental death and their mode of coping with it have taken primarily a clinical–descriptive form (Arthur & Kemme, 1964; Schowalter, 1975). However, a summary of relevant research has been provided by Black (1978), who pointed to a growing number of large-scale population studies that link parental death in childhood to later psychiatric disorder. Rutter (1979b, 1982), has performed a similar service for the role of deprivation, discord, and disruption (as opposed to death of a parent), as a correlate of several forms of psychiatric disorder in affected children.

There is a more focused literature devoted to bereavement in children and later psychiatric disorder (e.g., Munro & Griffiths, 1969; Rutter, 1966). These tend to be retrospective rather than prospective studies. Debate has arisen over the reported consistency with which maternal (but not paternal) loss in childhood tends to be associated with depressive states in the female offspring in adulthood. It is reported that neither schizophrenia nor anxiety states appear to be so related (Brown & Harris, 1978). Critics of the research, however, have viewed these symptomatic behaviors as transient "distress responses" (Tennant, Smith, Debbington, & Hurry, 1981). Other criticisms cited have included a failure to distinguish deaths from separations, the biasing effect of using psychiatric patients, and a failure to control for social variables (Tennant, Bebbington, & Hurry, 1980; Tennant, Hurry, & Bebbington, 1982).

In a recently published study (Tennant, Bebbington, & Hurry, 1982) of a random community sample, 5 % of the variance in adult psychiatric morbidity has been shown to be accounted for by loss and deprivation experiences. A low incidence in rate of breakdowns (5 %) has been reported in a recent study of psychiatric disorder in a sample of working-class women who were bereaved in childhood (Campbell, Cope, & Teasdale, 1983).

Groupings of children by age at time of separation or loss (0–4, 5–10, 11–15) indicate that the 5–10 age bracket seems to be the most vulnerable age of all, particularly if it occurred for a period exceeding a 6-month separation from both parents, siblings, and the family home. This ordinarily meant institutionalization, or placement in care, or in the homes of relatives or foster parents (Tennant, Bebbington, & Hurry, 1982). The occurrence of a significant loss to a child in this age bracket may be a marked "sensitizing" factor in adaptive difficulties of such children in adulthood. Other factors influencing the impact of bereavement on children include family closeness preceding the loss, the prior relationship between the affected child and the deceased parent, whether the parent is of the same or opposite sex of the child, the religious beliefs and social class background of the family, the suddenness as opposed to the gradual onset of the event.

On the side of "steeling" experiences there appears to be an attenuation of the impact of orphanhood or later mental disorder in adulthood if certain protective factors are present, of which one of the most important is the quality of care and support bereaved children receive following the parent's death. In general, the risk of psychiatric disorder in adults in relation to parental loss in childhood appears to be relatively low, but tends to be heightened by accumulated stressors, whether these occur in childhood or in adulthood.

There are many problems associated with interpretations of the effects of bereavement on children. Typically these are shortcomings attendant upon inadequate controls, low base rates, an emphasis on retrospection, and a dependency upon recall by respondents that raises questions of the veridicality of report that might arise from such recitals of the past.

Nevertheless, an interesting finding relates to what are presumed to be critical ages of the affected child when parental loss occurs. Thus for later depression, 10–14 years of age is also reported to be a particularly vulnerable age period. However, a more general statement may be warranted: Younger children grieve with less intensity than do older children. This is a consistent finding and it may be related to a child's cognitive understanding of the concept of death. Older children have a greater awareness of notions of causality and above all can comprehend the necessary abstraction of death as universal, inevitable, and irreversible. Younger children under 6 years of age do not understand the concept of universality, whereas by age 9 this is comprehended by most children. Irreversibility provides greater ambiguity in that some studies report confusion even in children up to the age 10 (Childers & Wimmer, 1971; White, Elsom, & Prawat, 1978).

However, others report that many children particularly by age 8 can understand that the dead do not return to life. Knowledge of such irreversibility
seems to be increased for children who have experienced the death of a
family member or of a pet. These data, however, are not inconsistent with a
maximization of the effect of loss in children between the ages 5 and 10 as
suggested by Tennant, Bebbington, and Hurry (1982).

The relationship between cognitive understanding of death and the
coping responses used by children in bereavement would appear to be a
fruitful area for systematic study.

Divorce

The subject of loss as a critical stressor has been accentuated by the
startling increase in divorce rates in the United States and Europe (Atkeson,
Forehand, & Rickard, 1982). In the United States nearly four in ten marriages end in dissolution through divorce. Wallerstein and Kelly (1980) noted
that for each year from 1972 to 1979 1 million new children below the age
of 18 experienced the trauma of family breakup through divorce. However,
in some areas of the country a dramatic increase is no longer evident and a
decline in the divorce rate has even made its appearance. Nevertheless,
there remains a growing acceptance of divorce as a likely possibility following marriage, with a marked increase in the number of persons who
have witnessed divorces in their immediate families (Caplow, Bahr, Chadwick, Hill, & Williamson, 1982).

With such a powerful psychosocial problem now evident one would
have expected an outpouring of research aimed at gaining an understanding of the impact of divorce on children. Unfortunately, this is not the case,
although the neglect has been tempered by two research programs, one
strongly clinical (Wallerstein, 1983; Wallerstein & Kelly, 1980), the other
strongly experimental/observational (Hetherington, Cox, & Cox, 1979a,
1979b, 1981). Both provide consistent results despite the differences in the
orientation and methods used by the investigators.

Wallerstein and Kelly's (1980) study began with clinical observations
made in the course of a 6-week divorce counseling program. Participants
consisted of 131 children and their parents from 60 predominantly white,
middle-class families living in Northern California. The study was
longitudinal with a 5-year follow-up after the separation, and a 10-year
follow-up of the offspring projected.

Wallerstein and Kelly perceive the existence of a stage sequence in
divorce. The initial stage following divorce proves to be "profoundly stressful" for almost all of the children and adolescents and for many of the
adults. Heightened conflict, pervasive unhappiness, and unrestrained sexual and aggressive behaviors mark the acute year-long period that follows
the breakup. After 1 year, children show recovery, typically in advance of

the parents, with girls recovering faster than boys. For some children, however, the symptomatic responses begin to follow a more chronic pattern, which the investigators attribute to long-standing stresses that were present prior to the parents' separation or to new stress experiences that have befallen the postdivorce family.

This transition period lasts for a span of 2 or 3 years, and its course is beset by changes in social, economic, and family circumstances. By the 5-year mark, some families have achieved stability, while others have maintained the earlier unhappy course.

The difficulty of final reconciliation is reflected in the authors' indication that many of the children had found the parental marriage more gratifying than did the parents. Over 50% of the children did not regard the postdivorce family as an improvement over the predivorce family. This is consistent with the observation by the authors that many of the children and adolescents as a group did not show an improvement in their psychological well-being at the termination of the initial follow-up period. An exception were those who had been physically separated by the divorce from a rejecting, critical, or a psychiatrically disturbed father.

One-third of the children were lively and well-adjusted at the 5-year mark, while approximately the same proportion still felt deprived, lonely, and rejected. Wallerstein and Kelly (1980) have emphasized that, in part, the reduced stature of the divorced family and its negative effect on economic, social, and psychological well-being (particularly the heightening of depression) may be an important contribution to the mental health problems of children of divorce.

Hetherington's study has a somewhat different cast, but she too finds many similar behavioral patterns in her children of divorce. She and her associates (Hetherington *et al.*, 1979a, 1979b, 1981) have provided a short-term longitudinal study of 48 middle-class preschool children (24 male, 24 female) from divorced families and 48 from matched control intact families who were studied at 2 months, 1 year, and 2 years following the divorce. In its experimental emphasis their study of the impact of divorce on the types of social or cognitive play of the children represents a unique contribution to the literature. Their children's average age was 3.9 years at the inception and 5.8 years at the conclusion of the 2-year period. Among the methods used to study the children's responses were free play and social interaction observations, peer nomination, and a related sociometric measure.

The results substantiate Wallerstein and Kelly's observation of the disruptive impact of divorce on the children. In the first year following divorce, the experimental children's play patterns were more fragmented, less cognitively and socially mature, evidencing less imaginativeness and a greater theme restriction. Their affective responses were more dysphoric, a pattern that continued for boys into the second year, but was reduced in girls. In their fantasy play boys were more restrictive, more egocentric, more aggressive, and more lacking in provider themes. Social interaction showed similar patterns, but the negative social behaviors rapidly disappeared from girls' social interactions. The investigators report that at year 2 following the parental divorce, the boys were unpopular with their peers, were restricted by them from participation in play groups and tended to play more with girls and younger peers.

The concordance of the children's behavior in home and in the laboratory setting was marked with regard to "observed noncompliance, negative demands, dependency, aggression, and sustained activity." Parent and teacher ratings obtained in the first year confirmed the comparability across the two settings for the children of divorce but not for the control children, who showed less behavioral stability across settings.

Behavioral variability within each study was markedly in evidence and was linked to such factors as a child's temperament characteristics, cumulative stress exposure, developmental status (i.e., the more limited the social and cognitive competencies of the young child the more limited the efficacy of the child's coping strategies), and gender (a more pervasive impact on boys than girls).

Despite the evidence of behavioral deficiencies in many of the children, Hetherington rejected the doom and gloom view of the single-parent family and called for a focus on positive functioning in such families and attention to support systems that could facilitate the social, emotional, and intellectual competence of the children.

Failure as Loss

Separation and loss of significant figures are recognized as among the most stressful experiences that individuals can sustain. The threat of failure seems to be something of a misfit among the great loss events, yet there is a linkage to be noted and it is found in the central theme of this volume. Depressive feelings often are a consequence of a pervasive sense of failure, and a theoretical link now has been forged between omnipresent attributions of worthlessness as a component of the self-concept of many who develop severe depressive disorders.

Failure touches the concept of loss in various other ways too. First, whereas loss and separation typically have an interpersonal context, failure is also a loss event, albeit an intrapersonal one. Second, ascriptions of failure are profoundly eroding of self-esteem, and self-esteem remains a key component of competent functioning. Failure experiences, if recurrent, inhibit the development of a sense of efficacy, which is also a constituent of competent functioning. Third, repetitive failure forms the base of anticipations of future ineffective performance, attributions of inadequacy, and loss of a sense of well-being.

All children have experience, in varying degrees, with successes and failures in performance. An important inquiry is related to the age at which the child begins to be shaped by such experiences. Although one must lean heavily on inference and interpretation in analyzing the behaviors of a responding infant, the suggested answer is that shaping of achieving behaviors can begin very early in life. Watson's (1966, 1967; Watson & Ramey, 1972) studies of the contingent activation (by a head movement) of an overhead mobile by a 3-week-old infant lying in its crib indicates not merely the acquisition of a head-turning response but the presence of positive affect (smiling and cooing) in response to the moving mobile. It is possible that precursors to the later development of effectance motivation may take place very early in life. Numerous researchers have commented on the possible roots in infancy of later mastery motivation (Dweck & Elliott, 1983; Harter, 1981; Izard, 1978, 1979). What is absent in the infant, of course, is the awareness of the requisites of personal competence that is essential to the satisfactory completion of a task, and in the longer run to the development of the self-concept.

DEVELOPMENTAL FACTORS IN RESPONSE TO FAILURE

That a sense of appraisal of possible failure develops in the second year of life is evident in the recent research of Kagan (1983). He has shown that in children 18–24 months of age a distress pattern implicating a critical self-appraisal of competence and the anticipation of failure can be evoked by the following simple experimental procedure:

> A child is playing happily with some toys while the mother sits nearby. A female examiner comes to the child and models three acts (e.g., the examiner picks up two plates and two dolls and makes the mother doll cook supper; she has a doll talk on a toy telephone; she picks up the animals and makes them go for a walk). The examiner then says, "Now it's your turn to play," and returns to the couch. (p. 201)

This procedure, notes Kagan, has been administered to two longitudinal and two cross-sectional samples of children, including a group of Fiji Island youngsters.

Manifest signs of distress following the instruction were evident in the marked clinging, crying, play inhibition, vocal protests, and requests to leave the setting that occurred in all groups after 17–18 months of age. In the U.S. sample, distress peaked just prior to the second birthday; in the Fiji sample, shortly after that age point. Kagan believes that these behaviors reflect two developmental processes in the young child. The first is the child's sense of an obligation to model the adult's behavior; the second is the cognitive act of comparison and evaluation of the act to be performed and the issue of personal competency to do so. The discrepancy between demand and ability evokes the distress inherent in the child's judgment that he or she lacks the ability to meet the required standard of performance. Thus the stressor is one that involves both an event and its individual interpretation rather than either one alone.

However, this task also reveals individual differences in temperament. Some children react with dysphoric affect and behavior, others show a milder degree of responsivity to the situation, while still others rarely show signs of distress. Unfortunately, the roots of these diverse reactions remain unknown.

With appraisal and self-evaluation in place one would anticipate the stressfulness of potential failure would also be evident in the responses of older children, but there are ameliorating factors that temper the response in children below the age of 4½ years.

Heckhausen (1967) has reported that children up to this age can cope with the conflict induced by their desire for achievement and the prospect of failure, provided that the probabilities of success and failure are equivalent. When the ratios are so aligned such children remain confident of their expectation of success. However, children from 3½ years of age onward are conflicted when faced with a task of increasing difficulty for which the likelihood of failure is marked.

An additional mediating factor is gender. Heckhausen also cited reports that girls, newly entering school, prefer to work at tasks they have already solved while boys try to master those that they have failed. Among 3- and 4-year-olds, girls try to overcome failure through persistence and independent action, whereas boys react affectively and inadequately. Whatever the strategy employed, success in overcoming such difficulties fosters achievement motivation, which may provide a protective factor against failure experiences and related stressors. Other positive influences include intactness of the family, medium family size, birth order, parental educational level, and achievement orientation of parents, whereas broken homes and weak parental ties have a negative effect on academic and occupational achievement drives.

Another gender difference relates to expectancies: girls tend to focus on negative information while boys look to the positive when constructing performance expectancies. Dweck and Elliott (1983) suggested that, in part, these differences might stem from the tendency of girls to rate tasks as more difficult than do boys. They see the combination in children of high ability and lowered expectancies as a possible risk factor for greater vulnerability to performance disruption by failure whether the failure is feared or actualized.

In general, younger children tend to view their abilities positively, underestimate the difficulty of tasks, and thus maintain high expectancies of success and low expectancies of failure. This optimism Dweck and Elliott

(1983) suggest is not always a sign of immaturity and inadequate processing abilities. It can in some instances reflect mastery motivation and an awareness of one's competence skills, but in many other cases young children lack the evaluative prerequisites for appraising successful or failed performance. Such appraisal requires a high degree of self-awareness for accomplishing four analytic tasks: awareness (1) that the success or failure outcome was self-produced, (2) that it was related to personal attributes of competence, (3) that both task difficulty together with the degree of personal competence required to perform it had been adequately evaluated, and (4) that there was some understanding of the role played by personal ability in directing the outcome that followed the expenditure of effort (Heckhausen, 1982).

This is a tall order for young children and the fragility of their optimism can be seen in the reduction of performance expectancy that takes place even with 4-year-olds if failure experiences are made more salient (Dweck & Elliott, 1983). In general, however, children up to age 3½ do not experience success or failure as related to personal attributes and do not engage in self-evaluation (see Heckhausen's 1982 review for supportive studies).

(For older children who have attained a higher degree of cognitive sophistication the recognition, monitoring, and assessment of task, ability, personal effort, and competence attributes can lead to a heightened concern with possible failure or to a heightened sense of confidence in successful performance of the task. Consistent success or consistent failure over tasks and over time can generate a determinate sense of efficacy or ineffectiveness by adolescence, which can prove to be quite resistant to change.)

Nevertheless, despite an absence of self-evaluation, success or failure in competitional laboratory tasks in children under 3½ years of age is evident in their stance and affective expression. Winners wear the look of triumph in their facial expression and bodily movements; losers are embarrassed and may even hide from the winner. By 4½, greater control is exercised by losers but they too betray their feelings by the forced smile, sighing, or voice tone.

Heckhausen (1982) reported that few children under 4½ admitted their failures; many lied or remained sullenly silent. Some covered up, made excuses, focused on earlier successes, were avoidant, stopped work, cheated, or tried various compensatory devices to attenuate losing.

Thus, the young child can engage in acts to deny negative self-evaluations. That becomes more difficult as children grow older. Nicholls (1975, 1978) asked children ages 5–13 to rank themselves in terms of class achievement. Younger children tended to rank themselves near the top of the class. More realistic appraisals appeared in the 9–10-year-old age group, while by age 13 self-rankings showed reasonably high correlations with teacher ratings.

These data were based on cross-sectional study. Needed are longitudinal studies of children who differ in terms of a success or a failure orientation, but these are few in number. One such study (Trudewind & Husarek, cited in Heckhausen, 1982) sought for the correlates of (German) first-grade children whose motivational patterns had undergone a change in orientation during the school year. One group had become very confident of success. The other had developed a pronounced fear of failure despite the fact that the two groups did not differ on demographic or ecological variables, intellectual development, or success/failure patterns upon entering school.

Among the correlates for this shift were differential patterns of maternal behavior in the two groups. Mothers of failure-motivated boys had high aspirations for their children, but granted them little autonomy or independence, showed inconsistent support of the children, were "neutral" in their reactions to their children's successes, but strongly negative to their failures, blamed performance inadequacies on lack of ability and effort, and used social comparison norms rather than individual norms for judging their child's achievements (cited in Heckhausen, 1982, p. 650).

Unfortunately, there is a lack of long-term longitudinal studies to evaluate whether there are stability, continuity, and consequences to such motive patterns into adulthood. Do such continuities exist? Are they related to later patterns of adaptation or maladaptation? Do early and excessive failure experiences enhance the likelihood of later depressive affects? These important questions cannot be answered at this point, but the potential of such negative motive orientations for later maladaptation constitutes a hypothesis in search of a test. Evidence from the therapeutic treatment of depression in adults is suggestive.

The formulation by Beck and his colleagues of the "cognitive triad"—three specific concepts that frame their cognitive model of depression—would suggest the potential power of such early failure events. The triad consists of (1) the self-perception of depressed patients as inadequate, blameworthy, defective, worthless, deficient, and self-critical, (2) a tendency by such patients to misinterpret in a negative direction their ongoing experiences, while avoiding use of more positive, more logical, and less biased alternative interpretations of an event or action, and (3) a negative, dysphoric view of the future that may lead to "psychomotor inhibition" (Beck, Rush, Shaw, & Emery, 1979, p. 12).

For Beck this triad is instrumental in the creation of "schemas"—the underlying stable cognitive patterns that frame the ways in which a person interprets a particular event or situation.

Beck et al. assume "that early experiences provide the basis for forming negative concepts about one's self, a view of the future and the external world." Such concepts, although latent, are capable of being potentiated by a specific disruptive event in later life. Although loss events have been accented as precipitants, a major failure can serve the same function, particularly if it is perceived as a symbol of past failures.

Confirmation of this model has been conducted within the narrow confines of the treatment room and is based on retrospective reconstruction of the patient's early experience. An alternative route, more truly developmental, is through a developmental–longitudinal study of children presumed to be at risk for later depression (Garmezy, 1981; Weissman, 1979). This would, of course, include attention to familial histories of depression in recognition of a genetic substrate as a vulnerability factor in the affective disorders. Such research projects are now getting underway (Beardslee, Bemporad, Keller, & Klerman, 1983) and the interrelatedness of loss, separation, failure, and depression may be more adequately explicated in future years by the extensive use of risk models of psychiatric disorder.

PROTECTIVE FACTORS IN CHILDREN UNDER STRESS

In a recent publication a number of studies that shed light on the nature of protective factors have been reviewed (Garmezy, 1985). These include

1. Studies associated with resistance to psychiatric disorder in children exposed to numerous risk factors associated with later psychopathology (Bleuler, 1978; Rutter, Cox, Tupling, Berger, & Yule, 1975; Rutter, Yule, Quinton, Rowlands, Yule, & Berger, 1975).
2. Research on adaptive behavior in adults who as infants and young children had been exposed to various disadvantaged circumstances including perinatal stress, poverty, family instability, limited parental education, and parental mental disturbance (Werner & Smith, 1982).
3. Longitudinal research on ego-resilient and ego-brittle children (Block & Block, 1980).
4. A review of competent black children reared in families marked by severe economic disadvantage (Garmezy & Nuechterlein, 1972).
5. Clinical research on adaptive children of divorce who had made substantial developmental progress when evaluated 5 years after family disruption (Wallerstein, 1983).
6. Studies of prosocial behavior in young children of severely depressed parents (Radke-Yarrow & Kuczynski, 1983).
7. The adaptation of children to war, disasters, and other markedly traumatic events (Garmezy & Rutter, 1985).

At best, this diverse array presents only clues to the emergence of resilience in children under stress. Nevertheless, there appear to be three recurring factors present in a number of these studies. These three broad categories of variables include (1) personality dispositions in the child, (2) a supportive family milieu, and (3) an external support system that encourages and reinforces a child's coping efforts and strengthens these by reinforcing the child's positive values.

Although these sound like homilies and one hesitates to offer them, they do reflect early efforts to comprehend that unique constellation of an adaptive child caught up in highly disadvantaging circumstances. What are the competencies of such children? How do these arise and what basic mechanisms underlie their manifestations? What are the protective factors that work to override the presence of risk and vulnerability indicators? These are the questions that call for programmatic research into the coping qualities of children under stress. Systematic research into resilience as a personal competence manifestation is a future requisite for understanding developmental changes in children's responses to separation, loss, and other stress experiences.

CONCLUSION

Summing up, a broad area of stress, namely, the effects of loss, separation, and failure and their consequences for children, has been described in this chapter. Developmental aspects of children's responsiveness to acutely traumatic events such as man-made and natural disasters are considered elsewhere (Garmezy & Rutter, 1985). The study of such developmental changes in response to stressors, accompanied by the discovery of factors that may heighten the prediction of vulnerability or resilience in exposed children, appears to be a significant aspect of future investigations of children who are at risk for physical or emotional disorders. By uniting clinical and experimental approaches in studies of the origins, manifestations, and modification of diverse adaptational patterns in children under stress, the growth of an interdisciplinary science of developmental psychopathology will be fostered.

ACKNOWLEDGMENTS

This chapter has been prepared with the aid of research grant support provided to the author by the William T. Grant Foundation, the National Institute of Mental Health, and a Research Career Award (NIMH, USPHS).

REFERENCES

Ainsworth, M., & Wittig, B. (1969). Attachment and exploratory behavior of one-year-olds in a strange situation. In B. Foss (Ed.), *Determinants of infant behavior* (Vol. 4, pp. 111–136). London: Methuen.

Arthur, B., & Kemme, M. L. (1964). Bereavement in childhood. *Journal of Child Psychology and Psychiatry, 5,* 37–49.

Atkeson, B. M., Forehand, R. L., & Rickard, K. M. (1982). The effects of divorce on children. In

B. B. Lahey & A. E. Kazdin (Eds.), *Advances in clinical child psychology* (Vol. 5, pp. 255–281). New York: Plenum Press.

Barnett, J. T. (1969). *Development of children's fears: The relationship between three systems of fear measurement.* Unpublished master's thesis, University of Wisconsin, Madison.

Beardslee, W. R., Bemporad, J., Keller, M. B., & Klerman, G. L. (1983). Children of parents with major affective disorder: A review. *American Journal of Psychiatry, 140*, 825–832.

Beck, A. T., Rush, A. J., Shaw, B. F., & Emery, G. (1979). *Cognitive therapy of depression: A treatment manual.* New York: Guilford.

Bergman, P., & Escalona, S. (1949). Unusual sensitivities in very young children. In *Psychoanalytic study of the child* (Vol. 3/4, pp. 333–352). New York: International Universities Press.

Black, D. (1978). Annotation: The bereaved child. *Journal of Child Psychology and Psychiatry, 19*, 287–292.

Bleuler, M. (1978). *The schizophrenic disorders: Long-term patient and family studies.* New Haven, CT: Yale University Press.

Block, J. H., & Block, J. (1980). The role of ego- centered and ego- resiliency in the organization of behavior. In W. A. Collins (Ed.), *Development of cognition, affect, and social relations* (pp. 39–101). Hillsdale, NJ: Lawrence Erlbaum Associates.

Bowlby, J. (1969). *Attachment and loss: Vol. 1. Attachment.* New York: Basic Books.

Brackbill, Y. (1971). Cumulative effects of continuous stimulation on arousal level in infants. *Child Development, 42*, 17–26.

Brown, G. W., & Harris, T. (1978). *Social origins of depression: A study of psychiatric disorder in women.* New York: Free Press.

Campbell, E. A., Cope, S. J., & Teasdale, J. D. (1983). Social factors and affective disorder: An investigation of Brown and Harris' model. *British Journal of Psychiatry, 143*, 548–553.

Caplow, T., Bahr, H. M., Chadwick, B. A., Hill, R., & Williamson, M. H. (1982). *Middletown families: Fifty years of change and continuity.* Minneapolis: University of Minnesota Press.

Childers, P., & Wimmer, M. (1971). The concept of death in early childhood. *Child Development, 42*, 1299–1301

Cohn, J. F., & Tronick, E. Z. (1983). Three-month-old infants' reaction to simulated maternal depression. *Child Development, 54*, 185–193.

Cox, T. (1978). *Stress.* London: Macmillan Press.

Crockenberg, S. (1981). Infant irritability, mother responsiveness, and social support influences on the security of infant-mother attachment. *Child Development, 52*, 857–865.

Dunn, J. (1977). *Distress and comfort.* Cambridge, MA: Harvard University Press.

Dweck, C. S., & Elliott, E. S. (1983). Achievement motivation. In P. H. Mussen (Ed.), E. M. Hetherington (Vol. Ed.), *Handbook of child psychology* (4th ed.): *Vol. 4. Socialization, personality and social development* (pp. 643–691). New York: Wiley.

Egeland, B., & Farber, E. A. (1984). Infant-mother attachment: Factors related to its development and changes over time. *Child Development. 55*, 753–771.

Emde, R. N., Gaensbauer, T. J., & Harmon, J. R. (1976). Emotional expression in infancy: A biobehavioral study. *Psychological Issues, 37*(1), 10.

Emde, R. N., & Robinson, J. (1976). The first two months: Recent research in developmental psychobiology and the changing view of the newborn. In J. Noshpitz & J. Call (Eds.), *Basic handbook of child psychiatry.* (Vol. I, pp. 72–105) New York: Basic Books.

Erickson, M. F., Sroufe, L. A., & Egeland, B. (in press). The relationship between quality of attachment and behavior problems in preschool in a high-risk sample. *Monographs of the Society for Research in Child Development.*

Eysenck, H. J., Arnold, W., & Meili, R. (Eds.). (1972). *Encyclopedia of Psychology* (Vol. 3). New York: Herder & Herder.

Freud, S. (1959). Inhibitions, symptoms and anxiety. In J. Strachey (Ed.), *The standard edition of the complete psychological works of Sigmund Freud* (Vol. 20, pp. 87–174). London: Hogarth Press (Original work published 1925–1926)

Garmezy, N. (1981). The current status of research with children at risk for schizophrenia and other forms of psychopathology. In D. A. Regier & G. Allen (Eds.), *Risk factor research in the major mental disorders* (DHHS Publication No. ADM 81–1068, pp. 23–40). Washington, DC: U. S. Government Printing Office.

Garmezy, N. (1985). Stress-resistant children: The search for protective factors. In J. E. Stevenson (Ed.), *Aspects of current child psychiatry research* (Journal of Child Psychology and Psychiatry Book Suppl. No. 4 pp. 213 233). Oxford: Pergamon Press.

Garmezy, N., & Nuechterlein, K. (1972). Invulnerable children: The fact and fiction of competence and disadvantage. *American Journal of Orthopsychiatry, 42,* 328–329, Abstract.

Garmezy, N., & Rutter, M. (Eds.). (1983). *Stress, coping, and development in children.* New York: McGraw-Hill.

Garmezy, N., & Rutter, M. (1985). Acute reactions to stress in children. In M. Rutter & L. Hersov (Eds.), *Child and adolescent psychiatry: Modern approaches* (2nd ed. pp. 152–176). Oxford: Blackwell Scientific Publications.

Geer, J. H. (1965). The development of a scale to measure fear. *Behaviour Research and Therapy, 13,* 45–53.

Harter, S. (1981). A model of intrinsic mastery motivation in children: Individual differences and developmental change. In A. Collins (Ed.), *Minnesota symposium on child psychology* (Vol. 14, pp. 215–255). Hillsdale, NJ: Lawrence Erlbaum Associates.

Hebb, D. O. (1955). Drives and the conceptual nervous system. *Psychological Review, 62,* 243–254.

Heckhausen, H. (1967). *The anatomy of achievement motivation.* New York: Academic Press.

Heckhausen, H. (1982). The development of achievement motivation. In W. W. Hartup (Ed.), *Review of child development research* (Vol. 6, pp. 600–668). Chicago: University of Chicago Press.

Hetherington, E. M., Cox, E. M., & Cox, R. (1979a). Family interaction and the social emotional and cognitive development of children following divorce. In V. Vaughn & T. Brazelton (Eds.), *The family: Setting priorities* (pp. 71–87). New York: Science and Medicine.

Hetherington, E. M., Cox, E. M., & Cox, R. (1979b). Play and social interaction in children following divorce. *Journal of Social Issues, 35,* 26–49.

Hetherington, E. M., Cox, E. M., & Cox, R. (1981). Effects of divorce on parents and children. In M. Lamb (Ed.), *Non-traditional families.* pp. 233–288 Hillsdale, NJ: Lawrence Erlbaum Associates.

Hutt, S. J., Lenard, H. G., & Prechtl, H. F. R. (1969). Psychophysiological studies in newborn infants. In L. P. Lipsitt & H. W. Reese (Eds.), *Advances in child development and behavior* (Vol. 4, pp. 127–172). New York: Academic Press.

Izard, C. E. (1978). On the development of emotions and emotion-cognition relationships in infancy. In M. Lewis & L. A. Rosenblum (Eds.), *The development of affect* (pp. 389–413). New York: Plenum Press.

Izard, C. E. (1979). Emotions as motivations: An evolutionary developmental perspective. In R. Dienstbier (Ed.), *Nebraska symposium on motivation,* 1978 (pp 163–200). Lincoln: University of Nebraska Press.

Izard, C. E., & Buechler, S. (1979). Emotion expressions and personality integration in infancy. In C. E. Izard (Ed.), *Emotions in personality and psychopathology* (pp. 447–472). New York: Plenum Press.

Jersild, A. T., & Holmes, F. G. (1935). *Children's fears.* New York: Teachers College.

Kagan, J. (1983). Stress and coping in early development. In N. Garmezy & M. Rutter (Eds.), *Stress, coping, and development in children* (pp. 191–216). New York: McGraw-Hill.

Lamb, M. E. (Ed.). (1981). *The role of the father in child development.* (2nd ed.). New York: Wiley.

Langmeier, J., & Matêjĉek, Z. (1975). *Psychological deprivation in childhood.* New York: Halstead Press.

Lindsley, D. B. (1960). Attention, consciousness, sleep and wakefulness. In J. Field & H. W. Magoun (Eds.), *Handbook of physiology* (Vol. 3, pp. 1553–1593). Washington DC: American Physiological Society.

Mason, J. W. (1975). A historical view of the stress field. Part II. *Journal of Human Stress, 1,* 22–36.

Miller, L. C., Barrett, C. L., Hampe, E., & Noble, H. (1972). Factor structure of childhood fears. *Journal of Consulting and Clinical Psychology, 39,* 264–268.

Munro, A., & Griffiths, A. B. (1969). Some psychiatric non-sequelae of childhood bereavement. *British Journal of Psychiatry, 115,* 305–311.

Nicholls, J. G. (1975). Causal attributions and other achievement-related cognitions: Effects of task outcome, attainment, value, and sex. *Journal of Personality and Social Psychology, 31,* 379–389.

Nicholls, J. G. (1978). The development of the concepts of effort and ability, perception of academic attainment, and the understanding that difficult tasks require more ability. *Child Development, 49,* 800–814.

Rachman, S. J. (1979). The concept of required helpfulness. *Behavior Research and Therapy, 17,* 1–6.

Radke-Yarrow, M., & Kuczynski, L. (1983). Perspectives and strategies in child-rearing: Studies of rearing by normal and depressed mothers. In D. Magnusson & V. Allen (Eds.), *Human development: An interactional perspective* (pp. 57–74). New York: Academic Press.

Radke-Yarrow, M., Zahn-Waxler, C., & Chapman, M. (1983). Children's prosocial dispositions and behavior. In P. H. Mussen (Ed.), E. M. Hetherington (Vol. Ed.), *Handbook of child psychology* (4th Ed.): *Vol. 4: Socialization, personality, and social development* (pp. 469–545). New York: Wiley.

Reese, H. W., & Lipsitt, L. P. (1970). *Experimental child psychology.* New York: Academic Press.

Rutter, M. (1966). *Children of sick parents: An environmental and psychiatric study.* London: Oxford University Press.

Rutter, M. (1979a). Maternal deprivation, 1972–1978: New findings, new concepts, new approaches. *Child Development, 50,* 283–305.

Rutter, M. (1979b). Protective factors in children's response to stress and disadvantage. In M. W. Kent & J. E. Rolf (Eds.), *Primary prevention of psychopathology: Vol. 3. Social competence in children* (pp. 49–74). Hanover, NH: University Press of New England.

Rutter, M. (1981). *Maternal deprivation reassessed.* (2nd ed.). Harmondsworth Middlesex, England: Penguin Books.

Rutter, M. (1982). Epidemiological-longitudinal approaches to the study of development. In W. A. Collins (Ed.), *The concept of development* (Minnesota Symposia on Child Psychology, Vol. 15, pp. 105–144). Hillsdale, NJ: Lawrence Erlbaum Associates.

Rutter, M., Cox, A., Tupling, C., Berger, M., & Yule, W. (1975). Attainment and adjustment in two geographical areas. I. The prevalence of psychiatric disorders. *British Journal of Psychiatry, 126,* 493–509.

Rutter, M., Yule, B., Quinton, D., Rowlands, O., Yule, W., & Berger, M. (1975). Attainment and adjustment in two geographical areas. III. Some factors accounting for area differences. *British Journal of Psychiatry, 126,* 520–533.

Schaffer, H. R. (1974). Cognitive components of the infant's response to strangeness. In M. Lewis & L. A. Rosenblum (Eds.), *The origins of fear* (pp. 11–24). New York: Wiley.

Scherer, M. W. & Nakamura, C. Y. (1968). A fear survey schedule for children: A factor analytic comparison with manifest anxiety. *Behaviour Research and Therapy, 6,* 173–182.

Schowalter, J. E. (1975). Parent death and child bereavement. In B. Schoenberg, I. Gerber, A.

Wiener, A. H. Kutscher, D. Peretz, & A. C. Carr (Eds.), Bereavement: Its psychosocial aspects (pp. 172–179). New York: Columbia University Press.

Selye, H. (1936). A syndrome produced by diverse nocuous agents. Nature (London), 138, 32.

Selye, H. (1946). The general adaptation syndrome and the diseases of adaptation. Journal of Clinical Endocrinology, 6, 117–230.

Spears, W. C., & Hohle, R. H. (1967). Sensory and perceptual processes in infants. In Y. Brackbill (Ed.), Infancy and early childhood (pp. 51–121). New York: Free Press.

Sroufe, L. A. (1979). The coherence of individual development. American Psychologist, 34, 834–841.

Sroufe, L. A., & Waters, E. (1977). Attachment as an organizational construct. Child Development, 48, 1184–1199.

Sulzer-Azaroff, B. & Pollack, M. J. (1982). The modification of child behavior problems in the home. In A. S. Bellack, M. Hersen, & A. E. Kazdin (Eds.), International handbook of behavior modification and therapy (pp. 917–958). New York: Plenum Press.

Tennant, C., Bebbington, P., & Hurry, J. (1980). Parental death in childhood and risk of adult depressive disorders: A review. Psychological Medicine, 10, 289–299.

Tennant, C., Bebbington, P., & Hurry, J. (1982). Social experiences in childhood and adult psychiatric morbidity: A multiple regression analysis. Psychological Medicine, 12, 321–327.

Tennant, C., Hurry, J., & Bebbington, P. (1982). The relation of childhood separation experiences to adult depressive and anxiety states. British Journal of Psychiatry, 141, 475–582.

Tennant, C., Smith, A., Bebbington, P., & Hurry, J. (1981). Parental loss in childhood. The relation to adult psychiatric impairment and contact with psychiatric services. Archives of General Psychiatry, 38, 309–314.

Thomas, A., Birch, H. G., Chess, S., Hertzig, M. E., & Korn, S. (1963). Behavioral individuality in early childhood. New York: New York University Press.

Wallerstein, J. S. (1983). Children of divorce: Stress and developmental tasks. In N. Garmezy, & M. Rutter (Eds.), Stress, coping and development in children (pp. 265–302). New York: McGraw-Hill.

Wallerstein, J. S., & Kelly, J. B. (1980). Surviving the breakup: How children and parents cope with divorce. New York: Basic Books.

Watson, J. S. (1966). The development and generalization of "contingency awareness" in early infancy: Some hypotheses. Merrill-Palmer Quarterly, 12, 123–135.

Watson, J. S. (1967). Memory and "contingency analysis" in infant learning. Merrill-Palmer Quarterly, 13, 55–76.

Watson, J. S., & Ramey, C. T. (1972). Reactions to response-contingent stimulation in early infancy. Merrill-Palmer Quarterly, 18, 219–227.

Weissman, M. M. (1979). Depressed parents and their children: Implications for prevention. In J. D. Noshpitz (Ed.), Basic handbook of child psychiatry (Vol. 4, pp. 292–299). New York: Basic Books.

Werner, E. E., & Smith, R. S. (1982). Vulnerable but invincible: A study of resilient children. New York: McGraw-Hill.

White, E. Elsom, B., & Prawat, R. (1978). Children's conceptions of death. Child Development, 49, 307–310.

Wolff, P. H. (1966). The causes, controls, and organization of behavior in the neonate. (Psychological Issues Vol. 5, No. 1, Monograph 17). New York: International Universities Press.

The Role of Shame in Depression

Helen Block Lewis

INTRODUCTION

Converging evidence about depression has now been collected under the guidance of Izard's differential emotions theory, Seligman's reformulated learned helplessness theory, psychoanalytic theory, and the construct of field dependence. A convergence of evidence collected from such widely divergent viewpoints is both unusual and a cause for optimism about the validity of the evidence. In this volume and elsewhere, Izard (1972) reports a robust finding that shame, in its shyness variant, plays a prominent role in the emotion profiles of depressed people. Seligman and Peterson's study, also in this volume, shows that depressed children (like depressed adults) are afflicted with an attributional style that interprets bad events as resulting from their own personal deficiencies (ISG attributions). This attributional style may be considered to reflect chronic low self-esteem or chronic shame. The children suffer, moreover, from a cognitive deficit that has some apparent similarity to field-dependent cognitive style. A substantial relationship between field dependence and depression is known to exist as well among adults (Crouppen, 1976; Levenson & Neuringer, 1974; Newman & Hirt, 1983; Patsioskas, Clum, & Luscomb, 1979; Witkin *et al.*, Witkin, 1965).

My own observations (Lewis, 1971, 1976), which were gathered under the guidance of psychoanalytic theory and in the course of research on field-dependent cognitive style, suggest the hypothesis that the affective–cognitive state of shame is prominent in both normal and clinical depres-

Helen Block Lewis. Department of Psychology, Yale University, New Haven, Connecticut.

sion. We now know also that there is a significant relationship between field dependence and shame in a sample of patients (Witkin, Lewis, & Weil, 1968). All four viewpoints thus seem to point to a network of congruent connections among a belief in personal helplessness, field dependence, the state of shame, and depression. All four viewpoints have independently adduced evidence that, when people confront trouble, attributional style, cognitive style, and "superego" style all predict depression.

Before returning to the evidence collected from differential emotions theory and from reformulated learned helplessness theory, let me briefly sketch the information on shame and depression that I obtained from psychoanalytic observations and research on field dependence.

SHAME IN PSYCHOANALYTIC THEORY

Over the past 20 years, I have developed a special focus in thinking about psychopathology, namely, the power of undischarged states of shame and guilt in symptom formation. I think this focus is useful for both children and adults. A few words are in order about the background of experiences out of which this focus grew. Over years as a practicing psychoanalyst, I became convinced that unanalyzed shame in the patient–therapist interaction is a frequent source of what is euphemistically called the "negative therapeutic reaction," that is, of treatment failure (Lewis, 1971). I have the hunch that some of the difficult cases Kohut (1971) and Kernberg (1975) call "narcissistic" personality are cases in which shame has been bypassed, with surprising and often florid sequelae into symptoms (Lewis, 1980).

There are many historical reasons for the neglect of shame in psychoanalytic thinking. Freud's original discovery was that hysterical symptoms somehow formed out of forbidden sexual longings. At the time of his discovery, however, he paid close theoretical attention not to the forbidding agency but to the nature of the sexual and aggressive instincts. The forbidding agency was simply called "shame, disgust and morality" (Freud, 1905). By the time Freud got around to inquiring into the origins of guilt, in *Totem and Taboo* (1913) he had already painted himself into a theoretical corner in which individualistic instincts were the prime movers of behavior. In this system, guilt was synonymous with internalized instinctive aggression. By the time he formulated his superego construct (1923), guilt had also become synonymous with the superego, to the neglect of shame.

Freud's theoretical model of the formation of guilt was based on the castration complex in men. The absence of the castration complex in women became his theoretical reason why women's superego was inferior in being "never so inexorable, so impersonal, so independent of its emotional origins as we require it to be in men" (Freud, 1925, pp. 257–258). The difficulties I encountered in fitting my observations about shame and guilt into existing psychoanalytic theory involved first separating the sexist implications of Freud's theory of guilt from the observations he made about sex differences in the experience of one's conscience. The idea that shame of the self, which often accompanies guilt for transgression, is more frequent in the experience of women was one way in which Freud's observations could be retained, while his theoretical framework was revised. In addition, Freud's theoretical framework needed to be enlarged to take account of the role of nurturance and empathy in superego formation. Attention to the role of these experiences in development also directs attention to the origin of shame as distinct from guilt. I have adopted the useful working assumption that shame and guilt should not be considered as if they formed either a cognitive or a moral hierarchy. I also assume that the two states develop in tandem, each fostering the other.

Development of Shame and Guilt

Woolf (1969) tells us that mothers learn to distinguish very early between their infants' "mad" cries (presumably resulting from the absence of cuddling) and cries resulting from "real" causes—physical distress or hunger. A process of shaming and of guilt induction begins with messages sent very early about "inappropriate" protests over cuddling. A system of messages is established in which the infant's crying over what he or she perceives to be "rejection" is "inappropriate" or shameful. The message that such crying is inappropriate implies that the child is able but unwilling to do without, in other words, a guilt message. The sequence: "rejection" → humiliated fury → guilt is thus a normal one and an adaptive one— provided it is experienced in interaction with a stably affectionate and appropriately judging mother, and later on, in a just world. Sroufe (1979) has evidence that competent nursery school children have been treated with a combination of sympathy for their humiliated protests over separation and firmness of discipline. The combinations and permutations that can arise in shame and guilt messages between mother and child are awesome in their number. I think a most illuminating line of research into this field is that of sex differences. We know that mothers' interaction with their girl babies is smoother than that with their boys (Moss, 1974), a finding that has a primate analog in the greater vulnerability of males to maternal deprivation (Sackett, 1974). This may be a basis for Rutter's finding, reported in this volume, that clinical depression in childhood is more frequent among boys than girls and that women's greater proneness to depression occurs only after puberty. Little girls discover, especially at puberty, that they are second-class citizens in a competitive world. In this context the humiliated fury into guilt sequence is not adaptive.

But, perhaps the most important difficulty in Freud's metapsychology is that he considered guilt and shame to be individual drive controls instead of mechanisms or dynamisms for the restoration of threatened affectional bonds (Lewis, 1981, 1983). I now reformulate as follows: When shame and guilt fail in their mission of restoring peace between the self and significant (internalized) others, psychiatric symptoms are formed. Specifically, when undischarged or unresolved shame is to the fore, hysteria and depression are likely to occur; when guilt is to the fore, obsessions, compulsions, and paranoia are likely (Lewis, 1976, 1978, 1979a, 1979b). The theoretical importance of considering the social bias for emotions, particularly the moral emotions of shame and guilt, is a point to which I shall return.

FIELD DEPENDENCE

A second source of the focus on shame and guilt was my work over the years with H. A. Witkin and others (Witkin et al., 1954) on field dependence. It is worth noting, in passing, that field dependence is a construct that was pursued partly because it was congenial to a psychodynamic view of perception. The idea that personality style might be reflected in characteristic mode of space orientation was developed as part of the New Look at cognition that characterized the late 1940s and the 1950s. Field dependence is a cognitive style that catches the self not only in relation to its physical surround but in relation to significant others.

During the 1960s Witkin, Edmund Weil, and myself (Witkin et al., 1968) planned and executed a study in which we predicted that field-dependent patients would be more prone to shame than to guilt in their first therapeutic encounters, while field-independent patients would be more prone to guilt than shame. The transcripts of the first two psychotherapy "pairs" of field-dependent and independent patients in treatment with the same therapist were assessed for their implied affective content by Gottschalk and Gleser's (1969) reliable and valid method. As predicted, field-dependent patients showed significantly more shame anxiety than guilt anxiety, while field-independent patients showed significantly more guilt than shame. The success of these predictions encouraged me to undertake a thorough phenomenological analysis of the experiences of shame and guilt with particular reference to the position and role of the self in both states. Smith (1972) has evidence for a connection between field dependence and shame.

Once the results on shame and field dependence were in place, several other well-known facts could be assembled to form a network of connection for predicting forms of psychopathology. Field dependence, as indicated earlier, had already been linked to depression. Field independence, as might be expected, is linked to paranoia (Johnson, 1980; Schooler & Silverman, 1969; Witkin, 1965; Witkin et al., 1954). There is a well-established sex difference in field dependence, which neatly parallels the established sex differences in depression and paranoia. Women are more field dependent and more prone to depression. Men are more field independent and more prone to paranoia, especially during the ages between 15 and 35 (Lewis, 1976, 1978). This congruence between sex differences in field dependence and in forms of pathology could now be connected to shame as possible mediator of women's greater proneness to depression.

Our study of field-dependent and independent patients in psychotherapy also yielded evidence that, as one might expect on an introspective basis alone, shame and self-directed hostility occur in conjunction with each other. Guilt, in contrast—and this had some surprise in it—occurred in our transcripts in conjunction with hostility directed both inward *and outward*, with about equal frequency.

The transcripts of 180 therapy sessions collected from nine patient–therapist pairs were the sources from which I made a phenomenological analysis of the states of shame and guilt, tracing symptom formation in statu nascendi from these evoked and undischarged states (Lewis, 1971).

PHENOMENOLOGY OF SHAME AND GUILT

I turn now to a very brief, condensed outline of the major phenomenological differences between the two states. At the same time I must repeat that the two states are dynamically close. They very often occur simultaneously when one is both guilty and ashamed of oneself for transgression. Both aim at the restoration of affectional ties. A brief word also on the subject of definition. I use "shame" to refer to a family of affection–cognitive states in which embarrassment, mortification, humiliation, feeling ridiculous, chagrin, disgrace, and shyness are among the variants. "Guilt" is a family of affective–cognitive states that shares the themes of responsibility, fault, obligation, and blame for specific events.

Stimulus to Shame/Guilt

The stimuli that evoke shame are multiple. Both one's transgressions *and* defeat, disappointments, or failure can evoke shame. Only one's own transgressions evoke guilt. Another way in which the multiple stimuli to shame have been described is to say that there is both moral and nonmoral shame (Ausubel, 1955). There is only one kind of (moral) guilt. When shame is evoked by the failure to keep the good opinion of the significant other— let me, for shorthand, call this unrequited love—it can quickly shift into guilt that finds a rational, specific basis for the rejection. Specific transgressions are reparable and less painful than the shame of the whole self. This is an observation that is captured in the "global" aspect of ISG attributions.

Its usefulness has been demonstrated also by Dweck's findings in this volume about the difference between instrumental versus global responses to failure.

The Self and the Other in Shame/Guilt

Shame is directly about the self. It is the vicarious experience of the other's scorn of the self. The self at the moment of shame is felt to be in the eye of a storm of disapproval. The metaphor "eye of the storm" is also literal. Shame can be evoked by being looked at, which speaks to the prominent imagery of the other in the experience of shame. Shame can also be relieved, although not always, by a positive glance from the other. In keeping with this imagery, absence of eye contact has been used as a measure of social anxiety or shame (for example, Exline, 1962).

While it is in a state of shame, the self feels helpless, as if paralyzed. This is particularly clear in embarrassment, which literally means impeded movement. The helplessness that is so characteristic a part of the ideation of depressed people may be understood as a consequence of their being in a state of shame.

In shame, the self is assailed by noxious body stimuli—blushing, sweating, and tears. This vulnerability to unwanted affective expressions increases the sense of helplessness in shame.

Shame, since it is "only" about the self, is simultaneously felt as an inappropriate, subjective reaction, which thus in turn evokes more shame. Especially in adults, but also in children, there is the shame of exposed "narcissism."

Guilt, in contrast, is about *things* done or undone in the world. Since the self is not focal in awareness, but the things done or undone, guilt has (Heider, 1958) an objective quality. It involves less disorganization of the self, more rational ideation, and the feeling that the self should do something to make amends. The other is less prominent in the imagery; when the imagery of the other is present, the other is injured and dependent upon the self for restitution. By implication, the self in guilt is *able,* not helpless.

This brief description of the self in relation to the other in shame and guilt is summarized in Table 1.

Anger in Shame and Guilt

Most important of all, shame evokes a particular kind of fury—*humiliated fury* or shame–rage, which is also felt as inappropriate. Humiliated fury, which is actually a first step of recovery of the self in shame, simultaneously is felt as inappropriate and unjust. Especially when it is directed at the significant other, humiliated fury involves the threat of further estrangement in response to unjust or inappropriate fury. *Righteous in-*

Table 1
Self and Other in Shame and Guilt

Shame experiences	
Self (unable)	**Other**
1. *Object* of scorn, contempt, ridicule; reduced; little	1. The *source* of scorn, contempt, ridicule
2. Paralyzed, helpless, passive	2. Laughing, ridiculing, powerful, active
3. Assailed by noxious body stimuli; rage, tears, blushing	3. Appears intact
4. Childish	4. Adult, going away, abandoning
5. Focal in awareness	5. Also focal in awareness
6. Functioning poorly as an agent or perceiver; divided between imaging self and the other; boundaries permeable, vicarious experience of self and other, especially in humiliation	6. Appears intact

Guilt experience	
Self (able)	**Other**
1. The *source* of guilt as well as of pity and concern; regret, remorse (virtue)	1. Injured, needful, suffering, hurt
2. Intact	2. Injured
3. Adult, responsible	3. Dependent, by implication
4. Occupied with guilty acts or thoughts	4. Subject of thoughts as *related* to guilt, otherwise other need not be involved
5. Functioning silently	5. Nothing comparable to vicarious experiences in shame, humiliation.

dignation, in contrast, is an appropriate reaction to guilt. As Nietzsche observed, guilt can even be an unconsciously agreeable state for the righteous one, in whom the consciousness of just anger can lead to a considerable feeling of moral elevation. In any case, there is an affinity between the helpless experiences of the self in shame and in depression, and an affinity between the mobilization of the self in guilt to *do* something, which is phenomenally similar to obsessive and compulsive states.

CONVERGENCE OF EVIDENCE

I return now to the way in which the information from Izard's work and from Seligman and Peterson's converges with these observations. As indicated earlier, Izard has found that shame in its shyness variant plays a prominent role in the emotion profiles of depressed people. This is an empirical finding that supports the phenomenological affinity between shame and depression.

As suggested in this volume, Izard and his colleagues have demonstrated that there are age-related changes in infants' responses to acute pain and that these changes serve a biological function. The infant's earliest response to pain is physical distress. The distress signal elicits the caretaker's tendency to satisfy the infant's physical needs. By 19 months, however, anger predominates over distress in infants' reactions to pain, suggesting that anger may be functioning to mobilize coping responses. Mothers' reactions to infants' anger are, however, likely to involve discipline and behavior control techniques, suggesting that mothers' anger has been evoked in response to the infants'. There is, indeed, a positive correlation between mothers' self-reported anger experiences with their 12-month-old infants and their infants' anger expressiveness at 19 months, the time when anger predominates over distress in response to pain. Izard and Huebner have evidence, moreover, that there are differences between infants in the speed with which their distress can be soothed. Infants slow to soothe show more anger expressiveness than infants who are quicker to soothe. Two contradictory views of anger thus emerge. On the one hand, anger serves a positive function in mobilizing coping responses; it certainly seems a more appropriate response than distress in a 19-month-old infant. On the other hand, anger can have a negative effect in making it harder for infants to be soothed after distress and in evoking mothers' anger, which in turn evokes the infants' anger. This contradiction readily reminds us of the difficulty we still encounter in trying to understand the role of anger in adult depression.

It is a commonly accepted clinical observation about anger in adult depression that its "repression" or suppression increases depression, while its expression relieves depression. My observations suggest that it is specifically humiliated fury that tends to be inhibited, from the sense of its inappropriateness and its injustice. Only righteous indignation immediately relieves depression. The failure to distinguish between these two very different forms of anger may be one reason why the cultivation of anger expression in therapy can have mixed results. In any case, my observations suggest that it is unresolved humiliated fury that underlies the inverse relation between anger and sadness.

Seligman and Peterson's finding of a cognitive deficit in depressives is congruent with the studies showing a correlation between field dependence and depression. Newman and Hirt's (1983) recent finding that field dependence is strongly related to level of distress and to level of inner-directed hostility as measured by Izard's DES + D scale is especially significant. Levenson and Neuringer (1974), using suicide as their ultimate criterion of depression, predicted and found that male suicides had significantly lower scores on the performance triad of the WAIS (Object-Assembly, Picture-Completion, and Block Design) than a comparable group of psychiatric patients. The authors describe suicides in cognitive terms as persons "lacking the problem-solving processes to re-orient [their] relationship to their environment" (p. 184). An equally appropriate formulation in terms of the field dependence construct would describe suicides as unable to separate themselves from significant others.

Field dependence has, moreover, more recently been associated with a set of positive attitudes toward others (Witkin, Goodenough, & Oltman, 1979). Witkin et al. speculate that the "greater recourse of field dependent people to external referents [meaning, in this case, others], stimulated the development of interpersonal competences but may be responsible for these peoples' lesser restructuring skills. Relatively field-dependent and field-independent people may be seen as making their main developmental investment in different domains" (p. 1139). What this formulation leaves unanswered, however, is why there should be an inverse relationship between social skills and cognitive skills, why the two differing domains of emotional and cognitive development should not proceed in a positive rather than a negative interaction. Why, for example, should women's ability to judge the warmth of other people's feelings go together with difficulty in cognitive restructuring (Rapaczynski, 1980). I do not suppose that I have the answer to this question, but I do propose that a distinction between the self as it organizes itself in its attachment to others, and the self as it organizes itself in relation to things is useful. A two-track segregation of self from nonself (others and things) characterizes development. It seems likely, and there is evidence, that the two tracks begin by interacting positively and stop doing so when socialization processes begin to require more cognitive restructuring skills from one gender and more interpersonal skills from the other.

In any case, the coincidence of a cognitive restructuring deficit and depression may be a product of the link between self-directed hostility and positive attitudes toward others. In this dynamic, the cognitive deficit occurs in order to maintain a positive attitude toward significant others in a hostile environment. This dynamic would, in turn, perpetuate the cognitive deficit. It might also be a more frequent dynamic among people who, for any reasons, including genetic ones, are more prone to develop a field-dependent cognitive style.

The most economical way I can find of reviewing the many connections I see between reformulated learned helplessness theory of depression and my own observations is to look at the way both psychoanalytic and helplessness theory profit from attention to the distinction between shame and guilt, more especially to the distinction between humiliated fury and righteous indignation.

It is a remarkable fact that neither Freudian theory nor helplessness theory has wrestled with the fact that women are more prone to depression than men. My own interpretation (Lewis, 1978) of this sex difference ascribes it two factors: (1) women's nurturant function, which fosters their attachment emotions and thereby renders them more vulnerable to the shame of rejection, and (2) women's second-class citizenship in the world of affairs, which also renders them prone to shame. My own opinion is that women's nurturant function is not the cause of their second-class citizenship, as many feminists, including De Beauvoir (1957) have argued, but this is another and still controversial story.

The absence of theoretical attention to the sex difference in proneness to depression seems to reflect the difficulty that scientific theory has in dealing with the attachment emotions as central motivators of behavior. The issues that trouble both psychoanalytic and behavior theory of depression arise out of a neglect of the attachment emotions.

Let us begin with Freud. An issue that he tackled was the accurate description of pathological depression. Freud described pathological depression as quite like normal grief or bereavement in its sadness, and loss of interest in the world, but different from bereavement in one salient characteristic, a fall in "self-regard" or "self-esteem." Since there is no actual bereavement, the puzzle became to account for this fall in self-esteem. Following Abraham's (1911/1960) lead, Freud accepted the idea that a person falls into depression when he "feels himself unloved and incapable of loving" (p. 138). The depressed person is dealing with "real slight and disappointment" (Freud, 1917/1968, p. 249) by someone close. Freud also made the acute observation, since many times confirmed clinically (for example, Cohen, Baker, Cohen, Fromm-Reichman, & Weigert, 1954), that depressives are overidentified with others. The content of their self-denigration is unconsciously meant for "someone whom the patient loves or has loved or should love" (Freud, 1917, 1968 p. 248). This description, which expects depression to follow "loss of love," thus anchors depression in the lost social tie.

However, Freud's theoretical formulation of the process by which loss of love becomes loss of self-esteem was cast in metapsychological terms: The original object cathexis, although strong, must really have been weak, that is, made on a "narcissistic" basis. The depressed person has made a narcissistically regressed, "oral" identification with the "object," such that the hostility unconsciously meant for the other is turned against the ego. In this theoretical system, humiliated fury or protest against the lost attachment was inherently pathological, not a normal process. Freud's failure, moreover, to distinguish between the self and narcissism led to the orthodox view that reacting to loss of love with depression is a symptom of the earliest, oral stage of narcissism, a form of "archaic" guilt even though the evidence suggests that depression is a more benign form of illness than schizophrenia. Depression's place in the hierachy of regressions was suited to the inferior place of its more frequent victims, women.

Freud's views of the "reality" behind the patient's self-abased views created considerable epistemological difficulty. On the one hand, the pa-

tient's estimate of himself is only keener than other people's and by implication more accurate. Freud wonders why a man has to fall ill in order to be
accessible to the "truth" about himself (p. 246). On the other hand, Freud
sees "no correspondence . . . between the degree of self-abasement and its
real justification" (p. 247). One can understand this contradiction of views
as depending upon whether shame or guilt is at issue in self-abasement.
Shame carries the cognitive message that it is subjective or only about the
self and in this respect an exaggerated or unreal response. Guilt, in contrast, carries with it an objective aura, which anchors it in specific deeds or
real events. In any case, Freud's difficulty in establishing the appropriateness of depressed people's lowered self-esteem is also a current problem in
behavior theory. It has been demonstrated, for example, that depressed
people may be more accurate—"sadder but wiser"—than nondepressed
controls in causal attributions of success and failure (Alloy & Abramson,
1979).

Freud's metapsychological formulation of depression as retroflected
hostility did not go unchallenged within psychoanalytic theory. Bibring
(1953), basing himself on the clinical observation of fall in self-esteem,
made clear that guilt is not the only stimulus to depression and insisted that
depression, rather than being the result of aggression turned inward, is "essentially independent of the vicissitudes of aggression" (p. 40). If anything,
aggression follows the breakdown of self-esteem rather than causing it.
Bibring suggested that the predisposing stimulus to depression is a "fixation of the ego to the state of helplessness" (p. 39). This formulation is
clearly similar to Seligman's two decades later.

As for the specifics of what the ego (self) is helpless to do, Bibring emphasizes its helplessness to maintain its narcissistic goals. A theory that
posits attachment emotions would reformulate this proposition to say that
the self is helpless to maintain its position as a loved person in its own and
other's eyes. Although behavior theorists do not necessarily agree with
Bibring as to these specifics, reformulated helplessness theory also pin-
points personal helplessness in comparison with others' competence as the
central state in depression.

A major point in the reformulation of learned helplessness theory is the
distinction that has been found necessary between universal and personal
helplessness (Abramson, Seligman, & Teasdale, 1978). People do not feel
depressed when they are unable to do what is not generally feasible, but
they can become depressed when they cannot do what others can. This is
an explicit statement of a social comparison basis for depression. Specifically, it may be assumed that what is evoked by personal helplessness is
the shame of envy, and humiliated fury, with the difficult sequel that I have
described.

Helplessness theory also deemphasizes the role of retroflected hostility
in depression, basing itself instead on the learning of a faulty negative at-

tributional style. In any case, both psychoanalytic theory and behavioral theory agree that depression is characterized by a lack of *overt* hostility. In fact, Seligman (1975) specifically includes "introjected hostility" in his list of symptoms common to learned helplessness and depression (p. 156).

Placing depression within the framework of the attachment emotions is particularly helpful for understanding the role of retroflected hostility in depression. We can assume that the sequel of lost love is humiliated fury or shame–rage, which is a communication to the other of protest at the broken tie. Bowlby (1980) suggests that "the principal issue about which a [depressed] person feels helpless is his ability to make or maintain affectional relationships" (p. 247). As is apparent, I am equating shame–rage with Bowlby's "bitter" protest on separation (1963). Humiliated fury is a particularly difficult state to resolve, since shame or humiliation is a vicarious experience of the self in the other's eyes. On the one hand, its sequel is "turning the tables" in an effort to humiliate the (beloved) other, which risks even further rejection in turn and also involves the self in guilt for retaliatory hostility. On the other hand, humiliated fury is "only about the self" and is thus perceived as inappropriate, which turns attention away from the fury. A fall in self-esteem, without full consciousness of fury, can thus operate to maintain the affectional tie. The recognition of humiliated fury as a particularly difficult feeling trap because affectional ties are threatened clarifies the social interaction behind retroflected hostility.

On the side of behavioral theory, a framework that posits the attachment emotions can also be helpful. Behavior theorists have come upon a cognitive paradox in depression: if depressed people are so helpless as they feel, logic dictates that they should not also feel self-reproaches for what they are unable to do (Abramson & Sackeim, 1977; Peterson, 1979; Rizley, 1978). This paradox vanishes, however, if we assume that depressed people are helpless to change the vicarious experience of another's negative feeling about the self—that is, to get out of a state of shame. Humiliated fury will not do it; expressing such fury is likely to get the self into even more trouble with the other, especially as humiliated fury is felt by the self to be inappropriate and blameworthy.

In a further refinement of ISG style, Peterson, Schwartz, and Seligman (1981) have found that depressed women undergraduates were more likely to blame their *characters* for bad events than they were to blame specific *behaviors*. (If anything, blame for behaviors was negatively correlated with depression.) If we equate blame of the self for its character with shame, and blame for behaviors with guilt, we may glimpse a convergence of evidence resulting from the accurate specification of the role of shame in depression. Indeed, the most hopeful sign of fruitful collaboration is the evidence recently provided by Peterson, Luborsky, and Seligman (1983) that depressive mood can be predicted from ISG attributions. Seligman (1975) and Beck (1967) both correctly point to the learning process by which faulty attributional style can perpetuate itself. What attention to shame suggests is that the maintenance of an affectional tie, even at some expense to self-esteem, may also contribute to the perpetuation of faulty negative attributions. There is even some experimental evidence for this dynamic produced on the behavioral side (see, for example, Forrest & Hokanson, 1975).

There is other indirect and direct evidence for a connection between shame and depression. Beck's (1967) study of depressed patients' dreams portrayed them as "recipients of rejection, disappointment, and humiliation" (p. 217). Blatt (1974) distinguishes between the anaclitic and introjective components of the depressive experience, a distinction that parallels shame and guilt. Smith (1972) predicted and confirmed a connection between shame and depression. One small finding of a behavioral study (Lamont, 1973) more than a decade ago seems to capture the essence of the connection between shame and depression. In this study, the following cognitive message was demonstrated to have a strong positive effect on dysphoric people. "We don't have that much control over other peoples' feelings [no shame at loss] and we don't have to feel responsible for how other people feel [no guilt]" (p. 320). (The brackets are my interpolations.)

A number of research strategies emerge from these considerations. Hoblitzelle (1982) has done preliminary work on developing a research tool for distinguishing between shame and guilt. She has also found a significant, sizable correlation between proneness to shame and depression. Some questions can now be tested empirically. Are people who are shame prone the same ones with a depressive attributional style? Do people who attribute bad events to their characters have a harder time expressing humiliated anger than people who attribute bad events to behaviors? Are the emotion profiles of humiliated anger different from the profiles of righteous indignation? Are women, who are known to be more prone to depression than men and more prone to affiliative attitudes (Maccoby & Jacklin, 1974), also more prone to shame, as many observers—including Darwin (1872)—have suggested?

REFERENCES

Abraham, K. (1960). Notes on the psychoanalytic investigation and treatment of manic-depressive insanity and allied conditions. In Selected papers on psychoanalysis. New York: Basic Books (Original work published 1911)

Abramson, L., & Sackeim, H. (1977). A paradox in depression: Uncontrollability and self-blame. Psychological Bulletin, 84, 838–857.

Abramson, L., Seligman, M., and Teasdale, J. Learned helplessness in humans: Critique and re-formulation. (1978). Journal of Abnormal Psychology, 87, 49–74.

Alloy, L., & Abramson, L. (1979). Judgments of contingency in depressed and nondepressed people. Journal of Experimental Psychology: General, 108, 441–485.

Ausubel, D. (1955). Relationships between shame and guilt in the socializing process. Psychological Review, 62, 378–390.

Beck, A. (1967). *Depression: Clinical, experimental and theoretical aspects.* New York: Harper & Row.

Bibring, E. (1953). The mechanism of depression. In P. Greenacre (Ed.), *Affective disorders: psychoanalytic contributions to their study* (pp. 13–48). New York: International Universities Press.

Blatt, S. (1974). Levels of object representation in anaclitic and introjective depression. *Psychoanalytic Study of the Child, 29,* 107–157.

Bowlby, J. (1963). Pathological mourning and childhood mourning. *Journal of the American Psychoanalytic Association, 11,* 500–542.

Bowlby, J. (1980). *Attachment and loss* (Vol 3). New York: Basic Books.

Cohen, M., Baker, G., Cohen, R., Fromm-Reichmann, F., & Weigert, E. (1954). An intensive study of manic-depressive psychosis. *Psychiatry, 17,* 103–137.

Crouppen, G. (1976). *Field dependence in depressed and normal males, as an indication of relative proneness to shame and guilt and ego functioning.* Unpublished dissertation, California School of Professional Psychology.

Darwin, C. (1872). *The expression of emotions in man and animals.* London: John Murray.

De Beauvoir, S. (1957). *The second sex.* New York: Knopf.

Exline, R. (1962). The effects of sex need for affiliation, and the sight of others upon initial communication in problem-solving groups. *Journal of Personality, 60,* 541–546.

Forrest, M., & Hokanson, J. (1975). Depression and autonomic arousal reduction accompanying self-punitive behavior. *Journal of Abnormal Psychology, 84,* 346–357.

Freud, S. (1953). Three essays on the theory of sexuality. In J. Strachey (Ed.), *The standard edition of the complete works of Sigmund Freud* (Vol. 7). London: Hogarth Press. (Original work published 1905)

Freud, S. (1923). The ego and the id. In J. Strachey (Ed.), *The standard edition of the complete works of Sigmund Freud.* London: Hogarth.

Freud, S. (1925). Some psychical consequences of the anatomical distinction between the sexes. In J. Strachey (Ed.), *The standard edition of the complete works of Sigmund Freud.* London: Hogarth.

Freud, S. (1913). Totem and taboo. In J. Strachey (Ed.), *The standard edition of the complete works of Sigmund Freud.* London: Hogarth.

Gottschalk, L., & Gleser, G. (1969). *The measurement of psychological states through content analysis of verbal behavior.* Berkeley: University of California Press.

Heider, F. (1958). *The psychology of interpersonal relations.* New York: Wiley.

Hoblitzelle, W. (1982). *Developing a measure of shame and guilt and the role of shame in depression.* Unpublished predissertation, Yale University, New Haven, CT.

Izard, C. (1972). *Patterns of emotion: A new analysis of anxiety and depression.* New York: Academic Press.

Johnson, D. (1980). *Cognitive organization in paranoid and non-paranoid schizophrenics.* Unpublished dissertation, Yale University, New Haven, CT.

Kernberg, O. (1975). *Borderline conditions and pathological narcissism.* New York: Jason Aronson.

Kohut, H. (1971). *The analysis of the self.* New York: International Universities Press.

Lamont, J. (1973). Depressed mood and power over other people's feelings. *Journal of Clinical Psychology, 29,* 319–321.

Levenson, M., & Neuringer, C. (1974). Suicide and field dependency. *Omega, 5,* 181–185.

Lewis, H. B. (1971). *Shame and guilt in neurosis.* New York: International Universities Press.

Lewis, H. B. (1976). *Psychic war in men and women.* New York: New York University Press.

Lewis, H. B. (1978). Sex differences in superego mode as related to sex differences in psychiatric illness. *Social Science and Medicine, 12B,* 199–205.

Lewis, H. B. (1979a). Shame in depression and hysteria. In C. Izard (Ed.), *Emotions in personality and psychopathology* (pp. 369–396). New York: Plenum.

Lewis, H. B. (1979b). Guilt in obsession and paranoia. In C. Izard (Ed.), *Emotions in personality and psychopathology* (pp. 399–414). New York: Plenum.

Lewis, H. B. (1980). "Narcissistic personality" or "shame-prone" superego modes. Comprehensive Psychotherapy, 1, 59–80.

Lewis, H. B. (1981). Freud and modern psychology (Vol. 1). New York: Plenum.

Lewis, H. B. (1983). Freud and modern psychology (Vol. 2). New York: Plenum.

Maccoby, E., & Jacklin, C. (1974). The psychology of sex differences. Stanford, CA: Stanford University Press.

Moss, H. (1974). Early sex differences and the mother-infant interaction. In R. Freidman, R. Reichert, & R. VandeWiele (Eds.), Sex differences in behavior (pp. 149–165). New York: Wiley.

Newman, R., & Hirt, M. (1983). The psychoanalytic theory of depression: Symptoms as a function of aggressive wishes and field articulation. Journal of Abnormal Psychology, 92, 42–49.

Patsioskas, A., Clum, G., & Luscomb, R. (1979). Cognitive characteristics of suicide attempters. Journal of Consulting and Clinical Psychology 47, 478–484.

Peterson, C. (1979). Uncontrollability and self-blame in depression: Investigations of the paradox in a college population. Journal of Abnormal Psychology, 88, 620–624.

Peterson, C., Luborsky, L., & Seligman, M. (1983). Attribution and depressed mood shifts: A case study using the symptom-complex method. Journal of Abnormal Psychology, 92, 96–104.

Peterson, C., Schwartz, S., & Seligman, M. (1981). Self-blame and depressive symptoms. Journal of Personality and Social Psychology, 41, 253–260.

Rapaczynski, W. (1979). Affect judgment and field dependence. Educational Testing Service Research report. Princeton, NJ: Educational Testing Service.

Rizley, R. (1978). Depression and distortion in the attribution of causality. Journal of Abnormal Psychology, 87, 32–48.

Sackett, G. (1974). Sex differences in rhesus monkeys following varied rearing experiences. In R. Friedman, R. Reichert, & R. VandeWiele (Eds.), Sex differences in behavior (pp. 99–123). New York: Wiley.

Schooler, C., & Silverman, J. (1969). Perceptual styles and their correlates among schizophrenic patients. Journal of Abnormal Psychology, 74, 459–470.

Seligman, M. (1975). Helplessness: On depression, development and death. San Francisco: Freeman.

Smith, R. (1972). The relative proneness to shame and guilt as an indicator of defensive style. Unpublished doctoral dissertation, Northwestern University, Chicago.

Sroufe, A. (1979). The coherence of individual development: Early care, attachment and subsequent developmental issues. American Psychologist, 34, 834–841.

Witkin, H. (1965). Psychological differentiation and forms of pathology. Journal of Abnormal Psychology, 70, 317–336.

Witkin, H., Goodenough, D., & Oltman, P. (1979). Psychological differentiation: Current status. Journal of Personality and Social Psychology, 37, 1127–1145.

Witkin, H., Lewis, H., Hertzman, M., Machover, K., Meissner, P., & Wapner, S. (1954). Personality through perception. New York: Harper & Row.

Witkin, H., Lewis, H., & Weil, E. (1968). Affective reactions and patient-therapist interactions among more and less differentiated patients early in therapy. Journal of Nervous and Mental Disease 146, 193–208.

Woolf, P. (1969). The natural history of crying and other vocalizations in early infancy. In B. M. Foss (Ed.) Determinants of infant behaviour. London: Methuen.

Psychobiological Markers:
Effects of Age and Puberty

Joaquim Puig-Antich

INTRODUCTION

In the context of this book on development of affect, attention should be paid to affective psychopathology during childhood. If the development of affect passes through several psychological stages, each one building upon those that preceded it (Piaget & Inhelder, 1969; Yarrow, 1979), the study of disorders appearing during these phases should be informative in its revealing of components that may be totally unavailable to observation in the normal state. The study of such abnormal affective states can also throw light on biological mechanisms involved in the regulation of affect. In adults, affective disorders are accompanied by a variety of biological abnormalities or markers, which are likely to reflect neuronal, chemical, or physiological mechanisms involved in the neuroregulation of normal and pathological mood and affect (Post & Ballenger, 1984). Together with the data that suggest an important role for heredity in the adult affective disorders (Nurnberger & Gershon, 1984), these constitute powerful arguments for a psychobiological approach to affect development. This does not mean that unrealistic dichotomies (such as psychological vs. biological, or genetic vs. environmental) should be allowed to organize our thinking. Instead, this viewpoint implies that every environmental influence is mediated by the brain, including the most subtle psychological interactions; that noxious effects can come as much from lack or warping of environmental influences as from the brain's inability to properly en-

Joaquim Puig-Antich. Division of Child Psychiatry. Western Psychiatric Institute, Pittsburgh, Pennsylvania.

code and interpret them. This viewpoint presupposes, therefore, that all psychological output and inner processes of the organism are a direct expression of brain function. In the case of childhood psychopathology this view offers a very exciting prospect, due to the explosive growth of basic developmental neurosciences and molecular genetics, and to the imminent availability for clinical research of noninvasive tools that can reveal the physico-chemical structure of living cells and tissues (Pettegrew, Woesner, Minshew, & Glonek, 1984).

This chapter provides an overview of recent psychobiological research in children and adolescents with affective disorders, evaluates these results in the light of current knowledge of biological markers in adult affective illness, and seeks to integrate these findings in a coherent fashion within the limits of what is known at present. This will, of necessity, involve some degree of speculation.

THE CONCEPT AND TYPES OF BIOLOGICAL MARKERS

Biological markers are characteristics that have been shown to be specifically associated to the disorder in question, during an episode, during the symptom-free intervals, or both. They are likely to reflect mechanisms involved in the pathogenesis of the disease in question. Biological markers are different from chromosomal markers, which are associated with the genetic transmission of particular disorders on the basis of chromosomal geography alone. Chromosomal markers in and of themselves do not have the potential to reveal pathophysiological mechanisms, unless the genes actually involved in the causation of the disorder in question are isolated and biochemically identified.

In order to clarify the discussion that follows, several definitions of types of biological markers are proposed below. A *state marker* is an abnormality that appears in close temporal relationship to the onset of the depressive episode and normalizes with the episode's outset. Initially, studies of biological markers were conducted in adult patients during an episode of depressive illness, comparing them to normal or sometimes pathological (nondepressed) control subjects. After identification of characteristics ("markers") that significantly differentiate depressives and controls, it is necessary to ask: Is this abnormality strictly related to the episode or does it remain abnormal after full recovery? Unless fully recovered drug-free patients are restudied during follow-up, we cannot know if a particular marker is a state marker. Finding an abnormality during the depressive episode is not tantamount to such abnormality being a state marker. A state marker should in addition normalize in loosely parallel chronological relationship to affective recovery.

A marker that remains abnormal after full recovery from the depressive episode should not ipso facto be considered to be a trait marker.

The fact that the abnormality remains after recovery can be due to three different possibilities:

1. The patient, although clinically recovered, is still too close in time to the clinical endpoint of the prior episode. Markers of illness do not necessarily normalize at the same time that the patient is declared clinically recovered. This is the most parsimonious explanation of persistently blunted thyroid stimulating hormone (TSH) responses to thyrotropin releasing hormone (TRH) in recovered, drug-maintained, adult depressives (Kirkegaard, Norlem, Lauridsen, Bjorum, & Christiansen, 1975; Kirkegaard et al., 1977). In such patients, such abnormality predicted clinical relapse in a relatively short period of time. In fact, persistent abnormality in state markers during maintenance antidepressant treatment may be a good indicator for the need to continue such treatment. It is on this basis that state markers have been proposed in the past as prognostic indicators. There is also evidence that some state markers may become abnormal shortly before the clinical onset of the next depressive episode (Bond, Dimitrakoudi, Howlett, & Jenner, 1975; Bond, Jenner, & Sampson, 1972; DeLeon, Jones, Maas, DeKirmenjian, & Fawcett, 1973; Greden et al., 1980). Thus, it is important that protocols include a sufficiently long period of sustained affective recovery, as well as an equally long follow-up period after retesting for all cases. Only patients who remain nondepressed during the follow-up should be accepted into data analysis for trait markers.

2. Another possibility is that the biological abnormality (marker) first appeared during the first depressive episode and it never normalized after recovery. In a way, it would be like a sequela from the first depressive episode, and its presence in a subject would be evidence of past episode(s) of depression. This would not be a true trait marker, but rather a marker of past depressive episode (or past state).

3. Finally, the abnormality may have been present long before the occurrence of the first depressive episode and may have remained unaltered throughout the subject's lifetime. Such abnormalities would allow for positive identification of subjects before their first depressive episode. These would constitute true trait markers.

All markers that remain abnormal after the episode may reflect the subject's predisposition to future episodes of depression, which is likely to be genetically determined. These distinctions are important as the potential significance of biological markers varies according to their respective type. The study of patients during the depressive episode only cannot possibly determine the type of marker. Finding significant differences between ill depressives and normals in a particular characteristic is a necessary but not sufficient condition for it to be considered a specific marker. In addition, results in other psychiatric disorders of similar severity should be significantly different than those in depressives. Otherwise, a biological abnormality may be general to all psychiatric disorders or to broad categories of psychiatric disorder (i.e., "psychoses") or be due simply to stress, and not to depressive illness.

Therefore, at least three conditions should be met for a marker to be identified as a marker of trait:

1. Persistently abnormal in fully recovered, drug-free, patients.
2. Present at a significantly higher rate in clinically normal (never mentally ill) subjects with a strong family history of major depressive disorder in first- and second-degree biological relatives than in normals without any affected biological relatives.
3. Long-term follow-up studies of depression-vulnerable informative pedigrees should produce increasing concordance with time between presence of the marker and lifetime history of major depressive disorder.

The research implications of trait markers are potentially great. True trait markers, which are evident before the first depressive episode, would signify the first preclinical manifestation of a genetic predisposition to future depressive episodes, independent of their timing. As such, they may be useful in the study of the mechanisms of familial transmission of these disorders, as a sensitive indicator of the probability of a particular subject displaying the affected phenotype in the future. The first application of true trait markers would be to make it possible to embark on solid prophylactic studies. Second, biological marker research in the affective disorders in children and youth can help to identify subgroups that may be quite different from each other on a neurobiological basis but not on a syndromic, clinical basis. By identifying the roots of at least some heterogeneity in this population, future research can be much more incisive. Thus, theoretically, the research potential and practical applicability of true (rigorously defined) trait markers are extraordinary, but the laborious path toward their identification is fraught with problems, although none are insurmountable.

THE NATURE OF CHILDHOOD AFFECTIVE DISORDERS

When the literature on depression in childhood up until 1977 is reviewed, it is quite obvious that there was an abundance of opinions coupled with a paucity of data. Assessment had never been standardized, the overwhelming majority of publications did not define the symptomatic criteria for the diagnosis and no single treatment study was properly designed and controlled. Although depression in adolescents was recognized, it was generally held to be "different" from adult depression, while the existence of prepubertal depression was widely questioned (Puig-Antich, 1980). Nevertheless, in the Isle of Wight Studies (Rutter, 1979; Rutter, Tizard, & Whitmore, 1970) depressive disorder was found in both children and adolescents, in spite of the fact that the assessment instruments did not fully tap many of the phenomena now regarded as critical for diagnosis of these conditions.

The introduction of standardized reliable assessment methods (Chambers et al., in press; Herjanic et al., 1975; Orvaschel, Puig-Antich, Chambers, Tabrizi, & Johnson, 1982; Poznanski et al., 1984) and the feasibility of using unmodified diagnostic criteria for adult major depressive disorder and other major psychiatric disorders (Puig-Antich, Blau, Marx, Greenhill, & Chambers, 1978; Strober, Green, & Carlson, 1982) in child and adolescent psychiatric populations provided for the possibility of selecting more clinically homogeneous samples. Also it allowed investigators in this field to use a single common language, thus increasing the chances of replicability of results across centers. This approach, although initially controversial, has been quite fertile in generating substantial amounts of research in a short period of time.

Briefly stated, the main advances in clinical aspects of child and adolescent affective disorders are as follows.

1. The basic phenomenology of major depression (Carlson & Cantwell, 1979, 1980; Cytryn, McKnew, & Bunney, 1980; Kuperman & Stewart, 1979; Poznanski, 1982; Puig-Antich et al., 1978; Strober et al., 1982; Weinberg, Rutman, Sullivan, Penick, & Dietz, 1973; Welner, Welner, McCrary, & Leonard, 1977), dysthymia (Kovacs et al., 1984a, 1984b) and/or that of manic disorder (Carlson & Strober, 1978) are quite similar from 6 years to senescence. Developmental variations do occur but they are minor compared to the steadiness of the symptomatology. This is true for both prepuberty and adolescence. Before 6 years, little has been done and very little is known. After 6 years, the semistructured interview technique of both child and parents is the most agreed upon assessment method.

2. Psychotic and endogenous forms of major depressive disorder do occur and are not a rarity. In a recent study, 40% of prepubertal children with major depressive disorders showed depressive hallucinations and 50% fit Research Diagnostic Criteria (RDC) for endogenous subtype (Chambers, Puig-Antich, Tabrizi, & Davies, 1982). Adolescent affective disorder studies where these symptoms were systematically assessed show very similar findings (Strober & Carlson, 1982; Strober et al., 1982).

3. Familial aggregation of a lifetime diagnosis of major depression in first-degree biological relatives studied by the family history or family study methods (Andreasen, Endicott, Spitzer, & Winokur, 1977) has been

reported to occur in studies of adult, adolescent, and prepubertal major depressive probands. Thus, in first-degree relatives of adult probands with major depression, the age-corrected lifetime morbidity risk for major depressive episodes has been reported to be between .18 and .30 (Gershon et al., 1976, 1977, 1982; Perris, 1974; Weissman, Gershon, Kidd, Prusoff, et al., 1984; Weissman, Kidd, & Prusoff, 1982), while in adolescents the same figure has been found to be between .35 in relatives of inpatient probands (Strober et al., in press) and .37 among those of mostly outpatients (Puig-Antich, unpublished manuscript,a). Among families of prepubertal children with major depression, the age-corrected morbidity risk for first-degree biological relatives over 16 years of age has been found to be .50 (Puig-Antich, unpublished manuscript,b). (If alcoholism and antisocial personality are added to major affective disorders, without age correction, 55% of all first-degree biological relatives of prepubertal probands were affected by at least one of these diagnoses. This was not found among families of adolescent probands.) There are some problems with the comparison of these morbidity risk data across age groups because the nature of the control groups in the different studies varies, and the methodologies although similar were not identical. Nonetheless, data in families of adult probands cited here were obtained by the more sensitive family study method (i.e., direct interview of every relative), while a substantial proportion of the data was obtained from families of child and adolescent probands using the less sensitive family history method (i.e., obtaining information from one relative about all the others). Therefore, finding higher aggregation among the earlier onset groups is contrary to the sensitivity of the methods used, a fact that lends credence to the hypothesis that there appears to be an inverse relationship between age of onset of the disorder and familial morbidity risks. This has been found also within samples of families of adult depressive probands (Weissman et al., in press). Adult probands with an age of onset below 20 years of age presented higher familial aggregation than those with later onsets. In addition there was aggregation for early age at onset among families.

Further evidence of familial aggregation of depressive disorders is provided by systematic studies of the child and adolescent offspring of adult probands (Beardslee, Keller, & Klerman, in press; Weissman et al., in press; Welner et al., 1977). So far, these studies tend to indicate that for offspring under 18 years the morbidity risk when only one parent has suffered from a major affective disorder is double that for offspring with neither parent affected. The risk quadruples for the offspring of dually affected parental matings. In another study of adult probands and relatives (Gershon et al., 1982), over 50% of dual parental mating adult offspring were shown to be affected. Only in a small study, Gershon et al. (unpublished manuscript) were no differences found between families of depressive children and those of controls, but both groups had unexpectedly high morbidity risks among their offspring. These discrepancies are likely to be secondary to small sample size, low assessment specificity, selection procedures of the control group that bias recruitment of control probands toward nonaffected parents from families with affectively loaded pedigrees, or a combination of all three. Most data do indicate familial aggregation in the offspring.

The familial aggregation of child, adolescent, and adult affective disorders; the likely relationship between both density of familial aggregation and age of onset rate of disorder in the offspring; together with the higher concordance for affective illness in adulthood of mono- over dizygotic twins (Gershon et al., 1976), all strongly suggest that inheritance is likely to play an important role in the familial transmission of affective disease.

4. Obviously the final and perhaps the most definitive piece of evidence will be long-term follow-up of prepubertal and adolescent depressives. Two ongoing studies are currently gathering these data. Kovacs' group has demonstrated the chronicity of prepubertal dysthymia with and without major depression (Kovacs et al., 1984a) and the continuity into adolescence of prepubertal depressive disorders (Kovacs et al., 1984b). These fundamental contributions do away with the up until recently commonly held belief that the depressive clinical pictures in children were transient and highly responsive to environmental events. As the characterization of affective illness in children is rather recent, no study has yet had the time to follow identified prepubertal depressive children up into adulthood, the key test of the continuity hypothesis. However, the preliminary results of the follow-up of adolescents with affective illness (Strober, 1983) attest to the continuity of these disorders over time. In fact, the results of the follow-up studies of prepubertal and adolescent onset depressive disorders, cited before, are largely parallel to the results of methodologically similar studies of adult major depressives (Keller, Shapiro, Lavori, & Wolfe, 1982a, 1982b; Keller, Lavori, Lewis, & Klerman, 1984). It is therefore likely that continuity across ages does exist.

To date, therefore, the available clinical research data point to the similarity, or possibly identity, of the nature of major depression in all age groups over 6 years of age, and generally support the point of view taken by DSM-III (American Psychiatric Association, 1980). There are not enough data, however, to differentiate between similarity or identity regarding different ages of onset. For example, it is conceivable that onset in childhood rather than in adult life of depressive illness may have serious implications for etiology, pathogenesis, course, and treatment. This is an area of inquiry that may be illuminated by further research into biological markers and genetics studies.

The evidence reviewed so far suggests that we should start to think about affective illness as a unitary syndrome across the life span. If the nature of depressive disorders is the same across ages, the first question that poses itself is what the effects of age and of sexual maturity and climacterium are upon the expression and the psychobiology of affective illness. At present we do not know whether affective disorders at all ages constitute a single disease, or whether as in diabetes we may have to distinguish a juvenile and an adult form. The fact that familial aggregation decreases to near base rates among adult probands with age of onset after 50 years suggests that phenocopies may be more frequent with increasing age. Thus, it is important to emphasize the importance of genetic marker and biological marker research in very early onset affective disorders, as this is the subgroup most likely to represent the most genetically determined form of the illness. Other advantages offered by the subgroup of affective disorders with very early age of onset for psychobiological research are the availability of at least three and frequently four preceding generations, the relatively short life span of the proband (which makes lifetime diagnoses more credible), the relative lack of exposure in most children to licit and illicit drugs, and the lower prevalence of chronic intercurrent diseases, which become more likely with advancing age.

BIOLOGICAL MARKERS IN AFFECTIVE ILLNESS: FROM ADULTS TO CHILDREN

The biological markers of major depressive disorders in adults can be classified into four general, but overlapping, areas: sleep EEG, neuroendocrine, biochemical, and cell receptors. Although most of them are peripherally measured, there is substantial evidence that each reflects more or less indirectly CNS function.

Sleep EEG

The evidence for polysomnographic markers occurring during the episode of major depressive disorder in adults is very strong. It has been repeatedly confirmed that adult primary major depressives present decreased first REM period latency (Gillin, Duncan, Pettegrew, Frankel, & Snyder, 1979; Kupfer, 1976; Vogel, Vogel, McAbee, & Thurmond, 1980), decreased slow-wave sleep (delta) time (Coble, Kupfer, Spiker, Neil, & Shaw, 1980; Kupfer & Foster, 1979); increased REM density (Coble *et al.*, 1980; Gillin *et al.*, 1979; Vogel *et al.*, 1980), decreased sleep efficiency (Gillin *et al.*, 1979; Kupfer & Foster, 1979), and abnormal temporal distribution of REM throughout the night (Vogel *et al.*, 1980).

The original purpose of the sleep studies of prepubertal depressives (Puig-Antich, Goetz, Hanlon *et al.*, 1982; Young, Knowles, MacLean, Boag, & McConville, 1982) was to validate or disprove the diagnosis of prepubertal major depressive disorder. In both studies, prepubertal children with this diagnosis, in spite of their multiple sleep complaints, did not differ in their polysomnograms from nondepressed neurotic or normal children. Thus, these data, taken at face value, did not support the validity of the diagnosis. None of the findings reported in adult major depressives appear to be characteristic of prepubertal children diagnosed as major depressive disorders of either subtype. There was no decrease in slow-wave sleep, no decrease in sleep efficiency, no shortening of latency to the first REM period, no increase in REM density, and no abnormality in the temporal distribution of REM sleep during the night.

However, the virtual lack of cross-sectional sleep architecture differences in prepubertal major depressives does not necessarily indicate that prepubertal and adult major depressive disorders are different conditions. This finding could also be interpreted as evidence of maturational differences in sleep correlates of the same depressive disorder at different ages. We have argued before (Puig-Antich, Goetz, Hanlon et al., 1982) that the evidence at hand in our studies and in those of others uniformly points to the likelihood that our sleep findings express a maturational (age) difference, and not a difference in the nature of prepubertal and adult major depression. Some of the evidence, other than biological markers, in favor of the similarity of prepubertal and adult major depressive disorders has already been summarized above.

There is evidence in the adult data that age has a fundamental influence on sleep EEG. Several studies have found strong relationships between age and sleep measures in adult depressives (over 18 years). This is also true of normative adult data. These age effects on sleep are so marked that norms are needed decade by decade within the adult age range. Ulrich, Shaw, and Kupfer (1980) reported that sleep efficiency, REM latency, and Stages 3 and 4 show strong correlations with age. Gillin, Duncan et al. (1979) found that in both depressed and normal subjects, total sleep time, Stages 3 and 4, sleep efficiency, REM sleep, and REM latency decreased as a function of age, while awake time increased. Coble et al. (1980) compared young adult with older endogenous depressives. Although there were practically no differences in severity of clinical picture, sleep efficiency was significantly lower in the older group ($p < .01$), SWS was also significantly lower in the older group ($p < .05$), REM latency was significantly shorter in the older group ($p < .05$), and REM density of the first REM period was significantly higher in the older group ($p < .01$). Normative data on SWS across ages from Williams, Karacan, and Hursch (1974) show that there is a progressive decrease of Stage 4 with age beginning in late adolescence not fully compensated by a minor increase in Stage 3. The same data show that REM latency normally decreases with age. Thus, negative sleep findings in prepubertal major depressives may be explained by maturational (age) differences in the nature of sleep, as their findings lie at the left-hand side of the regression line of age against sleep EEG variables in adult depressives.

Confirmation of this hypothesis is beginning to emerge from ongoing studies in adolescent major depressives. Preliminary findings by Lahmeyer, Poznanski, and Bellur (1983) showed shortened REM latency comparing 13 adolescent depressives with 13 controls, but the age of the sample was over 17 years (late adolescence/young adulthood). Puig-Antich and his group have compared at midpoint in their study adolescent endogenous and nonendogenous major depressives during the episode, and normal controls. Sleep continuity disturbances become evident as the depressive group enters adolescence. REM latency, on the other hand, only becomes abnormal in late adolescence. In addition, all major sleep variables under consideration are highly correlated with age in the predicted direction, while there are no sex effects. As we shall see later, there also is some evidence of mild sleep continuity disturbances in prepubertal major depressives when their records during the episode are compared to those during the recovered state.

In summary, using the same methods of data collection and reduction that are regularly used in adults, rigorously diagnosed prepubertal major depressives present none of the polysomnographic characteristics that are well established in adults with the same diagnosis. The same is likely to be true among younger adolescent major depressives, except for mild sleep continuity disturbance and shortening of REM latency beginning in late adolescence. It is therefore likely that the relative lack of sleep findings during the depressive episode in youngsters with major depression is secondary to maturational factors, which modify the expression of depressive illness. This hypothesis would imply that the nature of depressive illness is the same or quite similar in both groups. If true, the sleep findings characteristic of adult depressives would not only be due to depression, but secondary to an interaction between depressive illness and age. Therefore, REM advancement would constitute an epiphenomenon of adult depressive illness, neither necessary nor intrinsic to its pathophysiology. This would not detract anything from the use of sleep studies for diagnostic purposes in adult depressive illness, for which only association is necessary. But it may indicate that, at the time of trying to integrate the current knowledge on biological correlates of affective illness into a new quantum leap forward of theory building and generation of new hypotheses, markers highly related to age are likely to have substantially lesser roles than age-independent biological correlates, which are more likely to reflect pathophysiological mechanisms intrinsic to the disorder.

Paradoxically, therefore, although the EEG sleep studies of prepubertal and adolescent major depressive episodes show different results from those of adults with the same diagnosis, the results are quite consistent across age groups once the effects of age are taken into account. These age effects appear to be consistent through the life span. Sleep EEG during the depressive episode constitutes a prime example of an age-sensitive marker.

It should be noted that traditional data reduction methods in EEG sleep, although they have served clinical use well, are highly inefficient in that they disregard a lot of information that is likely to be quite important. The possibility remains that new, computerized, more sensitive methods, which are now available (Coble et al., 1984; Coble, Taska, Ulrich, & Kupfer, 1982), may reveal in children and adolescents during a depressive episode findings that were not detectable before.

Although circadian rhythm abnormalities have been reported in adult depressives (Wehr, 1984), there is no evidence that prepubertal children with the same diagnosis show any abnormality in that area except reported difficulty in falling asleep, which is most likely to be secondary to concomitant anxiety (Puig-Antich, Goetz, Hanlon et al., 1982). In contrast, clinical experience indicates that some adolescent depressives present with marked circadian shifts, which are demonstrably beyond their voluntary control or current peer group fad. The prepubertal data would again suggest that abnormal circadian shifts are not intrinsic to depressive illness and that theories that attempt to look at depressive illness as secondary to abnormalities of circadian regulation are bound to fail. The association of circadian abnormalities and affective illness in some adolescents and adults is not necessarily causal in that direction, in spite of the fact that sleep deprivation and imposed circadian advancement have been convincingly shown to induce transient clinical improvement in adult depressive illness (Kripke, 1984).

POLYSOMNOGRAPHY OF RECOVERED DEPRESSIVES

As noted above, recovery studies are required to determine whether abnormalities found during episodes of depression are correlates of active illness, or are true trait or past episode markers, which remain deviant during depression-free intervals. A study of EEG sleep during sustained, drug-free, recovered state in prepubertal children who had experienced a major depressive episode (Puig-Antich, Goetz, Hanlon et al., 1983) showed that even when there were no positive findings during the episode, a marker may become abnormal upon recovery.

Data on recovered drug-free adult depressives are contradictory. On the one hand, there are three studies that suggest normalization of REM latency in recovered adult depressives (Hauri, Chernik, Hawkins, & Mendels, 1974; Schultz & Trojan, 1979; Sitaram, Nurnberger, Gershon, & Gillin, 1982). In Hauri et al.'s study, remitted adult depressive patients, who had not been studied during their episodes, when compared to normal subjects were shown to present substantial sleep continuity abnormalities, greater difficulty falling asleep, and less delta sleep. However, REM sleep variables appeared to be no different from controls except for lower REM period fragmentation. Schultz and Trojan found a decrease in REM density progression in both ill and recovered adults with endogenous depression. M. Sitaram et al.'s studies (1980, 1982) found no differences in REM latency between remitted adult depressives and never-depressed controls. On the other hand, a variety of pilot studies that used depressives as their own controls (Avery, Wildshiodz, & Rafgelsen, 1982; Kupfer & Foster, 1973; Mendels & Chernik, 1973, 1975), as well as some unpublished data from ongoing studies (D. Kupfer et al., personal communication, 1984), suggest that sleep continuity measures tend to improve during recovery, whereas in some patients, REM measures, especially first REM period latency, tend to remain the same or improve to a small degree. Thus, the results of comparisons of the same subject across states (depressed/nondepressed) are not wholly concordant with comparisons for control groups in adult remitted depressive patients. This suggests heterogeneity.

Differences in presence and/or severity of residual symptoms of depression among patient groups studied may account for some discrepancies in sleep data. Hauri et al. (1974) report that, although remitted and functioning, the depressive group scored significantly higher than controls in all depression scales (Zung, Beck). This makes it even more surprising that REM findings were negative, as they have been noted as positive in dysthymic disorders (Akiskal et al., 1980). The definition of recovery may be a key factor to consider in the interpretation of every study. In addition, to our knowledge, no systematic data exist on drug-free polysomnographic measures during the 2–3 weeks preceding relapse or recurrence of a depressive episode, except in bipolar patients during the switch process (Bunney, Goodwin, Murphy, House, & Gordon, 1972; Gillin, 1977; Gillin & Wyatt, 1975; Mendelson, Gillin, & Wyatt, 1977), which is not relevant to this discussion. Given the decreased probability with time of a recurrent episode in adult depressives (Keller, Lavori, Lewis, & Klerman, 1984), it may be that those patients in whom REM latency continues to be short in spite of clinical recovery, are at highest risk and that this marker, like TSH response to TRH (Kirkegaard et al., 1977, 1978), expresses the current predisposition to relapse. An ongoing EEG sleep study of drug-free recovered adult depressive patients is likely to clarify many of these issues.

The combination of pharmacological dissection, understanding of receptor function, and polysomnography has revealed the likely importance of cholinergic mechanisms in the predisposition to affective illness. This group of studies also exemplifies the indirect demonstration of cell receptor abnormalities, but it is included here because EEG sleep is used as the dependent measure. In one study it was demonstrated that fully recovered adult endogenous depressives showed significantly faster advancement in the second REM period compared to never-depressed controls after an infusion of arecholine, a muscarinic receptor agonist, given 20 min after the outset of the first REM period (N. Sitaram, Nurnberger, Gershon, & Gillin, 1980). This effect also occurred, affecting the first REM period latency, when the infusion was given shortly after sleep onset (N. Sitaram, Moore, & Gillin, 1978a), when other muscarinic agonists, like physostigmine, were used (Gillin et al., 1978; B. Sitaram et al., 1976; N. Sitaram et al., 1977; N. Sitaram, Moore, & Gillin, 1978b), and it was blocked with pretreatment with scopolamine (Sagales, Erill, & Domino, 1975), a muscarinic receptor blocker that, like the other drugs just mentioned, crosses the blood–brain barrier. Furthermore, administration of 6 mg/kg of scopolamine for three consecutive mornings to nonaffective adult volunteers has been shown to induce progressively shorter REM latencies, and also other EEG sleep changes seen in depressive illness: increased REM density and sleep latency, with lower sleep efficiency and total sleep time (Gillin, Sitaram, & Duncan, 1979; N. Sitaram, Moore, & Gillin, 1979). Interestingly, mood changes in this experiment were minimal, suggesting a dissociation between neuroregulatory systems of sleep and affective phenomena. In view of the fact that scopolamine's actions are in the opposite direction and last no longer than 6 hr (Sagales, Erill, & Domino, 1975), it was concluded that the progressive sleep changes were due to scopolamine-induced muscarinic supersensitivity. These EEG sleep findings suggest that an excessive tendency to REM advancement does remain in recovered affective disorder adult patients even when abnormalities in REM latency are not demonstrable in the absence of pharmacological challenges, and that cholinergic mechanisms are likely to be at least a major mediator of such pathological tendency. It also is likely that decreased norepinephrine activity shortens REM latency as shown by a study using the tyrosine hydroxylase blocker α-methyl-para-tyrosine (AMPT), which depletes norepinephrine in the CNS (N. Sitaram, Gillin, & Bunney, 1984).

Puig-Antich, Goetz, Hanlon et al. (1983) have reported on the sleep and polysomnographic characteristics of 28 prepubertal major depressives (endogenous and nonendogenous) fully recovered from the depressive episode for at least 4 months and drug free for at least 1 month. The sleep measures in prepubertal recovered depressives were compared to the same measures in the same patients during illness and to baseline sleep studies of two control groups mentioned before, nondepressed psychiatric and normal.

Recovered prepubertal major depressives showed significantly shorter first REM period latency and significantly greater number of REM periods, when compared to themselves when ill and to both control groups. In addition, the sleep continuity of recovered depressives consistently and significantly improved on most relevant measures compared to the time when they were clinically depressed. Therefore, shortened first REM period latency may be a marker of trait or past episode, present in prepubertal major depressives during the recovered state, which may normalize during the depressive episode. No EEG sleep data are yet available from adolescents who have recovered from an episode of major depression.

In spite of their lack of polysomnographic abnormalities, most prepubertal children in the midst of a major depressive episode experience sleep difficulties (as reported by themselves and also by their parents), which do not substantially differ from those of adult depressives. Upon recovery, these complaints by and large disappear, in parallel with a small but significant improvement in sleep continuity variables. These findings suggest that children are very sensitive to small sleep disruptions, which in adults [except for pseudoinsomniacs (Borkovec, 1979)], would be accompanied by little or no subjective perception of sleep difficulty. The Stanford studies, which demonstrated the massive effects of sleep deprivation on daytime functioning of normal children support this interpretation (Anders, Carskadan, & Dement, 1980; Anders et al., 1978; Carskadan, Harvey, & Dement, 1981a, 1981b; Carskadan et al., 1980).

It is not clear whether or not the REM sleep results reported here in recovered depressive children are at variance with adult data, as too few data exist in adult recovered depressives. However, it does appear consistent with the tendency to REM advancement in recovered adult depressives after arecholine infusion (N. Sitaram et al., 1980). It is conceivable that shortened REM latency is more likely to persist (in adults) or appear (in prepuberty), during the recovered state, the younger the age of onset and/or the higher the familial aggregation. This hypothesis implicitly postulates a continuum between the concepts of marker of past episode and true trait marker. It is also tempting to speculate that what is constant from age group to age group in the recovered patients is a chronic state of central cholinergic (muscarinic) supersensitivity while lower norepinephrine activity in these younger age groups allows for the expression of the tendency to REM advancement without provocative tests. What remains a puzzle is why REM latency normalizes during the major depressive episode in prepubertal children.

Further research is obviously necessary at this juncture. Priority should be given to studying still unaffected prepubertal offspring of dual parental matings for affective illness, and to restudying already affected children serially during the recovered state and also during their next episode of depression, before treatment is instituted. The first strategy would address the question of whether or not shortened REM latency is a true trait marker for major depression in prepuberty. The second would focus on another question: Does REM latency remain abnormal in the recovered state with the passage of time? And, does it lengthen again to the age-corrected normal range in chronological relationship to the onset of the second depressive episode? In addition to REM latency and other standard variables, future studies should use new computerized techniques, which, by improving current data reduction methods, are likely to further our ability to understand brain function from electrophysiological measurements. Finally, the use of safe pharmacological probes may be indicated in order to advance our understanding of neuroregulation of sleep in depressed and nondepressed children.

In a recent study, Coble *et al.* (1984; personal communication), compared EEG sleep of normal prepubertal children with ($N=16$) versus without ($N=16$) a positive family history for affective illness. No differences were found in REM latency or measures of sleep continuity, but children with positive family history showed significantly higher REM densities (measured by computerized methods) than those without. These findings suggest that shortened REM latency found in the recovered state may be more a marker of past episode than a marker of trait, if the calculated risks in the first group, estimated from the affective density of their pedigrees, were shown to be very high, so that the anticipated rate of affected offspring at some point during their lifespan is close to 50%. Otherwise the correct hypothesis may be rejected even in not-so-small samples, because the group that will eventually develop the disorder would constitute only a relatively small proportion of the sample. The other alternative, which would only solve the problem partially, would be to add a long-term follow-up component to these studies. With small sample sizes and comparatively low risk rates, this design would not be assured of providing a valid informative answer even after several decades.

If the EEG sleep findings on the recovered state, reviewed in this chapter, were replicated, they would suggest that neuroregulation of affectivity and its psychobiological correlates, are different in prepuberty than in adulthood. There is abundant animal as well as clinical evidence to support this concept, which will be reviewed later in this chapter.

Neuroendocrine Markers

CORTISOL SECRETION

Abnormalities of cortisol secretion have been shown to be present regularly in a substantial proportion of adult patients with endogenous, and sometimes nonendogenous, major depressive disorder, compared to normal controls, using measures of cortisol secretion, plasma cortisol, or urinary-free cortisol (Gibbons, 1964; Sachar, Hellman, et al., 1973; Stokes et al., 1984). In about 40% of endogenously depressed adults, 24-hr mean serum cortisol has been shown to be in the hypersecretory range with more secretion, more secretory episodes, more minutes of active secretion and continued secretion in late evening and early morning hours, a period when normal secretion is minimal (Sachar, Hellman, et al., 1973), and shortened latency between sleep onset and rise of cortisol secretion (Jarrett, Coble, & Kupfer, 1983). Examining subsections of 24-hr serum cortisol samples in adult subjects, the mean plasma cortisol concentration of seven consecutive half-hourly samples in the afternoon was shown to correlate highly with mean 24-hr plasma cortisol (Halbreich, Zumoff, et al., 1982). The same measure was found to provide acceptable discrimination between depressives and normals for different 3-hr periods during afternoon and evening (Sachar *et al.,* 1985; E. J. Sachar *et al.,* unpublished manuscript). The examination of best sine wave fit for 24-hr secretory patterns for normals and depressives separately found no evidence of a shift of the diurnal rhythm of secretion.

These studies of cortisol secretion in adult major depressives indicated the presence of an abnormality reflected in higher plasma cortisol and urinary-free cortisol concentrations over the 24-hr period. Depending on the cutoff of mean plasma cortisol, this abnormality can be found in 30–50% of adult endogenous depressives. It may be tempting, therefore, to conceptualize cortisol hypersecretion as a phenomenon that is simply associated with some but not all endogenous or even major depressions. Nevertheless, studies on a variety of provocative tests of cortisol secretion (reviewed below) and on their interrelationships indicate that "spontaneous" cortisol hypersecretion may be only one of the manifestations of dysregulation of CRF–ACTH–cortisol secretion in adult depression.

The dexamethasone suppression test (DST) has been claimed to be a relatively sensitive and specific test for endogenous major depression (Carroll, Curtis, & Mendels, 1976a, 1976b; Carroll *et al.,* 1981). The 1-mg test has been shown to be more sensitive (60%) than the 2-mg test (40%) without unacceptably compromising specificity (96%) (Carroll *et al.,* 1981). Nevertheless, studies during the last few years have not replicated these figures consistently. Sensitivity has been reported substantially lower for outpatient endogenous and nonendogenous depressives [14% (Rabkin, Quitkin, Stewart, McGrath, & Puig-Antich, 1983); 26% (Amsterdam, Winokur, Caroff, & Conn, 1982)] and for inpatients with unipolar or bipolar major depression (32%) (Stokes *et al.,* 1984). Although claims have been made for higher sensitivity among some diagnostic subcategories (e.g., endogenous, psychotic, bipolar, pure familial unipolar), these have not been found consistently across studies.

Specificity has also been found to be lower than initially thought by several groups. Thus, DST nonsuppression rates among adult schizophrenics have been reported to be 0% by Schlesser, Winokur, and Sherman (1980) using an incomplete test, 30% by Dewan *et al.* (1982), and 17% by Stokes *et al.* (1976, 1984). Initially, Carroll (1972) reported an 18% nonsuppression rate among 108 nondepressed psychiatric inpatients. Anorexia nervosa is accompanied by both affective symptomatology and a rate of DST nonsuppression at least as highly as in major depression (Walsh, 1980). But specificity may be compromised further by certain aspects of depressive symptomatology. Thus, several recent reports point out the importance of weight loss. Diet-induced moderate weight loss in healthy adult volunteers has been shown to turn 1-mg DST suppression to nonsuppression (Berger, Doerr *et al.,* 1982; Berger, Krieg, & Pirke, 1982; Berger *et al.,* 1983; Edelstein *et al.,* 1983). The rate of nonsuppression among healthy adult volunteers has also varied between 4% and 16% (Amsterdam *et al.,* 1982).

Abnormal DST is not as sensitive or specific a test for major depression as initially reported. There is good reason to believe that this variability may be partially explained by assay variation from lab to lab (Meltzer & Fang, 1983) in the face of a tradition-honored cutoff value, and also by a too sporadic sampling routine in the face of considerable variability in patterns of nonsuppression found when 24-hr studies have been carried out (Sherman, Pfohl, & Winokur, 1984). Nevertheless, among adult psychiatric patients, it does occur more often among major depressives (and patients with anorexia nervosa) than among nonaffective psychiatric disorders. Therefore, the DST provides another measure of abnormal regulation of cortisol secretion in adult depressives. One may have anticipated that the degree of agreement between the two measures just reviewed would be very high. Nevertheless this is not so. Initially, Sachar et al. (1980) using the 2-mg test reported that the DST 2-mg escapers were mostly a subset of cortisol hypersecretors, especially if the mean 24-hr plasma cortisol cutoff is kept low. On the other hand, DST 1 mg is rather independent of cortisol hypersecretion. Only a subset of cortisol hypersecretors are DST 1-mg escapers, but in addition, a substantial proportion of cortisol normosecretors are also DST 1-mg escapers (Sachar et al., 1985). These findings have been confirmed by other reports (Rubinow, Post, Gold, Ballenger, & Wolff, 1984; Stokes et al., 1984).

Although the mechanism of action of dexamethasone suppression in endogenous depression is not fully understood, it is reasonable to speculate that a feedback loop mechanism involving at least some steroid receptors is involved. The relative independence of DST 1-mg and "spontaneous" cortisol hypersecretion in adult endogenous depressive disorder strongly suggests that they may be tapping slightly different sets of neuroregulatory mechanisms of cortisol secretion.

This tendency to hypersecrete cortisol and to escape dexamethasone suppression appears to be strictly a state marker that normalizes with affective recovery, and has found some applicability as an indicator of treatment success and risk to relapse (Greden et al., 1983). There is also little evidence that anxiety, agitation, or other clinical phenomena are involved in the pathogenesis of dysregulation of cortisol secretion in adult depression (Sachar, 1975). Clinical severity of the depression shows only a rather weak positive correlation to cortisol dysregulation, except intrasubject in longitudinal studies (Rubinow et al., 1984). In one study of adult major depressives, DST escapers were found to be significantly more likely than escapers to be older, have had an older age of onset of depressive illness, to have a recurrent form of the illness, and to improve regardless of treatment (W. A. Brown & Qualls, 1981). This relationship to age within samples of depressive adult patients has been found for cortisol hypersecretion (Asnis et al., 1981), dexamethasone nonsuppression (Asnis et al., in press), UFC (Stokes et al., 1984), and other measures of HPA overactivity (Sachar et al., 1985).

The poor degree of agreement between the different measures of HPA overactivity suggests that each measures a part of an elusive whole, and makes it imperative to attempt to use pharmacological dissection in order to clarify further the roles of different neurotransmitter systems. Carroll *et al.* (1980) demonstrated that physostigmine, a centrally active anticholinesterase that therefore stimulates cholinergic transmission, could turn DST to positive in normal volunteers. Thus, cholinergic overactivity may be involved in the lack of suppression to dexamethasone exhibited by a subgroup of depressed patients. This hypothesis is consistent with that of N. Sitaram *et al.* (1980), which posits muscarinic receptor supersensitivity as the basis of the excessive tendency to REM advancement as a marker of past episode or trait.

In another study from Sachar's group, intravenous infusion of D-amphetamine (.15 mg/kg) in the afternoon caused a reliable and substantial release of cortisol, increasing its plasma concentration above baseline in normals, while the same dose lowered or only minimally increased plasma cortisol from baseline in two-thirds of endogenously depressed patients (Sachar *et al.*, 1980, 1981). Further data on this test (DACT) by the same group (Sachar *et al.*, 1983) suggested high sensitivity for adult endogenous depression, and moderate for nonendogenous depressions (J. W. Stewart *et al.*, 1984). Positive tests in either spontaneous cortisol hypersecretion or DST in adult endogenous depression are strongly associated with abnormal DACT responses (Sachar *et al.*, 1985). Thus, it is reasonable to think that DACT taps a final common pathway in the abnormal regulation of cortisol secretion in adult endogenous depression.

Asnis *et al.* (in press) recently reported that desmethylimipramine (DMI) administered IM produced similar results on cortisol release as D-amphetamine in adult depressives and normal controls. This suggests that the effect of D-amphetamine in this paradigm is likely to be mediated by noradrenergic systems, almost as if these drugs, by increasing norepinephrine transmission, corrected cortisol hypersecretion in depressives.

Another pharmacological probe on the noradrenergic systems in the dysregulation of cortisol secretion in adult depressive illness has been achieved by using clonidine (Siever *et al.*, 1984). This drug stimulates presynaptic α-2 adrenergic receptors, inducing a decrease in presynaptic norepinephrine release. In addition, at somewhat higher doses, clonidine also stimulates the postsynaptic α-noradrenergic receptors. The IV administration of 2 μg/kg of clonidine hydrochloride was followed by a similar decrease in plasma cortisol to normal levels, as described with DMI and D-amphetamine. Although not entirely conclusive, the results of these studies suggest that cortisol dysregulation in adult depressives is likely to reflect a functional noradrenergic deficit.

A third set of experiments concerns the role of serotonergic systems in cortisol dysregulation in adult depressives. Meltzer, Unberkoman-Wilta et al. (1984) reported that adult patients with major depression (and also with mania) presented a significantly higher increase in plasma cortisol after oral ingestion of 200 mg of 5-hydroxy-tryptophan (5-HTP), a serotonin (5-HT) precursor, when compared to normal controls. Contrary to the work just reviewed with catecholaminergic agents, the response of 5-HTP was negatively correlated with baseline plasma cortisol. This correlation was significant in the controls, but was weaker, although still positive in the depressive group. Stated differently, the data suggest that this test is more likely to reveal abnormalities of neuroregulation of CRF–ACTH–cortisol secretion in adult depressives without spontaneous evidence of cortisol hypersecretion. High plasma cortisol response to 5-HTP in some adult depressives suggests serotonin receptor supersensitivity, which may be secondary to a deficit in 5-HT concentration in the synapse. The data also suggest that cortisol hypersecretion may be absent in adult depressives with functional serotonin deficiency. These are likely to be nonpsychotic depressives, who have committed suicidal acts, have a positive family history for major affective disorder, and are bipolar (Meltzer, Perline, Tricou, Lowy, & Robertson, 1984).

From the above discussion, it should be clear that the dysregulation of cortisol secretion in adult endogenous depressives is likely to be more widespread in these patients than the spontaneous plasma cortisol abnormalities and the DST alone would suggest. Furthermore, it is quite possible that dysregulation in different systems may cancel each other and result in what appears as normal cortisol secretion in the absence of provocative tests.

CORTISOL SECRETION IN CHILD
AND ADOLESCENT AFFECTIVE DISORDERS

Cortisol hypersecretion is found only occasionally (approximately 10% of the sample) when the circadian cortisol patterns of prepubertal children in a major depressive episode are compared to their own after recovery (J. Puig-Antich et al., unpublished data, 1979). Furthermore, no differences were found when cortisol secretion in children with major depression was compared to that of nondepressed psychiatric and normal control children. Therefore, the majority of these children have normal cortisol secretion during and after a major depressive episode. There is no change in cortisol latency either (Jarrett et al., 1983). Although at variance with the findings among adult endogenous depressives just reviewed, the findings in children are quite consistent with the influence of age on cortisol hypersecretion in adult endogenous major depressive patients (Asnis et al., 1981). In the latter, the older the patients the more likely they are to hypersecrete cortisol. Instead, in normal adults, there is a little relationship between mean plasma cortisol and age. Thus, the older the normal subject the lower the mean 24-hr plasma cortisol will be. This is quite consistent with our findings in prepuberty. The significance of the plasma cortisol contrasts between depressives and controls increases with the age of the sample. Thus simple age effects are probably responsible for the substantially lower rate of spontaneous cortisol hypersecretors in prepubertal endogenous depressives compared to older adults with the same diagnosis. As in the case of sleep EEG variables, it appears that age may be at least as important as major depression in the pathophysiological mechanisms resulting in cortisol hypersecretion in older depressed patients. Preliminary data from an ongoing study by the author suggest a low rate of cortisol hypersecretors among adolescent major depressives also, which provides further, if preliminary, support for the hypothesis of interaction between depression and age.

The published data on the DST in depressed children are contradictory. In a small outpatient controlled study of RDC endogenous prepubertal depressives, the DST showed a sensitivity of 63% and a specificity versus nondepressed psychiatric disorders of 90% (Poznanski, Carroll, Banegas, Sook, & Grossman, 1982). In an uncontrolled study of 10 outpatient children with the same diagnosis, only one escaped suppression (Geller *et al.*, 1983). Dosage was fixed (.5 mg) in the first study and weight corrected in the second, but in fact dosage differences were minor and unlikely to explain the discrepant results. In a third study, a nonsuppression rate of 70% was found in an inpatient sample of 20 children with major depression after 1 mg of dexamethasone (Weller, Weller, Fristad, & Preskorn, 1984). Although the study was not controlled, samples were obtained not only at 4 PM but also at 8 AM. Most 8 AM samples were suppressed, providing some indirect evidence that the dexamethasone pill was in fact ingested. Two other studies have addressed specificity questions. Targum, Chastek, and Sullivan (1981) found a 1-mg suppression rate of 89% among prepubertal inpatient conduct disorders, while Livingston, Reis, and Ringdahl (1984) found three of five children with separation anxiety and three of five children with major depression to escape suppression with a dose of 0.5 mg. In a recent study, now in the process of analysis, Puig-Antich found a very low rate of nonsuppression among all four groups of prepubertal children: endogenous and nonendogenous depressives, nondepressed psychiatric controls, and normal children. The study involved postdexamethasone hourly sampling for a full 24-hr through an in-dwelling catheter.

In adolescents the pattern of DST results appears to be quite similar to adults: among inpatients there is a 30–70% escape rate (Robins, Alessi, Yanchyshyn, & Colfer, 1982; M. Strober, personal communication), while the rate is much lower among outpatients (Puig-Antich, unpublished manuscript).

It is too early to come to conclusions regarding the DST in prepubertal and adolescent affective illness. Many questions regarding mechanisms, the role of weight loss (Berger, Doerr, Lund, Bronish, & von Zerssen, 1982; Berger, Krieg, & Pirke, 1982; Berger et al., 1983; Edelstein et al., 1983), and specificity are still unanswered, for children as well as for adults. Although Carroll et al. (1981) found no age effects whatsoever on the rate of escapers to DST 1 mg in adult endogenous depressives, other investigators have found substantial age influences (Asnis et al., 1981; Sachar et al., 1985).

As in the case of REM latency and other sleep variables, the regulation of cortisol secretion in depressive illness in prepuberty and adolescence should not be understood as "normal." The shortened REM latency in the recovered state, the positive DST studies, and the occasional cortisol hypersecretor suggest that such normality is likely to be illusory. With the deepening of our understanding of the extent and the different neuroregulatory mechanisms involved in depression in adults, we shall be able to ask more pointed questions and use more sophisticated techniques in order to answer them. Prepubertal children may normally have a lower noradrenergic tone in their CNS (Siefert, Foxx, & Butler, 1980; J. G. Young, Kyprie, Ross, & Cohen, 1980), and this may be related to lower rates of cortisol hypersecretion in depressives in this age group.

Growth Hormone Secretion

Studies of growth hormone (GH) secretion in endogenous depressives and controls highlight the effects of sex hormones on this particular marker. Sachar et al. (1970) suggested that the study of GH responses to some provocative tests could indirectly test the functional status of hypothalamic catecholaminergic systems in adult depressives. Among the different provocative tests investigated, the GH response to insulin tolerance test (ITT; insulin-induced hypoglycemia) was the first in generating evidence relating to this initial hypothesis. Thus, Sachar, Finkelstein, and Hellman (1971) and Mueller, Heninger, and MacDonald (1972) reported diminished GH responses to ITT in adult patients suffering from depressive illness. Nevertheless, the fact that estrogens have potentiating effects on GH responses to a variety of stimuli (Frantz & Rabkin, 1965; Merimee & Fineberg, 1971) and the inclusion in the samples of women of different ages and menstrual status presented some difficulties in the interpretation of these initial results. To eliminate the variable of estrogen status, Gruen, Sachar, Altman, and Sassin (1975) studied GH–ITT responses in postmenopausal depressed women and postmenopausal normal controls, and demonstrated GH hyposecretion in the depressive group. All normals had maximal GH values of 5 ng/ml or over, while in 60% of the depressives maximal GH values were under 5 ng/ml. Grégoire, Branman, DeBuck, and Corvilain (1977) reported similar results: about 50% of adult depressives had absent or very low (< 3.5 ng/ml) GH responses to ITT. In a more recent study, Koslow, Stokes, Mendels, Ramsey, and Casper (1982) did not replicate these findings, but their almost 50% exclusion rate due to insufficient hypoglycemia suggests that their results could be generalized only to the adult endogenous depressives with only minimal insulin resistance (Lewis, Kathal, Sherman, Winokur, & Schlesser, 1983; Mueller, Heninger, & MacDonald, 1972).

It is therefore likely that about one-half of unipolar endogenous patients present this characteristic GH hyporesponse. There is some agreement that bipolar patients tend to secrete GH normally in this test (Koslow, Stokes, Mendels, Ramsey, & Casper, 1982; Sachar, Frantz et al., 1973). Given that phentolamine (an α-adrenergic receptor blocker) (Blackard & Heidingsfelder, 1968) and also reserpine (Cavagnini & Perachi, 1971) block the GH response to ITT, and that neither apomorphine (a dopamine receptor agonist) (Frazier, 1975) nor L-dopa (Sachar et al., 1975) have been shown consistently to produce differences in GH responses in depressives versus controls once estrogen status is controlled for, a functional noradrenergic deficit in adult depressives was hypothesized.

The finding of GH hyporesponse to hypoglycemia has received further confirmation from the more recent reports in depressed adult patients of low GH responses to a variety of pharmacological agents, with the common property of increasing noradrenergic activity, like intramuscular or oral desmethylimipramine, a norepinephrine reuptake inhibitor (Checkley, Slade, & Shur, 1981; Laakman, 1979), clonidine, an α-2 adrenergic agonist (Charney et al., 1982; Checkley, Slade, & Shur, 1981; Matussek et al., 1980; Siever et al., 1982), and D-amphetamine (Langer Heinze, Rein, & Mattusek, 1976). Of these studies, the most interesting is the response to clonidine, which in contradistinction to the studies of other agents (Halbreich, Sachar, et al., 1982) has been experimentally controlled for the effects of age and estrogen status. As GH response to clonidine is completely blocked by an α-2 but not by an α-1 blocker, it has been suggested that the findings in depression indicate a decreased α-2 postsynaptic noradrenergic receptor sensitivity at the hypothalamic level (Uhde, Siever, & Post, 1984). The added finding that, within the depressive group patients with normal or high 3-methoxy-4-hydroxyphenylethylene glycol (MHPG) excretion were the same patients who hyposecreted GH in response to clonidine, increases the likelihood of receptor subsensitivity as the mediating mechanism.

Nevertheless, the neural regulation of GH secretion in the awake state is complex (Mendelson, 1982; Mendelson et al., 1979) and involves several neurotransmitter systems not well investigated as yet in endogenous adult depressives. Thus, both cholinergic (Mendelson et al., 1978, 1981) and serotonergic (Bivens, Lebovitz, & Feldman, 1973; Mendelson et al., 1975; Smythe & Lazarus, 1974) mechanisms normally increase GH response to ITT and may be abnormal in endogenous depressives. A very recent report (Casanueva et al., 1984) convincingly demonstrated that muscarinic blockade by atropine blocked GH responses to clonidine, exercise, and arginine. Furthermore, muscarinic blockade has been shown to suppress sleep-related GH secretion (Mendelson, Sitarem, Wyatt, Gillin, & Jacobs, 1978), as well as GH responses to opioids (Casanueva et al., 1980) in the dog, and glucagon (Delitala, Frulio, Pacifico, & Maioli, 1982) in humans, but not GH responses to insulin-induced hypoglycemia (Blackard & Waddell, 1969; Mendelson et al., 1978). Thus the interpretation of these data should recognize the possibility that cholinergic transmission may constitute the final common pathway of all GH responses except those to hypoglycemia and that, therefore, the status of cholinergic systems should be taken into account before proceeding to interpret GH responses to clonidine as reflecting NE status.

Endogenously depressed prepubertal children also have been shown to hyposecrete GH in response to insulin-induced hypoglycemia (Puig-Antich, Novacenko et al., 1984), as their postmenopausal adult counterparts, when compared to nonendogenous depressive children and nondepressed psychiatric controls. Since for ethical reasons the test could not be carried out in normal children, the possibility remains that prepubertal psychiatric patients hyposecrete GH in this test. Perusal of the literature (Frasier, Hilburn, & Matthews, 1967; Joss, Zuppinger, & Zahnd, 1970; Kaplan et al., 1968; Youlton, Kaplan, & Grunbach, 1969) indicates that plasma GH peaks after ITT of less than 6 or 7 ng/ml are suspect, and under 2–3 ng/ml are definitely abnormal when the test is used clinically to evaluate growth disorders. We used 3.5 ng/ml as a cutoff for abnormal GH secretion in response to ITT. Although GH hyporesponse to ITT has been reported in psychosocial dwarfism (G. M. Brown, 1976; Money, Annecillo, & Werlwas, 1976), these patients present abnormally short stature, severe sleeplessness (Wolf & Money, 1973), and their sleep, growth, and GH abnormalities are very quickly reversed by placement outside the home. None of these characteristics are true in prepubertal endogenous major depression.

The effects of estrogens on GH response to ITT have been known from the time of the first studies on this test in adult depressives (Frantz & Rabkin, 1965; Merimee & Fineberg, 1971). In the ongoing study of adolescent depression by Puig-Antich, there was a significant degree of hyposecretion of GH in the second hour among the endogenous group compared to the nonendogenous depressives; but, as expected, the findings in the first hour are negative. It is not yet clear if there will be significant differences between depressives and controls. In this particular test there seem to be no major age effects per se, but a strong pubertal effect, probably mediated by the estrogen potentiation of GH responsivity to all stimuli, as girls secreted significantly more GH than boys did in this test, regardless of diagnosis. Thus, only during prepuberty and after menopause does GH response to ITT seem to reflect neuroregulatory mechanisms involved in depressive illness. In adolescence and early adulthood the manifestation of these effects is probably blurred by estrogen overstimulation.

In prepubertal children the majority of GH secreted in a 24-hr period is released during the first few hours of sleep in conjunction with delta sleep (Finkelstein, Roffwarg, Boyar, Kream, & Hellman, 1972; Mace, Gotlin, & Beck, 1972). This chronological association with delta sleep has been found in all ages where delta sleep can be demonstrated (Takahashi, Kipais, & Daughaday, 1968). As pointed out by Mendelson in a recent review (1982), several instances of dissociation can be found in which pharmacological abolition of either GH secretion during sleep (Mendelson, 1982) or slow-wave sleep (Rubin, Govin, Arenander, & Poland, 1973) did not affect the associated phenomenon. On the other hand, when subjects are studied in an environment free of time cues (Weitzman, Czeisler, & Moore-Ede, 1981), and also when marked phase shifts in sleep–wake cycle are externally imposed (Parker et al., 1981), GH secretion continues to be chronologically associated with delta sleep.

The abnormalities of GH release found in adult endogenous depressives (Checkley et al., 1981; Grégoire et al., 1977; Gruen et al., 1975; Laakman, 1979; Matussek, 1979) and in children with the same diagnosis (Puig-Antich, Novacenko et al., 1984; Puig-Antich et al., 1981) are all phamacologically induced. The numerous provocative tests that result in significant GH differences between endogenous depressives and controls do not necessarily have a bearing on physiological (sleep) GH secretion, which is likely to be regulated through other neurotransmitter systems (Mendelson, 1982; Mendelson et al., 1979, 1981). Therefore, a thorough understanding of abnormalities of neuroregulation of GH secretion in depressive illness is not possible without studies to establish or disprove if major depressives differ from normal and nondepressed psychiatric controls in GH secretion during the sleep period. Prepubertal major depressive children present a unique opportunity to carry out this study because no differences of delta sleep time have been demonstrated between depressive and control children (Puig-Antich, Goetz, Hanlon, et al., 1982, 1983; W. Young et al., 1982).

Puig-Antich, Goetz, Davies, Fein, et al. (1984) studied sleep-related GH secretion in prepubertal major depressive children compared to prepubertal nondepressed emotional disorders and normal children. Prepubertal major depressives, regardless of endogenous features, were found to hypersecrete GH during sleep when compared to both control groups. As expected, most GH secretion occurred during the first 3 hr after sleep onset in all groups, in close relationship to delta sleep. Therefore, this neurohormonal abnormality appears to be specific to prepubertal major depressives (regardless of subtype) and not general to child psychiatric disorders.

Interestingly, both abnormalities persist in the sustained affectively recovered state, retested under drug-free conditions (Puig-Antich, Davies et al., 1984; Puig-Antich, Goetz, Davies, Tabrizi et al., 1984). Pre- and postcorrelations for both markers are in the order of .8. These findings raise again the possibility of the existence of trait markers in prepubertal major depression, subject to the same considerations and caveats described before regarding REM latency.

Work carried out very recently by D. B. Jarrett and D. J. Kupfer (unpublished manuscript) indicates that adult endogenous depressives hyposecrete GH during sleep, after controlling for delta sleep. Similar trends are found in Puig-Antich's ongoing adolescent major depression study, in the absence of significant differences in delta sleep. If the latter is confirmed at the end of the study, it would suggest a strong pubertal effect, which reverses the effect of major depression on the amount of GH secreted during sleep. There is also an age effect in the sense that after adolescence, with increasing age, there is a steady decrease of both delta sleep and sleep-related GH, but contrary to what was found in sleep EEG variables, these age and pubertal effects change the direction of the differences. Data on sleep GH secretion in recovered adolescent and adult depressives are not available as yet.

There is evidence that the GH response to ITT in recovered adult depressives normalizes (Kathol et al., 1984). Data from recovered adolescents are not yet available. It would be important to know if age of onset of affective illness and/or degree of familial aggregation influence the findings in adult depressives.

The regulation of sleep GH secretion is likely to be quite different from that of daytime secretion in response to provocative stimuli (Mendelson, 1982; Mendelson et al., 1979). Neither α-1 nor β-norepinephrine receptors (Lucke & Glick, 1971) or dopamine systems (Chihara, Kato, Maeda, Ongo, & Imura, 1976; Cime, Mendelson, & Loriaux, 1979; Takahashi, Kipais, & Daughaday, 1968) have been shown to have any influence on sleep-related GH secretion in normal adults. With the assumption that data from normal adult volunteers can be applied to prepubertal sleep–neuroendocrine regulatory mechanisms, there are three possible mechanisms of sleep GH hypersecretion:

1. A functional deficit of hypothalamic serotonin systems—as methysergide, a serotonin receptor blocker—increases sleep GH secretion (Mendelson et al., 1975).
2. An increase in cholinergic activity, be it due to receptor hypersensitivity or increase of acetylcholine release—as methoscopolamine, an antimuscarinic agent—dramatically inhibits sleep GH secretion (Mendelson et al., 1978).
3. Piperidine, a nicotinic receptor agonist, increases sleep GH secretion (Mendelson, Lantigua, Wyatt, Gillin, & Jacobs, 1981).

These speculations on mechanisms presuppose a parallelism between normal prepubertal and adult regulation of GH secretion, something that is by no means certain, needs to be addressed by future research, and will be reviewed briefly below.

Other Markers

Other neuroendocrine markers found in adult depressives, are actively studied at present in child and adolescent affective disorders, including thyroid stimulating hormone (TSH) response to thyrotropin releasing hormone (TRH) (Amsterdam et al., 1979; Asnis, Nathan, Halbreich, Halpern, & Sachar, 1980; Bjorum & Kirkegaard, 1979; Extein, Pottash, & Gold, 1980, 1981; Gold et al., 1980, 1981; Hollister, Kenneth, & Berger, 1976; Kirkegaard et al., 1977, 1978; Loosen & Prange, 1980; Loosen, Prange, Wilson, Lara, & Pettus, 1977; Mendelwicz, Linowski, & Brauman, 1979) and GH and cortisol responses to some of the agents mentioned before.

However, in addition, a variety of neurotransmitters or their metabolites, which have proven to be of some value in adults as part of the assessment of functional state of different neurotransmitter systems, can be measured in plasma and or urine. These include urinary excretion of tyramine after tyramine ingestion (Harrison et al., 1984), urinary excretion of phenyl acetic acid (Sabelli et al., 1983), urinary excretion and plasma concentration of MHPG (Beckmann & Goodwin, 1980; Charney et al., 1981, 1982; DeLeon-Jones et al., 1975; Jimerson et al., 1983; Koslow et al., 1983; Muscettola et al., 1984; Schildkraut, 1965; Schildkraut, Orsulak, LaBrie et al., 1978; Schildkraut, Orsulak, Schatzberg et al., 1978), and cerebrospinal fluid (CSF) metabolites of biogenic amines (Asberg, Traskman, & Thoren, 1976; Traskman et al., 1981), etc.

Furthermore, receptors to particular neurotransmitters exist in peripheral tissue cell and have been shown to parallel CNS receptor function in several animal studies (Garcia-Sevilla, Hollingsworth, & Smith, 1980; Paul, Rehavi, Rice et al., 1981). On this basis, their activity has been measured in depressive adult patients. Thus, serotonin uptake by platelets has been shown to be decreased in unmedicated adult depressives (Meltzer et al., 1981), platelet α-2 adrenergic receptors to be hypersensitive (Garcia-Sevilla et al., 1981), platelets ^{3}H-imipramine (IMI) binding sites to be decreased (Paul Rehavi, Skolnick et al., 1981), and cholinergic receptors in fibroblasts to be supersensitive (Nadi, Nurnberger, & Gershon, 1984).

AFFECTIVE DISORDERS AND DEVELOPMENT: NEW HYPOTHESES IN NEUROREGULATION OF AFFECTIVE DISORDERS

As mentioned above, there is abundant animal and clinical evidence to suggest that during the developmental period the balance between different neuroregulatory systems is not equivalent to that in adulthood. Thus, the maturational rates of different systems in the rat vary quite substantially from each other. For instance, catecholamine (CA) systems do not develop fully, anatomically, and functionally until the beginning of adulthood (Goldman-Rabik & Brown, 1982), while cholinergic (Ach) and serotonergic systems develop much earlier in the postnatal period (Lidor & Molliver, 1982; Shelton, Nadler, & Cotman, 1979).

In humans there is some clinical evidence that such physiological delay in CA function in the CNS also occurs (Siefert, Foxx, & Butler, 1980; J. G. Young et al., 1980). There is also in prepubertal children a body of clinical evidence quite consistent with this notion. For example, the normally short attention span of young children and the high prevalence of attention deficit (M. Stewart, Pitts, Craig, & Dieruf, 1966; Wender, 1971), which in many cases tends to improve over time (Minde, Weiss, & Mendelson, 1972; Weiss, Minde, Werry, Douglas, & Nemeth, 1971), points to low CA function during the early years. The lack of an excitatory, elated, or euphoric response to dextro-amphetamine in prepuberty (Rapoport et al., 1980), as well as the extreme rarity of mania (Puig-Antich, 1980), and even of elation [the few prepubertal depressives who in retrospect suffered hypomanic episodes were very irritable but not elated (M. Kovacs, personal communication, 1984)] suggest the same thing.

Several investigators have proposed the notion that Ach/adrenergic balance in the CNS, as well as serotonergic activity, may mediate the affective changes in manic–depressive illness (Janowsky, El-Yousef, & David, 1972; Meltzer, Unberkoman-Wilta et al., 1984; Traskman et al., 1981). Thus, there is evidence for a Ach overdrive, probably due to receptor supersensitivity, as a trait or past episode marker in major depression in adults (N. Sitaram et al., 1980; N. Sitaram et al., 1979). There is also evidence that low CA activity may precipitate depressive episodes among bipolar adults (N. Sitaram et al., 1984). Serotonin deficits seem also to be associated with some depressive episodes, especially nonpsychotic suicidal depressions (Meltzer, Perline et al., 1984).

The EEG and sleep GH secretion findings on recovery in prepubertal children are in principle consistent with the hypothesis of Ach supersensitivity.

Taking together the findings on GH response to ITT and to sleep in prepubertal major depressive disorders (Puig-Antich, Davies et al., 1984; Puig-Antich, Goetz, Davies, Fein et al., 1984; Puig-Antich, Goetz, Davies, Tabrizi et al., 1984; Puig-Antich, Novacenko et al., 1984), we initially hypothesized that a functional hypothalamic serotonin deficit may be a key pathophysiological mechanism underlying major depression in prepuberty. Such a deficit would explain the findings so far in a way that neither Ach hypothesis could. Both muscarinic (Mendelson et al., 1978) and nicotinic (Mendelson et al., 1981) systems tend to increase GH response to ITT. A serotonin deficit, on the other hand, would tend to decrease it slightly (Mendelson et al., 1975). In fact, the results from both GH–ITT and sleep GH secretion from the last study cited are strikingly similar to those on prepubertal major depressives.

Nevertheless, a closer look at the data revealed the complexity of the phenomena reviewed. There are no significant correlations among GH and REM latency variables in either of the control groups. On the other hand, the Spearman rho correlation of areas on the curve (AUC) of GH–ITT and GH sleep was .44 ($p < .03$) in the depressives during the episode, and .46 ($p < .09$) in the recovered state. Given that low AUC in GH–ITT is associated with depression, while, on the contrary, high AUC in GH sleep is depression related, a simple serotonin deficit alone can not explain the findings.

In addition, short REM latency in recovered depressive children correlates with inadequate response to ITT (.48; $p < .052$), and not with GH secretion during sleep, while it is clear that REM latency during the episode does not correlate with any other variable. Interestingly episode/recovery stability of the three variables was significant in each case, including REM latency (.46; $p < .02$). As indicated before, in nondepressed child psychiatric and in normal controls these variables are wholly unrelated to one another. Therefore, it is tempting to speculate that the predisposition to depressive illness in prepubertal children is associated with a particular constellation of neurotransmitter system dysfunction, which affects a variety of hypothalamic/midbrain regulatory functions in predictable fashion.

In addition, the data suggest that the onset of a depressive episode should be associated with a change in neurotransmitter systems that affects mostly REM latency, but also GH secretion to hypoglycemia, to a small degree. Furthermore, an understanding of CNS mechanisms should encompass the likely fact that some markers will be shown to change the direction of the differences upon puberty, and that others only become abnormal with increasing age. It should be apparent that the next stage of research will involve the systematic use of pharmacological probes as provocative tests with sleep, neuroendocrine, biochemical, and cell receptor variables, to determine the physiology and pathophysiology of these markers, in conjunction with familial–genetic strategies. Convergent progress in basic developmental neurosciences will be necessary for full interpretation of the findings.

CONCLUSION

The research reviewed in this chapter suggests that age and puberty factors have major effects in most psychobiological markers of depressive illness. In fact, for some of these markers, like sleep EEG, normative data should be broken down by decades during adult life span, in order to be able properly to interpret the data from patients.

What is most striking in this body of data is how prepubertal and adult work carry the potential of illuminating each other, with clear continuities of age effects can be found. If these are confirmed by ongoing adolescent studies, this probably will be very useful evidence ultimately to elucidate the neurochemical basis of the affective disorders at all ages. Without this biological grounding, attempts to organize our concepts on affect development are likely to prove ethereal.

REFERENCES

Akiskal, H. S., Rosenthal, T. L., Haykal, R. F., Lemmi, M. D., Rosenthal, R. H., & Scott-Strauss, H. (1980). Characterological depressions. *Archives of General Psychiatry, 37,* 777–783.

American Psychiatric Association (1980). *Diagnostic and statistical manual of mental disorders* (3rd ed.). Washington, DC: American Psychiatric Association.

Amsterdam, J. D., Winokur, A., Caroff, S. N., & Conn, J. (1982). The dexamethasone suppression test in outpatients with primary affective disorder and healthy control subjects. *American Journal of Psychiatry, 139,* 287–291.

Amsterdam, J. D., Winokur, A., Mendels, J., & Snyder, P. (1979). Distinguishing depressive subtypes of thyrotropin response to TRH testing. *Lancet, 2,* 904–905.

Anders, T. S., Carskadan, M., & Dement, W. C. (1980). Sleep and sleepiness in children and adolescents. *Pediatric Clinics of North America, 27,* 29–43.

Anders, T., Carskadan, M., Dement, W., & Harvey, K. (1978). Sleep habits of children and the identification of pathologically sleepy children. *Child Psychiatry and Human Development, 9,* 56–63.

Andreasen, N. C., Endicott, J., Spitzer, R. L., Winokur, G. (1977). Family history method using diagnostic criteria. *Archives of General Psychiatry, 34,* 1229–1233.

Asberg, M., Traskman, L., & Thoren, P. (1976). 5-HIAA in the cerebrospinal fluid: A biochemical suicide predictor? *Archives of General Psychiatry, 33,* 1193–1197.

Asnis, G. M., Nathan, R. S., Halbreich, U., Halpern, F., & Sachar, F. (1980). TRH tests in depression. *Lancet, 1,* 424–425.

Asnis, G. M., Sachar, E. J., Halbreich, U., Nathan, R. S., Novacenko, H., & Ostrow, L. C. (1981). Cortisol secretion in relation to age in major depression. *Psychosomatic Medicine, 43,* 235–242.

Asnis, G. M., Rabinovich, H., Ryan, N., Sachar, E. J., Nelson, B., Puig-Antich, J., & Novacenko, H. (in press). Cortisol responses to desipramine in endogenous depressives and normal controls: Preliminary findings. *Psychiatry Research.*

Avery, D., Wildshiodz, G., & Rafaelsen, O. (1982). REM latency and temperature in affective disorder before and after treatment. *Biological Psychiatry, 17,* 463–470.

Beardslee, W., Keller, M. D., & Klerman, G. L. (in press). Children of parents with affective disorder. *International Journal of Family Psychiatry.*

Beckmann, H., & Goodwin, F. K. (1980). Urinary MHPG in subgroups of depressed patients and normal controls. *Neuropsychobiology, 0,* 91–100.

Berger, M., Doerr, P., Lund, R., Bronish, T., & von Zerssen, D. (1982). Neuroendocrinological and neurophysiological studies in major depressive disorders: Are there biological markers for the endogenous subtype? *Biological Psychiatry, 17,* 1217–1242.

Berger, M., Krieg, C., & Pirke, K. M. (1982). Is the positive dexamethasone suppression test in depressed patients a consequence of weight loss? *Neuroendocrinology Letters, 4,* 177.

Berger, M., Pirke, K., Doerr, P., Krieg, C., & von Zerssen, D. (1983). Influence of weight loss on the dexamethasone suppression test. Letter. *Archives of General Psychiatry, 40,* 585–586.

Bivens, C. H., Lebovitz, H. E., & Feldman, J. M. (1973). Inhibition to hypoglycemia-induced growth hormone secretion by the serotonin antagonists cyproheptadine and methysergide. *New England Journal of Medicine, 289,* 236–239.

Bjorum, N., & Kirkegaard, C. (1979). Thyrotropin-releasing hormone test in unipolar and bipolar depression. *Lancet, 2,* 694.

Blackard, W. G., & Heidingsfelder, S. A. (1968). Adrenergic receptor control mechanism for growth hormone secretion. *Journal of Clinical Investigation, 47,* 1407–1414.

Blackard, W. G., & Waddell, C. C. (1969). Cholinergic blockade of growth hormone responsiveness to insulin hypoglycemia. *Proceedings of the Society for Experimental Biology and Medicine, 131,* 192.

Bond, P. A., Dimitrakoudi, M., Howlett, D. R., Jenner, F. (1975). Urinary excretion of the sulfate and glucuronide of 3-methoxy-4-hydroxyphenylethyleneglycol in a manic-depressive patient. *Psychological Medicine, 5,* 279–285.

Bond, P. A., Jenner, F. A., & Sampson, G. A. (1972). Daily variations of the urine content of 3-methoxy-4-hydroxyphenylglycol in two manic-depressive patients. *Psychological Medicine, 2,* 81–85.

Borkovec, T. D. (1979). Pseudo (experimental)-insomnia and idiopathic (objective) insomnia: Theoretical and therapeutic issues. *Behavioral Research and Therapy, 2,* 27–55.

Brown, G. M. (1976). Endocrine aspects of psychosocial dwarfism. In E. J. Sachar (Ed.), *Hormones, behavior and psychopathology.* New York: Raven Press.

Brown, W. A., & Qualls, C. B. (1981). Pituitary-adrenal disinhibition in depression: Marker of a subtype with characteristic clinical features and response to treatment. *Psychiatry Research, 14,* 115–128.

Bunney, W. E., Jr., Goodwin, F. K., Murphy, D. L., House, K., & Gordon, E. (1972). The "switch process" in manic-depressive illness. II. Relationship to catecholamines, REM sleep, and drugs. *Archives of General Psychiatry. 27,* 304–309.

Carlson, G. A., & Cantwell, D. (1979). A survey of depressive symptoms in child and adolescent psychiatric population. *Journal of the American Academy of Child Psychiatry,* 587–599.

Carlson, G. A., & Cantwell, D. (1980). Unmasking masked depression in children and adolescents. *American Journal of Psychiatry, 137,* 445–449.

Carlson, G. A., & Strober, M. (1978). Manic depressive illness in early adolescence. *Journal of the American Academy of Child Psychiatry, 17,* 138–153.

Carroll, B. J. (1972). The hypothalamic-pituitary-adrenal axis in depression. In B. M. Davies, B. J. Carroll, & R. M. Mowbray (Eds.), *Depressive illness: Some research studies.* Springfield, IL: Charles C Thomas.

Carroll, B. J., Curtis, G. C., & Mendels, J. (1976a). Neuroendocrine regulation in depression. I. Limbic system-adrenocortisol dysfunctions. *Archives of General Psychiatry, 33,* 1039–1044.

Carroll, B.J., Curtis, G. C., & Mendels, J. (1976b). Neuroendocrine regulation in depression. II. Discrimination of depressed from nondepressed patients. *Archives General Psychiatry, 33,* 1051–1058.

Carroll, B. J., Feinberg, M., Greden, J. F., Carroll, B., Feinberg, M., Greden, J., Tarika, J., Albala, A., Haskett, R., James, N., Kronfol, Z., Lohr, N., Steiner, M., deVigne, J. P., & Young, E. (1981). A specific laboratory test for the diagnosis of melancholia. *Archives of General Psychiatry, 38,* 15–23.

Carroll, B. J., Greden, J. F., Haskett, R., Feinberg, M., Albala, A., Martin, F., Rubin, R., Heath, B., Sharp, P., McLeod, W., & McLeod, M. (1980). Neurotransmitter studies of neuroendocrine pathology in depression. *Acta Psychiatrica Scandinavica, 61,* 183–199.

Carskadan, M. A., Harvey, K., & Dement, W. C. (1981a). Acute restriction of nocturnal sleep in children. *Perceptual and Motor Skills, 53*, 103–112.

Carskadan, M. A., Harvey, K., & Dement, W. C. (1981b). Sleep loss in young adolescents. *Sleep, 4*, 299–312.

Carskadan, M. A., Harvey, K., Duke, P., Anders, T., Citt, I., & Dement, W. (1980). Pubertal changes in daytime sleepiness. *Sleep, 2*, 435–460.

Casanueva, F. F., Grigerio, C., Cocchi, D., Cabezas-Cerrato, J., & Fernandez-Cruz, A. (1980). Growth hormone releasing effect of an enkephalin analog in the dog: Evidence for cholinergic mediation. *Endocrinology (Baltimore), 106*, 1239.

Casanueva, F. F., Villanueva, L., Cabranes, J. A., Cabezas-Cerrato, J., & Fernandez-Cruz, A. (1984). Cholinergic mediation of growth hormone secretion elicited by arganine, clonidine, and physical exercise in man. *Journal of Clinical Endocrinology and Metabolism, 59*, 526–534.

Cavagnini, F., & Perachi, M. (1971). Effect of reserpine on growth hormone response to insulin hypoglycemia and to arginine infusion in normal subjects and hypothyroid patients. *Journal of Endocrinology, 51*, 651–656.

Chambers, W. J., Puig-Antich, J., Hirsch, M., Paez, P., Ambrosini, P. J., Tabrizi, M. A., & Davies, M. (in press). The assessment of affective disordres in children and adolescents by semistructured interview: Test-retest reliability of the K-SADS-P. *Archives of General Psychiatry.*

Chambers, W. J., Puig-Antich, J., Tabrizi, M. A., & Davies, M. (1982). Psychotic symptoms in prepubertal major depressives. *Archives of General Psychiatry, 39*, 921–927.

Charney, D. S., Heninger, G. R., Sternberg, D. E., Redmond, D. E., Leckman, J. F., Mass, J. W., & Roth, R. H. (1981). Presynaptic adrenergic receptor sensitivity in depression. *Archives of General Psychiatry, 38*, 1334–1340.

Charney, D. S., Heninger, G. R., Sternberg, D. E., Hastad, K., Giddings, S., & Landis, H. (1982). Adrenergic receptor sensitivity in depression. *Archives of General Psychiatry, 39*, 290–294.

Checkley, S. A., Slade, A. P., & Shur, E. (1981). Growth hormone and other responses to clonidine in patients with endogenous depression. *British Journal of Psychiatry, 138*, 51–55.

Chihara, K., Kato, Y., Maeda, Y., Ohgo, S., & Imura, H. (1976). Suppressive effect of L-dopa on human PRL release during sleep. *Acta Endocrinologica (Copenhagen), 81*, 19–27.

Cime, E. D., Mendelson, W. B., & Loriaux, D. L. (1979). Neuroendocrine effects of haloperidol in an adolescent with Gilles de La Tourette's disease and delayed onset of puberty. *Journal of Nervous and Mental Disease, 167*, 504–507.

Coble, P. A., Kupfer, D. J., Spiker, D. G., Neil, J-F, & Shaw, D. H. (1980). EEG sleep and clinical characteristics in young primary depressives. *Sleep Research, 9*, 165.

Coble, P. A., Taska, L. S., Kupfer, D. J., Kazdin, A. E., Unis, A., & French, N. (1984). EEG sleep "abnormalities" in preadolescent boys with a diagnosis of conduct disorder. *Journal of the American Academy of Child Psychiatry, 23*, 438–447.

Coble, P. A., Taska, L. A., Ulrich, R. F., & Kupfer, D. J. (1982). Automated delta wave analysis in NREM sleep: Preliminary findings in normal health children. *Sleep Research, 11*, 80.

Cytryn, L., McKnew, D., & Bunney, W. (1980). Diagnosis of depression in children: Reassessment. *Americal Journal of Psychiatry, 137*, 22–25.

DeLeon-Jones, F. D., Maas, J. W., Dekirmenjian, H., & Fawcett, J. (1973). Urinary catecholamine metabolites during behavioral changes in a patient with manic-depressive cycles. *Science, 179*, 300–302.

DeLeon-Jones, F. D., Maas, J. W., Dekirmenjian, H., & Sanchez, J. (1975). Diagnostic subgroups of affective disorders and their urinary excretion of catecholamine metabolites. *American Journal of Psychiatry, 132*, 1141–1148.

Delitala, G., Frulio, T., Pacifico, A., & Maioli, M. (1982). Participation of cholinergic muscarinic receptors in glucagon- and arginine-mediated growth hormones, secretion in man. *Journal of Clinical Endocrinology and Metabolism, 55,* 1231.

Dewan, M. J., Pandurangi, A. K., Boucher, M. L., Levy, B., & Major, L. (1982). Abnormal dexamethasone suppression test results in chronic schizophrenic patients. *American Journal of Psychiatry, 139,* 1501–1503.

Edelstein, C. K., Roy-Byrne, P., Fawzy, F., & Dornfeld, L. (1983). Effects of weight loss on the dexamethasone suppression test. *American Journal of Psychiatry, 140,* 338–341.

Extein, I., Pottash, A. L. C., & Gold, M. S. (1980). TRH test in depression. *New England Journal of Medicine, 302,* 923–924.

Extein, I., Pottash, A. L. C., & Gold, M. S. (1981). The thyrotropin-releasing hormone test in the diagnosis of unipolar depression. *Psychiatry Research, 5,* 311–316.

Finkelstein, J. W., Roffwarg, H. P., Boyar, R. M., Kream, J., & Hellman, L. (1972). Age related change in the 24 hour spontaneous secretion of growth hormone. *Journal of Clinical Endocrinology and Metabolism, 35,* 665–670.

Frantz, A. G., & Rabkin, M. T. (1965). Effects of estrogen and sex difference on secretion of human growth hormone. *Journal of Clinical Endocrinology and Metabolism, 25,* 1470–1480.

Frasier, S. D., Hilburn, J. M., & Matthews, N. L. (1967). The serum growth hormone response to hypoglycemia in dwarfism. *Journal of Pediatrics, 71,* 625–638.

Frazier, A. (1975). Adrenergic responses in depression: Implications for a receptor defect. In J. Mendels (Ed.), *The psychobiology of depression.* New York: Spectrum.

Garcia-Sevilla, J. A., Hollingsworth, P. J., & Smith, C. B. (1980). ³H-Clonidine and ³H-yohimbine bind to alpha 2 receptors in human platelets, abstracted. *Pharmacologist, 22,* 284.

Garcia-Sevilla, J. A., Hollingsworth, P. H., & Smith, C. B., (1980). Alpha 2 adrenoreceptors on human platelets: Selective labelling by [³H]clonidine and [³H]yohimbine and competitive inhibition by antidepressant drugs. *European Journal of Pharmacology* (to be published).

Garcia-Sevilla, J. A., Zis, A. P., Hollingsworth, P. J., Greden, J., & Smith C. (1981). Platelet-adrenergic receptors in major depressive disorder. *Archives of General Psychiatry, 38,* 1327–1333.

Geller, B., Perel, H. M., Knitter, E. F., Lycak, H., & Farook, Z. (1983). Nortriptyline in major depressive disorder in children: Response, steady state plasma levels, predictive kinetics and pharmacokinetics. *Psychopharmacology Bulletin, 19,* 62–65.

Gershon, E. S., Bunney, W. E., Jr., Leckman, J. F., van Eerdewegh, M., & Debauche, B. A. (1976). The inheritance of affective disorders: A review of data and hypotheses. *Behavior Genetics,* 227–261.

Gershon, E. S., Hanovit, J., Guroff, J. J., Dibble, E., Leckman, J., Sceery, W., Targum, S., Nurnburger, J., Goldin, L., & Bunney, W. (1982). A family study of schizoaffective, bipolar I, bipolar II, unipolar, and normal control probands. *Archives of General Psychiatry, 39,* 1157–1167.

Gershon, E. S., McKnew, D., Cytryn, J., *et al.* (1900). Diagnosis in school-age children of bipolar affective disorder patients and normal controls. Unpublished manuscript.

Gershon, E. S., Targum, S. D., Kessler, L. R., Mazure, C. M., & Bunney, W. E. (1977). Genetic studies and biologic strategies in the affective disorders. *Progress in Medical Genetics, 2.*

Gibbons, M. L. (1964). Cortisol secretion rate in depressive illness. *Archives of General Psychiatry, 10,* 572–575.

Gillin, J. C. (1977). Electroencephalographic sleep alterations during the switch process. *Archives of Internal Medicine, 87,* 324–325.

Gillin, J. C., Duncan, W., Pettigrew, K. D., Frankel, B., & Snyder, F. Successful separation of depressed, normal and insomniac subjects by EEG sleep data. *Archives of General Psychiatry, 36,* 85–90.

Gillin, J. C., Sitaram, N., & Duncan, W. C., (1979). Muscarinic supersensitivity: A possible model for the sleep disturbance of primary depression? *Psychiatry Research, 1*, 17–22.

Gillin, J. C., Sitaram, N., Mendelson, W. B., & Wyatt, R. (1978). Physostigmine alters onset but not duration of REM sleep in man. *Psychopharmacology, 58*, 111–113.

Gillin, J. C., & Wyatt, R. J. (1975). Schizophrenia: Perchance a dream. *International Review of Neurobiology, 17*, 297–342.

Gold, M. S., Pottash, A. L. C., Extein, I., Martin, D., Howard, E., Mueller, E., & Sweeney, D. (1981). The TRH test in the diagnosis of major and minor depressions. *Psychoneuroendocrinology, 6*, 159–169.

Gold, M. S., Pottash, A. L. C., Ryan, N., Sweeney, D., Davies, R., & Martin, D. (1980). TRH-induced TSH response in unipolar, bipolar, and secondary depressions: Possible utility in clinical assessment and differential diagnosis. *Psychoneuroendocrinology, 5*, 147–155.

Goldberg, I. K. (1980). Dexamethasone suppression tests in depression and response to treatment. *Lancet, 1*, 92.

Goldman-Rabik, P. S., & Brown, R. M. (1982). Post-natal development of monoamine content and synthesis in the cerebral cortex of the rhesus monkeys. *Brain Research, 256*, 339–349.

Greden, J. F., Albala, A. A., Haskett, R. F., James, N., Goodman, L., Steiner, M., & Carroll, B. (1980). Normalization of dexamethasone suppression tests: A probable index of recovery among endogenous depressives. *Biological Psychiatry, 15*, 449–458.

Greden, J. F., Gardner, R., King, D., Grunhaus, L., Carroll, B., & Kronfol, Z. (1983). Dexamethasone suppression tests in antidepressant treatment of melancholia. *Archives of General Psychiatry, 40*, 493–500.

Grégoire, F., Branman, G., DeBuck, R., & Corvilain, J. (1977). Hormone release in depressed patients before and after recovery. *Psychoneuroendocrinology, 2*, 303–312.

Gruen, P. H., Sachar, E. J., Altman, N., & Sassin, J. (1975). Growth hormone responses to hypoglycemia in postmenopausal depressed women. *Archives of General Psychiatry, 32*, 31–33.

Halbreich, U., Sachar, E. J., Asnis, G. M., Quitkin, F., Nathan, R. S., Halpern, F., & Klein, D. (1982). Growth hormone response to dextroamphetamine in depressed patients and normal subjects. *Archives of General Psychiatry, 39*, 189–192.

Halbreich, U., Zumoff, B., Kream, J., & Fukushima, D. K. (1982). The mean 1300–1600 h plasma cortisol concentration as a diagnostic test for hypercortisolism. *Journal of Clinical Endocrinology and Metabolism, 54*, 1262–1264.

Harrison, W. M., Cooper, T. B., Stewart, J. W., Quitkin, F., McGrath, P., Liebowicz, M., Rabkin, J., Markowitz, J., & Klein, D. (1984). The tyramine challenge test as a marker for melancholia. *Archives of General Psychiatry, 41*, 681–687.

Hauri, P., Chernik, D., Hawkins, D., & Mendels, J. (1974). Sleep of depressed patients in remission. *Archives of General Psychiatry, 31*, 386–391.

Herjanic, B., Herjanic, M., Brown, F. et al. (1975). Are children reliable reporters? *Journal of the Association of Child Psychology, 3*, 41–48.

Hollister, L. E., Kenneth, L. D., Berger, P. A. (1976). Pituitary response to thyrotropin-releasing hormone in depression. *Archives of General Psychiatry, 33*, 1393–1396.

Janowsky, D. C., El-Yousef, M. K., & David, J. M. (1972). A cholinergic-adrenergic hypothesis of mania and depression. *Lancet, 2*, 632–635.

Jarrett, D. B., Coble, P. A., & Kupfer, D. J. (1983). Reduced cortisol latency in depressive illness. *Archives of General Psychiatry, 40*, 506–511.

Jimerson, D. C., Inssel, T. R., Reus, V. I., & Kopin, I. (1983). Increased plasms MHPG in dexamethasone-resistant depressed patients. *Archives of General Psychiatry, 40*, 173–180.

Joss, E. E., Zuppinger, K. A., & Kahnd, G. R. (1970). Diagnostic procedures in hypopituitary dwarfism. I. Evaluation of growth hormone deficiency. *Helvetica Paediatrica Acta, 25*, 371–381.

Kaplan, S. L., Abrams, C. A. L., Bell, J. J., Conte, F. A., & Grumbach, M. M. (1968). Growth and growth hormone. I. Changes in serum level of growth hormone following hypoglycemia in 134 children with growth retardation. *Pediatric Research, 2,* 43–63.

Kathol, R. G., Winokur, G., Sherman, B. M., Lewis, D., & Schlesser, M. (1984). Provocative endocrine testing in recovered depressives. *Psychoneuroendocrinology, 9,* 57–68.

Keller, M. B., Lavori, P. W., Lewis, C. E., & Klerman, G. (1984). Predictors of relapse in major depressive disorder. *Journal of the American Medical Association, 250,* 3299–3304.

Keller, M. B., Shapiro, R. W., Lavori, P. W., & Wolfe, N. (1982a). Recovery in major depressive disorder. *Archives of General Psychiatry, 39,* 905–910.

Keller, M. B., Shapiro, R. W., Lavori, P. W., & Wolfe, N. (1982b). Relapse in major depressive disorder. *Archives of General Psychiatry, 39,* 911–920.

Kirkegaard, C., Bjorum, N., Cohn, D., Faber, J., Lauridsen, U., & Nerup, J. (1977). Studies on the influence of biogenic amines and psychoactive drugs on the prognostic value of the TRH stimulation test in endogenous depression. *Psychoneuroendocrinology, 2,* 131–136.

Kirkegaard, C., Bjorum, N., Cohn, D., & Lauridsen, U. (1978). Thyrotropin-releasing hormone stimulation test in manic depressive illness. *Archives of General Psychiatry, 35,* 1017–1021.

Kirkegaard, C., Norlem, N., Lauridsen, U. B., Bjorum, N., & Christiansen, C. (1975). Protirelin stimulation test and thyroid function during treatment of depression. *Archives of General Psychiatry, 32,* 1115–1118.

Koslow, S. H., Maas, J. W., Bowden, C. L., Davis, J., Hanin, I., & Javaad, J. (1983). CSF and urinary biogemic amines and metabolites in depression and mania: A controlled univariate analysis. *Archives of General Psychiatry, 40,* 999–1010.

Koslow, S. H., Stokes, P. E., Mendels, J., Ramsey, A., & Casper, R. (1982). Insulin tolerance test: Human growth hormone response and insulin resistance in primary unipolar depressed bipolar depressed and control subjects. *Psychological Medicine, 12,* 45–55.

Kovacs, M., Feinberg, T. L., Crouse-Novak, M. A., Paulauskas, S., & Finkelstein, R. (1984a). Depressive disorders in childhood. I. A longitudinal prospective study of characteristics and recovery. *Archives of General Psychiatry, 41,* 229–239.

Kovacs, M., Feinberg, T. L., Crouse-Novak, M. A., Paulauskas, S., Pollock, M., & Finkelstein, R. (1984b). Depressive disorders in childhood. II. A longitudinal study of the risk for a subsequent major depression. *Archives of General Psychiatry, 41,* 643–649.

Kripke, D. F., (1984). Does a weak REM-NonREM oscillator cause depression? In R.M. Post & J. C. Ballenger (Eds.), *Neurobiology of mood disorders.* Baltimore: Williams & Wilkins.

Kupfer, D. (1976). REM latency: A psychobiological marker for primary depressive disease. *Biological Psychiatry, 11,* 159–174.

Kupfer, D., & Foster, F. G. (1973). Sleep and activity in a psychotic depression. *Journal of Nervous and Mental Disease, 156,* 341–348.

Kupfer, D., & Foster, F. G. (1979). EEG sleep and depression. In R. L. Williams & I. Karacan (Eds.), *Sleep disorders: Diagnosis and treatment* (pp. 163–203). New York: Wiley.

Kuperman, S., & Stewart, M. A. (1979). The diagnosis of depression in children. *Journal of Affective Disorders, 1,* 213–217.

Laakman, G. (1979). Neuroendocrine differences between endogenous and neurotic depression as seen in stimulation of growth hormone secretion. In E. E. Miller & A. Agnoli (Eds.), *Neuroendocrine correlates in neurology and psychiatry.* New York: North Holland.

Lahmeyer, H. W., Poznanski, E. O., & Bellur, S. N. (1983). EEG sleep in depressed adolescents. *American Journal of Psychiatry, 140,* 1150–1153.

Langer, G., Heinze, G., Rein, B., & Matussek, N. (1976). Reduced growth hormone response to amphetamine in endogenous depressive patients. *Archives of General Psychiatry, 33,* 1471–1475.

Lewis, D. A., Kathol, R. G., Sherman, B. M., Winokur, G., & Schlesser, M. (1983). Differentiation of depressive subtypes of insulin insensitivity in the recovered phase. *Archives of General Psychiatry, 40,* 167–172.

Lidor, H. G., & Molliver, M. E. (1982). An immunohistochemical study of serotonin neuron development in the rat: Ascending pathways and terminal fields. *Brain Research Bulletin, 8,* 389–340.

Livingston, R., Reis, C.J., & Ringdahl, I. C. (1984). Abnormal dexamethasone suppression test results in depressed and nondepressed children. *American Journal of Psychiatry, 141,* 106–107.

Loosen, P. T., & Prange, A. L., Jr. (1980). TRH test in psychiatric patients. *New England Journal of Medicine, 303,* 224–225.

Loosen, P. T., Prange, A. J., Jr., Wilson, I. C., Lara, P. P., & Pettus, C. (1977). Thyroid stimulating hormone response after thyrotropin-releasing hormone in depressed, schizophrenic and normal woman. *Psychoneuroendocrinology, 2,* 137–148.

Lucke, G., & Glick, S. M. (1971). Experimental modification of the sleep induced peak of growth hormone secretion. *Journal of Clinical Endocrinology and Metabolism, 32,* 729–736.

Mace, J. W., Gotlin, R. W., & Beck, P. (1972). Sleep related human growth hormone release: A test of physiological growth hormone secretion in children. *Journal of Clinical Endocrinology and Metabolism, 34,* 339–341.

Matussek, N. (1979). Neuroendocrinological studies in affective disorders. In M. Schou & E. Stromgren (Eds.), *Origin, prevention, and treatment of affective disorders.* New York: Academic Press.

Matussek, N., Ackenheil, M., Hippius, H., Müller, F., Schröder, H., Schultes, H., & Wasilewski, B. (1980). Effect of clonidine on growth hormone release in psychiatric patients and controls. *Psychiatry Research, 2,* 24–36.

Meltzer, H. Y., Arora, R. C., Baber, R., & Tricou, B. (1981). Serotonin uptake in blood platelets of psychiatric patients. *Archives of General Psychiatry, 38,* 1322–1326.

Meltzer, H. Y., & Fang, V. S. (1983). Cortisol determination and the dexamethasone suppression test. *Archives of General Psychiatry, 40,* 501–505.

Meltzer, H. Y., Perline, R., Tricou, B. J., Lowy, M., & Robertson, A. (1984). Effect of 5-hydroxytryptophan on serum cortisol levels in major affective disorders. II. Relation to suicide, psychosis, and depressive symptoms. *Archives of General Psychiatry, 41,* 379–390.

Meltzer, H. Y., Unberkoman-Wilta, B., Robertson, A., Tricou, B., Lowy, M., & Perline, R. (1984). Effect of 5-hydroxytryptophan on serum cortisol levels in major affective disorders. I. Enhanced responses in depression and mania. *Archives of General Psychiatry, 41,* 366–378.

Mendels, J., & Chernik, D. A. (1973). A follow-up study of the sleep patterns of three unipolar depressed patients. *Sleep Research, 1,* 142.

Mendels, J., & Chernik, D. A., (1975). Sleep changes in affective illness. In F. F. Flach & S. C. Draghi (Eds.), *The nature and treatment of depression.* New York: Wiley.

Mendelson, W. B. (1982). The clock and the blue guitar: Studies of human growth hormone secretion in sleep and waking. *International Review of Neurobiology, 23,* 367–389.

Mendelson, W. B., Gillin, J. C., Wyatt, R. J. (1977). *Human sleep and its disorders* (Chap. 7). New York: Plenum Press.

Mendelson, W. B., Jacobs, L. S., Gillin, J. C., & Wyatt, R. (1979). The regulation of insulin induced and sleep related human growth hormone secretion: A review. *Psychoneuroendocrinology, 4,* 341–350.

Mendelson, W. B., Jacobs, L. S., Reichman, J. D., Othmer, E., Cryer, P. E., Trivedi, B., & Daughaday, W.H. (1975). Methysergide: Suppression of sleep related prolactin secretion and enhancement of sleep related growth hormone secretion. *Journal of Clinical Investigation, 56,* 690–697.

Mendelson, W. B., Lantigua, R. A., Wyatt, R. J., Gillin, J. C., & Jacobs, L. S. (1981). Piperidine enhances sleep related and insulin induced growth hormone secretion: Further evidence for a cholinergic secretory mechanism. *Journal of Clinical Endocrinology and Metabolism, 52,* 409–415.

Mendelson, W. B., Sitaram, N., Wyatt, R. J., Gillin, J. C., & Jacobs, L. S. (1978). Methoscopolamine inhibition of sleep related growth hormone secretion. *Journal of Clinical Investigation, 61,* 1683–1690.

Mendelwicz, J., Linowski, P., & Brauman, H. (1979). TSH responses to TRH in women with unipolar and bipolar depression. *Lancet, 2,* 1079–1080.

Merimee, T. J., & Fineberg, S. E. (1971). Studies of sex based variation of human growth hormone secretion. *Journal of Clinical Endocrinology and Metabolism, 33,* 896–902.

Minde, G., Weiss, G., & Mendelson, M. (1972). A five-year follow-up study of 91 hyperactive school children. *Journal of the American Academy of Child Psychiatry, 11,* 595–610.

Money, J., Annecillo, C., & Werlwas, J. (1976). Hormonal and behavioral reversals in hyposomatotropic dwarfism. In E. J. Sachar (Ed.), *Hormones, behavior and psychopathology.* New York: Raven Press.

Mueller, P. S., Heninger, G. R., & MacDonald, R. K. (1972). Studies on glucose utilization and insulin sensitivity in affective disorders. In T. A. Williams, M. M. Katz, & J. A. Shield (Eds.), *Recent advances in psychobiology of depressive illnesses.* Washington, DC: U. S. Dept. of Health, Education, and Welfare.

Muscettola, G., Potter, W. Z., Pickar, D., & Goodwin, F. (1984). Urinary 3-methoxy-4-hydroxyphenylglycol and major affective disorders. *Archives of General Psychiatry, 41,* 337–346.

Nadi, N. S., Nurnberger, J. I., & Gershon, E. S. (1984). Muscarinic cholinergic receptors on skin fibroblasts in familial affective disorder. *New England Journal of Medicine. 311,* 225–230.

Nurnberger, J. I., & Gershon, E. S. (1984). Genetics of affective disorders. In R. M. Post & J. C. Ballenger (Eds.), *Neurobiology of mood disorders.* Baltimore, Williams & Wilkins.

Orvaschel, H., Puig-Antich, J., Chambers, W. J., Tabrizi, M. A., & Johnson, R. (1982). Retrospective assessment of child psychopathology with the Kiddie-SADS-E. *Journal of the American Academy of Child Psychiatry, 31,* 392–397.

Parker, D. C., Rossman, L. G., Pakary, A. E., Hershman, J. M., Kripke, D. F., & Gibson, W. (1981). Endocrine rhythms across reversal sleep-wake cycles. In L. C. Johnson, W. P. Coloquhoun, & D. I. Tepas (Eds.), *Biological rhythms, sleep, and shiftwork.* New York: Spectrum Books.

Paul, S. M., Rehavi, M., Rice, K. et al. (1981). Does high affinity [^{3}H]imipramine binding label serotonin reuptake sites in brain and platelet? *Life Science, 28,* 2253–2260.

Paul, S. M., Rehavi, M., Skolnick, P., Ballenger, J., & Goodwin, F. (1981). Depressed patients have decreased binding of triatiated imipramine to platelet serotonin "Transporter." *Archives of General Psychiatry, 38,* 1315–1317.

Perris, C. (1974). The genetics of affective disorders. In J. Mendels (Ed.), *Biological psychiatry.* New York: Wiley.

Pettegrew, J. W., Woessner, D. E., Minshew, N. J., & Glonek, T. (1984). Sodium-23NMR analysis of human whole blood, erythrocytes, and plasma. Chemical shift, spin relaxation, and intracellular sodium concentration studies. *Journal of Magnetic Resonance, 57,* 185–196.

Piaget, J., & Inhelder, B. (1969). *The psychology of the child.* New York: Basic Books.

Post, R. M., & Ballenger, J. C. (Eds.). (1984). *Neurobiology of mood disorders.* Baltimore: Williams & Wilkins.

Poznanski, E. O. (1982). The clinical characteristics of childhood depression. In L. Grinspoon (Ed.), *Psychiatry '82 annual review.* Washington, DC: American Psychiatric Association.

Poznanski, E. D., Carroll, B. J., Banegas, M. C., Sook, S. C., & Grossman, J. A. (1982). The dexamethasone suppression test in prepubertal depressed children. *American Journal of Psychiatry, 139,* 321–324.

Poznanski, E. O., Grossman, J. A., Buchsbaum, Y., Banegas, M., Freeman, L., & Gibbons, R. (1984). Preliminary studies of the reliability and validity of the Children's Depression Rating Scale. Journal of the Academy of Child Psychiatry, 23, 191–197.

Puig-Antich, J. (1980). Affective disorders in childhood: A review and perspective. In B. Blinder (Ed.), Psychiatric clinics of North America (Vol. 3). Philadelphia: Saunders.

Puig-Antich, J., Blau, S., Marx, N., Greenhill, L. L., & Chambers, W. (1978). Prepubertal major depressive disorder. A pilot study. Journal of the American Academy of Child Psychiatry, 17, 695–707.

Puig-Antich, J., Davies, M., Novacenko, H., Tabrizi, M. A., Ambrosini, P., Goetz, R., Bianca, J., & Sachar, E. J. (1984). Growth hormone secretion in prepubertal major depressive children. III. Response to insulin induced hypoglycemia in a drug-free, fully recovered clinical state. Archives of General Psychiatry, 41(5), 471–475.

Puig-Antich, J., Goetz, R., Davies, M., Fein, M., Hanlon, C., Chambers, W. J., Tabrizi, M. A., Sachar, E.J., & Weitzman, E. D. (1984). Growth hormone secretion in prepubertal major depressive children. II. Sleep related plasma concentrations during a depressive episode. Archives of General Psychiatry, 41, 463–466.

Puig-Antich, J., Goetz, R., Davies, M., Tabrizi, M. A., Novacenko, H., Hanlon, C., Sachar, E. J., & Weitzman, E. D. (1984). Growth hormone secretion in prepubertal major depressive children. IV. Sleep related plasma concentrations in a drug-free fully recovered clinical state. Archives of General Psychiatry, 41, 479–483.

Puig-Antich, J., Goetz, D., Davies, M., Kaplan, T., Davies, S., Ostrow, L., & Asmis, L. (1982). A controlled family history study of prepubertal major depressive disorder. Paper presented at the American Academy of Child Psychiatry.

Puig-Antich, J., Goetz, D., Davies, M. (1983). A controlled family history study of adolescent major depressive disorder. Paper presented at the American Academy of Child Psychiatry.

Puig-Antich, J., Goetz, R., Hanlon, C., Tabrizi, M. A., Davies, M., & Weitzman, E. (1982). Sleep architecture and REM sleep measures in prepubertal major depressives during an episode. Archives of General Psychiatry, 39, 932–939.

Puig-Antich, J., Goetz, R., Hanlon, C., Tabrizi, M. A., Davies, M., & Weitzman, E. (1983). Sleep architecture and REM sleep measures in prepubertal major depressives: Studies during recovery from a major depressive episode in a drug free state. Archives of General Psychiatry, 40, 187–192.

Puig-Antich, J., Novacenko, H., Davies, M., Chambers, W. J., Tabrizi, M. A., Krawiec, V., Ambrosini, P. J., & Sachar, E. J. (1984). Growth hormone secretion in prepubertal major depressive children. I. Sleep related plasma concentrations during a depressive episode. Archives of General Psychiatry, 41, 455–460.

Puig-Antich, J., Tabrizi, M. A., Davies, M., Chambers, W., Halpern, F., & Sachar, E. J. (1981). Prepubertal endogenous major depressives hyposecrete growth hormone in response to insulin-induced hypoglycemia. Journal of Biological Psychiatry, 16, 801–818.

Rabkin, J., Quitkin, F., Stewart, J., McGrath, P., & Puig-Antich, J. (1983). Dexamethasone suppression test with mild to moderately depressed outpatients. American Journal of Psychiatry, 140, 926–928.

Rappoport, J. L., Buchsbaum, M. S., Weingartner, H., Zahn, T., Ludlow, C., & Mikkelsen, E. (1980). Dextro-amphetamine: Its cognitive and behavioral effects in hyperactive boys and normal men. Archives of General Psychiatry, 37, 933–943.

Robins, D. R., Alessi, N. E., Yanchyshyn, G. W., & Colfer, M. (1982). Preliminary report on the dexamethasone suppression test in adolescents. American Journal of Psychiatry, 139, 942–943.

Rubin, R. T., Govin, P. R., Arenander, A. T., & Poland, R. (1973). Human growth hormone release during sleep following prolonged flurazepam administration. Research Communications in Chemical Pathology and Pharmacology, 6, 331–334.

Rubinow, D. R., Post, R. M., Gold, P. W., Ballenger, J. C., & Wolff, E. (1984). The relationship between cortisol and clinical phenomenology of affective illness. In R. M. Post & J. C. Ballenger (Eds.), *Neurobiology of mood disorders*. Baltimore: Williams & Wilkins.

Rutter, M. (1979). *Changing youth in a changing society*. London: Nuffield Provincial Hospitals Trust.

Rutter, M., Tizard, J., & Whitmore, K. (Eds.). (1970). *Education, health and behavior: Psychological and medical study of childhood development*. London: Longman.

Sabelli, H. C., Fawcett, J., Gusovsky, F., Javaid, J., Edwards, J., & Jeffries, H. (1983). Urinary phenyl acetate: A diagnostic test for depression? *Science, 220*, 1187–1188.

Sachar, E. J. (1975). Neuroendocrine abnormalities in depressive illness. In E. J. Sachar (Ed.), *Topics in psychoendocrinology*. New York: Grune & Stratton.

Sachar, E. J., Altman, N., Gruen, P. H., Glassman, A., Halpern, F., & Sassin, J. (1975). Human growth hormone responses to levodopa. *Archives of General Psychiatry, 32*, 502–503.

Sachar, E. J., Asnis, G. M., Nathan, R. S., Halbreich, U., Tabrizi, M. A., & Halpern, F. (1980). Dextroamphetamine and cortisol in depression. *Archives of General Psychiatry, 37*, 755–757.

Sachar, E. J., Finkelstein, J., & Hellman, L. (1971). Growth hormone responses in depressive illness: Response to insulin tolerance test. *Archives of General Psychiatry, 25*, 263–269.

Sachar, E. J., Frantz, A. G., Altman, N., & Sassin, J. (1973). Growth hormone and prolactin in unipolar and bipolar depressed patients: responses to hypoglycemia and L-dopa. *American Journal of Psychiatry, 130*, 1362–1367.

Sachar, E. J., Halbreich, U., Asnis, G. M., Nathan, R. S., Halpern, F. S., & Ostrow, L. (1981). Paradoxical cortisol responses to dextroamphetamine in endogenous depression. *Archives of General Psychiatry, 38*, 1113–1117.

Sachar, E. J., Hellman, L., Roffwarg, H. P., Halpern, F. S., Fukushima, D. K., & Gallagher, R. F. (1973). Disrupted 24-hour patterns of cortisol secretion in psychotic depression. *Archives of General Psychiatry, 28*, 19–24.

Sachar, E. J., Kanter, S. S., Buie, D., Engle, R., & Mehlman, R. (1970). Psychoendocrinology of ego disintegration. *American Journal of Psychiatry, 126*, 1067–1078.

Sachar, E. J., Puig-Antich, J., Ryan, N., Asnis, G. M., Rabinovich, H., Davies, M., & Halpern, F. S. (1985). Three tests of cortisol secretion in adult endogenous depressives. *Acta Psychiatrica Scandinavica, 71*, 1–8.

Sagales, T., Erill, S., & Domino, E. F. (1975). Effects of repeated doses of scopolamine on the electroencephalographic stages of sleep in normal volunteers. *Clinical Pharmacology and Therapeutics, 18*, 717–732.

Schildkraut, J. J. (1965). The catecholamine hypothesis of affective disorders: A review of supporting evidence. *American Journal of Psychiatry, 122*, 509–522.

Schildkraut, J. J., Orsulak, P. J., LaBrie, R. A., Schatzberg, A. F., Gudeman, J. E., O'Cole, J., & Rohde, W. A., (1978). Toward a biochemical classification of depressive disorders. I. Application of multivariate discriminant function analysis to data on urinary catecholamines and metabolites. *Archives of General Psychiatry, 35*, 1436–1439.

Schildkraut, J. J., Orsulak, P. J., Schatzberg, A. F., Gudeman, J. E., O'Cole, J., Rohde, W. A., & LaBrie, R. A., (1978). Toward a biochemical classification of depressive disorders. I. Differences in urinary MHPG and other catecholamine metabolites in clinically defined subtypes of depressions. *Archives of General Psychiatry, 35*, 1427–1433.

Schlesser, M. A., Winokur, G., & Sherman, B. M. (1980). Hypothalamic-pituitary-adrenal axis activity in depressive illness: Its relationship to classification. *Archives of General Psychiatry, 37*, 737–743.

Schultz, H., & Trojan, B. (1979). A comparison of eye movement density in normal subjects and in depressed patients before and after remission. *Sleep Research, 8*, 49.

Shelton, D. L., Nadler, J. V., & Cotman, C. W. (1979). Development of high affinity choline uptake and associated acetylcholine synthesis in the rat fuscia dentata. *Brain Research,* 164, 263–275.

Sherman, B., Pfohl, B., & Winokur, G. (1984). Circadian analysis of plasma cortisol levels before and after dexamethasone administration in depressed patients. *Archives of General Psychiatry,* 41, 271–278.

Siefert, W. E., Foxx, J. L., & Butler, I. J. (1980). Age effect on dopamine and serotonin metabolite levels in CSF. *Annals of Neurology,* 8, 38–42.

Siever, L. J., Uhde, T. W., Jimerson, D. C., Post, R. M., Lake, C. R., & Murphy, D. L. (1984). Plasma cortisol responses to clonidine in depressed patients and controls. *Archives of General Psychiatry,* 41, 63–71.

Siever, L. J., Uhde, T. W., Silberman, E. K., Jimerson, D. C., Aloi, J. A., Post, R. M., & Murphy, D. L. (1982). The growth hormone response to clinidine as a probe of noradrenergic receptor responsiveness in affective disorder patients and controls. *Psychiatry Research,* 6, 171–183.

Sitaram, B., Wyatt, R. J., Dawson, S., & Gillin, J. C. (1976). REM sleep induction by physostigmine infusion in normal volunteers. *Science,* 191, 1281–1283.

Sitaram, N., Nurmberger, J. I., Gershon, E. S., & Gillin, J. C. (1980). Faster cholinergic REM sleep induction in euthymic patients with primary affective illness. *Science,* 208, 200–201.

Sitaram, N., Nurnberger, J. I., Gershon, E. S., & Gillin, J. C. (1982). Cholinergic regulation of mood and REM sleep: A potential model and marker for vulnerability to depression. *American Journal of Psychiatry,* 139, 571–576.

Sitaram, N., Mendelson, W. B., Wyatt, R. J., & Gillin, J. C. (1977). Time-dependent REM sleep induction and arousal by physostigmine on normal human sleep. *Brain Research,* 122, 562–567.

Sitaram, N., Moore, A. M., & Gillin, J. C. (1978a). The cholinergic induction of dreaming in man. *Archives of General Psychiatry,* 35, 1239–1243.

Sitaram, N., Moore, A. M., & Gillin, J. C. (1978b). Induction and resetting of REM sleep rhythm in normal man by Arecholine: Blockade by scopolamine. *Sleep,* 1, 83–90.

Sitaram, N., Moore, A. M., & Gillin, J. C. (1979). Scopolamine induced muscarinic supersensitivity in man: Changes in sleep. *Psychiatry Research,* 1, 9–16.

Sitaram, N., Gillin, J. C., & Bunney, W. E. (1984). Cholinergic and catacholaminergic receptor sensitivity in affective illness: Strategy and theory. In R. M. Post & J. C. Ballenger (Eds.), *Neurobiology of mood disorders.* Baltimore: Williams & Wilkins.

Smythe, G. A., & Lazarus, L. (1974). Suppression of human growth hormone secretion by melatonin and cyproheptadine. *Journal of Clinical Investigation,* 54, 116–121.

Stewart, J. W., Quitkin, F., McGrath, P. J., Liebowitz, M. R., Harrison, W., Rabkin, J. G., Novacen, K. H., Puig-Antich, J., & Asnis, G. M. (1984). Cortisol response to dextroamphetamine stimulation in depressed outpatients. *Psychiatry Research,* 12, 195–206.

Stewart, M., Pitts, F., Craig, A., Dieruf, W. (1966). The hyperactive child syndrome. *American Journal of Orthopsychiatry,* 36, 861–867.

Stokes, P. E., Stoll, P. M., Koslow, S. H., Maas, J. W., Davis, J. M., Swann, A. C., & Robins, E. (1984). Pretreatment DST and hypothalamic-pituitary-adrenocortical function in depressed patients and comparison groups. *Archives of General Psychiatry,* 41, 257–270.

Stokes, P. E., Stoll, P. M., Mattson, M. R., & Sollod, R. N. (1976). Diagnosis and psychopathology in psychiatric patients resistant to dexamethasone. E. J. Sachar (Ed.), *Hormones, behavior and psychopathology.* New York: Raven Press.

Strober, M. (1983). *Follow-up of affective disorder patients.* Paper presented at the annual meeting of the American Psychiatric Association, New York.

Strober, M., Burroughs, J., Salkin, B., et al. (in press). Ancestral secondary cases of psychiatric illness in adolescents with mania, depression, schizophrenia and conduct disorder. *Biological Psychiatry.*

Strober, M., & Carlson, G. (1982). Bipolar illness in adolescent with major depression. *Archives of General Psychiatry, 39,* 549–558.

Strober, M., Green, J., & Carlson, G. (1982). Phenomenology and subtypes of major depressive disorder in adolescents. *Journal of Affective Disorder, 3,* 281–290.

Takahashi, Y., Kipais, D. M., & Daughaday, W. H. (1968). Growth hormone secretion during sleep. *Journal of Clinical Investigation, 47,* 2079–2090.

Targum, S., Chastek, C., & Sullivan, A. (1981). Dexamethasone suppression test in prepubertal conduct disorder. *Psychiatric Research, 5,* 107–108.

Traskman, L., Asberg, M., Bertilsson, L., Lars, S., & Ostranad, M. D. (1981). Monoamine metabolites in CSF and suicidal behavior. *Archives of General Psychiatry, 38,* 631–641.

Uhde, T. W., Siever, L. J., & Post, R. M. (1984). Clonidine: Acute challenge and clinical trial paradigms for the investigation and treatment of anxiety disorders, affective illness, and pain syndromes. In R. M. Post & J. C. Ballenger (Eds.), *Neurobiology of mood disorders.* Baltimore: Williams & Wilkins.

Ulrich, R., Shaw, D. H., & Kupfer, D. J. (1980). The effects of aging on sleep. *Sleep, 3,* 31–40.

Vogel, G. W., Vogel, F., McAbee, R. S., & Thurmond, A. J. (1980). Improvement of depression by REM sleep deprivation: New findings and a theory. Archives of General Psychiatry, 37, 247–253.

Walsh, B. T. (1980). The endocrinology of anorexia nervosa. In E. J. Sachar (Ed.), *Psychiatric clinics of North America* (Vol. 3). Philadelphia: Saunders.

Wehr, T. A. (1984). Biological rhythms and manic depressive illness. In R. M. Post & J. C. Ballenger (Eds.), *Neurobiology of mood disorders.* Baltimore: Williams & Wilkins.

Weinberg, W. A., Rutman, J., Sullivan, L., Penick, E. C., & Dietz, S. G. (1973). Depression in children referred to an educational diagnostic center: Diagnosis and treatment. *Journal of Pediatrics, 83,* 1065–1072.

Weiss, G., Minde, K., Werry, J., Douglas V., & Nemeth, E. (1971). Studies on the hyperactive child. VIII. Five-year follow-up. *Archives of General Psychiatry, 24,* 409–414.

Weissman, M. M., Gershon, E. S., Kidd, K. K., Brusoff, B. A., Leckman, J. F., Dibble, E., Hamovit, J., Thompson, W. D., Pauls, D. L., & Guroff, J. J. (1984). Psychiatric disorders in the relatives of probands with affective disorders. *Archives of General Psychiatry, 41,* 13–21.

Weissman, M. M., Kidd, K. K., & Prusoff, B. A. (1982). Variability in rates of affective disorders in relatives of depressed and normal probands. *Archives of General Psychiatry, 39,* 1397–1406.

Weissman, M. M., Leckman, J. F., Merikangas, K. R., et al. (in press). Depression and anxiety disorders in the children (ages 6–17) of parents with depression and anxiety disorders. Yale University School of Medicine. *Archives of General Psychiatry.*

Weissman, M. M., Wickramaratne, P., Merikangas, K. R., et al. (in press). Onset of major depression in early adulthood: Increased familial loading and specificity. *Archives of General Psychiatry.*

Weitzman, E. D., Czeisler, C. A., & Moore-Ede, M. C. (1981). Sleep-wake, endocrine and temperature rhythms in man during temporal isolation. In L. C. Johnson et al. (Eds.), *Biological rhythms, sleep and shiftwork.* New York: Spectrum.

Weller, E. B., Weller, B. A., Fristad, M. A., & Preskorn, S. H. (1984). The dexamethasone suppression test in hospitalized prepubertal depressed children. *American Journal of Psychiatry, 141,* 290–291.

Welner, Z., Welner, A., McCrary, M. D., & Leonard, M. A. (1977). Psychopathology in children of inpatients with depression: A controlled study. *Journal of Nervous and Mental Disease, 164,* 408–413.

Wender, P. (1971). *Minimal brain dysfunction in children.* New York: Wiley-Interscience.

Williams, R. L., Karacan, I., & Hursch, C. J. (1974). *Electroencephalography (EEG) of human sleep: Clinical applications.* New York: Wiley.

Wolf, G., & Money, J. (1973). Relationship between sleep and growth in patients with reversible somatrotropin deficiency (psychosocial dwarfism). *Psychological Medicine, 3,* 18–27.

Yarrow, L. J.: (1979). Emotional development. American Psychologist, 34, 951–957.

Youlton, R., Kaplan, S. L., & Grumbach, M. M. (1969). Growth and growth hormone: IV. Limitations of the growth hormone response to insulin and arginine and the immunoreactive insulin response to arginine in the assessment of growth hormone deficiency. *Pediatrics, 43,* 989–999.

Young, J. G., Kyprie, R. M., Ross, N. T., & Cohen, D. J. (1980). Serum dopamine hydroxylase activity: Clinical applications in child psychiatry. *Journal of Autism and Developmental Disorders, 10,* 1–13.

Young, W., Knowles, J. B., MacLean, A. W., Boag, L., & McConville, B. J. (1982). The sleep of childhood depressives: Comparison with age matched controls. *Biological Psychiatry, 17,* 1163–1168.

Developmental Factors in Child and Adolescent Suicide

David Shaffer

These notes are based on two premises: (1) that suicide is strongly related to disturbances of mood and (2) that suicide data are reliable. If these premises are accepted, the study of suicide, which while rare in childhood is increasingly common through adolescence, should offer a useful strategy for investigating the development of affect.

RATIONALE

Suicide and Depressed Mood

Studies in which the surviving relatives of representative groups of adult suicides are interviewed indicate that a majority of adult suicides were depressed before their death (Barraclough, Bunch, Nelson, & Sainsbury, 1974; Robins, Murphy, Wilkinson, Gassner, & Kayes, 1959). No precisely similar studies have been carried out among children or adolescents. However, Shaffer's (1974) study of completed suicide in children under the age of 15, which examined testimony given to coroners and medical, psychiatric, and educational records, indicated that a substantial proportion of the child victims had made self-denigratory remarks, had felt that people were against them, and had appeared withdrawn before death   clinical features consonant with a mood disturbance. These findings are supported by studies among children and

David Shaffer. New York State Psychiatric Institute, Columbia University College of Physicians and Surgeons, New York, New York.

adolescents who attempt suicide (see Shaffer, 1985), which indicate that depressive symptoms are also common in suicide attempters. However, depressed mood is not the only psychopathological correlate of suicidal behavior. Antisocial and interpersonal aggressive behaviors are probably more common among both completed (Shaffer, 1974) (see Table 1 below) and attempted suicides (Shaffer, 1982) than among nonsuicidal depressed patients, and in this respect young suicidal individuals are not typical of all patients with depression.

The Reliability of Suicide Statistics

The stigma attached to suicide and the complex procedures that lead up to certification may lead to systematic misreporting, especially in the case of children and adolescents. Misreporting may take the form of reporting bias following from variations in investigative and recording procedures or of underreporting. One research strategy for examining reporting bias has been to compare suicide rates among immigrants with rates in their countries of origin, the rationale being that the effect of different recording and certification procedures is likely to be particularly great across different nations. In studies in North America (Sainsbury & Barraclough, 1968) and Australia (Lester, 1972), the rank ordering of rates for different groups within the country of immigration was similar to the rank ordering of rates between the immigrants' countries of birth. This suggests that the effects of even quite large differences in reporting procedure are not sufficient to obscure variations that are known to occur across cultures. Barraclough, Holding, and Fayers (1976) and Sainsbury and Barraclough (1968) have further shown that the incidence of suicide within a particular coroner's or medical examiner's district is unaffected either by a change in

Table 1
Child and Adolescent Suicide in the United States, 1978

	Total population		Suicide	
Age group	No.[a]	(%)	No.[a]	(%)
0–9	32,273	(14.79)	2	(0.01)
10–14	18,589	(8.52)	151	(0.55)
15–19	21,013	(9.63)	1,606	(5.88)
19+	146,353	(67.06)	25,535	(93.56)
Total	218,228	(100.00)	27,294	(100.00)

Source. National Center for Health Statistics, Vital statistics of the United States, 1978: Vol. II. Mortality, Part B (unpublished); and U.S. Bureau of the Census, Current population reports (Series P. 25, No. 870). Washington, DC: U.S. Government Printing Office, 1980.
[a]In thousands.

coroner or by personnel changes among the police officers, pathologists, etc., who provide the information upon which coroners will base their verdicts. One may conclude from studies of this kind that idiosyncratic or biased reporting is not an important source of error.

Underreporting, on the other hand, is almost certainly a problem. Wilkins (1970), studying mortality among suicide prevention program contacts, concluded that the true suicide rate was probably two to three times greater than the recorded rate. A number of suicides are designated "undetermined whether death is accidental or purposefully inflicted." Shaffer (1974), reviewing coroners' records for a group of children aged 10–14 in whom an undetermined verdict had been given, concluded that most deaths in that category were probably suicides. The ratio of undetermined to suicidal verdicts appears to be greater among young children and adolescents (McClure & Gould, 1984; Shaffer & Fisher, 1981), so that underreporting is an especially significant factor in the young.

Barraclough (1973) has suggested that a combination of both suicide and undetermined verdicts is likely to be close to the "true" suicide rate. However, the number of undetermined verdicts, at least in the United States, from deaths due to firearms, strangulation, and falls from a height (the principal causes of suicidal death in this age group) is less than the number of determined suicides (Shaffer & Fisher, 1981). Although the tables provided below do not use this "combined" rate, had they done so the marked age gradient, which is the basis for these notes, would still have been apparent and the conclusions would not differ in any material way.

AGE TRENDS IN CHILD AND ADOLESCENT SUICIDE

As indicated above, suicide rarely occurs before the age of 10. The incidence then increases steadily through puberty and adolescence (see Fig. 1). The age-related increase is also reflected in the relatively small proportion of all suicides that are accounted for by children and adolescents (see Table 1). The increase in suicide through childhood and adolescence is unlikely to be due to idiosyncratic underreporting in the United States, since similarly low proportions are found in all other countries where reliable reporting procedures exist (see Table 2).

In summary, children enjoy considerable protection from suicide, but this protection is lost in a linear fashion through adolescence and young adulthood. This provides the basis for using suicide as a model with which to examine developmental factors in the genesis of depression. The notes that follow address specific possibilities that could account for this developmental phenomenon.

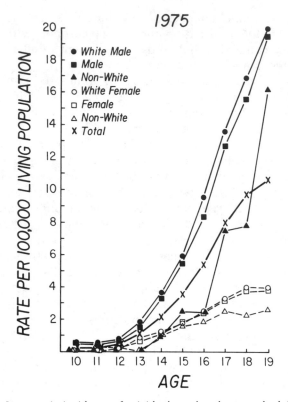

Fig. 1. *Increase in incidence of suicide through puberty and adolescence.*

Table 2
Percentage of All Suicides Committed by 5–14-Year-Olds

Country	Year	Percentage of total suicide rate
East Germany	1974	0.8
West Germany	1976	0.8
Switzerland	1977	0.6
United States	1976	0.6
Finland	1975	0.4
France	1976	0.4
The Netherlands	1977	0.4
Norway	1977	0.4
Denmark	1977	0.3
United Kingdom	1977	0.2
Sweden	1977	0.1

Source. World Health Statistics Annual. Geneva: World Health Organization, 1977.

INDIVIDUAL CHARACTERISTICS OF CHILD SUICIDES

Diagnosis

In a total population study of child suicides, Shaffer (1974) found both emotional symptoms and antisocial behavior to be common (see Table 3). As indicated above, controlled studies of adolescents who attempt suicide (see Cohen-Sandler, Berman, & King, 1982; Stanley & Barter, 1970) indicate that suicidal children and adolescents do not differ significantly from depressed nonsuicidal children except that they are less withdrawn and exhibit more interpersonal aggression. Developmental changes in these two forms of deviant behavior, that is, depression and antisocial behavior, could account for the increasing incidence of suicide from childhood through adolescence. While it appears that most children who show antisocial behavior already show some form of deviance at an early age (West & Farrington, 1977) the social consequences of that behavior (e.g., suspension and expulsion from school, arrest) probably become more severe with increasing age. The changing prevalence of depression has been studied in much less detail (see Shaffer, 1985) but it seems likely that prevalence increases with age and is greater in adolescence than before puberty.

Physical Characteristics

In Shaffer's study, children aged 12–14 who committed suicide were tall for their age (see Table 4). Height is highly correlated with puberty so that while, in general, children and young adolescents only commit suicide rarely, those who do tend to be physically precocious.

Cognitive Characteristics

In the same study, 12–14-year-old suicides were either more or less intelligent than average with the majority having a superior IQ (see Table 5).

Table 3
Psychiatric Symptoms in Childhood Suicide

	Boy	Girl	Total
Antisocial only	3 (14%)	2 (22%)	5 (17%)
Mixed antisocial, emotional/affective	14 (47%)	3 (33%)	17 (57%)
Emotional, affective		4 (45%)	4 (13%)
None	4 (19%)		4 (13%)

Source. Shaffer (1974).

Table 4
Height of Suicide Children (N = 20)

	No. (%)
< 50th percentile	2 (10%)
50–75th percentile	6 (30%)
75–97th percentile	5 (25%)
> 97th percentile	3 (15%)
Tall for age	4 (20%)

Source. Shaffer (1974).

Table 5
IQ of Suicide Children (N = 30)

	No. (%)
70–84	5 (17)
85–95	3 (10)
100–114	8 (27)
115–129	9 (30)
130+	3 (10)
Not known	2 (7)

Source. Shaffer (1974).

In summary, we see a somewhat mixed picture. Some of the known correlates of suicide, for example, the increasingly severe consequences of getting into trouble, are environmental correlates of growing up. Yet others, such as mental and physical precocity in younger suicides, suggest that biological processes increase vulnerability. While the increase in suicide with age could be a consequence of those effects, such a conclusion is not really very helpful—it merely begs the question of why affective changes should occur in a developmentally linked way.

SECULAR TRENDS—ENVIRONMENTAL EFFECTS

Another aspect of children's protection from suicide can be seen from their relative insensitivity to secular trends. Over the past decade suicide rates have increased in certain countries, notably in North America. However, children under age 15 and adults over age 30 have shown very small rate increases: the increase being greatest among young adults, with an intermediate increase in adolescents (see Figs. 2 and 3).

There has been a good deal of discussion about the nature of these secular trends. There are two general possibilities. The first is that it is a "period" effect, that is, during the period for which the increase has been

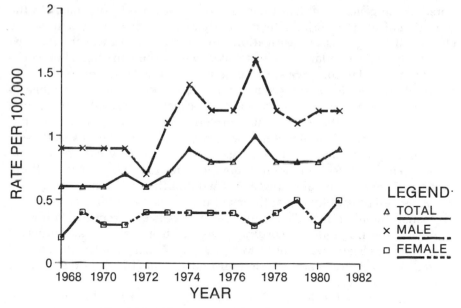

Fig. 2. *Suicide rate per 100,000 by sex, ages 10–14.*

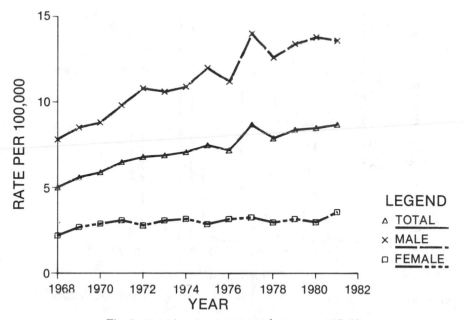

Fig. 3. *Suicide rate per 100,000 by sex, ages 15–19.*

noted, some general influence has led to an increase in suicide or in the reporting of suicide. Period effects usually result from some contemporary change in diagnosis, classification, or treatment. However, the age specificity of the secular increase speaks against such an effect. For example, it is difficult to conceive any treatment innovation that only benefits individuals in the 15–29 age group; and it is unlikely that any change in reporting procedures would selectively affect adolescents and young adults. Although there have undoubtedly been changes in the circumstances in which adolescents and young adults live their lives, the age span of 15 years, for the affected ages of 15–29, is so great and encompasses so many different types of life experience that it is difficult to think of a set of environmental changes that would affect the whole age group.

A second possibility is that the secular increases are part of a "cohort" or "generational" effect. The evidence for this is apparent if death rates from suicides are plotted according to year of birth and age at death (see Fig. 4) and has been argued for by Murphy and Wetzel (1980) on the basis of United States figures and by Solomon and Hellon (1980) on the basis of Canadian statistics.

The interest to the developmentalist of this cohort effect is twofold: (1) it again illustrates how younger children are different—whatever its cause

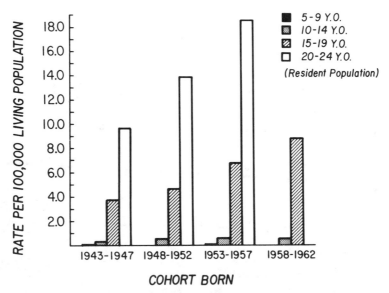

Fig. 4. *Suicide risk by birth cohort in the United States, 1952–1977. Source: National Center for Health Statistics,* Vital Statistics of the United States, *1952, 1957, 1962, 1967, 1972, and 1977, Volume II, Part A; and U.S. Bureau of the Census,* Current Population Reports Series *P-25, Nos. 310, 517, 721, and 820.*

it does not affect children in the 10–14 age group; (2) cohort effects usually reflect a long interval between cause and effect (Susser, 1973). Thus, the cause of the increase is probably operating during childhood but does not have its effect until later. What might this cause be?

Holinger and Offer (1982) have posited a secular "stress" factor. They suggest that the growth in the population—and in particular the "baby boom"—has resulted in increased pressure on educational and employment prospects, which selectively affect adolescents, and that this stress has led to an increase in suicide. This is an argument for a period rather than a generational effect; it ignores the wide age range that is being affected and it extends beyond the period when educational pressures are likely to be operative. In fact, increases are greatest in the 25–29 age group.

The plausibility of stress as a factor can also be examined by studying whether there are "protected" groups, other than the young, living within the same general society and if there are, whether they are relatively stress free.

There is one such group in the United States, southern blacks. As can be seen from Table 6, black adolescents living in the South Atlantic and the

Table 6

Adolescent (15–19-year-old) Suicide Rates in States in Which Blacks Account for More Than 95% of the Non-White Population (1970)

	No. of adolescent suicides		Adolescent population of Non-White	Adolescent suicides of Non-White
	All races	Non-White		
North–Central (Michigan, Illinois, Indiana, Ohio)	188	26	11.96	13.83
Mid-Atlantic (New Jersey, Pennsylvania)	82	5	10.74	6.09
South Atlantic (West Virginia, Virginia, Maryland, Washington, D.C., Delaware, North Carolina, South Carolina, Georgia, Florida)	151	21	25.34	13.9
East–South Central and Louisiana (Kentucky, Tennessee, Mississippi, Alabama)	56	9	26.47	16.07

Source. U.S. Bureau of the Census. (1970). *Census of the population. Characteristics of the population* (Vols. 2, 9, 10, 11, 12, 15, 16, 19, 20, 22, 26, 32, 35, 37, 40, 42, 44, 48, 51); National Center for Health Statistics (1970). *Vital statistics of the United States* (Vol. 11, Part B). Washington, D.C: U.S. Government Printing Office.

South Central States and Louisiana account for a much smaller proportion of adolescent suicides than would be expected if their suicide rate were proportional to their representation in the population of these areas. It is true that this discrepancy between the different races could rather be due to some genetic factor, but this is unlikely because the discrepancies do not hold with the same strength in all regions of the country. The protection enjoyed by southern blacks is unlikely to be due to that group enjoying a lesser degree of stress or educational and employment pressure. On almost every count, blacks within the United States will be experiencing more stress and will endure greater employment and educational pressures than whites. This makes a stress hypothesis unlikely.

Another possible explanation for the fact that blacks are less likely to commit suicide despite their greater exposure to stress follows from the psychoanalytic notion of there being a reciprocal relationship between inwardly and outwardly directed aggression. Black adolescents have high rates of delinquency, that is, outwardly directed aggression, and if the theory holds they may be expected to show a lower rate of suicidal behavior. However, Shaffer (1974) has shown that a majority of children who commit suicide manifest antisocial behavior before their death. More specifically, Breed (1970) found that a majority of blacks who attempted suicide had recently been in trouble with the law, that is, suicide is related directly rather than reciprocally to aggression.

A more probable explanation for the discrepancy is that some cultural factor or convention is operative. For example, Bush (1976) has suggested that blacks have more effective social support systems than whites. Other sociologists, such as Gibbs and Martin (1964), have suggested that "status integration" is enhanced by discrimination and by narrowed employment opportunities, and this could be expected to reduce the prevalence of suicide among blacks. These factors are likely to be most marked in blacks reared in a traditional setting and to break down with deculturation, which would in turn explain the geographical variation in black/white suicide ratios seen in Table 6.

The hypothesis that suicidal behaviors can be influenced by gross environmental factors is supported by other data. Phillips (1979; Bollen & Phillips, 1982) has shown that suicide rates vary with media coverage and that the front-page display of news of a suicide will have a temporary effect of increasing suicide rates within the area of distribution of that news. At a more detailed level, there is evidence for the communicability of suicide among young people who have attempted suicide. They are more likely to know and be close to others who have had and spoken about suicidal ideation or who have shown suicidal behavior than nonsuicidal patients (Kreitman, Smith & Tan, 1970; Tishler & McHenry, 1982).

Taken together, those observations suggest that cultural–environmental factors could be potent factors in the control if not the genesis of suicide

Table 7
Precipitants of Suicide in Children (%)

Disciplinary crisis	−37
Loss of face with peers	−23
Argument with parent	−13
Interaction with psychotic parent	−7
Career disappointment	−7
Recent bereavement	−7
Reading material	−7
Within 2 weeks of birthday	−23

Source. Shaffer (1974).

behavior, permitting an expression of depression/aggression that was previously taboo. That is, the secular effect operates through the expression of the condition rather than on its generation. One of the most dramatic secular changes has been the legitimizing of suicidal behavior in the societies affected by secular increases. Suicide was previously an illegal and profane act but is now more often viewed as a manifestation of mental illness.

There is other evidence for viewing this "release" hypothesis as being more plausible than other factors in constituting a "sufficient" cause of suicide. Controlled studies (Stanley & Barter, 1970) indicate that the external precipitants of nonlethal suicidal behavior are neither unique nor unusual, and the same appears to be true in uncontrolled studies of completed suicides (Shaffer, 1974) (see Table 7). We must therefore look to factors within the individual and particularly to those which might be subject to developmental change to understand the origins of the condition.

WHY SUICIDE MAY BE RARE AMONG CHILDREN

It is important to dismiss the idea that children do not know how to kill themselves. The methods that young children most often choose to threaten suicide—jumping from a window or throwing themselves in front of an automobile (Winn & Halla, 1966)—are surely lethal. Children do know how to kill themselves.

What then could account for the low suicide rate in childhood and early adolescence? The possibility that most suicides "require" depression and that if depression is rare in the prepubertal child then suicide will be rare have been discussed above. This simply begs the question of why there is a developmental gradient for depression. Two areas suggest themselves, one in the area of social support, the other in the sphere of cognition.

It has been argued that many successful suicides follow or take place in a context of social isolation. A feature of childhood is that the individual enjoys relatively little unsupervised time, but in practice, there are few children who are not left alone long enough to be able to implement a threat to say throw themselves out of a window or to jump in front of a moving automobile. A more plausible social effect may follow from the fact that children are generally well supported socially. Social support provides an opportunity for corrective discussions with friends or relatives, which might reduce the despair or correct the misperceptions or self-denigration of the potential victim. Children may be less likely to kill themselves because childhood is a period of life when there are rich, multiple social support systems that provide this help. If the system at home fails, then that at school may operate, and vice versa. The increasing self-consciousness of the older adolescent and the drive for individuation may weaken those support systems and increase vulnerability to suicide.

There are also a series of cognitive changes that coincide with the increased prevalence of suicide and that may be relevant. Most attention has been given to the development of the child's idea of death and in particular how many less mature children believe that death is reversible (Schilder & Wechsler, 1934). Somewhat unconvincingly, it has been suggested that because younger children believe in reversibility they are more likely to engage in suicidal behavior in the belief that it carries no risk of permanent death. This might be a convincing explanation if the phenomenon to be explained were an excess of suicidal behavior in young children. In fact, of course, the phenomenon to be explained is the reverse.

Beck, Kovacs, and Weissmann (1975) have suggested that despair is a critical construct for the contemplation or enactment of suicide. It may be that despair requires an ability to choose between various abstract life alternatives and to conclude that none are satisfactory. If this is the case, then it falls into the category of hypothesis setting and testing, mental activities that are said to characterize the stage of formal operations, which develops only in adolescence.

The cognitions associated with depression may also require that children have a well-developed ability to perceive themselves, albeit in a distorted fashion, with respect to the outside world, and that this is necessary for the feelings of isolation and helplessness, which are often alleged to occur in suicidal individuals.

Also in the domain of cognition, Kohlberg's "postconventional" child is more likely than a younger child or a child at an earlier stage of moral development to experience internalized distress after the commission of an antisocial act. If guilt rather than anxiety is a determinant of depressed and suicide facilitating affect, then this, combined with the increasingly grave social consequences of antisocial behavior, may account for the phenomenon of adolescents committing suicide when in trouble.

All of the above are in the nature of speculations and have no research backing. However, it is hoped that they present perhaps unrecognized clinical factors to a developmentally oriented group and that their expertise may orient research in that direction.

REFERENCES

Barraclough, B. M. (1973). Differences between national suicide rates. British Journal of Psychiatry, 122, 95–96.

Barraclough, B. M., Bunch, J., Nelson, B., & Sainsbury, P. (1974). A hundred cases of suicide. British Journal of Psychiatry, 125, 355–373.

Barraclough, B. M., Holding, T., & Fayers, P. (1976). Influence of coroners', officers and pathologists on suicide verdicts. British Journal of Psychiatry, 128, 471–474.

Beck, A. T., Kovacs, M. V., & Weissmann, A. (1975). Hopelessness and suicidal behavior. Journal of the American Medical Association, 234, 1146–1149.

Bollen, K. A., & Phillips, D. P. (1982). Imitative suicides: A national study of the effects of television news stories. American Sociological Review, 47, 802–809.

Breed, W. (1970). The Negro and fatalistic suicide. Pacific Society Review, 13, 156–162.

Bush, J. A. (1976). Suicide and blacks. Suicide Life-Threatening Behavior, 6, 216–222.

Cohen-Sandler, R., Berman, A. L., & King, R. A. (1982). Life stress and symptomatology; determinants of suicidal behavior in children. Journal of the American Academy of Child Psychiatry, 21, 178–186.

Gibbs, J. P., & Martin, W. T. (1964). Status integration and suicide. Eugene: University of Oregon Press.

Holinger, P. C., & Offer, D. (1982). Prediction of adolescent suicide: A population model. American Journal of Psychiatry, 139, 302–307.

Kreitman, N., Smith, P., & Tan, E. S. (1970). Attempted suicide as language; an empirical study. British Journal of Psychiatry, 116, 465–473.

Lester, D. (1972). Migration and suicide. Medical Journal of Australia, 1, 941–942 (letter).

McClure, G., & Gould, M. S. (1984). Recent trends in suicide among the young. British Journal of Psychiatry, 144, 134–138.

Murphy, G. E., & Wetzel, R. D. (1980). Suicide risk by birth cohort in the United States, 1949 to 1974. Archives of General Psychiatry, 37, 519–523.

Phillips, D. P. (1979). Suicide, motor vehicle fatalities, and the mass media: Evidence toward a theory of suggestion. American Journal of Sociology, 84, 1150–1174.

Robins, E., Murphy, G. E., Wilkinson, R. H., Jr., Gassner, S., & Kayes, J. (1959). Some clinical considerations in the prevention of suicide based on a study of 134 successful suicides. American Journal of Public Health, 49, 888–889.

Sainsbury, P., & Barraclough, B. (1968). Differences between suicide rates. Nature (London), 220, 1252.

Schilder, P., & Wechsler, D. (1934). The attitude of children toward death. Journal of Genetic Psychology, 45, 406–451.

Shaffer, D. (1974). Suicide in childhood and early adolescence. Journal of Child Psychology and Psychiatry, 15, 275–291.

Shaffer, D. (1982). Diagnostic issues in child and adolescent suicide. Journal of the American Academy of Child Psychiatry, 21, 414–416.

Shaffer, D. (1985). Depression and suicide in children and adolescents. In M. Rutter & L. Hersov (Eds.), Child and adolescent psychiatry: Modern approaches (2nd ed.). Oxford: Blackwell Scientific Publications.

Shaffer, D., & Fisher, P. (1981). The epidemiology of suicide in children and young adolescents. Journal of the American Academy of Child Psychiatry, 21, 545–565.

Solomon, M. J., & Hellon, C. O. (1980). Suicide and age in Alberta, Canada, 1951 to 1977. Archives of General Psychiatry, 37, 511–513.

Stanley, E. J., & Barter, J. T. (1970). Adolescent suicidal behavior. *American Journal of Orthopsychiatry, 40,* 87–96.

Susser, M. (1973). *Causal thinking in the health sciences.* New York: Oxford University Press.

Tishler, C. L., & McHenry, P. C. (1982). Parental negative self and adolescent suicidal attempts. *Journal of the American Academy of Child Psychiatry, 21.*

West, D. J., & Farrington, D. P. (1977). *The delinquent way of life.* London: Heinemann.

Wilkins, J. L. (1970). Producing suicides. *American Behavior Scientist, 14,* 185–201.

Winn, D., & Halla, R. (1966). Observations of children who threaten to kill themselves. *Canadian Psychiatric Association Journal, 11,* 283–294.

V

METHODS AND MEASUREMENT

Developmental Issues in the Classification of Depression in Children

Gabrielle A. Carlson
Judy Garber

INTRODUCTION

A major prerequisite to the advancement of knowledge concerning any psychiatric disorder is the clear delineation of a reliable and valid set of operationally defined criteria for classifying the disorder. The absence of a generally agreed-upon and objective set of guidelines for diagnosing depression in children has been a major obstacle to progress in the field, and has made generalizations across studies and communication among researchers difficult. With the burgeoning interest in this area over the past decade, however, much progress has been made toward diagnosing and understanding depressive disorders in children.

Historically, both theoretical and empirical work on childhood depression addressed questions of whether in fact children can become depressed, and if so, what form the depression takes. A brief review of this literature reveals that in a relatively short period of time, childhood depression has gone from being essentially overlooked (e.g., Kanner, 1957), to having its existence challenged and denied (Mahler, 1961; Rie, 1966; Rochlin, 1959), to being accepted as a distinct clinical entity whose defining characteristics are isomorphic with its adult counterpart (Cytryn, McKnew, & Bunney, 1980). Despite some early case studies (e.g., de Saussure, 1947), it really was not until 1952, when the journal *The Nervous Child* devoted a special issue to manic–depressive illness in childhood, that

Gabrielle A. Carlson. Department of Psychiatry, State University of New York at Stony Brook, Stony Brook, New York.

Judy Garber. Department of Psychology and Human Development, George Peabody College, Vanderbilt University, Nashville, Tennessee.

depression among elementary-school-aged children received any attention. The discussions that followed during the subsequent three decades focused primarily on attempts to clarify the diagnosis and classification of depression in children.

A first step in the clarification of the diagnosis of childhood depression is to note the distinctions among depression as a symptom, as a syndrome, and as a nosologic disorder. Sadness or depressed affect as a single symptom is a subjective state experienced by most people at various points in their lives, and by itself it is not necessarily pathological. In contrast, depression as a syndrome implies more than an isolated dysphoric mood, and occurs in combination with other symptoms to form a symptom-complex or syndrome. When this clinical syndrome is characterized by a particular symptom picture with a specifiable course, duration, outcome, response to treatment, and potential familial, psychological, and biological correlates, then it is referred to as a discrete nosologic entity or disorder.

The controversy in the literature surrounding the classification of childhood depression has been concerned primarily with the description and definition of the characteristic clinical symptomatology comprising the disorder of depression in children, rather than depression simply as a mood, expression, or symptom. What has emerged from the literature thus far has been essentially four major schools of thought. Each perspective presents a somewhat different view on the issue of the clinical picture of depressive disorder in childhood.

The first school of thought was represented by psychoanalytic theorists who seriously questioned whether the classical depressive disorders could occur in children because children lack a fully developed and well-internalized superego before adolescence (Rie, 1966; Rochlin, 1959). This school held that, "the familiar manifestations of adult nonpsychiatric depression are virtually nonexistent in childhood." Similarly, Mahler (1961) asserted that

> We know that the systematized affective disorders are unknown in childhood. It has been conclusively established that the immature personality structure of the infant or older child is not capable of producing a state of depression such as that seen in the adult. The ego cannot sustain itself without taking prompt defensive actions against object loss. It cannot survive in an objectless state for any length of time. (p. 339)

As a result of this theoretical perspective, childhood depression was basically ignored both clinically and empirically for many years.

The second perspective was that depression in children is "masked" or expressed in behavioral equivalents rather than being directly observable. Proponents of this view (Glaser, 1968; Toolan, 1962) argued that children do not manifest the signs and symptoms of depression in the same form as seen in adults, but rather have an underlying depression that is manifest in other behaviors and disorders instead—such as conduct problems (Burks & Harrison, 1962; Lesse, 1974), somatic complaints (Apley, 1959; Sperling, 1959), and delinquency (Toolan, 1962). Glaser (1968) asserted that although the child does not present with symptoms such as dysphoric mood and anhedonia that are typically associated with depression, the child's psychopathology features depressive elements that are dynamic forces influencing the child's functioning.

Critics of the concept of masked depression have emphasized the fact that the various disorders that have been characterized as "masking" depression include practically the full range of possible psychopathological disorders of childhood (Gittelman-Klein, 1977; Kovacs & Beck, 1977). Moreover, the connection between these various disorders and the presumed underlying depressive features is unclear. Criteria for establishing the presence of depression and for differentiating between disorders that mask depression from those with no such underlying depression have never been adequately delineated. Thus, over time the concept of "masked depression" has ceased to be useful.

The trend in the last decade espoused by the remaining two schools of thought has been to accept the existence of childhood depression as a real clinical phenomenon and to search for its defining characteristics. Early attempts to operationalize a set of diagnostic criteria sprang from the viewpoint that childhood depressive disorders have a number of similarities to the adult syndrome as well as having some additional unique features specific to children (Brumback, Dietz-Schmidt, & Weinberg, 1977; Ling, Oftedal, & Weinberg, 1970; McConville, Boag, & Purohit, 1973; Weinberg, Rutman, Sullivan, Penick, & Dietz, 1973). The proponents of this third perspective described childhood depression as including the core clinical symptoms that characterize the adult disorder such as sadness, anhedonia, low self-esteem, and the various vegetative symptoms. In addition, they enumerated several other symptoms that, although not necessarily part of the adult syndrome, may be uniquely manifested by children: somatic complaints, social withdrawal, aggression, negativism, conduct problems, and school refusal.

Cantwell (1983), however, pointed out that an important distinction should be made between what are the essential versus associated features of depression in children. He suggested that whereas the essential features of major depression may be identical for children, adolescents, and adults, there may be age-specific associated features for different ages and developmental levels. Puig-Antich, Blau, Marx, Greenhill, and Chambers (1978) and Puig-Antich (1982), for example, have reported a strong association between major depressive disorder and both conduct disorder and separation anxiety in prepubertal children. Further research examining the longitudinal course, biological and psychological correlates, and response to treatment are necessary in order to determine adequately to what extent these other symptoms and syndromes are *essential* features or secondary to depressive disorder in children.

As a result of all the disagreement and confusion in the literature, and the resulting proliferation of over a dozen different sets of criteria for diagnosing depression in children, a fourth perspective has emerged recently. In order to provide some standardization and uniformity in the field, proponents of this school of thought (Cytryn *et al.*, 1980; Puig-Antich *et al.*, 1978) have recommended the universal acceptance and use of the DSM-III criteria as the basis for diagnosing major affective disorders in children. According to this viewpoint, the clinical picture of depression in children is isomorphic with that manifested by adults. The advantage of this perspective is that it allows for comparison of findings across research settings and, thus, for the accumulation of a cohesive body of knowledge. However, these criteria are still in need of further empirical validation for use with children.

Thus, in a very brief period, the field has gone from the one extreme of denying the very existence of depression in children to the other extreme of asserting that depressive disorders in children and adults are identical. Recently, there has emerged a fifth school of thought concerning the classification of childhood depression that particularly challenges the latter viewpoint. Developmental psychopathologists (Cicchetti & Schneider-Rosen, this volume; Sroufe & Rutter, 1984) suggest that from a developmental perspective it is unrealistic to expect behavioral isomorphism in observed signs or symptoms of depression in individuals of different ages and developmental levels. That is, there are important differences in the developmental progression of children's cognitive, linguistic, and socioemotional capacities that will produce differences in their interpretation, experience, and expression of depressive symptomatology over time. Similar to the third school of thought described above, the developmental perspective asserts that the search for appropriate diagnostic criteria must incorporate age-specific manifestations of the symptomatology. Moreover, this viewpoint suggests that the classification of childhood psychopathology should go beyond the simple categorization of symptoms and behaviors and should include the broader notions of patterns of adaption and competence.

The major goal of this chapter is to examine the central issues involved in the construction of a set of criteria for the diagnosis and classification of depression in children, with a specail emphasis on this latter developmental perspective. First, a brief overview of the basic issues involved in the process of classification of childhood psychopathology will be presented. Next, we will review the current systems for classifying affective disorders in both adults and children. Finally, we will suggest how the developmental perspective for classifying childhood psychopathology can be used to improve the classification of childhood depression in particular.

ISSUES IN CLASSIFICATION

There are certain basic issues involved in the process of classification of psychopathology in general that are important to consider in our search for the appropriate criteria for classifying childhood depression. These include such questions as: What is the function or purpose of classification? What are the potential risks? What are the necessary criteria for an adequate and acceptable classification scheme? Although these questions are not unique to the classification of psychopathology in children, and have been adequately addressed elsewhere (Blashfield & Draguns, 1976a, 1976b; Cromwell, Blashfield, & Strauss, 1975; Hobbs, 1975a, 1975b; Rutter, 1965; Rutter & Gould, 1985; Zigler & Phillips, 1961; Zubin, 1967), a discussion of these key issues is an essential preliminary to any consideration of the specific application of classification to developmental psychopathology in general, and childhood depression in particular.

The major purposes of classification are communication, information organization and retrieval, description, prediction, and theoretical understanding (Blashfield & Draguns, 1976b). Classification facilitates communication among professionals by providing a uniform language without which there would be a professional "Tower of Babel" (Silberstein, 1969). Classification systems also serve an organizational function by summarizing, simplifying, and ordering large amounts of complex data, a descriptive function by characterizing the similarities and differences among homogeneous groups of individuals, and a predictive function by conveying new meaning and probability information associated with class membership. Assignment of a child to a relatively homogeneous category or dimension of psychopathology should allow one to make useful statements about the disorder with respect to its etiology, prognosis, and treatment based upon the child's membership in the category or placement on the dimension (Quay, 1979). Moreover, by isolating relatively homogeneous groups, we are better able to search for the significant etiological processes that underlie psychopathological disorders, and thereby, empirically test our theories of normal and abnormal development.

The primary clinical utility of classification is *control* in that it serves as an aid to the choice of the most appropriate treatment and prevention strategies for a specific disorder (Baldwin, 1969; Spitzer & Wilson, 1976). The primary research utility of classification is that it facilitates the replication, interpretation, and application of research results from investigations conducted in different laboratories and clinics around the world. Finally, classification also has important practical implications for social policy decisions by providing a uniform basis for categorizing and measuring disorders necessary for obtaining accurate estimates of the prevalence of childhood disorders and thus the need for intervention programs (Hobbs, 1975a).

Despite the apparent clinical, heuristic, and administrative utility of classification, however, there is not universal acceptance of the need for, nor desirability of, such an enterprise with respect to psychopathology. There seems to be an ongoing debate between "those who divide people into groups and those who do not" (May, 1979, p. 111), which rages even more poignantly with respect to the classification of childhood psychopathology. Indeed, there are those who question the very ethics of classifying at all (e.g., Hobbs, 1975a, 1975b).

Critics of traditional diagnostic practice have argued that classification is dehumanizing (Laing, 1967), that it constitutes an illegitimate exercise of social power to the detriment of the individual (Szasz, 1961), and that it is basically unnecessary because there really is only one mental illness that falls on a single continuum of psychopathology (Menninger, Mayman, & Pruyser, 1963). Others have expressed concern about the assumed etiological implications associated with the "medical model" (e.g., organic or intrapsychic pathology), and the resulting lack of attention to significant external factors such as family, school, community, and the constant interplay between the child and his/her environment (Hersch, 1968; Hobbs, 1975a; Kanfer & Saslow, 1965; Ullmann & Krasner, 1969).

A related antinosological argument is that classification involves the process of sterile "pigeonholing," and is used as a substitute for understanding the person, thereby neglecting the individual's uniqueness with respect to his or her strengths and weaknesses. Supporters of the idiographic position (Allport, 1937; Beck, 1953) have emphasized the importance of treating idiosyncratic aspects of the individual as pertinent rather than inconsequential data to be utilized in the process of obtaining a comprehensive view of the person as well as in the selection of the most appropriate treatment. May (1979) warned that "Diagnosis alone is not enough to make a clinical decision regarding treatment, nor is it the same as a full dynamic formulation of the mental mechanisms operative within the child" (p. 139).

Classification also has been criticized because it tends to be imprecise and unreliable (Bandura, 1969; Kanfer & Saslow, 1969). Empirical investigations of the reliability of existing schemes for classifying childhood psychopathology conducted with respect to DSM-III (Mattison, Cantwell, Russell, & Will, 1979), the WHO Multiaxial System (Rutter, Shaffer, & Shepherd, 1975), and the GAP (1966) classification system (Beitchman, Dietman, Landis, Benson, & Kemp, 1978; Freeman, 1971) have reported adequate interrater reliability (60–70%) for the broader categories of disorders, but only fair to poor reliability for the finer distinctions within these subcategories.

Proponents of psychiatric nosology (e.g., Eisenberg, 1969; Meehl, 1973; Rutter, 1965; Rutter & Gould, 1985; Rutter & Shaffer, 1980; Spitzer & Wilson, 1976), have responded to these arguments by pointing out that the criticisms are a result of the misunderstanding and misuse of classification systems, rather than there being any particular problems inherent in the process of classification itself. First, the assumption that psychiatric nosology automatically presumes the presence of "ubiquitous underlying organic causes" is erroneous (Gittelman-Klein, Spitzer, & Cantwell, 1978). Psychiatric classification merely suggests that relatively discrete sets of behavioral phenomena are represented in various categories; the etiology of these behavior disorders may range anywhere from a dysfunctional family system to biochemical abnormalities.

Second, if, as the idiographic position suggests, classification misses important information about the individual, then the system should be revised and expanded to include the relevant new dimensions, rather than simply be abandoned. Moreover, the diagnostic process is considered to be only an initial step in the process of understanding and eventually treating the child. The nosologic label, if it is doing its job, is *part* of understanding the individual, and is not intended to be the complete picture (Meehl, 1973).

Finally, the problem of the unreliability of psychiatric diagnosis may be reduced considerably by using broader diagnostic categories, requiring adequate clinical exposure to the patient and other significant information sources (e.g., parents and teachers), and employing well-trained clinicians who take seriously the diagnostic process (Blashfield & Draguns, 1976a; Meehl, 1973). Moreover, with the recent development of standardized, semi-structured clinical interviews such as the Schedule for Affective Disorders and Schizophrenia for School-aged Children (Kiddie-SADS) (Puig-Antich & Chambers, 1978) and the Diagnostic Interview for Children and Adolescents (DICA) (Herjanic & Campbell, 1977; Herjanic, Herjanic, Brown, & Wheatt, 1975), the reliability of the psychiatric diagnosis of children should begin to improve.

The antinosological argument most salient to the classification of childhood psychopathology concerns the issue of "labeling." Sociologists (e.g., Goffman, 1961; Lemert, 1967; Scheff, 1966) have argued that the use of labels implying deviance may lead to social rejection, loss of status, and coercive social control. Education specialists (e.g., MacMillan, Jones, & Aloia, 1974; MacMillan & Meyers, 1979) have asserted that the labeling of a child may result in lower self-esteem, peer rejection, academic underachievement, and biased responding by parents and teachers.

Empirical research demonstrating such anticipated negative effects of the labeling process, however, is inconclusive, although there is some evidence that labeling has important ramifications for children (Hobbs, 1975a, 1975b; Rutter & Madge, 1976). Studies examining the effects of labeling in the juvenile justice system, for example, have reported that the label of juvenile offender is positively associated with future delinquent acts (Farrington, 1977; Gold & Williams, 1969; McEachern, 1968). Owing to the various methodological complexities and flaws in this research, however, it is difficult to disentangle empirically the effects of the label from the child's prelabeling experience, postlabeling experiences, and the impact of the deviant behavior itself. Are the negative reactions and prejudices befalling these children a result of the label or the actual behavior observed?

The primary criticism of labeling is that it serves as a self-fulfilling prophecy. The concern is that others will treat the child in a way that is consistent with the label, and hence the child will live up to the label by becoming what it suggests (Aldrich, 1971). Thus, a vicious cycle is hypothesized to occur whereby behavior problems lead to a diagnostic label that, in turn, leads to responses on the part of parents, teachers, and peers that serve to maintain the undersirable behavior.

The widely cited study by Rosenthal and Jacobson (1968) on the Pygmalion effect of teachers' expectance of student change in IQ has provided empirical support for the notion that subjects' responses may be shaped to fit observers' expectations. These results, however, have been disputed on methodological grounds (Barber & Silver, 1968; Snow, 1969; Thorndike, 1968) and there has been some difficulty in replicating the effect empirically (Clairborne, 1969; Gozali & Meyer, 1970). Nevertheless, although the research is by no means conclusive, there is some evidence of a positive correlation between labels, teachers' expectations and behaviors, and the children's subsequent behavior and perceptions of themselves (Beez, 1968; Boekel, 1969; Brophy & Good, 1974; Davidson & Lang, 1960; Jones, 1972). It is important to note, however, that the effects of labeling are not *necessarily* negative; teachers may actually respond *more* favorably toward children labeled as low achievers by increasing their efforts to help them (Brophy & Good, 1974). Moreover, there also is evidence to suggest that individuals' attitudes may be influenced far more by the actual performance of the child than by the label assigned to him or her (Gottlieb, 1974).

One practical consequence of the concern about the potential dangers of stigmatizing children has been a tendency for clinicians to use more benign, albeit often less accurate, diagnoses. Several studies examining the utility of DSM-I (Dreger *et al.*, 1964; Rosen, Bahn, & Kramer, 1964), DSM-II (Cerreto & Tuma, 1977), and DSM III (Spitzer & Forman, 1979; Spitzer, Forman, & Nee, 1979) have found that between 30% and 40% of children seen in various clinics were given the less pejorative diagnosis of "adjustment reaction." These clinicians appear to have shown a clear preference for the milder label "adjustment reaction" because of their reluctance to stigmatize children with labels that will follow them after they leave the clinic (Nathan & Harris, 1980).

Not only is there a concern that the label will follow the children outside the clinic setting, but also that it will remain with them even after the problem ameliorates. In a critique of the use of traditional nosology with children, Santostefano (1971) notes that the assignment of a patient to a diagnostic category tends to be relatively permanent, and that the emphasis on relatively stable traits that define more or less static and non-overlapping categories is a serious limitation in the application of diagnosis to child psychopathology. He suggests, for example, that familiar traits such as impulsivity and hyperactivity once assigned to the child may persist even after the behaviors that define these traits disappear. Furthermore, the relatively static nature of diagnostic labels tends to discourage sensitivity to change in the child's condition. Kessler (1971) similarly has argued that diagnostic labeling is particularly inappropriate with children because of their growing and changing nature.

Classification systems, however, are not inherently typological. "Continua of personality or tempo of maturation may be classified just as 'illnesses' are" (Rutter, 1965, p. 163). Thus, psychiatric nosology does not necessarily imply static traits and discrete categories.

Moreover, in the diagnostic labeling of children, it is important to keep in mind that the object of classification is the child's behavior at a particular point in his or her development. Rutter (1965) proposed as a principle of classification that "the aim is to classify disorders, not to classify children. Just as children may have measles one year and scarlet fever the next, equally, it is possible that children may have one kind of psychiatric disorder at 5 years and another at 12 years" (p. 163). This perspective allows us to identify a specific disorder at a particular point in time, while at the same time recognizing the process of change and maturation. Thus the *child* is not hyperactive, but rather he or she is exhibiting hyperactive behaviors (e.g., restlessness and overactivity) at a particular time assessment.

In sum, critiques of traditional psychiatric nosology that are most relevant to the classification of childhood psychopathology have focused primarily on the potential dangers of labeling a child with stable "traits." Evidence supporting these concerns, however, is clearly mixed. Moreover, proponents of classification (e.g., Meehl, 1973; Rutter & Shaffer, 1980) have argued that we cannot afford to decide about the merits of a conceptual scheme on the basis of its being used improperly, such as when children, rather than disorders are classified. The problem is not with the concept or process of classification, but rather with its potential misuse.

The real issue concerning the classification of childhood psychopathology is not *whether* to classify but *how* to classify. Any use of words to describe behaviors or attributes of children necessarily implies an implicit classification. Such "informal" classifications differ from standard classifications in that they lack a set of clear rules and regulations specifying the number of categories or the meaning of the terms used, and hence, make it more difficult to compare classifications across individuals with respect to different children. This, of course, is the whole point of a standard classification; that is, to provide a set of rules that facilitates comparison and communication. Thus, an appropriate conclusion is not to abandon attempts at classifying childhood psychopathology, but rather to construct a system that minimizes the potential risks while meeting the criteria for "good" classification.

There is no one "correct way" to classify psychopathological disorders of childhood that exists in nature (Rutter & Gould, 1985). Traditional classificatory schemes have been based on the phenomenological manifestations of the disorders, their hypothesized etiology, probable outcome, potential response to treatment, or a combination of these. The ultimate utility of any classification system is dependent upon who is using it and the purpose for which it is being used. No one classification can ever satisfy the full range of possible uses to which the system can be applied (Anthony, 1969).

Nevertheless, there are some generally agreed-upon guidelines for the construction of any classificatory scheme. These criteria have been outlined by various authors (Blashfield & Draguns, 1976a; Cantwell, 1980; Cantwell & Carlson, 1983; Cromwell et al., 1975; Rutter, 1965; Rutter & Gould, 1985; Rutter et al., 1975; Soli, Nuechterlein, Garmezy, Devine, & Schaefer, 1981) and include operational definitions of terminology, reliability, coverage, validity, structural fidelity (Loevinger, 1957); specificity and mutual exclusivity; utility and acceptance; and flexibility in response to new data. One additional criterion that is central to the classification of psychopathological disorders in childhood is the need for a developmental framework (Cantwell, 1980) in order to accurately characterize the continuing processes of growth and change that children undergo. Such a developmental perspective has been suggested by Garber (1984a). Its particular application to the classification of childhood depression will be discussed in a later section of the chapter.

Classification of Depression in Adults

Although serious depression in humans has been recognized for several thousand years, and attempts to isolate homogeneous subtypes intuitively and empirically have been numerous, it is clear that no comprehensive system yet exists to classify persons with depressive syndromes. In the next few pages we will briefly review some of the existing classifications of adult depression, describe attempts that have been made to classify depression in children and finally discuss issues pertinent to the classification of depression in children.

In psychopathology, extremes of any entity are always clearer than the borders separating them. Hence, there are persons with clear-cut depressive syndromes whose illness is both more severe than and different from that seen in persons with occasional misery or grief. Delineating a system that will, with consistency and validity, distinguish all of the "normal" depressed from the "pathological" depressed has been so far impossible, however. Similarly, persons with clear-cut depressions are readily distinguishable from those with dementia, anxiety, or schizophrenia, yet the borders between all of those entities are imprecise and unsatisfactory. A major objective of diagnostic classification systems is to isolate a relatively homogenous group of people so that their disorder can be better studied and to establish a range of diagnoses broad enough to include everyone. It appears for depression, though, next to impossible to classify those disorders that fall on the boundaries without creating so many typologies as to be unwieldy.

Kendall (1976) and more recently Andreasen (1982) have thoroughly reviewed the dilemma of classification of depression. We will discuss only briefly the current categories of depression, with an eye to ultimately examining their relevance to the notion of childhood depression.

Table 1 summarizes some of the older and some of the more recent classification systems for depression in adults and reveals several consistencies in the descriptive and natural history categories:

1. *Episodic* depressions (manic–depressive types) are distinguished from other types of depression in both intensity and duration. This has been reflected in all of the APA classification systems. For example, in DSM-I and -II, manic–depressive psychosis–illness was classified separately from conflict or loss-related neurotic depressions. Currently in DSM-III, major affective disorder is separated from the more chronic or subsyndromal types, cyclothymic or dysthymic disorder.

2. In terms of the depressive episode itself, depressions characterized by psychomotor retardation, sleep and appetite disturbance, anhedonia, difficulty concentrating, a distinct quality of mood, and possibly mood-congruent hallucinations and delusions have been distinguished from those without these more severe features. For simplicity, Kendall (1976) has called the former "Type A" depressions and the latter "Type B" depressions. Although the features of Type A depressions are not totally agreed upon, there appears to be greater predictive value in terms of natural history and treatment of this construct than of the more heterogenous Type B depressions, which are those depressions remaining when the Type A group is removed (Andreasen, 1982). Even the empirically derived classification systems of Paykel (1971) and Overall and Zisook (1980) seem to break down to more severe (retarded) and less severe (anxious, hostile) types of depression, as Overall himself notes.

3. Type B depressions are reflected in various classifications as personality disorders, or subsyndromal "neurotic" disorders which depict both less severity and greater chronicity.

4. The use of a "precipitating event" to classify depressive subtypes, which formed the original basis of the differences between en-

Table 1

Some Attempts to Classify Depressive Disorders (Modified from Kendall, 1976)

I. Dimensional typologies
   A. Endogenous/Neurotic (Kiloh & Garside, 1963)
   B. Vital [Melancholic]/Personal (Van Pragg, Uleman, & Spitz, 1965)
   C. Psychotic/Anxious/Hostile/Personality Disorder (Paykel, 1971)
   D. Anxious/Agitated/Retarded/Hostile (Overall & Zisook, 1980)
II. Categorical typologies based on natural history and phenomenology
   A. Involutional/Manic-Depressive/Psychotic/Neurotic (DSM-I and II, American Psychiatric Association, 1952, 1968)
   B. Unipolar/Bipolar (Leonhard, 1959; Perris, 1966)
   C. Primary/Secondary (Woodruff et al., 1967)
   D. ICD–9 (World Health Organization, 1977)
      1. Affective psychoses (manic depressive disorders)
      2. Other nonorganic psychoses (depressive and excitative types)
      3. Neurotic disorders (neurotic depression)
      4. Personality disorders (affective personality)
      5. Stress reactions
      6. Adjustment reactions (brief or prolonged depressive reaction)
      7. Depressive Disorder (not elsewhere classified)
   E. DSM-III (American Psychiatric Association, 1980)
      1. Major Affective Disorders
         Bipolar disorder
         Major depression
      2. Other specific affective disorders
         Cyclothymic disorder
         Dysthmic disorder
      3. Atypical affective disorder
      4. Adjustment disorder with depressed mood
III. Family History Typologies (Winokur, 1979)
      Unipolar Depression
         Nonfamilial (no family history of depression)
         Pure (family history of depression only)
         Depressive Spectrum (family history of depression and/or alcoholism, antisocial personality, drug abuse, Briquet's Syndrome)

dogenous (no precipitating event) and reactive (precipitating event) depressions has been eliminated from the classification of major depressions, yet both ICD-9 and DSM-III have categories for adjustment reactions with depressive manifestations suggesting that some clinicians feel a separate category is still necessary.

In summary, depressions in adults can be said to fall into three groups: (1) severe, episodic (with a distinct quality of mood, vegetative symptoms, psychomotor retardation, diurnal mood variation, anhedonia, concentration difficulty); (2) less severe but either chronic or as part of a personality disorder; and (3) obviously stress-related but relatively short lived. As with impressionist paintings, however, it is obvious that closer inspection reveals less rather than greater clarity between these distinctions.

Classification of Depression in Children

We have already discussed the evolution of the current concept of childhood depression. It would appear, however, that the controversy regarding the existence of depression in children has not particularly centered on the Type B chronic or subsyndromal depressions. For instance, Anthony (1977) has quoted the following from Burton's 1621 text on melancholy: "Bad parents, step-mothers, tutors, masters, teachers too rigorous and too severe, or too remiss or indulgent on the other side, are often fountains and furtherers of this disease [depression]. Parents and such as have the tuition and oversight of children offend many times in that they are too stern, always threatening, chiding, brawling, whipping or striking; by means of which their poor children are so disheartened and cowed that they never after have any courage, a merry hour in their lives or take pleasure in anything. . . ." Children responding with depressive symptoms to chronically miserable environmental situations, whether they actually meet criteria for depressive illness or not, have been recognized for years.

An issue in the nosology of childhood depression is whether either a Type A or episodic "endogenous" depressive illness or the depressive component of bipolar disorder exists in children, and if it can be distinguished from misery, situational dysphorias, or appropriate withdrawal from noxious stimuli (Gittelman-Klein, 1977). Before going further, however, we need to clarify what is meant by "childhood." Until recently, adolescents were included in discussions of childhood psychopathology; however, regarding the phenomenology and natural history of depressive disorders, they appear more like adults. There is no question regarding the existence of "Type A" depression in postpubertal youngsters; these depressions became evident once they were systematically sought. Bipolar disorder (as manic–depressive illness, circular type is called in DSM-III) occurs not infrequently among adolescent inpatients (Carlson & Strober, 1978; Gammon et al., 1983; Hassanyeh & Davidson, 1980; Strober & Carlson, 1982). Endogenous/melancholic and mood-congruent psychotic symptoms are also identifiable in adolescent psychiatric patients subjected to structured interviews (Gammon et al., 1983; Strober & Carlson, 1982). Finally, major depressions beginning in adolescence have durations similar to those found with depressions in adults (M. Strober, personal communication, September, 1984) and similar predictors of a bipolar course (Strober & Carlson, 1982).

Difficulty identifying and classifying depressive symptoms in prepubertal youngsters brings us to direct confrontation with circumstances that make psychopathology in children different from adults. In addition to all of the definitional, reliability, and boundary problems attendant in the classification of adult depression, there are three additional complications which occur in children. The first problem is that of assessing symptoms and feelings in youngsters whose language abilities and concept formation are immature. Kovacs discusses these issues in another chapter, and it becomes especially relevant in discerning many of the symptoms of Type A depression, as we will see shortly. The second problem is whether symptoms that signify pathology at one age necessarily do so at another. Enuresis and fears of monsters under one's bed mean something very different at age 22 than they do at age 2. Depressive symptoms such as appetite change and sleep problems are not uncommon in preschoolers (Earls, 1980). Even if they co-occur with sad mood, irritability, and poor concentration, does this constellation describe a true depressive episode in a child of this age? The final problem that arises from application of adult classification systems to children may be that signs and symptoms unique to children may be missed.

Attempts to classify childhood depression have obviously paralleled the efforts to identify it. With each revision of the APA *Diagnostic and Statistical Manual* there has been a further refinement in the criteria and categories of childhood disorders.

DSM-III (American Psychiatric Association, 1980), for instance has tried to operationalize syndrome definitions. In its multiaxial approach, it incorporates developmental, personality and psychosocial variables into the diagnostic framework. However, depression as it may specifically occur in children is still given no special designation since at DSM-III's writing investigators either denied its existence or felt that the core psychopathologic symptoms present in adults were also present in children. There are, nevertheless, some symptom modifications for children: for example, for "Symptom" 1, "poor appetite or significant weight loss," "failure to make expected weight gains" is noted for children under age 6. In "Symptom" 3, hypoactivity rather than psychomotor agitation or retardation is allowed, and in "Symptom" 4, apathy rather than "loss of interest or pleasure in usual activities" is noted in children under age 6. Although they make clinical sense, even these modifications have not been validated since depression in children under age 6 is even harder to identify than in the somewhat more studied 7–17-year-old populations. As stated earlier, the implications of these symptoms at different developmental stages is not yet clear, nor are the childhood antecedents of some of the symptoms that have implications for adult depression. Rutter (this volume) has emphasized that symptom frequency is one area where stage of development seems to make a significant difference. However, the capacity of the developing organism even to manifest certain symptoms and the consequent change in phenomenology determined by changing maturational levels represents another interface of development and psychopathology.

Another classification system, that developed by the Group for the Advancement of Psychiatry (1966), has a specific category for psychoneurotic disorder, depressive type. In this nosology the description of the disorder explicity states that, "Depression in children and even adolescents may be manifested in ways somewhat different from those manifested in adults" (p. 236). Psychomotor retardation and some of the other biological signs of depression are considered to be less marked than in adults. This classification makes a distinction on the basis of age suggesting that symptoms such as low self-esteem, guilt, and ambivalence toward a loved person are more likely to be present in older children. Furthermore, chronic psychoneurotic depressive disorder is considered to be rare because the internalized conflicts and ambivalent feelings associated with it tend to be modified by the child's stage of development.

Finally, in the triaxial system of classification developed by the World Health Organization (Rutter et al., 1969) and used as something of a model for DSM-III, depressive disorders are described in the glossary under "neurotic disorders" as "emotional disorders in this category include states of disproportionate anxiety or depression" (p. 59). Rutter et al. (1969) suggested that a separate category for depressive reaction in children was not justified because symptoms of depression are often associated with a variety of other neurotic disorders. Moreover, they questioned whether depressive disorder in children was of the same nature as depressive illness in adults.

A number of typologies have addressed themselves specifically to childhood disorders. They might be said to fall into two subgroups: those that have used original "child-centered" categories which are based on phenomenology or age (e.g., depression in infancy, childhood, adolescence) and those that have superimposed the adult depression classification system onto child psychopathology. In most cases, data are derived from older reports that suffer both from inadequately defined populations and from lack of systematically acquired symptom information, so it is very difficult to know what psychopathological entities are actually being described. In some respects, knowledge of child development has been a handicap because clinicians presumed that children did not understand, did not feel, or did not think in ways that allowed for the possibility of a depressive syndrome.

CHILD-CENTERED CLASSIFICATIONS

A review of the "child-centered" classifications reveals that a number of authors (Cytryn & McKnew, 1972; Frommer, 1968; Malmquist, 1971; Stack, 1971), described basically similar categories: first are the acute, pure or simple depressions that seem to be the most easily identified, by adult criteria at least, and which seem to have a relatively good prognosis. The second group, or alternate forms of depression, subsume those "masked" disorders in which symptoms of anxiety predominate. These are the separation-type (Malmquist, 1971), phobic (Frommer, 1968) and psychosomatic depression (Eisen, 1973), or those in which "acting out" symptoms are most noticeable (Cytryn & McKnew, 1972). The third type are the chronic depressions, in which depression and misery seem to be accounted for by long-standing deprivation and learning problems or in which other problems (e.g., enuresis) are prominent (Cytryn & McKnew, 1972; Eisen, 1973; Frommer, 1968; Malmquist, 1971). This is a somewhat different breakdown from the Type A, Type B, and stress-related depression seen in the adult typologies and may suggest some major differences in phenomenology between childhood and adult depressions.

Only a little light can be shed on the relevance of "child-centered" classifications to current concepts of depression. Cytryn et al. (1980) reexamined their earlier classification system using DSM-III criteria and found considerable consistency (87%) between "acute" and "chronic" depressions and DSM-III major affective disorders with the chronic depressions being more likely recurrent. The children with "masked depression" were considerably more likely (71%) to have been diagnosed as having another disorder.

Specific developmental approaches to classification have been, for the most part, anecdotal or theoretical. Bemporad and Wilson (1978) have reviewed the relevance of anaclitic depression in infancy to childhood depression and conclude along with Sandler and Joffe (1965) that such depressive-like states are more likely a "basic psychobiological reaction to deprivation." The withdrawal, "psychomotor retardation," somber appearance and failure to thrive are, of course, symptomatically similar to depressive syndromes in adults. Here again, then, is the problem of whether similar symptoms and behaviors mean the same things at different ages.

The existence and manifestations of depressive syndromes in preschool children are also controversial. In the 1952 volume of The Nervous Child, devoted to manic–depressive disorders in children, several authors described cyclothymia and depression in 3–5-year-old children. More recently, Weinberg and Brumback (1976a, 1976b) and Brumback and Weinberg (1977) have presented case histories of episodes of depression and mania in preschoolers. From the material presented, however, it is difficult to separate notions of temperament and the episodic but normal developmental regressions described by Gesell (1940) and more recently Ames and Ilg (1976), from more serious psychopathology. Ushakov and Girich (1971) reviewed 100 children who had had at least one period of depression (84 were secondary to massive, traumatizing factors; 16 were recurrent depressions). In children under age 7 they felt that the "lack of contour and diffuseness" (and transience) of symptoms characterized responses which, when seen in older children, were better defined and more typically depressive. Certainly the cognitive and affectual limitations of the preoperational period suggest that different strategies are necessary to determine the presence of frank depressions or even "formes fruste" of the disorder.

Depression in school-aged children has been more thoroughly studied, and the child-centered classifications previously discussed are relevant to this age group. Suffice it to say, however, that children change enormously between the ages of 6 and 12—so much that it may not be relevant to lump them together in phenomenologic studies of psychopathology. In their study of depressive reactions, Ushakov and Girich (1971) found that the 24 7–10-year-olds differed from their younger counterparts in that (a) depressive symptoms were more clearly expressed and more persistent than in younger children who were easily diverted from their misery; (b) episodes of melancholy could be distinguished from a background of sadness and were recognized and complained of by the child; (c) symptoms of anxiety, which were more prominent especially toward night in younger children, were less so in the older group, though some children showed tics and obsessive–compulsive movements; (d) suicidal feelings were expressed for the first time but secondary to spiteful feelings rather than the feelings of self-reproach seen in adults.

Depressive symptoms in the 26 11–13-year-olds were "more fully expressed and pronounced." This group also differed from the 7–10-year-old children in their greater awareness of their illness and its cause, and in the further diminishing number of "anxiety, neurotic symptoms and behavioral deviations"; a few children were noted as having rudimentary depressive delusions. Thus, with advancing age through middle and later childhood, the diffuseness apparent at younger ages seems to concretize and become more recognizable as symptoms usually associated with depression.

In another study, McConville et al. (1973) examined the relationship of depressive symptom types to ages between 6 and 13 in 75 inpatients. These subjects were selected on the basis of having depressive symptoms noted in their records. Symptoms in the 6–8-year-olds were primarily of the "affectual type" and consisted of sadness, helplessness, occasional hopelessness, feelings of loneliness, and being withdrawn from peers. Slightly older children manifested more of the cognitive symptoms of depression—low self-esteem, worthlessness, and feelings of being unloved. The authors note, however, that many of these youngsters were continually experiencing loss in their environments; hence these feelings were not entirely illogical. Nonetheless, McConville et al. felt that the children's more advanced abilities to verbalize accounted for the more cognitive symptoms presented. The third pattern, seen in only a few older children, consisted of symptoms on a more delusional spectrum. These youngsters felt wicked, that they deserved to die, and auditory hallucinations were noted in two children. McConville et al. state that even in these children "thoughts lacked the intensity, attacking and sadistic quality experienced in adult depressive psychoses in which the patient tends to entertain absolute convictions of infinite and irrevocable wickedness." Thus, both the Russian and Canadian studies concur regarding the presence, albeit infrequent and immature, of delusional depressions (Type A depression?) but not until late childhood and early adolescence.

Finally, in a recent study of girls between the ages of 7 and 13 referred for psychological evaluation because of academic, behavioral, and/or emotional concerns, Garber (1984b) reported that there tends to be an increase with age in the frequency of depressive syndromes as well as in several of the individual depressive symptoms comprising the syndrome. Symptoms requiring more well-developed cognitive capacities such as hopelessness, guilt, and low self-esteem, in addition to other symptoms such as loss of interest, appetite problems, and hypoactivity were rated significantly higher (i.e., more severe) in the 12- and 13-year-olds as compared to the 7–11-year-olds. Thus, there is some support for the notion that the occurrence of depressive symptomatology changes with age and becomes more adultlike in its appearance as adolescence approaches.

ADULT TYPOLOGIES IN CHILDREN

Specific attempts to use adult typologies in children can be found in the older literature. Rarely, however, are *prepubertal* children described. Of the 18 cases of "manic–depressive psychosis" reported by Campbell (1953) only 5 were under age 13 at onset of depressive symptoms and one child was noted to be pubertal at age 10 when her symptoms began. All children had what would be now called major depressive episodes without a bipolar course. The level of impairment, lack of environmental precipitants, and presence of guilt, anhedonia, psychomotor retardation, and anorexia/weight loss described in the case reports qualified the 4 prepubertal children (ages 6, 7, 10, 12) for the endogenous type of depression under DSM-I and II terminology.

More recently, Cebiroglu, Sumer, and Polvan (1971) provided information about 10,661 children referred over 10 years to a university child psychiatry department in Istanbul. Eighty-five of these (.8%) were diagnosed as having depressive syndromes and although no information or case description is provided to delineate his criteria, the author found that 47 of these 85 (55%) had psychoneurotic (chronic) depression, 19 (22%) reactive depressions (stress related), 7 (8%) endogenous depression, 2 (2%) manic depressive psychosis, 3 (3.5%) anaclitic depression, and 7 (8%) schizoid depression. Obviously, the endogenous and manic depressive disorders are quite rare. Although not broken down into diagnostic subgroups, 5 children were between ages 3 and 6, 33 between ages 7 and 10, and 47 between ages 11 and 16. Boys and girls were equally represented.

Many investigators are currently systematically examining the nosology of depression in children with standardized interview schedules and specific criteria. It has not been difficult to isolate populations of children who by DSM-III or Research Diagnostic Criteria can be defined as having major depressive disorder, dysthymic disorder or adjustment disorder with depressed mood. This DSM-III typology in part parallels categories of the "child-centered" classification systems. The major depressions and adjustment reactions with depressed mood have relatively limited courses. Dysthymic disorder, like the chronic depressions, is more insidious and debilitating (Kovacs, Feinberg, Crouse-Novak, Paulauskas, & Finkelstein, 1984). The child-centered typologies did not identify Type A depressions and there seems to be some difference of opinion even now regarding the ease of finding either endogenously or psychotically depressed prepubertal youngsters.

As noted earlier, the current edition of the *APA Diagnostic and Statistical Manual* (DSM-III) recognizes the entity of endogenous depression under the classification of Major Depression with melancholia. Criteria include pervasive anhedonia and lack of reactivity to usually pleasurable experiences and three of the next six items: (a) depressed mood, perceived as qualitatively different from a loss experience, (b) depression worse in the morning, (c) early morning awakening (at least 2 hours earlier than usual), (d) marked psychomotor retardation or agitation, (e) significant anorexia or weight loss, (f) excessive or inappropriate guilt. Although there is currently a great deal of research in this area, little has yet been published regarding the frequency of these specific symptoms or the constellation of melancholia subtype per se in children. Chambers, Puig-Antich, Tabrizi, and Davies (1982) reported on 58 prepubertal depressive children and found that about half met Research Diagnostic Criteria for endogenous subtype. It is the opinion of this group that if interview questions are phrased properly the child will be able to articulate these features. E. O. Poznanski (personal communication, June 1984) and M. Kovacs (personal communication, June 1984) have found endogenous features to be considerably less frequent than 50% and are unclear whether this represents lower prevalence of endogenous subtypes in their populations or the limitations of adult criteria imposed onto younger children. Our own clinical experiences fall somewhere between these two extremes. There are some children, though not 50% of depressives, who fit the endogenous depression symptom cluster and who seem to have adult-type depressive features. In our experience they are exceedingly rare under 9 years of age. More frequent are children who can be said to have nonreactive mood, greater irritability in the morning, vegetative symptoms (though these are often chronic), and feelings of being "bad" if not guilty, who satisfy the letter but not the meaning of the criteria, so to speak. It is often the case even with adults who are floundering to describe their feelings that when you describe something they have experienced they can easily agree. When this does not happen with children, as in the case of some of the endogenous symptoms, it is difficult to know if the child has not experienced it, does not understand it, or the examiner simply has not phrased the question correctly. The questions, then, of the frequency of occurrence of endogenous depression in prepubertal children, and the developmental modifications that occur in symptomatology, have yet to be clarified.

Related to the concept of endogenous depression is that of psychotic depression. In the same study cited above, Chambers *et al.* (1982) reported that 38% of 58 prepubertal children had psychopathologically meaningful hallucinations though in only 39% of these cases were the hallucinations of a specific mood-congruent nature, and only in 29% of cases were hallucinations of sufficient severity to influence the child's behavior. On the other hand, delusions were very uncommon, occurring in only three children. Hallucinations are considerably less common in adolescents and adults with depression, and mood-congruent delusions account for more "psychosis" than hallucinations (Ianzito, Cadoret, & Pugh, 1974; Winokur, Clayton, & Reich, 1969). The relationship of age to the type of hallucination has not been analyzed, so whether the nonspecific hallucinations that characterized the majority of psychotic children represents the younger children is unknown. Do these nonspecific (i.e., mood-incongruent, less severe) but otherwise psychotic symptoms represent the "diffuseness and lack of contour" that seemed to characterize objective symptoms in younger children? Or do they represent distress in a nondiagnostic way? In any event, it is unlikely that psychotic depressions in these prepubertal children are continuous with adult psychotic depressions since the frequency seems to be so different in these age groups.

We have not specifically discussed the issue of mania in prepubertal children. It is relevant only insofar as it accompanies and subcategorizes certain kinds of depressive disorders. As has been summarized elsewhere (Carlson, 1983), cases of unequivocal bipolar affective disorder become more rare with every year below puberty. Many of the same developmental issues hold for mania as they do for depression. That is, do the seemingly grandiose, or hyperactive, silly, or expansive behaviors occasionally observed in some children mean the same things as they do in postpubertal children and adults? Many feel the absence of clear-cut episodes of mania in children below age 9 casts doubt on the existence of manic depressive or bipolar disorder and by extension, therefore, of Type A depression in young children.

IMPLICATIONS OF THE DEVELOPMENTAL PERSPECTIVE FOR THE CLASSIFICATION OF CHILDHOOD DEPRESSION

Thus far, we have outlined some of the general issues of classification and the specific subcategories within both adult- and child-oriented classifications of depression. Although there is a basic consensus concerning the

value of the process of classification itself, there is considerably less agreement as to how best to categorize and subdivide the disorder of depression
in both adults and children. Given that there is still some controversy concerning the various subtypes of depression in adults, it makes sense to proceed cautiously to examine the validity of these subtypes with respect to
childhood depression, particularly the categories of endogenous, psychotic, bipolar, and episodic versus chronic.

Beyond the issue of subtypes of depression, however, is the central
question of development and the classification of childhood depression
within a developmental framework. A developmental perspective involves
more than simply looking for isomorphisms in symptomatology across different ages. It is concerned with the entire question of the continuities and
discontinuities between normality and disorder, and between one developmental period and the next and the transitions between them (see Cicchetti
& Schneider-Rosen, this volume).

Briefly, this perspective suggests that development proceeds in an
orderly fashion from a state of relative globality and lack of differentiation
to a state of increasing complexity and hierarchic organization (Werner,
1948). Despite periods of reorganization, however, the coherence of the individual is maintained through the integration of the individual's earlier
structures with later ones. Moreover, these series of behavioral reorganizations take place around specific salient developmental issues, and the quality of the individual's adaptation is judged with respect to how well he or
she negotiates these tasks (Matas, Arend, & Sroufe, 1978). Finally, the various developmental issues are broadly integrative and cut across affective,
social, and cognitive domains. The individual's current level of functioning
is viewed in terms of the level of adaptation in each of these domains.

According to this developmental perspective, psychopathology results
when there is a lack of organization or integration of social, cognitive, or
emotional competences that influences the successful resolution of the salient developmental tasks that need to be accomplished within each domain
(Cicchetti & Schneider-Rosen, this volume). Maladaptation is defined in
terms of incompetence or deviation in the completion of developmentally
defined tasks (Sroufe, 1979), or the failure to deal with phase-appropriate
experiences (Greenspan, Lourie, & Nover, 1979).

Despite arguments to the contrary (Santostefano, 1971), the developmental model is not by definition antagonistic to nosology. Rather, the developmental perspective complements standard diagnostic classification
schema (Greenspan et al., 1979) by highlighting new dimensions, variables,
and parameters that need to be incorporated into a more inclusive and extensive developmentally relevant nosology. Moreover, the developmental
perspective provides a broader framework in which to address the issues of
the predictions origins and time course, and the clinical manifestations of
psychopathology over the course of development.

What are the implications of this developmental perspective for the classification of childhood depression? This question can best be addressed by examining further the more general issue concerning the continuity between childhood and adult psychopathology. Garber (1984a) recently outlined three important questions relevant to this continuity issue. First, are the diagnostic criteria that define adult psychopathology appropriate for use with children? Maturational differences may shape children's ability to experience or express certain affects, cognitions, and behaviors, and thus the manner in which symptoms are expressed may differ over the course of development. This issue has been at the heart of the controversy surrounding the diagnosis of depression in children. Although historically the tendency was to deny the existence of the syndrome in children or to assert that it only could be recognized in "masked" forms, the current trend is at risk of falling into the trap of "adultomorphism" (Phillips, Draguns, & Bartlett, 1975) by applying the adult criteria, essentially unmodified, to children.

Developmental psychopathologists have begun to question this current trend and argue that the "adult-based" diagnostic criteria are not developmentally oriented in that they do not take sufficient account of possible age-related differences in the defining attributes or manifest expression of the syndrome (Kovacs, this volume). Thus, one direct implication of the developmental perspective is that because development proceeds from diffuse and global to the more complex and differentiated, the very nature of the symptoms expressed at various ages may differ significantly.

Cicchetti and Schneider-Rosen (this volume) suggest further that we would not expect to find behavioral isomorphism in observed signs or symptoms of depression in children of different ages, and therefore it is futile to try to define symptom characteristics that comprise the diagnostic picture for depression that can be applied across ages. A major reason for this concern is that developmental advances in cognitive structures and functioning will influence the manner in which children experience, interpret, and express emotions at different ages.

An alternative, and somewhat less pessimistic view of the diagnostic enterprise is not that the search for symptomatic isomorphism is futile, but that it is insufficient. Using the developmental perspective as a guide, it may be possible to identify age-appropriate signs and symptoms that take into consideration the child's level of functioning within the various cognitive, affective, and social domains. The developmental perspective does not dictate that we abandon symptom-complex diagnosis, but rather that we go beyond it.

Thus, according to this developmental perspective we would search to identify additional phase-specific manifestations of the depressive syndrome while possibly eliminating or deemphasizing other symptoms that are age-inappropriate in view of the child's current level of functioning. For example, through empirical investigations we may discover that there are certain symptoms of the adult depressive syndrome (e.g., guilt, hopelessness) that require a higher level of cognitive functioning and therefore might not be expected to be manifested in younger children. Hence, these particular symptoms may not be appropriate for inclusion in the definition of the syndrome for this age group. On the other hand, there may be other symptoms not typically associated with the adult syndrome that are found to empirically cluster with the more familiar depressive syndrome and therefore should be added to it. Such symptoms as aggression and somatic complaints that may reflect children's less mature coping strategies and defensive styles are potential examples here.

An important implication of this view for the classification of childhood depression is that we may need to revise our current diagnostic criteria so as to reflect these developmental differences. For example, in DSM-III, four out of eight symptoms are currently required for a diagnosis of Major Depressive Disorder, and all symptoms are implicitly given equal weight. The developmental perspective suggests, however, that we may want to construct a somewhat more complex set of diagnostic rules involving a two-tiered process that takes into consideration different base rates as a function of age. The first tier would include a set of core indicators, consisting of those signs and symptoms that are found to occur with a similar frequency regardless of age. A certain required number of these symptoms would be necessary for the diagnosis of depression, similar to the system currently used in DSM-III. However, there would be a second set of indicators consisting of those symptoms found more rarely in children (e.g., guilt, suicidal ideation), that would contribute to the required number of symptoms if they were present, but would not alter the diagnosis if they were absent. Finally, there might be a third set of indicators that are found to be highly associated with depression in children (e.g., social withdrawal), but are not specifically listed among the adult criteria, that, if present, also would contribute to the required number of symptoms for the diagnosis. Thus, symptoms would be given a different weighting in the list of required criteria, as a function of their different base rates at different ages.

In addition, the actual number of symptoms required for the diagnosis may need to be reevaluated for the different age groups. Finn (1982) questioned the very use of fixed diagnostic rules because they fail to consider shifts in the base rates in different clinical settings. A similar concern would apply to the use of fixed diagnostic rules that do not consider different base rates as a function of age. As Meehl and Rosen (1955), among others, have pointed out, choosing an optimal cutting score to diagnose membership or nonmembership in a category requires consideration of not only the amount and type of diagnostic error one is willing to tolerate (e.g., Type I or Type II), but also the base rate of the category.

Another way of moving beyond the problem of the lack of behavioral isomorphism between the adult and child symptoms is to broaden the definitions of the symptoms to reflect developmental differences in phenomenology. It may be that the general areas of dysfunction associated with depression including the affective, cognitive, vegetative, and behavioral components are similar across development, but the specific symptoms and behaviors that characterize dysfunction may vary with age. Therefore, the definition of the symptom or area of dysfunction should be broad enough to include age-appropriate manifestations. A simple example is that anhedonia in adults typically is assessed in terms of loss of interest in sex or other leisure activities. For children, anhedonia is more appropriately defined in terms of sustained periods of boredom or loss of interest in usual sources of pleasure such as games or toys.

A somewhat more complex example concerns the affective component of depression. Whereas depressed adults typically give sadness as the predominant affect they feel, children, particularly younger ones, are less likely to verbalize such a feeling of sadness directly. Rather, they may *appear* sad or tearful in terms of their nonverbal behaviors, or they may use other terms to describe their affective experience in terms of feeling "bad" or "lousy" or "rotten." Before accepting any of these terms as equivalent to or at least related to sadness, we need to conduct normative developmental studies of children's expression of affect to see if this is their age-appropriate manner of expressing this symptom. Similar studies should be conducted to identify the age-appropriate manifestations of such other depressive symptoms as low self-esteem and morbid ideation. The ultimate test of the validity of these alternative developmental expressions of the various symptoms of depression is (a) whether the symptoms cluster together into a meaningful and internally consistent syndrome, and (b) whether this coherent syndrome forms a clinical entity with a particular etiology, course, prognosis, and response to treatment.

The second question derived from the continuity issue is concerned with whether or not there is a relationship between the childhood onset of a disorder and later adult psychopathology, and what are the implications for diagnosis and classification if no such continuity is found? Is depression during childhood necessarily a precursor to an emerging affective disorder in adulthood rather than an entity in its own right? Conversely, to what extent is adult depression preceded by the same disorder during childhood.

Follow-up studies of depressed adolescents in general have tended to show that a significant proportion of depressed adolescents have future episodes of depression (Garber, Koch, Kriss, & Lindholm, 1983; King & Pittman, 1970; Welner, Welner, & Fishman, 1970). Considerably less is known, however about the outcome of depressions with a prepubertal onset (Kovacs, Feinberg, Crouse-Novak, Paulauskas, & Finkelstein, 1984), the childhood psychiatric history of adult depressives (Orvaschel, Weissman, & Kidd, 1980).

Although since the time of Kraepelin (1883) the natural history and outcome of psychopathological conditions have been regarded as important validating features of diagnostic classification, it is not necessary for a disorder to persist into adulthood in order to be considered a valid entity in its own right during childhood. The issue of the continuity between childhood and adult depression is theoretically interesting and may have important implications for etiology and treatment, but it should not be considered as a necessary criterion for the diagnosis of depression during childhood. As Rutter (1965) has suggested, it is possible for a child to have one kind of psychiatric disorder at age 5 and another at age 12. This emphasis on the classification of disorders rather than the child allows for the diagnosis of disorders in the context of development.

This raises the third question derived from the continuity issue which is concerned with "continuity with respect to what?" If there is indeed little evidence of homotypic continuity—symptomatic isomorphism from early childhood (Kagan, 1971; Kohlberg, LaCrosse, & Ricks, 1976; Masters & Wellman, 1974; Mischel, 1968), then what are the proper choice of units for studying the coherence of the individual with development? According to an organizational–developmental perspective (Block & Block, 1979; Cicchetti & Rizley, 1981; Sroufe, 1979), a specific pattern of behaviors occurring as a particular developmental level and in a particular context is not necessarily predicted to recur in the same form or similar contexts at a later point in development. Rather, there tends to be some consistency in individuals' general adaptive or maladaptive patterns of organizing their experiences and interacting with the environment (Block & Block, 1979; Rutter, 1977; Sroufe, 1979). Thus, the continuity of development is expressed in organized patterns of behavior over time rather than in isolated behaviors.

The implications of such an organizational–developmental perspective for classification is that diagnostic models should emphasize adaptation and the organization of behavior at various developmental levels in addition to the more static notion of symptoms and signs. Psychiatric nosology with respect to childhood psychopathology should widen its focus to include the classification of levels of adaptation and competence with respect to the salient issues for the particular developmental period. Such an approach necessitates the categorizing of different types of healthy and maladaptive functioning as well as a cataloguing of the most salient age-appropriate tasks for each phase of development.

Once the salient developmental issues for the various age levels are identified and the modes of adaptation and maladaptation to them are categorized, these patterns of adaptation can be assessed and related to future psychopathology. In a study examining the relationship between childhood social competence and later psychopathological disorders, Lewine, Watt, Prentky, and Fryer (1980) found that children eventually hospitalized for schizophrenia in adult life were characterized by poor interpersonal skills long before symptom onset, whereas the social competence scores of individuals later manifesting psychotic depression were not significantly different from normals. It would be interesting to speculate about what might be the salient development issues relevant to the origin and maintenance of depression in children as well as adults. Such issues as coping with loss, the development of a sense of self, or attachment relationships may be particularly salient issues in the development of depression.

Thus, the developmental perspective suggests that the continuity between childhood and adult psychopathology lies in the link between early adaptation (or maladaptation) and later disorder rather than simply in the behavioral isomorphism of discrete symptomatology. This perspective allows us to examine individual coherence with respect to both failures in adaptation as well as nonpathological patterns that predict later pathology.

A final implication of the developmental perspective for the classification of childhood psychopathology concerns the importance of understanding normal development in each of the various affective, cognitive, and social domains in order to recognize and assess deviation from expected patterns at each age level. A classification that includes some notion of what is the normal progression of development in each of these various domains will facilitate the assessment of a child's current level of functioning and progress over time relative to an expected baseline. This system of classification will enable us to identify the type of impaired functioning associated with particular disorders, as well as to examine the impact of advances or lags in one domain upon another within both normal and atypical populations.

SUMMARY AND CONCLUSION

The major conclusion concerning the continuity between childhood and adult depression is that the same condition may present with a somewhat different clinical picture at different phases of development. These phenotypic differences are apparently a result of children's less mature and continually changing levels of functioning. We conclude, therefore, that the criteria used to diagnose a disorder may need to be altered somewhat in order to reflect these developmental differences.

There are two important questions that follow from this conclusion. First, how much overlap in manifest symptomatology is necessary in order to consider it the same disorder? One interesting perspective on this problem has been presented by Cantor, Smith, French, and Mezzich (1980). They have proposed a prototype view of categorization as an alternative to classical systems. This view essentially states that a prototype is "representative" of the category. Membership in the category is evaluated in terms of the overlap between the particular instance and the category prototype. Features are neither necessary nor sufficient. The advantage of this approach is that it permits heterogeneity and borderline cases.

The concept of prototypes is very similar to what Kraepelin, and before him Plato, referred to as "ideal types." According to Kraepelin, in the area of medicine, diseases are the ideal types, and each patient's symptoms are only an approximation to an essential "ideal" disease process (Blashfield, 1984). Thus, no real patient's symptoms perfectly characterize the ideal type. There are only degrees of overlap with the so-called ideal disorder.

The application of the concept of ideal types or prototypes to psychiatric nosology may be particularly useful for the comparison of child and adult depression. Rather than there being a specific set of necessary and sufficient defining features that both children and adults must manifest in order to be judged as a member of a category (e.g., depression), there could be a modal prototype from which there would be age-dependent variations. The degree of similarity between them could be judged in terms of the extent of overlap in features with the category prototype. Such a prototypic classification could facilitate the recognition of developmental differences in the same disorder.

The second, and essential question is, if the phenomenology of adult and childhood depressions are different and only approximate an "ideal" prototype, then how do we decide that the basic disorders are "the same?" Are there valid external criteria for determining whether the different phenotypic pictures of depression found for children and adults really comprise essentially the same disorder? The difficulty here is that in the area of Major Affective Disorders no unambiguous criteria exist.

There have been several attempts to identify biological markers of depression such as the dexamethasone suppression test (Carroll et al., 1981) or urinary MHPG (Schildkraut et al., 1978). Although a potentially promising approach, currently the use of biological markers as criterion suffers from the twin difficulties that: (a) the biological markers are not specific to depression even in adults (e.g., Berger, Pirke, Doerr, Krieg, & von Zerssen, 1983; Swartz & Dunner, 1982), and (b) the biological correlates of depression might not be the same in childhood as in adults (Puig-Antich et al., 1982).

Family history findings have been suggested as being useful in terms of implications for common genetic mechanisms, although mechanisms associated with a family history of depression can reflect environmental as well as genetic factors, and these also may differ between children and adults. Thus, being an offspring of a depressed parent has implications not only for one's genetic risk but also for alterations in patterns of parent–child interactions.

Response to antidepressant medication also has been considered, but the difficulty here is that antidepressants have multiple actions. For example, tricyclics are not only an antidepressant but they also reduce hyperactivity and enuresis, have a sedative effect, and affect sleep patterns (Petti, 1983). Finally, course and outcome may be useful, but these suffer from the limitations described in the earlier discussion of the continuity issue. That is, the validity of a psychopathological disorder during childhood is not necessarily dependent on there being future episodes of the disorder over the course of development into adulthood; and similarly, episodes of a disorder during childhood are not necessary for the validity of a disorder during adulthood.

Thus, in the absence of any one criterion, it appears that we must, instead, look for convergence across several different indicators. Similar to the construct validation approach used in test construction in which no one criterion is accepted as entirely adequate to define the construct to be measured (Cronbach & Meehl, 1955), we must set up a nomological network in order to validate the construct of depression in both children and adults. This network would consist of symptom description, etiology, course, outcome, treatment response, and biological and psychological correlates. Although none of these alone is sufficient for demonstrating validity, some combination of these components of the nomological net are required. Thus, once we have defined a set of symptom criteria that approximate a prototype of depression, allowing for some differences as a function of age, we then attempt to validate these criteria with respect to a similar etiology, course, response to treatment, and so on, as defined in our nomological network.

In sum, this chapter attempted to present the current state of knowledge regarding the classification of depressive disorders in children and to suggest the possible contributions of a developmental perspective to classifying this disorder. The most important conclusion to be derived from this review is that the classification and diagnosis of depression in children is by no means a *fait accompli*. Although beginning with the current adult criteria for major affective disorders and all of its various subtypes may be an appropriate initial strategy for studying the phenomenon in children, it is only a preliminary guide to empirical investigations. The validity of these adult diagnostic criteria applied to children must be evaluated further with respect to parallels in manifest symptomatology, etiology, course, prognosis, and treatment response.

However, these investigations must take into consideration the issues derived from the developmental perspective. When parallels between the child and adult syndromes are not found, it may be necessary to modify our current theories and descriptions of the disorder so as to more accurately reflect the processes of development. The few empirical studies that have examined the phenomenology of depression over the course of development have indeed suggested that important differences exist in symptomatology at different ages (Garber, 1984b; McConville et al., 1973; Ushakov &

Girich, 1971). Future investigations need to go even further from a developmental perspective by (a) broadening the existing definitions of symptoms to reflect developmental differences in phenomenology resulting from differing levels of cognitive, linguistic, and socioemotional functioning, and (b) widening the focus beyond symptoms to include the classification of adaptation and competence in the context of the salient issues at each developmental phase.

Finally, there is an obvious need for longitudinal research in order more directly to examine the issue of the continuity between childhood and adult psychopathology. Developmental theorists (Block & Block, 1979; Sroufe, 1979) have suggested that the coherence of the individual may be found in the organization of behavior over time rather than in terms of discrete behaviors. Thus, according to the developmental perspective, longitudinal studies designed to address the continuity question should go beyond the search for homotypic continuity of discrete behaviors, and rather should look for links between early patterns of adaptation and maladaptation to the salient developmental tasks at each developmental level and later forms of dysfunction and disorder.

REFERENCES

Aldrich, G. K. (1971). Thief. *Psychology Today*, 4, 66–69.

Allport, G. (1937). *Personality: A psychological interpretation*. New York: Holt, Rinehart & Winston.

American Psychiatric Association. (1952). *Diagnostic and statistical manual of mental disorders* (1st ed.). Washington, DC: APA.

American Psychiatric Association. (1968). *Diagnostic and statistical manual of mental disorders* (2nd ed.). Washington, DC: APA.

American Psychiatric Association. (1980). *Diagnostic and statistical manual of mental disorders* (3rd ed.). Washington, DC: APA.

Ames, L. B., & Ilg, F. (1976). *Your four year old: Wild and wonderful*. Gesell Institute of Child Development. New York: Dell.

Andreasen N C (1982). Concepts, diagnosis and classification. E. S. Paykel (Ed.), *Handbook of affective disorders*. New York: Guilford.

Anthony, E. J. (1969). Taxonomy is not one man's business. *International Journal of Psychiatry*, 7, 173–178.

Anthony, E. J. (1977). Depression in children. In D. Burrows (Ed.), *Handbook of studies on depression*. Amsterdam: Excerpta Medica.

Apley, J. (1959). *The child with abdominal pains*. Oxford: Blackwell Scientific Publications.

Baldwin, J. A. (1969). Statistical classification in psychiatry: A new international diagnostic code. *International Journal of Psychiatry*, 7, 378–381.

Bandura, A. (1969). *Principles of behavior modification*. New York: Holt, Rinehart & Winston.

Barber, T. X., & Silver, M. J. (1968). Facts, fiction and the experimenter bias effect. *Psychological Bulletin Monograph*, 70, 1–29.

Beck, S. (1953). The science of personality: Nomothetic or idiographic? *Psychological Review*, 60, 353–359.

Beez, W. V. (1968). Influence of biased psychological reports on teacher behavior and pupil performance. *Proceedings of the 76th Annual Convention of the American Psychological Association*. Washington, D.C.: APA.

Beitchman, J. H., Dietman, T. E., Landis, J. R., Benson, R. M., & Kemp, P. L. (1978). Reliability of the group for the advancement of psychiatry diagnostic categories in child psychiatry. *Archives of General Psychiatry, 35,* 1461–1466.

Bemporad, J. R., & Wilson, A. (1978). A developmental approach to depression in childhood and adolescence. *Journal of the American Academy of Psychoanalysis, 6,* 325–352.

Berger, M., Pirke, K., Doerr, P., Krieg, C., & von Zerssen, D. (1983). Influence of weight loss on the Dexamethasone Suppression Test. *Archives of General Psychiatry, 40,* 585–586.

Blashfield, R. K. (1984). *The classification of psychopathology.* New York: Plenum Press.

Blashfield, R. K., & Draguns, J. G. (1976a). Evaluative criteria for psychiatric classification. *Journal of Abnormal Psychology, 85,* 140–150.

Blashfield, R. K., & Draguns, J. G. (1976b). Toward a taxonomy of psychopathology: The purpose of psychiatric classification. *British Journal of Psychiatry, 129,* 574–583.

Block, J. H., & Block, J. (1979). The role of ego-control and ego-resiliency in the organization of behavior. In W. A. Collins (Ed.), *Minnesota symposium on child psychology* (Vol. 13). Hillside, NJ: Lawrence Erlbaum Associates.

Boekel, N. (1969). The influence of teacher expectations on the performance of the performance of the educable mentally retarded. *Focus on Exceptional Children, 1,* 6–10.

Brophy, J. E., & Good, T. L. (1974). *Teacher-student relationships: Causes and consequences.* New York: Holt, Rinehart, & Winston.

Brumback, R. A., & Weinberg, W. A. (1977). Mania in childhood II—Therapeutic trial of lithium carborate and further description of manic–depressive illness in children. *American Journal of Diseases of Children, 131,* 1122–1128.

Burks, H. L., & Harrison, S. I. (1962). Aggressive behavior as a means of avoiding depression. *American Journal of Orthopsychiatry, 32,* 416–422.

Campbell, J. D. (1953). *Manic depressive disease.* Philadelphia: Lippincott.

Cantor, N., Smith, E. E., French, R., & Mezzich, J. (1980). Psychiatric diagnosis as prototype categorization. *Journal of Abnormal Psychology, 89,* 181–193.

Cantwell, D. P. (1980). The diagnostic process and diagnostic classification in child psychiatry—DSM III. *Journal of the American Academy of Child Psychiatry, 19,* 345–355.

Cantwell, D. P. (1983). Depression in childhood: Clinical picture and diagnostic criteria. In D. P. Cantwell & G. A. Carlson (Eds.), *Affective disorders in childhood and adolescence: An update.* New York: Spectrum.

Carlson, G. A. (1983). Bipolar affective disorders in childhood and adolescence. In D. P. Cantwell & G. A. Carlson (Eds.), *Affective disorders in childhood and adolescence—An update.* New York: Spectrum.

Carlson, G. A., & Strober, M. (1978). Manic depressive illness in early adolescence; A study of clinical and diagnostic characteristics in six cases. *Journal of the American Academy of Child Psychiatry, 17,* 138–153.

Carroll, B. J., Feinberg, M., Greden, J. F., Tarika, A. A., Albala, R. F., Haskett, R. F., Norman, McI., J., Kronfol, Z., Lohr, N., Steiner, M., de Vigne, J. P., & Young, E. (1981). A specific laboratory test for the diagnosis of melancholia. *Archives of General Psychiatry, 38,* 15–22.

Cebiroglu, R., Sumer, E., & Polvan, O. (1971). Etiology and pathogenesis of depression in Turkish children. In A. L. Annell (Ed.). *Depressive states in childhood and adolescence* (pp. 133–136: Stockholm:) Almqvist & Wiksell.

Cerreto, M. C., & Tuma, J. M. (1977). Distribution of DSM II diagnosis in a child psychiatric setting. *Journal of Abnormal Child Psychology, 5,* 147–156.

Chambers, W. J., Puig-Antich, J., Tabrizi, M. A., & Davies, M. (1982). Psychotic symptoms in prepubertal major depressive disorder. *Archives of General Psychiatry, 39,* 921–927.

Cicchetti, D., & Rizley, R. (1981). Developmental perspectives on the etiology, intergenerational transmission, and sequelae of child maltreatment. *New Directions for Child Development, 11,* 31–56.

Clairborne, W. L. (1969). Expectancy effects in the classroom: A failure to replicate. *Journal of Educational Psychology, 60,* 377–383.

Cromwell, R. L., Blashfield, R. K., & Strauss, J. S. (1975). Criteria for classification systems. In N. Hobbs (Ed.), Issues in the classification of children. San Francisco: Jossey-Bass.

Cronbach, L. J., & Meehl, P. E. (1955). Construct validity in psychological tests. Psychological Bulletin, 52, 281–302.

Cytryn, L. & McKnew, D. H., Jr. (1972). Proposed classification of childhood depression. American Journal of Psychiatry, 129, 149–155.

Cytryn, L., McKnew, D. H., Jr., & Benney, W. E., Jr. (1980). Diagnosis of depression in children: A reassessment. American Journal of Psychiatry, 137, 22–25.

Davidson, H. H., & Lang, G. (1960). Children's perception of their teachers' feelings toward them related to self-perception, school achievement, and behavior. Journal of Experimental Education, 29, 108–118.

de Saussure, R. (1947). A case study. Psychoanalytic Study of the Child, 2, 417–426.

Dreger, R. M., Reed, M., Lewis, P., Overlade, D., Rich, T., Taffel, C., Miller, K., & Flemming, E. (1964). Behavioral classification project. Journal of Consulting Psychology, 28, 1–13.

Earls, F. (1980). The prevalence of behavior problems in three year old children: A cross national replication. Archives of General Psychiatry, 37, 1153–1157.

Eisen, P. (1973). As quoted in Anthony (1977).

Eisenberg, L. (1969). The role of classification in child psychiatry. International Journal of Psychiatry, 1, 179–181.

Farrington, D. P. (1977). The effects of public labeling. British Journal of Criminology, 17, 112–125.

Finn, S. E. (1982). Base rates, utilities, and DSM III: Shortcomings of fixed-rule systems of psychodiagnosis. Journal of Abnormal Psychology, 91, 294–302.

Freeman, M. (1971). A reliability study of psychiatric diagnosis in childhood and adolescence. Journal of Child Psychology and Psychiatry, 12, 43–54.

Frommer, E. A. (1968). Depressive illness in childhood. In A. Coppens & A. Walk (Eds.), Recent developments in affective disorders (pp. 117–136) Ashford, Kent: Headley Brothers.

Gammon, G., John, K., Rothblum, E. D., Mullen, K., Tishler, G., & Weissman, M. M. (1983). Use of a structured diagnostic interview to identify bipolar disorder in adolescent inpatients: Frequency and manifestations of the disorder. American Journal of Psychiatry, 140, 543–547.

Garber, J. (1984a). Classification of childhood psychopathology: A developmental perspective. Child Development, 55, 30–48.

Garber, J. (1984b). The developmental progression of depression in female children. In D. Cicchetti & K. Schneider-Rosen (Eds.), Developmental approaches to childhood depression. A special edition of New Directions for Child Development. San Francisco: Jossey-Bass.

Garber, J., Koch, M., Kriss, M., & Lindholm, L. (1983). Depression in adolescents: A follow-up study. Presented at the American Academy of Child Psychiatry annual convention, San Francisco.

Gesell, A. (1940). The first five years of life. New York, Harper & Row.

Gittelman-Klein, R. (1977). Definitional and methodological issues concerning depressive illness in children. In J. G. Schulterbrandt & A. Raskin (Eds.), Depression in childhood (pp. 69–81). New York: Raven Press.

Gittleman-Klein, R., Spitzer, R. L., & Cantwell, D. (1978). Diagnostic classifications and psychopharmacological indications. In J. S. Werry (Ed.), Pediatric psychopharmacology. New York: Brunner/Mazel.

Glaser, K. (1968). Masked depression in children and adolescents. Annual Progress in Child Psychiatry and Child Development, 1, 345–355.

Goffman, E. (1961). Asylums: Essays on the social situations of mental patients and other inmates. New York: Anchor.

Gold, M., & Williams, J. R. (1969). National study of the aftermath of apprehension. *Prospectus, 3,* 3–12.

Gottlieb, J. (1974). Attitudes toward retarded children: Effects of labeling and academic performance. *American Journal of Mental Deficiency, 79,* 268–273.

Gozali, J., & Meyer, E. L. (1970). The influence of the teacher expectancy phenomenon on the academic performances of educable mentally retarded pupils in special classes. *Journal of Special Education, 4,* 417–423.

Greenspan, S. I., Lourie, R. S., & Nover, R. A. (1979). A developmental approach to the classification of psychopathology in infancy and early childhood. In J. Noshpitz (Ed.), *Handbook of child psychiatry.* New York: Basic Books.

Group for the Advancement of Psychiatry, Committee on Child Psychiatry. (1966). *Psychopathological disorders of childhood: Theoretical considerations and a proposed classification* (Vol. 6, Report No. 62). New York: GAP.

Hamilton, M., & White, J. M. (1959). Clinical syndromes in depressive states. *Journal of Mental Science, 105,* 985–998.

Hassanyeh, F., & Davidson, K. (1980). Bipolar affective psychosis with onset before age 16. Report of 10 cases. *British Journal of Psychiatry, 137,* 530–539.

Herjanic, B., & Campbell, W. (1977). Differentiating psychiatrically disturbed children on the basis of a structured interview. *Journal of Abnormal Child Psychology, 5,* 127–134.

Herjanic, B., Herjanic, M., Brown, F., & Wheatt, T. (1975). Are children reliable reporters? *Journal of Abnormal Child Psychology, 3,* 41–48.

Hersch, C. (1968). The discontent explosion in mental health. *American Psychologist, 23,* 497–507.

Hobbs, N. (1975a). *The futures of children.* San Francisco: Jossey-Bass.

Hobbs, N. (Ed.). (1975b). *Issues in the classification of children.* San Francisco: Jossey-Bass.

Ianzito, B. M., Cadoret, R. J., & Pugh, D. D. (1974). Thought disorder in depression. *American Journal of Psychiatry, 131,* 703–707.

Jones, R. L. (1972). Labels and stigma in special education. *Exceptional Children, 38,* 553–564.

Kagan, J. (1971). *Change and continuity in infancy.* New York: Wiley.

Kanfer, F. H., & Saslow, G. (1965). Behavioral analysis: An alternative to diagnostic classification. *Archives of General Psychiatry, 12,* 529–538.

Kanfer, F. H., & Saslow, G. (1969). Behavioral diagnosis. In C. M. Franks (Ed.), *Behavior therapy: Appraisal and status.* New York: McGraw-Hill.

Kanner, L. (1957). *Child psychiatry.* Springfield, IL: Charles C. Thomas.

Kendall, R. E. (1976). The classification of depressions: A review of contemporary confusion. *British Journal of Psychiatry, 129,* 15–28.

Kessler, J. W. (1971). Nosology in child psychopathology. In H. E. Rie (Ed.), *Perspectives in child psychopathology.* Chicago: Aldine-Atherton.

Kiloh, L. G., & Garside, R. F. (1963). The incidence of neurotic depression and endogenous depression. *British Journal of Psychiatry, 109,* 451.

King, L. J., & Pittman, G. D. (1970). A six-year follow-up study of 65 adolescent patients: Natural history of affective disorders in adolescence. *Archives of General Psychiatry, 22,* 230–236.

Kohlberg, L., LaCrosse, J., & Ricks, D. (1976). The predictability of adult mental health from childhood behavior. In B. Wolman (Ed.), *Manual of child psychopathology.* New York: McGraw-Hill.

Kovacs, M., & Beck, A. T. (1977). An empirical-clinical approach toward a definition of childhood depression. In J. G. Schulterbrandt & A. Raskin (Eds.), *Depression in childhood: Diagnosis, treatment and conceptual models.* New York: Raven Press.

Kovacs, M., Feinberg, T. L., Crouse-Novak, M. A., Paulauskas, S. F., & Finkelstein, R. (1984). Depressive disorders in childhood. *Archives of General Psychiatry, 41,* 229–238.

Kraepelin, E. (1983). *Psychiatric.* Leipzig: Barth.

Laing, R. D. (1967). The study of family and social contexts in relation to the origin of schizophrenia. In J. Romano (Ed.), *Origins of schizophrenia.* Amsterdam: Excerpta Medica.

Lemert, E. M. (1967). *Human deviance, social problems and social control.* Englewood Cliffs, NJ: Prentice-Hall.

Leonhard, K., Korff, I., & Schulz, H. (1962). Temperaments in the families of monopolar and bipolar phasic psychoses. *Psychiatric Neurology, 143,* 416.

Lesse, S. (1974). Depression masked by acting-out behavior patterns. *American Journal of Psychotherapy, 28,* 352–361.

Lewine, R. R. J., Watt, N. F., Prentky, R. A., & Fryer, J. H. (1980). Childhood social competence in functionally disordered psychiatric patients and in normals. *Journal of Abnormal Psychology, 89,* 132–138.

Ling, W., Oftedal, G., & Weinberg, W. (1970). Depressive illness in childhood presenting as severe headache. *American Journal of Diseases of Childhood, 120,* 122–124.

Loevinger, J. (1957). Objective tests as instruments of psychological theory. *Psychological Reports, 3,* 635–694.

MacMillan, D. L., Jones, R., & Aloia, G. (1974). The mentally retarded label: A theoretical analysis and review of research. *American Journal of Mental Deficiency, 79,* 241–261.

MacMillan, D. L., & Meyers, C. E. (1979). Educational labeling of handicapped learners. In D. C. Berliner (Ed.), *Review of research in education* (Vol. 7). American Educational Research Association.

Mahler, M. S. (1961). On sadness and grief in infancy and childhood. *Psychoanalytic Study of the Child, 16,* 332–354.

Malmquist, C. (1971). Depressions in childhood and adolescence. *New England Journal of Medicine, 284,* 887–892, 955–961.

Masters, J. C., & Wellman, H. M. (1974). The study of human infant attachment. A procedural critique. *Psychological Bulletin, 81,* 218–237.

Matas, L., Arend, R. A., & Sroufe, L. A. (1978). Continuity of adaptation in the second year: The relationship between quality of attachment and later competence. *Child Development, 49,* 547–556.

Mattison, R., Cantwell, D. P., Russell, A. T., & Will, L. (1979). A comparison of DSM-II and DSM-III in the diagnosis of childhood psychiatric disorders. II. Interrater agreement. *Archives of General Psychiatry, 36,* 1217–1222.

May, J. G. (1979). Nosology and diagnosis. In J. D. Noshpitz (Ed.), *Basic Handbook of child psychiatry.* New York: Basic Books.

McConville, B. J., Boag, L. C., & Purohit, A. P. (1973). Three types of childhood depression. *Canadian Psychiatric Association Journal, 18,* 133–138.

McEachern, A. W. (1968). The juvenile probation system. *American Behavioral Scientist, 11,* 1–43.

Meehl, P. E. (1973). Why I do not attend case conferences. In P. E. Meehl (Ed.), *Psychodiagnosis.* New York: Norton.

Meehl, P. E., & Rosen, A. (1955). Antecedent probability and the efficiency of psychometric signs, patterns or cutting scores. *Psychological Bulletin, 52,* 194–216.

Menninger, K., Mayman, M., & Pruyser, P. (1963). *The vital balance: The life process in mental health and illness.* New York: Viking.

Mischel, W. (1968). *Personality and assessment.* New York: Wiley.

Nathan, P. E., & Harris, S. L. (1980). *Psychopathology and society.* New York: McGraw-Hill.

Orvaschel, H., Weissman, M. M., & Kidd, K. (1980). Children and depression. The children of depressed parents; the childhood of depressed patients; depression in children. *Journal of Affective Disorders, 3,* 1–16.

Overall, J. E., & Zisook, S. (1980). Diagnosis and the phenomenology of depressive disorders. *Journal of Consulting and Clinical Psychology, 48,* 626–634.

Paykel, E. S. (1971). Classification of depressed patients: A cluster analysis derived grouping. *British Journal of Psychiatry, 118,* 275–288.

Perris, C. (1966). A study of bipolar (manic-depressive) and unipolar recurrent depressive psychoses. *Acta Psychiatrica Scandinavica, 42.*

Petti, T. A. (1983). Imipramine in the treatment of depressed children. In D. P. Cantwell &

G. A. Carlson (Eds.), *Affective disorders in childhood and adolescence.* New York: Spectrum.

Phillips, L., Draguns, J. G., & Bartlett, D. P. (1975). Classification of behavior disorders. In N. Hobbs (Ed.), *Issues in the classification of children.* San Francisco: Jossey-Bass.

Puig-Antich, J. (1982). Major depression and conduct disorder in prepuberty. *Journal of the American Academy of Child Psychiatry, 21,* 118–128.

Puig-Antich, J., Blau, S., Marx, J., Greenhill, L. L., & Chambers, W. (1978). Pre-pubertal major depressive disorder: A pilot study. *Journal of the American Academy of Child Psychiatry, 17,* 695–707.

Puig-Antich, J., & Chambers, W. (1978). *The schedule for affective disorders and schizophrenia for school-age children (Kiddie-SADS).* New York: New York State Psychiatric Institute.

Puig-Antich, J., Goetz, R., Hanlon, C., Davies, M., Thompson, J., Chambers, W. J., Tabrizi, M. A., & Weitzman, E. D. (1982). Sleep architecture and REM sleep measures in prepubertal children with major depression: A controlled study. *Archives of General Psychiatry, 39,* 932–939.

Quay, H. C. (1979). Classification. In H. C. Quay & J. S. Werry (Eds.), *Psychopathological disorders in childhood* (2nd ed.), New York: Wiley.

Rie, H. E. (1966). Depression in childhood: A survey of some pertinent contributions. *Journal of the American Academy of Child Psychiatry, 5,* 653–685.

Rochlin, G. (1959). The loss complex. *Journal of the American Psychoanalytic Association, 7,* 229–316.

Rosen, B., Bahn, A., & Kramer, M. (1964). Demographic and diagnostic characteristics of psychiatric out-patient clinics in the U.S.A. *American Journal of Orthopsychiatry, 34,* 455–468.

Rosenthal, R., & Jacobson, L. (1968). *Pygmalion in the classroom: Teachers' expectation and pupils' intellectual development.* New York: Holt.

Rutter, M. (1965). Classification and categorization in child psychiatry. *Journal of Child Psychology and Psychiatry, 6,* 71–83.

Rutter, M. (1977). Individual differences. In M. Rutter & L. Hersov (Eds.), *Child psychiatry: Modern approaches.* Oxford: Blackwell Scientific Publications.

Rutter, M., & Gould, M. (1985). Classification. In M. Rutter & L. Hersov (Eds.), *Child and adolescent psychiatry: Modern approaches* (2nd ed.). London: Blackwell Scientific Publications.

Rutter, M., Lebovici, A., Eisenberg, L., Sneznevski, A. V., Sadoun, R., Brooke, E., & Lin, T-Y. (1969). A triaxial classification of mental disorders in childhood. *Journal of Child Psychology and Psychiatry, 10,* 41–61.

Rutter, M., & Madge, N. (1976). *Cycles of disadvantage.* London: Heinemann Educational.

Rutter, M., & Shaffer, D. (1980). DSM-III. A step forward or back in terms of the classification of child psychiatric disorders? *Journal of the American Academy of Child Psychiatry, 19,* 371–394.

Rutter, M., Shaffer, D., & Shepherd, M. (1975). *A multi-axial classification of child psychiatric disorders.* Geneva: World Health Organization.

Sandler, J., & Joffe, W. G. (1965). Notes on childhood depression. *International Journal of Psychoanalysis, 46,* 88–96.

Santostefano, S. (1971). Beyond nosology: Diagnosis from the viewpoint of development. In H. E. Rie (Ed.), *Perspectives in child psychopathology.* Chicago: Aldine-Atherton.

Scheff, J. (1966). *Being mentally ill: A sociological theory.* Chicago: Aldine.

Schildkraut, J. J., Orsulak, P. J., Schatzberg, A. F., Gudeman, J. E., Cole, J. Q., Rohde, W. A., & LaBrie, R. A. (1978). Toward a biochemical classification of depressive disorders. I. Differences in urinary excretion of MHPG and other catecholamine metabolites in clinically defined subtypes of depression. *Archives of General Psychiatry, 35,* 1427–1433.

Silberstein, R. M. (1969). Classification—The dilemma of the child psychiatrist. *International Journal of Psychiatry, 7,* 182–186.

Snow, R. E. (1969). Unfinished pygmalion. Contemporary Psychology, 14, 197–201.

Soli, S. D., Nuechterlein, K. H., Garmezy, N., Devine, V. T., & Schaefer, S. M. (1981). A classification system for research in childhood psychopathology. Part I. An empirical approach using factor and cluster analysis and conjunctive decision rules. In B. A. Maher (Ed.), Progress in experimental personality research (Vol. 10) New York: Academic Press.

Sporling, M. (1959). Equivalent of depression in children. Journal of Hillside Hospital, 8, 138–148.

Spitzer, R. L., & Forman, J. B. W. (1979). DSM-III field trials. II. Initial experience with the multi-axial system. American Journal of Psychiatry, 135, 818–820.

Spitzer, R. L., Forman, J. B. W., & Nee, J. (1979). DSM-III field trials. I. Initial interrater diagnostic reliability. American Journal of Psychiatry, 136, 815–817.

Spitzer, R. L., & Wilson, P. T. (1976). Nosology and the official psychiatric nomenclature. In A. M Freedman, H. I. Kaplan, & B. J. Sadock (Eds.), Comprehensive textbook of psychiatry (Vol. 2). Baltimore: Williams & Wilkins.

Sroufe, L. A. (1979). The coherence of individual development: Early care, attachment, and subsequent developmental issues. American Psychologist, 34, 834–841.

Sroufe, L. A., & Rutter, M. (1984). The domain of developmental psychopathology. Child Development, 55, 17–29.

Stack, J. J. (1971). Chemotherapy in childhood depression. In A. L. Annell (Ed.), Depressive States in Childhood and adolescence (pp. 460–466). Stockholm: Almqvist & Wiksell.

Strober, M., & Carlson, G. A. (1982). Bipolar illness in adolescents with major depression. Archives of General Psychiatry, 39, 549–555.

Swartz, C. M., & Dunner, F. J. (1982). Dexamethasone suppression testing in alcoholics. Archives of General Psychiatry, 39, 1309–1312.

Szasz, T. (1961). The myth of mental illness. New York: Harper & Row.

Throndike, R. L. (1968). Review of Rosenthal and Jacobson (1968). American Educational Research Journal, 5, 708–711.

Toolan, J. H. (1962). Depression in children and adolescents. American Journal of Orthopsychiatry, 32, 404–414.

Ullman, L. P., & Krasner, L. (1969). A psychological approach to abnormal behavior. Englewood Cliffs, NJ: Prentice-Hall.

Ushakov, G. K., & Girich, Y. P. (1971). Special features of psychogenic depression in children and adolescents. In A. L. Annell (Ed.), Depressive states in childhood and adolescence (pp. 510–516). Stockholm: Almqvist & Wiksell.

Van Pragg, H. M., Uleman, A. M., & Spitz, J. C. (1965). The vital syndrome interview. Psychiatria, Neurologia, Neurochirurgia, 68, 329–346.

Weinberg, W. A., & Brumback, R. A. (1976a). Mania in childhood. 5 case studies using adult type criteria-onsets from 20 months to 11 years. American Journal of Diseases in Children, 130, 380–385.

Weinberg, W. A., & Brumback, R. A. (1976b). Mania in childhood I—Case studies and literature review. American Journal of Disease of Children, 130, 380–382.

Weinberg, W. A., Rutman, J., Sullivan, L., Penick, E. C., & Dietz, S. G. (1973). Depression in children referred to an educational diagnostic center: Diagnosis and treatment. Journal of Pediatrics, 83, 1065–1072.

Welner, A., Welner, Z., & Fishman, R. (1970). Psychiatric adolescent inpatients. Archives of General Psychiatry, 35, 698–700.

Werner, H. (1948). Comparative psychology of mental development. Chicago: Follett.

Winokur, G. (1970). Familial (genetic) subtypes of pure depressive disorder. American Journal of Psychiatry, 136, 911.

Winokur, G., Clayton, P. J., & Reich, T. (1969). Manic depressive illness. St. Louis, MO: C. V. Mosby.

Woodruff, R. A., Murphy, G. E., & Herjanic, M. (1967). The natural history of affective disorders: I. Symptoms of 72 patients at the time of hospital admission. Journal of Psychiatry Research, 5, 255–263.

World Health Organization. (1977). *Manual of international statistical classification of diseases, injuries and causes of death (ICD-9).* Geneva: WHO.

Zigler, E., & Phillips, L. (1961). Psychiatric diagnosis: A critique. *Journal of Abnormal and Social Psychology, 63,* 607–618.

Zubin, J. (1967). Classification of the behavior disorder. *Annual Review of Psychology, 18,* 373–406.

A Developmental Perspective on Methods and Measures in the Assessment of Depressive Disorders: The Clinical Interview

Maria Kovacs

INTRODUCTION

In the last few years, the study of the depressive disorders in childhood has become increasingly empirical (Kashani, Husain, Shekim, Hodges, Cytryn, & McKnew, 1981; Puig-Antich, 1980). This movement has entailed, among others, a growing emphasis on uniform and multifaceted clinical evaluations (often by means of standardized interviews) and diagnosis of dysfunction according to operationally defined criteria. However, because the recently used tools and research paradigms have their roots in adult psychiatry, it has been questioned if it is appropriate to apply them to the study of children. Many workers have had reservations, for example, about the utility of the direct interview to diagnose juveniles. Another concern has been that the current psychiatric diagnostic criteria for depression are not developmentally oriented because they were derived on adult cohorts (see the introductory chapter by Rutter for developmental perspectives on childhood depression).

The present chapter focuses on one of the foregoing concerns, namely, on the use of the clinical interview for the diagnosis of depression in school-aged children and adolescents. The discussion is restricted to youngsters aged 6 and above because recent work has involved mostly this age group. The basic question addressed is whether the interview method of information gathering and the tools available for it are harmonious with presumably relevant developmental characteristics of juvenile informants.

Maria Kovacs. Department of Psychiatry, University of Pittsburgh School of Medicine, and Western Psychiatric Institute and Clinic, Pittsburgh, Pennsylvania.

The assessment of depression in children is examined from three perspectives in order to elucidate possible weaknesses of the interview method: (1) the general demands of the clinical interview, (2) interviewee competencies that are required specifically in the evaluation of depressive symptoms, and (3) research data on the development of presumably relevant individual abilities. Semistructured clinical and diagnostic interviews for children are then briefly reviewed in light of developmental considerations and in order to encourage the construction of better clinical tools.

THE CLINICAL INTERVIEW AND THE ASSESSMENT OF DEPRESSIVE DISORDERS

Background: The Diagnosis of Adults

In the field of adult psychiatry, the direct clinical interview of the patient and the process of diagnosis have gone hand in hand. The clinical interview has also played a central role in studies of classification and nomenclature and in investigations of the course and prognosis of major forms of mental illness. Some of its finest examples are still the early twentieth-century accounts of Kraepelin (1921).

The clinical diagnostic interview is a special case of interpersonal dialogue that has several distinguishing features. The latter not only define the nature of the dialogue but presumably make it easier for patients to be truthful about their problems. First, using the context of the patient's life history, the purpose of the interview is to elucidate the nature and patterns of past and current psychiatric problems in order to arrive at a diagnosis (e.g., MacKinnon, 1980; Sullivan, 1954). Second, the emphasis is on objective and historically accurate data about the patient's complaints, functioning, and premorbid adjustment. Therefore, this method of information gathering is also known as the direct examination or the face-to-face symptom-oriented interview. Third, the clinical interview typically involves an "expert–client" or "doctor–patient" dyad. Fourth, the purpose of the dialogue is explicit to both parties involved and the information gathered is usually protected by rules of confidentiality. The client, patient, or suffering party participates in the dialogue because of the desire for help or eventual relief; in turn, the interviewer is the expert who can elucidate and ameliorate the patient's intrapsychic and interpersonal problems (e.g., MacKinnon, 1980; Sullivan, 1954).

Table 1 schematizes salient attributes of the clinical interview. Although professionals generally assume that the special characteristics of the interview are critical to and facilitate the patient's self-disclosure, as Table 1 illustrates each of the attributes also signals an implicit demand on the patient. For example, the patient is expected to recognize that the role

Table 1
The Clinical Interview with the Adult

Definition/parameters[a]	Implied demand on the adult
A dyadic interaction	
On an expert–client (doctor–patient) basis	Recognition of expert's social status and role
Wherein the client/patient is the suffering party who expects to derive some benefit and desires relief	Self identification as a distressed person or patient, and self-referral
And the expert/doctor is expected to provide relief or elucidate problems	Helper attribute and helper competence recognition in providing relief
The interactive medium being one of vocal communication	Acknowledgement of/familiarity with vocal/verbal exchange as a means of problem resolution
Which should entail more or less full and voluntary disclosure on the part of the client/patient	Trust and confidence in the expert

[a]MacKinnon (1980); Sullivan (1954).

of an expert differs from the role of a patient; know that in the context of a clinical evaluation expertise signifies competence in psychological matters and a willingness to help in that regard; and be ready to confide in the examiner. In fact, if the clinical interview is wanting in any of the characteristics noted in Table 1 (e.g., when the patient is referred involuntarily; if there are cultural and expectational discrepancies between the two parties; survey-type mental health interviews that may not be protected by rules of confidentiality), the dialogue is not expected to yield optimal data.*

Assuming that the clinical interview has started off on good grounds and both parties understand their roles and act accordingly, the clinician/ doctor/expert must determine the nature of the patient's problem and its proper diagnosis. In order to accomplish that goal, the interviewer must rely on nosologic guidelines that specify what information must be sought and how it should be organized. At present, the clinician would probably keep in mind the official criteria for diagnosis from the *Diagnostic and Statistical Manual of the American Psychiatric Association,* 3rd Edition—the DSM-III (American Psychiatric Association, 1980). The DSM-III is the latest

---

*Besides these general attributes, obviously numerous other elements also play a role in the interview. For example, in the assessment of the adult, the adequacy of the interview and the quality of the resultant data also appear to be related to characteristics of the *interviewer,* such as his or her age, experience, and ability to establish rapport and communicate empathy (e.g., Cleary, Mechanic, & Weiss, 1981; Ianotti, 1975; MacKinnon, 1980; Rogers, 1975; Sullivan, 1954).

attempt to define diagnoses operationally. Together with its predecessors, the criteria of Feighner and associates (1972) and the Research Diagnostic Criteria (RDC) of Spitzer, Endicott, and Robins (1978), the DSM-III was designed to improve the reliability of psychiatric diagnosis.

The DSM-III criteria for an episode of major depressive disorder are summarized in Table 2. In order to give that diagnosis, the clinician must establish that the patient has suffered from (1) mood alteration in conjunction with (2) four or more of eight additional symptoms, all of which have lasted for at least 2 weeks, and (3) that the syndrome was not due to a nonaffective mental disorder or physical illness.

Table 3 summarizes the DSM-III guidelines for another category of depression called "dysthymic disorder." This condition, previously known as minor, neurotic, or reactive depression, likewise entails a set of symptoms and signs and a distinct time period within which the syndrome has been manifest. Parameters that exlude a condition from consideration are also specified.

As the information in Tables 2 and 3 indicate, the data which the interviewer needs for a diagnosis also place demands on the patient. The patient is expected, among other things, to recognize and properly label his or her emotional states, to have monitored and then to report orally certain changes in somatic functions, to describe complaints within a certain time perspective and to estimate symptom severity and frequency. In turn, the interviewer must ask the appropriate questions and frame them in a manner that is conceptually and culturally comprehensible to the patient. Also the interviewer must be sufficiently systematic that no relevant informa-

Table 2
DSM-III Diagnostic Criteria for Depressive Disorders:
Major Depressive Episode

A.   Depressed/sad/blue/hopeless/irritable mood or loss of interest or pleasure in all or almost all usual activities (must be prominent and relatively persistent)
B.   At least four of the following have been present nearly every day for at least 2 weeks (for children under 6, at least three of the first four):
  1. Appetite or significant weight change
  2. Insomnia or hypersomnia
  3. Psychomotor agitation or retardation (if under age 6, hyperactivity)
  4. Loss of interest or pleasure in usual activities (if under age 6, apathy)
  5. Loss of energy, fatigue
  6. Worthlessness, self-reproach, excessive/inappropriate guilt
  7. Diminished ability to think/concentrate
  8. Recurrent thoughts of death, wishes to be dead, suicidal ideation or attempt
C.   No evidence of predominant mood-incongruent delusions/hallucinations or bizarre behavior
D.   Not superimposed on schizophrenia, schizophreniform, or paranoid disorder
E.   Not due to organic mental disorder or uncomplicated bereavement

Table 3

DSM-III Diagnostic Criteria for Depressive Disorders: Dysthymic Disorder

A. In the past 2 years (1 year for children/adolescents), has been bothered most or all of the time by symptoms of the depressive syndrome that are not of sufficient severity and duration to meet major depressive episode criteria

B. The depression syndrome may be persistent or separated by normal mood of a few days to a few weeks, but no more than a few months at a time

C. When depressed, there is either marked depressed mood or loss of interest or pleasure in all or almost all usual activities and pastimes

D. During depressive periods, has at least three of the following:

1. Insomnia or hypersomnia
2. Low energy or chronic tiredness
3. Feelings of inadequacy, loss of self-esteem, or self-depreciation
4. Decreased effectiveness or productivity at school, work, or home
5. Decreased attention/concentration or ability to think clearly
6. Social withdrawal
7. Loss of interest or enjoyment in pleasurable activities
8. Irritability or excessive anger (in children, expressed toward parents or caretakers)
9. Inability to respond with apparent pleasure to praise or rewards
10. Less active or talkative than usual or feels slowed down/restless
11. Pessimism, broods about past or feels sorry for self
12. Tearfulness or crying
13. Recurrent thoughts of death or suicide

E. No psychotic features (e.g., delusions/hallucinations/incoherence)

F. If the disturbance is superimposed on a preexisting mental disorder, the depressed mood, by virtue of its intensity or effect on functioning, can be clearly distinguished from the person's usual mood

tion is missed and must be alert to the patient's facial and postural expression and general demeanor (e.g., Sullivan, 1954). The observational data can serve to clarify, validate, or falsify verbally delivered information.

In summary, the use of the clinical interview to diagnose a depressive disorder presupposes that the patient or client can comply with the general requirements of the dialogue and has the competencies to report on pertinent symptoms and functional issues. However, because of developmental considerations, it has been widely believed that school-aged children must be assessed and diagnosed in a different manner than has been customary in adult psychiatry.

The Diagnosis of Children

In child psychiatry, the clinical interview of the young patient and the process of diagnosis traditionally proceeded along separate lines (Puig-Antich, Chambers, & Tabrizi, 1983). The child psychiatric interview was used mostly to gather intrapsychic and conflict-oriented data in order to plan the treatment. On the other hand, the historic and symptomatic information necessary for a diagnosis were obtained primarily from parents, teachers, and other adults. As recently as 1981, Simmons stated that "it is neither possible nor desirable. . .to make these two. . .functions identical in process or aim" (p. 180). Therefore, in spite of the fact that Rutter and Graham (1968) demonstrated long ago that the direct interview of the child is feasible, reliable, and valid, the professional community has been slow to accept it as a vehicle for diagnosis.

According to the traditional child psychiatric stance, the direct examination of juveniles is unlikely to yield valid data about symptoms because young patients are limited in the cognitive, emotional, and linguistic domains. The direct examination is also constrained because the coercive nature of most child psychiatric referrals undermines confidence and trust in the examiner. Consequently, the traditional interview of the troubled child revolves around observation and interpretation. It entails mostly indirect data gathering procedures and much of the initiative is left to the child. For example, young patients are put into free-play situations. Then their constructions and behaviors are observed and interpreted as symbolic of the problems that they cannot or will not verbalize (Cramer, 1980; Simmons, 1981).

In contrast, the direct examination of children is increasingly advocated by research-clinicians, especially those who have used it to investigate affective disorders in the juvenile years (Carlson & Cantwell, 1982; Kovacs, 1983; Poznanski, 1982; Puig-Antich et al., 1983). These investigators contend that school-aged children can and should be interviewed directly about their symptoms and concerns; that such data are indispensable to the diagnostic process; and that free-play is a distraction rather than an aid in this regard. Advocates of the direct examination method also emphasize oral–vocal dialogue between the clinician and the young patient and the propriety of targeted questions about symptoms and complaints. However, because youngsters may not be able to label correctly their own affective states, the observation of nonverbal behavior is underscored (e.g., Kovacs, 1983; Poznanski, 1982; Puig-Antich et al., 1983).

Upon reflection, it is clear, however, that whether the goal of the child psychiatric examination is to elicit "dynamic" material or information about symptoms, the interview process makes demands on the young patient. Similar to its counterpart in the assessment of adults, the child psychiatric interview can proceed only if basic interpersonal parameters are satisfied. Namely, the young patient needs to recognize the "special" nature of the interview; that it is different from the usual child–adult interactions; and that its ultimate goal is to alleviate or remediate the problems that have resulted in the referral in the first place. Otherwise, it is highly unlikely that the clinician will be able to get the youngster to cooperate.

Table 4 schematizes important aspects of the child psychiatric in-

Table 4
The Clinical Interview with the Child

Definition/parameters[a]	Implied demand on the child
A dyadic interaction	
Wherein one party (doctor/clinician) is sincerely interested in helping	Recognition of doctor as a "helping" agent
The typically nonwilling child patient with his or her problems	Self-attribution as "having problems"
The interactive medium being one of in-indirect communication (e.g., free-play) or direct vocal communication	Acceptance of/familiarity with indirect communication or verbal exchange as a means of problem resolution
Which should eventually entail some de-gree of disclosure on the part of the child patient	Trust in the helping agent

[a]Cramer (1980), Simmons (1981).

terview as reflected in the descriptions of professionals. Although those interpersonal issues have been articulated most often in connection with the traditional examination, the attributes are just as salient in the conduct of a direct diagnostic interview. As noted in Table 4, even when the patient is a child, the dialogue does rest on an expert–client, doctor–patient basis. In the context of the child psychiatric interview, however, the expert or doctor is relabeled as a "helper"; it is this helping function that the youngster is particularly expected to recognize and appreciate. For example, parents have been advised to prepare the child for the interview by explaining that the examiner is "a person sincerely interested in helping" (Cramer, 1980) and that the examination will focus on the child's problems and difficulties (Simmons, 1981).

As a special case of interpersonal dialogue, the interview of the child and the adult do diverge in two important ways. First, children do not tend to identify themselves as patients or suffering agents and their help-seeking is therefore rarely voluntary. It is generally believed that, as a result, young patients tend to be distrustful and uncooperative and may even view the clinician as an object of fear (Simmons, 1981). Therefore, gaining the trust of the youngster may be a problem. It is nevertheless important to do so in order to ensure the young patient's cooperation. Toward that aim, Cramer (1980) has suggested that the child must be reassured early on that "the danger of trusting other adults does not exist with [the examiner]." Second, young patients cannot be guaranteed full confidentiality because of legal statutes and social convention. Thus, the notion of confidentiality does not play a highly salient role in the child psychiatric interview.

In summary, the child psychiatric interview has embedded in it a general set of professional expectations concerning the behavior and attitude of the young patient. It is assumed that if the child can comply with the expectations or demands for trust, cooperation, and recognition of the role of the doctor, he or she will experience the encounter as less stressful and may self-disclose more readily.* The clinical interview that has a diagnostic focus places further demands on the youngster. There is an expectation, for example, that the child is familiar and reasonably comfortable with verbal–oral interpersonal dialogue as a vehicle for problem identification. Because the child must provide responses to specific questions, the symptom-oriented interview also requires attention capacity. If the interview is designed for the diagnosis of a depressive disorder, the demands on the child become more extensive, as we shall now see.

Let us assume that the interviewer is about to conduct a direct, symptom-oriented examination and is faced with a reasonably cooperative and verbal child. In order to determine if the youngster has a diagnosable depressive disorder, the clinician may organize his or her inquiries according to one of three overlapping operational diagnostic systems: the criteria of Weinberg and associates (Weinberg, Rutman, Sullivan, Penick, & Dietz, 1973), the adult-based RDC (Spitzer *et al.*, 1978), or the DSM-III (American Psychiatric Association, 1980).

Although there has been some debate about the propriety of the DSM-III for various child psychopathologic conditions (Rutter & Shaffer, 1980), in this chapter it is assumed that the examiner will diagnose according to the rules depicted in Tables 2 and 3. As can be seen, the criteria make relatively few accommodations for the patient's developmental stage. In order to endorse or deny complaints, the youngster must have a command of various psychologic and cognitive processes. Self-recognition of many depressive symptoms requires monitoring and understanding one's inner experience as well as the ability to differentiate and correctly label affective states. To provide information about feelings of worthlessness or feeling sorry for oneself, the child needs to have a cognitive understanding of the self. And the patient also has to have some competence in the quantification of psychologic phenomena and a reasonably well developed time perspective. In turn, the examiner must be sensitive to the child's level of conceptualization, monitor if the inquiries are understood, and recognize when the child is experiencing a certain emotion but cannot identify it via linguistic symbols. The observation of nonverbal behavior is also critical

---

*Clearly, this represents an encapsulated view of the pediatric interview with a highlight on selected aspects. For example, the necessity to make the child comfortable in the assessment situation has been also emphasized (e.g., Cramer, 1980; Pogul, 1980; Simmons, 1981). The likely importance of an empathic interviewer and the child's ability to perceive this quality is also suggested by research on the relationship between teachers' empathy, and their students' behavior, cognitive performance, and attitudes toward themselves (for an overview, see Aspy, 1975).

because young patients may become easily tired, bored, or inattentive; such states may markedly influence their responses.

In summary, a developmental approach to the diagnosis of depression in children needs to take into consideration both the general, structural, interpersonal aspects of the interview method and its thematic focus. Are school-aged youngsters sufficiently mature to understand the interpersonal constructs that are called into play in a clinical interview? Can they act in accordance with their roles? Are young patients able to provide the information required for the diagnosis of a depressive disorder? Can they really understand the interviewer's questions about symptoms and complaints? An examination of some of these issues constitutes the thrust of the rest of this chapter.

THE GENERAL DEMANDS OF THE CLINICAL INTERVIEW ON THE CHILD: DEVELOPMENTAL CONSIDERATIONS

The foregoing section highlighted those aspects of the clinical interview that clearly make demands on young patients. Although professionals have suggested that parents or other adults should prepare youngsters for the examination (Cramer, 1980; Simmons, 1981), there is no compelling evidence that such preparation brings forth the desired result. In fact, the research evidence suggests that the stage of the child's cognitive and social development may be the limiting factor on the ability to acknowledge personal problems, to view the clinician as a competent and professional helping agent, and to trust the clinician.

Having a Problem

Telling a child beforehand that the purpose of the interview is to talk about and understand the child's problems and difficulties may not produce the expected cooperative stance. This is because the ability to conceptualize what constitutes a psychosocial problem unfolds gradually with age. And it is questionable if younger children view this construct the way in which clinicians do.

For example, even in regard to notions of *physical* illness, preschoolers and younger school-age children have relatively inadequate formulations. It is only around age 11 or 12 that children recognize that a disease is a distinct entity which entails two components—an internal process and a corresponding alteration in conventional role behaviors (Bibace & Walsh, 1979; Campbell, 1975). In a similar vein, the ability to recognize psychosocial deviance or psychopathology undergoes a developmental progression. One group of investigators found, for instance, that, when fourth- and sixth-grade students were presented with vignettes of imaginary peers, the older children were the ones who were more likely to detect the presence of emotional disturbance (Marsden & Kalter, 1976; Marsden, Kalter, Plunkett, & Barr-Grossman, 1977). Likewise, Coie and Pennington (1976) reported that when first-, fourth-, seventh-, and eleventh-graders were compared to one another, the youngest ones had the greatest difficulty in seeing psychopathology for what it was—namely, deviant behavior. Only the oldest subjects recognized that deviance reflected a person's failure to fulfill prevailing social definitions of psychologic stability.

Children's perceptions of the *causes* of deviance are subject to developmental progression as well. For example, it has been found that both 5- and 7-year-olds were likely to see intense sadness as elicited by external-physical events rather than by psychologic or interpersonal causes (Glasberg & Aboud, 1982). In a similar vein, it has been reported that 9- to 13-year-olds generally attributed the psychologic and behavioral problems of imaginary children to environmental and social factors such as watching too much TV or people being mean (Roberts, Beidleman, & Wurtele, 1981). Children and adolescents who attended outpatient clinics also felt that their own problems were due mostly to external causes, and they made such attributions to a greater extent than did their parents (Compas, Friedland-Bandes, Bastien, & Adelman, 1981). Likewise, in a study of fifth-through twelfth-graders, Dollinger, Thelen, and Walsh (1980) found that all their subjects conceptualized psychologic problems primarily from a social perspective, that is, as arising from familial, marital, or interpersonal conflicts. However, with increasing age, the subjects were more and more likely to define problems in terms of internal dimensions such as one's feelings, moods, and cognitions.

The data therefore suggest that when younger children are asked to talk about their problems, answers that appear to be "denial" may reflect their true understanding of the issues at hand, which is mediated by their stage of cognitive development. For the 6-, 7-, or 8-year-old, talking about "problems" probably signifies a recitation of undesirable external or physical events. According to the available evidence, only around age 10 or so is a child sufficiently mature to recognize that a personal problem implies salient internal events or psychological distress as well as external, observable correlates.

The Doctor or Clinician as a Helper

It has been assumed that preparing the child for the interview by a description of the doctor/clinician as a helping person will put the youngster at ease and facilitate cooperation. The putative usefulness of such information must be evaluated, however, in light of the child's notions of help and of a helping agent. In fact, the evidence indicates that the perceptions of children and the expectations of clinicians may be at odds.

At least two studies suggest that the ability to view the doctor or clinician as an expert helper is a function of developmental stage. Roberts et al. (1981) found that when their 9- to 13-year-old subjects did mention someone who could help children with psychological problems, they specified ministers or teachers rather than counselors, doctors, or the like. In a study by Barnett, Darcie, Holland, and Kobasigawa (1982), children were asked about the characteristics of good helpers. The results revealed that specific helper attributes were recognized only with increasing age. For example, 6-year-olds consistently cited global traits ("nice," "kind") and specific behaviors ("plays with me," "buys us stuff") as the characteristics of good helpers. References to competence ("knows what to do") began to appear among the third-graders. But the sixth-graders were the most likely to recognize that competence, willingness to help, and empathic ability were necessary attributes of a good helper.

The above-cited studies are even more relevant in the context of children's notions of effective interventions and may explain why talking about help may not make sense to them. The extant data suggest that, for the younger ones, "being helped" probably denotes some form of direct action. And only with increasing age do youngsters recognize that indirect methods, such as giving advice or discussing problems, are potent and appropriate ways to assist another. For example, when kindergarten, third-, and sixth-grade children were asked what would be the best helping strategy for several problem situations, the youngest ones typically reported direct action; only the older ones appreciated the importance of advice giving and other forms of indirect help (Barnett et al., 1982). In another study in which 9- to 13-year-olds were asked about desirable interventions for psychologically disturbed imaginary children, action in the form of self-help was still frequently cited (Roberts et al., 1981).

According to the research evidence, if a 6-year-old child has to be prepared for a psychiatric examination, it may not be inappropriate to liken the clinician to a familiar teacher or religious leader and to cite behavioral traits ("Dr. X is a nice person"). However, describing the interviewer as one who "wants to help" may not be useful until a youngster is about 10–12 years of age. Because younger children tend to identify problems in external–physical terms, it is not surprising that they view direct action as the most potent helping strategy. And yet, it is unlikely that the clinician will engage in direct action on behalf of the child. Therefore, it is unclear how the clinician's helping function could be translated into the conceptual schema of a 6- or 7-year-old.

The Notion of Trust

Although Selman and his associates have studied children's concepts of trust vis-à-vis their peers, it may be assumed that the findings have some generalizability to child–adult relationships. The evidence indicates that notions of trust progress developmentally from physicalistic, to behavioral, to interpersonal, and finally to psychologic–interpersonal definitions. It is questionable therefore if younger children view trust the ways in which adults do, or if they recognize its putative importance in the psychiatric interview. In fact, probably only adolescent or older patients are able to recognize that trust, as a psychologic construct, is an important part of a clinical interview.

According to the work of Selman, Jaquette, and Redman Lavin (1977), among very young children (3- to 5-year-olds), trust involves physical capability; thus, the child trusts a peer because "he or she won't break my toys." In the 5- to 11-year-old age group, trust involves one-way intentionality ("she'll do what you tell her"). Around ages 7 to 11, trust emerges as a concept that entails reciprocity, for example, "you'll do something for him and he'll do something for you." Between age 12 and adulthood, the notion of trust finally signifies intimacy and the sharing of personal and psychological concerns.

These findings suggest that although clinicians expect that trust will facilitate the child's self-disclosure, it may not be until age 12 or later that a youngster experiences trust as the sharing of personal concerns. Moreover, in the Barnett *et al.* (1982) investigation of how kindergarten, third-, and sixth-grade children conceptualized effective helping, trustworthiness as a helper attribute was not even cited. Thus, for the elementary-school-aged patient, the "adult" concept of trusting the expert is probably irrelevant to self-disclosure. It follows, therefore, that asking direct questions rather than waiting for the youngster to offer psychological information may be the most fruitful way to gather data.

In summary, professionals seem to assume that, in the psychiatric interview of the child, recognition that one has a problem, viewing the clinician as a helping person, and trusting the clinician facilitate self-disclosure and comfort. Research on normal children suggests however that the foregoing constructs undergo a developmental progression. In view of the fact that a 6- or 7-year-old, for example, is unlikely to appreciate or abide by these expectations in the "adult" sense, but that children of that age *can* be directly interviewed, it is possible that the parameters under discussion are not pertinent in the psychiatric examination of the *younger* patient. This question should be examined empirically. The results could alter current conceptualizations of the desirable and necessary attributes of the pediatric interview.

On the other hand, if the above-noted constructs are salient in the assessment of the young child and influence the outcome of the interview, it would be helpful to know if there are developmentally appropriate interpersonal strategies to facilitate the examination. For example, how could the clinician gain the trust of an 8-year-old besides doing what the child tells him or her? In order to be viewed by a 6-year-old as a "good helper," does the examiner have alternatives to playing with the child or buying the child things?

SPECIFIC INTERVIEWEE COMPETENCIES REQUIRED IN THE ASSESSMENT OF DEPRESSIVE DISORDERS: DEVELOPMENTAL CONSIDERATIONS

The young patient, as informant, needs to have a working command of various psychological, interpersonal, and intellectual concepts in order to give an account of salient depressive symptoms and complaints. The traditionalists have assumed that the emotional immaturity of children, namely, their denial, fear, or massive anxiety make it unlikely that they can provide direct data (Cramer, 1980; Simmons, 1981). However, there is considerable literature to suggest that many of the constructs implicated in the assessment of depression are subject to *normal* developmental vicissitudes. In the following section, three developmental dimensions are discussed that are relevant to the clinical diagnosis of depressive disorders.

Knowledge of Emotion and Mood

The cardinal feature of a depressive disorder is a disturbance of mood: sadness, tearfulness and crying, irritability or anger, and an inability to experience pleasure (anhedonia). Using age-appropriate language, the child is typically asked about each of these symptoms. Thus, the young patient is required to recognize and distinguish the various emotions, and to identify each by a proper semantic label.

According to the relevant literature, the understanding of affective experiences, including the ability to perceive, monitor, or symbolize them, constitutes one aspect of emotional development (for overviews, see Izard, 1984; Masters & Carlson, 1984; Schwartz & Trabasso, 1984). In general, the available data suggest that even preschoolers can differentiate basic emotions in others; can distinguish emotion words; and can properly identify causal events (Masters & Carlson, 1984; Schwartz & Trabasso, 1984). After the preschool years, there is continued development on several dimensions. For example, it is significantly easier for 8- and 11-year-olds than 6-year-olds to distinguish the emotions that pertain to the self ("*I* am glad") and those directed at others ("I love *him*"). However, it is only in the adolescent years that youth are typically able to locate the antecedents of emotional states within themselves (Schwartz & Trabasso, 1984).

Two studies are particularly pertinent because they examined children's understanding of *their own* emotions. Harris, Olthof, and Terwogt (1981) questioned 72 Dutch children about happiness, anger, and fear.

They found that between ages 6 and 11, there was a major shift from physicalistic to mentalistic understanding of inner experience, but there were no further changes in the adolescent years. To identify their own emotions:

1. Younger children were more likely to rely on situational cues than older ones ("it's my birthday"); 50% of the 6-year-olds but only 12% of the older children used such cues.
2. Physiological and behavioral cues ("I get a headache," "I bang the table") were used by similar portions of 6-, 11-, and 15-year-olds.
3. The private "inner mental aspects" of one's own emotional experiences were rarely recognized or acknowledged by 6-year-olds.

Overall, the younger children consistently focused on public, observable components of emotions; they also looked to external situational cues ("my birthday") to identify their emotions.

Using the theoretical framework of attributional-analysis, Weiner and Graham (1984) questioned 6- to 11-year-olds about incidents in their lives when they felt pity, guilt, or anger, and found that only the notion of guilt showed a developmental trend. Although all youngsters reported that they have felt guilty when they engaged in "wrongdoing," the 6- and 7-year-olds were much more likely than the older children to have felt guilty for uncontrollable or accidental outcomes, for example, for an unwitting mistake. However, for the older children, guilt was typically mediated by the intentionality or the controllability of events and outcomes.

The research data therefore suggest the following:

1. The diagnostic interview's demand concerning the differentiation of emotions should not be problematic for school-aged and older youth.
2. When the patient is a younger child, inquiries about sadness, irritability, and other affects should be posed in the context of specific environmental events or recent physical or somatic experiences.
3. Children aged 6 and 7 probably cannot distinguish mentally between "typical" sadness and an "autonomous" quality of dysphoria, a differentiation that is required for the DSM-III subtyping of a melancholic depression (American Psychiatric Association, 1980).
4. Finally, Weiner and Graham's (1984) work suggests that clinicians may need to have developmental guidelines about appropriate and inappropriate guilt for various ages because only the latter qualifies as a symptom for a depressive disorder. For example, based on these investigators' data, it would seem appropriate for a 7-year-old to feel guilty about a grandparent's death (that is, guilt being outcome-dependent), whereas in an 11-year-old, such a statement would be an age-inappropriate attribution.

It must be noted, however, that the findings concerning developmental competencies in normal children may not be readily generalizable to psychologically disturbed youth. In my ongoing, longitudinal, nosological study of depressed and psychiatrically maladjusted school-aged children, I have been continually surprised by some youngsters' inability to deal with (or have a command of) psychological constructs; particularly when such an inability was not predictable from the child's age or the literature on normal subjects. For example, although the extant work suggests that the ability to differentiate basic emotions is well formed by the preschool years, our considerably older, psychiatrically referred, nonretarded, out-patient research subjects have often mislabeled their own emotions.

Table 5 presents part of a verbal exchange from a semistructured clinical interview with one of our research subjects concerning depressed feelings and mood. The dialogue illustrates a possible "lag" in the ability to differentiate and label basic emotions. The content of the discussion in Table 5 also validates above-cited research that children younger than age 10 may have trouble identifying their own emotions in the absence of external cues. Finally, the exchange between the youngster and the clini-

Table 5
Which Feeling Are We Talking About? Interview Exchange with a 9-Year-Old Outpatient

Interviewer	Child
"One of the feelings that kids can have is feeling sad, unhappy, down in the dumps. Have you been feeling sad, unhappy?"	"Yeah."
"Have you been feeling sad all the time? Or many times? Or once in awhile?"	"Kind of—uhm—many times."
"Can other people tell when you are sad?"	(Child nods)
"How can other people tell when you are sad? How do you look?"	(Child makes a distinctly angry face)
"Tell me about the *last* time you were sad. What happened?"	"Well, it's like—like my sister always takes away my books and yells and she gets me real mad."
"Now, this is going to be a hard question. See if you can help me with it. When your sister takes . . . , the feeling you have, is it *sad* (interviewer makes appropriate facial expression) or *mad* (interviewer makes facial expression)? Or, is it like two feelings?"	"Uhm—it's more like mad."

cian also shows that it is important to "double-check" the child's oral responses to interview questions.

Understanding of the Self

In addition to a disturbance of mood, a depressive disorder typically encompasses self-depreciation, feelings of inadequacy or a sense of worthlessness, decreased ability to concentrate or to think clearly, and slowed thinking. The assessment of such symptoms presupposes (1) some competence in self-monitoring of psychological constructs using past (putatively normal) functioning as a baseline, and (2) that young patients can describe and judge themselves according to their own standards and in light of prevailing social norms. Consequently, there is an implicit demand for introspection and social perspective-taking. Inquiries about the quality of the child's own thinking require the youngster to reflect on his or her own cognitive processes, that is, to engage in metacognition.

As Damon and Hart (1982) noted, self-knowledge entails two important dimensions: cognizance of the psychological and physical self—the "me" attributes (all the qualities that define the self), and the aspect that organizes and interprets experience—the notion of "I," the self-as-knower. The available findings, as reviewed by Damon and Hart (1982), suggest that, among the very young, self is defined in terms of activity such as play; in early childhood, self is conceived in terms of physical characteristics or possessions ("I have blond hair," "I have a baseball bat"); by age 8, children begin to demonstrate that they understand the mental and volitional, that is, the psychological aspects of the self. Although children older than 8 do retain the physicalistic and action/behavior basis of self-definition, they use social-comparison information increasingly to define themselves. The latter phenomenon is manifest in the emerging use of interpersonal traits in self-descriptions (Damon & Hart, 1982). However, only as they reach higher levels of development do children make persistent use of social-comparison data in self-assessment. For example, Ruble, Boggiano, Feldman, and Loebl (1980) reported that the self-evaluations of only fourth-grade (but not second-grade or kindergarten) children were consistently affected by social-comparison feedback. Likewise, Ruble, Parsons, and Ross (1976) found that 10-year-olds were much more likely to feel "bad" than 6-year-olds when they received negative feedback about their task performance.

Therefore, the ability to evaluate oneself and to introspect do undergo developmental changes (Chandler, 1975; Elkind, 1974). Self-evaluations become more differentiated and less global with age (Mullener & Laird, 1971), and self-concept development appears to be related to the progressive refinement of the ideal self-image (Leahy & Huard, 1976). Selman and associates (1977) have also shown that social perspective-taking, including self-awareness, is subject to a developmental progression. However, only in adolescence emerges a conceptual integration of the dimensions of the self, stable social-personality characterizations, and true self-reflection (Damon & Hart, 1982; Selman et al., 1977). Finally, although the highly technical nature of much of the literature makes it difficult to translate the findings into clinically pertinent terms, there is considerable evidence that development also entails increased sophistication in metacognition, memory, and metamemory (e.g., Cavanaugh & Perlmutter, 1982; Siegler, 1978).

The above-cited data raise several issues concerning the presence of certain depressive symptoms in young children and about the proper clinical evaluation of others. First, because worthlessness implies a denigration of the self-as-knower, the "I," and suggests both a mentalistic conception of the self and a social-evaluative dimension, one wonders whether younger children can develop this symptom. Instead, the literature indicates that self-depreciation and lowered self-esteem, as "me" attributes probably manifest in different forms depending on the patient's developmental level.

For example, to assess self-depreciation in a 6-year-old, the clinician may be wise to focus on the child's physicalistic, action-related, or possession-connected descriptions. Probably only among 8- to 10-year-old or older patients is the clinician likely to elicit stable self-denigratory descriptions of a social-evaluative nature ("I am much more stupid than other kids") or self-perceived inability to live up to one's own expectations. It would also appear that, because a conceptual integration of various aspects of the self does not take place until adolescence, younger patients may provide inconsistent or contradictory responses to questions about their self-esteem. Finally, because metacognitive phenomena appear to be components of the self-as-knower, it would seem unlikely that a 6- or 7-year-old child could provide valid data about the quality of his or her own thinking (e.g., "slowed thinking").

On the other hand, however, it is appropriate to question if the findings on the developmental competencies of "normal" youth can be generalized to psychologically disturbed or clinically referred youngsters. There is some evidence, for example, that deviant children perform "below" age-matched normal peers on tasks of social cognition (e.g., Selman, 1976). However, it is unclear whether such findings reflect a true developmental "lag" or a temporary incapacity secondary to psychopathology. In either case, a clinical interviewer who is sensitive to developmental issues may need to downgrade his or her expectations of the young patient's cognitive sophistication and assess the child's self-report accordingly. As an example, Table 6 illustrates an exchange from a semistructured clinical research interview with an adolescent boy of normal intelligence who was referred to a guidance clinic because of behavioral problems and disobedience. Similar to the earlier-presented vignette, in view of this patient's age and the developmental literature on normal children, we would not have predicted that he would lack social-perspective-taking skills and fail to understand the relationship between emotions, behavior, and motivation.

Table 6
Can People Act One Way and Feel Another Way?
Interview Exchange with a 14-Year-Old Outpatient

Interviewer	Child
"Sometimes kids feel that nobody really loves them. They feel all alone. Have you been feeling that way in the last few weeks?"	"Yeah."
"Have you been feeling this way all the time? Many times? Sometimes?"	"Yeah—many times—I guess."
"Can you tell me what happens when you feel . . ? Does anything happen to make you feel . . .?"	"Yeah. It's because my mom keeps yelling at me all the time. She won't get off my back."
"So, when your mother . . . , you feel . . .?"	"Yeah."
"Does this just cross your mind, or do you really believe that your mother . . .?"	"Yeah, it's true, she really don't care. She always yells."
"Well, let me ask you this. Do you think it is *possible* that mom *does* love you? That she yells at you because she wants you to act in a certain way?"	"Uhm—no. She keeps yelling at me. So, she doesn't care about me."

Time Concepts and Memory

As the information in Tables 2 and 3 indicate, the diagnosis of a depressive disorder requires that the clinician establish the history and temporal co-occurrence of symptoms and the overall duration of the syndrome. In order to provide such data, the young patient must have a reasonably developed awareness of time. The latter construct and memory are interrelated because "remembering occurs within the frame of historical time and of one's own life history" (Wessman & Gorman, 1977, p. 42).

Explanations of the genesis and gradual unfolding of the concept of time have been most consistently formulated by the Piagetian school. As summarized by Wessman and Gorman (1977), Piagetians view "time" both as cognitive constructs and relational schemata that emerge gradually from one's own experiences and actions. Object recognition and object memory, two of the major accomplishments of infancy, constitute the foundations of time constructs. Because language serves as a vehicle to communicate about and to represent the past, the present, and the future, its emergence enlarges the child's schemata of time.

Overviews of research on the development of temporal awareness and time orientation suggest that, although even preschoolers can give adequate information about specific activities (e.g., "when do you go to bed?"), workable constructs of clock time and calendar time appear only around age 7–9 (Elkind, 1974; Wessman & Gorman, 1977). Likewise, it is not until children have reached this age range that they can correctly indicate the calendar year, the season of the year, or the day of the month (Fraisse, 1963; Friedman, 1978).

Children cannot truly conceive temporal order (that is, the succession of events) and temporal duration (the length of interval between events) until concrete operational thinking is well established, that is, around ages 8–9 (Friedman, 1978; Wessman & Gorman, 1977). For instance, when fourth- and sixth-graders were asked to order events according to whether they occurred "a long time ago" or a "short time ago," the children typically judged recent events ("last Christmas," "day I started kindergarten") much further back in time than warranted. And whereas 89% of the sample decided that "Bible times" occurred a long time ago, a similar portion (84%) also categorized the day they started kindergarten as an event long in the past (Doob, 1971). However, compared to 8-year-olds, 10-year-olds were found to be fairly consistent in how they ordered seasons and holidays using a scale that ranged from January to December (Friedman, 1978).

Studies of the ability to estimate lengths of time suggest that absolute judgments are genetically first to appear ("it takes long," "a short time"). But it is not until children are 12 years old or so that they can correctly estimate duration from marker events, such as how long it has been "since the holidays" (Fraisse, 1963). The developmental progression in the ability to estimate temporal duration has also been shown in the laboratory. For example, Voyat (1977) reported that none of the children under age 8, while only 27% of 8-year-olds and 33% of 9-year-olds were able to judge correctly two equal time durations. It has been also noted that, compared to adults, children are far more sensitive to the qualitative aspects of time. Thus, for example, they typically judge "empty time" as lasting significantly longer than "filled" time (Fraisse, 1963).

Although human beings of all ages tend to emphasize or live in the present, school children have a "shorter" future orientation than teenagers or adults (Doob, 1971). Moreover, an elaborated sense of personal and historical time emerges only around adolescence (Wessman & Gorman, 1977). Thus, developmental data on the concept of time are harmonious with the literature on self-understanding. Namely, young children invariably describe themselves in terms of the immediate present; only adolescents demonstrate an awareness of personal continuity in the sense of past and future selves (Damon & Hart, 1982). The typical present orientation of children also appears to characterize their memory and recall, as shown by Fitzgerald (1981), who examined autobiographical memory in response to various experimental prompts. It was found that, although among the 17- to 21-year-old subjects, date of the recalled memory and recall latency were related to the nature of the prompt (e.g., affective prompt), the 12- to 15-year-olds showed a uniform memory bias toward recent events.

Because young children understand absolute durations and their self-descriptions and recall are "here-and-now" oriented, it is reasonable to assume that even 6- to 9-year-olds can give reliable temporal information about current depressive symptoms. They are probably able to estimate, for example, if it takes a long or short time to fall asleep, or if a particular symptom has been present all day or all week. On the other hand, the research evidence suggests that, even if marker events are provided, 6- to 9-year-old patients are not likely to give correct data on the persistence (duration) of one symptom relative to another or estimate properly the overall duration of their complaints. The research data also appear to be quite convincing that only adolescent patients are likely to give temporally correct information about past episodes of depression or about the time of onset of chronic symptoms. However, because even among adolescents there appears to be a natural memory bias for recent events, accurate recall of autobiographical data may not be easy. It would therefore seem wise for

Table 7
When Did It Really Happen? Interview Exchange with a 10-Year-Old Outpatient

Interviewer	Child
"Sometimes when kids are unhappy or angry or upset, they think about killing themselves. Have you ever thought about killing yourself?"	"Uhmm."
"Do you remember the last time you thought about killing yourself, the last time this was on your mind?"	"Don't know."
"Well, was this a long time ago?"	
"Was it this week, or the week before?"	"A long time ago."
"Well, was this a *very* long time ago (interviewer gestures to indicate very long) or a little time ago (interviewer gestures again)?"	"Don't remember."
"I guess it's pretty hard to remember some things. Could you try *real* hard?"	
"Like the last time you thought . . . , were you as big as now? Were you in third grade? Were you real small?"	"Uhmm, I guess it was a long time ago. I was real small."

Note. This was a follow-up interview. The previous interview (6 months prior) showed that child admitted to several occasions of suicidal ideation around that time, an event that was also verified at the time by the child's mother.

the clinical interviewer to call on parents and collaterals for historical and temporal information about the young patient's depression.

The extant research on the genesis of temporal awareness has been subject to criticism, however, because most studies were done on small groups of typically bright and "advantaged" children (Doob, 1971). In more representative samples, one may conceivably find that the milestones emerge chronologically later than what has been documented. Any conclusions about depressed or otherwise maladjusted children's competencies vis-à-vis temporal awareness are further complicated by the fact that, at least in adult samples, it has been found that temporal orientation, time estimation, and content of recall were influenced by psychopathology (e.g., Fraisse, 1963). Nonetheless, the dialogue depicted in Table 7 with a research subject validates data cited above in regard to children's tendency to date recent events further back in time than warranted. The dialogue also instantiates the child's tendency to live in the present and documents that, in a temporal sense, the young patient is not likely to be a good informant about past history.

SEMISTRUCTURED CLINICAL INTERVIEWS FOR CHILDREN

Semistructured interview schedules are the "measures" that correspond to the clinical diagnostic interview. Interview schedules are measures or tools in the sense that they ensure a standard assessment format and systematic information coverage. For example, they specify what type of data must be collected; what questions should be asked in order to obtain the data; and how the information must be evaluated or quantified. These instruments thereby minimize some sources of error (e.g., information variance) and facilitate the collection of reliable data. Semistructured interviews were pioneered by researchers in adult psychiatry from among which the Schedule for Affective Disorders and Schizophrenia (SADS; Spitzer & Endicott, 1978) has remained one of the best known.

Just as its prototypes in adult psychiatry, an interview schedule for children must limit its symptomatic coverage and ensure a systematic way to gather the data. However, it must also reflect sensitivity to the developmental characteristics of young patients. Earlier in the present chapter, it was documented that both the general interview situation and the assessment of depression call into play interpersonal, psychologic, and cognitive constructs that are subject to development. Do the available instruments take into account such issues? Is it possible for an interview schedule to be sufficiently structured to ensure a standardized evaluation and yet, to be flexible enough to accommodate the various competencies of children?

There are three standardized interview schedules that are pertinent to the present chapter: namely, the SADS-"Kiddie" version (K-SADS) developed by Puig-Antich and colleague (Puig-Antich & Chambers, 1978), the Interview Schedule for Children (ICS) developed by the present author (Kovacs, 1978) and the Diagnostic Interview Schedule for Children and Adolescents (DICA) of Herjanic (1977). Each of the foregoing instruments reflects that it is possible to combine uniformity and flexibility in the psychiatric assessment of children. However, this is evident mostly in the specific semantic inquiries used to elicit data from young patients about their symptoms.

Perhaps because the schedules under consideration were developed for the purposes of research, for the most part they contain scant information on the general structural requirements of a "good" pediatric interview. For example, whereas each of the three schedules conveys implicitly or mentions explicitly that it is important to establish rapport with young patients, there are no detailed guidelines about ways to achieve that goal. In the introductory portions of the schedules, there is no mention as to whether (or how) a child should be prepared beforehand for the research interview. Neither are there explicit statements about the need to establish a trusting relationship with the young patient or that the youngster should be prepared to view the interviewer as a helping agent. Of course, a particular research interviewer may still entertain such notions. The latter proposition could be examined empirically with an emphasis on whether or not such an expectational set influences the conduct and outcome of a semistructured, symptom-oriented interview.

Although the interview schedules under consideration do not instruct parents to tell their children that the examiner will discuss problems and difficulties, references to a youngster's "problems" are embedded in the questions about specific symptoms. Because such references typically appear subsequent to a series of inquiries that set the stage for a symptom, the child's "problem" is therefore placed into various contexts. In light of the developmental literature that was reviewed earlier in this chapter, such context-related discussions of problems are probably more meaningful to younger children than general, pre-interview preparatory statements about the clinician's intent.

Because these interview tools were designed to facilitate the direct clinical examination of the child and emphasize phenomenologic description, they rely heavily on verbal–oral communication to elucidate complaints and symptoms. A perusal of the questions that serve to elicit the needed data suggest an attempt to be sensitive to the target population's variable linguistic, semantic, and conceptual levels. This sensitivity is evidenced in the generally simple sentence structures of the DICA questions, the relatively plain vocabulary and alternative symptom inquiries that are typical of the ISC and the K-SADS, and the "down-to-earth," direct approach to information-gathering that characterizes all three schedules. At the same time, however, the instruments do not maintain a consistently and uniformly low vocabulary level that would assure their ready use with 6-year-olds, for example.

As reviewed earlier, the available research evidence suggests that, with the exception of historic and chronologic data, school-aged children can provide information about many depressive symptoms. However, the examiner must be aware that even in that age group, young patients can differ considerably from one another in levels of cognitive and psychological development. How do semistructured clinical interviews handle inter- and intraindividual variations in developmental stages that may impact on the evaluation of the depressive syndrome? Because they were designed specifically for the clinical assessment of depression in the child, the answer to this question is now explored in relation to the K-SADS and the ISC.

First, both of the foregoing schedules require an initial interview with the parent about the child, and then a separate interview with the young patient. This strategy compensates for the child's inability to account correctly for all of his or her symptoms. It also provides the clinician a general historic framework within which to operate and makes it easier to decide which symptom areas must be probed further with the young patient.

With both the K-SADS and the ISC, the onset and duration of the child's disorder, the co-occurrence of depressive symptoms and signs, and past history are typically determined during the semistructured interview with the parent about the child. In light of the literature on the genesis and unfolding of temporal awareness, this procedure is sensible and appropriate. Moreover, by virtue of their perspectives, parents are also more likely to provide valid information about additional variables, such as the child's social and functional impairment.

As noted above, even the direct pediatric examination heavily relies on information from parents in order to arrive at a diagnosis. Therefore, it is reasonable to ask whether juvenile patients need to be interviewed at all. In light of clinical experience that parents are often unaware of certain symptoms in their children, the answer to this question is an unequivocal "yes." For example, parents frequently do not know that their children have had recurrent thoughts of wanting to die or suicidal ideation. Likewise, it is not uncommon for parents to underestimate the extent of a child's sleep disturbance (e.g., Puig-Antich et al., 1983).

Therefore, both the K-SADS and the ISC entail interview strategies to accommodate the variable abilities of children to report about themselves. For example, both schedules use serial, graded questions and actual, concrete examples of symptoms to elicit the needed data. The former approach is reflected in sets of inquiries that start with the simplest formulation of a construct and then progress to semantically and conceptually more complex levels. The latter strategy is exemplified by the manner in which the interviews approach the assessment of guilt. Instead of the mere use of the word "guilt," the young patient's attention is focused on exemplars; e.g., feeling bad about things one has done, or being bothered by feelings that one has caused bad things to happen. To determine if the child has had disturbances of mood, both semistructured interviews require situational examples to assure that the young patient is reporting on the emotion in question.

The ISC, for example, also takes into account the child's present orientation in the assessment of symptom frequency; the questions focus on whether the youngster has been bothered by a particular depressive symptom today, yesterday, the day before, and throughout the 2 weeks preceding the interview. Both the K-SADS and the ISC appear to be sensitive to children's difficulties in estimating the severity or duration of symptoms. The latter issues are handled by queries that require absolute or fairly crude judgments from the youngster (e.g., have you felt such and such "a lot," "a little," or "all day," "part of the day").

These instruments furthermore suggest that apparently sophisticated constructs can be assessed by the use of simple questions. For example, the question "Have you noticed any change in your thinking—are you pessimistic?" should prompt metacognitive processes and may not be comprehended by younger children. In contrast, a focus on specific content (e.g., "Do you think things will work out for you for the worst?") seems to tap simple self-report abilities and is more likely to elicit a valid reply from a younger child.

All in all, it appears that, based on clinical experience, educated intuition, and the literature, the originators of the available semistructured interviews for children have made headway in meeting developmental concerns. These tools should nonetheless by subjected to closer, impartial scrutiny because they could undoubtedly benefit from developmentally oriented refinements. For example, the K-SADS includes inquiries for all symptoms that require the child to report on them when the child's depression was the worst. Such questions demand a well-developed past time perspective, comparative judgments about severity of symptoms, and recall of information that may have occurred quite some time prior to the interview. In light of the pertinent literature, one wonders if such demands can be met by a 6- or 8-year-old. Likewise, although the ISC interview with the child is present focused, it requires the youngster to report on the presence and severity of affective and related symptoms for the past 2 weeks. It is possible that even that time interval is not meaningful to younger children and that, instead, they tend to report on the experiences of the past few days.

It also appears that the schedules have not specified that certain feelings or conceptualizations may be appropriate at some ages but not at others. The discussion about guilt in a previous section of this chapter is a case in point. According to the available data, it is age-appropriate for a young child to feel guilty about a negative event even though he or she did not cause it, nor could control it; for a 13-year-old, however, the same attribution is inappropriate. Interview schedules should therefore incorporate guidelines in that regard.

The vocabulary levels of the instruments could be also analyzed for uniformity and comprehensibility. However, there may be no proper way to ask a child about the notion of worthlessness if the child's developmental stage precludes an understanding of the self as "knower." Therefore, the extent to which interview items and salient psychological constructs are understood both by psychiatrically disturbed and normal children should be subjected to empirical study. The symptoms of the depressive syndrome could be examined more closely in order to assess whether their overt expression is subject to developmental vicissitudes. This is particularly important because, according to a recent study, none of the predicted developmental symptom trends could be observed among 8- to 13-year-old depressed children (Kovacs & Paulauskas, 1984).

One additional issue concerns the ways in which the clinical examiner can establish the child's stage of development on pertinent constructs. At present, such judgments are usually based on the intuition of the interviewer. And although a wide variety of developmental tasks are available, most of them are only marginally relevant to the psychiatric interview of the school-aged child. Therefore, there is a need for ways to assess children's cognitive and emotional development that can also serve to construct more sensitive clinical pediatric interviews.

THE INTERFACE BETWEEN THE TRADITIONAL INTERVIEW AND THE DIRECT EXAMINATION OF THE CHILD

Earlier in this chapter, a distinction was made between the "traditional" clinical interview and the typically research-oriented direct examination. As noted, the former method is generally geared to understand the individual youngster's problems and concerns. To achieve that aim, free play, observation, interpretation, as well as oral–verbal exchange are widely used and accepted interview strategies. In contrast, in the direct-examination method, oral-verbal dialogue is the primary means of information gathering, with a substantial reliance on the content of the young patient's oral responses. However, it would be an oversimplification to say that the traditional clinical interviewer does not talk to the child or ignores what the young patient says or, conversely, that the examiner who conducts a direct symptom-oriented interview ignores the child's behavior. The two methods do overlap in terms of strategies and contextual issues.

Although the direct diagnostic examination emphasizes the exchange of specific, objective information, attention is paid to the child's nonverbal interview behavior and affective display. As noted by Poznanski (1982), for example, the youngster's facial expression can provide clues to his or her emotional state; such observational data should be used to probe about recent affective experiences. A perusal of one semistructured interview, the ISC, also suggests that the child's nonverbal behavior is used to lead into specific symptomatic inquiries. For example, if the youngster looks sad, the questioning about depressed mood may start with "You seem to be feeling sad . . . did you have this feeling all day?" Furthermore, as the vignette in Table 5 suggests, even within the direct-examination model, the youngster's nonverbal display is used to validate or to falsify a particular response.

Many clinicians, particularly traditionally oriented ones, would argue that the emotions, feelings, and behaviors elicited in the interview are of diagnostic significance. However, in the assessment of depressive disorders such displays on their own, in isolation, do not usually provide sufficient data for diagnosis. For example, a young patient's sad expression could reflect a temporary emotion, it could be due to some event that occurred just prior to the interview, or it could signal a setting effect. To determine whether the child's overt sadness qualifies as a psychopathological symptom, its occurrence, persistence, and severity outside the interview must be ascertained.*

Opinions also differ about the helpfulness of adjunctive, nonverbal strategies in the clinical diagnostic examination of the child. Puig-Antich et al. (1983) found play techniques a distraction in their pediatric psychiatric interviews. In contrast, in the present author's projects, certain "play" activities have been used during the clinical examination. For example, we found it helpful to supply younger or nonverbal children with colored pencils or crayons so that they could draw pictures while the interview progressed. This has enabled some children to become more comfortable; and it is a sensible interview technique as long as the child's productions are not used as prima facie evidence of certain symptoms.

FINAL COMMENT

This chapter has attempted to bridge the fields of developmental psychology and clinical psychiatric assessment. A developmental approach to the clinical interview of the child was proposed with a specific emphasis on the diagnosis of depressive disorders. It was assumed that such a perspec-

---

*This point was raised by Dr. Martin Hoffman's comments at the SSRC–NIMH conference.

tive may lead to greater sensitivity about the method's implicit and explicit demands on young patients. Toward this aim, selected aspects of the clinical interview were emphasized and a portion of the pertinent developmental literature was reviewed.

The upsurge of interest in developmental psychopathology, as evidenced by this chapter and entire volume, is long overdue. But, the practical application of developmental principles requires that clinician–researchers have a working knowledge of developmental psychology, that developmental psychologists have an appreciation of clinical issues, or that the two professions develop collaborative enterprises. Nowhere is the need for integration more obvious than in the area of clinical assessment measures. Although the traditional skepticism about the direct examination of juveniles is based on the recognition of children's developmental immaturity, little attempt has been made to tease out the salient component processes or to examine clinicians' own contributions to the demands of the interview.

As a working model, it was proposed in this chapter that the structure of the direct-examination method and the information needed for diagnosis both require a certain level of linguistic, emotional, conceptual, and social maturity from the child. Thus, one researchable issue concerns the validity of arbitrarily dividing the impact of the clinical interview on the young patient into those arising from its structural aspects and those that can be traced to the diagnostic process. In this regard, it is of interest that standardized research interviews put little emphasis on the former. Therefore, it would be important to examine whether children's perceptions of clinicians as helping agents actually influence self-disclosure. Although it is generally accepted that, because youngsters do not self-identify as patients, they are less willing to "tell all," a closer study of this assumption could be worthwhile. If social-perspective-taking mediates self-labeling as a patient, that is, if one must view oneself from the vantage point of others in order to decide that one needs help, then even many adolescents may not be able to fulfill this particular clinical expectation.

Research is also needed on the extent to which youngsters at various ages and with different disorders are able to supply information about their difficulties and on whether the patient's developmental-stage affects diagnostic formulations. Developmentally oriented clinical research also needs to explore the interaction between psychopathology and the gradual unfolding of capacities. Does emotional and behavioral disturbance "mask" the child's emerging cognitive, emotional, and social competencies? If yes, what are the implications for the clinical diagnostic interview? For example, with respect to the vignette in Table 6, does the boy's lack of social-perspective-taking have diagnostic or developmental significance? In this case, the data's diagnostic implications are unclear because the young man demonstrated a similar lack of skills vis-à-vis other individuals. But there is a need for guidelines as to when chronological-age-incongruent cognitive performance is likely to have developmental significance.*

A related and already noted issue that requires collaboration between developmental and clinical researchers concerns the relationship between tested cognitive functioning and manifest ability. To what extent is it possible to extrapolate from "tested" cognitive-social-developmental stage to practically applied abilities? Are such extrapolations different for normal as opposed to depressed or otherwise psychiatrically distressed youth? If test abilities do not provide an index of the child's day-to-day skills, are there ways to assess the level at which the young patient actually functions? Answers to such questions would be helpful to the clinician examiner of the school-aged child and would vastly increase our understanding of the relationship between development, psychopathology, and its assessment.

ACKNOWLEDGMENTS

An earlier version of this chapter was delivered at the conference "Depressive Disorders: Developmental Perspectives," cosponsored by the Social Science Research Council (SSRC) and the National Institutes of Mental Health (NIMH), Philadelphia, April 21–23, 1982. Preparation of this chapter was supported by Grant No. MH-33990 from the National Institutes of Mental Health, Health and Human Services Administration.

REFERENCES

American Psychiatric Association. (1980). *Diagnostic and statistical manual of mental disorders* (3rd ed.). Washington, DC: Author.

Aspy, D. N. (1975). Empathy: Let's get the hell on with it. *Counseling Psychologist, 5*(2), 10–14.

Barnett, K., Darcie, G., Holland, C. J., & Kobasigawa, A. (1982). Children's cognitions about effective helping. *Developmental Psychology, 18*(2), 267–277.

Bibace, R., & Walsh, M. E. (1979). Developmental stages in children's conceptions of illness. In G. C. Stone, F. Cohen, N. E. Adler, & Associates (Eds.), *Health psychology—A handbook: Theories, applications, and challenges of a psychological approach to the health care system* (pp. 285–301). San Francisco: Jossey-Bass.

Campbell, J. D. (1975). Illness is a point of view: The development of children's concepts of illness. *Child Development, 46*, 92–100.

Carlson, G. A., & Cantwell, D. P. (1982). Diagnosis of childhood depression: A comparison of

---

*This is not to say that interview behavior is relatively unimportant. In fact under certain conditions or for some diagnoses, the patient's actions, demeanor, and general stance communicate crucial information. For example, the criteria for schizotypal personality disorder permit "inadequate rapport" in the interview to be counted as a positive diagnostic sign. Likewise, a patient's behavior during the examination may be so overtly and grossly deviant as to indicate clearly the presence of psychosis and/or the need for immediate hospitalization. Also, the observation of the young patient may allow the clinician to formulate tentative working hypotheses about differential diagnosis that can be then pursued by direct questioning.

the Weinberg and DSM-III criteria. *Journal of the American Academy of Child Psychiatry, 21*(3), 247–250.

Cavanaugh, J. C., & Perlmutter, M. (1982). Metamemory: A critical examination. *Child Development, 53*, 11–28.

Chandler, M. J. (1975). Relativism and the problem of epistemological loneliness. *Human Development, 18*, 171–180.

Clearly, P. D., Mechanic, D., & Weiss, N. (1981). The effect of interviewer characteristics on responses to a mental health interview. *Journal of Health and Social Behavior, 22*, 183–193.

Coie, J. D., & Pennington, B. F. (1976). Children's perceptions of deviance and disorder. *Child Development, 47*, 407–413.

Compas, B. E., Friedland-Bandes, R., Bastien, R., & Adelman, H. S. (1981). Parent and child causal attributions related to the child's clinical problem. *Journal of Abnormal Child Psychology, 9*(3), 389–397.

Cramer, J. B. (1980). Psychiatric examination of the child. In H. I. Kaplan, A. M. Freedman, & B. J. Sadock (Eds.), *Comprehensive textbook of psychiatry/III* (3rd ed., Vol. 3, pp. 2453–2461). Baltimore: Williams & Wilkins, 1980.

Damon, W., & Hart, D. (1982). The development of self-understanding from infancy through adolescence. *Child Development, 53*, 841–864.

Dollinger, S. J., Thelen, M. H., & Walsh, M. L. (1980). Children's conceptions of psychological problems. *Journal of Clinical Child Psychology, 9*, 191–194.

Doob, L. W. (1971). *Patterning of time.* New Haven, CT: Yale University Press.

Elkind, D. (1974). *Children and adolescents. Interpretive essays on Jean Piaget* (2nd ed.). New York: Oxford University Press.

Feighner, J. P., Robins, E., Guze, S. B., Woodruff, R. A., Winokur, G., & Munoz, R. (1972). Diagnostic criteria for use in psychiatric research. *Archives of General Psychiatry, 26*, 57–63.

Fitzgerald, J. M. (1981). Autobiographical memory: Reports in adolescence. *Canadian Journal of Psychology, 35*(1), 69–73.

Fraisse, P. (1963). *The psychology of time.* New York: Harper & Row.

Friedman, W. J. (1978). Development of time concepts in children. In W. H. Reese & L. P. Lipsett (Eds.), *Advances in child development and behavior* (Vol. 12, pp. 267–298). New York: Academic Press.

Glasberg, R., & Aboud, F. (1982). Keeping one's distance from sadness: Children's self-reports of emotional experience. *Developmental Psychology, 18*(2), 287–293.

Harris, P. L., Olthof, T., & Terwogt, M. M. (1981). Children's knowledge of emotion. *Journal of Child Psychology and Psychiatry, 22*, 247–262.

Herjanic, B. (1977). *Diagnostic interview for children and adolescents (Ages 9–17)(DICA).* Unpublished manuscript. (Available from B. Herjanic, Washington University School of Medicine, St. Louis, MO)

Iannotti, R. J. (1975). The nature and measurement of empathy in children. *Counseling Psychologist, 5*(2), 21–25.

Izard, C. E. (1984). Emotion–cognition relationships and human development. In C. E. Izard, J. Kagan, & R. Zajonc (Eds.), *Emotions, cognition, and behavior* (pp. 17–37). New York: Cambridge University Press.

Kashani, J. H., Husain, A., Shekim, W. O., Hodges, K. K., Cytryn, L., & McKnew, D. H. (1981). Current perspectives on childhood depression: An overview. *The American Journal of Psychiatry, 138*, 143–153.

Kovacs, M. (1978). *Interview schedule for children (ISC) Form C.* Unpublished manuscript. (Available from M. Kovacs, Western Psychiatric Institute and Clinic, Pittsburgh, PA)

Kovacs, M. (1983). *The interview schedule for children (ISC): Interrater and parent-child agreement.* Unpublished manuscript. (Available from M. Kovacs, Western Psychiatric Institute and Clinic, Pittsburgh, PA).

Kovacs, M., & Paulauskas, S. L. (1984). Developmental stage and the expression of depressive disorders in children: An empirical analysis. In D. Cicchetti & K. Schneider-Rosen (Eds.), Childhood Depression. New Directions for Child Development, No. 26. San Francisco: Jossey-Bass.

Kraepelin, E. (1921). Manic-depressive insanity and paranoia. (G. M. Robertson, Ed. and R. M. Barclay, Trans.). Edinburgh: Livingstone.

Leahy. R. L., & Huard, C. (1976). Role taking and self-image disparity in children. Developmental Psychology, 12(6), 504–508.

MacKinnon, R. A. (1980). Psychiatric interview. In H. I. Kaplan, A. M. Freedman, & B. J. Sadock (Eds.), Comprehensive textbook of psychiatry/III (3rd ed., Vol. 1, pp. 895–905). Baltimore: Williams & Wilkins.

Marsden, G., & Kalter, N. (1976). Children's understanding of their emotionally disturbed peers. I. The concept of emotional disturbance. Psychiatry, 39(3), 227–238.

Marsden, G., Kalter, N., Plunkett, J. W., & Barr-Grossman, T. (1977). Children's social judgments concerning emotionally disturbed peers. Journal of Consulting and Clinical Psychology, 45(5), 948.

Masters, J. C., & Carlson, C. R. (1984). Children's and adults' understanding of the causes and consequences of emotional states. In C. E. Izard, J. Kagan, & R. Zajonc (Eds.), Emotions, cognition, and behavior (pp. 438–463). New York: Cambridge University Press.

Mullener, N., & Laird, J. D. (1971). Some developmental changes in the organization of self-evaluations. Developmental Psychology, 5(2), 233–236.

Pogul, L. J. (1980). Psychological testing in childhood. In J. R. Bemporad (Ed.), Child development in normality and psychopathology (pp. 477–508). New York: Brunner/Mazel, Inc.

Poznanski, E. O. (1982). The clinical characteristics of childhood depression. In L. Grinspoon, (Ed.), Psychiatry 1982. The American Psychiatric Association Annual Review. Washington, DC: American Psychiatric Press.

Puig-Antich, J. (1980). Affective disorders in childhood: A review and perspective. In B. Blinder (Ed.), Psychiatric clinics in North America (Vol. 3, pp. 403–424). Philadelphia: W. B. Saunders.

Puig-Antich, J., & Chambers, W. (1978). Schedule for affective disorders and schizophrenia for school-age children (6–16 years). Kiddie-SADS (K-SADS). Unpublished manuscript. (Available from J. Puig-Antich, Department of Child and Adolescent Psychiatry, New York State Psychiatric Institute, New York, NY).

Puig-Antich, J., Chambers, W. J., & Tabrizi, M. A. (1983). The clinical assessment of current depressive episodes in children and adolescents: Interviews with parents and children. In D. Cantwell & G. Carlson (Eds.), Childhood depression (pp. 157–179). New York: Spectrum.

Roberts, M. C., Beidleman, W. B., & Wurtele, S. K. (1981). Children's perceptions of medical and psychological disorders in their peers. Journal of Clinical Child Psychology, 10, 76–78.

Rogers, C. R. (1975). Empathic: An unappreciated way of being. Counseling Psychologist, 5(2), 2–10.

Ruble, D. N., Boggiano, A. K., Feldman, N. S., & Loebl, J. H. (1980). Developmental analysis of the role of social comparison in self-evaluation. Developmental Psychology, 16(2), 105–115.

Ruble, D. N., Parsons, J. E., & Ross, J. (1976). Self-evaluative responses of children in an achievement setting. Child Development, 47, 990–997.

Rutter, M., & Graham, P. (1968). The reliability and validity of the psychiatric assessment of the child. I. Interview with the child. British Journal of Psychiatry, 114, 563–579.

Rutter, M., & Shaffer, D. (1980). DSM-III: A step forward or back in terms of the classification of child psychiatric disorders? Journal of the American Academy of Child Psychiatry, 19, 371–394.

Schwartz, R. M., & Trabasso, T. (1984). Children's understanding of emotions. In C. E. Izard,

J. Kagan, & R. Zajonc (Eds.), *Emotions, cognition, and behavior* (pp. 409–437). New York: Cambridge University Press.

Selman, R. L. (1976). Toward a structural analysis of developing interpersonal relations concepts: Research with normal and disturbed preadolescent boys. In A. Pick (Ed.), *Minnesota symposia on child psychology* (Vol. 10, pp. 156–200). Minneapolis: University of Minnesota Press.

Selman, R. L., Jaquette, D., & Redman Lavin, D. (1977). Interpersonal awareness in children: Toward an integration of developmental and clinical child psychology. *American Journal of Orthopsychiatry, 47*(2), 264–274.

Siegler, R. S. (Ed.). (1978). *Children's thinking: What develops?* Hillsdale, NJ: Lawrence Erlbaum Associates.

Simmons, J. E. (1981). *Psychiatric examination of children* (3rd ed.). Philadelphia: Lea & Febiger.

Spitzer, R. L., & Endicott, J. (1978). *Schedule for affective disorders and schizophrenia-lifetime version (SADS-L)* (3rd ed.). Unpublished manuscript. (Available from R. L. Spitzer, New York State Psychiatric Institute, New York, NY).

Spitzer, R. L., Endicott, J., & Robins, E. (1978). Research diagnostic criteria: Rationale and reliability. *Archives of General Psychiatry, 35*, 773–782.

Sullivan, H. S. (1954). *The psychiatric interview.* New York: Norton.

Voyat, G. (1977). Perception and concept of time: A developmental perspective. In B. S. Gorman & A. E. Wessman (Eds.), *The personal experience of time* (pp. 135–160). New York: Plenum Press.

Weinberg, W. A., Rutman, J., Sullivan, L., Penick, E. C., & Dietz, S. G. (1973). Depression in children referred to an educational diagnostic center: Diagnosis and treatment. *Journal of Pediatrics, 83*(6), 1065–1072.

Weiner, B., & Graham, S. (1984). An attributional approach to emotional development. In C. E. Izard, J. Kagan, & R. Zajonc (Eds.), *Emotions, cognition, and behavior* (pp. 167–191). New York: Cambridge University Press.

Wessman, A. E., & Gorman, B. S. (1977). The emergence of human awareness and concepts of time. In B. S. Gorman & A. E. Wessman (Eds.), *The personal experience of time* (pp. 3–55). New York: Plenum Press.

VI

SOME OUTSTANDING ISSUES

When Is a Case a Case?

Leon Eisenberg

Ideological debates between those committed to "caseness" and those arguing for "continuum" have been recurrent themes in the discussions in this volume. The two views have been presented as though they were mutually exclusive and as though the first were the property of biomedicine and the second the domain of psychology. The discussion has been burdened by the incorrect view that the difficulty in distinguishing between the pathological and the normal is peculiar to psychiatry in contrast to general medicine, where (it is assumed) diseases are not only readily agreed upon but also more "real." The essentialist view (which takes disease to be an entity that causes illness) is just as debatable in physical as in psychological medicine.

Disease definitions are social constructs. In so stating, I do not imply that they are simply arbitrary and without relation to events in the world. To the contrary, disease concepts are elaborated in the effort to make sense out of, in order to alleviate, complaint patterns patients bring to physicians. However, our definitions of disease change historically as they are influenced by new observations, new methods of investigation, and new scientific ideas. As definitions change, patients formerly included as cases are reassigned to other diagnostic categories; others, previously not recognized as belonging to the "species," now are so diagnosed. As knowledge increases, definitions based on clinical signs and symptoms are replaced by pathological, etiological, or combined classifications (e.g., cirrhosis of the liver, vivax malaria, and pneumococcal pneumonia, respectively).

Leon Eisenberg. Department of Social Medicine and Health Policy, Harvard Medical School, Boston, Massachusetts.

However, this should not be mistaken for a process approaching truth as an asymptote. Agent Y, which causes clinical disease in patient A, may be present in individual B without producing disease—as in the instance of hemolytic streptococci in the throat, which result in severe pharyngitis in A but no symptoms in B, who is a carrier. Laboriously acquired knowledge that high levels of blood calcium can result from a disorder of the parathyroid gland and can produce incapacitating illness does not tell us how to interpret high levels of blood calcium found incidentally in the course of a hospital work-up now that automated blood chemistry analyses are done routinely (Heath, Hodgson, & Kennedy, 1980; Mundy, Cove, & Fiskin, 1980; Paterson & Gunn, 1981). Furthermore, the symptoms that patients experience even in the course of diseases where the anatomical substrate is known are not explicable solely in terms of the observable pathology (Eisenberg, 1977).

Let me provide a historical vignette that sets forth the way the definition of a particular hematologic disease has evolved. Fifty years ago, Cooley and Lee (1925) separated out, from the broad category of childhood anemia, five children with enlarged livers and spleens, pigmented skin, thick bones, and odd-looking red cells, which showed decreased osmotic fragility. A decade later, the disorder was renamed thalassemia by Whipple and Bradford (1936) because of the observation that the children came from families of Mediterranean origin. That the disorder is genetic was established by Wintrobe, Mathews, Pollack, and Dobyns (1940), among others, when they identified less severe forms of the anemia among carriers (heterozygotes). When Kunkel and Wallenius (1955) discovered the normal minor hemoglobin component, hemoglobin A_2, and showed that it was elevated in persons with thalassemia minor, they provided a marker for genetic studies. A veritable explosion of research on the hemoglobin molecule has led to the recognition of more than 50 combinations of genetic errors (structural gene deletions, nucleotide substitutions in intervening sequences, and nonsense mutations in codons) that can result in the thalassemia phenotype (Weatherall & Clegg 1981).

Consider what has happened to "Cooley's anemia" in the course of this history. In the first edition of Wintrobe's *Clinical Hematology* (1942), the reader was told that thalassemia "is characterized by chronic progressive anemia commencing early in life, well-marked erythroblastosis in the peripheral blood, a characteristic facies, splenomegaly, and a familial and racial incidence" (p. 507). Thirty years later in the current edition of that standard textbook (Wintrobe et al., 1974), the reader learns that "thalassemia comprises a heterogeneous group of inherited disorders of hemoglobin synthesis. Indeed, it can no longer be said that the presence of hypochromic, microcytic red corpuscles, which are not the result of iron deficiency and whose osmotic fragility is decreased, is the sine qua non of thalassemia. The morphologic picture varies in the different thalassemia syndromes, *even to the point of total absence of morphologic features or clinical manifestations* in some heterozygotes [!]" (pp. 855–856).

The evolution of the disease process began with two astute clinical observers who recognized, among a large clinical population of anemic patients, five children who seemed to share common features. Later observers noted that the children came (largely) from Italian and Greek families. This prepared the ground for pedigree studies and the identification of the heterozygote. Progress in basic hemoglobin biochemistry, applied to a clinical problem known to be genetic and therefore expected to be biochemical, permitted the identification of the molecular pathology underlying the clinical phenomena. With the new laboratory methods, it became possible to recognize persons who have a genetic defect in globin chain synthesis but who have few or no clinical features. What had appeared to be a single clinical entity has been revealed to be heterogeneous to an extent undreamed of and to be the result of any one or more of 50 genetic errors, which can alter α- or β-globin chain synthesis.

In this sequence of events, the definition of thalassemia has been put on its head. Originally limited to individuals in desperate need of help because of the morbidity and mortality caused by their condition, the label has been extended to individuals who are entirely asymptomatic and enjoy a normal life span; the latter are included because they have inherited a gene that results in an unusual pattern of globin chain synthesis, even though it has no clinical consequences. Such an individual is hardly to be considered a "case" in the sense in which we have employed the term in this volume. If the inclusion of nonpatients in the redefinition troubles philosophic purists, it does not gainsay the enormous progress in disease control made possible by biomedical research. Because the methods of molecular biology have permitted the prenatal diagnosis of some subtypes of thalassemia (Orkin, 1982), public health programs based on amniocentesis and abortion have been able to reduce markedly the prevalence of thalassemia in populations at risk (Alter, 1981). Even greater advances are visible on the horizon. Kan's research group (Temple, Dozy, Roy, & Kan, 1982) has come close to the dream of "gene therapy"; they have been able *in vitro* to insert a suppressor gene into *Xenopus* oocytes in order to "correct" a nonsense mutation in β^0-thalassemia mRNA. The "treated" oocytes were then able to produce the β-globin chain! This elegant laboratory experiment is many steps away from clinical application but it indicates that a general solution is possible in principle.

What was originally thought to be a "species" (a clinical syndrome sui generis) has been shown to be more in the nature of a genus comprised of many species. The definition has been restricted in one sense (to inherited disorders of hemoglobin synthesis) and broadened in another (no longer limited to a particular patient population). If we consider the present status of our understanding of depression as a syndrome, we are at one and the same time working to characterize *a* syndrome (akin to Cooley's anemia) and to identify unequivocal neurobiological stigmata (akin to defective globin synthesis). We can be confident of only one thing: What appears to be homogeneous (to some clinicians) will not prove to be so as more data are gathered.

Other aspects of the history of disease are illustrated by secular changes in the prevalence of tuberculosis. Nineteen eighty two was the centenary of that exciting moment in the history of medical science when Robert Koch isolated the tubercle bacillus from patients with clinical disease and demonstrated that the organism could be stained, grown in culture, and shown to produce disease in laboratory animals. By the early years of this century, the bitter nineteenth-century debate about the nature and cause of tuberculosis had been superseded by general agreement among scientists that the tubercle bacillus was the necessary cause for the production of the disease. Only slowly did it become evident that it was not a sufficient condition. We know now that, of individuals infected by the tubercle bacillus as evidenced by a positive tuberculin test, only 5–15% ever become clinically ill with tuberculosis, as evidenced by signs, symptoms, X-ray findings, and positive cultures. Susceptibility in populations varies with age, sex, race, and social class as well as with HLA phenotype (Glassroth, Robbins, & Snider, 1980). Although resistance to infection with the tubercle bacillus (BCG type) has been shown to be under genetic control in mice (Gros, Skamene, & Forget, 1981), inheritance has never been demonstrated unequivocally in humans, though the differences in mortality between endogamous human subgroups have suggested a genetic basis for susceptibility, perhaps by differential survival of resistant individuals among highly urbanized groups (Motulsky, 1979). The understandable elation at identifying a cause for the white plague had obscured the equally important role of host resistance, which determines outcome in interaction with the virulence of the pathogen.

No one would deny that tuberculosis is a "biological" disease. However, social and psychological factors are powerful determinants of the number and distribution of those who are victimized by the pathogen. The mortality rate from tuberculosis in the United Kingdom fell from 400/100,000 in 1840 to 200/100,000 by 1880—2 years before the tubercle bacillus was identified by Koch (McKeown, 1976). Moreover, it had fallen to 60/100,000 by the mid-1940s, before effective medical interventions had been discovered. McKeown has argued persuasively that improved nutrition, sanitation, and living conditions account for this striking change in the susceptibility of the British population to tuberculosis (mortality rates for other infectious diseases show similar benefit). However, knowledge of the infectious origin and transmission of tuberculosis did permit useful public health measures (case identification and isolation).

The introduction of chemotherapy in 1947 markedly accelerated the pace of change. By 1980 in the United States (Centers for Disease Control, 1982), the mortality rate had fallen to less than 1/100,000. If one extrapolates the rate of decline that obtained before the introduction of chemotherapy to the period after it, the rate in 1980 would have been 20 times higher than that observed. Thus, tuberculosis provides a prime example of the interaction between the social and biomedical determinants of the prevalence of a disease.

As I read this history, it illustrates the folly of dichotomous thinking in the biological and social investigation of childhood depression. If further research succeeds in identifying reliable biological correlates of depression, such evidence will not preclude the possibility of effective intervention by social measures. Nor does the demonstration of social correlates for depressive symptoms (or for cases of depression) exclude a biological pathway for the expression of the interaction between social stress and individual vulnerability.

The examples of thalassemia and tuberculosis are illustrations of "progress," an increase in knowledge leading to greater control over disease. There are other instances in which disease concepts, prematurely entertained, come undone but only after creating mischief.

As a medical student, I was taught about "chronic brucellosis," a disease that accounted for persistent illness in patients likely to be dismissed as having "neurasthenia" unless a careful history was taken and appropriate laboratory tests performed (Evans, 1947). It had been known since the turn of the century that several species of *Brucella* microorganisms can produce an acute infectious illness; some patients, after recovery from an acute episode, go on to display continuing ill health (weakness, fatigue, migratory aches and pains, low-grade fever, depression) in the absence of abnormal physical findings. In patients seen long after an initial infection (and even when there was no clear history of an initial infection), the diagnosis was said to be established by a positive serum agglutination test against the microbes.

There is, however, a serious flaw in this line of reasoning. Agglutins may persist for many years in recovered as well as chronically ill patients. The two groups seem the same in all respects other than complaint pattern. Is it possible that chronic brucellosis is a spurious disease construct that legitimates (and therefore serves to perpetuate) chronic illness behavior?

Cluff, Trever, Imboden, and Canter (1959) studied 24 patients known to have had acute brucellosis, in 16 of whom symptoms had persisted for 4 – 8 years. They were unable to distinguish between the recovered and the ill patients by physical or laboratory examination. However, mental status examination revealed clear evidence of emotional disturbance, particularly depression, in those who were symptomatic. Since the chronic patients had been ill for many years, it remained possible that the psychiatric findings were the "result" rather than the "cause" of illness.

To test the hypothesis that prolonged convalescence from an acute infection is a function of preexisting personality traits, the Hopkins team (Imboden, Canter, & Cluff, 1961) assessed 600 individuals on the MMPI in order to identify those who were depression prone. The testing was done by design shortly before an epidemic of influenza was predicted to strike the area. During the flu season, the rate of infection, as determined by serological testing, was no greater in depression-prone persons than in others (40 vs. 34%) but rates of *illness,* as registered by clinic visits, did differ significantly (17 vs. 3%). Moreover, almost all the patients who exhibited prolonged convalescence from flu (3 weeks or more vs. 2 weeks or less) were, as predicted, in the depression-prone group. What is still called by many physicians "chronic brucellosis" appears to be a pattern of illness behavior fashioned out of the experience of an acute infection in psychologically predisposed individuals, a pattern reinforced by medical responses that sanction complaints by ascribing them to "disease."

The history of "chronic brucellosis" suggests caution before invoking an organic explanation for a congeries of symptoms just because an immunologic (or endocrine or biochemical) abnormality accompanies the syndrome. Deficiency in human growth hormone (HGH) is a typical feature of hypopituitary dwarfism; yet HGH deficiency is also found in psychosocial dwarfism, a condition secondary to severe emotional deprivation (Powell, Brasel, Raiti & Blizzard, 1967). In the former, HGH deficiency is permanent and dwarfism can only be averted by hormone replacement therapy; in the latter, it is rapidly reversible following removal from the pathologic environment when catch-up growth occurs (Guilhaume, Benoit, Gourmelen, & Richardet, 1982). Thus, the endocrine abnormalities found in depressed children reported in this volume by Puig-Antich are important research results, but they do not yet suffice to establish either the mechanism or the cause of the pathologic behavior (or its caseness).

The problems we encounter in exploring so murky an area as depression in childhood tempt us to reason by analogy from diseases currently better understood than the syndromes we are dealing with. Unfortunately, analogy is as likely to be misleading as it is to be insightful.

Those who believe depression to be an inherited condition express puzzlement that it is so much less common in childhood than adolescence and adulthood. Should that surprise us? Take the example of Huntington's disease (Chase, Wexler, & Barbeau, 1979), a degenerative neurological disorder, characterized by involuntary movements and progressive dementia. Clinical symptoms begin when the patient is between 30 and 50 years of age, although the disease has been shown to be transmitted as a dominant autosomal trait. Thus far, careful study has been unable to identify any premorbid characteristics to distinguish the child who is destined to be victimized from the one who will remain healthy within a sibship known to be at risk because of an affected parent (Martin, 1982). On the other hand, the presence of the "same" disease in childhood and adulthood does not establish identity of cause and character. Patients with juvenile-onset and adult-onset diabetes exhibit qualitatively similar disorders of glucose metabolism and insulin production; yet juvenile- and adult-onset diabetes differ, not only in severity, but in cause (Cudworth, 1978; Zimmet, 1982). Present evidence indicates that the juvenile- but not the adult-onset form results from an autoimmune process directed against the insulin-producing beta cells of the pancreas—probably triggered by environmental factors in a genetically susceptible individual (Kahn, 1982). Thus, our puzzlement about childhood depression is not illuminated by an appeal to known medical disorders.

Finally, there is something perverse about insisting on exalting either a caseness or a continuity model. To the contrary, it is the creative use of both methods simultaneously that is the most likely to increase understanding.

If we consider the Gaussian curve we obtain by plotting the heights of members of a population against the number of individuals who have attained each height, we discover at each end of the distribution more instances of shortness and tallness than we would expect to find on the theory of a normal distribution. If we examine the individuals who are more than 2 SD below the mean in height, we shall find, in addition to normal variants, a variety of dwarfs who differ qualitatively (i.e., show "caseness") from the normal population; that is, we shall discover that some exhibit abnormalities in the growth of long bones but normal torsos, others show proportionate reductions in all dimensions but have deficient hormone secretion, etc. However, it is not height per se that distinguishes the "pathologically" short from the "normally" short. It is the other associated features that will enable us to identify them if we are shrewd enough to use the proper study methods. An investigator who starts with a population sample at the extreme end of the distribution of a characteristic of interest increases the likelihood of finding cases: qualitatively different and functionally impaired phenotypes. Proper study of individuals at the extremes of the distribution may then permit the identification of the determinants of the population distribution (e.g., variation in growth hormone, in nutrition, in chondrogenesis).

Thus, a dimensional or continuous model can be of great assistance to the very investigator who is searching for caseness because a population survey provides an enriched vein to tap. If being 2 SD or more beyond the mean on the measured psychopathological dimension is not associated with a higher probability for caseness, then one must conclude that the clinician and the psychometrist are looking at different phenomena for which they are incorrectly using the same name. Before we can conclude that Martin Seligman's conclusions about learned helplessness based on a classroom sample apply to clinically depressed children—or that Monroe Lefkowitz' correlations between depression and other measured characteristics apply to cases—we shall need to know the degree of correspondence between psychometric depression as measured by their instruments and the diagnosis of depression by clinicians. I do not suggest the latter constitute the canonical criterion group. If the correspondence is poor, it may well be that each group is measuring important but nonoverlapping dimensions of affect or that the methods of the clinician no less than those of the psychometrician lack validity.

To summarize, caseness and continuity models have heuristic value in generating research hypotheses. They become impediments when they serve to "justify" hegemony for psychometricians (continuity) or for clinicians (caseness) and when they are elevated to dogma. The dialectic between them can become a source of creativity when they are used in a complementary fashion.

The world is more complex than some of us would like it to be. Let me conclude with a telling example of the futility of what Adolf Meyer once characterized as "doctrines of exclusive salvationism."

Vivax malaria occurs only in persons whose blood is positive for the Duffy antigen. Duffy blood group status is genetically controlled. Therefore, vivax malaria must be a genetic disease. Right? Wrong!

Vivax malaria is found only in individuals whose red cells are infested with *Plasmodium vivax* organisms. *P. vivax* is an infectious parasite transmitted by mosquitoes. Therefore, *P. vivax* is the cause of vivax malaria. Right? Wrong!

Present evidence indicates that *P. vivax* is able to penetrate the surface of the red cell in Duffy-positive individuals by attaching directly to the Duffy antigen (Miller, Mason, Dvorak, McGinnis, & Rothman, 1975; Miller, Mason, Clyde, & McGinnis, 1976) or another structurally related characteristic (Mason, Miller, Shiroishi, Dvorak, & McGinnis, 1977). Individuals who are Duffy negative are resistant to *P. vivax* infection because the plasmodium is unable to penetrate the red cell membrane. This difference has evolutionary consequences. West African blacks, who inhabit a geographic zone where *P. vivax* is endemic, are almost 100% Duffy negative as the result of selection of the resistant genotype.

To summarize, vivax malaria requires (1) genetic susceptibility and (2) exposure to an inoculum of the parasite; it is "genetic" and "infectious." What is necessary is not sufficient. Both causes must be present at one and the same time in order for disease to occur. Thus, in working with a disorder like depression, so far less defined than malaria, we should abjure causal conclusions on the basis of preliminary physiological or psychological findings.

If I argue so vehemently against premature closure to the debate about the nature and causes of childhood depression as a clinical entity, it is because I recall the naive neurologizing about the psychological sequellae of brain damage in childhood (Eisenberg, 1957). As Michael Rutter and his colleagues have demonstrated in an elegant follow-up study (Brown, Chadwick, Shaffer, Rutter, & Traub, 1981; Chadwick, Rutter, Brown, Shaffer, & Traub, 1981) children suffering from head injury are, indeed, at greater risk for intellectual impairment and psychiatric disorder; further, degree of risk is related to the severity of the injury. All well and good. However, the psychiatric consequences of brain damage also vary with (1) the preinjury behavior of the child, (2) psychosocial circumstances, and (3) cognitive level. "In spite of claims to the contrary, there appear to be rather few specific cognitive or behavioral sequellae of brain injury" (Rutter, 1981, p. 1542).

The lessons of our recent history clearly warrant caution before drawing large conclusions. Hypotheses must be stated in such fashion as to be capable of disconfirmation by clearly designed and carefully described empirical studies.

REFERENCES

Alter, B. P. (1981). Prenatal diagnosis of haemoglobinopathies: A status report. Lancet, 2, 1152–1155.

Brown, G., Chadwick, O., Shaffer, D., Rutter, M., & Traub, M. (1981). A prospective study of children with head injuries. III. Psychiatric sequelae. Psychological Medicine, 11, 63–78.

Centers for Disease Control. (1982). Bicentennial: Koch's discovery of the tubercle bacillus. Morbidity and Mortality Weekly Report, 31, 121–123.

Chadwick, O., Rutter, M., Brown, G., Shaffer, D., & Traub, M. (1981). A prospective study of children with head injuries. II. Cognitive sequelae. Psychological Medicine, 11, 49–61.

Chase, T. N., Wexler, N. S., & Barbeau, A. (Eds.) (1979). Huntington's disease. Advances in Neurology, 23.

Cluff, L. E., Trever, R. W., Imboden, J. B., & Canter, A., (1959). Brucellosis II. Medical aspects of delayed convalescence. Archives of Internal Medicine 103, 393–405.

Cooley, T. P., & Lee, P. (1925). A series of cases of splenomegaly in children with anemia and peculiar bone changes. Transactions of the American Pediatric Society, 37, 29.

Cudworth, A. G. (1978). Type I diabetes mellitus. Diabetologia, 14, 281–291.

Eisenberg, L. (1957). Psychiatric aspects of brain damage in children. Psychiatric Quarterly, 31, 72–92.

Eisenberg, L. (1977). Disease and illness. Culture, Medicine and Psychiatry, 1, 9–23.

Evans, A. C. (1947). Brucellosis in the United States. American Journal of Public Health, 37, 139–151.

Glassroth, J., Robbins, A. G., & Snider, D. E. (1980). Tuberculosis in the 1980's. New England Journal of Medince, 302, 1441–1450.

Gros, P., Skamene, E., & Forget, A. (1981). Genetic control of natural resistance to mycobacterium bovis (BCG) in mice. Journal of Immunology, 127, 2417–2421.

Guilhaume, A., Benoit, O., Gourmelen, M., & Richardet, J. M. (1982). Relationship between sleep stage IV deficit and reversible HGH deficiency in psychosocial dwarfism. Pediatric Research, 16, 299–303.

Heath, H., Hodgson, S. F., & Kennedy, M. A. (1980). Primary hyperparathyroidism. New England Journal of Medicine, 302, 189–193.

Imboden, J., Canter, A., & Cluff, L. E. (1961). Convalescence from influenza. Archives of Internal Medicine, 108, 393–399.

Kahn, C. R. (1982). Autoimmunity and the etiology of insulin-dependent diabetes mellitus. *Nature (London)*, *299*, 15–16.

Kunkel, H. G., & Wallenius, G. (1955). New hemoglobin in normal adult blood. *Science, 122*, 288.

Martin, J. B. (1982). Huntington's Disease: Genetically programmed cell death in the human central nervous system. *Nature (London)*, *299*, 205–206.

Mason, S. J., Miller, L. H., Shiroishi, T., Dvorak, J. A., & McGinniss, M. H., (1977). The Duffy blood group determinants: their role in susceptibility of human and animal erythrocytes to *P. Knowlesi* malaria. *British Journal of Haematology, 36*, 327–335.

McKeown, T. (1976). *The role of medicine: Dream, mirage, or nemesis?* London: The Nuffield Provincial Hospitals Trust.

Miller, L. H., Mason, S. J., Clyde, D. F. & McGinnis, M. H., (1976). The resistance factor to *Plasmodium vivax* in blacks. The Duffy blood group genotype FyFy. *New England Journal of Medicine, 295*, 302–304.

Miller, L. H., Mason, S., Dvorak, J. A. McGinnis, M. H., & Rothman, I. K. (1975). Erythrocyte receptors for *(Plasmodium knowlesi)* malaria: Duffy blood group determinants. *Science, 189*, 561–563.

Motulsky, A. G. (1979). Possible selective effects of urbanization on Ashkenazi Jews. In R. M. Goodman & A. G. Motulsky (Eds.), *Genetic diseases among Ashkenazi Jews* (pp. 301–312). New York: Raven Press.

Mundy, G. R., Cove, D. H., & Fiskin, R. (1980). Primary hyperparathyroidism. *Lancet, 1*, 1317–1320.

Orkin, S. H. (1982). Genetic diagnosis of the fetus. *Nature (London)*, *296*, 202–203.

Paterson, C. R., & Gunn, A. (1981). Familial benign hypercalcemia. *Lancet, 2*, 61–63.

Powell, G. F., Brasel, J. A., Raiti, S., & Blizzard, R. M. (1967). Emotional deprivation and growth retardation simulating idiopathic hypopituitarism. II. Endocrinologic evaluation. *New England Journal of Medicine, 276*, 1279–1283.

Rutter, M. (1981). Psychological sequelae of brain damage in children. *American Journal of Psychiatry, 138*, 1533–1544.

Temple, G. F., Dozy, A. M., Roy, K. L., & Kan, W. Y. (1982). Construction of a functional human suppressor tRNA gene: An approach to gene therapy for beta-thalassaemia. *Nature (London) 296*, 537–540.

Weatherall, D. J., & Clegg, J. B. (1981). *The thalassemia syndromes.* Oxford: Blackwell Scientific Publications.

Whipple, G. H., & Bradford, W. L. (1936). Mediterranean disease—thalassemia (erythroblastic anemia of Cooley); associated pigment abnormalities simulating hemochromatosis. *Journal of Pediatrics, 9*, 279–311.

Wintrobe, M. M. (1942). *Clinical hematology* (p. 507). Philadelphia: Lea & Febiger.

Wintrobe, M. M., Lee, G. R., Boggs, D. R., Bithell, J. C., Athens, J. W., & Foerster, J. (1974). *Clinical hematology* (7th ed., pp. 855–856). Philadelphia: Lea & Febiger.

Wintrobe, M. M., Mathews, E., Pollack, R., & Dobyns, B. M. (1940). Familial hematopoetic disorder in Italian adolescents and adults resembling Mediterranean disease (thalassemia). *Journal of the American Medical Association, 114*, 1530–1538.

Zimmet, P. (1982). Type 2 (non-insulin dependent) diabetes—an epidemiological overview. *Diabetologia, 22*, 399–411.

Stress, Development, and Family Interaction

Judy Dunn

Several chapters in this volume highlight issues of very general developmental significance—issues that are important not only in relation to clinical problems, but more broadly in relation to our understanding of children's emotional development. I shall focus on three of these issues: (1) the notion of stress, (2) the relation of cognitive maturity to childhood depression and to children's response to stress, and (3) the relation of stress to developmental change.

STRESS AND INDIVIDUAL DIFFERENCE

Garmezy (this volume) begins with the problem of defining and using the notion of stress. While he comments on the difficulties involved, he finds appropriate a definition of stress that focuses on change in the environment, which "in the average person" induces emotional tension and disrupts normal patterns of response. But is it useful to consider stress, or the emotional tension that different changes in the environment induce, as a unitary phenomenon? In relation to childhood depression at least, Rutter has argued forcibly that it is not (Rutter, 1981b). He reviewed evidence that the effects on children of divorce, bereavement, separation from the mother, or periods in hospital are different, and argued that the questions that we now have to elucidate are specific rather than general. What is it about particular life events that makes them predispose children to par-

Judy Dunn. M.R.C. Unit on the Development and Integration of Behaviour, University of Cambridge, Cambridge, England.

ticular disorders? What kinds of disorder follow which kinds of events at which stages of development? Neither a general notion of stress nor an itemization of the general factors associated with vulnerability or resilience that Garmezy delineates can help us greatly toward answering these questions. What must be emphasized is that the effects of the different kinds of stressful change in the family are different not only in the form of children's response, but probably also in the form of parental response as well, and by implication in the processes linking event and outcome.

Beyond this general criticism—that we are now at a stage of asking precise and specific questions about the consequences of particular events at different stages of children's lives—there are two particular problems involved in relating a general notion of stress to children's development. The first concerns individual differences. The notion of what is a stressful happening in early childhood is closely linked to the issue of individual differences, not only in children's responses to the event, but in the response of parents and in each family member's response to the others' altered behavior. It is not simply the point that some children find particular experiences stressful and others do not, but a more complicated matter, involving family patterns of response. Garmezy argues convincingly for the importance of individual differences in children's temperament in his discussion of resilience. We now have evidence that temperamental differences between children are closely related not only to the way in which they respond to changes in their environment, but to the persistence of behavior problems following such changes (Dunn & Kendrick, 1980). However, it is clear that we should not regard such temperamental differences as completely independent of the quality of the relationship between child and parent. Although temperamental differences are not simply attributable to differences in parent perception of the child, they are closely related to differences in parental behavior. This means that it cannot be assumed that the link between temperamental differences and childrens' responses to stressful events is one that does not involve differences in parental behavior.

In considering the association between individual differences in children's responses to stressful events and family patterns of interaction, we face then a central question about the processes linking stressful events to behavior disorders. How far and in what ways are changes in family interaction implicated in the development of disorder? With the birth of a sibling, for instance, the development of behavior problems was found to be linked not only to the children's temperament, but also to the marked changes in the interaction between mother and firstborn that accompanied the sibling birth (Dunn & Kendrick, 1982). Not only did the children become more difficult, miserable, or withdrawn, but their mothers tended to become more restrictive and punitive and less playful and attentive. In any attempt to understand the process linking the initial event—in this case the sibling birth—to the later behavior problems we should take account of not only the child's initial response, but the parental behavior related to that response. This point—that the consequences of stressful events for a child's development will depend on the patterns of family interaction that follow—illustrates one way in which the "transactional" processes emphasized by Emde, Harmon, and Good (Chapter 4 of this volume) may be important. They draw attention to the high incidence of children with depressive feelings in families with depressed mothers—an association that is confirmed in several recent studies, such as those of Seligman and Peterson (this volume), and Mills and Puckering (1984). The question of which particular processes and patterns of influence are implicated in this association is raised by Emde and his colleagues, and clearly it is a crucial one. To emphasize the mutual influence of mother and child is not new: It is the clinical significance of the link between maternal and child behavior in these studies that makes it all the more crucial that we should begin to trace the patterns of influence within the family with more accuracy—not simply refer to mutual effects.

A second problem with the notion of stress is closely related to this issue of changed patterns of family interaction. Does the notion of stress refer to a "happening" and "event," or does it apply to chronic circumstances that continue over time? The concept is frequently used in a confusing way with regard to the distinction between a *life event*, and *difficult circumstances*. It is interesting that the notion of "coping" is seen as adaptation over time, while stresses are sometimes seen as on–off events. This may be very misleading, however: It could well be that what links the initial environmental change with the development of behavioral disorder or depression is a long-term change in family interaction. Many stressful changes in children's lives, such as the separation or divorce of parents or the loss or illness of one parent, are also very likely to involve marked and long-term changes in the interaction between parent and child. After divorce, for instance, the behavior of both the parent who has custody of the child, and the parent who does not, changes toward the child (see Hetherington, Cox, & Cox, 1976). Two studies of attempted suicide have shown that the association between early loss of parent and suicidal ideation is strongly linked to the long-term consequences of the loss of family organization:

> Our data indicate that when the family has accommodated successfully to loss or has been adequately reconstituted through remarriage or the presence of alternative surrogate parental figures, suicidal trends are unlikely to develop. On the other hand, when the disruption has resulted in major and longstanding family disorganization, a predisposition to suicidal thinking is very probable and the likelihood that this could result in suicidal behaviour later in life is high. (Adam, 1982, p. 286)

It seems very probable that differences in the way in which family interaction patterns are affected are implicated in the different consequences of divorce, bereavement, separation, and so on. Furthermore, the link between initial event and long-term change in family interaction patterns could well be important in understanding "sleeper-effects"—why, for example, the immediate grief reactions of very young children to bereavement may be very short term, although the long-term effects may be marked (Rutter, 1981b).

It is, then, surely important to examine the relation between specific events and chronic difficulties. To an observer following families longitudinally, it is the relentlessly repeated nature of what appear to be punitive stressful exchanges for the child that is so impressive. If family patterns of interaction are importantly implicated in the development of disorder, then the notion of stressful circumstances rather than happenings must be taken seriously.

It is interesting to note here that in Hinde's experiments on the effects on rhesus monkeys of separation from the mother every independent variable that affected infant rhesus depression also affected mother–infant interaction (Hinde & McGinnis, 1977). However, there is so much that we do not know about children's response to chronic stressful circumstances. Are children less affected than adults by day-to-day frustrations and difficulties? They certainly behave in the immediate context as if such frustrations were very difficult to bear. Are they less or more likely than adults to respond to such difficulties with "learned helplessness"? How does this change with age? The importance of understanding the relation of a child's cognitive maturity—what he or she understands about the events and behavior of people of his world—is the second main topic that I wish to consider. It is an issue that is emphasized in Garmezy's discussion of failure as loss, in Shaffer's review (Chapter 13 of this volume) of the incidence of suicide in childhood and adolescence, and in Seligman and Petersen's account of the relation between children's attributional style and depression (Chapter 8 of this volume); it is an issue central to any consideration of developmental changes in childhood depression.

COGNITIVE MATURITY, DEPRESSION, AND SUICIDE

In the work on adult depression (Brown, Harris, & Bifulco, Chapter 9 of this volume) increasing attention has been given to the meaning of life events to the person involved—the "thoughts we have about the world and ourselves." However, there are obvious difficulties in relating this notion to the behavior of very young children, and any attempt to do so raises absolutely central questions about our understanding of children and their development. Our inferences about the meaning of events to children depend on our assumptions about the nature of children's understanding of the world and themselves, and for young children this is a very contentious issue. Disagreements about children's capabilities, particularly in the area of social cognition and the understanding of emotions, are marked, and the view that we have systematically underestimated children's understanding is increasingly widely held (Donaldson, 1978).

The disagreements, however, are not easily resolved: the difficulties facing the researcher here are enormous. How do we address the question of the meaning of an event or set of circumstances to an 18-month-old, let alone to a rhesus monkey? How can we begin to understand the child's thoughts or feelings?

Emde, Harmon, and Good emphasize that it is important to focus upon the feelings of the child, rather than solely upon the behaviors that until now have received most attention, such as facial and vocal expression or behavioral regulation. This is indisputably a valid and important point, but how can we gain access to these feelings, in a small child, who cannot yet articulate them to us? Emde and his colleagues suggest two strategies that we could use to understand children's feelings more clearly. First, they suggest that we can use our own empathy, and that of the caregiver. Clearly clinicians can (or as Emde and colleagues emphasize, should) use such sensitivity to a child's feelings, but how accurate are their inferences, and on what precisely are they based? How well do such inferences predict the child's later behavior? It would be helpful if such inferences were studied systematically, so that their basis and their usefulness could be described and assessed. The difficulty with the other suggestion—that we should use the caregiver's empathy and understanding of the child—is all too clear. Without doubt the caregiver's perception and interpretation of the child's feelings are important. However, it would not be very satisfactory if, in our attempt to understand the tangle of emotions between a depressed mother and a difficult or depressed child, our chief source of information was the mother's own account of the child's feelings.

Emde, Harmon, and Good's second suggestion is that we can make use of longitudinal studies of individual differences in mood states. The problem here is that, as Emde and his colleagues themselves argue, it is very important to be precise in our description and assessment of emotions. However, while the research on the expression of discrete emotions has, as they show, been concerned with exactly this issue, the longitudinal studies of temperament and mood have been far more impressionistic in their approach. It is, surely, important not to blur the distinction between "negative mood," as used by the temperament researchers, and depressive feelings. At present the longitudinal data of temperament research are too imprecise to be used as a source of information on children's feelings.

One point is clear from Garmezy's discussion of "failure," from Shaffer's review of suicide rates and from the studies of Seligman and Peterson (Chapter 8 of this volume) and Dweck (see Dweck & Elliott, 1983). The part played by children's sense of their own efficacy or helplessness is of major importance in the way they respond to stressful events. What is so interesting and so important about Shaffer's discussion is that it highlights a whole series of developmental questions on these issues—questions to which we do not as yet have very satisfactory answers. How do young children recall and anticipate pain and joy? How does their sense of mastery and attribution of failure change during the middle childhood years? Garmezy quotes Kagan's work demonstrating children's pleasure in mastery around the end of the second year, and indeed other work has shown us that children display a delight in their own efficacy far earlier (Harmon, Glicken, & Culp, 1982). If children are delighted by mastery, if they are frustrated and distressed at their own failure by 2 years old, and if they have a clear sense of what they can and cannot do by 4 years, then what precisely are the changes in response to failure or stress over the next 5 or 6 years?

As Garmezy comments, we do have some evidence on the age changes in children's understanding of the irreversibility of death. We must, however, be wary of making a single jump from such evidence to, for instance, assumptions about the consequences of parental loss. For if parental loss has its maximum effects on later behavior if it occurs before 10 years (see discussion by Garmezy, Chapter 10 of this volume), this suggests that the consequences are not a simple function of the limits of the child's understanding of the loss. [And see Rutter (1981a) for evidence that the long-term effects may be greatest if the child was bereaved at 2–3 years old.]

Two points must be distinguished here. The first is that to be deprived of the company and support of a parent can have emotionally damaging effects whether or not the child initially understands that the deprivation is permanent, or understands why it is so. It is scarcely surprising that this form of trauma should be more acute among children under 10 than among children from 10 to 15 years. The second point concerns the schema of beliefs and feelings with which the loss is interpreted by the child. What matters is not just comprehension of the nature of the loss of event, but the child's interpretation of what can be done about it, and his or her sense of his or her own ability to cope with it. To investigate the changes in children's conceptions of life and death, cross-cultural developmental work would be especially valuable. How people conceive of their lives is an issue that is strongly culturally dependent; the conception of life as a whole is likely to be an ideological rather than a biological matter. The differences in suicide rates of different cultures, which are particularly clear among adolescents, support such an argument.

The changes in children's conceptualization of life and death are presumably related to the changes documented by Piaget in his account of the transition to formal operations—the child's development of the ability to conceive of a state that does not exist and to use this as a means of solving a problem. Suicide is apparently not often seen as a means of solving a problem by children younger than 10. [It should be noted, however, that suicidal thoughts, threats, and actions are reported to occur in one-tenth to one-third of children aged 6–12 referred to psychiatric clinics (Hawton, 1982; Lukianowicz, 1968; Pfeffer, Conte, Plutchik, & Jerret, 1980).] A recent study by Kosky (1983) of 20 children under 14 years of age who had made suicidal attempts showed clearly that children can form and act on suicidal intent at a very young age. The youngest child in this group was 5 years, 2 months, 15% of the sample were less than 11 years, and the mean age was 11.0 years. The suggestion that the rarity of suicide in children under 10 is due to an inability to plan effectively, in the sense of carrying out the necessary actions, is unconvincing. Children below 10 are well able to plan to deceive, to steal, and to manipulate, and could certainly carry out the necessary sequence of actions for suicide. More relevant, surely, is the evidence that change and reorganization in children's sense of self-esteem and self-concept occur around the beginning of adolescence.

Such evidence is, again, limited in scope and open to different interpretations. While some researchers emphasize the slow and gradual nature of the changes in self-concept during adolescence (Dusek & Flaherty, 1981) others stress the important qualitative changes in organization of concepts (Hill, 1981; Livesley & Bromley, 1973). More longitudinal studies of the transition to adolescence are, as Hill argued, clearly needed.

The issue of individual differences is, here again, of central importance. What is the nature and the range of individual differences in young children's and adolescents' attribution of failure and their susceptibility to hopelessness? How are these differences related to the children's self-concept? What are the origins of such differences? Seligman and Peterson's studies are of real significance in relation to these questions. They show not only that childhood depression as measured on the CDI is both relatively common and stable in 9–10-year-olds, but that it is linked to the child's attributional style and to the mother's attributional style and depressive symptoms. This is a demonstration that will surely stimulate further research, as well as influence clinical practice. Seligman and Peterson's conclusions about the causal direction of the link between children's and mothers' attributional style are that attributional style "causes" later depression. On the basis of the data presented so far, this suggestion seems open to question. The correlations given do not allow us to conclude definitely if children's attributional style leads to depression, if maternal depression leads to children's depression, or if maternal attributional style influences children's attributional style. However, the close link between the attributional style and depressive symptoms of both mothers and children suggests that one fruitful way to pursue the origins of childhood depression might be to look at the conversations between even younger children and their mothers. One hint that the processes involved may begin very early in children's lives comes from the analysis of family conversations in the sibling study already cited (Dunn & Kendrick, 1982). This showed, first, that young children, even those of 3 years and under, were interested in psychological causality, but that there were marked differences in how the mothers responded to this interest and in the extent to which they discussed the motives, intentions, and feelings of others. In those families in which the mother discussed the newborn baby as a person with feelings, wishes, and intentions, the children behaved with far more friendliness toward their siblings 1 year later than the children in those families in which such discussion had not taken place. While the analysis did not bear directly on the attribution of failure, the results suggest that mothers' interpretation of and beliefs about the behavior of their babies may have a direct influence on the behavior of their other children, and that such processes begin extremely early.

This brings us back to the very general notion of parental transactional effects discussed by Emde, Harmon, and Good. They comment that parental depreciation of children can be shown either by "stressing the child's inadequacy or worthlessness or by indicating a lack of respect, involvement, or caring," or through overprotection. The claim is that both such very different parental styles are implicated in the development of children's depressive feelings. It is a claim that should be examined further: we should now try to describe and to trace with precision the process involved in the naturally occurring conversations of mothers and their children, employing systems of analysis such as that developed by Seligman and Peterson.

STRESS AND DEVELOPMENTAL CHANGE

My final point concerns the relation between stress and developmental change. Garmezy ends with a discussion of resilience: It is both a helpful and an encouraging way to consider children's response to change. He brings together results from a number of careful studies to stress the "triad of protective factors," arguing that the same three factors may provide protection against the consequences of a range of different stressful experiences. There is a further point to be considered here. It is important to recognize that stressful events can lead not only to coping, but also to developmental advances. We are, however, very far from understanding what processes may be involved in these changes (see Rutter, 1981b). In the study of children's responses to the birth of a sibling, over half the children made remarkably rapid developmental advances in the period immediately following the sibling birth (see also Legg, Sherick, & Wadland, 1974; Trause et al., 1978) and it was argued that the changes in the children's world that the birth involved—in particular, the change in caregiver for the days surrounding the birth—could well have contributed to these developmental advances:

It is certainly plausible that a shift in the routine of the child, and in what is expected of him by the care giver, might lead the child to discover for himself that he *can* do certain things, and that such achievement is enjoyable, whether it be mastering a difficult task like putting on a shoe, or conquering his fear of going to the toilet alone, or discovering that he has resources for play within himself.

There are three different possibilities here that need to be distinguished: the first is that with a different care giver different requirements are placed on the child: the second is that the new care giver has different expectations and beliefs concerning the child. He or she attributes intentions and interprets the child's behavior differently than the mother does. With both these interpretations the explanation for the changed behavior lies in the molding by the *adults* of the child's actions. A third possibility is to view the altered behavior as essentially a response by the *child* to an altered environment: if you greatly change the world of a child (or indeed of an adult), the chances are that you will not only draw his attention to new possibilities in the world, but also to new possibilities in himself as an actor in that world. It may be that with a change in care giver both the first two effects are operative. With either kind of change in the care giver, though, the consequence is likely to be a change in the child's feelings, beliefs, and ways of acting in the world. (Dunn & Kendrick, 1982, p. 56)

The individual differences between children in the nature and extent of these developmental advances were marked, and clearly this is an important area for further research. Are there some stages of development when particular experiences of change may be helpful to particular children? It is already known that the experience of routine separation from the mother during the first 2 years of life may buffer the child against the traumatic consequences of major separations from her. It seems likely that to understand why some experiences lead to an increase in "coping" or to rapid developmental change we need to study not only the individual children but their whole families' response to the change—just as we need to study the whole family in order to understand the processes linking event to disorder. Seligman and Peterson's work suggests that one aspect that could be important is the attributional style of family members. The clinicians' work on the consequences of stressful change has an important lesson for developmental psychologists here. It raises the question of what role sharp changes in the social environment may play in "normal" development. How far, for instance, are the changes in self-concept at adolescence, discussed in relation to suicide, linked to the changes in schooling and the social world that are experienced by adolescents in the United States and Europe? Would such changes be apparent in cultures in which the pattern of social experience of adolescents is very different? Cross-cultural studies that examined the relation between the timing of changes in adolescent social experience, such as initiation rites and the transition to the adult world, and changes in self-concept would be very useful.

It is ironic that discontinuities in the early development of children should so often be attributed to maturational change—the impact of parents, the main environmental influence on children's development being assumed to be continuous—while biologists have shown the profound importance of sharp environmental transitions—weaning for instance—in contributing to discontinuities in development (Bateson, 1981). The discontinuities in social experience and expectation imposed by changes from home to preschool, from home to school, from junior to senior high school, must surely have profound effects on children's views of themselves, their families, and other people. Research on childrens' responses to stressful change then not only addresses questions of major clinical importance, it reminds us that changes in the social environment may be centrally important in accounting for transitions in normal development.

REFERENCES

Adam, K. S. (1982). Loss, suicide and attachment. In C. Murray-Parkes & J. Stevenson-Hinde (Eds.), *The place of attachment in human behavior*. New York: Basic Books.

Bateson, P. P. G. (1981). Discontinuities in development and changes in the organization of play in cats. In K. Immelman, G. W. Barlow, L. Petrinovich, & M. Main (Eds.), *Behavioral development*. London: Cambridge University Press.

Donaldson, M. (1978). *Children's minds*. London: Fontana, Collins.

Dunn, J., & Kendrick, C. (1980). Studying temperament and parent-child interaction: A comparison of information from direct observation and from parental interview. *Developmental Medicine & Child Neurology, 22*, 484–496.

Dunn, J., & Kendrick, C. (1982). *Siblings: Love, envy and understanding*, Cambridge, MA: Harvard University Press.

Dusek, J. B., & Flaherty, J. F. (1981). The development of the self-concept during the adolescent years. *Monographs of the Society for Research in Child Development, 46* (4, Serial No. 191).

Dweck, C. S., & Elliott, E. S. (1983). Achievement Motivation. In E. M. Hetherington (Ed.), *Socialization, personality, and social development: Vol. 4. Mussen's handbook of child psychology* (4th ed., pp. 643–691). New York: Wiley.

Harmon, R. J., Glicken, A. D., & Culp, A. M. (1982). *Assessment of mastery motivation in term and preterm infants*. Paper presented at the International Conference on Infant Studies, Austin, Texas.

Hawton, K. (1982). Attempted suicide in children and adolescents. *Journal of Child Psychology and Psychiatry, 23*(4), 497–503.

Hetherington, E. M., Cox, E. M., & Cox, R. (1976). Divorced fathers. *Family Coordinator, 25*, 417–428.

Hill, J. P. (1981). Commentary in: The development of the self-concept during the adolescent years (Dusek & Flahery, 1981).

Hinde, R. A., & McGinnis, L. (1977). Some factors influencing the effects of temporary mother-infant separation: Some experiments with Rhesus monkeys. *Psychological Medicine, 7*, 197–212.

Kosky, R., (1983). Childhood suicidal behavior. *Journal of Child Psychology and Psychiatry, 24*(3), 457–468.

Legg, C., Sherick, I., & Wadland, W. (1974). Reactions of preschool children to the birth of a sibling. *Child Psychiatry and Human Development, 5*(1), 3–39.

Livesley, W. J., & Bromley, D. B. (1073). *Person perception in childhood and adolescence*. New York: Wiley.

Lukianowicz, N. (1968). Attempted suicide in children. *Acta Psychiatrica Scandinavica, 44,* 415–435.

Mills, M., & Puckering, C. (1984). What is it about depressed mothers that influences their children's functioning? In J. Stevenson (Ed.), *Aspects of current child psychiatry research*. Oxford: Pergamon Press.

Pfeffer, C. R., Conte, H. R., Plutchik, R., & Jerret, J. (1980). Suicidal behavior in latency age children: An outpatient population. *Journal of the American Academy of Child Psychiatry, 19,* 707–710.

Rutter, M., (1981a). *Maternal deprivation reassessed,* (2nd ed.). Harmondsworth: Middlesex, England: Penguin Books.

Rutter, M., (1981b). Stress, coping and development: Some isues and some questions. *Journal of Child Psychology and Psychiatry, 22*(4), 323–356.

Trause, M. A., Boslett, M., Voos, D., Rudd, C., Klaus, M., & Kennel, J. (1978). A birth in the hospital: The effect on the sibling. *Birth and the Family Journal, 5,* 207–210.

Depressive Feelings, Cognitions, and Disorders: A Research Postscript

Michael Rutter

INTRODUCTION

As discussed in earlier chapters of this volume, during the last decade there has come a general recognition of the importance of the phenomena of affective development and affective disorders during childhood. As part of that recognition it has become appreciated that two major features have to be taken into account. First, there is no doubt that children experience a range of affects and that overt depressive disorders can and do occur in childhood. Second, however, it is clear that there are major changes with age in the styles of affective expression and equally marked variations in the rates of at least certain kinds of affective disorders. It is evident that we are some distance from an adequate understanding of the developmental processes that are involved; equally it is apparent that such an understanding is of crucial importance for both developmentalists and clinicians. Hence, the motivation for a volume that would provide an interchange between disciplines and an opportunity for developmentalists and clinicians to learn from each other in their common interest in the concepts and findings of developmental psychopathology (Rutter & Garmezy, 1983; Sroufe & Rutter, 1984).

It is never an easy matter to bring together markedly diverse theoretical and empirical approaches. It is not just that the types of explanation used are disparate, although they are. Thus some chapters in this volume are concerned with brain chemistry, others with internal psychological proc-

Michael Rutter. Department of Child and Adolescent Psychiatry, University of London, Institute of Psychiatry, London, England.

esses, and yet others with social circumstances and external stressors. Nor is it only that the measures used are not the same, although certainly that poses considerable problems. Some of the research described here is based on questionnaire measures of "depression," whereas other investigations concern seriously ill children who have been admitted to hospital. Do they both refer to comparable phenomena that differ only in severity or to phenomena that differ in kind? It is necessary to appreciate that behind these variations in measures and in theoretical explanations lie differences in concepts of what is meant by "depression" as a feeling state, as a cognition, and as a disorder. In this final chapter, there is an attempt to make overt the issues involved in order to consider the research implications and some of the possible ways forward in seeking to resolve the key controversies as they apply to psychopathology.

CONCEPTS OF DEPRESSIVE CONDITIONS

Depression as a Symptom

It is necessary to begin by considering just what is involved in psychiatric concepts of depressive disorders. The first point that requires emphasis is that the concept of depression (as a symptom or a syndrome) is not synonymous with sadness or unhappiness. Moreover, even when present to a severe degree, sadness does not necessarily constitute depression (M. Hamilton, 1982). It is true that dysphoria is universally regarded as a necessary element in depression, but it is not a sufficient criterion. Also, although sadness is a very common component of the dysphoric mood associated with depression, it is by no means a universal feature. Thus, the negative mood of depression may be represented more by a loss of interest or pleasure, an emotional emptiness, a lack of responsiveness to ongoing activities, or a feeling of "flatness" (M. Hamilton, 1982). Although some pediatric specialists have laid emphasis on the clinician's empathic response to depression, probably this emphasis confuses sadness and depression. It is true that another person's misery evokes empathy, but the hostile withdrawal and lack of response to comfort so often found with depression is as likely to be felt as rebuffing. Adults with a major depressive disorder frequently draw a sharp distinction between the 'black cloud' of depression and the sadness or unhappiness they feel at times when they are not ill, maintaining that the two emotions do not feel the same (M. Hamilton, 1982).

More importantly, the concept of depression includes certain key cognitive features, as well as mood components (Beck, 1976). Thus, emphasis tends to be laid on feelings of self-blame, self-reproach, and guilt; on thoughts of self-depreciation and worthlessness; on helplessness in the face of a life situation felt to be oppressive; and on hopelessness about the future. In other words, depressed persons' thoughts include three key elements: (1) a concept of themselves as in some way unworthy or to blame for their own or other people's plight; (2) a belief that there is nothing that they can do to change the situation; and (3) a view that things will not get better in the future. Beck (1976) put these notions in terms of a cognitive triad comprising a negative view of oneself, a negative view of the world, and a negative view of the future.

It will be appreciated that these cognitive ideations may be present in depressive mood disturbances that are not part of any overt depressive disorder; that the cognitions do not necessarily amount to psychopathological symptoms of guilt; that there is individual variation in the extent to which these cognitive components dominate depressive thinking; and that these thoughts are not a necessary part of even very severe sadness. Thus, when a much loved pet dies, a person may be very sad and greatly distressed, may well be tearful, and may even lie awake thinking about the pet's death. Nevertheless, probably the person will not regard himself or herself as unworthy, feelings of helplessness will be restricted to the loss of pet situation, and the future will not seem black or hopeless. On the other hand, it would not be correct to see grief as qualitatively distinct from depression; bereavement commonly gives rise to a depressive state (Clayton, 1982). Most bereaved persons accept their depression as a normal response to death—emphasizing that the phenomenon of depressive feelings is part of the normal range of human emotions and reactions.

Depression as a Psychiatric Condition

The second point with respect to concepts of depression is that the phenomenon (or symptom) and the syndrome or condition are not synonymous. Many people feel depressed (in terms of both dysthymia and depressive cognitions) when they experience task failure, a personal rebuff, or some other life stress. Indeed, depressive feelings may also occur in the absence of any obvious environmental precipitant. Autochthonous mood swings are relatively common and may be a prominent feature in individuals with a cyclothymic or depressive personality.

In adult psychiatry, three main criteria tend to be used to determine when there is a depressive condition, as distinct from a depressive symptom: associated phenomena, social impairment, and persistence. M. Hamilton (1982) argued that loss of interest and anxiety (shown not only by apprehension but also by irritability, forgetfulness, inability to concentrate, and tension) are almost universal; and that difficulty falling asleep or early morning waking, loss of appetite, lack of energy and fatiguability, psychomotor retardation (or agitation), and suicidal thoughts are very common. Loss of libido and hypochondriacal preoccupations, too, are relatively frequent. DSM-III (American Psychiatric Association, 1980) provides much the same list of depressive symptoms but specifies that only four out of eight need be present. Studies of the covariance over time of depressive symptoms confirm the close association between sadness, retardation, and an inability to feel (i.e., a lack of interest in hitherto pleasurable activities), as well as the links with pessimism, tension, and poor concentration (Hibbert, Teasdale, & Spencer, 1984). Impairments in appetite and sleep disturbance are less closely associated with changes in other features of depression. Similarly, it has been found that the cognitive features of unworthiness, helplessness, and hopelessness are prominent features of clinically significant depression, and that these cognitions change strikingly as the depression remits or responds to treatment (Blackburn & Bishop, 1983; E. W. Hamilton & Abramson, 1983; Norman, Miller, & Klee, 1983; Raps, Peterson, Reinhard, Abramson, & Seligman, 1982).

Curiously, DSM-III does not demand any assessment of degree of social impairment—presumably on the grounds that those with the required number of symptoms are likely to be significantly affected in their day-to-day activities. However, most investigators studying nonpatient populations have required the presence of social impairment of a degree easily recognized by others (e.g., Gershon *et al.*, 1982; Weissman, Gershon, Kidd *et al.*, 1984).

DSM-III has rather minimal criteria for persistence in requiring only that the symptoms have been present "nearly every day for a period of at least 2 weeks" (p. 213) but, again, many researchers have demanded a duration of at least 4 weeks (Weissman, Gershon, Kidd, *et al.*, 1984).

Differentiation from Normality

It might be thought that the criteria of multiple depressive phenomena, persisting over time and associated with substantial social impairment, should be sufficient to differentiate depressive disorders from normality, but this has been disputed. The controversies center around three main issues: (1) depression versus "demoralization," (2) depression versus normal grief (or other stress) reactions, and (3) depression versus "distress" reactions to physical illness.

The criteria for a depressive condition outlined above apply to major depressive disorders, but DSM-III (and other schemes of classification such as the World Health Organization's, 1978, ICD-9) also recognize the existence of lesser, but chronic, depressive disorders—termed "dysthymic disorders" or "depressive neuroses." The phenomena are regarded as generally similar to those found with major depressive disorders but are less severe and less pervasive. However, to be included, the disorder must have been present chronically or recurrently for at least 2 years, according to DSM-III. A category of "atypical depression" is provided for those disorders that fall between the stools of major depression and dysthymic disorders.

The dispute has focused on the depressive disorders very commonly found in women in community surveys. For example, Brown and Harris (1978) found that 17% of women in their London surveys were definite "cases" and a further 19% were "borderline." Rates of depression among working-class women were even higher (22% definite cases). It has been argued that those highly prevalent depressive disorders found in the general population are not the same as those seen in psychiatric clinics or hospitals (Tennant & Bebbington, 1978) and that it is better to conceptualize them as "demoralization" rather than a psychiatric condition of depression (Link & Dohrenwend, 1980). However, Finlay-Jones et al. (1980) have shown that community survey diagnoses of depression, when obtained through systematic interview methods, do accord with the operational criteria applied to patients using either the Feighner, Robins, Guze, Woodruff, and Winokur (1972) or the Wing, Cooper, and Sartorius (1974) criteria. Accordingly, the issue is better considered in terms of the links or lack of links between major depressive disorders and mild dysthymic disorders (see below).

The differentiation between depression and "normal" grief or stress reactions raises rather different issues. It is accepted that many grief reactions fulfill the diagnostic criteria for major depressive disorders, but it is argued that they should be regarded as "normal" phenomena rather than illnesses because they are both common and understandable (Clayton, 1982). While at first sight an apparently persuasive argument, it is clear that such a position serves, by edict, to rule out psychosocial features as common causes of psychiatric conditions. We do not follow this convention with physical causes or physical illness (to a substantial extent we understand how the influenza virus causes influenza and influenza is exceedingly common, but we do not thereby regard influenza as "normality") Therefore, why should we do so for psychosocial causes of psychiatric disorders? That does not seem a logical approach. Instead, the matter is better approached by asking whether depressive disorders that follow bereavement or some other acute stress differ from other depressive conditions in their correlates, course, or response to treatment. The evidence on these points, however, is so far contradictory and inconclusive (Brown & Harris, 1978; Parker, 1983; Paykel, 1982). Tennant, Bebbington, and Hurry (1981) found that neurotic disorders in the community were more likely to remit if precipitated by an acute stress, but remission was also a function of recent onset and recent peaks of disorder; it is not clear whether outcome was influenced by the presence of stress precipitation after taking account of the existence of the disorder. It appears that life events may trigger the onset of all manner of depressive conditions, and may also precipitate mania. If there are differences in the type of depression according to psychosocial causation, they are likely to be matters of degree or frequency rather than of kind. That conclusion, however, applies to conditions that meet the full criteria for a depressive disorder. Stress or adjustment reactions that do not meet such criteria may have a substantially better prognosis (Kovacs, Feinberg, Crouse-Novak, Paulauskas, & Finkelstein, 1984; Kovacs, Feinberg, Crouse-Novak, Paulauskas, Pollack, & Finkelstein, 1984) but this may be a function of their mildness and acuteness rather than their mode of causation.

Broadly comparable issues with respect to the diagnosis of affective disturbance that occurs in the context of a physical illness. Lloyd and Cawley (1983) found that one-third of adult patients suffering their first acute myocardial infarction showed psychiatric morbidity 1 week after admission; in half of those, the psychiatric problems had been precipitated by the infarction. Of that half (N = 19), only one-quarter showed psychiatric morbidity 4 months later. It was concluded that most acute psychiatric symptoms precipitated by a severe physical illness are better viewed as a normal stress response than as a psychiatric disorder. Once again, it is clear that acute stress reactions, whether precipitated by psychosocial or physical stresses, tend to have a good prognosis. There appear to be grounds for differentiating them from depressive disorders, but it is not clear whether the stress constitutes a significant independent differentiating feature, once acuteness and symptom features have been taken into account.

"Primary" and "Secondary" Depression

It is widely recognized that symptoms of depression can arise in many different forms of psychiatric illness. Thus, depressive symptoms occur in about half of schizophrenic disorders (D. A. W. Johnson, 1981). However, because schizophrenia and affective disorders have been shown to differ with respect to both family history findings and long-term prognosis (see, e.g., Tsuang, Winokur, & Crowe, 1980; Tsuang, Woolsam, & Simpson, 1981), the presence of depression does not give rise to an additional diagnosis if there is a clear-cut clinical picture of schizophrenia. Rather, it is assumed that the depressive symptoms are part of the schizophrenia. Thus, DSM-III specifies that major depressive disorder should not be diagnosed if the depressive syndrome is superimposed on schizophrenia.

However, the same issues also arise with respect to other clinical conditions, as it is relatively common for depressive syndromes to accompany alcoholism, anxiety states, hysteria, anorexia nervosa, and personality disorders. The usual convention here has been different from that employed with schizophrenia; that is, with these other psychiatric conditions both tend to be diagnosed (i.e., depression and the other disorder).

However, it has been argued by some researchers that these cases of "secondary" depression should be differentiated from "primary" cases in which there is no antecedent nondepressive psychiatric disorder (Guze, Woodruff, & Clayton, 1971). While it seems reasonable to suppose that primary and secondary depression might well differ in many important respects, so far it has not been well validated (Andreasen, 1982; Stancer, Persad, Jorna, Flood, & Wagener, 1984). On the whole, the two groups have differed rather little in terms of course, response to treatment, or familial clustering.

In summary, although great progress has been made in the differentiation and diagnosis of depressive disorders as they occur in adult life, it is evident that many issues still await resolution.

SUBCLASSIFICATION OF DEPRESSIVE DISORDERS

As already noted, DSM-III draws a distinction between major depressive episodes and minor dysthymic disorders. In addition, however, a differentiation is made between bipolar and unipolar affective disorders (i.e. those in which there have and those in which there have not been manic episodes). A further subclassification is provided to note the presence of psychotic features and "melancholic" characteristics (see also Chapter 14). The latter approximate to what others have termed "endogenous" features (Spitzer, Endicott, & Robins, 1978), namely, lack of reactivity to usually pleasurable stimuli, a depressive mood that differs in quality from that normally experienced, early morning waking and intensification of depression, marked psychomotor retardation or agitation, significant anorexia or weight loss, and excessive or inappropriate guilt. Schizoaffective disorders (i.e., those with an admixture of major depressive symptomatology and mood-incongruent psychotic features) are not included with affective conditions in DSM-III; anxiety disorders, too, are classified separately.

ICD-9 has a rather more complex approach to the subclassification of affective disorders. As the respects in which it differs from DSM-III are not empirically validated, they will not be considered further here.

Several rather different research strategies have been employed in order to test the validity of these nosological distinctions. First, genetic family studies have been used to determine whether or not the familial loading differs in pattern between the hypothesized different varieties of depressive disorder. Most attention has been paid to the unipolar–bipolar distinction (Perris, 1982)—sometimes with the further differentiation of bipolar into Types I and II according to whether or not the manic pole involved a history of frank mania (Type I) or just hypomania (Type II). The findings are reasonably consistent in showing that bipolar illness in the probands is associated with an increased rate of both bipolar and unipolar disorders in the relatives; whereas unipolar illness in the probands is associated with a high rate of unipolar, but not bipolar, disorders in first-degree relatives (see, e.g., Gershon et al., 1982; Weissman, Prusoff, et al., 1984). However, there is continuing uncertainty on whether the findings are better interpreted in terms of a continuum of underlying multifactorial vulnerability (with bipolar disorder the most severe variant), or in terms of two genetically distinct (but overlapping) types of affective disorder.

The same family studies suggest that at least some forms of schizoaffective disorder (a condition over which there is considerable disagreement on definition; Brockington & Leff, 1979), minor depressive conditions, and anxiety states (especially panic disorders) are genetically associated with major depression. However, the findings are by no means conclusive and it is clear that further research using the genetic family study strategy is required. In that connection, three major requirements are evident: (1) Comparisons between possibly overlapping conditions (such as depression and anxiety, or depression and personality disorder) are needed. (2) Family risk must be determined systematically for both depressive and supposedly nondepressive conditions. (3) A nonhierarchical approach to diagnosis must be followed (Leckman, Weissman, Merikangas, Pauls, & Prusoff, 1983). Until recently, most investigators have imposed hierarchic schemes in order to aid clarity, but it seems that the procedure may have obscured genetic relationships between supposedly different conditions.

A variety of biological measures have been used to test the validity of the bipolar–unipolar distinction; on the whole these have tended to show differences (with the bipolar more "abnormal"). However, the results have shown substantial overlap between the groups with some inconsistency in findings between studies (Andreasen, 1982; Perris, 1982). Nonsuppression on the dexamethasone suppression test (DST) has been proposed as an important feature differentiating depressive from nondepressive disorders and, within depression, melancholic from nonmelancholic conditions (Carroll, 1982). However, as data have accumulated, it has become clear that the DST provides only a moderate depression versus nondepression differentiation and very little differentiation within the range of depressive disorders (see, e.g., Coppen et al., 1983; Mendlewicz, Charles, & Franckson, 1982; Stokes et al., 1984).

Response to treatment and long-term course have, however, tended to provide a better separation of subgroups of depressive disorders. Endogenous or melancholic features have been found to predict a good response to both antidepressant medication and to electroconvulsive therapy (ECT), as well as a better long-term outcome (Andreasen, 1982). However, it seems that the presence of delusions suggests resistance to tricyclic antidepressants but responsiveness to ECT (Clinical Research Centre, 1984). Bipolar disorders differ to some extent from unipolar disorders in terms of an earlier age of onset, more frequent episodes of illness, and greater social impairment.

Symptom clustering, too, has been used to subdivide depressive disorders. On the whole, the results have separated a group with severe psychotic or endogenous depression but the findings have not been at all consistent in delineating other groupings (Andreasen, 1982). It should be noted, incidentally, that although bipolar disorders differ from unipolar disorders in several respects, the clinical picture of the depressed phase in the two types seems much the same (Brockington, Altman, Hillier, Meltzer, & Nand, 1982). In other words, the bipolar group cases are differentiated by the history of manic episodes rather than by the features of the depressive state.

In summary, it has proved clinically useful to make various distinctions within the broad group of depressive disorders. That between unipolar and bipolar disorder is the best established, but also there is support for a differentiation according to the presence of endogenous or melancholic features (although it may be that this is done better in dimensional than categorical terms). Delusional depression, too, warrants separation. However, it remains quite uncertain whether these types refer to different conditions or rather variations within the same condition. Also, there is continuing doubt on where to draw the boundaries of depression—especially with respect to schizoaffective disorders, conditions with predominant anxiety, and minor but chronic mood disturbances.

DEPRESSION IN CHILDHOOD AND ADOLESCENCE

It may be assumed that the problems already discussed in relation to the diagnosis and classification of depressive disorders in adults are likely also to apply to those arising in childhood. However, there are a variety of other issues that need consideration with respect to childhood depression.

Age Differences in Depressive Phenomena

To begin with, it is clear that there are important and large age differences in the occurrence of depressive and depression-related conditions. The data on such age differences are limited and inadequate in many respects; indeed, they cannot be really satisfactory until the methodological issues outlined below are resolved. Nevertheless, the available findings are sufficiently striking to raise a host of crucial questions.

1. General population surveys suggest that depressive feelings are more prevalent in adolescence than in earlier childhood (Kaplan,

Hong, & Weinhold, 1984; Rutter, Graham, Chadwick, & Yule, 1976), and that the rise may be more a function of puberty than chronological age (Rutter, 1979/1980).

2. Clinical data suggest that overt depressive disorders also become more frequent during adolescence with a possible parallel shift in the sex ratio from a male preponderance before puberty to a female preponderance after puberty (see Chapter 1).

3. Mania also becomes more frequent during the teenage years, although less commonly it can occur before puberty (Anthony & Scott, 1960; Hassanyeh & Davison, 1980; Loranger & Levine, 1978; Lowe & Cohen, 1980).

4. Immediate grief reactions following bereavement tend to be both milder and of shorter duration in young children compared with those in adolescents or adults (Bowlby, 1980; Kliman, 1968; Rutter, 1966; van Eerdewegh, Bieri, Parilla, & Clayton, 1982).

5. Suicide is excessively rare before puberty but shows a massive rise over the adolescent years (see Chapter 13)—although the rate continues to rise through adult life into old age (Eisenberg, 1980; Kosky, 1982; McClure & Gould, 1984; Shaffer, 1974; Shaffer & Fisher, 1981).

6. Attempted suicide, or parasuicide, also exhibits a huge increase in frequency during adolescence (Hawton & Goldacre, 1982)—although it differs from suicide in reaching a peak in early adult life rather than in old age.

7. Finally, within psychiatric clinic samples, suicidal ideation increases in frequency during adolescence (Carlson & Cantwell, 1982).

These findings raise a multitude of rather varied questions. To begin with, of course, there is the problem that the data are not as systematic and standardized as one would wish. It is possible that some of the age effects may be a consequence of referral artifacts or of different modes of assessment at different ages. On the other hand, that explanation carries little weight with regard to the findings on suicide and attempted suicide. It should not, however, necessarily be assumed that all the age trends for the different phenomena are due to the same causes. Perhaps some of the age effects for suicide derive from variations in readiness of access to suicidal means or variations in the determination or ability to carry through a suicidal act.

A second issue concerns the measurement of depression. Insofar as the diagnosis of a major depressive disorder requires the reporting of complex emotions and cognitive ideations, it might be that young children are not able to report, or to experience, these in the form usual in adults (see below). If that is the case, does that mean that major depressive disorders cannot be diagnosed so readily in early childhood, or should one expect that depression will be manifest in somewhat different ways in younger age groups? If the latter applies, how is one to know that it is "truly" equivalent to adult depression (see below)? Indeed, what is the aspect of adult depression to which equivalence should be required? It will be appreciated that recourse to the widely adopted strategy of requiring the use in childhood of adult criteria provides no solution to this problem. Of course, it is important that it has been demonstrated that adult-type depressive conditions do occur in childhood, but still the issue of age trends requires consideration of the possibility of age-related variations in the manifestations of depression.

In that connection it would be unduly restricting to focus exclusively on the apparent increase in depression during adolescence. There is the additional feature of infant's protest–despair–detachment responses to institutional admission to consider. These reactions are seen in many toddlers admitted to hospital or to a residential nursery (Bowlby, 1969, 1980) but are most likely to occur from 6 months to 4 years old (Rutter, 1981). Naturally, in children as young as that it would be extremely difficult to elicit verbal reports of adult-type depressive ideations. Nevertheless, Bowlby (1980) has argued that they represent depressive equivalents. That claim is arguable but it cannot be denied that they constitute some form of dysthymic affective state. If protest–despair–detachment responses are not depressive, a rather different explanation may be required for these early age trends in affective reaction than that applicable to the adolescent increase in major depressive disorders. However, if these early dysthymic responses are depressive, there is the question of why depressive phenomena should fall in frequency during the early school years only to rise again at puberty.

If further research should confirm the reality of age differences in depressive conditions and in the expression of depressive phenomena, as well it might, it will be necessary to determine the reasons for the age trend. A variety of quite different types of explanations could be proffered (see Chapter 1). Perhaps, to a large extent major depressive disorders are genetically determined and perhaps the genes do not usually "switch on" until later childhood or adolescence (in the way that Huntington's chorea, although due to a dominant gene, does not become manifest until adult life). Or perhaps sex hormones play a role in the vulnerability to depression in that the increase in sex hormones at puberty increases susceptibility to depression. Alternatively, it could be suggested that depression becomes more frequent during the teenage years because the stressors or loss events that predispose to depression become more prevalent at that time (we lack good data on age-related changes in the experience of stressors). Similarly, it could be argued that depression rises in frequency during adolescence because family supports and other protective factors become less operative or less available at that time. Different types of explanations stem from considerations of cognitive sets. It could be that experiences during later childhood and adolescence increase the likelihood of a set of learned helplessness (Dweck, Davidson, Nelson, & Enna, 1978). Or it might be that there are developmental changes in children's ability to make depressive-type cognitive attributions (Rholes, Blackwell, Jordan, & Walters, 1980), so that younger children may be less susceptible to feelings of helplessness because they tend not to view failure as implying a stable and lasting limitation on their performance. Perhaps, too, the age-related changes in depression reflect developmentally mediated alterations in children's concepts of emotions, in their awareness of emotions in others, and in their appreciation of the emotional connotations of social situations.

It is all too obvious that the relevant data to test these hypotheses are lacking. It is also apparent that their testing is likely to raise quite difficult methodological issues.

Age Trends in Depression-Related Cognitive Ideations

Insofar as depression involves thoughts of guilt, helplessness in the face of task failure, and hopelessness about the future, it is important to consider how far children possess the ability to experience such cognitions. There is a surprising lack of knowledge on these matters, but some limited evidence is available (see Chapters 1 and 3).

Many theorists place great weight on the effects of loss of a love relationship as a precipitant of depression (Bowlby, 1980; Brown & Harris, 1978). Hence, the age at which children are able to experience selective attachments to particular people would seem relevant. There are good data indicating that this capacity usually becomes manifest during the second half of the first year of life (Rutter, 1980, 1981). If children are to experience guilt, feelings of unworthiness, and a sense of failure, presumably it is necessary that they appreciate the meaning of standards, that they are able to compare themselves with others, and that they can understand the concept of failure to achieve particular standards of performance. Kagan's (1981, 1982) data suggest that these self-concepts related to the capacity to feel guilt arise at about the age of 2 years. However, depressive cognitions involve more than a sense of specific task failure—they require that the sense of failure be experienced as generalized and that it be projected into the future.

Less is known on the developmental changes in these aspects of social cognition as they apply specifically to depressive ideation, but something is known on the broader aspects of such thought processes. Thus, for example, at about the age of 5 or 6 years there is an increase in children's ability to differentiate accidental and intentional behavior shown by others (Shantz, 1983). At first there is some tendency to assume that bad outcomes are unintended, but the bias begins to wane during the early elementary school years. Also, at about the age of 7 years children begin to shift from a view of task performance and skills as specific to a conception of general abilities that are global, stable, and persistent (Dweck & Elliott, 1983). Probably, too, this is accompanied by an increasing tendency for children to use social comparisons to evaluate their own competence. Young children tend to have an overoptimistic view of their own competence and it is only during the early years of schooling that they begin to adjust their self-perceptions as a consequence of task failure. Perhaps this tendency accounts for Rholes *et al.*'s (1980) finding that young children are less likely to have learned helplessness in response to repeated (experimentally induced) task failure. Children as young as age 4 or 5 years are aware that other people may feel proud or ashamed of them but it is not until 8 years or so that most children talk about being proud or ashamed of themselves (Harter, 1983). Self-awareness in the form of marked self-consciousness probably increases during adolescence (Rosenberg, 1979). Also, it seems that anxieties about the future may increase during the teenage period (Coleman, 1974; Coleman, Herzberg, & Morris, 1977). Young children do not think much about the long-term future, nor do they conceptualize actions in terms of distant consequences. Probably it is only during later childhood and early adolescence that future perspectives come to the fore. It would seem that such perspectives may be important in the development of feelings of hopelessness about the rest of life.

It is clear that there is much more to be learned about the development of children's social cognitions and self-perceptions, and we are only just beginning to study the possible links between that development and the emergence of depressive phenomena.

Children's Reporting of Depressive Feelings

In addition to the question of children's abilities to experience depressive affects and cognitions, there is the further issue of their ability to report them—a crucial matter with respect to the clinical assessment of depressive states. The limited available data on developmental competencies relevant to children's reporting of depression have been well summarized by Kovacs (in Chapter 15). She, like other researchers, concluded that much can be gained by direct interviewing of the child with specific questions about mood and functioning. However, she also noted young children's limitations with regard to reporting on certain key features required for DSM-III diagnosis of major depressive disorder. Specifically, she drew attention to the difficulties experienced by children up to the age of 8 years or so in considering their own affect separate from particular environmental contexts, and in differentiating normal sadness from authochthonous dysphoria. Probably the ability to locate the antecedents of emotional states within themselves is not achieved until adolescence. Concepts of guilt, too, show important developmental trends, with young children normally feeling responsible for many events outside their control.

The gradual development of metacognition, that is, children's ability to reflect on their own cognitive processes, will constrain their capacity to report (as well as to experience) depressive cognitions. It seems that a conceptual integration of the dimensions of the self, the use of stable personality characterizations, and true self-reflection emerge only in adolescence (Damon & Hart, 1982; Selman, Jaquette, & Redman, 1977). Accordingly, it is unlikely that children as young as age 6–7 years could provide valid reports on features of their own thinking (such as "slowness" or "emptiness"). Moreover, it is probable that during the middle years of childhood it will be difficult to get meaningful reports regarding feelings of worthlessness, helplessness, and hopelessness.

A further consideration concerns children's abilities to report either depressive feelings in the past or the duration of present feelings. The evidence indicates that although young children have some sense of time, their capacity to give accurate accounts of the past and to provide estimates of absolute duration are severely limited. Accounts of these features will need to be obtained from parents when the children are below the age of 10–12 years. However, it is likely that children will vary greatly in these (and other) cognitive skills; also, it may be that the presence of psychiatric disorder will itself alter the children's abilities to conceptualize time dimensions (see Chapter 15).

Measures of Depression in Childhood

During the last decade or so there has developed quite a range of questionnaire and interview methods for the assessment of depression in childhood (Carlson & Cantwell, 1980a; Chambers et al., in press; A. J. Costello, Edelbrock, Dulcan, Kalas, & Klavic, 1984; E. J. Costello, Edelbrock, & Costello, 1984; Edelbrock, Costello, Dulcan, Kalas, & Conover (1985); Kazdin, 1981; Kazdin, French, Bourgondam, & Saleeby, 1983; Kazdin & Petti, 1982; Weissman, Orvaschel, & Padian, 1980). They provide a set of usable instruments that can be employed to diagnose depressive phenomena and syndromes in children and adolescents. However, important problems remain:

1. The test–retest reliability is least satisfactory for the crucial cognitive components of depression and for the differentiation between normal sadness and authochthonous dysthymia. This is especially so with the younger children.

2. There is generally only low to moderate agreement between parent and child on depressive features. The finding that the agreement is lower in adolescence than in childhood suggests that, at least in

part, this may be a function of parent's lack of appreciation of their teenager's feelings—a feature noted also in earlier epidemiological studies (Rutter *et al.*, 1976). Nevertheless, it is noteworthy that at least so far as self-report questionnaires are concerned, parental measures provide a better differentiation of clinically diagnosed depressed and nondepressed groups than do child measures (Kazdin *et al.*, 1983).

3. Little is known on the degree to which different measures tap the same features or give rise to the designation of comparable syndromes. However, it is clear that there is only moderate agreement between different sets of operational criteria (Cantwell, 1983).

4. The available structured interviews for children do not give rise to reliable measures of depression; the clinical-type interviews seem to be more satisfactory for this purpose.

5. In trying to make assessments more applicable for use with children, there is a danger that the meaning of items is changed. For example, Chambers *et al.* (in press), using the K-SADS-P, reported that the quality of depressive mood could be assessed more reliably if children were asked about missing someone or feeling lonely. It seems dubious, to say the least, that loneliness and depression are synonymous. Similarly, the Weinberg criteria for depressive disorder treat "negative and difficult to please" as indicative of dysphoric mood, and "desire to run away or leave home" as evidence of self-depreciatory ideation (Cantwell, 1983). But are they?

6. Finally, there is the vexed question of the validity of these measures. Some studies have shown poor and some good differentiation between patients diagnosed as depressed and nondepressed, but what is the validity of the clinical diagnoses (see below)? Also when it is found many patients with other psychiatric disorders or with learning disabilities meet the operational criteria for major depressive disorder (as has often been the case; see, e.g., Frommer, 1968; Hendren, 1983; Puig-Antich, 1982; Puig-Antich & Gittelman, 1982; Weinberg & Rehmet, 1983), does this imply that the measure of depression has poor validity or rather does it mean that depression frequently coexists with other disorders?

Variations in the Manifestations of Depression

It is now accepted that children and adolescents can show major depressive disorders that fully meet the diagnostic criteria used with adults. So far as those disorders are concerned, the main issues are the same as those that apply to depressive conditions arising in adult life (see above). However, there is an additional interest in whether the very early age of onset carries with it any specific implications. For example,

Weissman, Wiekramartne, et al., (1984) found that the familial loading for major depression was highest when the depressive disorder had an onset before 30 years of age; Puig-Antich, Goetz, Davies, et al., (in press) found that the familial aggregation of depressive disorders was particularly high in children with a major depressive disorder. Perhaps depressive disorders with an onset in childhood represent those with the strongest genetic loading. In adults various sleep EEG abnormalities have been found to be present during episodes of depression, but Puig-Antich et al. (1982) failed to find them in a controlled study of severely depressed children. Does this mean that the type of depression seen in childhood differs from that in adult life or rather does it mean that there are developmentally mediated effects on sleep that alter the sleep phenomena in depression? In adults there is a fair amount of evidence (although not without its problems; Mindham, 1982) that depression showing endogenous or melancholic features usually responds to tricyclic antidepressants. The limited evidence on the drug treatment of depressive disorders in childhood shows little difference between active drug and placebo (Kramer & Feguine, 1981; Puig-Antich, Lupatkin, Chambers, et al., 1984). The apparently weaker drug effect in childhood requires confirmation (or refutation) but, if confirmed, it could reflect either a greater placebo effect in early life or a weaker drug effect. The latter possibility might be a consequence of age-related differences in drug response, rather than any difference in depressive disorder. Thus, prepubertal children seem to lack the euphoriant response to dextroamphetamine seen in adults (Rapoport et al., 1980). For all these reasons, and others of a similar kind, further research is necessary into "classical" major depressive disorders arising in childhood.

However, in addition, there is a particular need to study further those depressive disorders in childhood that fail fully to meet the adult criteria for major depressive disorder or that meet the criteria in circumstances that give rise to doubts about their comparability. These fall into six main groups:

1. It is common for depression to be associated with other psychiatric conditions. Thus, Puig-Antich (1982) found that one-third of boys fitting research diagnostic criteria (RDC) for major depressive disorder also fitted DSM-III criteria for conduct disorder; the majority showed pathological levels of separation anxiety (Puig-Antich & Gittelman, 1982) and most exhibited major difficulties in interpersonal relationships (Puig-Antich, Lukens, et al., 1985). Weinberg and Rehmet (1983) reported that over half the children admitted to a school for children with specific learning disabilities had a depressive disorder; Hendren (1983) found that among patients meeting DSM-III criteria for anorexia nervosa over half also met the criteria for a major depressive disorder, and a third met the criteria for

an endogenous depression. Do depressive syndromes have the same meaning when they occur in conjunction with other psychiatric disorders?

2. In some cases the criteria are met only by making inferences about the meaning of particular child behaviors that are not isomorphic with those in adult depressive disorders (see above). Are these inferences valid?

3. What is the meaning of the dysthymic states seen in middle childhood and adolescence that fall short of the criteria for a major depressive disorder? Many of these are quite long-standing without the clear onset more typical of acute depressive conditions. The one study with good data on the long-term outcome of these dysthymic states (Kovacs, Feinberg, Crouse-Novak, Paulauskas, & Finkelstein, 1984; Kovacs, Feinberg, Crouse-Novak, Paulauskas, Pollack, & Finkelstein, 1984) showed that two-thirds developed a major depressive disorder over the next 5 years. The findings provide a strong pointer to the likely link between chronic dysthymia and major depressive disorder, but the interpretation of the finding is not free from ambiguity (see below).

4. What is the meaning of the protest–despair–detachment syndromes seen in some preschool children following institutional admission, and of the rarer "anaclitic depression" of infancy (Harmon, Wagonfeld, & Emde, 1982; Spitz, 1946)? Is this the form that major depression takes in early childhood or does it constitute a response to institutional care and separation from family that has little in common with the major depressive disorders of adult life?

5. Is there any validity to the notion of "masked depression" or "depressive equivalents" in which such features as enuresis, somatic complaints, or conduct disturbance are thought to stem from depression even though overt depressive manifestations are absent? Interest in this concept has greatly diminished since it has been shown that many of the children with these clinical pictures in fact do show overt depression (Carlson & Cantwell, 1980b). Nevertheless, it is possible that the manifestations of depression might be greatly modified in early childhood (McConville, Boag, & Purohit, 1973).

6. What are the consequences of the DSM-III practice of not including social impairment in the criteria for depressive disorders? The available evidence suggests that depressive disorders are diagnosed surprisingly frequently in supposedly normal populations. Does this mean that such disorders are indeed very common in the community, or rather does depression in the absence of social impairment has a different meaning?

7. Lastly, does major depression have the same significance when it occurs in the context of severe environmental stress or adversity and when it remits rapidly following removal from the stress environment? This applies to most of the cases of anaclitic depression described by Spitz (1946) and to many of the cases of masked depression described by Cytryn and

McKnew (1972). However, it also applies to many acute syndromes of major depression.

Doubts about the comparability of these various depressive syndromes with the major endogenous-type depressive conditions of adult life have led to some skepticism about the true frequency of depressive conditions in prepubertal children (Graham, 1981). The issues remain unresolved and in the remainder of this chapter I consider how they might be tackled.

RESEARCH APPROACHES TO CHILDHOOD DEPRESSION

Developmental/Epidemiological Studies

In many respects, perhaps the most basic need of all is to determine how the manifestations of depression vary with age. In frustrating fashion, the satisfactory investigation of developmental trends awaits the availability of reliable and valid measures of depressive affect and cognition, while in parallel the methodological problems inherent in the creation of measures applicable to all age groups await knowledge on the developmental features that influence the manifestations of depression. The dilemma cannot be circumvented; it is necessary to grasp the nettle and to seek to deal with the substantive and methodological issues in tandem. For that to work effectively, it is essential clearly to separate children's reports, parental accounts, observations of the child, and inferences based upon each. This means, for example, that the inference that loneliness is the equivalent of depression must be tested rather than assumed. Also it requires that information be sought from the child independently from that obtained from the parent, rather than with that foreknowledge as has been the pattern in most clinical studies so far. Questions need to be raised, too, regarding the consequences of using different types of instrument. For example, the highly structured questionnaire-type interview epitomized by the DISC (A. J. Costello *et al.*, 1984) differs from the more clinically oriented semistructured interview such as the K-SADS (Chambers *et al.*, in press; Puig-Antich *et al.*, 1983) in at least two rather different respects. First, the latter allows the use of observations as well as verbal reports. Second, it relies on detailed personalized cross-questioning and the obtaining of examples in order for the interviewer (rather than the interviewee) to be confident that a rating can be made. A systematic comparison of the two types of interview method, as measures of depression, is needed. This should also aim to determine how far the differences stem from the type of questioning (i.e., a comparison using ratings based on typescripts) and how far from the observations of the child.

Crucial to the developmental/epidemiological study of depression, of course, is the use of instruments that discriminate within the different elements of depressive mood (such as sadness, emptiness, and loss of

pleasurable response), within the different elements of depressive cognition (such as feelings of guilt or unworthiness, helplessness about the life
situation, and hopelessness about the future), and between the affective
and cognitive domains. For the reasons already given, it will be necessary
both to use measures across age groups that are directly comparable and to
seek to make adaptations that reflect developmental variations in
children's cognitive capacity. (The latter should also be used in adolescents
and adults in order to provide a part-check on their comparability with the
traditional adult measures.)

CLINIC POPULATIONS

Probably it is best to apply these developmental approaches in the first
instance to clinic populations. This seems desirable because this is the only
way to ensure an adequate sample of major depressive disorders and
because there is the continuing uncertainty (with adults as well as with
children) regarding the parallels between the more severe depressive
disorders seen in hospital practice and the less severe disorders found in
community surveys (although clearly the two overlap). The necessary
assumption underlying the suggested clinical studies is that, insofar as
there are any age-related psychiatric referral biases, they will not differ
between depressive and nondepressive psychiatric conditions. That seems
a not unreasonable assumption, but still the need to test it makes it essential to go on to apply comparable methods in general population surveys.

The prime question to be asked in such clinical studies is whether the
different manifestations of depression, together with their patterning and
correlates, vary with age. Of course, it would be desirable in such studies to
relate the findings to some specific biological "marker" of depression. Unfortunately, such unambiguous markers have not as yet been found (see
Chapter 12). Nevertheless, it may be desirable to use the nearest approaches that are available—such as a familial loading of depressive
disorders (with the data obtained blind to the child's age and diagnosis) and
nonsuppression on the DST (Carroll, 1982; Leckman, 1983), using salivary
estimations of cortisol level (Woolston, Gianfredi, Gertner, Pangas, &
Mason, 1983). The point of such measures would be to determine whether
or not indices of depression that are separate from the child's symptomatology vary with age. If they do, this would suggest that depressive
disorders truly vary in frequency with age. If they do not, but if the frequency of operationally defined depressive syndromes varies, this would
suggest that depression changes with age in its clinical manifestations.

GENERAL POPULATION STUDIES

The clinic studies are required in order to derive and test valid
measures of depressive affect and cognition. General population studies
are required to test the assumptions required in the clinic studies (see

above). However, more importantly they are needed in order to obtain valid measures of possible age trends in depressive phenomena in children without, as well as those with, overt socially handicapping psychiatric disorders. Obviously, it would be important at the same time to obtain data on age changes in the various features that might possibly explain age differences in depression (see above), such as frequency of stressors or availability of social supports. Ideally, such epidemiological strategies should be combined with a longitudinal follow-up in order to examine age changes in the same individuals.

Natural History Studies

A second, rather different research approach is provided by the natural history or follow-up strategy applied to clinically diagnosed depressive conditions in childhood. The rationale here is that major depressive disorders tend to be recurrent conditions (Coyrell & Winokur, 1982). This is particularly the case with bipolar disorders both in adulthood and in adolescence (Strober & Carlson, 1982). Thus, the validation (or rather part-validation) of depressive syndromes in childhood relies on the demonstration that depressed children are more likely than children with other forms of psychiatric disorder to develop major depressive disorders in adult life. There is no published study that does just that but there are some that provide important pointers. Kovacs, Feinberg, Crouse-Novak, Paulauskas, and Finkelstein (1984) and Kovacs, Feinberg, Crouse-Novak, Paulauskas, Pollack, and Finkelstein (1984) undertook a 5-year follow-up of child patients with a major depressive disorder, a dysthymic disorder, an adjustment disorder with depressed mood, and some other psychiatric condition. The findings are striking in showing that recovery was fastest in the case of major depressive disorders and adjustment reactions, but that the development of subsequent episodes of major depression was virtually confined to children with major depressive disorders and dysthymic disorders (about two-thirds by 5 years of follow-up in both groups). There are four main limitations to this important well-planned study: (1) It seems that the follow-up assessments were not made blind to the original diagnosis. (2) The nondepressive comparison group was not closely matched on symptomatology (it was defined solely in terms of absence of dysthymic mood as such). (3) The follow-up did not extend into adult life. (4) The published findings do not as yet provide data on the outcome with respect to nondepressive disorders.

The relevance of this last limitation is shown by the evidence that depressed children often also show other forms of psychiatric disturbance (see above) and that this may persist after recovery from the initial depressive eposide (e.g., Eastgate & Gilmour, 1984; Poznanski, 1981; Puig-Antich, 1982). Moreover, in a systematic study of Maudsley Hospital patients seen both as children and as adults, Zeitlin (1983) found substantial continuity in the phenomena of depression as operationally defined, but considerable variations over time in the other psychiatric phenomena with which it was associated. A systematic follow-up study from childhood to adult life of matched depressed and nondepressed psychiatric patients, which deals with the limitations of the research to date, would be most informative.

Genetic Family Studies

As already noted, research with adult patients has shown that those with major depressive disorders differ from those with other psychiatric conditions in the rate of depression in first-degree relatives. The possible relevance of this to the study of depression in childhood is shown both by the high familial loading for depression (Puig-Antich, Goetz, Davies, et al., in press) and by the high rate of psychiatric problems, especially depression, in the offspring of adults with major depressive disorder (Beardslee, Bemporad, Keller, & Klerman, 1983; Weissman, Prusoff, et al., 1984; see also Chapters 5-7). However, in planning research strategies it is necessary to appreciate that parental depression constitutes an environmental as well as a genetic risk factor for the children, and that the risk is for nondepressive as well as depressive disorders in the offspring (Quinton & Rutter, 1985). Moreover, parental mental illness is a common occurrence with a wide range of child psychiatric problems (Rutter, 1966). It also appears that there may be a familial loading for nondepressive as well as depressive conditions in children with depressive states (Puig-Antich, Goetz, Davies, et al., in press). This may arise as a result of the overlap with other psychiatric disorders but, whatever the explanation, it needs to be taken into account.

What is required is a genetic family study of depressive and nondepressive disorders in childhood (matched on nondepressive symptomatology), in which there is systematic direct assessment of psychiatric conditions in relatives (Leckman, Shulomskas, Thompson, Bélanger, & Weissman, 1982; Orvaschel, Thompson, Bélanger, Prusoff, & Kidd, 1982; Thompson, Kidd & Weissman, 1979; Thompson, Orvaschel, Prusoff, & Kidd, 1982), that is undertaken blind to the child's diagnosis. In such a study it would be essential to determine the familial risk for both depressive and nondepressive conditions in relatives. If such a study could be combined with a follow-up from childhood to adult life (see above), it would be advantageous to assess the familial risk separately for depressive disorders arising in childhood, for those recurring in adult life, and for those present in both age periods.

Biological Correlates

There is a substantial body of research into the biological correlates of depression in adult life (see Åsberg, Mårtensson, & Wägner, in press; McKinney & Moran, 1982; Sachar, 1982; Zis & Goodwin, 1982) and equivalent data for children are accumulating (see Chapter 12). Unfortunately, so far the biological correlates of depression have but moderate sensitivity and specificity. Moreover, most represent markers of state rather than trait (that is to say, they are abnormal during the depressive episode but return to normal after recovery). However, there are some promising leads from research in adults that warrant following up and these should be accompanied by comparable research in childhood. As already noted, it will, of course, be necessary in such research to take account of possible age-related changes in biological functioning.

Drug Response

Potentially, a specific drug response to antidepressant medication might prove to be useful in the study of depressive conditions in childhood. However, up to now it has been of very limited utility in the study of the classification of depressive and nondepressive conditions. This is because of three main limitations. First, there is no drug as yet available that has a certain, or even near-certain, effect in major depressive disorders in adults. Hence, a lack of drug response is no indication that the disorder is not depressive in origin. Second, the antidepressant drugs in general use have an astonishingly wide range of pharmacological effects. Thus, for example, the tricyclics have been shown to relieve enuresis and to be of benefit in the treatment of attention deficit disorders (see Taylor, 1985). Accordingly, any beneficial effect may stem from the drugs' nonantidepressant as well as antidepressant properties. Third, there may be age-related differences in the way in which individuals respond to drugs (see above). In addition, there are the practical problems in the assessment of drug response that stem from children's noncompliance in taking drugs.

Stress Correlates

In adults, there is a good deal of evidence that depressive disorders are commonly precipitated by stress events, perhaps especially those involving loss or the breaking of important (love) relationships (Brown & Harris, 1978; Paykel, 1982). There is also some preliminary evidence that the type of life events associated with depression may differ from those associated with anxiety states (Finlay Jones & Brown, 1981). Thus, it might be supposed that one useful approach to the study of childhood depression would be the determination of possible associations with stress events of different kinds—once more making systematic comparisons with nondepressive disorders. Indeed, that would be a useful strategy. However, certain constraints need to be borne in mind. First, there is uncertainty over the extent to which there is specificity in the kinds of stressors associated with depression (Paykel, 1982). Second, loss events have been shown to lead to quite a range of disorders, both somatic and psychic (Craig, in press; Weiner, in press). Third, the study of stress in childhood is in its infancy (Garmezy & Rutter, 1983 & 1985; J. H. Johnson, 1982; see Garmezy, Chapter 10 of this volume); adequately tested instruments are not yet available and it remains uncertain how far the life events that constitute stressors to adults pose a similar risk to children. In particular, it remains to be determined how far the risks impinge directly on the child and how far they operate through effects on the parents and the family. Nevertheless, in spite of these limitations there is no doubt that this is a research strategy well worth pursuing.

CONCLUSIONS

In discussions concerning the difficulties involved in the diagnosis and classification of depression in childhood it is sometimes assumed that all is well with respect to the nosology of depressive disorders as they occur in adults. It is evident that this is far from the case, although equally a good deal is known. This final chapter has sought to provide a brief overview of the conceptual and measurement issues that apply to all age groups as well as those that apply specifically to children. An outline has been provided of some of the research strategies that might be employed in attempts to resolve the remaining issues. It is evident that such strategies include both those that derive from developmental approaches and those that stem from clinical methodologies.

REFERENCES

American Psychiatric Association. (1980). *Diagnostic and statistical manual of mental disorders—DSM-III* (3rd ed). Washington, DC: American Psychiatric Association.

Andreasen, N. C. (1982). Concepts, diagnosis and classification. In E. S. Paykel (Ed.), *Handbook of affective disorders* (pp. 24–44). Edinburgh & London: Churchill-Livingstone.

Anthony, J., & Scott, P. D. (1960). Manic-depressive psychosis in childhood. *Journal of Child Psychology and Psychiatry, 1,* 53–72.

Åsberg, M., Mårtensson, B., & Wägner, A. (in press). On the psychobiology of depression and suicidal behavior. In D. Magnusson & A. Öhman (Eds.), *Psychopathology in the perspective of person-environment interaction.* New York: Academic Press.

Beardslee, W. R., Bemporad, J., Keller, M. B., & Klerman, G. L. (1983). Children of parents with major affective disorder: A review. *American Journal of Psychiatry, 140,* 825–832.

Beck, A. T. (1976). *Cognitive therapy and the emotional disorders.* New York: International Universities Press.

Blackburn, I. M., & Bishop, S. (1983). Changes in cognition with pharmacotherapy and cognitive therapy. *British Journal of Psychiatry, 143,* 609–617.

Bowlby, J. (1969). *Attachment and loss. I. Attachment.* London: Hogarth Press.

Bowlby, J. (1980). *Attachment and loss. III. Loss, sadness and depression.* New York: Basic Books.

Brockington, I. F., Altman, E., Hillier, V., Meltzer, H. Y., & Nand, S. (1982). The clinical picture of bipolar affective disorder in its depressed phase: A report from London and Chicago. *British Journal of Psychiatry, 141,* 558–562.

Brockington, I. F., & Leff, J. P. (1979). Schizoaffective psychosis: Definition and incidence. *Psychological Medicine, 9,* 91–99.

Brown, G. W., & Harris, T. (1978). *Social origins of depression.* London: Tavistock Press.

Cantwell, D. P. (1983). Depression in childhood: Clinical picture and diagnostic criteria. In D. P. Cantwell & G. A. Carlson (Eds.), *Affective disorders in childhood and adolescence: An update* (pp. 3–18). Lancaster, England: MTP Press, Ltd.

Carlson, G. A., & Cantwell, D. P. (1980a). A survey of depressive symptoms, syndrome and disorder in a child psychiatric population. *Journal of Child Psychology and Psychiatry, 21,* 19–25.

Carlson, G. A., & Cantwell, D. P. (1980b). Unmasking masked depression in children and adolescents. *American Journal of Psychiatry, 137,* 445–449.

Carlson, G. A., & Cantwell, D. P. (1982). Suicidal behavior and depression in children and adolescents. *Journal of the American Academy of Child Psychiatry, 21,* 361–368.

Carroll, B. J. (1982). The dexamethasone suppression test for melancholia. *British Journal of Psychiatry, 140,* 292–304.

Chambers, W. J., Puig-Antich, J., Hirsch, M., Paez, P., Ambrosini, P. J., Tabrizi, M. A., & Davies, M. (in press). The assessment of affective disorders in children and adolescents by semistructured interview: Test-retest reliability of the K-SADS-P. *Archives of General Psychiatry.*

Clayton, P. J. (1982). Bereavement. In E. S. Paykel (Ed.), *Handbook of affective disorders* (pp. 403–415). Edinburgh & London: Churchill-Livingstone.

Clinical Research Centre, Division of Psychiatry. (1984). The Northwick Park ECT trial; predictors of response to real and simulated ECT (1984). *British Journal of Psychiatry, 144,* 227–237.

Coleman, J. C. (1974). *Relationships in adolescence.* London: Routledge & Kegan Paul.

Coleman, J. C., Herzberg, J., & Morris, M. (1977). Identity in adolescence: Present and future self-concepts. *Journal of Youth and Adolescence, 6,* 63–75.

Coppen, A., Abou-Saleh, M., Miller, P., Metcalfe, M., Harwood, J., & Bailey, J. (1983). Dexamethasone suppression test in depressive and other psychiatric illness. *British Journal of Psychiatry, 142,* 498–504.

Costello, A. J., Edelbrock, C. S., Dulcan, M. H., Kales, R., & Klavic, S. H. (1984). *Report on the NIMH diagnostic interview schedule for children (DISC).* Report to the National Institute of Mental Health, Bethesda, MD.

Costello, E. J., Edelbrock, C. S., & Costello, A. J. (1984). Validity of the NIMH diagnostic interview schedule for children: A comparison between pediatric and psychiatric referrals. (Submitted for publication)

Coryell, W., & Winokur, G. (1982). Course and outcome. In E. S. Paykel (Ed.), *Handbook of affective disorders* (pp. 93–106). Edinburgh & London: Churchill-Livingstone.

Craig, T. K. J. (in press). Stress and contextual meaning: Specific causal effects in psychiatric and physical disorders. In D. Magnusson & A. Öhman (Eds.), *Psychopathology in the perspective of person–environment interaction.* New York: Academic Press.

Cytryn, L., & McKnew, D. H. (1972). Proposed classification of childhood depression. *American Journal of Psychiatry, 129,* 149–155.

Damon, W., & Hart, D. (1982). The development of self-understanding from infancy through adolescence. *Child Development, 53,* 841–864.

Dweck, C. S., Davidson, W., Nelson, S., & Enna, B. (1978). Sex differences in learned helplessness. II. The contingencies of evaluative feedback in the classroom. III. An experimental analysis. *Developmental Psychology, 14,* 268–276.

Dweck, C. S., & Elliott, E. S. (1983). Achievement motivation. In E. M. Hetherington (Ed.), *Socialization, personality, and social development: Vol. 4. Mussen's handbook of child psychology* (4th ed., pp. 643–691). New York: Wiley.

Eastgate, J., & Gilmour, L. (1984). Long-term outcome of depressed children: A follow-up study. Developmental Medicine and Child Neurology, 26, 68–72.

Edelbrock, C., Costello, A. J., Dulcan, M. H., Kalas, R., & Conover, N. C. (1985). Age differences in the reliability of the psychiatric interview of the child. Child Development, 56, 265–275.

Eisenberg, L. (1980). Adolescent suicide: On taking arms against a sea of troubles. Pediatrics, 66, 315–320.

Feighner, J. P., Robins, E., Guze, S. B., Woodruff, R. A., & Winokur, G. (1972). Diagnostic criteria for use in psychiatric research. Archives of General Psychiatry, 26, 57–63.

Finlay-Jones, R. A., & Brown, G. W. (1981). Types of stressful life events and the onset of anxiety and depressive disorders. Psychological Medicine, 11, 803–815.

Finlay-Jones, R. A., Brown, G. W., Duncan-Jones, P., Harris, T., Murphy, E., & Prudo, R. (1980). Depression and anxiety in the community: Replicating the diagnosis of a case. Psychological Medicine, 10, 445–454.

Frommer, E. A. (1968). Depressive illness in childhood. In A. J. Coppen & A. Walk (Eds.), Recent developments in affective disorders (British Journal of Psychiatry Special Publication No. 2). Ashford, England: Headley Bros.

Garmezy, N., & Rutter, M. (Eds.). (1983). Stress, coping, and development in children. New York: McGraw-Hill.

Garmezy, N., & Rutter, M. (1985). Acute reactions to stress. In M. Rutter & L. Hersov (Eds.), Child and adolescent psychiatry: Modern approaches (pp. 152–176). Oxford: Blackwell Scientific Publications.

Gershon, E. S., Hamovit, J., Guroff, J., Dibble, E., Leckman, J. F., Sceery, W., Targum, S. D., Nurnberger, J. P., Jr., Golden, L. R., & Bunney, W. C. S., Jr. (1982). A family study of schizoaffective, bipolar I, bipolar II, unipolar and normal controls. Archives of General Psychiatry, 39, 1157–1167.

Graham, P. J. (1981). Depressive disorders—a reconsideration. Acta Pedopsychiatrica, 46, 285–296.

Guze, S. B., Woodruff, R. A., & Clayton, P. J. (1971). "Secondary" affective disorder: A study of 95 cases. Psychological Medicine, 1, 426–428.

Hamilton, E. W., & Abramson, L. Y. (1983). Cognitive patterns and major depressive disorder: A longitudinal study in a hospital setting. Journal of Abnormal Psychology, 92, 173–184.

Hamilton, M. (1982). Symptoms and assessment of depression. In E. S. Paykel (Ed.), Handbook of affective disorders (pp. 3–11). Edinburgh & London: Churchill-Livingstone.

Harmon, R. J., Wagonfeld, S., & Emde, R. N. (1982). Anaclitic depression: A follow-up from infancy to puberty. Psychoanalytic Study of the Child, 37, 67–94.

Harter, S. (1983). Developmental perspectives on the self-system. In E. M. Hetherington (Ed.), Socialization, personality, and social development: Vol. 4. Mussen's handbook of child psychology (4th ed., pp. 275–385). New York: Wiley.

Hassanyeh, F., & Davison, K. (1980). Bipolar affective psychosis with onset before age 16 years: Report of 10 cases. British Journal of Psychiatry, 137, 530–539.

Hawton, K., & Goldacre, M. (1982). Hospital admissions for adverse effects of medicinal agents (mainly self-poisoning) among adolescents in the Oxford region. British Journal of Psychiatry, 141, 166–170.

Hendren, R. L. (1983). Depression in anorexia nervosa. Journal of the American Academy of Child Psychiatry, 22, 59–62.

Hibbert, G. A., Teasdale, J. D., & Spencer, P. (1984). Covariation of depressive symptoms over time. Psychological Medicine, 14, 451–456.

Johnson, D. A. W. (1981). Studies of depressive symptoms in schizophrenia. British Journal of Psychiatry, 139, 89–101.

Johnson, J. H. (1982). Life events as stressors in childhood and adolescence. In B. B. Lahey & A. E. Kazdin (Eds.), Advances in clinical child psychology (Vol. 5, pp. 219–253). New York: Plenum Press.

Kagan, J. (1981). The second year. Cambridge, MA: Harvard University Press.

Kagan, J. (1982). The emergence of self. Journal of Child Psychology and Psychiatry, 23, 363–382.

Kaplan, S. L., Hong, G. K., & Weinhold, C. (1984). Epidemiology of depressive symptomatology in adolescents. Journal of the American Academy of Child Psychiatry, 23, 91–98.

Kazdin, A. E. (1981). Assessment techniques for childhood depression: A critical appraisal. Journal of the American Academy of Child Psychiatry, 20, 358–375.

Kazdin, A. E., French, N. A., Bourgondan, M. V., & Saleeby, N. (1983). Assessment of childhood depression: Correspondence of child and parent ratings. Journal of the American Academy of Child Psychiatry, 22, 157–164.

Kazdin, A. E., & Petti, J. A. (1982). Self-report and interview measures of childhood and adolescent depression. Journal of Child Psychology and Psychiatry, 23, 437–458.

Kliman, G. W. (1968). Psychological emergencies of childhood. New York: Grune & Stratton.

Kosky, R. (1982). Suicide and attempted suicide among Australian children. Medical Journal of Australia, 1, 121–126.

Kovacs, M., Feinberg, T. L., Crouse-Novak, M. A., Paulauskas, S. L., & Finkelstein, R. (1984). Depressive disorders in childhood. I. A longitudinal prospective study of characteristics and recovery. Archives of General Psychiatry, 41, 229–237.

Kovacs, M., Feinberg, T. L., Crouse-Novak, M. A., Paulauskas, S. L., Polláck, M., & Finkelstein, R. (1984). Depressive disorders in childhood. II. A longitudinal study of the risk for a subsequent major depression. Archives of General Psychiatry, 41, 643–649.

Kramer, A. D., & Feigune, R. J. (1981). Clinical effects of amitriptyline in adolescent depression. Journal of the American Academy of Child Psychiatry, 20, 636–644.

Leckman, J. F. (1983). The dexamethasone suppression test. Journal of the American Academy of Child Psychiatry, 22, 477–479.

Leckman, J. F., Shulomskas, D., Thompson, W. D., Bélanger, A., & Weissman, M. M. (1982). Best estimate of lifetime psychiatric diagnosis: A methodological study. Archives of General Psychiatry, 39, 879–883.

Leckman, J. F., Weissman, M. M., Merikangas, K. R., Pauls, D. L., & Prusoff, B. A. (1983). Panic disorder and major depression: Increased rate of major depression, alcoholism, panic and phobic disorders in families of depressed probands with panic disorder. Archives of General Psychiatry, 40, 1055–1060.

Link, B., & Dohrenwend, B. P. (1980). Formulation of hypotheses about the true prevalence of demoralization in the United States. In B. P. Dohrenwend, B. S. Dohrenwend, M. S. Gould, B. Link, R. Neugebauer, & R. Wunst-Hilzig, R. (Eds.), Mental illness in the United States: Epidemiological estimates (pp. 114–132). New York: Praeger.

Lloyd, G. G., & Cawley, R. H. (1983). Distress or illness? A study of psychological symptoms after myocardial infarction. British Journal of Psychiatry, 142, 120–125.

Loranger, A. W., & Levine, P. M. (1978). Age at onset of bipolar affective illness. Archives of General Psychiatry, 35, 1345–1348.

Lowe, T. L., & Cohen, D. J. (1980). Mania in childhood and adolescence. In R. H. Belmaker & H. M. van Praag (Eds.), Mania: An evolving concept (pp. 111–117). New York: Spectrum.

McClure, G., & Gould, M. S. (1984). Recent trends in suicide among the young. British Journal of Psychiatry, 144, 134–138.

McConville, B. J., Boag, L. C., & Purohit, A. P. (1973). Three types of childhood depression. Canadian Psychiatric Association Journal, 18, 133–138.

McKinney, W. T., & Moran, E. C. (1982). Animal models. In E. S. Paykel (Ed.), Handbook of affective disorders (pp. 202–211). Edinburgh & London: Churchill-Livingstone.

Mendlewicz, J., Charles, G., & Franckson, J. M. (1982). The dexamethasone suppression test in affective disorder: Relationship to clinical and genetic subgroups. British Journal of Psychiatry, 141, 464–470.

Mindham, R. H. S. (1982). Tricyclic antidepressants and amine precursors. In E. S. Paykel (Ed.), Handbook of affective disorders (pp. 231–245). Edinburgh & London: Churchill-Livingstone.

Norman, W. H., Miller, I. W., & Klee, S. H. (1983). Assessment of cognitive distortion in a clinically depressed population. *Cognitive Therapy and Research, 7,* 133–140.

Orvaschel, H., Thompson, W. D., Belanger, A., Prusoff, B. A., & Kidd, K. K. (1982). Comparison of the family history method to direct interviews: Factors affecting the diagnosis of depression. *Journal of Affective Disorders, 4,* 49–59.

Parker, G. (1983). *Parental overprotection: A risk factor in psychosocial development.* New York: Grune & Stratton.

Paykel, E. S. (1982). Life events and early environment. In E. S. Paykel (Ed.), *Handbook of affective disorders* (pp. 146–161). Edinburgh & London: Churchill-Livingstone.

Perris, C. (1982). The distinction between bipolar and unipolar affective disorders. In E. S. Paykel (Ed.), *Handbook of affective disorders* (pp. 45–58). Edinburgh & London: Churchill-Livingstone.

Poznanski, E. (1981). Childhood depression: The outcome. *Acta Pedopsychiatrica, 46,* 297–304.

Puig-Antich, J. (1982). Major depression and conduct disorder in prepuberty. *Journal of the American Academy of Child Psychiatry, 21,* 118–128.

Puig-Antich, J., Chambers, W. J., & Tabrizi, M. A. (1983). The clinical assessment of current depressive episodes in children and adolescents: Interviews with parents and children. In D. P. Cantwell & G. A. Carlson (Eds.), *Affective disorders in childhood and adolescence: An update* (pp. 157–179). Lancaster, England: MTP Press, Ltd.

Puig-Antich, J., & Gittelman, R. (1982). Depression in childhood and adolescence. In E. S. Paykel (Ed.), *Handbook of affective disorders* (pp. 379–392). Edinburgh & London: Churchill-Livingstone.

Puig-Antich, J., Goetz, D., Davies, M., Kaplan, T., Davies, S., Ostrow, L., & Asmis, L. (in press). A controlled family history study of prepubertal major depressive disorder. *Archives of General Psychiatry.*

Puig-Antich, J., Goetz, R., Hanlon, C., Davies, M., Thompson, J., Chambers, W. J., Tabrizi, M. A., & Weitzman, E. D. (1982). Sleep architecture and REM sleep measures in prepubertal children with major depression: A controlled study. *Archives of General Psychiatry, 39,* 932–939.

Puig-Antich, J., Lukens, E., Davies, M., Goetz, D., Brennan-Quattrock, J., & Todak, G. (1985). Psychosocial functioning in prepubertal major depressive disorder, I. Interpersonal relationships during the depressive episode. *Archives of General Psychiatry, 42,* 500–507.

Puig-Antich, J., Lupatkin, W., Chambers, W. J., King, J., Tabizi, M. A., Davies, M., & Goetz, R. (1984). Imipramine affectiveness in prepubertal major depressive disorders. II. A double blind placebo-controlled study. (Submitted for publication)

Quinton, D. & Rutter, M. (1985). Family pathology and child psychiatric disorder: A four year prospective study. In A. R. Nicol (Ed.), *Longitudinal studies in child psychology and psychiatry: Practical lessons from research experience* (pp. 91–134). Chichester: Wiley.

Rapoport, J., Bucksbaum, M., Weingartner, H., Zahn, T., Ludlow, C., Bartko, J., & Mikkelsen, E. J. (1980). Dextroamphetamine: Cognitive and behavioral effects in normal and hyperactive boys and normal adult males. *Archives of General Psychiatry, 37,* 933–943.

Raps, C. S., Peterson, C., Reinhard, K. E., Abramson, L. Y., & Seligman, M. E. P. (1982). Attributional style among depressed patients. *Journal of Abnormal Psychology, 91,* 102–108.

Rholes, W. S., Blackwell, J., Jordan, C., & Walters, C. (1980). A developmental study of learned helplessness. *Developmental Psychology, 16,* 616–624.

Rosenberg, M. (1979). *Conceiving the self.* New York: Basic Books.

Rutter, M. (1966). *Children of sick parents: An environmental and psychiatric study.* (Institute of Psychiatry Maudsley Monographs No. 16). London: Oxford University Press.

Rutter, M. (1979). *Changing youth in a changing society: Patterns of adolescent development and disorder.* London: Nuffield Provincial Hospitals Trust. (Cambridge, MA: Harvard University Press, 1980.)

Rutter, M. (1980). Attachment and the development of social relationships. In M. Rutter (Ed.), *Scientific foundations of developmental psychiatry* (pp. 267–279). London: Heinemann.

Rutter, M. (1981). *Maternal deprivation reassessed* (2nd ed.). Harmondsworth, Middlesex, England. Penguin Books.

Rutter, M., & Garmezy, N. (1983). Developmental psychopathology. In E. M. Hetherington (Ed.), *Socialization, personality, and social development: Vol. 4. Mussen's handbook of child psychology* (4th ed., pp. 775–911). New York: Wiley.

Rutter, M., Graham, P., Chadwick, O., & Yule, W. (1976). Adolescent turmoil: Fact or faction? *Journal of Child Psychology and Psychiatry, 17,* 35–56.

Sachar, E. J. (1982). Endocrine abnormalities in depression. In E. S. Paykel (Ed.), *Handbook of affective disorders* (pp. 191–201). Edinburgh & London: Churchill-Livingstone.

Selman, R. L., Jaquette, D., & Redman, L. D. (1977). Interpersonal awareness in children. Toward an integration of developmental and clinical child psychology. *American Journal of Orthopsychiatry, 47,* 264–274.

Shaffer, D. (1974). Suicide in childhood and early adolescence. *Journal of Child Psychology and Psychiatry, 15,* 275–292.

Shaffer, D., & Fisher, P. (1981). The epidemiology of suicide in children and young adolescents. *Journal of the American Academy of Child Psychiatry, 20,* 545–565.

Shantz, C. (1983). Social cognition. In J. H. Flavell & E. M. Markman (Eds.), *Cognitive development: Vol. 3. Mussen's handbook of child psychology* (4th ed., pp 495–555). New York: Wiley.

Spitz, R. (1946). Anaclitic depression. *Psychoanalytic Study of the Child, 2,* 313–342.

Spitzer, R. L., Endicott, J., & Robins, E. (1978). Research diagnostic criteria: Rationale and reliability. *Archives of General Psychiatry, 35,* 773–782.

Sroufe, A., & Rutter, M. (1984). The domain of developmental psychopathology. *Child Development, 58,* 17–29.

Stancer, H. C., Persad, E., Jorna, T., Flood, C., & Wagener, D. (1984). The occurrence of secondary affective disorder in an in-patient population and severe and recurrent affective disorder. *British Journal of Psychiatry, 144,* 630–635.

Stokes, P. E., Stoll, P. M., Koslow, S. H., Maas, J. W., David, J. M., Swann, A. C., & Robins, E. (1984). Pretreatment DST and hypothalamic-pituitary-adrenocortical function in depressed patients and comparison groups. *Archives of General Psychiatry, 41,* 257–267.

Strober, M., & Carlson, G. (1982). Bipolar illness in adolescents with major depression: Clinical, genetic, and psychopharmacologic predictors in a three- to four-year prospective follow-up investigation. *Archives of General Psychiatry, 39,* 549–555.

Taylor, E. (1985). Drug treatment. In M. Rutter & L. Hersov (Eds.), *Child and adolescent psychiatry: Modern approaches* (pp. 780–793). Oxford: Blackwell Scientific Publications.

Tennant, C., & Bebbington, P. (1978). The social causation of depression: A critique of the work of Brown and his colleagues. *Psychological Medicine, 8,* 556–576.

Tennant, C., Bebbington, P., & Hurry, J. (1981). The short-term outcome of neurotic disorders in the community: The relation of remission to clinical factors and to 'neutralizing' life events. *British Journal of Psychiatry, 139,* 213–220.

Thompson, W. D., Kidd, J. R., & Weissman, M. M. (1978). A procedure for the efficient collection and processing of pedigree data suitable for genetic analysis. *Journal of Psychiatric Research, 15,* 291–303.

Thompson, W. D., Orvashel, H., Prusoff, B. A., & Kidd, K. K. (1982). An evaluation of the family history method for ascertaining psychiatric disorders. *Archives of General Psychiatry, 39,* 53–58.

Tsuang, M. T., Winokur, G., & Crowe, R. R. (1980). Morbidity risks of schizophrenia and affective disorders among first degree relatives of patients with schizophrenia, mania, depression and surgical conditions. *British Journal of Psychiatry, 133,* 497–504.

Tsuang, M. T., Woolsam, R. F., & Simpson, J. C. (1981). An evaluation of the Feighner criteria for schizophrenia and affective disorders using long-term outcome data. *Psychological Medicine, 11*, 281–288.

van Eerdewegh, M. M., Bieri, M. D., Parilla, R. H., & Clayton, P. (1982). The bereaved child. *British Journal of Psychiatry, 140*, 23–29.

Weinberg, W., & Rehmet, A. (1983). Childhood affective disorder and school problems. In D. P. Cantwell & G. A. Carlson (Eds.), *Affective disorders in childhood and adolescence: An update* (pp. 109–128). Lancaster, England: MTP Press, Ltd.

Weiner, H. (in press). Human relationships in health, illness and disease. In D. Magnusson & A. Öhman (Eds.), *Psychopathology in the perspective of person-environment interaction.* New York: Academic Press.

Weissman, M. M., Gershon, E. S., Kidd, K. K., Prusoff, B. A., Leckman, J. F., Dibble, E., Hamovit, J., Thompson, N. D., Pauls, D. L., & Guroff, J. J. (1984). Psychiatric disorders in the relatives of probands with affective disorders: The Yale University: National Institute of Mental Health collaborative study. *Archives of General Psychiatry, 41*, 13–21.

Weissman, M. M., Orvashel, H., & Padian, N. (1980). Children's symptoms and social functioning self-report scales: Comparison of mothers' and children's reports. *Journal of Nervous and Mental Diseases, 168*, 736–740.

Weissman, M. M., Prusoff, B. A., Gammon, P. D., Merikangas, K. R., Leckman, J. F., & Kidd, K. K. (1984). Psychopathology in the children (ages 6–18) of depressed and normal parents. *Journal of the American Academy of Child Psychiatry, 23*, 78–84.

Weissman, M. M., Wiekramaratne, P., Merikangas, K. R., Leckman, J. F., Prusoff, B. A., Caruso, K. A., Kidd, K. K., & Gammon, G. D. (1984) Onset of major depression in early adulthood: Increased familial loading and specificity. *Archives of General Psychiatry, 41*, 1136–1143.

Wing, J. K., Cooper, J. E., & Sartorius, N. (1974). *The measurement and classification of psychiatric symptoms.* London: Cambridge University Press.

Woolston, J. L., Gianfredi, S., Gertner, J. H., Pangas, J. A., & Mason, J. W. (1983). Salivary cortisol: A nontraumatic sampling technique for assaying cortisol dynamics. *Journal of the American Academy of Child Psychiatry, 22*, 474–476.

World Health Organization. (1978). *International classification of diseases* (9th rev. ed.). Geneva: World Health Organization.

Zeitlin, H. (1983). *The natural history of psychiatric disorder in children.* Unpublished doctoral thesis, University of London.

Zis, A. P., & Goodwin, F. K. (1982). The amine hypothesis. In E. S. Paykel (Ed.), *Handbook of affective disorders* (pp. 175–190). Edinburgh & London: Churchill-Livingstone.

Author Index

Mendels, J., 169, 185n., 351, 352, 356, 362,
366, 369n., 370n., 373n., 374n., 375n.
Mendelson, M., 109, 131n., 228, 247n., 367,
376n.
Mendelson, W. B., 46, 70n., 352, 353, 362,
363, 364, 365, 367, 371n., 373n., 375n.,
376n., 379n.
Mendlewicz, J., 21, 26n., 165, 185n., 366,
376n., 498, 516n.
Menninger, K., 404, 431n.
Merikangas, K. R., 199, 204n., 346, 380n.,
498, 506, 511, 516n., 519n.
Merimee, T. J., 361, 363, 376n.
Metcalf, D., 146, 157n.
Metcalfe, M., 498, 514n.
Meyer, E. L., 406, 430n.
Meyers, C. E., 405, 431n.
Mezzich, J., 424, 428n.
Michael, S. T., 254, 294n.
Mikkelsen, E., 367, 377n., 506, 517n.
Miller, I. W., 230, 248n., 494, 517n.
Miller, J., 80, 131n.
Miller, K., 406, 429n.
Miller, L. C., 307, 322n.
Miller, L. H., 476, 478n.
Miller, P., 498, 514n.
Miller, W. R., 228, 229, 248n.
Mills, M., 481, 489n.
Minde, G., 367, 376n.
Minde, K., 367, 380n.
Mindham, R. H. S., 506, 516n.
Minshew, N. J., 342, 376n.
Minturn, M., 209, 219n.
Mirsheidaie, F., 172, 185n.
Mischol, W., 237, 248n., 423, 431n.
Mock, J., 228, 247n.
Molliver, M. E., 367, 375n.
Money, J., 363, 376n., 381n.
Monroe, S. M., 21, 26n., 93, 128n., 209,
216, 218n.
Monteiro, K. P., 41, 61, 67n.
Moore, A. M., 166, 187n., 353, 367, 379n.
Moore-Ede, M. C., 364, 380n.
Moran, E. C., 511, 516n.
Morris, C. A., 165, 186n.
Morris, M., 503, 514n.
Moss, H., 327, 339n.
Motti, F., 35, 41, 70n., 86, 87, 133n.
Motulsky, A. G., 472, 478n.
Mrazek, D., 207, 219n.
Mueller, E., 366, 373n.
Mueller, P. S., 361, 362, 376n.

Mullen, K., 411, 429n.
Mullener, N., 450, 464n.
Müller, F., 362, 375n.
Mundy, G. R., 470, 478n.
Munoz, R., 438, 463n.
Munro, A., 309, 322n.
Murphy, D. L., 166, 170, 182n., 183n., 352,
358, 362, 370n., 379n.
Murphy, E., 253, 254, 294n., 295n., 495,
515n.
Murphy, G. E., 383, 390, 395n.
Myers, J. K., 168, 169, 185n., 187n.
Muscottola, G., 366, 376n.

N

Nadi, N. S., 164, 166, 183n., 185n., 366,
376n.
Nadler, J. V., 367, 378n.
Nakamura, C. Y., 307, 322n.
Nand, S., 499, 513n.
Nathan, P. E., 406, 431n.
Nathan, R. S., 357, 358, 359, 361, 362, 366,
369n., 373n., 378n.
Nauta, W., 79, 112, 131n.
Neale, J. M., 172, 187n., 206, 207, 208, 209,
210, 211, 215, 216, 218n., 219n., 220n.
Nee, J., 406, 433n.
Negri, F., 165, 187n.
Neil, J. F., 172, 182n., 207, 215, 218n., 348,
349, 371n.
Nelson, B., 15, 26n., 357, 358, 369n., 383,
395n.
Nelson, R. E., 237, 248n.
Nelson, S., 22, 27n., 502, 514n.
Nemeth, E., 367, 380n.
Nerup, J., 343, 352, 374n.
Neuringer, C., 325, 332, 338n.
Newman, R., 325, 332, 339n.
Nicholls, J. G., 316, 322n.
Nixon, J. M., 254, 295n.
Noble, H., 307, 322n.
Norlem, N., 343, 374n.
Norman, McI. J., 425, 428n.
Norman, W. H., 230, 248n., 494, 517n.
Norman, W. T., 209, 219n.
Novacen, K. H., 358, 379n.
Novacenko, H., 170, 186n., 357, 358, 359,
361, 363, 364, 367, 369n., 377n.
Nover, R. A., 419, 430n.
Nuechterlein, K. H., 318, 321n., 408, 433n.
Nurnberger, J. I., Jr., 164, 165, 166, 167,

Subject Index